CO-ATV-533

INTRODUCTION TO COMPUTER INFORMATION SYSTEMS

INTRODUCTION TO COMPUTER INFORMATION SYSTEMS

BARRY SHORE
University of New Hampshire

H O L T • R I N E H A R T • A N D • W I N S T O N , I N C.

New York   Chicago   San Francisco   Philadelphia
Montreal   Toronto   London   Sydney   Tokyo

Publisher: Ted Buchholz
Acquiring Editor: David Chodoff
Production Manager: Paul Nardi
Project Manager: Rachel Hockett, Cobb/Dunlop Publisher Services, Inc.
Interior Design: Keri Keating
Illustrations: David Weisman
Original Chapter-Opening Art: Deborah Phillips
Composition: Science Press
Printing and Binding: Von Hoffmann Press

Copyright © 1988 by Holt, Rinehart and Winston, Inc.

All rights reserved. No part of this publication may be reproduced or transmitted in any form by any means, electronic or mechanical, including photocopy, recording, or any other information storage and retrieval system, without permission in writing from the publisher.

Requests for permission to make copies of any part of the work should be mailed to: Permissions, Holt, Rinehart and Winston, Inc., 111 Fifth Avenue, New York, New York 10003.

8 9 0 1   032   9 8 7 6 5 4 3 2

Printed in the United States of America

ISBN 0-03-004348-4

Library of Congress Cataloging-in-Publication Data

Shore, Barry.
  Introduction to computer information systems.

  Includes index.
  1. Electronic digital computers.   2. Management information systems.   I. Title.
QA76.5.S495   1987   658.4′038   87-19732
ISBN 0-03-004348-4

Holt, Rinehart and Winston, Inc.
The Dryden Press
Saunders College Publishing

PREFACE

Functionality and end-user computing—these are two frequently heard terms in the computer industry today that provide a shorthand description of important ideas. It isn't good enough for a new computer or a new software product to represent a technological breakthrough. It isn't good enough for it to be faster, more powerful, or even cheaper than its predecessors. It must be functional, and to be functional it must meet the needs of the people who will depend on it—the end-users—and meet those needs more effectively than its competition. If it can't, it won't sell.

The stress on functionality translates into a shift in focus from the technical aspects of hardware and software to their practical applications. This shift, which began in industry, is working its way into the classroom. Courses on information systems are increasingly shifting their focus from technology to applications and end-users, creating a need for a textbook that reflects this trend. This textbook is intended to meet that need.

ABOUT THE TEXTBOOK

Introduction to Computer Information Systems is about the role of computer systems in organizations. It focuses on the transaction systems that support the day-to-day operations of an organization and on the management information and decision support systems that help business professionals plan, organize, and control the organization's activities. It meets the guidelines for the first course in information systems by the Data Processing Management Association (DPMA).

As much as possible, this textbook emphasizes functionality, applications, and the end-user. Several features reflect this emphasis:

■ Basic coverage of hardware and systems software is confined to a single overview chapter (Chapter 2). This chapter provides students with the technical concepts they need to work with computer systems in an organizational setting without burdening them with technical detail they won't use.

■ Microcomputers are discussed throughout the text in a way that stresses their role in integrated systems that serve the business professional. They are *not,* as they are in many other texts, relegated to a separate chapter and treated simply as stand-alone hardware.

■ Chapters 3, "How Computer Information Systems Are Used," 4, "Computers in the Transaction Process," and 5, "Computers in the Decision-Making Process," present an extensive overview of the way in which computers are used in organizations, thus making the argument for functionality early in the book.

■ Vignettes and case studies illustrate concepts from the business professional or end-user's point of view. The vignettes are woven into the text.

- Chapters 6 through 10, which cover word processing, spreadsheets, and database management systems, stress the way these productivity tools are used in organizations.

- The book contains extensive coverage of graphics packages and expert systems and how they are used.

- The chapters on systems analysis (12) and system design (13) stress the involvement of management and other end users in the design of large scale systems. These chapters also provide guidance for end-users who need to develop stand-alone microcomputer applications using productivity software.

In addition to the emphasis on functionality, applications, and the end-user, the key features of *Introduction to Computer Information Systems* include its extensive use of vignettes and cases, its chapter learning aids, and its flexible organization.

VIGNETTES AND CASES

One goal of the end-user orientation of this text is to make the material relevant, interesting, and, I hope, exciting for students. Vignettes and cases are an important tool for achieving that goal.

The vignettes, which are really minicases, are interspersed within every chapter. They provide concrete examples to illustrate the concepts presented in the paragraphs that precede them. Fictionalized accounts based on real situations, they bring life to the text and reinforce learning by demonstrating how important concepts apply to organizations.

The book also includes ten extended cases that appear at the end of Chapters 1, 2, 4, 5, 7, 10, 12, 13, 15 and 17. These cases illustrate the key points of the chapter in a real-world setting. They can be used in several ways: for review of the major concepts of the chapter after the material has been covered in class; to *introduce* the concepts covered in the chapter; to stimulate class discussion; or as written exercises.

LEARNING AIDS

Each chapter contains a number of learning aids to help students master the material. These include:

- *Chapter Objectives*

- A *Chapter Outline*

- *Questions* for review in the middle and at the end of the chapter.

- *Key Terms* in boldface type

- A *Summary* with key terms

- A list of *Key Terms*

- Discussion Questions (called *For Discussion*)

- *Hands-on Projects* that suggest projects for students out of the classroom

FLEXIBLE ORGANIZATION

The text is divided into five parts:

Part One   How Computers Work
Part Two   Computer Information Systems
Part Three   Tools for the Business Professional
Part Four   Designing Information Systems
Part Five   Computers in Society and the Workplace

Although I recommend that Parts One and Two be covered first and in sequence, the remaining parts can be covered in any order. Some instructors might choose to present the systems development concepts in Part Four before the applications software material in Part Three, whereas others might prefer the sequence in the book.

Part One (Chapter 1, "Introduction," and Chapter 2, "How Computer Systems Work: Hardware and Software") provides an overview of information systems and concise coverage of the basic concepts of hardware and systems software.

Part Two (Chapter 3, "How Computer Information Systems Are Used"; Chapter 4, "Computers in the Transaction Process"; and Chapter 5, "Computers in the Decision-Making Process") shifts from the technical aspects of computer information systems to their functionality. In this section students will learn to differentiate systems by the way they are used.

Part Three (Chapter 6, "Office Automation and Word Processing"; Chapter 7, "Spreadsheets"; Chapter 8, "Data Storage and File Processing"; Chapter 9, "Data Management and File Managers"; Chapter 10, "Database Management Systems"; and Chapter 11, "More Productivity Tools") focuses on productivity software. Instructors who teach the use of specific software packages in conjunction with their course will probably want to link their labs with these chapters. However, the text is not tied to any particular type of software, and can be used to teach the concepts of productivity software whether or not a lab accompanies the course. In fact, the material in these chapters goes well beyond the kind of information found in a software manual to show how productivity packages are used in real-world settings.

Data management (Chapters 8, 9, and 10) is treated differently in *Introduction to Computer Information Systems* than in most other texts. First, Chapter 8 introduces the basics of data storage and retrieval. Then Chapter 9 turns to data management and file managers. This chapter illustrates, in a very simple way, the issues in data management. For courses with labs, this chapter would complement exercises with simple file management software such as PFS File® or Perfect Filer®. Finally, Chapter 10 covers database management systems and would complement labs using such DBMS packages as dBase III® and Rbase: 5000®.

Part Four (Chapter 12, "Systems Analysis"; Chapter 13, "Systems Design and Program Development"; Chapter 14, "Data Communication"; and Chapter 15, "Distributed Data Processing") covers systems analysis and design, a topic that has taken on increasing importance with the growing emphasis on end-user computing. Software development tools, fourth-generation languages, local area networks, and micro-mainframe links are making ever greater resources available to end-users and requiring them to understand the system development process to effectively manage their firms' information resources and develop their own applications.

Part Five (Chapter 16, "Computer Crime and System Security"; Chapter 17, "Computers and Society"; and Chapter 18, "Careers in Information Systems") covers such social issues as computer crime, security, privacy, and the effect of computers on employment. These topics raise important ethical questions that anyone responsible for computer resources in an organization should be aware of.

INSTRUCTIONAL SUPPORT PACKAGE

Introduction to Computer Information Systems is accompanied by a complete set of support materials for both instructors and students. These include a student *Study Guide*, a *Computerized Study Guide*, an *Instructor's Manual*, a *Test Bank* available in both printed and computerized form, *Transparency Masters*, and a variety of software packages.

STUDY GUIDE

The *Study Guide*, by Jerry Ralya and myself, contains a variety of resources to help students master the text material and challenge them to extend their grasp over the subject matter of the course. In addition to chapter summaries and a variety of self-testing questions, it contains a section called "Applications" for every chapter that asks students to apply the concepts they have learned.

COMPUTERIZED STUDY GUIDE

The computerized study guide to accompany *Introduction to Computer Information Systems* allows students to take a self test, see how well they did, review the questions they missed, and consult substantial blocks of text about the answers to those questions. Students can also skip the self test and review subjects of their own choosing.

INSTRUCTOR'S MANUAL

The *Instructor's Manual* provides chapter outlines, teaching suggestions, answers to chapter discussion questions, suggestions for using cases in the classroom, and other resources for enhancing classroom presentation.

TEST BANK

The *Test Bank* contains over 2000 questions in a variety of formats, including true/false, multiple-choice, fill-in, and essay. It is available in printed form and on disk for the IBM PC and Apple II family. The computerized form allows you not only to generate tests, but also to edit questions and create your own.

TRANSPARENCY MASTERS

The 125 *Transparency Masters* include both figures from the book and original illustrations. The *Instructor's Manual* suggests when to show each transparency and lists points to make about them.

SOFTWARE PACKAGES

Holt, Rinehart and Winston offers a variety of software packages to accompany this text, ranging from educational versions of popular commercial programs to Joe, a full-powered, full-featured Lotus® 1-2-3® workalike. For details, contact your Holt sales representative.

CASES IN MANAGEMENT INFORMATION SYSTEMS

In addition to the instructional package, described above, that was prepared specifically for *Introduction to Computer Information Systems,* Jerry Ralya and I have written a case book, *Cases in Management Information Systems,* with forty additional cases like the end-of-chapter cases in the textbook. Lotus® templates and a simple general ledger software package accompany the case book.

ACKNOWLEDGMENTS

As with any complex project, this text has benefited from a team approach and frequent "management" reviews. My team included many capable faculty from a wide variety of schools, the staff at Holt, Rinehart and Winston, and the production team at Cobb/Dunlop. Faculty reviewers included the following:

William Baker   Brigham Young University
Richard Bernardin   Cape Cod Community College (MA)
Warren Boe   University of Iowa

Eli Cohen	California State University Sacramento
Hiram Crawford	Olive Harvey College (IL)
Patrick Fenton	West Valley College (CA)
Bernice Folz	College of St. Thomas (MN)
Joyce Hamilton	Henry Ford Community College (MI)
Rod Heisterberg	Austin Community College (TX)
Thomas Ho	Purdue University
Hillary Hosmer	Bentley College (MA)
Peter Irwin	Richland College (TX)
Mo Khan	California State University Long Beach
Jim LaBarre	University of Wisconsin
Koon Lam	Los Angeles Southwest College
Kurt Mikan	University of Montevallo (AL)
Marilyn Moore	Indiana University, Northwest
Leonard Schwab	California State University Hayward
Rod Southworth	Laramie County Community College (WY)
Anthony Verstraete	Pennsylvania State University
Sue Zulauf	Sinclair Community College (OH)

I would like to give special thanks to Leonard Schwab and Anthony Verstraete for their painstaking and detailed reviews.

At Holt, two people especially deserve thanks: David Chodoff, the editor on the project, whose guidance played a significant role in the book's organization and development, and Deborah Moore, whose original vision convinced me to write it in the first place. Paul Nardi at Holt provided valuable advice on the book's design.

Special thanks also to Jerry Ralya and Shelly Langman who both provided invaluable editorial advice and assistance.

Rachel Hockett, of Cobb/Dunlop Publisher Services, kept the complex production process involved in this book running smoothly and efficiently. I would also like to thank Keri Keating for the book's handsome design, and David Weisman for the illustrations.

My family has been especially supportive through this three-year project. Words can't begin to express my appreciation to my wife, Carol, whose optimism and encouragement have been the raw material from which this finished product was created. My loving thanks to my daughters Tonnie and Denise: Tonnie, who, as a student in my classroom, encouraged me to write the book, and Denise, whose dedication as a student helped me too. Special thanks to Elizabeth and George Rubin, who have followed my progress from week to week, and have been an important source of encouragement.

I would also like to thank the University of New Hampshire for providing me the leave that allowed me to write this book.

Barry Shore

BRIEF
CONTENTS

DETAILED
CONTENTS

**PART TWO
COMPUTER INFORMATION SYSTEMS   63**

INTRODUCTION
TO
COMPUTER
INFORMATION
SYSTEMS

HOW COMPUTERS WORK

1
INTRODUCTION

OUTLINE

OBJECTIVES

After studying this chapter you should understand the following:

■ *The importance of information technology to the modern organization.*

■ *Where computer systems are used in organizations, how they are used, and who uses them.*

■ *How computer systems work.*

■ *The distinction among microcomputers, minicomputers, and mainframes.*

■ *How business professionals use computers for word-processing, spreadsheets, and data-management applications.*

In the last 20 years, organizations have undergone sweeping changes. From the board of directors to the first line of professionals, and even to entry-level positions, few people find it possible to escape the consequences of changes in management style, in the domestic and international competitive environment, and in government policies. Small and large organizations have been affected, ranging from manufacturers to service, government, and nonprofit organizations.

Today, products are manufactured in different ways; new and old services are delivered using new techniques; people approach work in a different manner; and decisions are made based on up-to-the-minute information.

Perhaps the greatest change of all is in the role that computer information systems now play in organizations (Figure 1-1). What

Figure 1-1.
The computer has changed the ways that organizations collect, process, store, present, and use information. For example, a sophisticated inventory control system allows a soda manufacturing company to track inventory automatically from the warehouse to final delivery at retail stores, a hospital lab management system keeps track of patient tests and lab records, and a stock exchange's order entry system gives brokers and traders up-to-the-minute information on trades. All such systems provide the vital information managers need to do their jobs.

exactly is a **computer system?** It consists of a computer, all the support equipment necessary to use it, instructions that specify how the computer will perform certain tasks, procedures that people must follow to use the computer, and the people who use the system.

Computer information systems are a particular kind of computer system. A computer information system is a system used to collect, store, process, and present information to support an organization's information needs.

This book is about computer information systems: how they are designed, developed, and used by organizations to operate more efficiently and to help them make better-informed decisions.

Many books in print today focus on these issues. What makes this book different is that it takes the *user's* point of view. It examines and explains computer information systems from the standpoint of the business professional using the systems, rather than from the perspective of the hardware expert, software expert, or computer history devotee. We assume throughout the book that the business professional will be an active rather than a passive user of computer information systems. And because many professionals will interact with their information systems through a microcomputer, this book also pays special attention to the integral role of microcomputers in today's computer information systems (Figure 1-2).

Figure 1-2.
Business professionals often interact with the organization's information system through a microcomputer.

This chapter is an introduction to the text, explaining why computer information systems have become so important, where and how they are used, and how they work.

THE IMPACT OF COMPUTER INFORMATION SYSTEMS ON ORGANIZATIONS

WHAT ARE THE BENEFITS AND COSTS?

Twenty years ago it still would have been possible for an organization and its staff of business professionals to ignore computers. But today such an attitude would be considered organizational suicide. The benefits of computer information systems are so great that if they are ignored, profits will surely suffer. Without a computer, in fact, many companies could even fail.

The range of benefits is wide, generally including one or more of the following categories:

- Higher efficiency.

- Tighter control over operations.

- Lower costs.

- Fewer errors.

- Improved customer service.

- Better planning and organization of operational and distribution activities.

- Better-informed decisions.

- Less reliance on labor-intensive clerical processes.

Some companies use computer information systems to obtain a **strategic advantage** over their competitors. These companies use computers to provide new or improved products or services that would be impossible without the use of computer technology.

But using a computer does not automatically guarantee such benefits. Some applications fail. To ensure that computer information systems are used successfully, they must be well designed, carefully developed, and properly used. Only then can the risk of failure be minimized.

Computer information systems are expensive. Although the cost of computer equipment has dropped dramatically over the years, most organizations are now designing larger and more ambitious systems, and their cost can run into the millions of dollars. Furthermore, once a computer system is purchased, the costs have only begun. Large professional staffs are often required to keep the system running and maintained and to develop new applications. Moreover, in time the hardware will become obsolete, and the instructions that are used to run the computer may need to be changed frequently to meet the organization's changing needs.

WHERE ARE THEY USED?

Computer information systems can be used in every functional area of an organization, including accounting, sales, operations, personnel, distribution, marketing, and finance (Figure 1-3). Within these functional areas, information systems are used to support both routine transaction processes and more complex problem-solving and decision-making processes. Because this is an important distinction, let's look at it a bit more closely.

Transaction Systems **Transaction systems** are those computer systems used to process the routine information flows in an organization. For example, many transaction systems can be found in the accounting function, including general ledger, billing, accounts receivable, accounts payable, and payroll. In fact, these accounting transaction systems are considered to be the backbone of a company's computer information system, and often they are the first segment of a business to be automated. Later, in Chapters 3 and 4, we will learn more about these applications.

Other applications that can be classified as transaction systems include

Figure 1-3.
Computers on the factory floor help keep manufacturing costs low.

Figure 1-4.
Supermarkets use optical scanning systems to speed the checkout process and to update inventory records.

■ A sales-order entry system used by a catalog merchandiser to process telephone and mail orders.

■ A reservation system used by a regional airline to process reservations and billing data.

■ An optical scanning system used by a supermarket chain to process customer orders and update inventory records (Figure 1-4).

These systems share with other transaction systems their support of relatively routine and repetitive procedures.

MIS and DSS   Besides processing routine data flows, computer information systems are also used to help organizations plan, organize, direct, and control their resources. These systems, discussed in Chapters 3 and 5, can be classified as Management Information Systems or Decision Support Systems. They draw on the information provided by transaction systems to perform analyses.

A **Management Information System** (MIS) is an information system that offers the kind of information that business professionals will predictably need to manage the organization and make decisions. A monthly financial statement or production schedule, for example, are the products of an MIS.

A **Decision Support System** (DSS) is an information system that offers the kind of information that may not be predictable, the kind that business professionals may need only once. These systems do not produce regularly scheduled management reports. Instead, they are designed to respond to a wide range of requests that the designers of the computer information system did not find necessary to formalize in the MIS.

Although in the past, Management Information Systems and Decision Support Systems were clearly distinguished, today this distinction in some settings, especially the popular press, has become less clear. So it is not unusual for both of these terms to refer to any system that supports an organization's problem-solving and decision-making activities. In this text, however, the distinctions described above will be followed.

Both MIS and DSS differ from transaction systems in that they are used to help solve problems or make decisions when solving the problem or reaching the decision does not necessarily follow a routine or repetitive sequence of steps. Clearly, computing a person's pay—a transaction process—is different from deciding what products to manufacture next month. Deciding what to produce is never repetitive or routine, as the nature of the problem changes from month to month.

Examples of systems which help business professionals solve problems and make decisions include:

■ A sales information system used by marketing to help allocate advertising dollars.

■ An investment system used by a regional bank to select and monitor its bond portfolio.

■ A staffing system used by a large metropolitan hospital to schedule nurses.

Figure 1-5.
A microcomputer used in the budgeting process. Computers of all sizes are employed in MIS and DSS applications.

■ A system used by a doughnut chain to help identify new locations based on an analysis of regional data.

Such applications may suggest large-scale systems. But as the following two examples suggest, many smaller problems are also solved by computer (Figure 1-5).

IN A TWO-YEAR PROGRAM TO REDUCE PRODUCT REJECT RATES, Ann Shine, a quality-control specialist employed by a large electronics firm, developed an application on her microcomputer to collect and analyze reject data from over 100 manufacturing cost centers. Using these data as the basis for identifying and correcting manufacturing trouble spots, Shine was successful in reducing reject rates from 17 to 12 percent. This reduction helped the company maintain its profit margins despite intense competitive pressure, which saw the price of its product fall 20 percent in just a few months.

IN ANOTHER APPLICATION, Steve Larkin, an accountant for one of the "big eight" accounting firms, takes along his portable computer when visiting clients. For one client, he uses the system to develop short- and intermediate-range plans. For another client, he uses the system to prepare cash budgets. And for a third, he compares the company's performance with that of other firms in the same industry.

WHAT DOES A USER NEED TO KNOW?

There is a big difference between what an airline reservation clerk, who enters a reservation into the computer, needs to know about computer systems and what a business professional, who uses the computer to prepare a budget, needs to know.

Transaction systems are used primarily by clerical personnel, who are usually trained to follow certain clearly defined and limited procedures. They make reservations, enter sales-order data, update inventory records, and post accounting transactions. And as long as they follow standard procedures—all of them anticipated by the system's designers—these clerks need not know much about computer systems.

But business professionals seldom perform strictly clerical tasks. They often use a computer system in more complex situations to solve problems and make decisions. Thus, they must know more about the computer system. For example, a product line manager may need a list of all the West Coast distributors who have exceeded their sales quotas by more than 20 percent. Or a sales representative may need to access the sales budget and compare it with current performance. To obtain

Figure 1-6.
Business professionals must understand how computer systems work because they may often need to use them in unanticipated ways. To the business professional, a computer is a general-purpose tool.

this information from most computer information systems, users would probably not find an existing set of procedures that could routinely give them the information needed. Instead, they would have to understand enough about how the computer system works so that they could phrase their request in a way that the computer could understand. It follows that although transaction users typically use a system for predetermined purposes, professional business users may make requests that have never been made before and probably will never be made again. Business users, then, are likely to use the system in ways unanticipated by its designers (Figure 1-6).

There is another compelling reason that business professionals need to understand how computer information systems work. Earlier in the chapter, we mentioned the risks associated with developing a computer application. One way to minimize such risks is to include in the development process the people who will ultimately use the system. And if business professionals are to be involved, then they must be knowledgeable, active participants in the process.

HOW THESE SYSTEMS WORK

The **computer** itself is an electronic device that accepts inputs, processes these inputs, produces outputs, and stores data. This sequence of activities is also referred to as the **data processing cycle** (Figure 1-7).

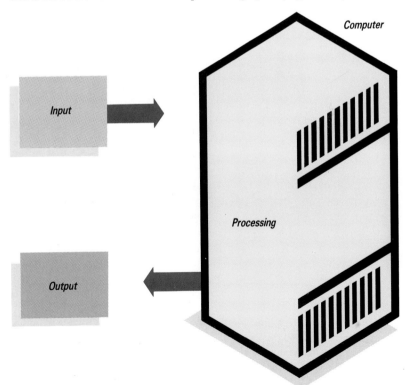

Computer

Input

Processing

Output

Figure 1-7.
The data processing cycle.

COMPUTER INPUT

The data processing cycle begins with data entry. **Data** are the raw facts entered into the computer. Employee names, inventory withdrawals, and sales figures are examples of raw facts or data. For example, in the payroll system illustrated in Figure 1-8, the data entered into the system are employee name, social security number, hourly pay rate, number of dependents, and hours worked.

In a sales-order entry system, the data entered into the system would include the purchaser's name and address, the items purchased, and their prices. And in an airline reservation system, the data entered into the system are the passenger's name, telephone number, flight number, date, flight class, and credit-card number.

Although some data entered into a system are static, other data are dynamic. Static data—such as a person's name and social security number—change infrequently, if at all. But dynamic data—such as the number of hours worked each week—change regularly (Figure 1-8).

Data also differ from information. Data are the raw facts. But **information** is data that have been processed into a useful form. For

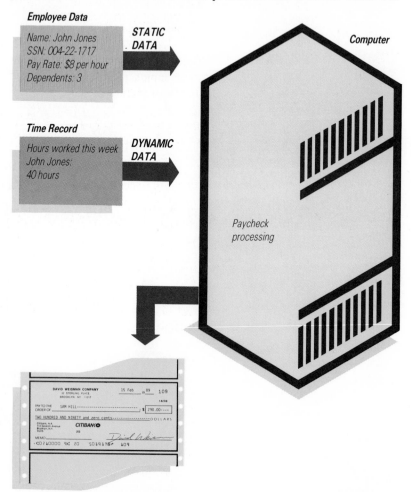

Figure 1-8.
In a payroll system, the input includes static data, such as the hourly rate of pay, and dynamic data, such as the number of hours worked.

example, the 250 exam grades for members of a class might be raw data, whereas the class average would be considered information, as it is data that have been manipulated and put into a more meaningful form.

Data are often entered into the computer through a **keyboard,** a device like a typewriter through which letters, numbers, and symbols can be entered. If you have used an automatic teller machine, then you are familiar with this method of data entry. In these systems, the user enters deposit or withdrawal information by pressing the appropriate keys on the keyboard (Figure 1-9).

COMPUTER OUTPUT

Figure 1-9.
This automatic teller machine uses a keyboard for input and both a display screen and printer for output.

Several methods are used to present output. Most people are familiar with display screens. A **display screen** or **monitor** is the same type of device that is used to display TV pictures. Automatic teller machines and airline reservation systems both rely heavily on them. But in addition, these systems also use printers to prepare "hard copy," a record that can be retained after the screen image fades; for example, automatic teller machines print receipts, and reservation systems print tickets (Figure 1-10).

Figure 1-10.
Printers are often used to provide "hard copy."

PROGRAMS AND SOFTWARE

A computer operates under the direction of a program. A **program** is a set of step-by-step instructions to solve a processing problem in a sequence and format that the computer understands.

Figure 1-11 suggests how a payroll program might be written. Although this example has been greatly simplified for our purposes, it conveys the principle that a program must break down a complex process into a series of simple steps.

If this program is used to process a weekly payroll, then the following sequence of events will take place: First, the program is entered into

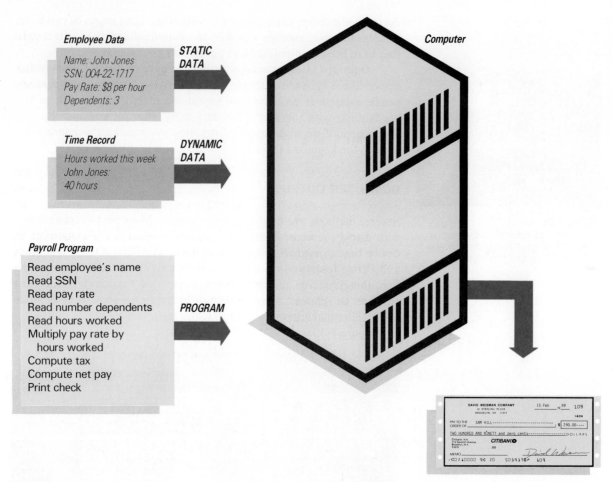

Figure 1-11.
Programs and both static and dynamic data are entered into the CPU. Then the program tells the computer what to do with the data.

the computer. Next the static data, including the employee's number of dependents and pay rate, are entered for the first employee to be paid. Then the dynamic data, including the hours worked, are entered. Next, these data are processed through the program; and finally a paycheck for that employee is printed. The sequence is then repeated for each remaining employee on the payroll.

Although this payroll example used only one program, most applications rely on several. **Software** consists of one or more computer programs, together with related procedures and documentation, that pertain to the operation of a computer information system. A complete payroll software system would then include several programs together with documentation explaining how the system is to be used.

THE CENTRAL PROCESSING UNIT

A computer system's physical equipment is known as the **hardware.** It comprises the computer and all of its associated devices. The computer itself is also called the **central processing unit** or CPU (Figure 1-12). It accepts and stores the program and data in an area called **main memory**

Figure 1-12.
The CPU is where processing takes place.

or **primary storage.** Once the program and data (or enough of them) are stored, the CPU executes, step by step, the instructions specified in the program. These activities are often referred to as **processing.**

Data and programs are stored only temporarily in the CPU. Once the processing has been completed, they are cleared from main memory, which is then ready for the next job.

DATA STORAGE AND RETRIEVAL

The central processing unit stores data and programs only while a job is in progress, but both can be retained on a more permanent basis in **secondary** (or **auxiliary**) **storage.** Although most secondary storage is on disk, some are on tape.

Magnetic tape is a flexible, flat plastic ribbon on which data can be stored using a magnetic process and from which data can be retrieved (Figure 1-13). **Magnetic disk** is a flat, circular platter on which data can be stored using a magnetic process and from which data can be retrieved (Figure 1-14). Tape drives are the devices that record or read the data on tapes, and disk drives record or read the data on disks.

Figure 1-13.
A magnetic tape library.

Figure 1-14.
Magnetic disks with the mechanism used to store and retrieve data.

Once they have been stored on magnetic tape or magnetic disk, data can be either erased or updated. So, if inventory data are stored on disk and if there is an inventory transaction, the balance of the item can be updated. The next time these data are accessed, the updated balance will then be retrieved.

Consider how disk storage would be used in our payroll example. Employee data and the payroll program would be stored on disk. When it was time to run the weekly payroll, both would be read from the disk and entered into the computer's main memory. In addition, the number of hours that each employee had worked during the recent pay period would also be entered. Once all of these data were available to the CPU, the program would be run and the paychecks printed (Figure 1-15).

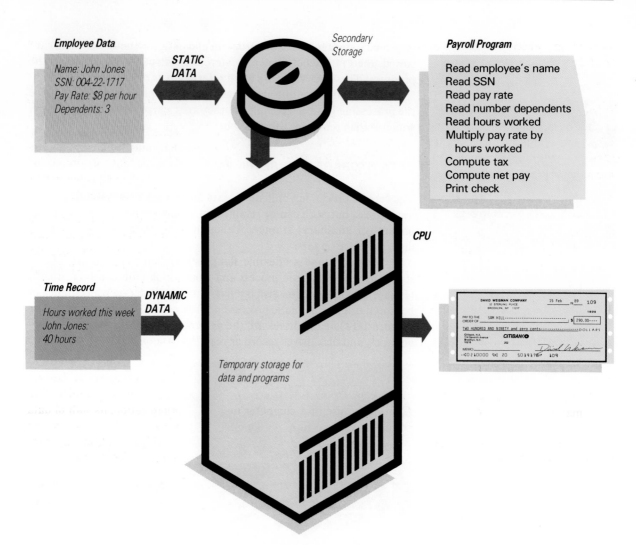

Figure 1-15.
Data and programs can be stored for long periods of time on tape or disk. When they are needed, they can be retrieved and entered into the CPU's temporary memory.

As you can see from the process just described, the benefit of secondary storage is that the payroll program and employee data (static data) need be entered only once and stored on disk. Thereafter, both can be accessed whenever the payroll is run. They will need to be updated only when changes are made in programs or in the static data.

● ●

E N D · U S E R   H I N T S

WHEN SHOULD A COMPUTER INFORMATION SYSTEM BE USED?

No doubt you have heard about people who use the computer at every opportunity. And you have

probably also heard of skeptics who believe that computers are a curse of modern technology, to be avoided at whatever cost. The truth lies somewhere in between.

When to Use the Computer

If one or more of the following conditions is true, the chances are that computer information systems should be considered:

1. The cost of performing the job manually is too high.

2. The data obtained using a manual system would be available too late to be useful.

3. The volume of data to process is so high that any other approach would be unthinkable.

4. The data stored by the computer system can be used to maintain tighter control over a process, an organization, or one's own professional activities.

5. Data from computer-based sources both inside and outside an organization need to be accessed.

6. Data stored in a computer system will improve decision-making and problem-solving processes.

7. It is necessary to communicate with others using a technology known as electronic mail (covered in Chapter 6).

8. The computer information system can be used to achieve a strategic advantage over other firms.

When Not to Use the Computer

Conversely, use of a computer information system may not be appropriate when one or more of the following conditions apply:

1. The time and cost to obtain the data exceed the value of the information.

2. The effort required to maintain the data stored in a computer information system, and keep them up-to-date, is out of proportion with the benefits obtained by users of the system.

3. It would be too costly to obtain the hardware, software, and professional support necessary to develop an application.

4. The way the information would be used, once available, is only vaguely understood.

5. The application is beyond the current capabilities of an organization, its staff of data processing specialists, or the capabilities of contemporary computer technology.

● ●

MAINFRAMES, MINIS, AND MICROS

Computers come in many sizes, but they all accept data, process them through programs, produce output, and store data. They range from large, multiuser mainframe computers down to small, portable computers.

MAINFRAMES

Mainframes have the largest main memories, the fastest processing times, and the capacity to support the largest secondary storage systems (Figure 1-16). As you would expect, they are also the most expensive, often costing several million dollars. These systems are frequently found in large organizations such as banks, insurance companies, manufacturing firms, federal and state agencies, airlines, and universities. The most powerful mainframe computers are known as **supercomputers.**

Figure 1-16.
Mainframes, like this IBM 3090 system, are the largest and fastest computers.

MINICOMPUTERS

Minicomputers (minis) process data more slowly, have smaller main memories, and have less secondary storage capacity than do mainframes. Although they cost less than mainframes do, the price of a complete system still may range from a hundred thousand to several hundred thousand dollars.

Minicomputers are found in both large and medium-sized companies. A large company might use several minicomputers, distributing them among its divisions and linking them with a communication system. A **communication system,** which we will discuss in Chapter 14, provides the necessary hardware and software to permit data to be sent from one geographic location to another. When a communication system is used to connect more than one computer, the result is often referred to as a *distributed system* (the topic of Chapter 15).

MICROCOMPUTERS

Microcomputers (micros or **personal computers)** are small, self-contained computers, which usually contain one or more disk drives for the secondary storage of programs and data (Figure 1-17). The prices of these systems begin at several hundred dollars.

Figure 1-17.
Microcomputers are reasonably priced and can perform many helpful and sophisticated tasks.

Microcomputers can be used singly, on what is called a **stand-alone basis,** or they can be tied together with other computers in a **local area network (LAN),** a type of distributed network serving users in a limited geographic area. Sometimes the local area networks are even linked to minis and mainframes. Networks will be discussed in Chapter 15.

The smallest of the micros are also known as portables, lugables, or laptop computers. Several manufacturers make laptop computers that weigh less than ten pounds and can run on rechargeable batteries. They are especially popular among professionals who are frequently away from their offices but need to keep in touch.

Whether used as a stand-alone computer or linked to others, the microcomputer brings a host of useful tools to the business professional's desk. But regardless of the size of computer used, three types of applications above all have shaped the face of contemporary computing for business professionals: word processing, spreadsheets, and data management. The use of these applications is one focus of this text.

Figure 1-18.
Word-processing systems are simple to learn and improve office productivity.

HOW PROFESSIONALS USE COMPUTERS

WORD PROCESSING

Word processing refers to the use of computer technology to create, edit, store, and print documents (Figure 1-18). Business professionals use word-processing software to write letters and memos, and as a student you will find word processing useful for writing reports and term papers.

To use a word-processing system, you first enter a word-processing software package into the computer. You will then see a blank area of the screen that functions much like a blank piece of paper. When you type words onto the keyboard, they are automatically stored in a temporary storage area. Then, by using codes and commands, you can change words, correct errors, move sentences and paragraphs, and make insertions or deletions. When you finish your document, you can save it on a secondary storage device and then print it (Figure 1-19).

Although word-processing packages vary in how difficult they are to use, most are not hard to learn. Often it takes a few hours of instruction to become familiar with enough commands to begin using the system. Later, you can learn more powerful commands. Once you are comfortable with the word-processing software, you will discover that it not only makes the process of writing easier but that it also improves the

Figure 1-19.
Using word-processing software, documents can be written, edited, saved, and printed.

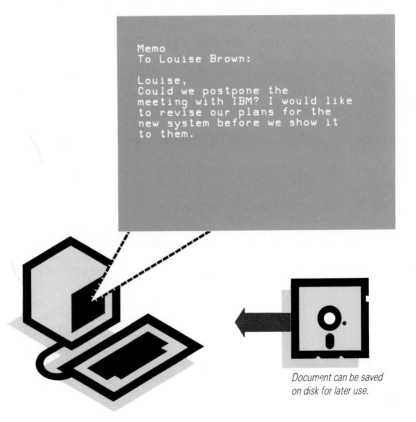

```
Memo
To Louise Brown:

Louise,
Could we postpone the
meeting with IBM? I would like
to revise our plans for the
new system before we show it
to them.
```

*Document can be saved
on disk for later use.*

quality of the finished document, because you can make corrections and changes more easily and use sophisticated typefaces and layouts.

The ability to write better documents, however, is not the only reason that a knowledge of word processing is useful. Word-processing skills are also useful for modern electronic mail systems. **Electronic mail** refers to a system in which documents are instantly transmitted from one user's microcomputer or other input device to one or more other microcomputers or output devices in an organization. In many applications the user prepares a document on a word-processing system and then sends it, by electronic mail, to appropriate staff members throughout the organization.

Word processing therefore is often at the center of the **automated office,** an environment that relies on the computer for many functions that improve productivity in the workplace. In Chapter 6, we will take a closer look at this automated workplace and at word processing.

SPREADSHEETS

Electronic spreadsheets were developed to replace the rows and columns of handwritten data that accountants often prepare when summarizing

Figure 1-20.
Electronic spreadsheets are composed of rows and columns into which labels and numbers are placed. The spreadsheet software can be instructed to perform arithmetic operations on the numbers.

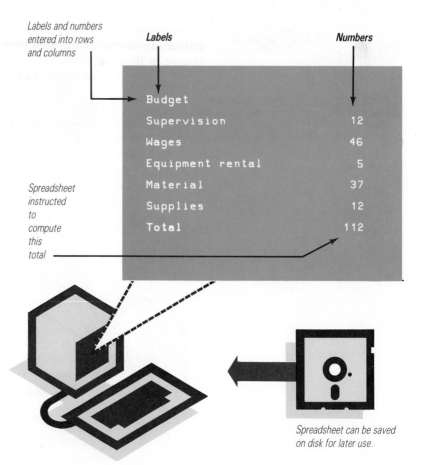

Labels and numbers entered into rows and columns

Labels

Numbers

Spreadsheet instructed to compute this total

Budget	
Supervision	12
Wages	46
Equipment rental	5
Material	37
Supplies	12
Total	112

Spreadsheet can be saved on disk for later use.

and analyzing data. Before spreadsheets, the columns and rows had to be summed by hand, and if errors were made or numbers had to be changed, the recalculations were time-consuming to complete.

But electronic spreadsheets eliminate these problems. An **electronic spreadsheet** is a software package that accepts data in the form of columns and rows and facilitates their manipulation and presentation. With electronic spreadsheets, data are entered through the computer's keyboard; computations are automatically performed; and data are summarized and presented. Time-consuming mathematics becomes a thing of the past.

Figure 1-21.
Some spreadsheet systems allow you to present the results of calculations graphically.

Figure 1-20 illustrates how an electronic spreadsheet is used for budgeting. When the spreadsheet first appears on the screen, it consists of only an empty table with columns and rows. Then, to transform it into a useful budget tool, appropriate labels such as "budget" are entered across the first row. Next, budget categories such as "supervision" and "wages" are entered down the first column. Then the dollar budget estimates are entered down the second column. In the last row, the spreadsheet is instructed to compute the total for all expenses by summing each of the numbers, from supervision to supplies.

After the estimates have been entered, they can be changed, and every value that is derived from them will automatically be recalculated. As a result, the user can easily analyze and compare different versions to see how these changes will affect the results. For example, if the wage estimate in our budget increases from $46 to $55, the user can enter this change in the table. Then the software will automatically recalculate profit. In fact, it is this ability to explore "what if" questions that is considered to be one of the most useful features of spreadsheets.

Once the data have been entered into the spreadsheet, they can be saved on disk and retrieved for use at a later time. Thus, a budget, for example, can be started in one work session, saved at the end, and then retrieved and modified during another session. In addition, spreadsheet software often has graphic capabilities that enable users to print data in the form of bar charts, pie charts, and line graphs. These offer a meaningful representation of the information (Figure 1-21). Because of these and many other features, spreadsheets have become an indispensable tool for analyzing, summarizing, and presenting data.

DATA MANAGEMENT

Perhaps the most common requirement in managing and operating a business's day-to-day activities is for an efficient and accessible system to store, process, and retrieve data. But building and using such a system can be very difficult, and if it is too difficult to build, it probably won't be. And if it has already been built but is too difficult to use, it probably won't be used, either, especially by business professionals.

Data management problems are so central to businesses that software developers have found it very profitable to create programs that simplify the development and use of data storage and retrieval systems.

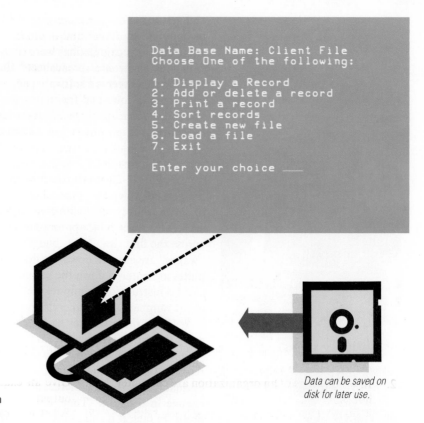

```
Data Base Name: Client File
Choose One of the following:

1. Display a Record
2. Add or delete a record
3. Print a record
4. Sort records
5. Create new file
6. Load a file
7. Exit

Enter your choice ____
```

Data can be saved on disk for later use.

Figure 1-22.
Microcomputers can be used to manage data. Here a user can choose from a menu of data management functions.

These programs are known as **data management systems.** Some microcomputer data management systems make it so easy, in fact, that a new user can design and build a simple but useful system in just a few hours (Figure 1-22).

■■■■■■■■■■■■■■■■■■■■■■■■■■■■■■■■■■■■■■■

AS GEORGE DODGE EXPLAINED, "I never could get the information I needed. So out of frustration, I built my own system." Dodge, a salesperson for an auto parts manufacturer, uses a data management system called a file manager. A **file manager** is a category of software that facilitates the storage and retrieval of data. In less than a week, Dodge learned how to use the software and had his system running. Now at the end of each day, he updates the records of those companies to whom he made a sale. Then at the end of each week, he writes several reports, one summarizing the total sales for each customer and another summarizing the total sales for each product in the line. Dodge is very happy with his system. "Not only do I feel in control," he admitted with a smile, "but with this information I am better able to manage my time, service my customers, and increase my productivity."

■■■■■■■■■■■■■■■■■■■■■■■■■■■■■■■■■■■■■■■

Although in some applications it may be more appropriate for a user to build a microcomputer data management system and to assume all of the responsibility for managing the data, most data management systems are developed and maintained by a professional information system staff. But even in this case, business professionals can usually access the data and transfer or "download" them to their own micro. Then, the data can be analyzed or used in a spreadsheet or for a document created by word-processing software.

Most business professionals interact with the computer system through the word processing, electronic spreadsheet, and data management applications that we have briefly described. Later we will learn how other transaction, MIS, and DSS applications are used in the organization. Taken together, these applications play a significant role in the operation and management of the modern organization. Indeed, it would be incomplete to study business without developing an understanding of how computer systems work and how these applications are used.

? Q U E S T I O N S ?

1. What are some of the ways that computer information systems help an organization?
2. In which areas of an organization are computer information systems used?
3. Are computer information systems used differently by clerks and by business professionals? Explain.
4. What is the data processing cycle?
5. Identify the following as either data or information, and explain your choice.
   a. A list of all employees and their salaries.
   b. A list of all supervisory employees who have successfully completed a company's training program.
   c. The names of all vendors from whom a company purchases parts used in the manufacturing process.
   d. A list of all vendors who supply a particular part.
6. Give an example of both computer input and output.
7. What is a computer program?
8. What is the function of the CPU?
9. How does a computer system store data permanently?
10. Describe the differences among a mainframe, minicomputer, and microcomputer.
11. What is the purpose of word-processing software and how is it used?
12. Compared with using pencil and paper, what advantage does using an electronic spreadsheet have?
13. Is the need for data management systems fairly common or fairly rare?

S U M M A R Y

■ A **computer system** consists of a computer, support equipment, software, procedures, and users.

■ A **computer information system** is a computer system used to collect, store, process, and present information to support an organization's information needs. This book focuses on computer information systems and the way that business professionals work with these systems. Special emphasis is placed on the microcomputer, which many business professionals use to interact with computer information systems.

■ Organizations use computer information systems to increase their efficiency, tighten control, lower costs, reduce errors, improve service, help plan and organize, improve decisions, and automate. Some companies use computer information systems to obtain a **strategic advantage.** Organizations can use computer information systems in all of their functional areas, from accounting to personnel.

■ Clerks, who use **transaction systems,** see computers as special-purpose devices capable of a limited range of repetitive activities. Business professionals, who use **Management Information Systems** and **Decision Support Systems,** see computers as general-purpose devices capable of being used in unanticipated ways.

■ A **computer** is an electronic device that accepts inputs, processes these inputs, produces outputs, and stores data. This sequence of activities is known as the **data processing cycle.**

■ **Data** are the raw facts entered into a computer. **Information** is data that have been processed into a useful form. Data are often entered into a computer through a **keyboard,** and information is often output on a **display screen** or **monitor.**

■ A **program** is a set of step-by-step instructions that tells a computer what to do with the data. **Software** consists of one or more programs together with related procedures and documentation.

■ **Hardware** is a computer system's physical equipment. The computer itself is known as the **central processing unit (CPU).** It accepts programs and data in **main memory** (or **primary storage**) and then proceeds with the **processing,** during which it executes program instructions step by step. When not actually in use, data and programs can be stored in **secondary** (or **auxiliary**) **storage. Magnetic tape** and **magnetic disk** are common secondary storage media.

■ Computers can be ranked by size. **Mainframes** are the largest. The most powerful mainframes are known as **supercomputers. Mini-computers (minis)** are smaller than mainframes; sometimes minis or other computers are linked together through a **communication system. Microcomputers (micros** or **personal computers)** are the smallest type of computer. They can be used singly on a **stand-alone basis** or linked together into **local area networks (LANs).** The smallest microcomputers are laptop computers.

■ Microcomputers bring a host of useful tools to the business professional's desk, including word processing, spreadsheets, and data management.

■ **Word processing** is the use of computer technology to create, edit, store, and print documents. Word processing is often used in connection with **electronic mail** and is prominent in the **automated office.**

■ **Electronic spreadsheets** accept data in the form of columns and rows and facilitate the manipulation and presentation of these data. A useful feature of spreadsheets is their ability to respond to "what if" questions.

■ **Data management systems** are used to store and retrieve data. A **file manager** is one type of data-management system.

K E Y • T E R M S

The following list shows the key terms in the order in which they appear in the chapter.

Computer system (p. 4)
Computer information system
  (p. 4)
Strategic advantage (p. 6)
Transaction system (p. 6)
Management Information System
  (MIS) (p. 7)
Decision Support System (DSS)
  (p. 7)
Computer (p. 9)
Data processing cycle (p. 9)
Data (p. 10)
Information (p. 10)
Keyboard (p. 11)
Display screen or monitor (p. 11)
Program (p. 11)
Software (p. 12)
Hardware (p. 12)
Central processing unit (CPU)
  (p. 12)

Main memory (primary storage)
  (p. 12)
Processing (p. 13)
Secondary (or auxiliary) storage
  (p. 13)
Magnetic tape (p. 13)
Magnetic disk (p. 13)
Mainframe (p. 15)
Supercomputer (p. 15)
Minicomputer (mini) (p. 16)
Communication system (p. 16)
Microcomputer (micro or
  personal computer) (p. 16)
Stand-alone basis (p. 16)
Local area network (LAN) (p. 16)
Word processing (p. 17)
Electronic mail (p. 18)
Automated office (p. 18)
Electronic spreadsheet (p. 19)
Data management system (p. 19)
File manager (p. 20)

F O R   D I S C U S S I O N

1. How have computer information systems affected you?
2. Why is an understanding of how computers work and how they are used so important to business professionals?

3. Why do you think the accounting function is usually the first place in an organization where a computer is used?

4. Some people feel that tools such as word processing, electronic spreadsheets, and data management systems have drawn computer professionals and end-users closer together. Do you agree? Why or why not?

HANDS-ON PROJECTS

1. Describe a computer system with which you are familiar. What data are entered into the system, and what output is made available? Describe the processing steps. Does the system need secondary storage? Explain.
   Suggestions: Supermarket checkout and inventory systems, airline reservation systems, school registration systems, Ticketron.

2. Find a computer magazine or business periodical in your library, and reproduce an advertisement for a micro, mini, or mainframe. Do you think the advertisement describes the machine's features in terms that an end-user can understand? What do you think an end-user wants to know about a computer?
   Suggestions: Computerworld, Business Week, Datamation, PC Week.

3. Interview a business professional, and write a short paragraph describing how that individual uses word-processing, spreadsheets, and data-management systems.

CASE · STUDY

NATIONAL BANK AND TRUST: AN INTRODUCTION TO END-USER COMPUTING

"Tim, do you think we could collect these data sooner and take less time to draw these graphs?"

"It's possible," replied Tim Hudson. "When you get a chance, talk to Harriet Brown in central data processing. She might have some ideas."

Sally Filmore was talking with Tim Hudson. Both work for the National Bank and Trust Company, a large regional bank with over $1 billion in assets. Filmore, a recent business school graduate, was hired by the company to work in the commercial loan department.

One of Filmore's responsibilities is to prepare several loan portfolio reports on the first and third Monday of every month. The information she needs was not available from any one source, and so she has to use several reports, each prepared by central data processing. And it is from these reports that Filmore draws her graphs.

She uses four graphs to illustrate the performance of the bank's loan portfolio. The first graph shows the number of loans that are 30, 60, 90, and over 90 days late (Figure 1-23). The second graph shows the dollar amount that is 30, 60, 90, and over 90 days late (Figure 1-24). Both graphs are used to monitor the bank's exposure to bad or "nonperforming" loans.

In the third graph, the total dollar amount of all loans past due is plotted for each weekly period. Filmore uses this graph to show trends over time. Several weeks ago, in fact, an upward trend in the series became noticeable (Figure 1-25).

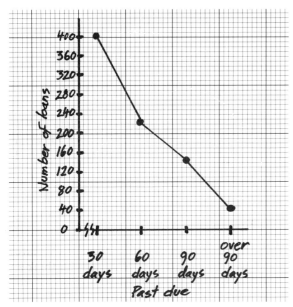

Figure 1-23.
Number of National Bank and Trust loans past due.

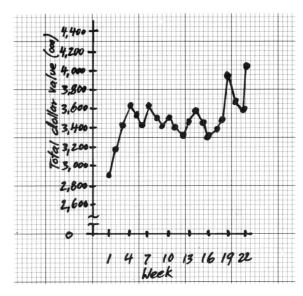

Figure 1-25.
Performance of bad loans over time.

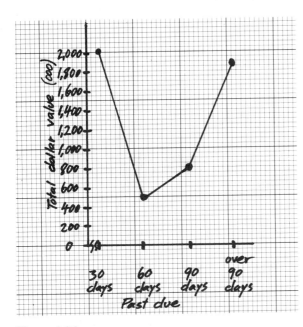

Figure 1-24.
Dollar value of loans past due.

The fourth graph shows the number of loans past due, broken down by the size of the loan (Figure 1-26). From this graph Filmore can determine whether or not the problem loans are limited to a few large loans or many small loans.

As the chart in Figure 1-25 shows, the performance of the bank's loan portfolio is deteriorating. Figure 1-26 suggests that several large loans are past due. Indeed, the bank is now exposed to losses that could be as great as $10 million.

Although the charts that Filmore compiled in the past were helpful in monitoring the portfolio's performance, the graphs were often too late to be useful. The vice-president of corporate loans, for example, felt that if the graphs had been more up-to-date, the bank's current problems could have been recognized earlier, and steps could have been taken to cut the bank's potential losses.

The vice-president had spoken earlier with Filmore, and it was this conversation that prompted her conversation with Hudson.

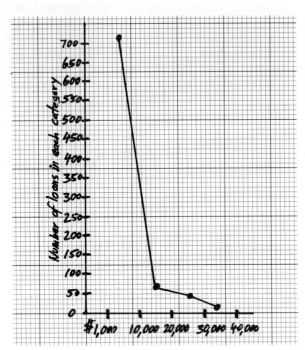

Figure 1-26.
Number of loans past due in each size category.

As Hudson suggested, Filmore walked over to central data processing, where she found Brown working on a credit-card billing project. Brown told her that the changes she was making in the credit-card software were necessary to accommodate the bank's new billing procedures.

After Brown briefly described what she was doing, Filmore explained the urgency of her problem. "Is it possible," asked Filmore, "for the mainframe computer to give me up-to-date graphs directly?"

Brown asked Filmore for some of the details. "Your request seems reasonable to me. The data you need are already in our mainframe. All we have to do is figure out a way to collect the data from the separate sources, combine them, and print the results as a graph."

"The problem, however," continued Brown, "is that we are up to our necks in work. Our backlog is well over a year's worth of work, and most of that backlog includes rush jobs like the one I'm working on now. We have to make these changes for the new credit-card billing system right now, and we have to get it running in the next few months. And then before we make these changes permanent, we have to test them. A project like yours just doesn't have the

same urgency, and I doubt that my manager would give it a very high priority. In fact, there's a good chance we might never get to it."

"What about the new microcomputer center?" asked Filmore. "Do you think they could help me?"

"I've never been over there. Don't have the time. But it's worth a try."

Two days later, Filmore went to the new microcomputer center, located about a mile from her office, in a building that was leased by the bank. Walking through the door into a space that had been at one time a retail store, she immediately detected an entirely different environment from the one at central data processing. She counted at least sixteen microcomputers arranged in small clusters of four units each. Along one wall she noticed a library of computer literature, and at the opposite end a video cassette recorder with a large screen monitor. But instead of computer professionals at these terminals, she saw many familiar faces. One of them was Frank Nahigian's, a classmate of hers in business school and now working in the bank's audit department.

"Frank, what are you doing here?"

"My boss suggested that I learn how to use spreadsheets."

"How did it go?" asked Filmore.

"Better than expected," was the answer. "I even discovered that the microcomputer center has software that allows us to access the bank's central database. With access to the data we need and the ability to load them into one of these spreadsheets, it looks like we'll be able to solve some of our information-processing problems ourselves."

"But don't you rely on central data processing for most of your needs?" asked Filmore.

"Yes, and they will probably continue to meet them, but they have been so tied up with the big number-crunching jobs lately that they just don't have any time for the kind of management-support applications we desperately need. My manager says that we'll just have to learn to use these systems ourselves. He calls it 'end-user computing.' By doing it ourselves, he feels, we'll be more likely to develop applications that meet our needs. And I agree. What about you, Sally? What are you up to?"

"Big crisis. We need loan performance data faster than we can now get them. Central data processing is too busy, so I thought I'd give this place a try."

Before she could explain the details to Nahigian, they were interrupted. "Excuse me, I'm Jeff

Gilbreath, one of the microcomputer consultants. Is there something I can help you with?"

Filmore explained her problem to Gilbreath. He listened carefully, interrupting only to ask a few questions, one of which concerned the type of graphs she needed. In response, Filmore drew sketches of the graphs. After they had been talking for about an hour, Gilbreath had to leave for a meeting. He asked Filmore to return next Wednesday morning at ten o'clock to continue their conversation.

When Filmore returned, Gilbreath had some new information. "Sally, I called central data processing, and they told me that the data you need are already part of our new data management system."

"But how does this do me any good?" she interrupted. "Central data processing made it clear they don't have time to help me."

"Well, the fact that it is on our new data-management system actually does make a big difference in this case. Using our microcomputers and communication software, we can access these centrally stored data ourselves and download them into a spreadsheet on the micro. Once the data are available on the micro, we have software packages that can help process them in any way you like. You can even produce your reports and graphs. And the most important thing here is that you won't have to rely on central data-processing personnel. You can do it yourself. And because you will be the one designing the system, you can change the reports or graphs any time you feel there is a better way. And another advantage is that you can access the database whenever you want. Every day, if necessary. And those graphs will be up-to-the-minute."

"But wait a minute, Jeff. Aren't you forgetting something?"

"What's that?"

"I know almost nothing about computers. Most of what Brown talked about when I went to see her sounded like a foreign language. How can I possibly build my own system?"

"First, you won't be on your own. We're here to help. Nahigian is a good example. He was in your shoes three weeks ago, and now he is well on his way to building a very useful system. Second, new user-friendly computer software really makes the job a lot easier than you think.

"Why don't you spend a few minutes right now getting acquainted with the kinds of computer systems we use," Jeff suggested. "Most people find that this introduction begins to alleviate their fears about computers. Then if you decide to go ahead with the project, I assure you that in a few weeks you will surprise even yourself."

Questions

1. Describe the charts that Filmore prepared twice each month. How does she now obtain the data used to draw the graphs?
2. How would National Bank and Trust benefit if this application is computerized?
3. What is meant by end-user computing, and how does the case suggest that it differs from the centralized computing environment in which Brown is employed?
4. Why couldn't the central data-processing department help Filmore with her problem? Do you think this situation might also be found in other companies?
5. Do you think that the way Filmore would use a microcomputer in this application would differ from the way an inventory clerk or secretary would use a computer? Explain.
6. Describe Filmore's application in terms of the data-processing cycle.
7. Give an example of computer input in Filmore's application.
8. Give an example of output.
9. Are the data that Filmore needs an example of static or dynamic data?
10. What are the roles played by hardware, software, and people in the design of the new system?
11. Would you classify Filmore's application as a transaction-processing system, Management Information System, or Decision Support System?
12. How does this case illustrate that a transaction system is the backbone of an MIS or a DSS?
13. Do you think the conflicts between computer professionals in central information processing departments and end-user groups in the functional business areas are inevitable?
14. There are many who feel that tools such as word-processing, spreadsheets, and database systems have drawn computer professionals and end-users closer together. Does this case suggest that this is true? In general, do you think this is true?
15. Even though several of the professionals in Filmore's department are computer literate, others are not. Do you think computer-literate professionals have an advantage in an organization? Explain.

2
HOW COMPUTER SYSTEMS WORK: HARDWARE AND SOFTWARE

O U T L I N E

O B J E C T I V E S

After studying this chapter you should understand the following:

■ *The way data are represented in a computer and how data are entered into the system.*

■ *How the central processing unit stores data and programs, performs operations, and controls the system.*

■ *The types of secondary storage that computer systems use.*

■ *System software's role in managing a computer system's resources.*

■ *The different options available for presenting output.*

Chapter 1 introduced information processing, how computers work, and how they are used. In this chapter we will take a closer look at how computers work. But this chapter does not take a highly technical or engineer's point of view. Instead, it takes a business professional's view, which recognizes that business users need to know only enough about how computers work to use them properly.

In Chapter 1 we learned that business professionals use computers as a general-purpose tool. This means that they must be prepared to use the computer in unanticipated ways or perhaps even become involved in the design of a new system. As a result, they need to have a general understanding of

- data and data-entry methods.

- how data are stored.

- how the CPU processes data.

- alternative output choices.

These are the topics of this chapter.

Figure 2-1.
Data are the raw facts entered into the computer. Here, data from the stock exchange floor are quickly entered into a computer system, making them available to investors, analysts, and the media.

DATA AND DATA ENTRY

As we stated earlier, **data** are the raw facts that are entered into the computer. They can be a person's name, a withdrawal of funds from a bank account, an airline reservation, the depletion of stock from inventory, or cost estimates in a quarterly budget (Figure 2-1).

The first step in understanding how a computer system works is to learn more about data. We will examine the way that data are viewed and described, how data are represented in a computer system, and the different methods of data entry. First we will discuss the way data are viewed and described.

HIERARCHY OF DATA

A common way to view data is to describe them hierarchically from the smallest data component, called a field, to the largest aggregate form, called a database (these terms will be defined in a moment). This is how we, as humans, think about data.

But this differs from the way that computers view data. Whereas the human or "logical" view of data focuses on the relationships we use to describe data, the computer or "physical" view focuses on how the data are actually stored in the computer system. In some simpler systems there is actually a close correspondence between the logical and physical views: The way that we would describe the data corresponds fairly well to the way that they are stored. In other, more complex systems, however, the data are stored in the computer in a manner that is very different from the way we would describe them. (The "Data Representation" section later in this chapter will give more details about the computer's view.)

Field   In the hierarchy of data, the lowest level is called a field (Figure 2-2). A **field** can include one or more related characters, where a character can be a letter of the alphabet, a number from 0 to 9, or a symbol such as *, +, or −. For example, the catalog part number A1425 has five related characters, and the customer name "Anderson" has eight related characters.

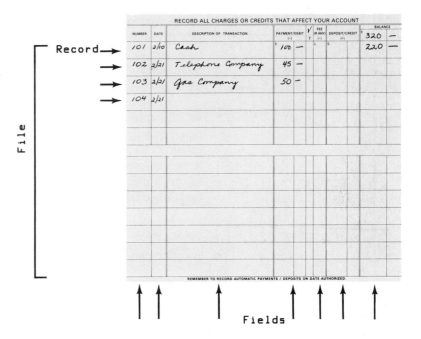

Figure 2-2.
Hierarchy of data in a checkbook.

Not only does a field consist of a collection of related characters, but it also represents the smallest unit of meaningful data in a computer system. Thus the characters "John Smith" are a field of data not only because the characters are related but also because a person's name certainly is meaningful data. The characters "15 Main St." also are a field of data because the field includes both related characters and meaningful data.

Fields are commonly given a name. The field in the first example might be called a NAME field, and that in the second example might be called an ADDRESS field.

Most data systems distinguish among several different types of fields. If the field contains letters, numbers, and symbols, then it is said to be an alphanumeric field. But if the field only contains numbers, it is called a numeric field.

Record   A **record** is a collection of related fields. This is the next step up the hierarchy. An inventory record, for example, might include several related fields, such as the part number, part description, vendor from whom the part was purchased, cost, and current balance. A savings account record might include a person's name, address, telephone number, social security number, account number, and current balance.

File A **file** is a collection of related records. For example, an inventory file would contain a full set of inventory records, and a savings account file would contain a full set of depositor records. Your checkbook and address book would be considered files.

Database At the top of the data hierarchy, a **database** is a collection of all the data stored in one or more files. The database maintained by a manufacturer of catamaran boats, for example, might include inventory, purchasing, production scheduling, personnel, payroll, and accounting data. Together, all of these data comprise the company's database.

In many modern database systems, as will be shown in Chapter 10, an individual record or data item is physically stored in only one location, regardless of how many applications share it. For example, an inventory balance may be physically stored in one location on a disk, but it may be used in purchasing, inventory control, sales-order entry, and finance applications. In the next section, we will explain how this physical storage takes place.

DATA REPRESENTATION

The building block for the physical representation of data in the computer is called a bit. The term **bit** is an abbreviation for "binary digit." There are two binary digits, 0 and 1, which are combined to form representations of binary numbers (such as 1110). This is similar to the way we combine our everyday decimal digits—0, 1, 2, 3, 4, 5, 6, 7, 8, and 9—to form decimal numbers (such as 14). Combinations of binary digits can be used to represent decimal digits.

The binary number system is central to understanding how a computer works. Computers are composed of electronic devices that can be instructed to be in only one of two states. When placed in one state, called the "on" state, the electronic device represents a binary 1. When in the other state, called the "off" state, it represents a binary 0. These binary devices are used throughout a computer system to both store and process data.

The operation of a light bulb can help us understand how these devices store binary digits and how combinations of these digits can then be used to represent decimal digits, letters, and symbols. Light bulbs, like the electronic binary devices, can be only "on" or "off." If a bulb is on, it can represent a binary 1, and if it is off, it can represent a binary 0.

Figure 2-3 shows eight light bulbs, or binary devices, arranged in a single column. Suppose we agree that if the last two bulbs are turned on, they will represent the decimal number 3. In this way we can use a set of

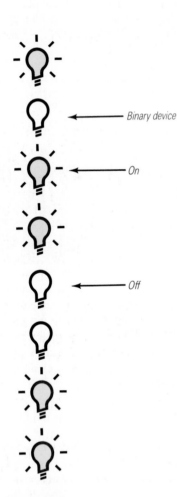

Binary device

On

Off

Figure 2-3.
Eight binary devices are used to store a single letter, number, or special character. The on-off pattern shown here represents storage of the ASCII code (Figure 2-4) for the number 3.

eight binary devices to represent eight bits. These bits are then combined to represent a single decimal digit.

Bits can also be combined to represent data. A **byte** is a group of adjacent bits that represents a decimal digit, a letter, or a symbol. There are usually eight bits in a byte. Consequently, the eight binary devices illustrated in Figure 2-3 can be said to represent one byte of data.

Two standard codes are used to determine which bits to turn on and which to turn off to represent letters, numbers, and symbols. One is called EBCDIC (pronounced "ib-see-dick") and is an acronym for Extended Binary Coded Decimal Interchange Code. The other is called ASCII (pronounced "ask-key") and is an acronym for American Standard Code for Information Interchange. Although most microcomputers use ASCII, mainframe systems may use ASCII or EBCDIC.

As shown in the ASCII table in Figure 2-4, any number or letter, as well as many symbols, can be represented using this code. Returning to our use of light bulbs to illustrate this process, the binary representation of the address 123 Main St. is shown in Figure 2-5.

Character	ASCII Code	Character	ASCII Code
A	11000001	S	11010011
B	11000010	T	11010100
C	11000011	U	11010101
D	11000100	V	11010110
E	11000101	W	11010111
F	11000110	X	11011000
G	11000111	Y	11011001
H	11001000	Z	11011010
I	11001001	0	10110000
J	11001010	1	10110001
K	11001011	2	10110010
L	11001100	3	10110011
M	11001101	4	10110100
N	11001110	5	10110101
O	11001111	6	10110110
P	11010000	7	10110111
Q	11010001	8	10111000
R	11010010	9	10111001

Figure 2-4.
The ASCII code.

Computers, of course, do not use light bulbs to store a bit of information. Instead they use solid-state or magnetic-media technology to store bits. Solid-state devices are employed in the computer's main memory, and magnetic media are used on disk and tapes. Both methods store data in binary form; consequently, computers are often referred to as binary or digital computers.

Now that you have a general idea of how data are represented, we will turn to the way in which they are entered into the machine.

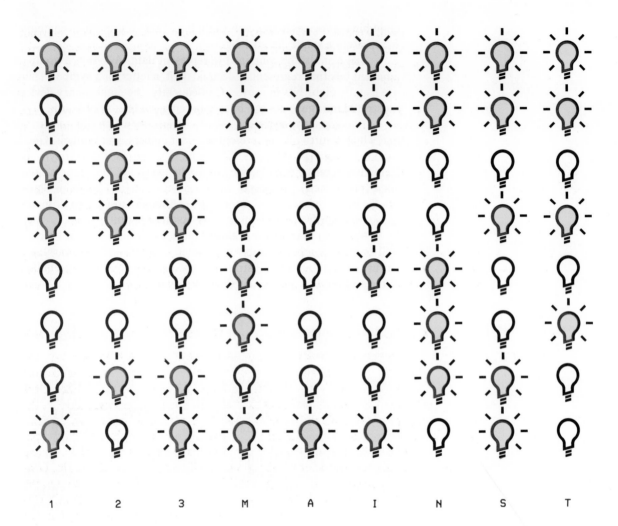

Figure 2-5.
Storage of "123 Main St." represented in ASCII using eight binary devices.

DATA ENTRY

The data processing cycle begins with the entry of data into the computer information system. In fact, the volume of data that some large corporations enter into their systems is so large that data entry represents a significant portion of their information-processing budget. Banks, airlines, hotels, and department stores often enter tens of thousands of transactions in one day.

To maintain control of data entry and data-entry costs requires an understanding of the available alternatives and an awareness of emerging data-entry technology. Several alternatives are described in the following paragraphs.

Punched Cards   Early systems used punch cards—cardboard cards with holes punched in them—to represent data. With this data-entry method, keypunch operators read data from a source document, such as a bill, and punched them into a card using a keypunch machine. A group of cards was then fed into a card reader, and the data contained in the cards were sent to the computer. This approach is very slow and does not allow mistakes to be corrected; instead, the card that contains the error must be destroyed, and a new one made in its place. Punched cards are seldom used today.

Key-to-Disk and Key-to-Tape Systems Key-to-disk and key-to-tape systems are a significant improvement over punched-card technology. In key-to-disk and key-to-tape systems, data are entered through a keyboard and then are held for a short time in a small memory area. During this time the data are checked for errors. If any are found, they are corrected. Once approved, the data are recorded on either magnetic disk or magnetic tape. Then, at periodic intervals, the database is updated with the contents of the disk or tape. In most modern applications, key-to-disk has replaced key-to-tape equipment.

But a major problem with both of these methods is that they rely heavily on data-entry clerks. Although in some applications this labor-intensive activity cannot possibly be avoided, in others it can, as we will see.

■■■■■■■■■■■■■■■■■■■■■■■■■■■■■■■■■■■■■■

THE ROCKINGHAM MUTUAL LIFE INSURANCE COMPANY EMPLOYS 150 DATA-ENTRY CLERKS, most of whose time is devoted to processing monthly premium payments received from policyholders. Each clerk enters the data onto magnetic disk with a key-to-disk device, and at the end of the shift, the data from the disk are entered into the central computing facilities. For almost two years, central data processing has been pressuring the vice-president of finance to include in the data processing budget funds to automate this process. In the last several months, however, data entry has grown into a full-scale crisis. Unemployment in the region from which Rockingham draws its employees is less than 4 percent, and at the wage they are paid—$6.50 per hour—Rockingham has had little luck in attracting new employees. Over 24 positions have yet to be filled, and the uncompleted backlog of work is growing each day. Claudette Wolf, Rockingham's personnel director, asserts that not only is the pay too low, but most people find the job boring. She too is a supporter of the automation project.

■■■■■■■■■■■■■■■■■■■■■■■■■■■■■■■■■■■■■

There is no question that labor-intensive data-entry methods, like those used at Rockingham Mutual, can be inefficient and costly. As a result, more and more organizations are turning to the automated methods described in the following sections.

Magnetic Ink Character Recognition If you look at the bottom of your canceled checks (Figure 2-6), you will find a series of numbers that includes such information as the bank's identification number, your bank account number, the check number, and the check amount. These numbers have been printed with a special ink that contains finely ground particles of a magnetic substance. The technology used to record and

DAVID WEISMAN COMPANY	15 Feb 19 89 109
32 STERLING PLACE	
BROOKLYN, NY 11217	1-8/210

PAY TO THE   SAM HILL------------------------------ $ | 290.00----

TWO HUNDRED AND NINETY and zero cents------------------DOLLARS

Citibank, N.A.   **CITIBANK✛**
114 Seventh Avenue
Brooklyn, N.Y.
11215   202

MEMO_____

⑆⑉0210000 9⑉ 20   5039378⑈ ⑈109

Magnetic Ink Character Recognition ——▶
(MICR) characters

Figure 2-6.
Magnetic ink character recognition is
used on checks to speed their processing.

read data encoded in this way is known as **magnetic ink character recognition (MICR).**

MICR technology represents one approach to **source data automation,** which is the collection of data as near as possible to the time and
place of their origination with minimal human intervention. This saves
labor and cuts down drastically on errors.

With MICR, the only human intervention required is for a clerk to
print the dollar amount on the bottom of the check using a magnetic
character inscriber. After the check amount has been printed, all of the
information contained in the line of magnetic data is automatically read
by a magnetic ink reader and entered into the computer system.

Optical Character Recognition   Although banks rely on MICR technology, other organizations use different methods of source data automation to reduce the need to use clerks during the data-entry process. Many
have turned to **optical character recognition (OCR),** in which data that
have been written by hand or printed by machine are optically read by
input devices.

Three types of OCR involve optical marks, bar coding, and optical
characters. With optical mark technology, the data-entry equipment is
capable of recognizing the presence or absence of a mark. Multiple-
choice tests often use this method. Answers to test questions are marked
with a soft pencil on an answer sheet; the answer sheet is then read by an
optical mark reader; and the results are entered into a computer, which
totals the correct and incorrect answers for the test. Optical mark technology has not found widespread use outside testing, because there are
few applications in which the data entered into a computer are simple
enough to be represented by check marks.

But the use of another familiar OCR technology has exploded in
recent years. Bar code technology is now used in applications from
supermarket checkout to inventory control and mail routing (Figure 2-
7). In this approach a bar code—which consists of identification data in
the form of printed lines of varying thicknesses—is affixed to an item. A
laser-reading device, sometimes called an optical wand, is then used to
read the bars and enter the data directly into the computer system.

Figure 2-7.
The use of bar code technology is rapidly gaining acceptance as one of the
most economical means of data input.

Supermarkets have used this technology for over a decade. They find that it not only speeds customer checkout but also leads to fewer errors. In addition, because the data for every item sold are now accessible, they can be used to update inventory records.

■■■■■■■■■■■■■■■■■■■■■■■■■■■■■■■■■■■

TRUEMED, a distributor of hospital and surgical supplies located in New Orleans, has used bar code technology as a basis for a paperless order-entry system. In this system each of their customers receives a catalog with a bar code next to each item. To place an order, customers scan the items desired with an optical wand and transmit these data by telephone directly to the distributor's mainframe computer. This information is then entered into TrueMed's order-entry system. One of the principal benefits of this system is that it has virtually eliminated most order-entry errors.

■■■■■■■■■■■■■■■■■■■■■■■■■■■■■■■■■■■

Figure 2-8.
With optical character recognition, data can be read and entered into the computer with limited human intervention.

But bar codes cannot be affixed to everything; sometimes it is easier to simply read optical characters using a technique known as character recognition. With character recognition, data are printed in conventional rather than magnetic ink characters. The style of characters used is legible and unambiguous so that machines can read them easily (Figure 2-8). Utility companies often use this approach. The bills they send include a stub with the customer's name, account number, and amount due. This information is printed with optical characters. When the stub is returned with the customer's payment, the information is read by OCR equipment, fed directly into the computer system, and the account is updated.

Sometimes OCR devices can also read handwritten characters. For this to work, the person writing the data must follow certain guidelines in forming the letters and numbers. The post office uses OCR devices to read handwritten addresses on letters. But because the error rate in these systems can be high, the technology has not won widespread acceptance.

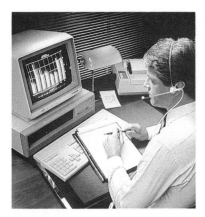

Figure 2-9.
In this voice-input system, the operator can use a limited number of spoken commands to give instructions to the computer.

Voice Input   Voice input is a relatively new and exciting technology. It promises to improve the efficiency of data entry for a wide range of applications, especially those that find other automated means of entry cumbersome, impossible, or too costly (Figure 2-9).

At the present time, voice-input systems generally recognize only a small vocabulary of words, up to several hundred. In addition, most systems must be "trained" to understand their users. To train a system the user enters the words in a normal speaking voice. The computer then "digitizes" the sound of each spoken word and stores the digitized pattern in its memory. When the system is used, it compares the spoken word with the stored patterns. If there is a match, then the word will be recognized. But if the user pronounces the words differently or if another person uses the system, it may recognize few words.

The future for voice input, nevertheless, is promising. Someday it may even be possible to call an airline and place a reservation directly through a computer system capable of understanding your instructions. Such a system—one that need not be trained—is still a few years away. Present-day voice-input technology has already earned its stripes, however, by providing a means for blind and vision-impaired personnel to enter data, send messages, and write programs.

Terminals Many applications, however, cannot rely on key-to-disk, key-to-tape, MICR, OCR, or current voice-input technology. Airline reservation systems and bank automatic teller machines, for example, are applications that still rely on keyboards for data entry. Keyboards are used with microcomputers, minicomputers, and mainframes.

With a microcomputer, the keyboard is either built into the same physical unit with the computer or is located a short distance away, and is almost always the main device used for entering data. Microcomputers also include a display screen or monitor so that the data entered through the keyboard can be checked before they are processed. The screen is also used for output.

Mainframes and minicomputers use terminals for the same purposes. A **display terminal,** or **terminal** for short, is a device used for both entering data via a keyboard and receiving output via a display screen. Unlike microcomputers, terminals are not actual computers designed to perform processing tasks; rather, they are input and output devices linked to a computer that does the processing and that may be in the next room or halfway around the world (Figure 2-10).

In most cases the terminals are located close to the source of the data being entered—in the warehouse for inventory data, in the bank for automatic teller machines, and at the admissions desk for hospital record-keeping systems. Terminals located at the data source are sometimes referred to as *point-of-entry terminals.*

Terminals come in many guises, but all perform the same input and output functions. *Smart terminals* (or *intelligent terminals*) contain some memory and processing circuitry to help perform such tasks as formatting the data being entered; *dumb terminals* contain no such aids.

Figure 2-10.
Many applications rely on the entry of data through remote terminals. Here an inventory clerk enters data on stock depletions into the central computer.

?   **Q U E S T I O N S**   **?**

---

1. What are data? Give an example of some of the data that might be entered into a hospital's medical record system.

2. Describe the differences among a character, field, record, file, and database, and explain where they fit into the data hierarchy.

3. Your school maintains a file of student grade records. Describe the fields that might be included in each record.

4. What is the purpose of the ASCII and EBCDIC codes?

5. How do punched cards represent data? Why do you think they have become obsolete?

6. What is a key-to-disk device?

7. How does a magnetic ink character recognition system work?

8. Give an example of how optical character recognition is used. Why might this be a better method for entering data than key-to-disk technology is?

9. Explain how bar codes are used to input data. Think of some applications for which bar code technology might offer an effective means of data entry.

10. What are the limitations of handwritten character recognition?

11. Are there any problems with current voice-input systems?

12. What is the difference between a smart terminal and a dumb terminal?

CENTRAL PROCESSING UNIT

Programs and data are brought together in the **central processing unit (CPU),** which is the computer itself. Here the instructions specified in the programs are executed. The three main functions of the CPU are to

■ Temporarily store data and programs.

■ Perform arithmetic and logical operations.

■ Control the computer system.

Each of these functions corresponds to a section of the CPU (Figure 2-11). Main memory (or primary storage) accepts and stores the data and programs. The arithmetic/logic unit (ALU) performs arithmetic and logical operations on the data. The control unit controls the computer system. Let's examine these three sections of the CPU more closely.

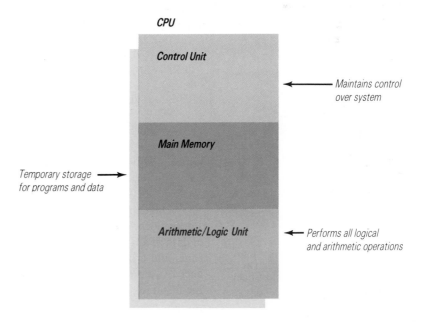

Figure 2-11.
The central processing unit and its functions.

MAIN MEMORY

The purpose of **main memory** (also called **primary storage**) is to provide temporary storage in the CPU itself. This storage serves many needs:

■ It accepts program instructions and data entered through input and secondary storage devices.

■ It acts as a source and destination for intermediate results needed by the arithmetic/logic unit.

■ It holds processed information until it can be sent to output devices.

To perform these varied functions, main memory must have an adequate storage capacity.

Storage Capacity   The storage capacity of smaller computers is measured in "K," or kilobytes, with 1 K (1 kilobyte) representing 1024 bytes. Microcomputers, for example, usually have a storage capacity ranging from 256 K to 640 K. A 512-K computer can store 524,288 characters of data and program instructions in its main memory at any one time. This is equivalent to the length of a short paperback novel.

At the upper extreme, the capacity of large mainframe computers is measured in "M," or megabytes, with a megabyte equal to 1000 K. A large computer, for example, may have from 32 M to 256 M of main memory, enough to store up to five hundred short novels.

Main memory must be large enough to accommodate both program instructions and data. Suppose a microcomputer with 256 K of main memory is to be used for a spreadsheet application. If the spreadsheet itself requires 128 K of main memory, and the data require another 150 K, then the system will be unable to accommodate both at once. A larger system must be used, or the data must be introduced in smaller quantities at a time.

Storage Locations   Data and programs are stored in main memory, and the process by which they are stored is similar to the way in which mail is stored in post office boxes. Each of the post office boxes shown in Figure 2-12 has its own location or address, and this address must be used whenever mail is placed in or removed from a box. Similarly, data and programs stored in main memory are placed into and removed from their respective storage locations or addresses. Each location, depending on the system, may store one character or several characters. To store or retrieve data, the correct address in main memory must be known.

One way to measure a computer's capability is by the size of each storage location. A 16-bit machine is able to store and process two bytes of data at a time. A 32-bit machine can store and process four bytes at a time, and a 64-bit machine is able to store and process eight bytes at once. As a rule, the more bits that can be stored and processed at a time, the faster and more powerful the machine is.

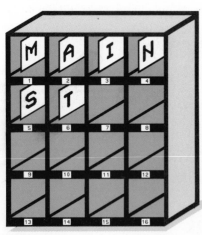

Figure 2-12.
Numbered storage locations in main memory can be conceptualized as post office boxes used to store data and programs.

Figure 2-13.
Microminiaturized integrated circuits contained on silicon chips are used for storage devices in most of today's computers.

Storage Devices　The storage locations in most modern computers are located in a miniature integrated circuit (IC), such as the one shown in Figure 2-13. These devices are made of silicon chips and store data in areas called bit cells. When an electrical current is passed through a bit cell, the cell is placed in the "on" state, and when no current is present, the cell is in the "off" state. So, by controlling the current that flows through eight bit cells, one character can be stored.

When the bit cells in main memory can be addressed, changed, and accessed, the memory is referred to as **random access memory,** or RAM. Sometimes RAM is also called *read and write memory*.

Although the larger part of memory in most systems is made up of RAM, some computers permanently store programs in main memory. These programs can only be read and cannot be changed or erased. Memory used in this way is known as **read only memory,** or ROM. Programs contained on ROM are often referred to as *firmware* (rather than software). Laptop computers, for example, often store word-processing programs in ROM. The benefits of ROM storage are that the software is always available when needed and cannot be changed or destroyed by the user. The disadvantage, however, is that this space is not available for other applications.

ARITHMETIC/LOGIC UNIT

The function of the **arithmetic/logic unit** (ALU) is to carry out the instructions specified within a program. The ALU does the actual computing from which computers derive their name. But the ALU can only add, subtract, multiply, divide, and compare. Programs therefore must be written in such a way that complex processing tasks are broken into simple sequences that rely only on these mathematical and logical operations. These restrictions are part of what makes the job of programming a challenging one.

For example, one employee credit union, associated with a large manufacturer of household appliances, uses software that includes a program that can locate a particular member's record and add a deposited amount to the balance. Several programming steps in this process involve the ALU. First, the ALU *compares* the member's name with each record in the file until it finds the correct one. Second, the ALU *adds* the deposited amount to the old balance. Although this example is greatly simplified, it illustrates two typical ALU functions: comparison and addition.

CONTROL UNIT

The **control unit** is responsible for exercising control over the CPU. Like the control tower at a busy airport, a computer's control unit must coordinate all of the demands made on the functions that the system performs.

In response to the program's instructions, the control unit may cause a number of actions to take place in the computer, such as

Routing of data to appropriate locations in main memory.

■ Entry of programs into main memory locations.

■ Sequential access of programming steps from main memory and the initiation of the appropriate functions in the CPU.

■ Transfer of data from main memory to the arithmetic/logic unit when the program requires arithmetic or logical steps to be executed.

■ Temporary storage of the results from the arithmetic/logic unit in main memory locations.

■ Response to a program's request for output by finding the data in the appropriate memory locations and sending the data to the correct output device.

SECONDARY STORAGE

Main memory is relatively expensive and therefore not available in unlimited quantity. In addition, it is "volatile"—that is, data and programs can be stored in memory only as long as the proper electrical currents are supplied to the storage devices. If the current should be interrupted, the data will be instantly lost. Many people discover this when the plug is accidentally pulled from their microcomputer!

Because of the expense and volatility of main memory, data and programs are kept in **secondary** (or **auxiliary**) **storage** when not in use. There are several different kinds of secondary storage media. Three of the most common are magnetic disk, magnetic tape, and optical disk.

MAGNETIC DISK STORAGE

Magnetic disk is the most widely used secondary storage medium. Magnetic disk is a flat, circular platter on which data can be stored using a magnetic process and from which data can be retrieved. Two types of magnetic disks are hard and floppy disks. A hard or rigid disk has a stiff aluminum base on which a magnetic medium has been deposited. This medium is composed of metallic oxide particles that align themselves in one direction to represent a binary 0 and in another direction to represent a binary 1. Data on these disks are stored on concentric "tracks." As the disk rotates, a read/write head moves in and out, either reading from or writing to particular tracks (Figure 2-14).

The second type of magnetic disk is a floppy or flexible disk. These disks are made from a pliable mylar plastic and are most commonly used in microcomputer systems (Figure 2-15). The advantage of floppy disks is that a user can accumulate an extensive library of them. When a particular program and data combination are needed, the appropriate disks can be inserted into the computer's disk drives. A disadvantage, however, is that floppy disks have a smaller storage capacity than do hard disks, thus making it necessary to store large databases or programs on several floppy disks. And retrieving data is much slower from floppy disks than from hard disks.

Figure 2-14.
Hard disks store programs and data in a binary format. Storage is on concentric tracks that are read, as the disk rotates, by a read/write mechanism.

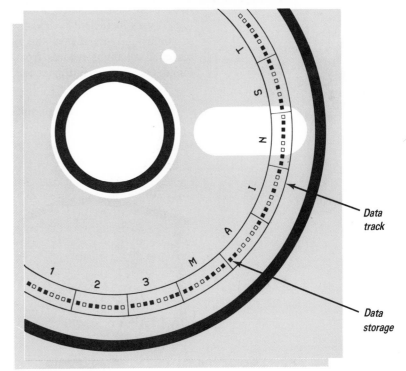

Figure 2-15.
Floppy disks usually consist of a mylar disk with a magnetic surface encased in a protective sleeve. Data are recorded as magnetic spots on concentric tracks. Reading and writing are done through the small oval opening.

The major advantage of magnetic disk technology is that the data stored on either hard or floppy disks can be accessed directly. This is known as **direct access.** It is similar to the way in which the arm of a turntable in your stereo music system can be lifted and moved to any cut on a record: Those cuts that the listener chooses not to play can be skipped. So, if a bank uses disk technology to store depositor data, it is not necessary to proceed through every account in the file before a particular account is updated. The system can be instructed to proceed directly to the right account.

MAGNETIC TAPE STORAGE

Although its use has fallen sharply, earlier computer information systems relied heavily on magnetic tape for secondary storage. **Magnetic tape** is a flexible, flat plastic ribbon on which data can be stored using a magnetic process and from which data can be retrieved. Magnetic tape is contained in either a large reel or a smaller cartridge or cassette. It is coated with metal oxide particles that can be arranged, through the recording process, to represent binary digits. Figure 2-16 shows eight spots on the tape, arranged across the width of the tape. These spots are used to store one byte of data.

Tape has several advantages. It is cheaper than disk storage; large databases can be stored in less space; and tapes can often be loaded onto tape drives more conveniently than disks can be loaded onto disk drives. But magnetic tape has a major shortcoming: Data can be accessed only sequentially. Using **sequential access** to reach a particular record, all of the records that precede it must first be processed. Sequential access thus is very inefficient for most applications. Imagine calling an airline to confirm a reservation and waiting while its tape storage system searched all flight records from the beginning until your record was found. Or imagine waiting at an automatic teller machine while a tape is

Figure 2-16.
Data and programs can be stored on magnetic tape. Each column shown here stores one byte of data.

Storage of one byte in each column

Figure 2-17.
Optical disks are a recent development in storage technology.

searched for your deposit record. Clearly, competitive pressures would prevent airlines or banks from using such slow and inefficient methods. Instead, time-critical applications rely on disk storage methods, which provide direct access to a record.

Does this mean that magnetic tape has little use as a secondary storage medium? Absolutely not. In systems with enormous quantities of data, tape is preferred because disk storage would be prohibitively expensive. Magnetic tape is also used to maintain inexpensive backup copies of data contained on disk storage.

OPTICAL DISKS

Optical disk technology is relatively new and holds the promise of increasing the capacity of disk storage well beyond what is possible with magnetic disks (Figure 2-17). Data are stored in microscopic patterns and are read by reflecting light off the disk's surface. Some optical disks are prerecorded with data and cannot be erased or rewritten; compact stereo disks are an example. On other optical disks the user can record data just once but can read them countless times; these disks are called "read-only-write-once" disks. Still other optical disks, only recently available, can be erased and can therefore be used like a magnetic disk.

?   **Q U E S T I O N S**   **?**

---

1. Explain the role, use, and limitations of main memory.
2. How is the storage capacity of main memory measured?
3. How does ROM differ from RAM?
4. What are the functions of the arithmetic/logic unit? How would it be used to find all students whose grade point average is above 3.0?
5. What function does the control unit perform?

6. Why are data and programs kept in secondary storage when not in use?
7. Explain how data are stored on magnetic disk.
8. Explain how data are stored on magnetic tape.
9. Compare the advantages and disadvantages of magnetic tape and disk storage.
10. How does optical disk storage compare with magnetic tape and disk storage?

SYSTEM SOFTWARE

Two major categories of software are used in a computer system: application software and system software.

Application software consists of programs that direct the computer to perform user-related tasks. In business, application software specifies how computers process a payroll, update accounting records, or make a reservation.

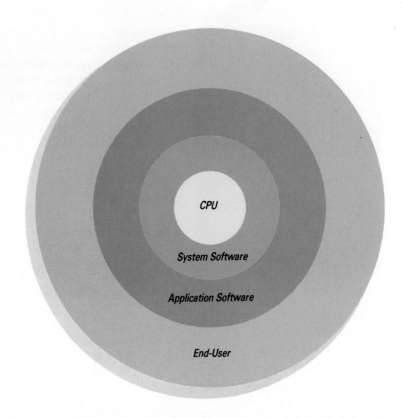

Figure 2-18.
System software acts as the intermediary between the CPU and the application software. Together, both categories of software comprise the interface between the CPU and the end-user.

System software is a collection of programs that manages the equipment resources of the computer system and provides supporting functions for application programs. It can be visualized as an intermediate level of software existing between the application software and the CPU (Figure 2-18).

System software can be divided into three categories: (1) the operating system, (2) language translators, and (3) utility programs. The operating system manages the resources of the computer system. The language translators convert programming instructions into a language that the machine can understand. And utility programs perform tasks commonly needed by many programs during the processing of data.

OPERATING SYSTEM

An **operating system** manages and coordinates the functions performed by the computer hardware, including the CPU, input/output units, secondary storage devices, and communication and network equipment. The operating system software must keep track of each hardware resource, determine who gets what, determine when the user will have access to the resource, allocate how much of the resource the user will be given, and terminate access at the end of the use period.

Operating systems vary in complexity from those that support single-user microcomputers to those that handle multiple-user mainframes. Their complexity depends on the computer system's size and scope, together with the type of performance provided to its users. A single stand-alone microcomputer will have a relatively simple operating system, whereas a mainframe that supports hundreds of users accessing the system simultaneously will have one that is far more complex.

Even the most simple operating system in a mini or mainframe performs a number of resource management tasks or functions. These functions include job management, batch processing, on-line processing, data management, virtual storage, and input/output management. Let's take a brief look at each.

Job Management   Job management software manages the jobs waiting to be processed. It recognizes the jobs, identifies their priorities, determines whether the appropriate main memory and secondary storage capacity they require is available, and schedules and finally runs each job at the appropriate moment.

Batch Processing   System software is available to support different methods of processing a job. With **batch processing,** the most basic method, data are accumulated and processed in groups. Payroll, for example, is often processed this way. Once every week, hourly records are grouped and the payroll software is run. Most microcomputer users are doing batch processing, whether or not they are aware of it.

Figure 2-19.
In this on-line application, the code for a product is entered into point-of-sale terminals; the central computer is accessed; and the current price is returned to the terminal's screen. In addition, the central inventory records are updated to reflect the sale of the item. All of this occurs in a matter of seconds.

On-Line Processing   A more sophisticated way to process jobs is called **on-line processing** (Figure 2-19). In this approach data are processed instantaneously. For example, a salesperson may need to find out whether a particular item requested by a customer is in stock for immediate shipment. Using an on-line system, the request for information will be instantly acknowledged by the on-line software, and the appropriate steps will be taken to access the central database on disk and return the requested information to the terminal from which the request was made. All of these steps take less than a few seconds, at most.

Most on-line operating systems also support multiuser and multitasking access. In multiuser access, many users can share the same computer simultaneously, whereas in multitasking, these users can be performing different tasks. In an on-line, multiuser, multitasking system, then, we might find an inventory clerk retrieving inventory data, a sales-order entry clerk entering the data for a sale, and an accountant entering accounting data. It is the responsibility of on-line system software to see that these requests are accommodated quickly and do not interfere with one another.

■ ■

WHEN URBAN CHIC, a clothing designer and manufacturer, was selecting a new computer, it decided to upgrade from a batch system, which it was currently using, to an on-line system. The sales staff was especially enthusiastic about the new on-line system's ability to keep them directly in touch with inventory levels. With the old system, inventory reports were always out of date, and the sales staff never did know exactly what was in or out of stock. And customers were often sold goods that never were delivered. With the new system, however, salespersons would be able to tell a customer how many of a style were in stock as well as how many of each size and color. George Rubin, a veteran salesman with 20 years' experience, was sure that the new system would give him an advantage over the competition. At the very least, he said, it would make fewer enemies of the firm's customers.

■■■■■■■■■■■■■■■■■■■■■■■■■■■■■■■■■■

Data Management   In the process of managing the resources of the computer system, operating system software also manages the storage and retrieval of data. Because the system software handles many of the details associated with this process, such details are not a primary concern for users or programmers writing application programs.

Virtual Storage   The operating system also manages the allocation of main memory to specific jobs. Some operating systems have a feature called *virtual storage.* With this software it is possible to increase the capacity of main memory without actually increasing its size. This is accomplished by breaking a job into sequences of instructions, called *pages* or *segments,* and keeping only a few of these in main memory at a time; the remainder are kept on secondary storage. As a result, relatively large jobs can be processed by a CPU that in fact contains a relatively small memory.

Input/Output Management   Operating systems also manage the input to and output from a computer system. This applies to the flow of data among computers, terminals, and other devices such as printers. Application programs use the operating system extensively to handle input and output devices as needed.

LANGUAGE TRANSLATORS

At the beginning of this chapter we stated that data are stored in the computer in binary format. It should therefore come as no surprise to learn that data are also processed by the arithmetic/logic unit in binary format. Fortunately, however, programs need not be written in binary format. In fact, application programs are written in English-like programming languages. But this means that these English-like programming languages have to be translated into a language the computer can understand.

An application programming language is translated into a machine language through a language translator. One such language translator, illustrated in Figure 2-20, is called a compiler. A **compiler** translates an entire program before it is executed. Another type of language translator, an **interpreter,** executes each statement of a program as it is translated.

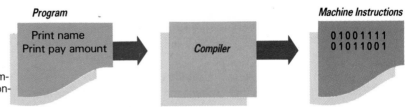

Figure 2-20.
A compiler is one of the software components of an operating system. It converts English-like programs into machine-usable instructions.

UTILITY PROGRAMS

The system software also includes **utility programs,** which perform frequently required tasks in a computer system. In a microcomputer operating system, for example, utility programs copy the contents of one disk to another and format a new disk so that it has the correct structure to store data. In large computer systems, utility programs sort data according to user-specified criteria, merge files, and copy data from disk to tape.

● ●

E N D · U S E R   H I N T S

WHAT TO LOOK FOR WHEN CHOOSING END-USER SOFTWARE

Although the involvement of end-users in selecting or designing the software used in large-scale applications, such as payroll or accounting, will often be limited, their involvement in selecting the software that they will actually use will be more direct. End-users will often become involved in the evaluation and selection of such categories of software as

■ Word processing

■ Electronic spreadsheets

■ Data management

Since there are several hundred different commercial software packages to choose from, it may be necessary to compare a fair number of programs before making a final selection. Several factors influence this choice:

■ Functionality

■ Compatibility

■ Cost

■ Usability

Functionality
Before you can begin to select software, you must be able to specify what it is the software needs to do. For example, if you need to write several hundred letters, each containing the name and address of a customer, then it would be important for the word-processing program to be able to automatically obtain names and addresses from a mailing list. Or if you need to obtain a graphic illustration of the data in a spreadsheet application, then the software must have this feature.

The next step is to identify several software alternatives, and to determine whether or not they can perform these functions. This can be done by referring to the software firm's promotional literature, consulting a current user of the software, or arranging a demonstration. Demonstrations are preferable—they make it possible to test the exact use to which the software would be put.

Compatibility
In large organizations, an overriding consideration in the choice of a software package will often be its compatibility with other packages already in use in the organization. This is especially important when data may be exchanged between users. It is usually difficult, if not altogether impossible, for most users to exchange data between com-

puters and software that are not compatible, if not identical.

Cost

Cost is a consideration in a few applications, but it is seldom the overriding consideration. Software costs are often in the range of $100 to $500, and the other costs—including the end-user's time—often overwhelm the direct cost of the software. Sometimes, however, these "other costs" are ignored. They shouldn't be.

Usability

Since most end-users in a business environment are business professionals rather than computer professionals, it is important for the software to be easy to use. Software that is easy to use is referred to as "user-friendly." To be user-friendly, the software must lead the user through every step in a simple, direct, and easy-to-follow manner. In addition, the software must be accompanied by a manual that provides clear instructions.

Above all, good end-user software should not need lengthy study before users can put it to work.

OUTPUT HARDWARE

Computer output can take many different forms. At a travel agency a printer writes an airline ticket; at a supermarket an electronic cash register prints a sales receipt; in a marketing department a terminal displays a sales graph in color; and in a secretary's office a word processor prints a letter.

In general, there are three types of output: (1) printed or hard-copy output, (2) display output, and (3) voice output. We will consider each in the next sections.

PRINTED OUTPUT

Printers are devices for producing permanent output on paper. Such output is sometimes referred to as *hard copy;* it includes reports, address lists, tickets, checks, maps, charts, and anything else that can be placed on paper. Printers can be classified according to the printing speed, the quality of output produced, and the printing method.

The printing speed varies widely. As with a person typing on a keyboard, serial printers can print only one character at a time. There are also line printers, which can print all the characters of a line as a unit. Serial printers can print as fast as 900 characters per second, and some line printers can pass speeds of 4000 lines per minute. At the latter rate, a short book could be printed in three minutes. Fast enough? Not necessarily, for high-volume applications. The very fastest printers, page printers, can attain speeds of over 40,000 lines per minute.

The quality of the work that printers produce can be classified as either draft quality or letter quality (Figure 2-21). Draft quality represents the output that would be acceptable for internal memos and some letters. Letter quality, on the other hand, is appropriate for typed correspondence sent outside the company.

Printers use several different methods for printing. Impact printers work like a typewriter. Letters are formed by bringing a type element

```
Draft-quality printing
```

letter-quality printing

Figure 2-21.
An example of draft-quality and letter-quality printing.

into contact with the paper. Nonimpact printers work without any physical contact or impact between the printer and paper. They use thermal, chemical, electrostatic, and ink-jet technologies. In the next two sections we will examine the types of impact and nonimpact printers available today.

Impact Printers   There are four main types of impact printers: dot-matrix, daisy-wheel, chain/train, and band printers. The printing mechanism in a **dot-matrix printer** uses a movable print head that encases a set of wires. When each wire is activated, the end of the wire presses against the ribbon and prints a small dot. Combinations of dots are used to represent characters (Figure 2-22).

Figure 2-22.
Dot-matrix printer and print element.

Printers using this technology are relatively slow, as they print only one character at a time. Although the quality is generally in the draft category, some dot-matrix printers are capable of printing very high quality characters by overstriking and packing the dots closely together. This technique, however, slows the printing process even more. Despite their better quality, the edges of the letters formed by many dot-matrix printers are still fuzzy and do not compare with the quality of the letters formed by printers using other technologies.

Daisy-wheel printers use a removable wheel that has a raised letter on the end of each spoke (Figure 2-23). To print a particular letter, the wheel rotates to the appropriate position and a hammer strikes the letter. Because the letter on the end of the spoke is engraved, the resulting image deposited on the paper is a solid one; hence daisy-wheel printers produce letter-quality results. Although daisy-wheel printers produce significantly higher quality output than do dot-matrix printers, their speed is considerably slower.

Figure 2-23.
Daisy-wheel printers use a removable wheel on which the letters are embossed. A hammer strikes the letter and leaves the image on the paper.

In general, dot-matrix and daisy-wheel printers are used when the volume of printed output is low. Now let's turn to the faster machines.

In a chain/train printer, the characters are connected to a chain that revolves at very high speed in front of the paper (Figure 2-24). When the appropriate letter passes by, the hammer is released, strikes the letter, and prints the image on the paper. Hammers are located at each possible print position across the width of a page, and as a result, letters can be rapidly printed as a group.

A band printer operates like a chain printer, but the characters are on a rotating metal belt or band. These machines are often used in small and medium-sized computer installations.

Nonimpact Printers   Nonimpact printers do not strike the paper in order to form characters. The two main categories are ink-jet printers and laser printers.

An ink-jet printer uses nozzles that spray liquid ink on a page. These printers produce very high quality output at top speed. Some ink-jet printers can produce output in several different colors and can be used to reproduce a color graphics display from a screen.

Figure 2-24.
Chain/train printers can handle large volumes of output at relatively high speeds.

Laser printers are a recent development in printing technology. Laser printers convert information into a beam of light that is then used to create characters on a drum. The characters are then treated with a "toner" and transferred to paper. This process is similar to that used by copy machines. It can also produce graphical output. Laser printers produce exceptionally high quality printing. In fact, the output is close to the quality obtained with a professional printing job. As a result, laser printing has brought professional printing capabilities to the user of nearly every computer system (Figure 2-25).

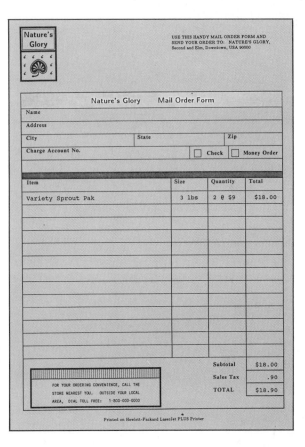

Figure 2-25.
Laser printers produce professional-quality printing. The ability to produce forms like the one shown here eliminates the need—and the cost—of ordering them from a professional printer.

Plotters Some of the printers we have mentioned can produce graphical output in addition to letters and numbers. High-speed laser printers, for example, can produce the forms for a particular application right along with the data that fill out the forms. Inexpensive dot-matrix printers are available for use with microcomputers that can produce colorful charts and graphs.

In addition to printers that handle graphics, plotters are available. **Plotters** are devices that produce hard-copy graphical output. These devices vary in the technique they employ and in the quality of their output. One common variety uses mechanically directed pens to draw on a paper that lies flat in a frame; another type draws on paper that rotates around a cylinder. The resulting sales projection, engineering design, or weather map can approach the quality produced by a professional graphic artist.

DISPLAY OUTPUT

Figure 2-26.
Graphic output is usually easier to interpret than is text output.

In addition to hard-copy output, a significant share of the output produced by a computer system appears visually on the display screen (or monitor) of a microcomputer or of a display terminal. Usually, in fact, the same screen is used for input and output, but there is a basic conceptual difference between input and output. The input process often collects only raw facts from the environment. This is a straightforward process. But the purpose of producing output is to communicate information as effectively as possible. Sometimes this can best be done graphically—for which display terminals (along with plotters and some of the printers mentioned earlier) are ideally suited (Figure 2-26).

Some computers include windowing/multitasking software as part of their operating system. This software permits the screen to be divided or split into sections (Figure 2-27). Different application software can be run by the user simultaneously (multitasking), and the results of each are displayed on the split screen (**windowing**). Using word-processing software, for example, text can be displayed on one section of the screen; using spreadsheet software, a table can be displayed on another section; and a memo combining the text and data can be displayed on a third section of the screen.

VOICE OUTPUT

Figure 2-27.
With windowing, different application software can be run at the same time, and the outputs will be visible on a split screen.

In some situations it is effective to use **voice output.** This is true, for example, for blind and vision-impaired persons or for persons who must gain access to data over nonvisual media (such as a telephone). Unlike the problem of voice input—where it is difficult for machines to understand more than a limited vocabulary, voice output is relatively simple.

In voice-output systems, the user hears synthesized speech over headphones, a loudspeaker, or the telephone. Telephone companies use voice output for directory assistance requests, and some banks use voice output to give depositors their bank balances over the telephone.

EQUITY FUNDS, a large financial services company, gives by telephone the most recent yields on several of its mutual funds. The caller simply dials the company's number using touch-tone equipment and, when the line is answered, enters the appropriate code to identify the mutual fund of interest. A synthesized voice then promptly responds with the current yield.

? Q U E S T I O N S ?

1. What is the difference between system software and application software?
2. Describe the function of an operating system.
3. What are the benefits of on-line processing?
4. Suppose a program requires at least 2 megabytes of main memory, but the computer has only 1 megabyte available. What operating system feature would help solve this problem?
5. What is the function of a language translator?
6. What are the three general categories of output?

7. What is the difference among a serial printer, a line printer, and a page printer?
8. Describe how impact printers and nonimpact printers work.
9. How does a dot-matrix printer form its characters? Is it able to produce letter-quality results?
10. Give an example of a type of nonimpact printer. Do nonimpact printers have any advantages over impact printers?
11. Name some devices that can produce hard-copy graphical output.
12. Is voice output more feasible than voice input? Explain.

S U M M A R Y

- **Data** are the raw facts entered into a computer.

- People view data in terms of a hierarchy. The hierarchy begins at the lowest level with the **field,** which includes one or more related characters. Alphanumeric fields contain letters, numbers, and symbols, whereas numeric fields contain only numbers.

- Moving up the data hierarchy, a **record** is a collection of related fields; a **file** is a collection of related records; and a **database** is a collection of all the data stored in one or more files.

- Within the computer, data are physically represented in **bits,** or binary digits. A **byte** is a group of adjacent bits that represent a decimal digit, letter, or symbol. Two standard codes, **EBCDIC** and **ASCII,** are used to represent a decimal digit, letter, or symbol.

- Early computer systems used punched cards to enter data. Key-to-disk and key-to-tape systems are an improvement, temporarily storing and correcting data before they are sent to the computer.

- **Magnetic ink character recognition (MICR),** used by banks, is one approach to **source data automation. Optical character recognition (OCR)** is another; techniques include optical mark technology, bar code technology, and character recognition.

- **Voice input** is a promising new means of entering data, but the capabilities of current systems remain limited.

■ **Display terminals** (or **terminals**) are a common device used for both entering data via a keyboard and receiving output via a display screen. Point-of-entry terminals are located at the data source. Smart terminals (or intelligent terminals) help with such tasks as data editing; dumb terminals do not.

■ The computer itself, known as the **central processing unit (CPU),** consists of main memory, the arithmetic/logic unit, and the control unit.

■ **Main memory** (or **primary storage**) accepts and stores input data and programs, intermediate results during processing, and processed information waiting to be output. Miniature integrated circuits are used for storage in most modern computers. **Random access memory (RAM),** which can be changed as well as read, makes up the larger part of memory. **Read only memory (ROM),** which can be read but not changed, is sometimes used to contain important programs, which in this form are referred to as firmware.

■ The **arithmetic/logic unit (ALU)** carries out the instructions given by a program. But it only adds, subtracts, multiplies, divides, and compares; therefore, programs must break down all processing tasks into these operations.

■ The **control unit** controls the flow of activities in the central processing unit.

■ Because of the expense and volatility of main memory, data and programs are kept in **secondary** (or **auxiliary**) **storage** when not in use.

■ **Magnetic disk** is the most common secondary storage medium. Two types are hard or rigid disks, which have a large storage capacity, and floppy or flexible disks, which are used mainly with microcomputers. Both types permit **direct access** to data.

■ **Magnetic tape** is cheaper and in some respects easier to use than a magnetic disk but offers only **sequential access** to data.

■ **Optical disks** represent a relatively new technology and are capable of storing very large quantities of data.

■ Computer systems use two main categories of software: **application software,** which performs user-related tasks, and **system software.**

■ System software consists of operating systems, language translators, and utility programs.

■ **Operating systems** manage the resources of the entire computer system. Among the operating systems' functions are handling **batch processing,** in which data are collected in batches and processed in one session, or **on-line processing,** in which data are processed instantaneously. Some operating systems employ virtual storage to extend the apparent capacity of main memory.

■ Language translators translate programs from English-like programming languages into machine languages. A **compiler** translates an entire program before it is executed, whereas an **interpreter** executes each statement of a program as it is translated.

■ **Utility programs** perform frequently required tasks in a computer system.

■ Information can be obtained from a computer as printed output, display output, or voice output.

■ **Printers** produce hard copy. Speeds increase from serial printers to line printers to page printers. Impact printers form characters by contacting a type element with the paper; nonimpact printers do not use contact.

■ Impact printers include **dot-matrix printers,** daisy-wheel printers, chain/train printers, and band printers. Most dot-matrix printers produce draft quality, whereas daisy-wheel printers produce letter-quality documents; both print only one character at a time. Chain/train printers and band printers operate at higher speeds, printing a group of letters at a time.

■ Nonimpact printers include ink-jet printers and laser printers. Both produce highly professional output, and both can handle graphics.

■ **Plotters** are specialized devices for producing hard-copy graphics output.

■ When hard-copy output is not required, display output can be used. This appears visually on a display terminal or a microcomputer display screen. Display output is sometimes best presented graphically. Some computers have a **windowing** capability.

■ **Voice output** is effective in some situations and is a simpler technology than voice input.

K E Y • T E R M S

The following list shows the key terms in the order in which they appear in the chapter.

Data (p. 30)
Field (p. 31)
Record (p. 31)
File (p. 32)
Database (p. 32)
Bit (p. 32)
Byte (p. 33)

EBCDIC (p. 33)
ASCII (p. 33)
Magnetic ink character
    recognition (MICR) (p. 36)
Source data automation (p. 36)
Optical character recognition
    (OCR) (p. 36)

F O R   D I S C U S S I O N

1. Give an example of a character, field, record, and database in your school's grade-reporting system.
2. If you have used a computer system, briefly explain the role of each of the following in the application:
   input
   output
   processing
   system software
   application software
3. What is ASCII? What purpose does it serve in a computer system?
4. Why might it be important to have quick access to data on a terminal?
5. Justify the shift from traditional data-entry methods, such as keypunch machines and key-to-tape devices, to source data automation.
6. Why has voice input found only limited application?

H A N D S - O N   P R O J E C T S

1. Find a computer magazine in your library and locate an advertisement for a disk drive. Make a copy of the advertisement. Describe

the drive. What is its capacity? How fast can it access data? *Suggestions: PC Week, PC, Byte, Datamation.*

2. Take a tour of a minicomputer or mainframe computer facility. Identify the CPU, data-entry, output, and storage devices. How much main memory does the system have? What type of secondary storage is used (tape or magnetic disk)? How much secondary storage is there? What application software packages are commonly used?

3. Go to your local retail computer store and "shop" for a personal computer. What types of computers does the store carry? For a particular system, what is the capacity of main memory? How many floppy disk drives does the system have? How much does a hard disk drive cost? What type of operating system is used? Select three application packages that can be used with the computer. What type of printer does the store recommend for draft-quality reports? For letter-quality reports? How much does the entire system cost?

C A S E · S T U D Y

EAGLE CARDS

With sales of over $100 million, Eagle Cards is one of the largest manufacturers of playing cards, puzzles, and board games. Since 1972, Eagle had been owned by Spencer Entertainment, Inc., a diversified company with seven divisions in the leisure and entertainment industry. But one month ago, Eagle was sold to a group of independent investors. At the time of the sale, it was made clear that in six months Spencer would cease providing all services.

Information Processing at Spencer
Although Eagle produces its products in a totally automated factory, it has no business data processing facilities at its plant. All of its computer data processing services are provided by Spencer's corporate headquarters in Chicago. According to the sales agreement, these are among the services Spencer will no longer provide. This places Eagle in a difficult position.

Spencer currently processes all of Eagle's accounting and payroll data. Eagle submits written forms each day to Spencer, where the data are then entered using key-to-disk machines; the corporate da-

tabase is updated; and customer billing, monthly invoices, and financial statements are produced on a routine basis.

Although Spencer assumes the responsibility for processing accounting and payroll data, Eagle processes its own sales-order and inventory data. Both of these systems, however, are manual. When a customer calls to place an order, for example, a sales-order entry clerk enters the details of the order onto a form and sends the form through the company's mail system to the credit department for credit approval. After credit has been approved, the paperwork is sent to the shipping department. When the order arrives, the shipping department reads the instructions on the form, assembles the order, and sends it to the customer. Once shipped, the paperwork is sent to Spencer, where the appropriate accounting entries are made and an invoice is sent to the customer.

A New System
Without Spencer's accounting and payroll services, Eagle could not operate. The need, therefore, is to develop a new system by the cutoff date.

Eagle's new investors realize that few people on its staff know much about computers. To overcome this shortcoming they recently hired Bill Lenhart, a computer professional with over ten years of experience. His job is to have the system ready in time.

Upon his arrival two weeks earlier, the new owners suggested to Lenhart that it would be short-sighted to devise a new accounting and payroll system without also considering automation of the manual information systems at Eagle. Accordingly, they asked him to develop a system capable of accounting, payroll, sales-order entry, and inventory control. To accomplish this task, they gave him a budget of $500,000.

Lenhart has decided that the new system should be primarily an on-line system, with the capability of running a few batch-processing jobs as well. He learned, for example, that once every month Spencer's data processing department mails statements summarizing the amount owed by each of Eagle's customers. The job is now processed in the batch mode, and Lenhart feels that there is no reason that this should change with the new system. But he agrees with the new investors that many of the accounting functions and certainly all of the inventory and sales-order entry activities should be on-line. As the new owners explained in a recent memo, "An on-line system will speed order processing, shipping, and customer billing. This will not only make us more competitive, but lower production costs and improve our profit margins."

One of the systems that Lenhart is considering is a minicomputer with 5 megabytes (or 5 million bytes) of main memory and 256 megabytes of magnetic disk storage. He is also considering an optical disk system for long-term historical data storage, such as for old invoices, and a cartridge tape system for routine backup purposes.

The minicomputer's operating system makes it possible to perform either batch processing or on-line processing. In the on-line mode it can support up to one hundred terminals. Initially, Lenhart sees a need for fifty-two terminals, positioned at manufacturing and administrative locations throughout the facility. He would like eight printers: one laser printer for letter-quality correspondence and seven dot-matrix printers for internal paperwork. The cost of this system falls just within the budget of $500,000.

Data Entry

To keep the new system's data-entry costs as low as possible, Lenhart plans to have the sales-order entry clerks enter the order data directly at the terminals. But he believes that the solution to the data-entry problem in the inventory area is not clear. He would prefer to use bar code technology. Bar codes would be affixed to inventory items, and when an item was removed from stock, an optical wand would be used to read the bar code and enter the data into the system. When the data had been entered, the computer would update the inventory balance.

The inventory control manager, Andy Wasalik, said he would prefer to rely on his inventory clerks to enter the data manually. He would like them to be responsible for entering part numbers and quantity depleted. Wasalik pointed out that a bar code could not be affixed to every inventory item. "How," he asked, "can you put a bar code label on a nut or bolt?"

Secondary Storage

A problem that remained unresolved was the amount of secondary storage that should be purchased. To help make an informed estimate, Lenhart asked the managers of the order-entry and inventory departments to estimate the quantity of data that they would store in the system. Wasalik studied his needs and concluded that he would like to store 31 data fields, such as product ID number and balance, for each inventory item. Lenhart then asked him to estimate the number of characters associated with each of these data fields, and the number of items in stock. Within a few days, Wasalik sent a memo to Lenhart stating that he needed to store 655 characters of data for each of the 10,000 items in stock.

Lenhart figured that Wasalik needed 6.55 megabytes of storage for data, and he estimated that another 15 megabytes would be required for inventory software.

Using a similar approach, it was determined that the order department needed 75 megabytes of storage for data and software; and after several calls to Spencer's data processing department, it became clear that at least 80 megabytes of storage would be needed for accounting and payroll.

With a total requirement of at least 177 megabytes, Lenhart tentatively decided that a 256-megabyte disk drive would be adequate to store not only the data and application programs but also the system software.

The system software would require about 25 megabytes of secondary storage. But the exact amount of storage capacity was still uncertain, because Lenhart had not yet decided on some of the system software that he felt might be needed. He did, however, feel that virtual storage capability would be required, so that the size of programs would not be limited by the computer's 5 megabytes of main memory.

Outside Opinions

While designing this system, Lenhart relied heavily on sales representatives from the major computer companies. They gave him advice on the kind of equipment they felt was needed and arranged demonstrations of the accounting, payroll, order-entry, and inventory software that could be purchased with their machines.

Although Lenhart wanted to keep the cost of the system within his $500,000 budget, several of the sales representatives warned him that the system he had in mind would have a capacity only close to the organization's current needs. One representative said that after the users became familiar with the new system's capabilities, they would come up with new applications to help them in their jobs—and these new applications would demand a larger system. He therefore recommended a system with more primary memory and a 1-gigabyte magnetic disk drive. This would cost another $100,000.

Another rep also had some advice for Lenhart. She said that to attempt to install a complex system with accounting, payroll, sales-order entry, and inventory applications at the same time would be very difficult for any organization; and because few people at Eagle had any computer experience, it would be almost impossible. She therefore recommended purchasing the equipment necessary to implement the entire system but focusing on only the accounting applications until it was running smoothly. Payroll, she said, could be run by an independent service agency. This would be more expensive than an in-house solution, but it would remove a burden from Eagle's deadline, now less than five months away.

Questions

1. Identify each of the pieces of hardware and software that the new system will need.
2. Explain how data will be entered into the new system. Will the data-entry methods be the same for all applications?
3. The sales-order entry system will collect such data as customer's name and address, the items ordered, the quantity ordered, and the price. Describe these data using the following terms: *character, field, record,* and *database.*
4. Explain how data will be represented in the CPU of the computer that will be used with this system.
5. What methods of source data automation could be used in the new system?
6. How will the new system store data? Use the following terms: *main memory, integrated circuits, secondary storage, magnetic disk,* and *optical disk.*
7. Give an example of how the arithmetic/logic unit would be used when the CPU processes an inventory transaction.
8. Describe two functions that the operating system will perform.
9. Do you think that Lenhart should listen to the sales rep and consider a 1-gigabyte disk drive, or should he stay within the present budget? Why?
10. How will output be produced by the system? Do you see any applications for graphics?
11. Explain how an on-line system will speed order processing.
12. Should Lenhart continue with his plans to bring a system capable of processing accounting, payroll, orders, and inventory into operation within the next five months? Is this too ambitious? What would you recommend?

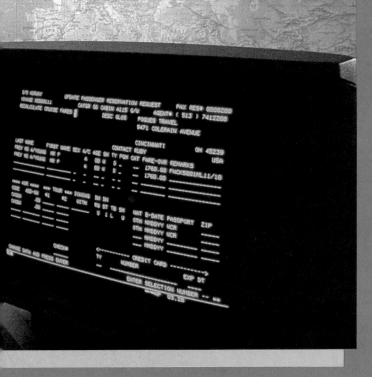

PART · TWO

COMPUTER
INFORMATION
SYSTEMS

3
HOW COMPUTER INFORMATION SYSTEMS ARE USED

O U T L I N E

O B J E C T I V E S

After studying this chapter you should understand the following:

■ *How to classify and describe information systems according to the hierarchical, structured/unstructured, and functional views.*

■ *How information systems are used at different levels in the management hierarchy.*

■ *Some of the differences and similarities among information system applications.*

■ *Key trends in the historical evolution of computer information systems.*

In Chapter 1 we saw that organizations use computer information systems for applications ranging from transaction processing to problem solving and decision making. This range of applications is so wide that those at one end of the scale are very different from those at the other. The software certainly is different; the hardware often is, too; the cost of supporting the applications is different; the applications are designed for different categories of users; and the users receive different kinds of benefits.

If we compare an accounting application such as payroll processing with a finance application such as budgeting, these differences will become apparent. First, the software needed to support a payroll package is quite different from a spreadsheet software package to support the budgeting process. The accounting application usually requires minicomputer or mainframe hardware, together with large-capacity disk storage to store employee payroll data; the budgeting process, in contrast, may use an inexpensive microcomputer.

The costs to support a payroll system may be high, especially if the organization writes its own software and employs a staff of computer programmers to maintain the programs. But the microcomputer spreadsheet software should not require much attention, if any. Users of these systems are certainly different, too: Clerks use the payroll system, and business professionals use the budgeting software. Finally, the benefits from a payroll system—which would include more efficient payroll processing—certainly differ from the benefits of a budgeting process, which might include better management and control over the organization's planning process.

Although the differences between applications are not always as dramatic, what we mean to make clear is that grouping all systems into one category can oversimplify the uses of computer information systems. This oversimplification can, in turn, confuse your understanding of how these systems are designed and used. Accordingly, this chapter will devise a framework to help identify the differences among applications. At the end of the chapter, we will present a capsule history of how today's computer information systems evolved.

THREE VIEWS

Three different views can be used to classify and describe computer information systems: the hierarchical, structured/unstructured, and functional views. The **hierarchical view** focuses on the level of the organization in which an information system, or even part of a system, is used. In this view, the lowest level uses information systems that process routine, everyday activities such as bank transactions or sales orders, and the highest level uses systems that support much less routine activities such as planning new products or studying the effects of corporate mergers.

The **structured/unstructured view** focuses on the characteristics of the problem or decision itself that a computer information system is intended to support. Structured problems are those that follow a sequence of well-defined steps to reach a clearly defined processing objective. In payroll processing, for example, the objective is to produce a paycheck, and this is accomplished by following a series of steps in which the gross pay is computed and deductions are taken from this amount. Because the steps to be followed are reasonably clear, the process is considered structured. With an unstructured problem, however, it may not always be clear which steps must be followed. When planning for new products, for example, it is simply not possible to follow a routine sequence of steps and expect to discover which product the firm should introduce to its product line.

The third view is called a **functional view,** in which a computer information system is categorized by the particular business area that uses the system. These areas include accounting, finance, marketing, personnel, manufacturing and operations, sales, and distribution.

Using the functional view to describe an information system, a payroll application would be part of the accounting information system; a sales-order entry application would be part of the sales information system; and a manufacturing scheduling system would be part of the manufacturing information system.

Although all three views help us to understand how information systems are used, our primary focus in this chapter will be the hierarchical view.

HIERARCHICAL VIEW

THE MANAGEMENT HIERARCHY

The hierarchical view of computer information systems closely parallels the management levels in an organization. As you can see in Figure 3-1, the lowest level in the organization is the one on which day-to-day activities occur. On this level the necessary steps are undertaken to provide goods and services to the organization's customers. Here we would find sales-order entry, accounting, manufacturing, and inventory record-keeping activities and the delivery of goods and services to the firm's customers.

On the next level, called the tactical management level, the focus shifts to the management and control of the activities in the lowest level. Here managers must plan and control the activities to meet price, quality, and output objectives.

Next up the hierarchy comes middle management. Here budgets are formulated, rules and procedures are established, and controls imposed to monitor the performance of the activities carried out at the tactical management level.

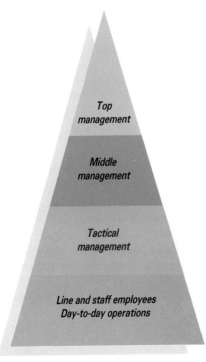

Figure 3-1.
The management hierarchy.

Figure 3-2.
The information systems hierarchy.

At the highest level, top management formulates long-range goals and objectives and establishes plans to meet them.

THE INFORMATION SYSTEMS HIERARCHY

An organization's information needs, and the systems that serve them, are closely related to the management activities at each level of the management hierarchy. At the base of the information systems hierarchy (Figure 3-2) are the systems that support the organization's transaction-processing needs. Then come systems that support operational planning and control needs. On the next level, we find systems that support management planning and control needs. And on the highest level are the systems that support strategic planning.

A Caveat   Sometimes it may be difficult to place an application in a single category in the information systems hierarchy. Inventory systems, for example, can be classified as transaction systems when they are used to maintain records of stock balances. Yet these same inventory systems would be classified as management planning and control systems when they produce reports used by middle management to control the firm's inventory investment. Perhaps the best way to classify such complex applications is that some components are representative of a transaction system and other components are representative of a management planning and control system. Bear in mind, in other words, that the classification schemes presented here are not iron-clad.

The characteristics of each of the four categories of computer information systems will be examined more closely in the following sections.

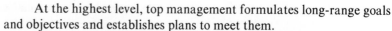

TRANSACTION-PROCESSING SYSTEMS

Figure 3-3.
Computer systems used to authorize credit-card purchases can be categorized as transaction-processing systems.

Transaction-processing systems (or **transaction systems**) are familiar to many of us because we often come into contact with them on the job or when purchasing goods and services (Figure 3-3). Transaction-processing systems keep records of routine business activities. Banks use these systems to process deposits and produce monthly statements; telephone companies use them to process long-distance charges and prepare monthly bills; the Internal Revenue Service uses them to handle tax returns; universities use them to record grades and produce transcripts; and most companies use them to process weekly payrolls.

The computer systems used at this level share certain characteristics. These systems:

■   Help the organization carry out its routine business efficiently.

■   Are operated by people at the lower level of the organization, who generally have little or no management responsibility.

■   Require few, if any, decisions from the people who operate them.

■   Handle a high volume of detailed data generated by the daily activities of the business.

■   Are in constant use.

We next will discuss these characteristics.

ROUTINE DAY-TO-DAY DATA FLOWS

Transaction-processing systems process the routine day-to-day data that flow through an organization. And because these data are routine, standard operating procedures establish exactly how the data should be entered into the system and processed by the computer. Consequently, almost every transaction system can be classified as a structured information system.

A sales-order entry system, for example, is clearly a transaction system. As orders are received from customers, they are entered into the system by order-entry clerks who have been trained to follow standard order-entry procedures. Once entered, the orders are then processed by computer programs, which also follow standard operating procedures.

An airline reservation system is another example of a transaction system. Reservation clerks follow standard operating procedures when requesting information from the computer database (asking, for example, whether there is a seat available on the Friday morning flight to Chicago) and also follow these procedures when entering reservations.

In both of these examples, the computer is used for a narrow range of information-processing activities. Those who use transaction systems would not consider the computer a general-purpose tool.

Sales-order entry and airline reservations are, of course, only two of the many transaction systems in use. Others are accounting, inventory, payroll, distribution, medical record-keeping, and banking systems (Figure 3-4).

Figure 3-4.
When an automatic teller machine is used, the customer in effect becomes the data-entry clerk and so must follow the standard operating procedures specified on the terminal's screen.

■■■■■■■■■■■■■■■■■■■■■■■■■■■■■■■■■■■■

AT THE CENTERVILLE NATIONAL BANK, customers can process deposits or withdrawals either at the teller windows or at one of the bank's 125 automatic teller machines (ATMs). The ATMs are located at branch banks as well as shopping centers and supermarkets throughout the city.

The user of an ATM actually takes on the role of the data-entry clerk and enters the data for the transaction. Because these users are not trained, the bank's system is designed to lead each user through the standard operating procedures necessary to complete a transaction. This is accomplished by presenting a sequence of instructions on the ATM's screen. After the user enters the data into the transaction system, the computer processes them through a sequence of standard steps, updates the user's account, provides a receipt, and dispenses cash if it is appropriate to do so.

■■■■■■■■■■■■■■■■■■■■■■■■■■■■■■■■■■■■

USED BY CLERKS

Transaction systems are used primarily by clerks or by those with little or no management responsibility. Inventory transaction systems, for example, are used by stockroom and production personnel; hotel reservation systems are used by reservation clerks; and sales-order entry systems are used by sales clerks. Seldom are transaction systems (or the transaction-processing portions of more complex systems) used by managers or decision makers.

FEW DECISIONS REQUIRED

Because transaction systems follow standard operating procedures, users are rarely called on to interact with the system's output and to solve a problem or make a decision that would be of any consequence to the firm. For example, an airline reservation clerk would never schedule another flight because one has just been filled. Nor would an order-entry clerk decide to issue a production order for an item that is selling well.

HIGH VOLUME OF DETAILED DATA

Transaction systems usually process a high volume of data in a relatively short period of time. Airlines, telephone companies, and banks are just a few of the companies that process thousands of transactions every hour (Figure 3-5).

In addition to their volume, the data entered into these systems usually include a significant degree of detail. Sales-order data, for example, must specify the person or organization placing the order, describe each of the items ordered, and spell out shipping and billing instructions.

Figure 3-5.
Transaction systems must be able to process great volumes of data.

The data entered into transaction-processing systems must be accurate and timely, because they often represent financial or physical assets. Errors in accounts receivable, cash, inventory, or sales data cannot be tolerated, for they would jeopardize a firm's financial integrity.

The information contained in the transaction-processing system is the data that Management Information Systems and Decision Support Systems use. So it is also for this reason that the data need to be accurate and timely.

CONSTANT USE

Because transaction systems are tied to a firm's routine day-to-day activities, they are in constant use. In many environments, in fact, it is not unusual to find the users of transactions systems, such as reservation clerks, relying on the systems to support most of the activities associated with their jobs.

Figure 3-6.
Operational planning and control systems support the planning and control of operational processes.

OPERATIONAL PLANNING AND CONTROL SYSTEMS

At the next higher level in the information systems hierarchy are those systems that help plan and control operational processes (Figure 3-6). An **operational process** is an ongoing group of activities that produce the goods or services that a firm delivers to its customers. Production lines, distribution systems, bank loan departments, and the kitchen in a restaurant all are examples of operational processes. In contrast with transaction systems, which focus on routine data-processing activities, **operational planning and control systems** focus on the decisions that must be made to run the operational processes. Computer systems at this level

- Help with the day-to-day planning and control of operational processes.

- Are operated by low-level managers and other business professionals responsible for daily operations.

- Interact with users and require them to make a choice.

- Handle a high volume of reasonably detailed but very timely data derived from daily operations.

- Are used weekly or daily.

Let's take a closer look at each of these characteristics.

DAY-TO-DAY PLANNING AND CONTROL

Operational planning and control systems provide decision makers with the information they need to plan and exercise control over the day-to-day operations of an organization. As a planning tool, these systems are used to organize and schedule the work force, materials, facilities, and funds needed to meet the short-run demand for an organization's products or services. Usually these plans extend over a time period of perhaps several weeks.

In manufacturing, operational planning and control systems support the process of developing a daily production schedule. In inventory management, they support the process of deciding when reorders should be placed and how many items to order. In finance, they support the process of managing daily cash flows.

Operational information systems also provide managers and business professionals with the information needed to maintain control over a firm's daily activities. Often this information is in the form of standard reports that summarize the status of a process or activity. In a production-scheduling environment, for example, the scheduling department might use a report to monitor the status of jobs behind schedule, or a sales representative might use a marketing report to monitor the difference between the sales actually booked and the sales quota for the month. Often such regularly scheduled and routine management information is referred to as the output from a Management Information System (MIS). In addition to routine reports, **exception reports** are also produced by an MIS. They call attention to data that might suggest some activities in the day-to-day operation of the firm are beyond the range of what is expected.

SUPPORTS OPERATIONAL DECISION MAKING

The planning and control process requires that problems be solved and decisions be made, and in this process, it is often necessary to interact with environments more complex than those in which transaction applications are found. Although most modern transaction systems are considered structured processes, operational decision-making processes are less structured, and the steps followed to reach decisions and solve problems in this more complex environment are less straightforward. Therefore the systems used to support operational decision making are viewed as semistructured systems.

Problem solving and decision making in an operational environment can be complex because many interactive events are set into motion whenever choices are made. For example, if just one extra job is inserted into a production schedule, many of the current jobs, machines, workers, and parts stored in inventory may be affected as this change works its way through the system. So to be an effective source of information during the operational decision-making process, the system must provide users with information concerning these consequences.

■■■

THE AIRPORT OF A MEDIUM-SIZED CITY WAS EXPERIENCING A SEVERE WINTER BLIZZARD. The airport had already been closed for over fourteen hours, and thousands of passengers were left without transportation. During the storm the scheduling group at Mercury Airways was faced with a steadily worsening situation. Not only were thirteen of their planes grounded and hundreds of their passengers stranded at the airport, but Mercury's passengers at other airports were already waiting for these same planes to arrive in order to reach other destinations.

When the storm ended, a new schedule would be needed. Perhaps some of the aircraft at other airports could be temporarily rerouted to relieve the bottleneck. But if this were done, what would be the effect on other scheduled flights?

To solve this scheduling problem Mercury Airways used a computer information system. Its system took into account the interactions among the aircraft, crew, and passengers and produced a schedule that was then reviewed by the airline's scheduling staff.

■ ■

This aircraft-scheduling example illustrates a management decision problem involving a complex interactive network of events. If just one flight were changed, it would have affected other flights, passengers, and airline crews, both at the snowed-in airport and at other connecting airports. One event influences other events in a complex web of interactions. Without a computer information system, it would be much more difficult—if not impossible—to come up with a revised schedule in a reasonably short time (Figure 3-7).

Figure 3-7.
Airline scheduling affects the aircraft, crews, and passengers. Computers are used to help airline staff make scheduling decisions.

■ ■

FARMCO, a major manufacturer of farm equipment, has received a request from a Latin American country to bid for fifty pieces of farm machinery. Several of the larger pieces requested by the secretary of agriculture's office, however, require customized manufacturing sequences. Usually orders of this kind take a year to process from date of order to delivery. But the country wants them in six months.

Farmco's task is to determine how processing this order will affect those already scheduled. Clearly, some orders will be delayed, as all the manufacturing facilities are shared. The exact length of the delay, however, cannot be determined until the proposed changes are entered into the manufacturing information system. This production planning and control system, called a **Manufacturing Resource Planning System (MRP),** is used by many manufacturers. With this system, Farmco can determine how tens of thousands of parts, thousands of manufacturing steps, hundreds of workers, and dozens of vendors who supply parts for its products will be affected by this proposed change in its schedule. Only then can Farmco's management decide whether or not to bid for the order.

■■■■■■■■■■■■■■■■■■■■■■■■■■■■■■■■

INTERACTION WITH USERS

Many operational planning and control systems are designed to permit the user to interact with the system while solving a problem. This is especially important when the decision-making environment is so complex that a final decision can be reached only after several tentative solutions have been examined and compared. A person preparing a production schedule, for example, may examine the consequences of one possible computer solution, make adjustments, reenter the data, examine the new solution, and continue this process until deciding on a satisfactory solution.

■■■■■■■■■■■■■■■■■■■■■■■■■■■■■■■■

AT ST. MARY'S HOSPITAL, a 200-bed facility, a computer information system is used to assign staff to each of the hospital's departments (Figure 3-8). These include the emergency room, surgery, recovery, intensive care, obstetrics, pediatrics, general wards, and outpatient departments.

The demand for each of these departments changes daily. Every

Figure 3-8.
Computers are used to schedule nurses' shifts at large hospitals.

evening, the nursing administrator enters the proposed staffing assignments for each shift on the following day as well as the expected patient census for that day. Then several reports are printed, including one that identifies where and when shortages are likely to occur. If the shortages are significant, then the administrator will revise the plan and reenter the staffing assignments into the computer information system. The new report will suggest whether or not the changes have helped. When necessary, the administrator will make additional passes until a satisfactory solution can be found.

■■■■■■■■■■■■■■■■■■■■■■■■■■■■■■■

DETAILED AND TIMELY DATA

Because operational problems are often linked in a complex web of interactive events, operational planning and control systems must handle a huge volume of detailed data. And it is essential that the data be timely and accurate: Last week's data have much less decision-making value than do today's. Although the data need not be as precise as transaction data, as the error rate begins to increase, a costly chain reaction of time delays, higher expenses, lost sales, and poor service will be set in motion.

USED WEEKLY OR DAILY

Operational planning and control systems are used less often than are transaction systems. Nonetheless, they are often used daily or weekly. In production scheduling, for example, the system may be used daily to change the production schedule and may be used weekly as new schedules are developed. A transaction system, on the other hand, may be used 24 hours a day.

MANAGEMENT PLANNING AND CONTROL SYSTEMS

Further up the information systems hierarchy, **management planning and control systems** serve a higher level in the management organization. In contrast with operational planning and control systems, which focus on the day-to-day decisions needed to run the organization, a management planning and control system focuses on the intermediate-range decisions needed to manage the firm's resources. The process of compiling a quarterly budget, for example, may be supported by a management planning and control system.

Management planning and control systems

■ Support the intermediate-range planning process—involving a time period of from one to six months into the future—and provide information on the organization's performance.

- Are used by middle managers responsible for planning and control.

- Require users to make independent judgments.

- Consider the uncertainty in the planning environment.

- Work with summarized (aggregate) data that come from both the organization and outside sources.

- Are used regularly but not as frequently as are operational planning and control systems.

We will briefly examine each of these characteristics.

INTERMEDIATE-RANGE PLANNING AND CONTROL

Perhaps the most significant difference between operational planning and control systems, and management planning and control systems is that to the latter the details of an organization's day-to-day operations are less important. When used for planning, management planning and control systems focus on the intermediate horizon, typically one to six months in the future. Consequently, they are not concerned with today's problems as much as they are with those coming in the next few months (Figure 3-9).

In addition to their role in the planning process, management planning and control systems are also used by decision makers and professionals to supply them with the information needed to monitor and control the activities for which they are responsible. But these systems focus on the control of organizational units larger than operational planning and control systems. A sales manager, for example, may request a graph showing sales by product line for an entire division, or a production manager may request a report listing reject rates for all major product cate-

Figure 3-9.
Management planning and control systems focus on longer-range problems than do operational planning and control systems.

Figure 3-10.
Business professionals use management planning and control systems to help them make decisions.

gories. The use of these systems for control purposes generally focuses on the department, division, or corporate level.

USED BY MIDDLE MANAGEMENT

Management planning and control systems are used by middle management or by professionals with problem-solving or decision-making responsibilities (Figure 3-10). In general, these individuals occupy positions between the first level of supervision and the higher ranks at the division or corporate level.

A management planning and control system can also be classified as an MIS or a DSS. When a management planning and control system is used to provide the routine and periodic reports that management needs, it is referred to as a Management Information System (MIS). But when management uses such a system to obtain information that is not routine, it is referred to as a Decision Support System (DSS).

INDEPENDENT JUDGMENTS

The decision-making environment at this higher level in the hierarchy becomes even more complex than at the operational planning and control level. Here problems are even less structured and seldom can use a step-by-step procedure to solve them. These systems, then, are considered semistructured.

To accommodate such ambiguity in the decision-making environment, management planning and control systems are designed to permit the user to interact with the systems during the decision-making process. Furthermore, the decision-making process at this level relies more on the decision maker's judgment and intuition than on the facts and figures from the information system. If such a system were used in the quarterly budgeting process, for example, the decision maker might well revise the budget several times before approving a final version. And the final version might be influenced more heavily by the decision maker's judgment than by the data obtained from the computer information system.

UNCERTAINTY IN THE PLANNING ENVIRONMENT

When a management planning and control system is used for planning purposes, it often looks months into the future. Since the future is unknown to us, planning systems must provide some mechanism for acknowledging this problem. Some include forecasting capabilities, and others make it easy for the user to explore the consequences of a wide variety of decision choices.

AGGREGATE DATA

Unlike transaction or operational planning and control systems, management planning and control systems use sources of data other than the firm's central database (Figure 3-11). Data are frequently obtained from others in the organization. It may be necessary, for example, to ask the sales manager how sales would be likely to respond to a new promotional campaign or to ask a production supervisor how the manufacture of a changed product might affect work-force levels. Sometimes useful data can be obtained from customers, market surveys, and trade organizations.

Rarely do management planning and control systems depend upon large volumes of detailed data. For example, while preparing a budget, a manager may review the total sales for each department over the most recent months, but not necessarily the daily sales totals, as often aggregate data are all that are required.

Figure 3-11.
Data used in the management planning and control process may be obtained through interaction with others within or outside the organization.

■■■■■■■■■■■■■■■■■■■■■■■■■■■■■■■■

WINSLOW'S IS A LARGE DEPARTMENT-STORE CHAIN IN THE MIDWEST. Founded in 1904, the company remained at its single downtown location until 1962 when the founder's grandson undertook a major expansion. In 1975, Winslow's was bought by a large department-store chain with headquarters on the East Coast. Since 1962, sales have increased over twentyfold, and the company now operates thirty stores in shopping malls and downtown locations.

Maintaining financial control over an operation with locations in four states proved to be a problem. Last year the vice-president of operations decided to install a network of minicomputers distributed among the thirty stores. He explained his reason for the purchase: "These computers should help us control our costs better. Until now, headquarters discovered problems long after they could do anything about them. For example, just before we put in this system, the labor costs in one of our stores skyrocketed. When we finally saw the data, the problem had already cost us over fifty thousand dollars. But with the new system we can do something before a situation like this becomes too costly."

Each store has been divided into departments such as children's wear, men's wear, and cosmetics. The new machines, together with spreadsheet software, are used to collect budgets from the managers of each department. One such monthly budget, for the housewares department of Winslow's largest store, is shown in Figure 3-12. Notice that the budget contains only aggregate data. Wages, for example, is given as a single category. Exactly how the payroll is divided among the department's employees is not shown.

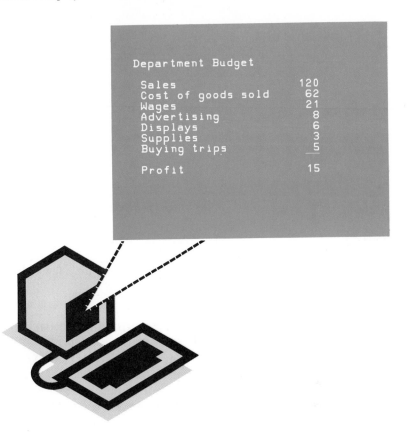

Figure 3-12.
The budget for the housewares department at Winslow's.

After the budgets for each department are calculated, they are combined into a store budget. Then the store manager communicates with the minicomputer located at corporate headquarters and enters the store budget into the system. When the staff at corporate headquarters has received the budgets for all thirty stores, their minicomputer combines the data into the overall corporate budget, which is illustrated in Figure 3-13.

When Janet Wilcox, a manager at one Winslow store, was asked about the new system, she mentioned several benefits. "My department managers now can access the expense data from earlier periods, and this certainly helps them draw up more realistic budgets. The system also can pull together department budgets into a storewide budget very quickly. But the biggest benefit is that a budget update made by a department manager can instantaneously be incorporated in our store-

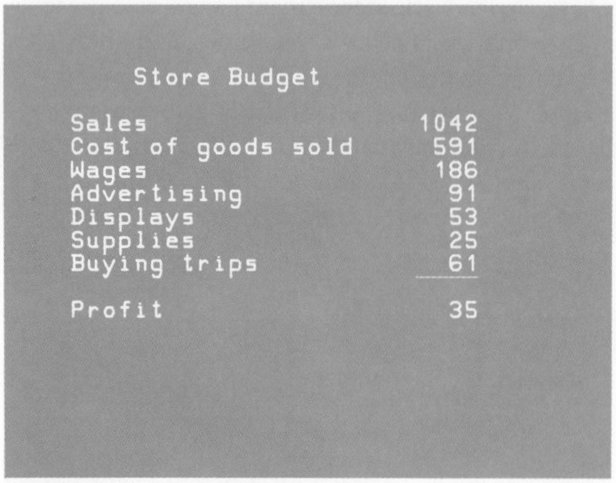

```
        Store Budget

Sales                    1042
Cost of goods sold        591
Wages                     186
Advertising                91
Displays                   53
Supplies                   25
Buying trips               61
                         ____

Profit                     35
```

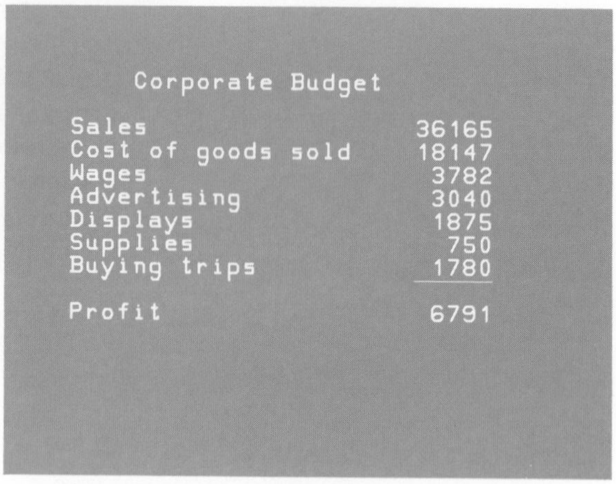

```
        Corporate Budget

Sales                   36165
Cost of goods sold      18147
Wages                    3782
Advertising              3040
Displays                 1875
Supplies                  750
Buying trips             1780
                        _____

Profit                   6791
```

Figure 3-13.
The budget for one store in the Winslow chain and the aggregate budget for all stores in the corporation.

wide and companywide budgets. There is absolutely no question that we now have more financial control over the company's operations."

■■■■■■■■■■■■■■■■■■■■■■■■■■■■■■■■■■■■■

USED REGULARLY

Although operational planning and control systems are used daily or weekly, management planning and control systems are used less frequently, perhaps just a few times each week or month.

■■■■■■■■■■■■■■■■■■■■■■■■■■■■■■■■

A GARMENT MANUFACTURER LOCATED ON SEVENTH AVENUE IN NEW YORK CITY FOUND THAT TO ACHIEVE A $2-MILLION QUARTER, the company would have to borrow $150,000 in working capital, hire four more cutters, require employees to work six hours of overtime each week, and subcontract ten thousand pieces to another garment manufacturer on 37th Street. These were the results of the company's monthly microcomputer planning analysis to determine the kind of resources needed to meet a certain level of demand. Although this plan showed much less detail than a daily production schedule would, it provided the kind of information needed for intermediate-range planning (Figure 3-14).

"The real advantage of this system," said Nelson Aurelio, the company's vice-president of finance, "is that it gives us a chance to explore the consequences of sales levels both higher and lower than the level we most expect. Ours is a risky business, and so we must be prepared for several possible outcomes, some of them not so good."

To examine the different possible outcomes for this quarter, the company entered several additional sales estimates. For example, it learned that if sales were only $1.75 million, the company would not require any overtime; it would need to subcontract only 3000 pieces; and it would need no short-term financing. But if sales reached $2.25 million, then the company would need at least fifteen new employees; would

Month	Sales forecast in units	Proposed production in units	Cash flow
Jan	145	150	-$150
Feb	175	150	- 50
Mar	65	100	+ 200
April	180	150	+ 175
May	200	150	+ 300
June	105	100	+ 475

Production Plan

Figure 3-14.
A garment manufacturer plans production over the next several months.

have to increase overtime to ten hours each week; would have to subcontract 25,000 pieces; and would have to arrange $250,000 in short-term financing.

STEVE CHEN USED A SECURITY ANALYSIS SOFTWARE PACKAGE TO MANAGE HIS PERSONAL STOCK PORTFOLIO. Through his microcomputer he accesses a financial database and obtains a variety of information, ranging from the most recent price quotation to news that a company has just released over business news wire services.

His system also helps him analyze price movements by producing various up-to-the-minute graphs. By watching these graphs and recognizing trends, Chen can determine which stocks he should buy and which ones he should sell.

But Chen knows that any system designed to support decision-making behavior does not guarantee better results. He is also aware that many investors who use these systems lose money.

STRATEGIC PLANNING SYSTEMS

Strategic decisions are made at the highest levels in an organization and often have the greatest impact on its future course. **Strategic planning systems** provide information to help top-level managers make these vital decisions. Computer systems used at this level

- Help solve long-term strategic problems.

- Are used by top-level managers responsible for deciding on the organization's overall goals and objectives.

- Require users to make independent judgments.

- Work with summarized data and use outside sources.

- Are used infrequently on an as-needed basis.

Let's take a close look at these characteristics.

LONG-RANGE PLANNING

Strategic planning systems are used primarily by top-level decision makers to support those decisions whose focus is on the issues affecting the organization's long-term ability to compete profitably in the marketplace for goods and services. Some of these decisions concern the firm's financial structure, the products and services that customers will demand, and the firm's ability to produce and deliver these products and services. And in most circumstances such decisions will not have an impact on the firm's day-to-day operations for at least one to five years into the future.

Strategic planning systems may be used, for example, by a company's board of directors to produce graphs that project market trends so that they can decide whether or not the product mix should be altered. Or the vice-president of finance may use them to examine the consequences of new methods of financing. A manager of manufacturing may explore the benefits and costs associated with different production methods.

Because the planning focus is so far into the future, the decision need not be encumbered with resource constraints. There is enough time to build new plants, purchase new equipment, and hire and train new personnel. So there is greater freedom of choice associated with decisions at this level than with those at the lower levels in the organization hierarchy.

USED BY TOP-LEVEL DECISION MAKERS

When the focus extends beyond a year, many of these decisions bear directly on issues relating to the organization's overall goals. Accordingly, information systems at this level often play an important role in setting financial, product, market share, sales, cost, and work-force

Figure 3-15.
Strategic planning systems are used by decision makers at the top levels of the management hierarchy.

goals (Figure 3-15). Although there are situations in which routine and periodic reports are used by top-level managers in support of the problems they must solve, most of the situations are not routine and special requests for data must be made. Accordingly, many of the systems at this level can be classified as Decision Support Systems.

INDEPENDENT JUDGMENTS

As with the management planning and control systems described earlier, the users of strategic planning systems can rely on these systems only for support. But the decision-making environment at the strategic level is almost always unstructured; as a result, the computer can certainly not be relied upon to present the decision maker with a step-by-step approach to solving a problem. Almost all decisions at this level must rely more on independent judgment than decisions at any of the lower levels.

SUMMARIZED AND EXTERNAL DATA

The corporate database usually contains data that are more detailed than needed for strategic decision making. The specific parts stored in inventory or the sequence of jobs waiting to be processed through a machine shop is hardly the data needed to plan an organization's future course.

Furthermore, nearly all of the stored data are historical. Sometimes these data are used. But at the strategic level only the most aggregate data are of interest to decision makers. Of greater interest are the kinds of data often obtained from commercial database services, which provide forecasts based on various economic, demographic, and industry statistics (Figure 3-16).

Although uncertainty is an issue at the management planning and control level, it is of even greater concern here. Strategic problems usually look so far into the future that forecasts or estimates are likely to fall wide of the mark. As a result, the risks associated with alternative courses of action can be great, and so any information system used at this level must provide some mechanism for addressing these risks.

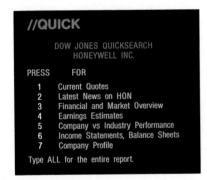

```
//QUICK

         DOW JONES QUICKSEARCH
              HONEYWELL INC.

PRESS      FOR
  1    Current Quotes
  2    Latest News on HON
  3    Financial and Market Overview
  4    Earnings Estimates
  5    Company vs Industry Performance
  6    Income Statements, Balance Sheets
  7    Company Profile

Type ALL for the entire report.
```

Figure 3-16.
Information available from Dow Jones Market Monitor, a commercial database service.

USED INFREQUENTLY

We've seen that transaction systems are used the most frequently; many systems in fact process thousands of transactions per hour. Strategic planning systems, on the other hand, are used the least often. Sometimes months will go by between one use and the next. Often a particular application will never recur. And this nonrecurring nature of stategic decision making suggests that the data collected by these systems may also find infrequent use.

One reason that such systems are used so seldom is that the problems confronted by upper-level managers are always changing. Thus, an application developed to support the problems of today may be totally inappropriate for those faced tomorrow. An especially difficult burden imposed on these computer systems, then, is that they must be changed or modified for each new application. In Chapter 13 we will see how natural language–processing systems enable the end-users to design many applications themselves. These systems allow a user to work with the computer using everyday language and obtain the needed information without the help of data processing professionals.

The following example illustrates how one organization developed an application to support an important strategic decision.

■■■■■■■■■■■■■■■■■■■■■■■■■■■■■■■■■■■■■

VACATIONS INTERNATIONAL IS A MAJOR DEVELOPER IN THE RESORT TIME-SHARE INDUSTRY. For ten years it has purchased large resort properties, converted the rooms into apartments, and then sold the right to own each apartment for a specific one week time slot during the year. Recently, the managing partner, Dan Binney, discovered an opportunity with extraordinary potential. A large resort hotel in the Azores was for sale and appeared to be an ideal candidate for conversion into time-share units. Once converted, the units could be sold to the European yachting community.

Binney estimated that the project could generate a net profit of roughly $2 million. But because several other developers were interested in the property, Vacations International had to act quickly. Binney called several investors and two bankers, suggesting they all meet in two days. But Vacations International needed a complete financial plan before the investors would seriously consider the project.

Using his microcomputer and a commercial spreadsheet package, Binney identified and estimated over 150 revenue and expense items that would be incurred over the project's three-year life. Using these data, he constructed a cash-flow model and financial statements. Because these flows were single estimates and because the risks were so high, Binney repeated the analysis for several different assumptions regarding income and expenses, ranging from a pessimistic to an optimistic outcome. In this way, he created a comprehensive picture of the risks associated with the project.

■■■■■■■■■■■■■■■■■■■■■■■■■■■■■■■■■■■■

• •

E N D · U S E R H I N T S

HOW TO MAKE SENSE OF AN APPLICATION

The first time you look closely at any computer application, it can be a confusing experience. Hardware, software, data, procedures, and people—how do they all fit together? What exactly is going on?

Because the equipment appears to be responsible for the "magic" that takes place, there is the unavoidable temptation to describe a computer information system by its hardware: "The mainframe is an IBM 3090 with 24 megabytes of main memory, 6000 megabytes of disk storage, 120 terminals, 30 dot-matrix printers, and 4 laser printers."

Hardware is important, true. But consider for a moment *why* the equipment was purchased. Without exception, the money was spent for "functionality"—the ability of the system to perform business applications. So when you look at a system for the first time, or when you are trying to explain it to others, it makes more sense to describe it in terms of what it does.

Finding out what it does may not be as easy as it sounds. The experience is worthwhile, however, for it helps to bring the concepts you are learning about computer information systems into focus. Try answering these questions as a guide:

■ In which functional area is the system used—account-ing, finance, operations, or marketing?

■ Who is using the system—clerks, business professionals, managers, or executives?

■ What task is performed by the application—sales-order entry, inventory control, accounting, payroll, production scheduling and control, decision support, supplying management information, or something else (describe)?

■ Does the user have to make any complex or nonroutine decisions?

■ If decisions are made, describe them. What risks are involved?

■ If it is a transaction system, describe a transaction. What volume of data does the system handle, low or high?

■ How often is the system used—constantly, weekly, seldom, or just once?

■ How far into the future does the system look—today, the next few days or weeks, the next few months, or long-range?

■ Are the data that are collected, stored, and presented detailed or aggregate?

■ How does this system help the firm meet its business objectives?

Working out the answers to these questions should help you understand most business applications. Remember, not all applications will fit neatly into one of the categories described in this chapter. Nonetheless, the framework is still useful for developing a way of thinking meaningfully about applications.

? QUESTIONS ?

1. What are the three ways of viewing a computer information system?
2. Which view describes an application as an accounting system?
3. Why can all transaction-processing systems also be classified as structured systems?
4. An investment firm that manages several hundred million dollars is deciding whether or not to place some of its funds in long-term government bonds. How would you classify the system that helps make this decision?
5. In reference to Question 4, describe briefly three transaction systems that an investment firm might use to help meet the day-to-day demands.
6. Compare the characteristics of an operational planning and control system with those of a management planning and control system.
7. When are strategic planning systems used?
8. Give one example each, from this chapter, of a transaction-processing, an operational planning and control, and a strategic planning system.
9. Where do Decision Support Systems fall in the information systems hierarchy?
10. Where do Management Information Systems fall in the information systems hierarchy?

THE HISTORICAL EVOLUTION OF INFORMATION SYSTEMS

All of the information systems that we have described reflect the ways in which computer systems are used today. Of course, before the introduction of the computer, firms used manual information systems, but they were far less powerful than present-day computer systems. The introduction of the computer has revolutionized information systems. A review of the highlights in the historical development of the computer will help us understand how this revolution unfolded.

COMPUTER GENERATIONS

One of the earliest milestones in the development of modern-day computers was Dr. Herman Hollerith's creation of a data processing technique in the 1880s. Hollerith's method used punch cards and mechanical tabulators and proved successful in reducing the time needed to process the results of the 1890 census. After a merger and a name change, the company Hollerith founded became the International Business Machines Corporation (IBM).

After Hollerith's tabulating machines came a host of more complex electromechanical accounting machines. These were not computers, but they could sort, merge, and summarize data on punch cards. By the late 1930s, electromechanical punch-card technology was widely used by government and industry. Then an electromechanical computer appeared in 1944, the MARK I; this machine was monumental in size and very limited in its computational ability, but it did accept data on punch cards and produce output on paper tape. Electronic computers soon followed. The ENIAC (short for Electronic Numerical Integrator and Calculator), a famous early electronic computer, relied on thousands of vacuum tubes to process and store data (Figure 3-17). With the earliest of these machines, including the ENIAC, "programming" was done by setting switches and connecting wires. The first computers were one-of-a-kind articles produced for research or for use by the military. Even if a business had found a use for computers in the 1940s, they were not available for purchase.

First Generation   Not until 1951 did the first general-purpose electronic computer, the UNIVAC I (Universal Automatic Computer), manufactured by Sperry Rand, become available for purchase (Figure 3-18). Three were installed at the U.S. Census Bureau. In 1953 IBM introduced its first commercial computer, the IBM 701. These first commercially available electronic computers marked the advent of the computer generations. Ever since then, we have been counting generations.

First-generation computers relied on vacuum-tube technology. The vacuum tubes functioned as binary devices and were used to store and process binary data in the computer's CPU. In addition to punch

Figure 3-17.
The ENIAC, one of the first electronic computers.

Figure 3-18.
The UNIVAC I, the first general-purpose computer used to process business transactions.

cards for data input, these computers also used magnetic drums for secondary storage. Some first-generation computers were programmed by setting switches and connecting wires. Other machines accepted programs as input and stored them, as today's computers do. But the programs had to be written in binary-coded machine languages or in assembly languages, which use symbols in place of binary numbers but are still extremely complex to use. Only dedicated computer experts could program a first-generation computer.

Second Generation   In the late 1950s computers began to use the transistor, developed in 1948 by scientists at Bell Labs, in place of vacuum tubes. Transistors were much smaller than vacuum tubes, much more reliable, and faster. Computers took a quantum leap forward. Computers using transistors were called **second-generation computers.** The IBM 1401 was a popular second-generation machine.

Magnetic tape was also widely used in the second generation. With this technology, data could be read some 50 to 75 times faster than was possible with punch cards. In addition, tape was inexpensive and made the storage of data less cumbersome and easier to maintain.

The second generation also saw the introduction of high-level programming languages, principally FORTRAN (short for FORmula TRANslation) and COBOL (Common Business-Oriented Language), both of which are still extensively used today. It is easier and faster to program in these languages than in machine or assembly languages, but a familiarity with how computers work is still required. Magnetic disks were introduced in 1956 with the IBM 305 disk storage unit. This product marked the beginning of direct-access technology, a development that eventually had a profound effect on the use of computers in transaction processing and especially in decision-support applications. The first disk systems were slow and expensive, but this technology improved at an astonishing rate. Indeed, product improvements have advanced every decade by a factor of eleven.

Third Generation   **Third-generation computers** were born in the mid-1960s. These systems relied on a process that could put hundreds of electronic components on a single silicon chip measuring less than an eighth of an inch square. These integrated circuits made the third-generation computers even faster and more reliable than the second-generation computers had been. Magnetic disk storage also became faster and less expensive and had a greater capacity. A popular third-generation computer was the IBM 360 (Figure 3-19).

Third-generation machines also saw the first sophisticated operating systems. Some could handle not only batch processing but also on-line processing, in which data are processed instantaneously. The popu-

Figure 3-19.
The IBM 360, a third-generation computer.

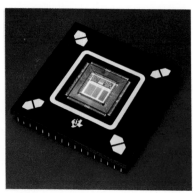

Figure 3-20.
In very large scale integration, a chip with thousands of circuits is designed on a scale many times larger than its final size. Then the design is photographically reduced, and finally the chips are manufactured.

lar BASIC (Beginner's All-Purpose Symbolic Code) computer language was developed, designed for ease of use by the beginning programmer.

Fourth Generation In the 1970s, ever-more components were loaded onto a silicon chip in what is called **large-scale integration (LSI).** In the late 1970s, **very large scale integration (VLSI)** began, which today has led to electronic circuits that can store more than one million bits (1 megabit) on a single chip no larger than a fingernail (Figure 3-20). These highly miniaturized silicon chips are characteristic of **fourth-generation computers.** The fourth generation is still in progress.

The microcomputer is a product of the fourth generation. The first popular micro was the Apple II. Advances in microcomputer chips have made possible a desktop micro with a main memory of 512 K—about thirty-two times the capacity of the average 16-K machine typical of second-generation computers—and available for a fraction of the cost.

Although the fourth generation is associated mainly with advancements in hardware, the advancement in software cannot be ignored. Fourth-generation languages make it faster and easier to program computers than did earlier languages such as BASIC and COBOL. In addition, a host of prepackaged software has made using computers considerably easier for noncomputer experts, as we will see in a moment.

The Future Advancements in both hardware and software can be expected to continue in the same directions. Faster computers with larger main memories, and secondary storage devices with faster access times and greater storage capacities, will permit software developers to write even more sophisticated programs. Computers will also offer steadily more power and ease of use to the business professional.

FROM TRANSACTIONS TO DECISION SUPPORT

The third-generation computers developed in the 1960s were used mainly in transaction environments, but infrequently for Management Information Systems and Decision Support Systems. The problems were the following: First, the cost of developing most third-generation systems using a programming language such as COBOL was so high that only the high-volume applications found in transaction processing could justify it. Second, the centralization of corporate computing centers separated the information resources from the user. Third, third-generation technology and complex programming languages such as COBOL prevented nonprofessional programmers from directly interacting with an information system. End-users thus had few opportunities to use these systems directly.

Management indeed found computer use up to the mid-1970s to be frustrating. Although the potential benefit that computers could bring to decision makers was acknowledged, the link between these users and complex computer systems had yet to be clearly established.

THE MICRO AND USER-FRIENDLY SOFTWARE

The frustration of the 1970s began to change with several technological innovations, in particular, microcomputer technology and user-friendly languages.

The microcomputer made its debut in the mid-1970s. Like larger machines, microcomputers were first used in transaction environments. Most were used by small organizations for which larger and more costly computers were beyond reach. To decision makers in large organizations, the microcomputer at this stage in its development was of little use in the MIS or DSS process and, consequently, was of little concern.

But this changed. In the late 1970s a new type of micro software was created and gained the attention of a pioneer group of users. This new software was an electronic spreadsheet named VisiCalc. One of the most significant features of VisiCalc and the many programs that followed it was the ease with which they could be learned and used. In just a few hours a new user could be solving a practical problem. This was a major breakthrough: It was no longer necessary to become an expert before using a computer to solve business problems. And spreadsheet software is credited with the birth of **end-user computing**—solving problems using a computer oneself without involving programmers or other computer professionals.

The widespread success of VisiCalc led to a parade of user-friendly decision-support software including word-processing, data management, and project-planning packages. In addition, a host of other spreadsheet packages soon followed VisiCalc, many of them even better than the original.

In 1981 there was another major breakthrough: IBM announced the IBM Personal Computer, or PC. This giant company, with a major share of the mainframe data processing market, had legitimized the use of microcomputers in corporations. As everyone expected, the IBM PC and its operating system became the standard for microcomputing. Other microcomputer manufacturers and software developers quickly learned that in order to sell their products to corporations, they had to make their products compatible with the IBM microcomputer line. These computers are often called "clones." Products that are not compatible do still sell, but they represent only a small percentage of total corporate sales.

COMPUTER NETWORKS

The original microcomputers were used only singly as stand-alone machines. They functioned as if the central data processing facilities of the organization did not even exist. But in the early and mid-1980s, microcomputers began to be linked together in networks using modems, communication software, and networking software. Once tied together, they could share data, programs, and printers and, above all, access central minicomputers and mainframe systems and their all-important centralized databases (Figure 3-21).

Finally, the microcomputer had placed the business professional at the center of the organization's information resources.

Figure 3-21.
Micros, minis, and mainframes all can be linked together in an integrated network.

?   Q U E S T I O N S   **?**

1. How were the earliest computers, such as the ENIAC, "programmed"?

2. In what year did the first general-purpose electronic computer become available for purchase? What company built this machine?

3. Describe some of the main differences between first- and second-generation computers.

4. What are the characteristics of a third-generation computer?

5. When were magnetic disk storage devices introduced? Have they improved since then? How fast have they improved?

6. In what generation is present-day computer technology?

7. Why were computers of the first through third generations seldom used for Management Information Systems and Decision Support Systems?

8. List some of the factors that helped in the introduction of microcomputers into large organizations.

9. Back off a bit from dates and machines, and try to describe the evolution of the computer as a decision-making support tool.

S U M M A R Y

- Three views of computer information systems are the hierarchical view, the structured/unstructured view, and the functional view.

- The **hierarchical view** categorizes computer information systems according to the level in the organizational hierarchy that the system supports.

- The **structured/unstructured view** categorizes a computer information system according to the nature of the decision itself. Structured problems are those that follow a sequence of well-defined steps in order to reach a clearly defined processing objective. Payroll processing is an example. Unstructured problems offer no such clear, cut-and-dried solutions. Planning a research and development project is an example.

- The **functional view** categorizes a computer information system according to the particular business area in which the system is used. Such areas are accounting, finance, marketing, personnel, manufacturing and operations, sales, and distribution.

- This chapter focused on the hierarchical view of computer information systems, which closely parallels the four management levels in an organization. Starting at the bottom, the systems that serve these levels are transaction-processing systems, operational planning and control systems, management planning and control systems, and strategic planning systems.

- A **transaction-processing system** (or **transaction system**) focuses on day-to-day routine information flows that follow standard operating procedures. Accounting systems fall into this category.

- An **operational process** is an ongoing group of activities that produces the goods or services that a firm delivers to its customers.

Operational planning and control systems concentrate on the decisions necessary for the firm's operation, producing routine reports as well as **exception reports** calling attention to potential problems. A **Material Requirements Planning System** (MRP) is an example of an operational planning and control system.

■ **Management planning and control systems** support the management of a firm's resources and operational systems. These intermediate-range planning problems extend one to six months in the future. Budgeting falls into this category.

■ **Strategic planning systems** help top-level managers make decisions concerning problems extending a year or more into the future. New product–planning decisions fall into this category.

■ Computers have revolutionized information systems. Before the early 1950s, no computers were available for purchase by private industry. Since then, computers have been divided into generations based on their technical characteristics.

■ **First-generation computers** used vacuum tubes for their circuitry, punch cards for input, and magnetic drums for secondary storage. They were programmed with great difficulty by setting switches and connecting wires or with programs coded in cumbersome machine and assembly languages.

■ **Second-generation computers** used transistors in their circuitry, and magnetic tape and, in some cases, magnetic disk for input/ output and secondary storage. They were programmed somewhat more easily in high-level programming languages.

■ **Third-generation computers** used integrated circuits and magnetic disk and magnetic tape for input/output and secondary storage. They had the first sophisticated operating systems and more advanced programming languages.

■ **Fourth-generation computers** employ **large-scale integration** (LSI) and **very large scale integration** (VLSI) to pack many components onto a silicon chip. The microcomputer is a product of the fourth generation, which is still in progress. Programming languages are available to simplify programming, and prepackaged software can be used without any programming required at all.

■ Even through the third generation, businesses used computers mainly for transaction processing. But this changed with the fourth-generation microcomputers and the rise of **end-user computing.** The introduction of microcomputer software with which new users can solve practical problems in just a few hours, IBM's "legitimization" of the corporate use of microcomputers, and advances in constructing networks with microcomputers place today's business professional at the center of the organization's information resources.

K E Y • T E R M S

The following list shows the key terms in the order in which they appear in the chapter.

Hierarchical view (p. 66)

Structured/unstructured view (p. 67)

Functional view (p. 67)

Transaction-processing system (transaction system) (p. 68)

Operational process (p. 71)

Operational planning and control system (p. 71)

Exception report (p. 72)

Material Requirements Planning System (MRP) (p. 74)

Management planning and control system (p. 75)

Strategic planning system (p. 82)

First-generation computers (p. 86)

Second-generation computers (p. 88)

Third-generation computers (p. 88)

Large-scale integration (LSI) (p. 89)

Very large scale integration (VLSI) (p. 89)

Fourth-generation computers (p. 89)

End-user computing (p. 90)

F O R   D I S C U S S I O N

1. The Oak Valley Aluminum Company, a distributor of sheet and extruded aluminum products, is considering placing terminals in its customers' plants. The terminals would be connected to Oak Valley's central computer and capable of accessing inventory, sales-order entry, and accounts receivable systems. Customers could then use these terminals to determine whether Oak had an item in stock, to place orders, and to find out how much they owed the company. Where in the hierarchy of information systems would these applications be placed? Do you think that offering these services to its customers would give Oak Valley a strategic advantage over other aluminum suppliers? Do you think it likely that other information used at higher levels in the management hierarchy would be made available to the firm's customers?

2. The product-line managers in the marketing department of a consumer goods company receive both weekly inventory status reports and a weekly sales report. Although the reports are accurate, the product-line managers feel that the reports do not meet their needs. What would you guess is the problem? How might it be solved?

H A N D S - O N   P R O J E C T S

1. Find an example of a computer system application in a computer or business magazine. Explain in your own words how this application is used. Where does this application fit in the hierarchical view of information systems?
    Suggestions: PC Week, Computerworld, Business Computer Systems, Business Week, Fortune.
2. Visit the computer center at a hospital, school, or local government office. Describe an application. Where does this application fit in the hierarchical framework?

4
COMPUTERS IN THE TRANSACTION PROCESS

O U T L I N E

O B J E C T I V E S

After studying this chapter you should understand the following:

■ *What a transaction-processing system is and how it is used.*

■ *How data are entered, processed, and output in a transaction-processing system.*

■ *The difference between batch and on-line transaction processing.*

■ *How transaction-processing systems are used in accounting, operations, manufacturing, and sales.*

If you walk into a large firm's computer center filled with impressive hardware and busy computer operators, the odds are that most of what is going on is transaction processing. Computers spend the lion's share of their time in transaction processing. Management Information Systems and Decision Support Systems do indeed help managers guide the *direction* of a business, but transaction-processing systems support the actual *work* of the business. To make an analogy, if Management Information Systems and Decision Support Systems are the delicate appetizers and tempting desserts that begin and end a meal, transaction-processing systems are the vegetables and meat of the main course. As we will see, however, even these can be cut and prepared in some remarkable ways.

Few computer applications are as essential to an organization as its transactions systems are (Figure 4-1). Without them, efficiency would most certainly suffer, operating expenses would increase, and profits would fall. Companies such as airlines would be unable to operate. Imagine a telephone company of today processing billing data without a computerized transaction system. Charges for long distance, information services, basic service, and taxes all would have to be processed manually by an army of clerks. Errors would skyrocket. Some customers would be charged for calls they never made, and calls they did make might be billed incorrectly. In today's competitive environment, with cost pressures on long-distance carriers, no carrier could survive.

Few would suggest a return to the manual methods that predated transaction-processing systems. The evidence from over two decades of computerized transaction-processing systems in a wide range of applications has demonstrated the advantage of using these systems. Most automated record-keeping systems reduce errors and lower costs. In the end, not only is a company more efficient and better able to compete, but the benefits of automation are often passed on to the consumer as lower prices.

There is another benefit. A well-conceived transaction-processing system is the foundation on which a complete corporate information sys-

Figure 4-1.
Transaction-processing systems are essential to the performance of most companies. Shown here is a dispatching system used by a trucking company.

tem is built (Figure 4-2). We learned in the last chapter that the information systems hierarchy consisted of transaction-processing systems at the lowest level, operational planning and control systems at the second level, management planning and control systems at the third, and strategic planning systems on top. Without effective transaction-processing systems, the MIS and DSS applications from the operational planning and control to the strategic planning levels may not be able to exist (Figure 4-3).

In this chapter we will take a close look at computerized transaction-processing systems, and examine several applications in accounting, operations, sales, and marketing.

Figure 4-2.
Transaction-processing systems provide a foundation on which to build a complete corporate information system. Here a manager reviews product sales data obtained from a transaction-processing system.

Figure 4-3.
The place of transaction systems in the information systems hierarchy.

WHAT IS A TRANSACTION SYSTEM?

Chapter 3 stated that a **transaction-processing system** (or **transaction system** for short) keeps records of routine business activities, follows standard operating procedures, and does not require complex decision making. These systems also depend on accurate and detailed data and must be able to process large volumes of data in short periods of time. Examples of transaction systems are accounting, inventory, sales-order entry, banking, and airline reservation systems. All of these applications follow a **transaction-processing cycle,** which begins by entering the data, continues by processing the data, and concludes by presenting the output. In the next three sections we will look more closely at these stages.

TRANSACTION DATA ENTRY

Data can be entered into a computer system in many ways. At a bank, customers can enter their transactions through an automatic teller terminal. At a supermarket, prices may be read by an optical scanning device. At a travel agency, airline reservations are entered through a terminal. Regardless of the method used, the data must be entered accurately as well as efficiently.

DATA ACCURACY

If the transaction data are inaccurate, the applications that use the data may suffer; users may abandon the transaction system; and the organization's financial health may even be jeopardized. Although accuracy is the goal, many databases are plagued by bad data. The following example illustrates how careless data-entry practices can turn an otherwise well-designed system into an ineffective one.

■■■■■■■■■■■■■■■■■■■■■■■■■■■■■■■■■■■■

THE END OF THE MONTH IS USUALLY A VERY BUSY TIME FOR THE GROVE-WOOD COMPANY, a manufacturer of kitchen appliances. Finished goods are rushed out the back door to meet monthly shipping quotas. Often in the rush of the last few hours many depletions from stock are not even entered into the computer information system. The thought uppermost in everyone's mind is reaching the quota. But as a result of these practices, the inventory records maintained by the information system seldom contain accurate information. In fact, anyone who needs an accurate balance for an item knows that the only way to get it is to walk to the stockroom and count the items on the shelf! Few people, however, are willing to take responsibility for this problem. Rather, they blame it on the computer, insisting that a better data-entry system would solve the problem.

To some extent these critics are right. Grovewood's inventory system requires every user to type several pieces of data into a terminal every time a unit is withdrawn from stock. This data entry takes time and is tempting to skip. So, in the rush at the end of the month, few people take the time to do it properly or at all.

■■■■■■■■■■■■■■■■■■■■■■■■■■■■■■■■■■■■

DATA-ENTRY METHODS

To maintain accurate data in a database, the way in which data are entered into the system must be carefully controlled. This control over

Figure 4-4.
Data-collection hardware is often located as close as possible to the data's source.

the data's accuracy or "integrity" is maintained, to some extent, by the software that accepts the data. In Chapter 13 we will see exactly how software can be used to police data entry.

In addition to data-input procedures that are designed to control data entry, companies are turning to **source data automation,** collecting data as near as possible to the time and place of their origination with minimal human intervention (Figure 4-4). Reading prices from products passed over an optical scanner at the supermarket checkout stand is one example of source data automation. This and other source data automation techniques were discussed in Chapter 2.

Collecting data near their source rather than forwarding them to a central group of data-entry clerks has several advantages:

■ Users entering the data know more about them than would data-entry clerks.

■ Data enter the database more quickly.

■ The database is more up-to-date.

■ Data-entry costs can often be passed on to the user.

There is also a disadvantage to moving the data entry to the data source. Central control over data collection will be lost, and the system may become vulnerable to unauthorized access by people at remote locations. The advantages of decentralized access, however, usually outweigh its disadvantages.

■■■■■■■■■■■■■■■■■■■■■■■■■■■■■■■■■■■■

PACKAGE EXPRESS IS A NATIONAL DELIVERY SERVICE THAT ADVERTISES TWENTY-FOUR-HOUR DELIVERY TO ANY LOCATION IN THE UNITED STATES. Its fleet of delivery vans picks up and delivers the packages locally, and its fleet of aircraft transports the packages across the country.

To track the progress of each package, Package Express uses a complex information system. Each delivery vehicle is equipped with a terminal into which the driver enters pickup and delivery data. These data are in turn passed on to local dispatch stations via radio. From the dispatch stations the data are relayed to the corporate mainframe, where the status of the package is updated. Data-entry terminals are also located at distribution centers and airports. Optical reading devices at these locations read the data and update the database to reflect the presence of particular packages at given locations.

This system relies on source data entry. As a result, the database always contains the current whereabouts of every package. Therefore, when a customer calls Package Express and requests delivery information, the exact location of the package can be identified. The ability to provide this information gives Package Express a strategic advantage over many of its competitors, and it emphasizes this advantage in most of its advertisements and TV commercials.

■■■■■■■■■■■■■■■■■■■■■■■■■■■■■■■■■■■■

Figure 4-5.
In this batch-processing application, data are entered into a terminal, stored on disk, and periodically transmitted to a central computer.

PROCESSING TRANSACTION DATA

Once the data have been entered into a transaction system, they must be processed. Two ways of handling data are batch and on-line processing.

BATCH PROCESSING

In **batch processing** the data are collected for a given period of time, and the resulting "batch" of data is processed as a single job (Figure 4-5). Batch processing is useful when most of the records in a large database must be processed at the same time.

■■■■■■■■■■■■■■■■■■■■■■■■■■■■■■■■■

COHEN ASSOCIATES, a Boston accounting firm, subscribes to a service that automatically processes income tax returns. As Sid Cohen explained, "Our accountants enter information for each client into one of our IBM PCs. The data are stored on a disk, and then, at the end of the day, we send the contents of the disk—which may include the data for a dozen or more clients—through our modem to the service bureau's central database. Within forty-eight hours we receive the completed tax returns by mail."

■■■■■■■■■■■■■■■■■■■■■■■■■■■■■■■■■

Many organizations also use batch-processing methods for billing. Telephone, gas, electric, and cable TV companies, for example, prepare their bills using batch processing. Even payroll—whether processed weekly, biweekly, or monthly—is almost always handled by batch processing.

ON-LINE PROCESSING

Although batch processing is still used for some applications, today an increasing number of companies choose **on-line transaction-processing (OLTP)** systems. On-line systems can reduce data-processing costs, offer better customer service, and provide a strategic advantage over competitors (Figure 4-6).

In on-line systems (briefly described in Chapter 2), data are processed instantly by the CPU. As a result, whenever a user wishes to enter or access data, the request is accommodated within a few seconds. Unlike batch processing, each request is processed individually—there is no waiting while groups of requests are batched and processed together. On-line systems are thus preferred when only selected records must be processed at any one point in time or when the user and computer system must interact.

Because on-line transaction-processing systems can access data instantly and because many transaction systems must accommodate large volumes of data, larger systems generally include several disk

Figure 4-6.
In this on-line manufacturing system at Rockwell's Graphic Systems Division, remote terminals are used to collect data on the status of each job, job costs, and payroll.

drives with capacities of several billion bytes (gigabytes) of data. Tapes and optical storage, if used at all, serve as a backup medium, storing additional copies of the data in the event that those stored on disk are lost or damaged.

But an OLTP system that brings data within instantaneous reach can also, if it breaks down, bring many of an organization's activities to a screeching halt. Imagine the consequences of a failure in a bank deposit system. Not only would it be difficult, if not impossible, to continue serving customers, but the cost to the bank for even a few hours of service interruption could be very high.

Because many organizations have become so dependent on OLTP systems and because failures can be dramatically disruptive, some firms have chosen to purchase **fault-tolerant computer systems** (Figure 4-7). These systems use additional hardware and software to help avoid a system failure. One key ingredient is the use of *disk mirroring,* a scheme in which the system maintains a mirror image of critical disk data on two physically separated disk drives. Whenever data are entered into the system, they are automatically entered into both devices; in the event of a disk failure, the system will automatically retrieve the data from the working disk. In addition, fault-tolerant systems can, through hardware and software, circumvent portions of the hardware if the electronic circuitry breaks down.

As we stated in Chapter 2, two other important characteristics of an OLTP are its multiuser and **multitasking** capabilities. A multiuser, multitasking OLTP serves many users, each executing a different job, at what appears to be the same time. For example, it allows several people to sit at terminals scattered throughout an organization and work on problems that may be totally unrelated to one another. One user may be entering accounts receivables transactions; another may be entering accounts payables; and a third may be producing an inventory report. Each user has the impression that no one else is using the system, thanks to complex on-line operating system software that keeps the separate uses of the system disentangled.

Figure 4-7.
In this fault-tolerant on-line transaction-processing system, the system's reliability is close to 100 percent.

OUTPUT FROM TRANSACTION-PROCESSING SYSTEMS

Once the data have been entered and processed, the system gives the users the appropriate output. Output from a transaction-processing system can take many forms. It can be displayed on a screen, printed on paper, or spoken in a simulated voice. Output can be internal for users within the organization or external for the organization's customers and clients. Although most correspondence that leaves an organization is printed on paper, most output used within a firm is displayed on the screen. This practice has led to the term **paperless office** or **paperless factory** (Figure 4-8). Although a totally paperless office may not be possible, a sharp reduction in paperwork may be a design goal in many applications. Organizations often find that many of their paper documents can be replaced by electronic documents, which are easier to file and retrieve. Furthermore, the use of electronic documents reduces the need for duplication.

■■■■■■■■■■■■■■■■■■■■■■■■■■■■■■■■■■

BEFORE THE H.J. WILCOX COMPANY INSTALLED AN OLTP SYSTEM, six documents accompanied each scheduled job through the firm's production facilities. With the new system only one document—the manufacturing specifications—is actually sent with the job. The other documents can be retrieved and displayed whenever they are needed, by using terminals located throughout the production facility. By using a printer, even hard copy is available. According to a spokesperson for the production scheduling group, switching to an OLTP system has cut paperwork at least in half.

■■■■■■■■■■■■■■■■■■■■■■■■■■■■■■■■■■

Figure 4-8.
In manufacturing there is a growing trend toward display screen output and a consequent reduction in the use of paper.

?   Q U E S T I O N S   ?

1. What are the characteristics of a transaction-processing system? How does a transaction-processing system differ from the systems found at higher levels in the information systems hierarchy?

2. What characteristics are shared by data processed in a transaction system?

3. What are the three stages of the transaction-processing cycle?

4. What are some advantages of source data automation? Does it have any disadvantages?

5. How does a batch-processing system work? When is such a system used?

6. How does an on-line transaction-processing system work? When is such a system used?

7. What is multitasking?

8. How can paperwork in an office be cut down? Do you think a totally paperless office or factory is possible?

APPLICATIONS IN ACCOUNTING

DIFFERENCES FROM OTHER TRANSACTION SYSTEMS

Accounting systems collect, store, process, and present an organization's accounting data. Although these systems share the characteristics of all transaction-processing systems, they are also characterized by the fact that they:

■ Process transactions involve the firm's assets and liabilities.

■ Are often the target of computer crime.

■ Must maintain, in many circumstances, absolutely accurate data.

■ Include the data used to report a company's performance to the IRS, other governmental agencies, and company investors.

Let's look a bit more closely at each of these characteristics.

Assets and Liabilities Accounting systems maintain records and process data that control the flow of a firm's assets and liabilities. *Assets* are items of value to the firm such as cash and property, and its *liabilities* are its debts or sums owed to other businesses or individuals.

Vulnerability to Unauthorized Access The records of a firm's assets include not only cash accounts—such as a checking or cash account at a bank—but also accounts that keep data regarding the money that customers owe the firm and the money that the firm owes its suppliers. Because money is involved, these systems are particularly vulnerable to criminal activity, and as a result, security is an important issue in the design and use of accounting systems. But preventing unauthorized access can be difficult, as the firm's accounting database is often accessible from terminals distributed over a broad geographic area. Indeed, the intention behind distributing terminals is to make it easier for authorized users to gain access to financial data. Unfortunately, this strategy also makes it easier for unauthorized users to gain similar access. Chapter 13 will cover techniques that can be used to control access to a system and make it more secure. Nonetheless, accounting systems remain more vulnerable than most other applications are.

Accuracy   Data in any system should be accurate. In accounting systems, they must be accurate, down to the penny. Cash, sales, and credit data cannot be subject to errors. No company can tolerate the problems created by inaccurate cash balance data, nor will customers tolerate errors in billing data.

To protect the accuracy of data, the computer information system must ensure as best it can that the data are entered correctly and that once entered, their accuracy is maintained. This can be especially difficult in applications in which data are sent between remote locations over communications media such as telephone lines.

Basis of External Reporting   Accounting systems are unique in that they collect the information needed to pay taxes and report on a company's financial status to its stockholders. Every month, quarter, and end of year, companies must file reports with the Internal Revenue Service and various other federal, state, and even local government agencies. Every quarter and year end they must also send financial reports to their stockholders. In addition, publicly held companies must file quarterly reports with the Securities and Exchange Commission.

TYPES OF ACCOUNTING SYSTEMS

At least five different types of accounting systems can be found in most organizations:

- General ledger systems
- Billing systems
- Accounts receivable systems
- Accounts payable systems
- Payroll systems

In the following sections we will briefly discuss each.

GENERAL LEDGER SYSTEMS

At the heart of an accounting system is the **general ledger system,** a collection of accounts for maintaining records of all of an organization's accounting transactions, including the cash, accounts receivable, and accounts payable accounts. Whenever cash is received, purchases made, wages paid, or dividends issued, the data to record these events are entered into the appropriate accounts.

A general ledger system is primarily a bookkeeping system. Although in theory, manual general ledger systems may still be used, a computerized one has many advantages. A computerized general ledger system is more efficient, can provide timely information for maintaining greater control over the accounting process, and can help control the organization's operations.

In the computerized general ledger system illustrated in Figure 4-9, accounting transactions are first entered through a terminal. In the next step, the computer accesses the correct account in the database, loads that account record from the disk into main memory, updates the account, and finally writes the new balance back to the database. Output from the general ledger system can take many forms. The status of an account can be displayed on a screen, and financial statements and special reports can be printed.

Figure 4-9.
A general ledger system accepts accounting transactions as input, updates account records, and produces financial reports.

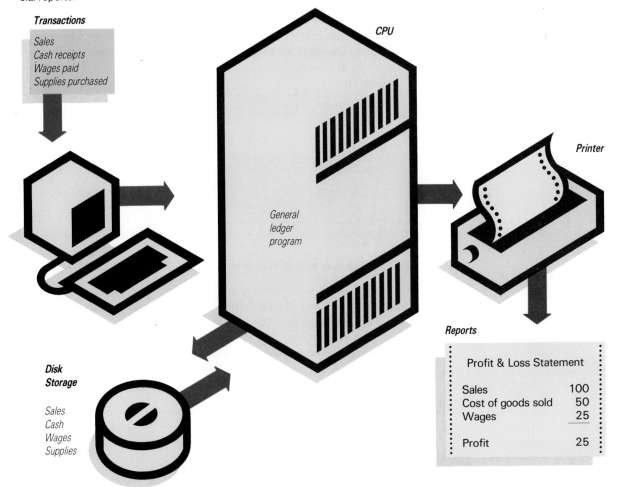

Transactions

Sales
Cash receipts
Wages paid
Supplies purchased

CPU

General
ledger
program

Printer

Disk Storage

Sales
Cash
Wages
Supplies

Reports

Profit & Loss Statement

Sales	100
Cost of goods sold	50
Wages	25
Profit	25

Developing a System   Large companies with specialized requirements will sometimes develop and write their own general ledger software. This process, however, may take a team of professionals months or even years to complete. Many organizations find this approach too expensive and choose instead to purchase a commercial general ledger package. Most commercial packages are designed in such a way that users can "customize" or alter the system to accommodate their own particular operations.

If a company buys a commercial package, it must be initialized, a process that prepares the system to accept the company's data. In this process, the following steps are undertaken:

■   Establish a chart of accounts.

■   Enter the chart of accounts into the system.

■   Design financial statements.

■   Enter opening balances.

The accounts in a general ledger system into which accounting transactions are entered are collectively referred to as the **chart of accounts.** One account may be the cash account, another the sales account, and a third the wages account. Several such accounts are listed in Figure 4-10. A properly chosen chart of accounts is more than a record-keeping system; it can also be used as a control system.

Figure 4-10.
The chart of accounts represents the categories into which the accounting transactions are entered.

Cash

Sales

Cost of goods sold

Wages

Selling expenses

General expenses

Taxes

Figure 4-11.
These twelve separate accounts enable closer control over three profit centers.

AT THE SANBORN COMPANY, a manufacturer of medical electronic equipment, the accounting system divides the manufacturing process into three profit centers, the fabrication, assembly, and inventory centers. Each profit center has its own general ledger accounts (Figure 4-11), into which expenses are entered. Wages incurred in the fabrication profit center are entered in an account called "Wages-F," wages in the assembly profit center in the "Wages-A" account, and wages in the

Wages-F	*Wages-A*	*Wages-I*
Materials-F	*Materials-A*	*Materials-I*
Supervision-F	*Supervision-A*	*Supervision-I*
Supplies-F	*Supplies-A*	*Supplies-I*

inventory profit center in the "Wages-I" account. Other expense categories such as materials, supervision, and supplies are also broken down by profit center.

One advantage of using this approach is that the expenses for each profit center can be printed separately in report form. Then management can use each report to compare the performance of the profit centers. If the expenses for all profit centers were not kept separately but were combined into one account, management would not be able to determine how each center was performing.

■■■■■■■■■■■■■■■■■■■■■■■■■■■■■■■■■■■

Once the chart of accounts has been determined, each account name is entered into the general ledger software package. This is usually a straightforward process in which the user responds to prompts on the display screen and enters the account titles one at a time at the keyboard.

After the accounts have been entered, the financial statements are designed. One such statement, the **profit-and-loss (P&L) statement,** expresses an organization's profit (or loss) over a specific operating period. This financial statement is designed by specifying the name of the sales and expense accounts that will be used in the report and, in some cases, specifying the physical layout of the report itself.

Once it has been designed, a user can request a P&L statement at any time. When it is requested, the software automatically accesses the appropriate general ledger accounts and places the balance of the accounts in the specified P&L format, such as the one shown in Figure 4-12.

In the final initialization step, the opening balances are entered into the system. So if the cash balance of the company is $6,534.55, this number—together with the other general ledger account balances—is entered into the system. Once all opening data have been entered, the system is ready to use. The next case illustrates how one organization acquired, initialized, and used a general ledger system.

■■■■■■■■■■■■■■■■■■■■■■■■■■■■■■■■■■■

UPPERCUT IS A BEAUTY PARLOR LOCATED IN A SUBURBAN SHOPPING MALL. It employs twelve full-time and eight part-time hairdressers. All of Uppercut's accounting is done on an IBM microcomputer which the owner, Jackie Thomas, purchased several years ago.

Although Thomas bought one of the more popular accounting packages, it took her almost three months to bring the system into full operation. "I bought this software without knowing the first thing about accounting," she said. "For three thousand dollars I thought the computer would solve all my problems. But I was wrong! When I unpacked the system, I discovered that there were lots of new problems to be solved before the computer could solve my old ones. I had to decide on a chart of accounts; I had to figure out how to set the system up so that it knew what these accounts were; and I had to learn how to construct profit-

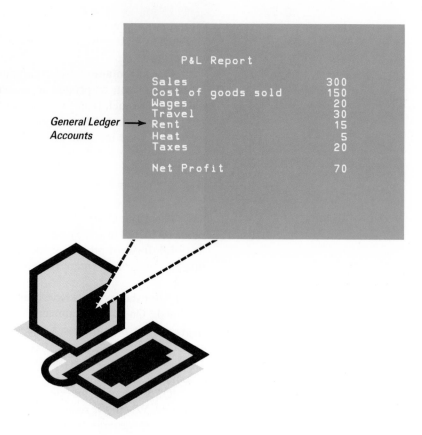

General Ledger → Accounts

```
              P&L Report

        Sales                    300
        Cost of goods sold       150
        Wages                     20
        Travel                    30
        Rent                      15
        Heat                       5
        Taxes                     20

        Net Profit                70
```

Figure 4-12.
The profit-and-loss statement is designed by identifying the general ledger accounts to be included in the report.

and-loss and balance sheet statements. What an education! It's hard to believe I actually did it."

The chart of accounts that Thomas eventually entered is shown in Figure 4-13. Once the software was initialized, it was ready for use. Now at the end of each day Thomas summarizes her sales slips and makes the appropriate entries into the system.

Thomas has found the system to be very helpful. She especially likes the financial reports she can obtain at the close of each month. Before she bought her computer, her accountant prepared financial statements only twice each year, and even then these reports were usually eight to ten weeks late. One of the reasons they were so late was that it took her accountant several days to summarize all the data and prepare the reports. Now, using her computer, she can prepare the reports in a few hours.

After one year, however, Thomas has become somewhat critical of the system. All expenses—whether they are for linen service, paper products, shampoos and conditioners, equipment, or maintenance supplies—are charged to a single general-expense category. Although this produces a simple chart of accounts, there was little that could be learned from the data. At the end of the month, for example, Thomas cannot determine how much was spent on the individual categories, in order to see whether usage was heavy or light. In short, the data have little value for management control purposes.

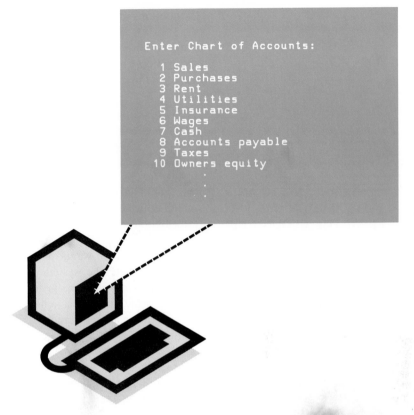

Figure 4-13.
Uppercut's chart of accounts. Every company has its own unique chart of accounts, specified during the software initialization process.

So Thomas has decided to separate this category into twenty-five new accounts. After the new version of her system is finished, at the end of the month she will be able to obtain a P&L with sufficient detail to determine exactly how her money was spent—and do something about it.

BILLING SYSTEMS

When a large company offers credit to its customers, a bill is usually prepared on a computerized **billing system** shortly after the customer's order is filled. The description of the items purchased, their cost, and customer data are entered into the system. The system then prepares and mails the bill or "invoice."

As is the case with accounting systems, some large companies may write their own billing software. Most, however, find it less expensive to purchase billing software developed by commercial software vendors. And if commercial software is chosen, it must be initialized in a process that is similar to that followed when general ledger systems are initialized.

Billing systems may or may not be tied directly to the general ledger system. In some billing systems, an automatic entry is made into the accounts receivable account in the general ledger system as well as in the accounts receivable system (described in the next section). In other systems, however, such entries are not automatically made. Copies of the invoices are sent to the appropriate person in the accounting department, and manual entries are made to both of these systems.

● ●

E N D · U S E R   H I N T S

UNDERSTANDING AN INFORMATION SYSTEM FROM THE GROUND UP

The foundation of many information systems is the transaction system, which captures data at their source. Although business professionals are seldom responsible for entering transaction data into the system, learning how the system works in general terms will be necessary if the business professional is to obtain a better understanding of the organization's information processing system.

Sometimes you can learn a lot by watching an experienced clerk use the system. In other cases it may be necessary to learn by asking computer professionals or by reading the documentation supplied with the software. Whichever way you learn, following certain steps makes the job easier.

Start with the output of the system. This will tell you what the system is attempting to do. If the application is a reservation system for an entertainment facility, then you should be able to tell from the screen that the system will provide information about the status of a seat. Then, if the seat is available and the customer wants to purchase a ticket, the system will make the reservation, print a ticket, and process a charge against the customer's credit card number. By studying this output, you begin to learn what the computer is doing.

Next, determine what the system requires the clerks to do. What data must they enter? Are some data, such as the date, automatically entered? Are checks and balances imposed on the data as they are entered, or is it possible for the clerks to enter wrong data? As a result of these observations, how reliable do you think the data in the system are?

Then study the processing function of the system. What steps are taken when the data are processed? In a sales-order entry system, a credit authorization may be automatically obtained when the computer dials the credit card authorization center. In an accounting application, the computer may have to maintain a detailed record of every person who uses the system.

Now turn to the hardware and software. Is batch processing used? If so, how often are the data updated? Is an OLTP system used? How many terminals are connected to the computer? How is access obtained? How are data stored? What is the capacity of the system? Is the system near its maximum capacity, or does it have room to grow? Is access time fast enough for most users?

Understanding the transaction system, from input to output, is essential if the business professional is to rely on the reports and data produced by Management Information and Decision Support Systems. Only by understanding the underlying transaction system can the user truly have confidence that the data used to solve problems and make decisions are timely and reliable.

● ●

ACCOUNTS RECEIVABLE SYSTEMS

Another accounting system is the **accounts receivable system,** which keeps track of the amounts owed by, and the payments received from, customers who make purchases on credit.

The input to an accounts receivable system (Figure 4-14) begins when a sale is made and the customer is billed for the products or services. When the details of the new purchase are entered into the system, the software searches for the customer's record in a customer master file, which contains data about all of the customers and is stored on disk. Then the new sales data are added to this record. Similarly, the master file is updated when payment is made.

Regularly, usually once a month, the accounts receivable system generates monthly statements which are mailed to the customers. These statements list those invoices that have been paid since the last statement, those that have not, and the total amount due. One such statement is shown in Figure 4-15. In addition, accounts receivable systems produce several reports used in the credit and collection process. One report, called an **aged trial balance report,** is especially useful for controlling receivables, as it lists those customers who have not paid their bills for more than 30, 60, and 90 days (Figure 4-16).

What benefits do users receive from a computerized accounts receivable system? First, it sends invoices regularly until the bill is paid.

Figure 4-14.
Credit sales are entered into an accounts receivable system; the database is updated to reflect the new balance owed by the firm's customers; and monthly statements and reports are produced as output.

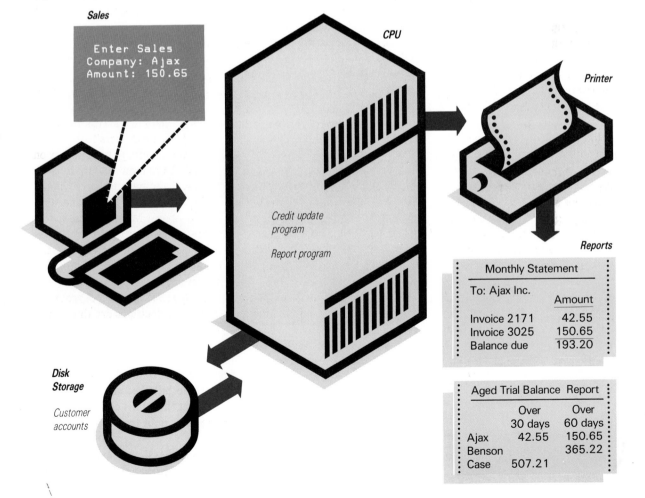

Monthly Statement	
To: Ajax Inc.	Amount
Invoice 2171	42.55
Invoice 3025	150.65
Balance due	193.20

Aged Trial Balance Report		
	Over 30 days	Over 60 days
Ajax	42.55	150.65
Benson		365.22
Case	507.21	

```
                         Statement


     Ajax Company
     10411 South Main St
     East Bridgewater, Idaho
                                           Amount

     Invoice   2171                         42.55
     Invoice   3025                        150.65


     Balance Due                           193.20
```

Current	Over 30 days	Over 60 days	Over 90 days
—	42.55	150.65	

Figure 4-15.
An accounts receivable statement.

```
                Aged Trial Balance Report
                    Over        Over        Over
                  30 days     60 days     90 days

     Ajax          42.55      150.65

     Benson                   365.22

     Case         507.21

     Denix                                1237.42

     Fargo         82.50

     Standard                 221.30      651.75

                  632.26      737.17     1889.17
```

Figure 4-16.
An aged trial balance report.

Second, the company uses an aged trial balance to focus attention on the collection of overdue accounts before these bills become impossible to collect. Third, those who are slow in paying their bills can be identified, and their credit rating adjusted, before their debt from additional purchases becomes too high.

Most computerized accounts receivable systems perform well. As a result, the total amount of outstanding receivables is often less with a computer system than when processed manually. When receivables are low, the firm's need for funds decreases, and borrowing costs drop. The result is higher profits.

Although some larger companies prefer to write their own accounts receivable software, many do not. Instead, they choose from a wide variety of commercial software packages. An initialization process similar to the one followed with general ledger systems is required before the accounts receivable software is ready for actual use.

ACCOUNTS PAYABLE SYSTEMS

An **accounts payable system** maintains records of purchases made from vendors. Data entry into this system begins when a bill from the vendor arrives. The vendor's record is located and data are entered for the goods received, including the items purchased, their cost, and the date on which the bill is due. In addition, an entry is also made to the general ledger to record the dollar amount of the outstanding bill.

An accounts payable system produces reports that regularly inform the accounting department when payments to vendors are due. Using this system, the accounting department will not miss the discounts often given by vendors to those companies that pay their bills on time. In addition, by paying its bills on time, the company can maintain a good credit rating.

PAYROLL SYSTEMS

Most organizations of all types, apart from the very simplest, use payroll systems. In a **payroll system** the hours that each employee works are entered into the computer system, and static data—such as the employee's wage rate, number of dependents, and payroll deductions—are retrieved from secondary storage when the payroll is run. Using both the static and dynamic data, a payroll system computes each employee's pay, prints a paycheck, and in most cases makes the appropriate entries in the general ledger system. In addition, the computer system can store historical payroll data that can be used to prepare reports and forms required by federal, state, and local government agencies.

The relationship among these different types of transaction systems is shown in Figure 4-17. Together they work to organize, manage, and control the firm's assets and liabilities.

APPLICATIONS IN OPERATIONS AND MANUFACTURING

Most operations and manufacturing facilities depend on routine transaction data to make schedules, control schedules, order raw materials, assign employees, control inventories, and respond to unexpected problems. Without the information provided by these computer systems,

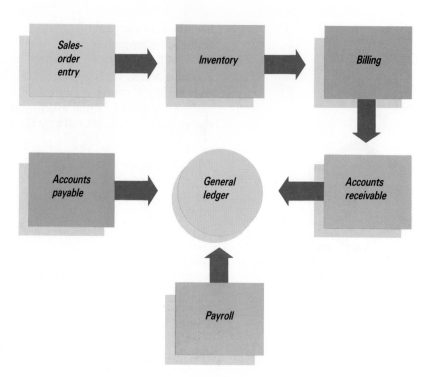

Figure 4-17.
The relationship among several transaction systems in an organization.

manufacturing costs would almost certainly rise, deliveries slip, and customer service deteriorate.

Because this type of software is so complex to develop, most small companies, and even some larger ones, find it more economical to use prepackaged software for these applications. But there are many large firms with central data processing staffs that develop their own. They insist that their problems are unlike those found in other companies, and that a more general software system designed to accommodate a wide range of users is not for them.

In the following sections we will describe three common transaction applications in operations and manufacturing: inventory, purchasing, and reservations.

INVENTORY SYSTEMS

The primary objective of an **inventory system** is to provide accurate and timely data on the status of every item in stock, so that the items will be available when needed. The items are often called *stockkeeping units*. The system maintains a record for each stockkeeping unit, updating the record whenever stock is added or depleted (Figure 4-18).

When stock is depleted, for example, the user enters the stockkeeping number that identifies the item and the number of units taken from inventory. Next the inventory system finds the record for this item in the database, transfers the contents of the record to the CPU, updates the balance amount, and writes the new balance back to the disk.

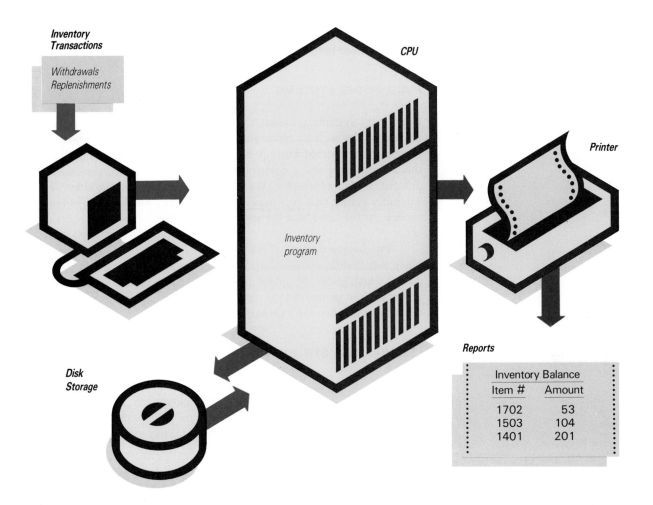

Figure 4-18.
Inventory transactions are entered into the inventory system, and the balance of the item is updated. When requested, the system also produces inventory reports.

Inventory systems are not only used in manufacturing or distribution environments, but as the following case illustrates, they also are used in marketing.

FRANK BENNET, a salesman for Tabco Inc., an industrial manufacturer, carries a portable computer to each sales call and uses it for inquiries. When a customer places an order, Bennet connects his computer to the customer's phone, accesses his company's finished goods inventory database, and determines which of the items can be shipped from current stock and which items will have to be back ordered.

In addition to updates and inquiries, inventory systems also provide management with reports. Usually considered part of the Management Information System, the reports may include the total dollar amount invested in inventory, list the inventory by categories, or identify those items that need to be reordered.

PURCHASING SYSTEMS

Purchasing systems are used to produce the paperwork necessary to place an order with a vendor and to monitor the status of items that a company has ordered but has not yet received. The data entered into these systems include a description of the items ordered, the quantity ordered, shipping instructions, and the vendor's name and address. The computer system then produces a purchase order, which is mailed to the vendor. At the same time the system updates the database to reflect the order.

Purchasing systems also keep track of the vendor's history (reliability, return rate, and so on) and which items are sold by particular vendors at which prices. The purchasing system can help structure purchase orders so as to minimize total cost (item prices plus shipping) within the constraints of when the items are needed.

RESERVATION SYSTEMS

Reservation systems are used mainly by car-rental firms, hotels, and airlines. They help make, cancel, and track reservations. These systems—airline reservation systems in particular—are perhaps the most complex of all on-line transaction-processing systems. They may support a large number of users, are often available around the clock, and are usually vital to the business they serve.

In an airline reservation system, a central database stores data on the availability of seats for each flight. Usually this database can be accessed by ticket agents and travel agencies around the world. Agents can make inquiries to the database, such as which flights are scheduled between two airports on a given date at a given time. When the customer makes a decision, a reservation is entered. This involves the on-line updating of the central database, reducing the number of available seats, and creating a passenger name record containing such data as the passenger's name and phone number.

Airline reservation systems are characterized by massive databases, an enormous number of terminals, and very high transaction volume. One medium-sized international carrier, for example, uses 144 disk drives, each with a capacity of 300 million bytes; supports over 12,000 remote terminals; and, at peak periods, handles more than 200 transactions each second.

APPLICATIONS IN SALES AND MARKETING

In today's business environment, where the ability to respond quickly to competitive situations is a must, many companies find their computer

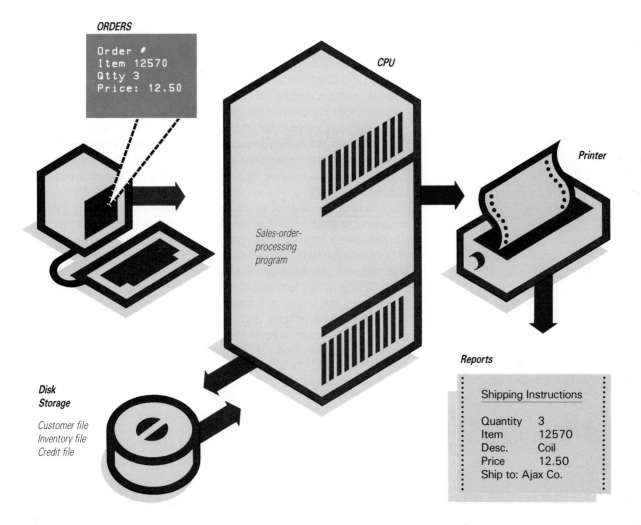

Figure 4-19.
Orders are entered into a sales-order entry system. Several files are checked to determine whether a customer record has already been established, which items are available for immediate shipment, and whether the dollar value of the order is within range of the customer's credit limit.

sales and marketing systems indispensable. One of these systems, **sales-order entry** (Figure 4-19), is an application that not only speeds the order process and enables the company to serve its customers faster but also is the basis for collecting data that can be used to analyze sales patterns. The purpose of a sales-order entry system is to process incoming orders as quickly and efficiently as possible (Figure 4-20). This often requires access to several different categories of centralized data, including inventory and customer credit data.

■■■■■■■■■■■■■■■■■■■■■■■■■■■■■■■■■

HIGHTECH SUPPLY IS A DISTRIBUTOR OF COMPUTER SUPPLIES, such as paper, printer ribbons, and floppy disks. Its customers include commercial accounts that the company is committed to serve as quickly and efficiently as possible. In fact, Hightech advertises that it ships most orders within twenty-four hours. To offer such efficient service, Hightech has three toll-free telephone lines through which its customers place orders, as well as a computerized sales-order entry system to accept the orders.

Figure 4-20.
Sales data can be entered directly from the field using this portable data system that transmits the data to a remote central computer.

When a customer places a call, a sales representative asks for the customer's company name. The company name is entered into a terminal, and the computer system then searches the customer database to find the company's record. If it cannot be found, the caller is switched to a new account representative who sets up an account.

When the correct account is located, the system displays several data items on the sales representative's screen, including the buyer's name. So, within a few seconds after entering the company's name, the representative can respond with a personal greeting: "Good morning, is this Alice Brooks?"

In the next stage of the order process, the representative asks for the name, product identification number, and quantity of each item in the customer's order. As the representative obtains these data they are entered into the terminal. Once the entries are completed, the computer then consults the inventory database to determine the status of each item. Within a few seconds the representative can tell the customer which items can be shipped, which must be back ordered, and how long it will take to receive those that are back ordered.

If the customer accepts the delivery terms, the sales-order entry system will again access the inventory system and determine the price for each item. Then this price is multiplied by the quantity ordered, and the total cost of the order is computed. Next, the software accesses the customer's available credit to see whether the current order falls within its limits. After the credit is approved, the order is entered into the sales-order entry file. This file is usually accessed by inventory personnel within four hours, when they pick the orders from stock, make the appropriate entries into the inventory computer system, and ship the orders.

■■■■■■■■■■■■■■■■■■■■■■■■■■■■■■■■■■■■■■

As should be clear, a sales-order entry system speeds the processing of orders from receipt until shipment. And once the sales-order entry data become part of the company database, they can be used to support marketing and sales activities (Figure 4-21), as the following example illustrates.

■■■■■■■■■■■■■■■■■■■■■■■■■■■■■■■■■■■■■■

AT THE HILLSBORO COMPANY, distributors of imported gourmet foods, sales representatives carry portable computers and enter each order into the computer when they make a sale. At the end of the day the orders are sent through a modem over telephone lines to the company's mainframe. Once received, the data are entered into the order-entry system and are shortly thereafter accessed by inventory personnel who begin to pack the order.

The data in the sales-order entry database are also used every morning to produce a report that summarizes the sales of each product in the line. And once every week, on Monday morning, several additional reports are produced. One lists weekly and year-to-date sales by

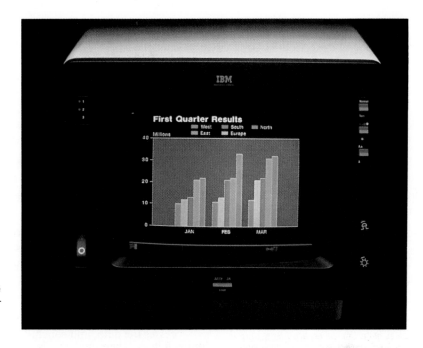

Figure 4-21.
Sales data collected and processed promptly by an information system are an effective vehicle for better management control of marketing and sales activities.

product line and compares these figures with sales goals and with those of last year. Another report compares the sales of each representative with the sales goals. Using these reports, the marketing strategies, sales promotions, and incentive programs used to support Hillsboro's twelve-person sales force are reviewed and revised when necessary.

Some companies may use commercial software for sales-order entry, but most large companies are likely to develop their own software. This allows them to design a system that will meet their own needs and, in particular, that will produce the kinds of reports most useful to the sales and marketing staff.

?   Q U E S T I O N S   ?

1. How do accounting systems differ from other transaction-processing systems?
2. What is the purpose of a general ledger system?
3. How is a commercial general ledger system customized for a particular application?
4. Explain how a general ledger system can be designed so that it can be used to monitor and control the expenses in a particular profit center.
5. How does a computerized accounts receivable system work? What are the benefits of using such a system?
6. What is the primary function of an inventory system?

7. Describe how an airline reservation system works. Why would these systems be classified as OLTP systems?

8. What steps are followed in the sales-order entry system described in the chapter?

9. For which types of applications would a large company be likely to write its own software rather than purchasing it prepackaged?

S U M M A R Y

- **Transaction-processing systems** (or **transaction systems** for short) keep records of routine business activities, follow standard operating procedures, do not require complex decision making, depend on accurate and detailed data, and process large volumes of data in short periods of time.

- The **transaction-processing cycle** begins by entering the data, processes the data, and concludes by presenting the output.

- **Source data automation**—collecting data as near as possible to the time and place of their origination with minimal human intervention—is used more and more often for data entry.

- With **batch-processing** systems, data are collected for a given period of time, and the resulting "batch" is processed as a single job. Billing is a typical application.

- With **on-line transaction processing** (OLTP) systems, data are processed instantly, and there is no waiting while groups of requests are batched and processed together. But because of the dramatic consequences when such systems fail, **fault-tolerant computer systems** are often employed to help avoid failures.

- An important characteristic of OLTP systems is **multitasking,** whereby the computer system serves many users, each performing a different job, at what appears to be the same time.

- Output from a transaction-processing system can take many forms. A trend toward using documents stored and displayed electronically is leading toward the **paperless office** or **paperless factory.**

- **Accounting systems** collect, store, process, and present an organization's accounting data. Such systems process transactions involving the firm's assets and liabilities, are often the target of computer crime, must maintain absolutely accurate data, and include data reported to governmental agencies and investors.

- At the heart of an accounting system is the **general ledger system,** a collection of accounts for maintaining records of all of an organization's accounting transactions, including the cash, accounts receivable, and accounts payable accounts.

■ In a general ledger system, the accounts into which accounting transactions are entered are collectively referred to as the **chart of accounts.**

■ An important statement produced by the general ledger system is the **profit-and-loss (P & L) statement,** which gives an organization's profit (or loss) over an operating period.

■ Many organizations use **billing systems** to prepare their customer's bills.

■ An **accounts receivable system** keeps track of the amounts owed by, and the payments received from, customers who buy on credit. The **aged trial balance report,** produced by the system, helps track customers who have not paid their bills.

■ An **accounts payable system** maintains records of purchases made from vendors.

■ **Payroll systems** compute pay, print checks, and store data for reports to governmental agencies.

■ **Inventory systems** provide accurate and timely data on the status of every item kept in stock, so that the items will be available when needed.

■ **Purchasing systems** produce the paperwork necessary to place orders with vendors and to monitor the status of items on order.

■ Car-rental firms, hotels, and airlines use **reservation systems.** Airline reservation systems, in particular, are perhaps the most complex OLTP systems.

■ **Sales-order entry** is an application that not only speeds the order process and enables companies to serve their customers faster but that also is the basis for collecting data helpful in analyzing sales patterns.

K E Y • T E R M S

The following list shows the key terms in the order in which they appear in the chapter.

Transaction-processing system
(transaction system) (p. 99)
Transaction-processing cycle
(p. 99)

Source data automation (p. 101)
Batch processing (p. 102)
On-line transaction processing
(OLTP) (p. 102)

FOR DISCUSSION

1. Suppose a new manufacturing company is developing a computer information system. Would you recommend that it begin with an accounting system or with a system to help place orders for raw materials? Explain your choice.

2. The Beacon Company currently has transaction-processing systems for inventory, shipping, billing, and accounts receivable. These systems are separate from one another, and data are entered in them in separate areas of the company by different people. A recently hired employee has suggested that these systems be tied together and that entries from one system be made automatically to another. Explain why this might make sense. Can you see any disadvantages to such a system?

HANDS-ON PROJECTS

1. Visit your local supermarket, and observe the transaction system used to process orders through the checkout stand. How are data entered into the system? Is this an example of source data automation? What do you think is the sequence of steps in processing each transaction? How is the output presented? Would you classify this as a batch or an on-line system?

2. Interview an accountant (or a student majoring in accounting) and ask him or her what the two main advantages and disadvantages of computerized general ledger systems are.

■■■

C A S E · S T U D Y

CASCADE SPORTS

Two months ago, Del King was hired by Cascade Sports as its new marketing manager. King had worked for a major retailer in San Francisco and was hired by Cascade to bring additional strength to a catalog sales business that was growing faster than the sales made in Cascade's two retail stores.

The catalog was started four years ago, and for the first two years, it was sent to Cascade's regular customers. But when Cascade began advertising the catalog in national magazines, its circulation increased dramatically, as did its sales from the catalog. During its recent peak selling season (July to December), Cascade processed from one thousand to three thousand orders each day.

Herman Feist, the president of Cascade, is especially excited about the potential of the catalog business. He pointed to the fact that between 30 and 50 percent of North American households ordered from catalogs of some sort last year and that this segment of the retail business is growing at an annual rate of 10 percent. It is Feist's feeling that these gains are due to a shifting society in which more women were working, thereby increasing family income but reducing time available for shopping. And at the retail level, the cost of labor is so high that retailers are cutting back on the service at their stores. A combination of such factors suggests that the catalog sales industry has a bright future.

Cascade is in the sporting goods business. It sells outdoor apparel and equipment and is known especially for goose-down sleeping bags, vests, jackets, and parkas. Cascade's sales last year totaled $55 million, 60 percent of which was from the catalog and 40 percent from the two retail locations.

Computer Facilities

Seven years ago Cascade bought a minicomputer to handle payroll, accounts payable, and inventory control. The inventory software, which used the batch-processing method, kept records of the items in stock and on order. Four remote terminals located in the distribution and shipping warehouse were used to enter additions and depletions from inventory. These entries were saved on disk, and at the close of the workday, the inventory database was updated.

Weekly reports were produced listing the stock levels for all items in inventory. Although the system was useful to those in the inventory and purchasing departments, it was not to those in the catalog order department, as it was impossible to obtain on-line access to current inventory levels. So, when a customer called and asked whether an item was in stock, the order clerk could only refer to the most recent inventory stock report, which did not reflect what was on the shelves at the moment.

A New System

Shortly after his arrival, Del King made it clear that he needed access to timely data from which he would make the kind of decisions that would chart Cascade's future. He needed to know how certain items were selling, where sales were coming from, and even the buying history of particular customers.

In his second week, King arranged to meet with Phil Woods, the MIS manager, and Nancy Green, the supervisor of catalog sales-order entry. At that meeting King began to explain the kinds of data he sought. He needed to know the advertisements and catalogs from which orders were received. He needed to have instant access to the order database, so that he could determine which items were selling. He needed to be able to summarize data into groups and into regions of the country, and he needed to know what percentages of sales were credit-card and cash sales, and to isolate certain regular customers so that they could be sent special mailings.

While he explained his needs, Green became increasingly concerned. When King finished, she explained that her department was already overworked and that it would be impossible for her to collect the data that King wanted.

Order entry was currently processed through a manual system. Operators took an order, entered the data on a three-part form, and sent the form to the credit department, where credit clerks totaled the order and received the proper authorization from the credit-card companies.

When Green objected to the increase in workload, Woods interrupted. "I think this supports the position I have taken for the last year," he said. "We've outgrown our current computer, and we must bite the bullet and buy a larger one."

King asked what he had in mind and how it might help.

"We basically need a new on-line transaction-processing system," replied Woods. "From my knowledge of other companies like ours, I would guess the computer we need would have about four megabytes of main memory, about one gigabyte of disk storage, a backup tape drive, two printers for internal paperwork that could print about six hundred lines per minute, and two laser printers for faster output. About forty-five work stations would be enough. I expect that inventory would take five of them, sales-order entry about twenty, and the rest would be spread among marketing, accounting, and administration."

King was confused. "Phil, all that technology doesn't mean much to me. Maybe it will help Nancy, but it's not clear how it will help me."

"First we've got to build a strong transaction system," Woods said. "Only then can we overlay an MIS system like the one you need. Let me give you an example. In the transaction system I envision, the order-entry clerks will get order data from the customers over the phone and enter these data directly into the system. Once the customer's name, address, items purchased, and prices are entered, the system will automatically dial up for a credit-card authorization, and the order will be sent to the terminals in the shipping department where a packing ticket and customer invoice will be printed. The shipping clerks will then pack the order and send it on its way. Finally, the system will process the credit-card data so that Cascade's bank account can be credited with the amount of the sale as soon as possible."

"Not only would such a system cut processing time," Woods continued, "which now is about seven working days, but it also would offer some benefits. For example, the software that we would use, called a database management system, would enable you or your marketing people to request data. You could find out how our subzero sleeping bags have sold in the last month. Or you might ask for a graph of cookstove sales for the last three years."

"It just occurred to me how you could solve another one of my problems," said King. "Suppose

we use a different last letter on a product's code to represent the catalog or newspaper advertisement from which a customer placed the order. For instance, product number 2345A might represent product 2345 advertised in the *Sunday Times*, and 2345B might represent the same item advertised in our fall gift catalog."

"Excellent idea," said Woods. "You now see why the careful development of a transaction-processing system is so important. The Management Information System is only as good as the transaction system."

Green had been listening intently to the exchange of ideas. "Phil," she said, "one of our problems is that customers usually want to know whether an item is in stock before they place their order. With the old system, we have outdated data and can't give them an accurate answer. Do you think your new system could help?"

"Absolutely," replied Woods. "We could design the terminal's screen to automatically display the stock position of an item whenever a clerk entered an order. Then if the screen showed the item as out of stock, the clerk could ask the system to display the date the order is expected to arrive in stock."

King was excited. "Nancy, I think you have hit on something that could help us give better service to our customer and give us an advantage over our competitors. I like it."

King then turned to Woods. "Phil, how can we sell this to management? A quarter of a million dollars isn't small change, and we'll probably get a lot of resistance to replacing a five-year-old system."

Questions

1. Describe Cascade's problem.
2. What is the new system's transaction component?
3. Although part of the proposed system is a transaction system, other components of the system will be used differently. What are these uses, and how can they be classified?
4. Could King's needs be accommodated by a new and completely separate marketing information system, or do you feel that a new transaction-processing system is needed as a foundation for the information King needs?
5. Compare the differences between the older batch processing of orders and the proposed on-line

processing of orders. What are the benefits of on-line processing?

6. Could automated source data entry be considered for sales orders?

7. What are the advantages to having the sales-order clerks enter the data from terminals, rather than having centralized data-entry clerks—who might be faster typists—enter the data from a centralized location?

8. How would the proposed system benefit the accounting department?

9. Would the system affect the organization's cash flow?

10. Would the operating system have to have multi-tasking capabilities? Explain.

11. Do you think Cascade should consider a fault-tolerant computer system to solve its problem? Why or why not?

12. Assume that you have been chosen to make a presentation to Cascade's top management team. Prepare a statement that justifies your recommendation of a new computer system.

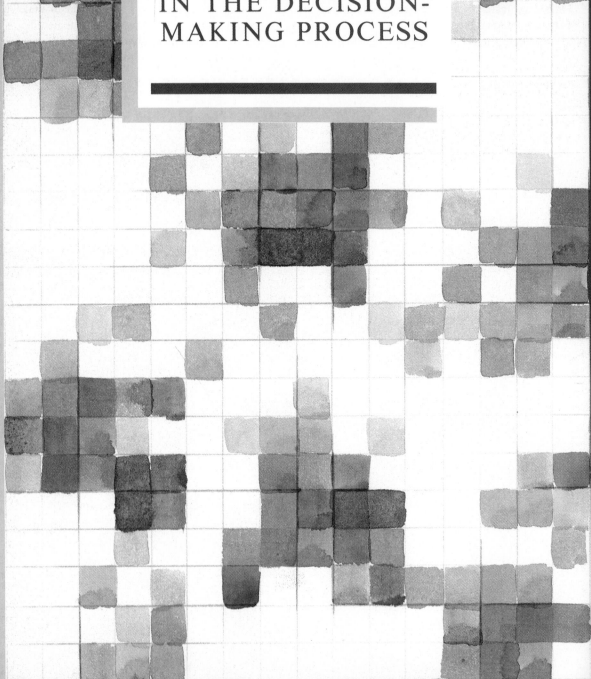

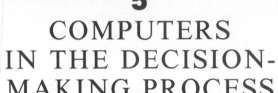

5
COMPUTERS
IN THE DECISION-
MAKING PROCESS

O U T L I N E

O B J E C T I V E S

After studying this chapter you should understand the following:

- *The stages of the decision-making process.*

- *How problems in an organization are recognized.*

- *The uses for internal and external data in the decision-making process.*

- *How alternative solutions to problems are identified and compared.*

- *How decisions are made.*

- *How computers can support the decision-making process.*

Figure 5-1.
The place of higher-level systems in the information systems hierarchy.

Figure 5-2.
All decisions, including this investment decision, pass through similar stages before a course of action is chosen.

Chapter 4 illustrated how transaction-processing systems are used to accommodate the day-to-day flow of routine data in an organization. Transaction systems, which occupy the lowest level of the information systems hierarchy, differ from the higher-level systems that focus on operational planning and control, management planning and control, and strategic planning. Probably the greatest difference is that information systems at the higher levels are used to support problem-solving and decision-making activities (Figure 5-1).

To understand how these higher-level systems are used, we need to know the steps in the **decision-making process** (or **decision process** for short). This chapter will examine each of the steps and illustrate how computer information systems can be used to help make better decisions.

THE DECISION-MAKING PROCESS

On the surface, the decisions people make seem to have little in common. How can a decision to schedule a nursing staff, for example, have much in common with a decision to allocate advertising dollars? The nursing decision will consider patients, staff, and facilities, whereas the advertising decision will weigh consumer buying habits, competitor strategies, media, and advertising costs. But when examined more closely, these different decisions do have similarities: Each proceeds through parallel stages to analyze and solve the problem (Figure 5-2).

In fact, nearly all decision-making processes follow five stages (Figure 5-3).

1. Recognizing the problem.

2. Identifying alternatives.

3. Evaluating alternatives.

4. Choosing a solution.

5. Implementing the solution and following up.

In the next sections we will take a closer look at each of these stages.

PROBLEM RECOGNITION

HOW PROBLEMS ARE RECOGNIZED

The first stage in the decision-making process begins when a problem is first recognized or an opportunity is uncovered. Although it is not necessary for a computer to be involved this early in the decision process, one often is. The following example illustrates how a computer information

Figure 5-3.
Stages in the decision-making process.

system, using data from a company's database, helped a manager uncover both a problem and an opportunity.

MILAN CHAN WAS MARKETING MANAGER OF WOOL-INNS, a sportswear manufacturer. When Chan arrived at work each Monday, she requested a report that displayed the sales totals for the previous week. Presented as a graph on the screen of her microcomputer, the report showed sales figures for each Wool-inns product line, enabling her to determine which clothing lines were meeting their targets and which were not. Within the last six months this report had brought two situations to her attention.

In the first situation, sales of a summer clothing line had begun to fall off prematurely (Figure 5-4). After a few calls to her sales force, Chan found that demand for the product was strong but that the factory was slow in sending reorders of the clothing line to their retail accounts. Chan quickly arranged a meeting the next morning to discuss the problem with factory personnel.

In the second situation, the Monday morning report showed a particularly strong sales response to a marketing strategy used by an advertising agency that the company had recently hired. Chan decided to use this opportunity to increase the number of clothing lines handled by the new agency and to terminate a contract with another agency whose performance had been marginal for some time.

Figure 5-4.
When sales begin to fall, there is likely to be a problem that needs to be solved.

As this case suggests, many problems come to light when data are reviewed and differences observed between what is and what should be. Such a review might indicate that sales are falling, inventory levels are high, manufacturing costs are rising, a vendor is consistently missing delivery dates, receivables are growing faster than sales are, or product quality is deteriorating. Negative symptoms like these suggest that a problem exists.

SOURCES OF DATA

The data used to recognize a problem or opportunity can be obtained from sources both within the organization, called **internal data sources,** or outside the organization, called **external data sources.**

Internal Data Sources   An organization collects and maintains internal data while providing goods and services to its customers. Internal data can be classified as either centralized or local.

Centralized data are maintained in the organization's central data processing facilities, usually in a minicomputer or mainframe. The data are almost always collected as part of the transaction-processing and operations planning and control process. In many systems, centralized data can be requested using English-like commands (Figure 5-5). As the following case suggests, when the data are summarized and reviewed, they may warn that a problem is about to surface.

Figure 5-5.
Centralized data can often be obtained by using simple commands.

List Eastern Division
Sales by product
by date.

■■■■■■■■■■■■■■■■■■■■■■■■■■■■■■■■■■

FIZZLE BEVERAGES, a soft drink bottler located near Denver, uses a centralized database system to monitor the progress of new products introduced into test market areas. One product, a diet chocolate fudge soft drink, has been introduced into three such markets. As the test progresses, data are collected and entered weekly into the company's central computer. These data include the price of the product, promotional data, and sales figures for each of the test sites. At the end of every week, sales reports are prepared and distributed to the marketing department.

During the third week of the test, the output from the computer system shows that sales in one of the three test markets are beginning to fall. The marketing group suspects that it is not the product itself that is responsible for this fall, but some other factor.

After making several phone calls and collecting additional information, Fizzle's marketing group discovers that one of its competitors has not only lowered the price of its competing product but has also increased its promotional efforts. Once this is known, it is just a matter of hours before Fizzle's marketing team has revised its pricing and promotional strategy and has begun putting this new plan to work. They know that without a quick response, their market test would produce misleading data.

What the bottling firm and many other companies have discovered is that the availability of timely marketing data can have a significant impact on a company's ability to uncover a problem and respond quickly to market changes. In this example, the data prevented a competitor from sabotaging a test for a new product.

■■■■■■■■■■■■■■■■■■■■■■■■■■■■■■■■■

Local data are another source of information. **Local data** are collected and used in a limited environment, which may be an individual, a group, or a department. Some local databases are built around a microcomputer and used by one person. But in many applications a local database is maintained and used by a group of individuals, each having access to the data through a network of interconnected terminals or microcomputers. An example is a quality-control database containing inspection data on equipment being manufactured. Anyone in the manufacturing department can consult the data to help spot and resolve problems.

External Data Sources   Sometimes the data used to uncover a problem or opportunity must be obtained from sources outside an organization. Several commercial database services offer a variety of industry, government, and financial statistics.

■■■■■■■■■■■■■■■■■■■■■■■■■■■■■■■■■

LOUIS SANCHEZ, a funds manager at a southern savings bank, manages a trading portfolio of $50 million in treasury securities. To help make buy-and-sell decisions, he subscribes to a commercial database service.

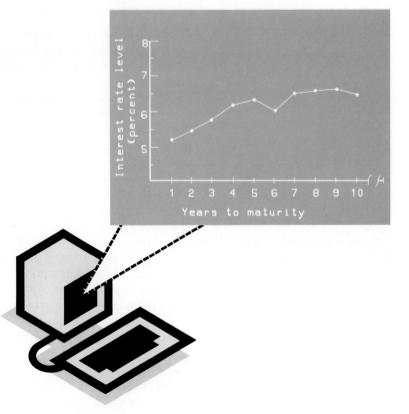

Figure 5-6.
Identifying trading opportunities from the yield curve. The yield curve represents the rate of return available to investors if they buy government securities of varying maturities. For example, if an investor buys a five-year note, the yield according to the curve will be approximately 6½ percent. Notice that the yield curve drops for securities that mature in six years. To a trader, this irregularity might suggest that the security could be traded in the short run and the position held until the rate on six-year notes moves back in line with the rest of the curve.

Every morning he accesses the interest rate data for some twelve treasury instruments and enters the data into his microcomputer. He then requests a plot of the data on the screen (Figure 5-6) and uses this information to determine whether the interest rate for any given issue is out of line with his expectations. Combining this information with price quotations, information about Federal Reserve policy, and expected treasury activity, Sanchez then identifies possible trading opportunities—and acts on them.

One commercial database service, Dialog, offers users access to both data and written material covering such topics as science, medicine, business, economics, and current events. Using this system it is possible to obtain an abstract of the literature written on a specific topic or to consult a database of different types of statistical and demographic data for fifty countries. You can find, for example, the population, GNP, per-capita income, employment, production, or usage of major materials, as well as other economic, demographic, industrial, and product data, for the major countries of Latin America. Many organizations routinely scan data like these to uncover opportunities that they might otherwise fail to notice.

Data Used in Other Stages   Although internal and external data are often needed to recognize problems, both sources are also used in the remaining stages of the decision process. In the next section we will discuss how data are used to identify alternatives.

IDENTIFYING ALTERNATIVES

There are often many ways to solve any problem. Early in the decision process, the decision maker should identify these choices.

In a production-scheduling decision, for example, the alternatives may be the different sequences in which products can be released to the production shop. In an investment decision, these alternatives may be the different stocks and bonds that can be bought or sold. In a media-selection problem, the alternatives may be the different categories of advertising media that can be selected.

The number of alternatives varies greatly for different problems. In a loan-granting decision, for example, there are only two alternatives: to approve or not to approve the loan (Figure 5-7). But in a media-selection decision, there may be hundreds of newspapers, magazines, and television and radio stations from which to choose.

Whether there are few or many potential alternatives, the computer can often be helpful in the process of identifying them. For example, software exists that can uncover alternative production schedules, identify investment choices, list appropriate advertising media, and as the next case illustrates, identify possible expansion sites.

Figure 5-7.
This loan officer is examining the data before deciding whether or not to approve a customer's request for a loan. Computers are often used when alternatives must be compared and one chosen.

FOX LUMBER COMPANY, a building materials supplier in the Pacific Northwest, is planning an expansion program. At least one new location is to be chosen. To help identify possible sites, Fox is using a commercial database service, accessing both general economic and housing-start data for several Standard Metropolitan Statistical Areas. From these data Fox will identify rapidly growing areas suitable for the company's expansion.

But the computer—especially when it is used to support decisions at the higher levels in the hierarchy—may not play a major role in the identification of alternatives. At these levels decision makers may have to rely solely on their own abilities and resources. The more knowledgeable, open-minded, and experienced the decision maker is, the broader will be the range of choices uncovered.

Computers are also used to find alternatives in many applications outside business. In sports, for example, football teams routinely rely on computerized game analyses (Figure 5-8). Using graphics and printed output, computers identify formations, define pass patterns, summarize players' movements, and analyze blocking patterns. While preparing for a game, the output from a system used by one NFL team suggested that between the 20-yard line and the goal line its next opponent lined up in

Figure 5-8.
Football plays analyzed by computer can be used to help identify alternative strategies that can be used against an opponent.

the same formation 70 percent of the time. Using this information, the team created a play to exploit this defensive lineup. As a result, the team was able to score three touchdowns and one long gain using that single play. These systems have been so successful that one NFL coach uses a computer to plan the first twenty plays of every game even before the opposing team arrives in the stadium.

EVALUATING ALTERNATIVES

Once the possible alternatives for solving a problem have been identified, the next stage of the decision-making process is to evaluate these alternatives; that is, the expected outcome for each alternative must be determined, which can often be a complex process.

RISK

If there were no unknowns in making a decision, it would be fairly simple to determine the outcome of an alternative. But most decisions are made in uncertain environments (with some amount of **risk**), and as a result, a choice may lead to several possible outcomes (Figure 5-9).

To accurately predict the outcome of a particular production-scheduling strategy, for example, is nearly impossible. Raw materials may not be delivered on time; employees may be absent; machines may break down; and bottlenecks may occur on the production floor. As a result, it is difficult to determine exactly when jobs will be completed and exactly how much it will cost to complete them.

The difficulty, then, is that alternatives do not necessarily have a single outcome, they can have many (Figure 5-10). It is this range of possible outcomes that represents the risk to which decision makers are exposed. Two techniques used to better understand risk are sensitivity analysis and forecasting.

Figure 5-9.
The outcome of an alternative is hard to predict. This retail store has decided to stock a certain quantity of merchandise for the holiday season. The risk is that the stock level could be either too high or too low.

	Alternative	Optimistic Outcome		Pessimistic Outcome	
1	Choose newspaper advertisements only	Revenue Media cost	650 50	Revenue Media cost	300 50
2	Choose TV advertisements only	Revenue Media cost	1060 500	Revenue Media cost	500 500
3	Choose both TV and newspaper advertisements	Revenue Media cost	1400 550	Revenue Media cost	650 550

Figure 5-10.
Alternatives usually have several possible outcomes.

SENSITIVITY ANALYSIS

Risk cannot be eliminated from the decision-making environment, but the consequences of risk can be explored before the decision maker decides whether or not the risk associated with a particular alternative is worth taking. In some computer information systems, risk can be analyzed using a technique known as **sensitivity analysis.** A series of "what if" questions is asked, and then the effect of each new condition on the alternative's outcome is examined.

For example, the risk associated with a real estate investment can be analyzed by examining the consequences of different construction costs, interest rates, rents, operating expenses, and resale prices on the project's profitability. Or if a children's toy company is considering the development of a new product, sensitivity analysis might be used to analyze the profitability of this product for several different levels of sales.

Although sensitivity analysis offers business professionals a vehicle for analyzing the consequences of different conditions, the decision maker can often predict with some degree of confidence which outcome is most likely to occur. These predictions are often based on a combination of experience, intuition, and judgment. But sometimes predictions can be based on a more formal forecast.

FORECASTING

When the appropriate data (internal or external) are available, **forecasting** is often used to help narrow the range of possible outcomes that must be considered for an alternative. A mobile home manufacturer could use a forecast of housing starts to help determine the profitability of an investment in new plant and equipment. A gift importer might employ a sales forecast to help determine the profits that can be expected if a contract is signed with a Hong Kong manufacturer. In both cases a forecast is used to narrow the range of possible outcomes that need be considered.

Most forecasting methods project historical data into the future, assuming that patterns in the past will hold in the future. But because this may not always be true, forecasts must be used cautiously.

Forecasting software is sometimes used to make the forecast. A statistical forecasting model is a set of procedures that accepts historical data as input and provides as output a projection of trends. Many different statistical forecasting packages are available for microcomputers, minicomputers, and mainframes.

Some applications may not require a formal statistical forecast. Instead, the user may simply use the data from a spreadsheet to plot a graph of the historical data on the screen and informally extend—by eye—the trend into the next period (Figure 5-11). Although this is a very informal approach, it will often be effective if the trend is obvious to the naked eye. It will, of course, be less helpful when no clear-cut trend can be seen.

Frequently the external data used for forecasting are general economic data on such categories as interest rates, housing starts, and disposable income. For most companies it is not cost effective to collect and maintain such data in their database but is more economical to subscribe to a commercial database service. Data Resources, Inc., is one such commercial database service, which collects and maintains current data on over 100 million different time series. A *time series* is a series of data points, like interest rates, that extends over a number of time periods. In addition to accessing the time series data, a subscriber to this service can also access several different types of forecasts based on the data.

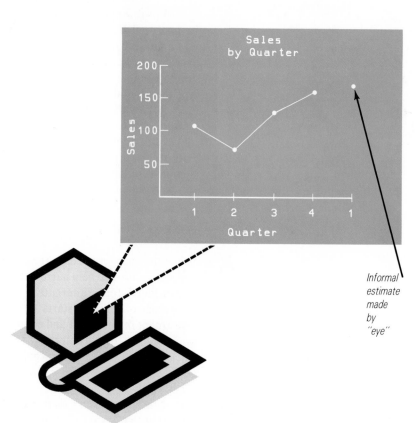

Informal estimate made by "eye"

Figure 5-11.
In this example of an informal forecast procedure, spreadsheet data are plotted on the screen. The user then simply visualizes a line through the points and extends this line into the future.

COMPUTATION

When determining the outcome for a particular alternative, it may be necessary to access data and perform calculations. As can be expected, computers are especially useful at this stage. Spreadsheets can be used to automatically compute the outcomes for alternatives that the user specifies (Figure 5-12).

■ ■

ATLAS TRUCKING COMPANY, a contract carrier, hauls paper, beer, and other consumer goods over a twelve-state region along the Atlantic seaboard. Each day it receives several requests to bid for jobs. Before spreadsheets were used, prices were quoted on the basis of the sales manager's experience and judgment. But often the prices were either overstated or understated by a wide margin, and it was not unusual for the company to lose money on a job. As the president, Joe O'Brien, said, "Before we used spreadsheets we never knew what it cost us to deliver a load."

Figure 5-12.
Spreadsheets are a convenient way of computing the outcome of an alternative.

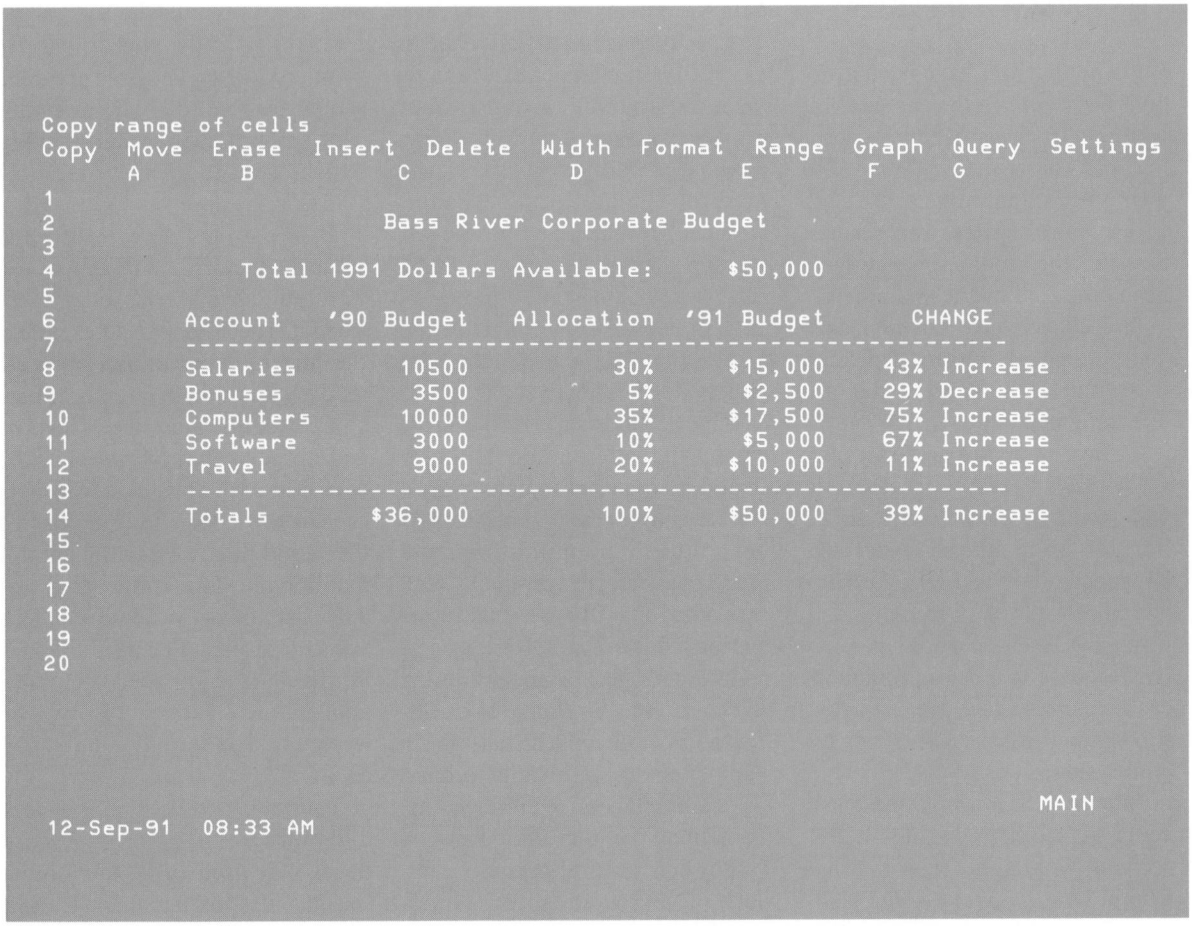

```
Copy range of cells
Copy   Move  Erase   Insert   Delete   Width   Format   Range   Graph   Query   Settings
       A     B                C        D       E        F       G
1
2                     Bass River Corporate Budget
3
4           Total 1991 Dollars Available:         $50,000
5
6      Account    '90 Budget   Allocation   '91 Budget      CHANGE
7      ------------------------------------------------------------------
8      Salaries      10500         30%       $15,000      43% Increase
9      Bonuses        3500          5%        $2,500      29% Decrease
10     Computers     10000         35%       $17,500      75% Increase
11     Software       3000         10%        $5,000      67% Increase
12     Travel         9000         20%       $10,000      11% Increase
13     ------------------------------------------------------------------
14     Totals     $36,000        100%       $50,000      39% Increase
15
16
17
18
19
20
                                                                MAIN

12-Sep-91  08:33 AM
```

Now, when Atlas receives a request for a bid, the detailed data on the shipment—including origin, destination, type of cargo, weight, pickup date, and delivery date—are entered into its computer system. Next the expected profits for three different levels of bids are computed. These computations consider more than twenty expense categories, including fuel, wages, repairs, insurance, and tolls. Finally, after examining each of the bid possibilities and weighing the bids that its competition is likely to make, Atlas submits a bid to the customer.

O'Brien feels that there is much less guesswork in the bidding process. "When we submit a bid," he said, "we now know how much profit we're going to make."

E N D · U S E R   H I N T S

USING AN EXECUTIVE INFORMATION SYSTEM

Imagine that you have been away on a business trip for one week, it is nine o'clock on Monday morning, and you have just returned to your office. Your desk is piled high with memos, letters, and reports. Some of the reports, in fact, have been produced by the MIS.

Indeed, you have too much data and not enough information. Like most middle managers, you are drowning in data.

In fact, there are probably only a few key pieces of information you would need in order to be brought up-to-date on what has happened since you left. Perhaps you need a graph of weekly sales, inventory levels, new-order activity, response to a sales promotion, cash balances, stock market activity, competitive pricing trends, or quality control data.

Whatever it is you need, if you could glance at it for just a few seconds, you might feel somewhat caught up. An *Executive Information System (EIS)* would provide

you with access to just this kind of data.

Executive Information Systems are really an offshoot of Management Information Systems. They provide managers with the predictable information they will need to keep up-to-date. The difference, however, is that an EIS regularly monitors the "critical" and "most important" pieces of data in a user's environment and makes these data available both "easily" and "effectively."

A good EIS is simple to use. To obtain the information the user should be required to enter only a few keystrokes, and the information, often in graphical form, will then appear on the terminal.

A good EIS also presents information effectively. Often several related data groups are presented on the screen. A graph, for example, might not only display daily shipments but also daily orders. To communicate combined information like this effectively, a well-designed EIS will employ a variety of presentation techniques. Graphs may be in color to empha-

size certain data items, and when data are presented in lists or tables, they should appear only in summary form. The user of an EIS should be able to obtain a significant amount of information without the need to spend a long time studying the data.

Before an EIS is developed, the critical factors that must be watched have to be identified. Then it is necessary to determine if the current information system already collects these data, or if new data streams must be collected and stored by the system. Once the data are available, a decision is needed on how to summarize them, and on how often the EIS will monitor the data stream and update that data. In some applications the system may need to monitor the data continuously; in other applications hourly, daily, or weekly monitoring may be enough.

Because each user may have a different group of critical data items that need to be monitored, the EIS must be customized to each user. Consequently, an EIS must be flexible enough to accommodate the needs of a wide variety of users. Since the business environment is a rapidly changing one, an EIS also must be flexible, so that new types of information can be made available when needed.

Some software vendors sell EIS software. Most companies, however, develop their own. Companies that develop their own often use the same software with which MIS and DSS applications are developed. But an EIS focuses on just those critical factors that the user needs to monitor on a regular basis. One way to categorize an EIS, then, is as a subset of a Management Information System. Furthermore, most EIS applications focus on the operational planning and control, and management planning and control levels in the information hierarchy.

MAKING THE CHOICE

SPECIFYING CRITERIA

Once the outcomes for each alternative have been determined, the alternatives are compared in order to choose a solution. But in this process it must be clear to the decision maker which criteria will guide the final choice. The criteria depend, of course, on the situation and the problem. The criteria may be to maximize profits, minimize costs, improve product quality, improve product delivery, reduce manufacturing times, or increase market share. Although this list is certainly not complete, it illustrates the many criteria that may be considered. In fact, it is not unusual for several criteria to be considered at once, some in conflict with one another.

THE DIAMOND MANUFACTURING COMPANY MANUFACTURES INDUSTRIAL FASTENERS. Before it finalizes a production schedule, specifying in which order the jobs will be processed through the shop, the company considers several criteria. The first is to choose a schedule that will minimize the costs of producing the orders. The second is to choose a schedule that will minimize the possibility that jobs will be shipped late.

Usually these criteria lead to conflicting schedules. Several recent jobs, for example, would have been scheduled in one sequence if minimizing costs were the goal and in another sequence if minimizing the possibility of a late shipment were the goal. When the decision was finally made, a compromise schedule was chosen that primarily minimized the likelihood of a late shipment. Unfortunately, the costs were higher with this schedule, because several automatic machines had to be used. These machines produced the job faster but raised the per-unit cost of producing each piece in the order.

THE DECISION

Based on the criteria, the decision maker must make a choice. Now, the next job to be released to production is chosen; the particular stock or

Figure 5-13.
At the higher levels in the information pyramid, less emphasis is placed on the role of the computer in the decision-making process.

bond is purchased; or the loan application is approved or denied. Sometimes the choice is relatively simple.

But the choice is easy only when the risks are not too high, the differences among the alternatives are wide, and the criteria used are simple and clear. But when risks are high, the differences among alternatives, are either narrow or difficult to estimate, or several conflicting criteria must be considered, then the choice may be difficult. And the latter is usually the situation at the management planning and strategic levels of decision making.

The computer's role during this final stage of the decision process varies considerably. Simpler decisions, such as placing a routine order for an out-of-stock part, may require little or no human intervention. But most decisions do, to a varying degree. Higher-level decisions—those made at the organization's management planning and control and strategic planning levels—almost always rely on the computer less than will decisions at the operational planning and control level (Figure 5-13). And when computers are used at these higher levels they play only a supporting role. The final choice is always the decision maker's responsibility.

IMPLEMENTATION AND FOLLOW-UP

Once a choice has been made, the course of action chosen must be set into motion, or *implemented*. Management needs to determine when implementation will take place and who will be responsible. Once implemented, regular performance reviews must be scheduled (Figure 5-14). If a review suggests that a plan is not progressing as expected, then corrective action should be taken.

ORDER OF STEPS

Figure 5-14.
Once a plan has been implemented, periodic performance reviews are necessary to ensure that it is being properly carried out. Here the design team for a computerized manufacturing planning system interviews a user of the system.

We have described the decision process as moving from recognizing the problem, to identifying alternatives, to evaluating alternatives, to making a choice, and finally to implementing it and following it up. Rarely, however, does the decision process follow such a linear sequence. Often the process must return to an earlier stage before a decision can be made, as in the following example.

■ ■

THE PORTFOLIO SELECTION COMMITTEE at the Southern Life Insurance Company had just picked the new stocks and bonds to be included in its investment portfolio, when it learned from an advisory service of several problems that could affect the earnings of one company on the list. On the basis of this information, the committee decided to eliminate this choice, and to find another alternative.

■ ■

THE HUMAN FACTOR

Although the computer may indeed be an important part of the decision-making process, a person is responsible for making the final decision. Exactly what that person may decide is difficult to predict. Everyone will respond differently to the data supplied by the computer system. In addition, when it is time to finally make the decision, data will often be considered that were not supplied by the computer system.

■■■■■■■■■■■■■■■■■■■■■■■■■■■■■■■■■

WHEN THE COMPUTER-GENERATED PRODUCTION SCHEDULE AT THE THOMASTON SHOE COMPANY, a manufacturer of athletic shoes, is delivered to Alice Murphy, she routinely makes several changes in the schedule. These changes reflect product promotions, last-minute sales trends from the information she receives from the marketing department, recent bottlenecks on the production floor, likely changes in the production work force, possible delays in the receipt of parts and materials necessary to meet the schedule, and delivery changes requested by customers.

Although Murphy uses these last-minute data when she finalizes the schedule, many of her changes are also based on her own intuition. This intuition was gained from over five years as Thomaston's chief scheduler. Other people in the production department often see things differently and would make other changes. And in a few situations the others have turned out to be right. Murphy, nonetheless, has shown that in most cases her decisions have been good ones.

■■■■■■■■■■■■■■■■■■■■■■■■■■■■■■■

WHEN DOES MORE INFORMATION HELP?

Because the last step in the decision-making process is a human one, and because in this stage individuals respond differently to data, it is often difficult to determine exactly how many data should be made available. In some situations—especially at the operational planning and control level—more detailed data may be better. In production, for example, a shop-floor control system must have access to all of the details, including the location of jobs, due dates, processing times, machine status, work-force status, and capacity data. Using these data, decisions can be made to establish a reasonable degree of control over the system.

But as decision making moves from the operations to the management planning and control and the strategic planning levels, the information requirements change dramatically. Less rather than more detail is needed. In fact, at each of these higher levels it is certainly possible to burden the decision maker with too much information. **Information overload** occurs when so many data or so much information is supplied that it serves only to confuse or obscure the issue (Figure 5-15). As a result, decision performance may not only fail to improve but may also

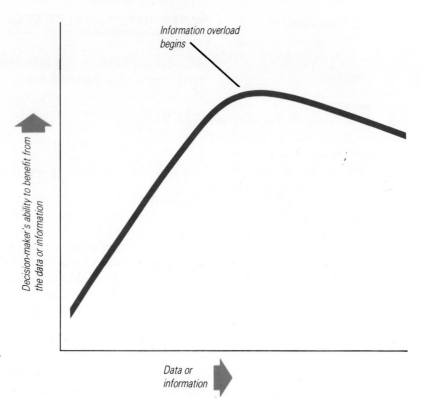

Figure 5-15.
Information overload. As more and more data or information is made available to the decision maker, that person's ability to benefit from it will eventually diminish.

actually deteriorate. Thus when designing an information system, more information may not necessarily be better than less information. Consequently, before deciding to increase the quantity of data or information in the Management Information System or Decision Support System, the use of the information and the actual need for it must be carefully justified.

THE ECONOMICS OF COMPUTERS IN THE DECISION-MAKING PROCESS

As we have discovered in this chapter, there are many ways in which a computer-based Decision Support System can be used. First, it can help uncover potential problems by reviewing and comparing internal and external data. Second, it can be used to help identify alternative choices. Third, it can be used to evaluate the outcomes associated with each alternative. Fourth, it can be used to choose among the alternatives.

Unless it contributes to one of these areas, the computer information system may not lead to either faster or better decisions, and as a result there may be little economic payoff to the organization. Without a significant payoff, more information may not necessarily be better than less.

? Q U E S T I O N S ?

1. Describe the five stages in the decision-making process.
2. How might the following problems be discovered? Is it likely that a computer information system would be involved? Would internal or external data be involved?
   a. Drop in sales of a product line.
   b. Increase in consumer dissatisfaction with a company's product.
   c. Higher-than-normal reject rates in a manufacturing department.
3. What is the difference between centralized and local data?
4. What makes data more accessible or less accessible?
5. Define "external data," and explain how they might be used in the decision-making process.
6. Identify the alternatives that might accompany the following decision problems:
   a. Investing the funds received by a union pension fund.
   b. Adding a new retail store to a cosmetic chain with thirty-five stores.
   c. Choosing a production schedule.

   d. Placing an order to replenish stock for a supermarket chain.
7. Why might it be important to expand the decision maker's range of choices?
8. What might be the criteria in the following situations? If more than one criterion is appropriate, will they conflict with one another?
   a. Scheduling patients through a hospital's X-ray facility.
   b. Choosing advertising media.
   c. Selecting a vendor to supply parts for a new product.
9. What is the risk to which decisions are exposed?
10. Identify the risk in the following situations:
    a. Investing money in the stock market.
    b. Selecting a vendor to supply parts for a new product.
    c. Choosing courses during registration week.
11. How is sensitivity analysis used to explore risk?
12. How does a forecast help a decision maker?
13. How can too many data affect a decision maker's performance?

S U M M A R Y

■ Higher-level information systems are used to support the **decision-making process** (called the **decision process** for short).

■ There are five stages in the decision-making process: (1) recognizing a problem, (2) identifying alternatives, (3) evaluating alternatives, (4) choosing a solution, and (5) implementing a solution and following up.

■ Problems are often recognized when data are reviewed and differences observed between what is and what should be. Data may be from an **internal data source** or an **external data source.**

■ Internal data can be **centralized data,** which are maintained in an organization's central data processing facility, or **local data,** which are collected and used in a more limited environment.

■ External data are often obtained from commercial database services offering a variety of industry, government, and financial statistics.

■ There are many ways to solve any problem, and computers can be useful in uncovering these alternatives.

■ Alternatives can be evaluated by examining their expected outcomes. Two techniques used to analyze **risk** are **sensitivity analysis** and **forecasting.**

■ Comparison of alternatives is necessary to choose a solution. The difficulty in making a decision increases as the risks increase and when conflicting criteria must be considered.

■ Once a choice has been made, the course of action chosen must then be set into motion or implemented. After it is implemented, the plan should be regularly reviewed.

■ As a rule, the decision-making process does not follow the five steps rigidly.

■ Most final decisions are made by humans, not computers. Different people react differently to the same data supplied by a computer system. In addition, data that the computer system never provided are often used to make the decision.

■ The quantity and detail of data provided should be tailored to the decision-making level. The higher the level is, the less detail will be required. **Information overload** can take place when so many data or so much information is supplied that it serves only to confuse or obscure the issue.

K E Y • T E R M S

The following list shows the key terms in the order in which they appear in the chapter.

F   O   R   D   I   S   C   U   S   S   I   O   N

1. You have just received a computer printout that shows the location of two thousand manufacturing jobs currently being processed at forty different manufacturing locations in your plant. Fifteen of these jobs are already behind schedule, and so you would like to locate these jobs and rush them through their next steps. The format of the computer output, however, is by machine center rather than by job. Would you classify this output as data or information? Under what circumstances could it be referred to as information? What changes would you recommend?

2. When you make plans for a weekend, what criteria guide your choice of activities? Do the criteria conflict with one another? Would you place more weight on one criterion than another? Do you think the criteria change over time?

3. An investor is considering the purchase of several hundred shares of common stock in IBM. What are the risks to which this investor is exposed, and what can be done to better understand them? Can these risks be eliminated? Would a better understanding of these risks help the decision maker formulate an investment strategy? Would an understanding of the risks lead to higher profits in IBM stock?

H   A   N   D   S - O   N   P   R   O   J   E   C   T   S

1. Go to a library and find an article that describes how a computer information system was used to support a business decision. Write a brief paragraph summarizing the application.
    Suggestions: Business Week, Fortune, Wall Street Journal, Computerworld, PC Week, Business Computer Systems

2. Does your school subscribe to, or have access to, any computer-based external data sources? If so, find out what types of data are available. How might industry use these data in the decision-making process?

■■■

C A S E · S T U D Y

SWEATS, INC.

While Sweats, Inc. has always emphasized the role of management and planning, and downplayed the role of technology, they nonetheless have developed one of the more sophisticated computer information systems in the sporting goods business.

Development of this information system began over six years ago. It was planned in response to increasing paperwork costs and a lack of control over operations. First, accounting applications were introduced; then sales-order entry, inventory control, and production planning and control applications were added.

Until recently the benefits from these applications played a significant role in management's ability to maintain healthy profit margins while growing at a rate exceeding 25 percent per year. Shortly after these computer applications became operational, inventory levels dropped 25 percent, lead times shortened by 50 percent, and in some production areas employment was reduced by 30 percent. And all of these improvements without sacrificing customer service!

Now, however, the computer no longer seems to be helping. Costs are rising and profits falling.

Product Line

Sweats manufactures a line of exercise equipment, which includes exercise machines, treadmills, stationary bicycles, and rowing machines. The lower priced consumer line is sold through major department stores, while the higher priced commercial line is sold directly to commercial gyms, universities, exercise centers, sweat palaces, and, in growing numbers, to companies that are constructing physical fitness facilities for their employees.

A new line of interactive exercise equipment introduced six months ago has sold especially well in the commercial market. Perhaps the most distinguishing feature of this new line is the computer built into each piece of equipment. It supports a database system that is capable of storing historical workout records for 7000 people. So those who regularly use one machine can enter their names and see their past performance record on the screen. In addition, these computers use artificial intelligence to determine a workout schedule based on the person's most recent sessions. The computer even has voice output. So when a person is struggling to complete an exercise, it can offer encouragement: "Bill, you're halfway there." And when each exercise is completed, and again at the end of the session, the computer scores the workout on a scale of 0 to 100.

Accounting System

The accounting system at Sweats—the first function which they computerized—is an on-line transaction processing system which includes general ledger, accounts receivable, and accounts payable software. The general ledger system has over 250 accounts, designed in such a way to support cost center accounting so that the accounting data can be used to prepare reports which show how actual costs in different cost centers compare with the budget for these areas and also how the costs compare with those incurred in the previous year. It also, of course, supports routine accounting transactions and produces P&L and balance sheets.

Inventory

The inventory system maintains data on the stock levels of some 15,000 items—called stock-keeping units or SKUs—used in the manufacture of the exercise equipment. And it also maintains data on the stock levels for over 275 different finished products which Sweats has in their line.

Terminals are located in the stock room and shipping area. Whenever a part or finished product is removed from stock, a clerk makes an entry into the system. Users in other areas, such as the purchasing or production scheduling departments, can also inquire about the status of an inventory item from terminals in their area. They can find out how many items are in stock, how many are on order, and when the items ordered are due.

Periodic inventory reports are also available from central data processing. One report prints the items which are out of stock, another lists inventory investment for each category of SKU, while another even summarizes those items for which there has been little or no demand.

Manufacturing Planning

Sweats can be classified as a made-to-stock manufacturer. This means that manufactured items are produced for the purpose of replenishing stock in the finished goods warehouse. When sales are made, the order entry department fills orders from these finished goods. This manufacturing method is different from the made-to-order method used by furniture and automobile manufacturers, for example, who manufacture to a specific order. A customer who is purchasing an automobile can order a car with certain options, and then this order is forwarded to an automotive assembly plant where this specific car is assembled. In contrast, a customer ordering an exercise machine from Sweats orders from finished goods inventory. No special orders are filled.

Every month the scheduling department at Sweats prepares a master production schedule (MPS) on the computer. The schedule specifies the finished products to be manufactured and the date they must be finished and available in finished goods inventory. To prepare this plan they refer to computer reports to determine what is already available. Inventory reports are used to identify what is presently in stock, while in-process reports are used to identify what products are currently in progress on the shop floor and when they will be finished. Next, scheduling personnel determine what their needs will be. This information is obtained from two sources. The first source is a forecast. Here a graphics package is used to plot the demand pattern for each product over the last 24 months. Then the graphics package is used to help estimate demand for the next several months. The second source is a computer file, called the back-order file, which stores orders for equipment that has been ordered by customers but not yet shipped. Finally, the net demand is computed by subtracting the in-stock and in-process from the demand forecast plus back orders.

In the next step the production department uses the computer to translate net demand for finished products into a detailed production schedule. This schedule will specify when parts must be ordered from vendors, when parts must be manaufactured in Sweats' own production facilities, and when assembly must take place. And the dates on the schedule assure that these steps begin at the right time and in the correct sequence so that the finished product will be completed on schedule.

What complicates the development of this detailed schedule is that each of the finished products is comprised of hundreds of parts and several subassemblies (a subassembly is an assembly of parts). A bill-of-materials file organizes this detail. The file, which is stored on disk, not only identifies the parts and subassemblies for a given product, but it shows the order in which they are assembled, and also includes the length of time to complete each step in the process.

When the detailed scheduling process begins, the bill-of-materials file is accessed. Using this file as a reference, a software package, called the manufacturing resource planning system (MRP), works backward from the planned completion date to determine when each item, subassembly, or finished assembly must be started so that the due date for the product will be met. The outcome of the MRP system then becomes the detailed production schedule.

Sales-Order Entry

Sweats has an automated sales-order entry system. When an order arrives the order data is entered into one of the terminals in the sales department. The order-entry software then accesses the inventory database and checks to see if the item is in stock. If it is, then the item or items are allocated to the customer, and after the appropriate computerized credit checks, the order is forwarded to the shipping department and shipped. If the items are not in stock, then the order clerk can query the production scheduling system and determine when they will be available. If the customer approves the expected shipping date, then the order is entered into the back-order file.

Capacity Planning Problems

The management staff at Sweats keeps in touch with performance through several regularly scheduled reports, including monthly sales performance charts and profit-and-loss statements. But they can also keep in touch by accessing the database using an English-like query language. With this language they can obtain information to solve an unusual problem, or to monitor a potentially troublesome area for which regular reports are not available.

In the last three months the monthly profit-and-loss statement has begun to show signs that Sweats is in trouble. Manufacturing costs are on the increase and profits on the decrease.

Lou Garrety, president, called a staff meeting to discuss the problem. At the meeting Bob Bass, manager of production planning, complained that beyond the general financial data that Lou presented, there wasn't enough hard data to pinpoint the problem. Garrety agreed with Bob and asked several of the staff to submit performance reports for their areas. "Let's get back here tomorrow at nine and see if we can't figure out how to reverse the trend," Garrety said.

Alice Jackson, a manufacturing cost control specialist, used her microcomputer to access the central database and prepare several graphs for the meeting. These graphs showed that per-unit manufacturing costs for all but the new interactive exercise line—manufactured by new automatic manufacturing equipment—had been on the rise in the last six months. And this increase was accelerating in the last three months.

Bob Bass passed the request on to one of his staff. Using the English-like query features of the information system, a report was produced which showed that jobs were now missing their due dates by as much as one or two weeks, and that the backlog of jobs at each machine and at each assembly station was growing longer. At the morning meeting he explained, "This means our production floor is more congested than it has ever been and as a result our efficiency has gone down the drain. That's why our costs are out of control."

Sally Friedman from customer service also produced some data using the English-like query feature of the system. Her data showed that customer complaints and returns during the warranty period were on the rise. "If this continues," she said, "our reputation for high-quality equipment will be in jeopardy."

Towards the end of the morning meeting, Alice tried to sum up the problem. "It looks to me like we have a capacity planning problem. If we continue to raise our production levels in response to higher sales, then costs, backlogs, processing time, profits, and product quality will suffer even more. What we need to do is increase our capacity." She then asked a question which had been on her mind for some time. "Why can't we solve this problem by adding a second shift, or by subcontracting with local job shops to manufacture and assemble the overload?"

Bob Bass disagreed. "Sally, it makes no sense to stay with inefficient production methods. We need to automate our production methods. Look at the results from the automated line that produces our new universal equipment. We produce those units in half the time and at two-thirds the cost."

"Bob, we just don't have the budget for an undertaking like that," was Garrety's quick reply.

While Garrety realized that capacity was a real problem, he was unwilling to make a decision now, especially one that would involve the cost to automate most of the factory. "Alice, do you think you could collect some cost data that would show us the consequences of your choices?"

"I can try."

To organize her analysis, Alice constructed a spreadsheet for the choices she had recommended. The spreadsheets were like cost tables. And for each spreadsheet she included five columns in which she included cost estimates for the next five years. While some of the data was obtained from the accounting database, other data, for evaluating the subcontracting alternative, were obtained from local subcontractors.

When she was through, she showed Garrety the results. "It looks to me like the two-shift operation is not such a bad idea," he concluded. "The costs will be high in the beginning but if we continue to grow at our current rate, your spreadsheet shows that we will be operating efficiently in the second year."

Alice agreed. "The reason I like that option is that we can get back to the high quality we're known for, and we don't have to use outside manufacturing resources that could turn out to be unreliable."

Garrety wanted the group to take a look at the analysis, and called a meeting on Friday at 1:00 p.m.

Bob Bass was critical of the plan. "What bothers me is the possibility that growth may slow and we will be saddled with the higher costs of a second shift operation."

"Good point," was Garrety's response. He turned to Alice. "Before we make a decision, could you go back to your computer and change these data so we can see what the impact of slower growth would be?"

Questions

1. Describe the business that Sweats is in.
2. What impact did the development of a computer information system have on their performance when it was first installed?
3. Classify their computer applications by business function.

4. Describe the accounting system.

5. Which applications can be categorized as MIS? Explain how the transaction system is a backbone for the accounting MIS.

6. Which computer applications support operational planning and control decisions?

7. Which computer applications support management planning and control decisions?

8. Describe the inventory system. How many items are covered by the system? What are these items called? How are transactions entered?

9. Can the inventory system be classified as a transaction system or an MIS, or does it support both uses? Explain.

10. Is Sweats a made-to-order or made-to-stock manufacturer? Explain the difference.

11. What is the first step in the production scheduling process? Is a computer used?

12. Explain how net demand is determined. Is the computer used? How would you classify the computer application that supports this process? Is it a transaction, operations planning and control, or management planning and control system?

13. What is the bill-of-materials file, and how is it used by Sweats in the scheduling process?

14. Explain the purpose of MRP. What input data are needed? What output does it produce?

15. Explain the sales-order entry process. Would it be classified as a transaction system or MIS?

16. How does management at Sweats keep in touch with performance?

17. How was the current problem recognized? What was the source of data?

18. Describe the performance reports submitted by Jackson, Bass, and Friedman. What type of system produced these reports? Would you classify it as a transaction, operational planning and control, or management planning and control system? Explain.

19. Describe the alternative solutions to the capacity problem.

20. How was the computer used to organize the data needed to compare the alternatives?

21. Were internal or external data used? Do you think these data needed to be detailed data?

22. What is the risk in selecting one of these alternatives? Was the computer used in exploring the consequence of this risk? Explain.

23. Do you think that the sales data in the sales-order entry database might be accessed to produce a sales forecast which could then be used to understand better the risks that would be taken if a second shift were initiated? Would this help?

24. If you were in Garrety's position, what would be your next step?

25. In general, do you think that the use of the computer to support decision-making behavior at Sweats can be economically justified? Do the benefits exceed the costs?

■ ■

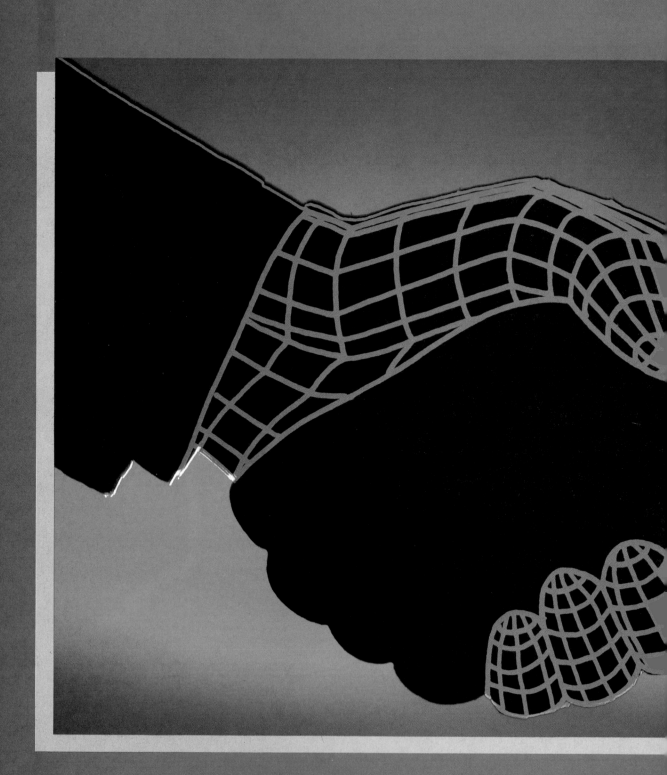

PART THREE

TOOLS FOR THE BUSINESS PROFESSIONAL

6
OFFICE AUTOMATION AND WORD PROCESSING

O U T L I N E

O B J E C T I V E S

After studying this chapter you should understand the following:

- *Why office automation plays an important role in information processing.*

- *The fundamentals of word processing, including the creation storage, editing, and printing of documents.*

- *How electronic filing occurs in an office environment.*

- *How electronic mail is used.*

- *How electronic conferencing can help people communicate.*

In the previous chapters you learned how computer systems work and how they are used in transaction and decision-making environments. Such systems are much in evidence at the workplace. In some offices, in fact, a terminal or microcomputer can be found on every desk.

Starting with this chapter, we will zero in even more closely on the office. We will discuss how word processing, electronic filing, electronic mail, and electronic conferencing can be used to automate and integrate many of the information-related activities carried out in virtually every office. **Office automation,** or OA, refers to the use of information-processing and communication technologies for writing, collecting, storing, organizing, retrieving, and communicating office data (Figure 6-1). From clerks to executives, it is changing the way people work. It affects the job itself, the flow of information through an organization, the process of management, and even the corporate structure.

Figure 6-1.
The flow of information is a dominant characteristic of the office. Office automation facilitates this process.

WHY OFFICE AUTOMATION?

The office has been one of the last places in organizations to benefit from computer information systems. Until recently, there have been few improvements in office productivity. Whenever the workload increased, the tendency was to hire more people. As a result, office costs—of which wages and salaries are the largest part—have increased significantly over the decades. Factory productivity, in contrast, has steadily improved through the use of automated manufacturing processes.

The spread of word-processing and spreadsheet applications was the first step toward office automation. Now other applications, made possible by newer hardware and software and developed specifically for

Figure 6-2.
Office automation significantly increases office productivity.

this market, are regularly used. And with their help, office productivity is on the rise. Jobs take less time to complete; office personnel can handle more work; managers perform more functions; and in some cases fewer levels in the organization's hierarchy are needed to get the job done (Figure 6-2).

■■■■■■■■■■■■■■■■■■■■■■■■■■■■■■■■■■■■■

INTERSTATE BANK AND TRUST CORPORATION, one of the largest commercial banks in the country, recently installed a new office system. The commercial banking group found that it improved customer service, made account and customer information available more quickly to its corporate clients, and at the same time enabled Interstate to reduce its staff. These changes had a significant impact on the composition of the group: Before the change, 70 percent of the workers were clerical, but after the change, this figure dropped to 30 percent.

■■■■■■■■■■■■■■■■■■■■■■■■■■■■■■■■■■■

THE OBSTACLES TO OFFICE AUTOMATION

One of the reasons that office automation was slow to take hold, and is still difficult to implement successfully, is that it supports a wide variety of applications. These applications range from structured tasks such as writing letters to unstructured tasks such as selecting advertising media. Indeed, the range is so wide that it is almost too simplistic to include these applications under the title of office automation. This is quite a contrast with transaction systems such as payroll and inventory processing, oriented toward specific, well defined methods and procedures.

Another reason that OA has been slow to take hold is that user support for this technology is widely diffused. First, an office is likely to include hardware and software obtained from several different vendors, and the kinds of support for these different pieces of equipment and software may vary widely: Seldom will the support a user feels is necessary be available. Furthermore, a direct consequence of this multivendor environment is that the equipment may be incompatible. Users who want to share hardware, software, or documents may find that sharing is impossible.

Also contributing to problems with office automation is the fact that it is often unclear where the end-user should go in the organization for help. Some support may come from the central data processing group, and other support may be available from a special OA support staff, but in most organizations there are always fellow employees who develop into self-made experts and are quick to offer advice.

For these reasons, organizations often find that they lack consistent policies regarding office automation. And perhaps this helps explain why the hardware and software available to end-users may be underutilized, why incompatability problems occur, and why many become frustrated and angry with the computer.

One solution is to formalize and administer an organizationwide policy regarding the development and use of office automation. This policy should focus on the kinds of hardware and software to be purchased and even extend to the type of training for all users before an application is authorized. But a companywide policy like this is sometimes difficult to introduce and enforce, as many departments will want the freedom to select the hardware and software they feel are best suited to their needs.

Although office automation has many advantages, the obstacles cannot be ignored. Creating an acceptable office automation environment is difficult and complex. And when we examine the details of office automation applications, it is important to realize that the success of these applications will depend on how well they are managed.

WORKSTATIONS

The place in the computerized office where most of these automated activities converge is called the **workstation.** Sometimes the use of this term is confusing, because it implies that a workstation is a specialized piece of office equipment. Although this is true in a few applications, a workstation is usually just a microcomputer with applications software, or in some systems a terminal tied to a minicomputer or mainframe, that is dedicated to office activities or performs them together with other tasks (Figure 6-3). **Departmental computing** refers to a collection of workstations tied together in a network or tied to a larger minicomputer system. These workstations usually support the information-processing needs of a group of offices in a specific department.

Figure 6-3.
The workstation is the focal point in an office automation system.

As in any computer system, it is the software that makes the difference. Workstations are no exception. They use various types of software and provide the following functions:

- Word processing
- Electronic filing
- Electronic mail
- Electronic conferencing
- Spreadsheets
- Graphics
- Project management

In the following sections of this chapter we will take a closer look at word processing, electronic filing, electronic mail, and electronic conferencing. In later chapters we will explore spreadsheets, graphics, and project management software.

WORD PROCESSING

Figure 6-4.
Word processing simplifies the initial creation of a document. The memo this executive produces on the train will be printed and distributed as soon as he gets to his office.

Word processing refers to the use of computer technology to create, edit, store, and print documents. Word processing has changed the way in which memos, letters, and documents are created. In fact, if you compare the creation of a written document on a word processor with the creation of the same document using a typewriter, you will find the difference to be dramatic.

If you used a typewriter, you usually would type your first draft from your original, handwritten copy. Then you would review the draft and make any changes in pencil. Next, you would retype the revised draft, incorporating the changes. And even then, there still might be a few typographical and other minor errors, making it necessary for you to retype it again. If you have kept count, that is three passes through the typewriter!

Word processors not only avoid having to type the drafts of a document over and over again, but they also simplify its initial creation (Figure 6-4).

The advantages of word processing can be attributed to eight functions performed by most systems:

- Document creation
- Storage
- Editing
- Formatting
- Printing

- Spelling checking

- Thesaurus

- Mail merge

Let us look at each function.

DOCUMENT CREATION

When word-processing software is first "loaded," or entered, into the computer, information appears on the display screen. The information shown on a display screen at a given time is referred to as a **screen.** The screen shown in Figure 6-5 is like that of many word-processing systems.

This screen is called the *opening menu;* a **menu** lists the program options that you can select. Although it is helpful for a beginner to see this menu of options, many systems permit the experienced user to eliminate the menu area, thereby leaving more room for text. Some systems do not usually show menus but can call them up when needed.

To create a new document, using the software illustrated in Figure 6-5, you select "D," and the screen shown in Figure 6-6 appears. This screen is divided into three sections: (1) a status line, (2) the menu area, and (3) the text area.

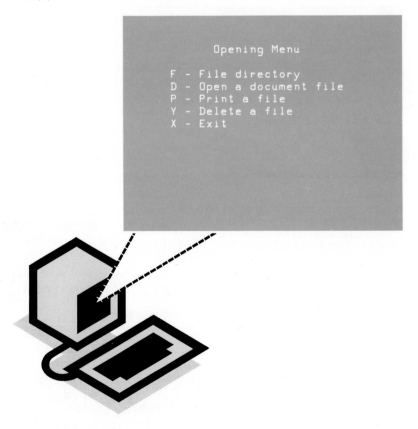

```
                    Opening Menu

         F - File directory
         D - Open a document file
         P - Print a file
         Y - Delete a file
         X - Exit
```

Figure 6-5.
An example of an opening menu in a word-processing system.

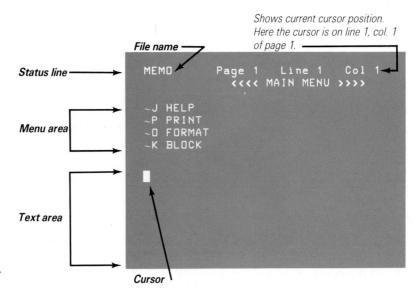

Figure 6-6.
This screen is ready to accept a document. Entry from the keyboard will appear at the cursor position in the text area. The status line informs the user of the document name and the exact cursor position. The menu area lists the options that can be used while creating the document.

The **status line,** at the top of the screen, shows the name of the document and the position on the screen where the cursor is currently located. In some systems the status line identifies the current page number of the text shown on the screen. The **cursor** is the small, often blinking, symbol that shows where you are; it generally points to the location where the next character you type in will appear.

The next section is called the **menu area.** At the initial stage in creating a document, the main menu will appear, listing the program options. These include obtaining help if you are confused about using the system (Option J), printing the document (Option P), changing the format of the document (Option O), or moving large blocks of data to other locations in the document (Option K).

When you make a selection from the main menu, additional *sub-menus* may appear in the menu area. They provide additional options from which the user may choose. Submenus are often referred to as *pull-down menus.*

Below the menu comes the **text area,** the portion of the screen where the text is entered. It is like a blank sheet of paper. The cursor marks the exact location on the screen into which the text entered from the keyboard will be placed.

To enter a text, you simply begin to type. To illustrate how to do this, we will enter the memo shown in Figure 6-7. Notice that it contains several errors. We will enter these errors to show you how easily word-processing software can be used to correct them.

The first two lines (beginning MEMO and TO) are entered, and after each one, the RETURN key is pressed. This is referred to as a **hard return.**

When the main content of the memo is entered, it is not necessary to press the RETURN key when the typed words reach the end of the screen. The software knows exactly how many characters are in a line,

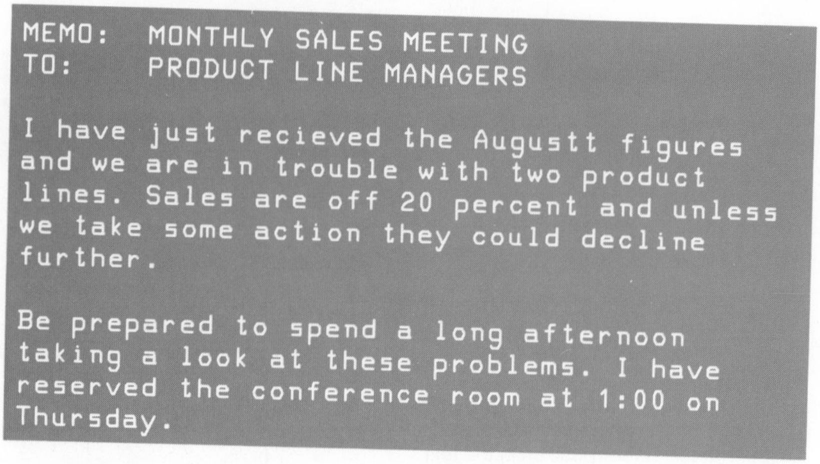

```
MEMO:   MONTHLY SALES MEETING
TO:     PRODUCT LINE MANAGERS

I have just recieved the Augustt figures
and we are in trouble with two product
lines. Sales are off 20 percent and unless
we take some action they could decline
further.

Be prepared to spend a long afternoon
taking a look at these problems. I have
reserved the conference room at 1:00 on
Thursday.
```

Figure 6-7.
The first draft of a memo entered from the keyboard.

and when a word exceeds this number, the entire word is automatically moved to the next line. This feature, referred to as **wordwrap,** frees you from having to watch the right-hand margin. The only time that a hard return is required during text entry is when a line must be skipped or a paragraph ends.

DOCUMENT STORAGE AND RETRIEVAL

While a document is being created, it is stored only in main memory. To save it on disk, you must use an explicit save command found in one of the pulldown menus. It is advisable to save a document at regular intervals during its creation, perhaps as often as every two pages. This will prevent losing a lot of work if the plug is accidentally pulled from the computer or if the power is otherwise temporarily interrupted. Saving at regular intervals hardly interrupts the flow of work. You enter the save command; the document is saved on disk; and after a few seconds the cursor is waiting at the same place in the document from which the save command was entered for the user to continue.

You can retrieve text files by selecting the appropriate command from the pulldown menu. You may save and retrieve a file many times. For example, when you enter a long document, you will often need several work sessions to complete it. At the end of the first session the text is saved. Then at the beginning of the next session, you will retrieve the old file, enter additional text, and save the new, larger text—and so on until you have completed the entire document.

EDITING

One of the biggest advantages of a word processor is the ability to edit, or revise, text after it has been entered into the computer. Editing usually involves the following activities:

- Deleting text

- Inserting text

■ Moving text

■ Searching for text and/or replacing text

To illustrate each of these editing features we will use the memo in Figure 6-7 to show how the corrections illustrated in Figure 6-8 are made. In the first sentence the word *August* has two *t*s. We can use the computer's DELETE key to remove one of them. First, however, we must know how to move the cursor to the appropriate place in the document. Most computers have cursor movement keys, marked by arrows, which, when pressed, move the cursor in one of four possible directions: up, down, left, or right. Macro cursor movements, using specially designated keys, allow the cursor to be moved over a wider range of the document, such as a word or a paragraph at a time, from the beginning to the end of the document, or to any designated page in the document.

Using the appropriate keys, we now move the cursor to the second *t* in *August*. Then we press the DELETE key to delete the letter.

The fourth word in the memo, *recieved,* is spelled incorrectly. To correct it, we first move the cursor to the *i* and delete it. Next we delete the *e* following the *i*. Finally, we insert the *e* and *i* in their right order by typing them on the keyboard. We could also make this correction by using a *find-and-replace* feature. We would ask the word processor to find the word *recieved* and replace it with *received*.

As you can see from Figure 6-8, the word *immediate* in the first paragraph (between *some* and *action*) would make the memo clearer. To insert a word, we simply move the cursor to the appropriate location in the text and enter the letters through the keyboard. The software will automatically move the words that follow, making room for the new word. In this example, you need only position the cursor after the word *some* and then enter the word *immediate.*

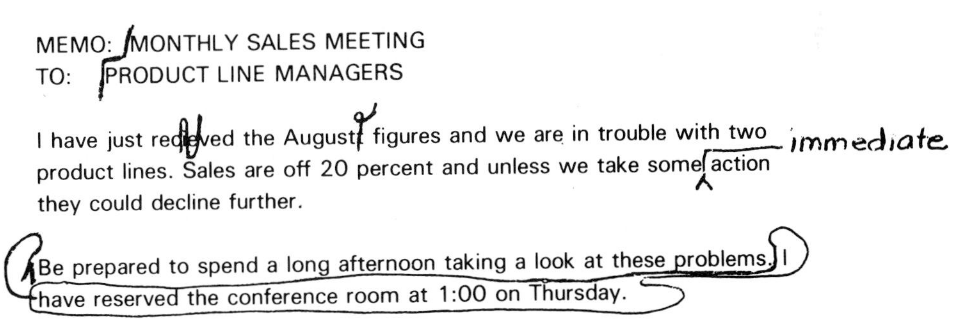

MEMO: MONTHLY SALES MEETING
TO: PRODUCT LINE MANAGERS

I have just recieved the August figures and we are in trouble with two _ *immediate*
product lines. Sales are off 20 percent and unless we take some action
they could decline further.

Be prepared to spend a long afternoon taking a look at these problems. I
have reserved the conference room at 1:00 on Thursday.

Figure 6-8.
The first draft of the memo in Figure 6-7 printed out and marked for correction. The editing features of word-processing software are used to make these changes in the memo.

The last correction in Figure 6-8 is to reverse the final two sentences so that they make more sense. To do this we can use another feature, often called *block commands.* This feature allows you to move or copy text from one location in the document to another. Sometimes this is referred to as *cut and paste.* Three steps are required. First, you identify or "mark" the segment of the text, or block, to be cut. Next, you move the cursor to the block's new location. Finally, you issue the command that "pastes" the marked segment. The completely revised memo is shown in Figure 6-9.

The find-and-replace feature is also useful in long text files that require repetitive word replacement. For example, suppose that a long memo has been entered into the computer and that the author wants to be sure that the product mentioned in the memo is referred to by its new name, "64K buffer board," instead of its old name, "32K buffer board." Rather than reviewing the entire document on the screen, the author can use the *find* command to uncover each instance of the old name. When this command, also called a *global command,* is used, the cursor will instantly appear next to the first occurrence. The software will then

```
MEMO:    MONTHLY SALES MEETING
TO:      PRODUCT LINE MANAGERS

I have just received the August figures
and we are in trouble with two product
lines. Sales are off 20 percent and unless
we take some immediate action they could
decline further.

I have reserved the conference room at
1:00 on Thursday. Be prepared to spend a
long afternoon taking a look at these
problems.
```

Figure 6-9.
The revised memo, ready to print.

allow the author to make the change by entering the new name through the keyboard. Then the search can continue for more instances of the old name. A more efficient variation of this global command is the find-and-replace command, which will automatically replace each occurrence of "32K buffer board" with "64K buffer board."

Again, remember to periodically enter the save command while you are editing and again at the end. Otherwise your changes will not be stored on disk.

FORMATTING

Another benefit of word processing is the ability to control, through the use of commands, how the printed output will look. This feature is called *formatting.* Some systems permit on-screen formatting, in which the text displayed on the screen looks exactly the same as the printed output will look.

Every word-processing system contains commands to establish a document's format. They control text layout characteristics such as

- Left and right margins

- Top and bottom margins

- Single or double spacing

- Automatic centering of text on a page

- Tab stops to create tables

- Paragraph indentation

Some systems have very powerful formatting capabilities. But it is not necessary to use the commands that control these characteristics. When no instructions are given, the system's standard or **default values** will automatically be used. Often these default values produce a perfectly acceptable document.

PRINTING

Once a document has been created, edited, and formatted, it can be printed. A print command is selected from the menu, and the printing begins.

Most word-processing systems have commands that will determine how characters are printed. Different from the formatting commands mentioned in the last section, these may include

- Boldface

- Underlining

- Italics

- Subscripts

- Superscripts

- Strike-out

- Font selection

The quality of the finished document depends, of course, on the printer as well as on the word-processing software. In Chapter 2 we explored a range of printer possibilities, including dot-matrix, daisy-wheel, ink-jet, and laser printers. For some applications the draft quality of a dot-matrix printer will suffice, but for others only a letter-quality printer— either a daisy-wheel or laser printer—will do. Some dot-matrix printers can produce *near letter-quality* output when the dots printed on the page are close to one another and each letter is struck twice.

SPELLING CHECKING

Many word-processing systems contain **spelling checkers,** software that includes a dictionary of approximately 100,000 words and checks the spelling of words in a document against this dictionary. Many spelling checkers also allow the user to add the correct spelling of names or special terms to the dictionary.

Spelling checkers can be used in two ways. In the first, the spelling of a word is checked when the word is entered in the document. If the spelling is incorrect, the user will be notified instantly on the terminal's screen, and he or she can correct the error before continuing.

In the second method, the spelling of words is checked for an entire text file after the text has been entered. Some prefer this method because it does not interfere with the writer's train of thought.

THESAURUS

Most of us have had the problem of searching in our mind for a word to use in place of one that does not sound quite right or one that has already been used many times in the last few paragraphs. A **thesaurus** is a software package that will automatically perform this search. Usually it offers several substitutes, or synonyms. These commercial software packages include a database of words, some with as many as 200,000 entries. When a substitute is needed, the cursor is placed over the word and the appropriate command is entered. The software then will find a synonym.

MAIL MERGE

Another useful feature of many word-processing systems is the ability to create mailing lists and to produce form letters. The format for a form letter contains a standard text that will be written to each recipient. In addition, it includes codes that allow the insertion of special characters—such as name and address—to "personalize" the letter. To produce these letters, the standard text file is merged with another file, such as a name-and-address file. The mail-merge software then prints personalized letters.

■ ■

SEVERAL YEARS AGO THE DIXON COMPANY, a distributor of dental supplies, bought a word-processing system complete with a mail-merge software. Today it has a mailing list of over five thousand dentists. Once every month a letter introducing a new product in Dixon's line is mailed to each dentist. The system automatically addresses the letter to the dentist and, in addition, refers to the dentist by name in at least one paragraph of the letter. Dixon's marketing vice-president has found that the dentists appreciate this informative letter, and he believes that it has generated much goodwill for the company.

■ ■

INTEGRATION

Often it is necessary to combine the output from several different applications into one document. An **integrated package** is a software package that includes word processing, data management, electronic spreadsheet, graphics, and perhaps other capabilities in one software package. Its advantage is that the user can move easily among applications and data can be shared.

For example, data can be accessed from a database and used in an electronic spreadsheet. Then the spreadsheet data can be used to construct a graph. In the next step, the spreadsheet and graph can be integrated with the text of a memo. Finally, the document can be printed.

■ ■

WHEN FAY KELLY WAS ASKED BY HER BOSS TO WRITE A REPORT SUMMARIZING A RECENT MARKET SURVEY SHE HAD COMPLETED, she turned to her microcomputer. She began by writing the first draft of her report on the word-processing system. While writing the draft, she realized that it would help to include the survey statistics.

After she finished writing the text, she switched to the spreadsheet software in her integrated package. This package already stored data from the market survey. Kelly, however, decided to summarize the data, as they were too detailed for this particular report.

Once she had condensed and summarized the data, she inserted the spreadsheet table into the body of her first-draft memo. Then she read the draft again and made some changes. But while she was making these changes, she wondered whether the addition of a pie chart would help emphasize her conclusions. So Kelly turned to the graphics software in her integrated system. She selected the data to be graphed and gave the commands to create a pie chart using the data.

Next, Kelly returned to her memo and incorporated the graph into her text and spreadsheet output. After making just a few more changes, she printed a copy of the report on a laser printer. Pleased with the report's contents and appearance, she sent it to her boss by electronic mail.

■ ■

DESKTOP PUBLISHING

The term **desktop publishing** refers to the use of hardware and software to produce hard copy of a quality similar to that obtained by commercial printing. It requires both a software package capable of combining text and graphics and formatting capabilities powerful enough to accommodate a wide range of layout possibilities. Desktop publishing also requires a laser printer.

Usually, but not always, a microcomputer is used. When the document is entered into the keyboard, it is displayed on the screen in the same format as the desired finished product, including graphics, if any. Then the laser printer is used to print high-quality copies of the exact image that is on the screen. Desktop publishing can be used to produce internal reports, newsletters, brochures, flyers, letterheads, and even advertising copy. Indeed, it has significantly reduced many organizations' reliance on commercial printing.

● ●

E N D · U S E R   H I N T S

IMPROVE YOUR WRITING WITH A WORD PROCESSOR

Once you have learned how to use a word-processing system, you then have a tool that can be used to improve the way you write. Although readers may be interested in the *content* of what you write, how you express it may encourage them to read on or stop. Here are some steps to follow to improve your writing.

1. Write a rough draft. Get your thoughts entered into the computer. At this point do not worry at all about spelling, punctuation, grammar, clarity, or style. This is your chance to be creative!

2. Review your work on the screen, or print it out.

3. Now focus on your thoughts and their clarity. Does the rough draft say what you want it to say? If not, use the editing features of the word-processing software. Delete words, add words, move paragraphs around. Review your work again. Is it better?

4. Now focus on style.

   ■ How does it read?

   ■ Is it stuffy? Use every-day speech.

   ■ Does your opening paragraph set the theme for the paper?

   ■ Do the ideas follow logically?

   ■ Are these ideas expressed clearly?

   ■ Have you been too wordy?

   ■ Can some words be deleted?

   ■ Are your sentences too long?

   ■ Are your paragraphs too long?

   ■ Do your thoughts flow smoothly from one paragraph to the next?

   ■ Is your closing paragraph strong?

5. You can improve the impact and readability of your work by using such techniques as bulleting, underlining, tables, and graphics. Bulleting is useful for:

   ■ Emphasis

   ■ Lists

   ■ Variety

   Underlining draws attention to important ideas. Spreadsheet tables and graphics produced by integrated software packages and combined with your text can provide variety and reduce the need for wordy and often complex explanations.

6. Be prepared to write several drafts. Few if any writers can produce effective work at one sitting. As a rule, the more drafts, the more effective the finished product.

7. Now check spelling and grammar. If available, use the word processor's spelling checker software.

● ●

?   Q U E S T I O N S   ?

1. Define office automation.
2. How can office automation help reduce office-related costs?
3. What is a workstation?
4. What are the eight major functions performed by a word-processing system?
5. What is the purpose of the status line and menu area?
6. How does wordwrap help the person entering a document?
7. What effect does a RETURN have in a word-processing system?
8. Explain how a document is saved and retrieved using a word processor.
9. How is text deleted and inserted?
10. How is text moved from one place in a document to another?
11. When is the find-and-replace feature used?
12. What options are available to format a document?

13. How are a spelling checker and a thesaurus used?
14. Can a word processor produce a form letter using the mail-merge feature that is more personalized than one that is photocopied? Why?
15. What is an integrated package?
16. What is desktop publishing, and how does it help an organization?

ELECTRONIC FILING

Office workers must frequently collect, store, update, and retrieve data. In the past they did this at the file cabinet; today they do it at the terminal.

Data storage and retrieval activities are not limited to the office but also are part of a firm's operational processes. Data must be collected, stored, updated, and retrieved in transaction systems as well as in systems used to manage and control such operational activities as order processing, inventory control, and distribution.

In Chapters 8 to 10 we will examine data management and how such systems can be used in a wide variety of applications. Here, however, we will focus on only the procedures that would be followed if a computer were to replace the functions of a file cabinet in the office.

Accordingly, we will define **electronic filing** as the use of the computer to collect, store, update, and retrieve the data that flow through an office environment. The purpose of electronic filing is to increase the efficiency of the paper-handling process and make data accessible to users in ways not possible with manual filing methods.

FILE STRUCTURE

So that users will find electronic filing systems familiar and easy to use, many are designed to perform like office filing cabinet systems. The data that the electronic files contain can be divided into *files* and *records*. For example, to establish a filing system for customer feedback on products, the user creates a file labeled *customer feedback*. This file is like a drawer in a file cabinet. Once this file has been created, records are then established, which are like the folders in a drawer (Figure 6-10). Each record represents a specific product in the product line. Whenever customer feedback is received, a new entry is made to the appropriate record.

FILE SECURITY

Sometimes it is important to limit the number of people who can access the data in these systems. Consequently, when a file is established, several levels of restricted access may be specified. At the highest level, only the person who created the file can access it; no one else will even know that the file exists. At a lower security level, the file can be shared with a limited number of people by providing them with a *password,* a code

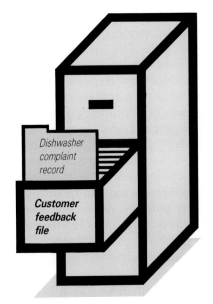

Figure 6-10.
An electronic filing system is used in the same way that a file cabinet is used. One major difference, however, is that records can be retrieved from files very quickly in an electronic system.

Dishwasher complaint record

Customer feedback file

that when identified by the computer permits access to the data. For example, secretaries can be given a password that will give them access to only those files they need to use.

Files can also be made public, but even then, the owner may limit access privileges. Options the owner can specify include

■ Read—everyone can read the data in the file but cannot change or remove them.

■ Append—everyone can read and add new data but cannot change or delete them.

■ Unlimited—everyone has full access to read, change, add, and delete data.

Security will be considered in greater detail in Chapter 16.

SEARCHING

One of the most useful features of an electronic filing system is that it can find data very quickly. Sometimes the user may retrieve data directly by specifying the record in which the data are stored—for example, "list all customer complaints received for our dishwasher model 1106." But sometimes the user does not know exactly where the needed data are filed. These systems then allow the user to search for the data by specifying a category (or field), such as a keyword, a document name, or the date when the document was created—for example, "list all customer complaints received after May 1 for every product in the product line."

In addition to locating data that have been stored in the office electronic filing system, terminals or microcomputers can also be used to access an organization's central computer facilities. As a result, data from its functional areas—including operations, finance, accounting, marketing, and sales—can be used by office personnel. Beginning in Chapter 8 we will examine these centralized database systems.

BENEFITS

There are several ways that the use of electronic filing technology affects the office:

■ The data—regardless of where they are stored or who owns them—are no farther away than the terminal or microcomputer on a desk.

■ Because the process of entering or retrieving data is now more efficient, many professionals no longer need to rely on clerks or secretaries to do this; they can do it themselves.

■ The availability of information is likely to reduce the time it takes to make decisions and, in many cases, to improve their quality.

■   Because the data are so accessible, information is now available to all levels in the organizational hierarchy, which helps explain why some companies have been able to reduce the number of layers in the organization.

■■■■■■■■■■■■■■■■■■■■■■■■■■■■■■■■■■■■■

MANAGING THE PAPERWORK IN A CONGRESSIONAL OFFICE IS AN ENORMOUS TASK, and so most of these offices rely heavily on office automation technology. At any time a congressman or congresswoman must keep track of dozens or even hundreds of pieces of legislation as they move through Congress and in addition manage the flow of data to and from thousands of constituents.

One congressman from the Southwest maintains a staff of eight people in his Washington office. He has no secretaries. Nine microcomputers, one on each desk (one is his own), are used for all of the paperwork.

When a constituent writes a letter to the congressman, it is assigned to a staff member, who reads the letter and writes a reply using the word-processing system. After the letter is finished, the voter file—which maintains personal data for each voter in the congressman's district—is searched to determine whether there is a record for that voter. If there is not, then one will be established. Then the file is updated, summarizing the purpose of the correspondence.

Because the filing system contains valuable data about many of the voters, it is often used to identify constituents with common interests. Recently, for example, the congressman felt that he should write to voters in his district about pending Medicaid legislation that would decrease some benefits. He composed a letter on the word-processing system that expressed his strong opposition to the bill. Then the electronic filing system was searched to find the addresses of all those who had mentioned this issue in their letters, and over seven thousand letters were mailed.

When asked about the effectiveness of his office system, the congressman explained, "It helps in two ways. First, it helps keep each voter segment informed about issues of specific concern to them without the need to send them long and largely irrelevant newsletters. Second, by targeting an audience you get their attention. And once you get their attention they will take the time to consider you as a candidate. That surely doesn't hurt at election time. In fact, I heard a political consultant claim that these systems can lead to as much as a 2-percent increase in the vote. Because many elections are won by only 5 percent, a system like this could mean the difference between winning or losing. I would rather win."

■■■■■■■■■■■■■■■■■■■■■■■■■■■■■■■■■■■■■

ELECTRONIC MAIL

Time spent communicating—especially the time spent on the telephone—can be very inefficient. In fact, the person called is often not available. So a message is left to call back. But when the call is returned, the original caller may now be away. So a message is left to try again. This game of "telephone tag" can go on and on. In fact, it is not unusual for up to six calls to be placed before the called party is finally reached.

Electronic mail promises to replace some but not all of these wasted efforts. **Electronic mail** refers to the use of computers to send messages, memos, letters, and other forms of office correspondence. It is best suited for short communications that do not require any personal interaction.

In many electronic mail systems, memos, letters, reports, and even illustrations are entered into a terminal or microcomputer, sent to a central computer facility, and then forwarded to one or more destinations where they are accessed by the person, or group of persons, to whom they are addressed. Because messages in these systems are stored and then forwarded by a central computer, the computers are often referred to as *store-and-forward message-switching systems.*

When electronic mail must be sent over long distances, telecommunication facilities must be used. **Telecommunication** is the transmission of data between computers at different locations. Some telecommunication occurs over the telephone lines we use every day, and other telecommunication occurs over microwave and fiber-optic cables—technologies we will examine in Chapter 14. Perhaps one of the greatest advantages of these systems, as the following case suggests, is that the recipient need not be at his or her desk.

■■■■■■■■■■■■■■■■■■■■■■■■■■■■■■■■■■■

WHEN ROBERT WILLIS, an accounting manager for an international consumer products firm, needs to send a report to the five members of his budget committee, he sends it through the company's electronic mail system. The committee members find the report waiting when they query their microcomputers for messages. Within two hours most if not all of the members will have read the report.

For most of the electronic mail users at this firm, the ability to access a message when it is most convenient is an important feature of their system. It means fewer interrupted meetings and work sessions, and when communications span several time zones, there is less concern for communicating only during those few hours when both parties are at work.

■■■■■■■■■■■■■■■■■■■■■■■■■■■■■■■■■■■

Although some electronic mail systems are limited to those locations served by the firm's computers and linked by its telecommunication system, others interface with major commercial electronic mail systems offered by such companies as MCI, Western Union, and General

Electric Information Services. Using these systems, electronic mail can be sent from a company's private system to anyone in the world, provided that a microcomputer, a modem, and a telephone line are available.

ELECTRONIC CONFERENCING

Although electronic mail is most effective for one-way communication—such as sending a memo to department heads—electronic conferencing is most effective when people must exchange ideas in an ongoing dialogue or when a face-to-face meeting is desirable but not feasible. Two forms of electronic conferencing are used today: computer conferencing and teleconferencing.

COMPUTER CONFERENCING

Often an additional feature in an electronic mail system, **computer conferencing** permits users at different locations to participate in an ongoing discussion. Using the software that supports computer conferencing, a conference is established among users at different locations, and those who are interested in the topic are invited to participate (Figure 6-11). There is no requirement that they meet face-to-face, and they can direct their attention to the problem whenever it is convenient for them to do so. That is, they do not have to participate in the conference at the same time.

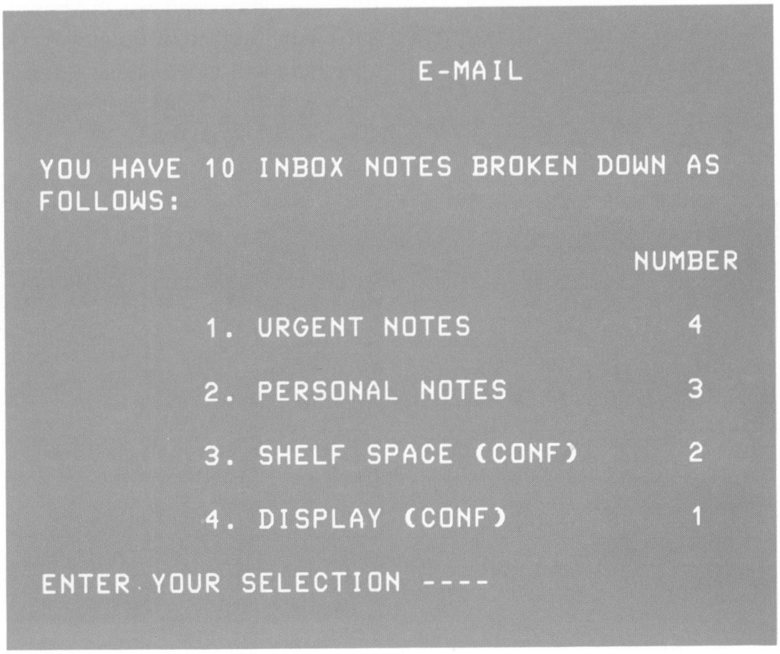

Figure 6-11.
A user of electronic mail with conferencing capabilities might see the screen shown here. The first two categories are electronic mail, and the last two are ongoing conferences.

```
                            E-MAIL


        YOU HAVE 10 INBOX NOTES BROKEN DOWN AS
        FOLLOWS:

                                                NUMBER


                1. URGENT NOTES               4

                2. PERSONAL NOTES             3

                3. SHELF SPACE (CONF)         2

                4. DISPLAY (CONF)             1

        ENTER YOUR SELECTION ----
```

■■■■■■■■■■■■■■■■■■■■■■■■■■■■■■■■■■■■

RALPH JOHNSON, an advertising executive at a soft drink company, spoke with several sales representatives about the problem of obtaining retail shelf space at supermarkets and other retail stores for a new soft drink. Many people had good ideas. Because all of these reps, located throughout the country, used microcomputers, Johnson decided to establish a computer conference so that their ideas could be shared.

To start the conference, Johnson identified the topic, which he called "shelf space," and then entered a memo describing the problem and the objectives of the conference. Next, the memo was sent to all sales reps in North America. At the end of the memo, he invited them to join the conference by contributing memos that they felt were constructive.

Within one week, several reps had joined and were added to the conference mailing list. As memos were contributed, they were automatically routed to all members. One participant even established a subconference to exchange ideas about in-store displays.

■■■■■■■■■■■■■■■■■■■■■■■■■■■■■■■■■■■■

TELECONFERENCING

Sometimes face-to-face communication in the same room is preferable, but logistics may make it impossible for everyone to attend a meeting at the same time. To remedy this, there are several options for **teleconferencing,** visually linking people at separate locations. One alternative is to install video workstations. In addition to performing the office automation functions of a standard workstation, a video workstation can offer full-color video and voice communications (Figure 6-12). Besides the hardware that conventional workstations require, these workstations also include a video camera and an audio system. When a network of video workstations is connected, two or more users can talk and see each other at the same time.

Figure 6-12.
Video workstations can be used for video, voice, or data.

Figure 6-13.
This teleconferencing facility enables distant groups to see and hear one another simultaneously.

A more complex teleconferencing option is one in which several large groups are able to see and hear one another at the same time (Figure 6-13). Teleconferencing facilities such as this can be expensive to install and maintain. Some large hotel chains rent out facilities complete with all of the necessary teleconferencing equipment. So, at both ends of the link, the conference participants merely go to a local hotel and begin their conference. By using such facilities, costly business trips can often be avoided.

Computer conferencing and teleconferencing are clearly not interchangeable. Teleconferencing does allow people to see and hear one another, but it also requires them to be available at the same time. When the participants do not need to converse directly, and the primary information to be shared is text, many organizations turn to computer conferencing. Not only is computer conferencing cheaper, but those using it can postpone their attention to the topic and catch up on it later.

?   Q U E S T I O N S   ?

1. What are the benefits of electronic filing?
2. Describe some of the different access options common to electronic filing systems.
3. Explain how electronic mail might be a more

effective way to deliver a message than a telephone would be.

4. What is the difference between computer conferencing and teleconferencing?

S U M M A R Y

■ **Office automation** refers to the use of information-processing and communication technologies to improve the process of writing, collecting, storing, organizing, retrieving, and communicating office data.

■ The **workstation** is the place where most automated activities converge. Sometimes workstations are joined in a network for **departmental computing.**

■ Software can be used at workstations for such functions as word processing, electronic filing, electronic mail, electronic conferencing, spreadsheets, graphics, and project management.

■ **Word processing** refers to the use of computer technology to create, edit, store, and print documents.

■ Like other types of software, word-processing software employs **screens** containing such information as **menus** listing program options.

- Word-processing screens are commonly divided into the **status line,** which gives the name of the document and the screen position where the **cursor** is located; the **menu area,** which contains the current menu; and the **text area,** which is in effect a blank page for typing.

- As text is entered, it can be placed at the start of a new line or paragraph by hitting the RETURN key—a **hard return.** Complete words will automatically be placed on a new line through a software feature known as **wordwrap.**

- Once created, documents can be saved on disk and retrieved later for change, expansion, or printing.

- One of the biggest advantages of a word processor is the ability to edit text by performing such functions as deleting, inserting, moving, searching for, and replacing text.

- Formatting commands can be used to control the way printed output from a word processor will appear. When formatting commands are omitted, **default values** will be followed.

- Options are also available to control the way a word processor prints characters. The final quality, of course, depends on the printer.

- Many word-processing systems use **spelling checkers,** to check the spelling of words in a document, and a **thesaurus,** to find substitutes for words in the text.

- Mail merge is a word-processing feature used to create mailing lists and produce form letters.

- An **integrated package** is a software package that includes word processing, data management, electronic spreadsheet, graphics, and perhaps other capabilities.

- **Desktop publishing** is used when professional printing quality is required.

- With **electronic filing,** the computer can collect, store, update, and retrieve data that flow through an office environment.

- **Electronic mail** refers to the use of computers to send messages, memos, and letters. **Telecommunication** is used to transmit the data between computers or terminals at different locations.

- Electronic conferencing is useful for two-way communications. Two forms are computer conferencing and teleconferencing.

- **Computer conferencing** permits users at different locations to participate in an ongoing discussion by sharing written messages.

- **Teleconferencing** offers several options for permitting people to see and hear one another while they communicate.

K E Y · T E R M S

The following list shows the key terms in the order in which they appear in the chapter.

Office automation (p. 156)	Wordwrap (p. 162)
Workstation (p. 158)	Default value (p. 165)
Departmental computing (p. 158)	Spelling checker (p. 165)
Word processing (p. 159)	Thesaurus (p. 166)
Screen (p. 160)	Integrated package (p. 166)
Menu (p. 160)	Desktop publishing (p. 167)
Status line (p. 161)	Electronic filing (p. 169)
Cursor (p. 161)	Electronic mail (p. 172)
Menu area (p. 161)	Telecommunication (p. 172)
Text area (p. 161)	Computer conferencing (p. 173)
Hard return (p. 161)	Teleconferencing (p. 174)

F O R   D I S C U S S I O N

1. Do you think that as data become easier to enter and retrieve, the need for secretaries and administrative assistants will diminish? Will professionals do more of their own work? Is this in fact the best use of a professional's time?
2. Compare writing a term paper using a typewriter and writing it using a word processor.
3. What problems do you think people have in adjusting to the office of the future?

H A N D S - O N   P R O J E C T S

1. Interview a secretary or administrative assistant, and find out the types of office automation technology that they regularly use. Find out how that person has benefited from office automation. What problems has he or she encountered? How would this individual improve the current system? Would electronic filing or electronic mail (if not already employed) be useful?
2. Use a word-processing program to prepare an assignment for another class in which you are currently enrolled. How did using this aid affect your finished output? Did it improve it? What features of the word processor did you like best?

7
SPREADSHEETS

O U T L I N E

O B J E C T I V E S

After studying this chapter you should understand the following:

■ *What a spreadsheet is and why it is useful.*

■ *How to construct a spreadsheet.*

■ *The ways that spreadsheets are used as decision-support tools.*

In the preceding chapter we discussed how software, from word processors to electronic filing, has affected the way some office activities are performed. Another software category that has had a similar impact is the electronic spreadsheet.

Although many office automation processes (see Chapter 6) affect clerical activities, electronic spreadsheets have a greater impact on problem-solving and decision-making activities. Some activities—such as budgeting—are seldom undertaken today without using a spreadsheet. And spreadsheets are used in many other applications, from the factory floor to the sales office.

The purpose of this chapter is to help you understand what a spreadsheet is, to show you how to create your own spreadsheets, and to explain how several companies use commercial spreadsheet packages to solve business problems.

Many commercial spreadsheet software packages are available, all nearly identical in concept but somewhat different in how they work and how they can be used. Rather than concentrate on any one commercial software package, this chapter will focus on the concepts behind all electronic spreadsheets and the features they share. Many of the details will be left to the user manuals that accompany the individual packages.

WHAT IS A SPREADSHEET?

An **electronic spreadsheet,** or **spreadsheet** for short, is a table with rows and columns into which data are entered. Spreadsheet software makes it possible to enter data into a table format, manipulate them, store them, and print reports. All of this can be done with relative ease compared with working by hand with the same rows-and-columns of data.

Whenever a problem or situation can be organized into rows and columns, a spreadsheet can be used. In the following example you will see how one problem fits into this format.

As part of the annual budgeting process for Amdex Corporation, product-line managers must submit a budget for each of the next four quarters. One such budget is summarized in the worksheet shown in Figure 7-1. This worksheet is a table with rows and columns. The rows are identified by numbers (1 through 8), and the columns by letters (A through F). The table can be described as follows:

- The labels in the left-hand column, column A, identify the categories of the data in each row.

- The labels in the top row, row 1, identify each of the four quarters in the budget.

	A	B	C	D	E	F
1		First	Second	Third	Fourth	
2	Expenses					
3	Wages	32	35	41	36	
4	Material	12	13	15	14	
5	Supplies	4	4	6	5	
6	Utilities	2	2	3	3	
7	Repairs	2	2	4	3	
8	Total	52	56	69	61	238

Figure 7-1.
A budget worksheet for four quarters.

■ The budget data for the first quarter are in column B, rows 3 through 7. The budget data for the remaining quarters are in columns C through E.

■ The computed totals for each quarter are in row 8, columns B through E.

■ The intersection of row 8 and column F contains the computed total budget amount for the year.

Because this budget can be organized as a table, spreadsheet software can be used.

■ ■

In the next section we will describe the characteristics of spreadsheet software. Later in the chapter we will explain how spreadsheet applications can be entered into a computer system.

CHARACTERISTICS OF A SPREADSHEET

Although spreadsheet software organizes data in rows and columns, it has many other characteristics a user must understand before developing an application and using it as a problem-solving or decision-making tool. These characteristics include

■ Table format

■ Data forms

- Recalculations
- Storage and retrieval
- Presentation
- Standard format

Let us look at each characteristic.

TABLE FORMAT

When spreadsheet software is first loaded into the computer, a screen similar to the one shown in Figure 7-2 appears. The screen shows an empty table with designations for columns and rows. The intersection of a row and column is referred to as a **cell.** The location or *address* of a cell can be identified by the column and row that intersect to form the cell. The shaded rectangle in Figure 7-2, for example, can be referred to as cell B2.

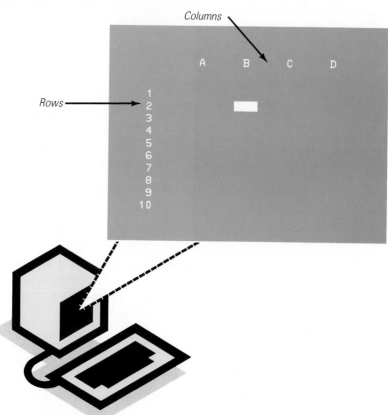

Figure 7-2.
An empty spreadsheet, with the rows and columns awaiting data.

DATA FORMS

Three different kinds of data can be entered into a spreadsheet: (1) labels or titles, (2) numbers, and (3) calculated entries.

Labels or Titles A **label** is a description. In the Amdex example (Figure 7-1), wages, materials, and supplies are labels, as are the designations for the quarters—first, second, third, and fourth. Figure 7-3 identifies all of the labels in that example.

Numbers **Numbers,** which the user enters directly into a cell, are the second kind of data in a spreadsheet. For example, the entry in cell B3, illustrated in Figure 7-3, is a number representing wages for the first quarter.

Calculated Entries The totals found in row 8 of Figure 7-3, cells B8 through E8, are called **calculated entries.** The software calculates these totals by adding up the numbers in the columns above each of these cells. For example, the entry in cell B8 is obtained by summing the entries in cells B3 through B7. The entry in F8 is also a calculated entry. Users do not enter calculated entries.

Calculated entries are computed by using a **formula,** an instruction that specifies the steps to obtain the desired mathematical result. The user enters formulas into the cells in which the results will be displayed. For example, when the spreadsheet is developed, the following formula will be entered into cell B8:

$$+B3+B4+B5+B6+B7$$

The formula specifies that the contents of cells B3, B4, B5, B6, and B7 be added, with the result displayed in cell B8. It is important to realize

	A	B	C	D	E	F
1		First	Second	Third	Fourth	
2	Expenses					
3	Wages	32	35	41	36	
4	Material	12	13	15	14	
5	Supplies	4	4	6	5	
6	Utilities	2	2	3	3	
7	Repairs	2	2	4	3	
8	Total	52	56	69	61	238

Figure 7-3.
The entries in a spreadsheet can be classified as labels, numbers, or calculated entries.

Labels
Numbers
Calculated entries

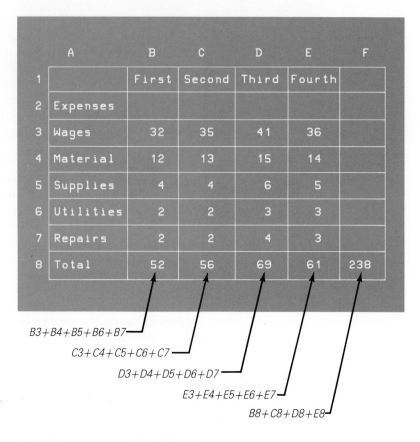

	A	B	C	D	E	F
1		First	Second	Third	Fourth	
2	Expenses					
3	Wages	32	35	41	36	
4	Material	12	13	15	14	
5	Supplies	4	4	6	5	
6	Utilities	2	2	3	3	
7	Repairs	2	2	4	3	
8	Total	52	56	69	61	238

B3+B4+B5+B6+B7

C3+C4+C5+C6+C7

D3+D4+D5+D6+D7

E3+E4+E5+E6+E7

B8+C8+D8+E8

Figure 7-4.
Formulas instruct the spreadsheet software to perform calculated results.

that although the formula is entered into the cell when the spreadsheet is designed, the *result* of the formula, not the formula itself, is displayed in that cell when it is used. Figure 7-4 shows all of the formulas for our example, including the total for all four quarters in F8.

RECALCULATIONS

Once the labels, numbers, and formulas have been entered, the spreadsheet software can automatically compute the calculated results. And results can be recalculated when revised numbers are entered.

    For example, suppose the person preparing the budget presented in the earlier figures wants to determine the consequence of an increase in wages in the first quarter. The new estimate, shown in Figure 7-5, can be entered into cell B3. Immediately after this entry, the software will automatically recalculate the new total for the first quarter.

    As we mentioned in Chapter 5, sensitivity analysis is one method of exploring the risk in a decision problem. Changing selected numbers in a spreadsheet and observing the consequences enables us to use a spreadsheet model as an especially effective vehicle for this type of analysis.

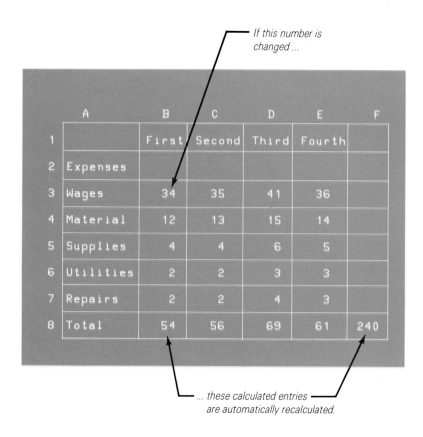

If this number is changed ...

... these calculated entries are automatically recalculated.

Figure 7-5.
When numbers are changed, spreadsheet software instantly recalculates the results.

STORAGE AND RETRIEVAL

The ability to store and retrieve data is central to any business information system. Consequently, an important feature of spreadsheet software is its ability to store and retrieve the data with which it works.

In a budget application, for example, the spreadsheet may be stored on a hard or floppy disk and retrieved several times during the budgeting process. Each time, one or more of the budget categories may be changed. It may also be useful to retrieve the budget again several weeks or months into the budget period, to compare actual costs with those expected when the budget was first developed.

PRESENTATION

Most users need to present the results of their analysis in a way that communicates the information as effectively as possible. Sometimes a simple printout of all or a section of the spreadsheet will suffice. In these cases, the spreadsheet's row-and-column format is considered satisfactory.

But spreadsheet users are turning with increasing frequency to the use of graphics when they want to present information in a more effective format. Several commercial spreadsheet packages have capabilities that make it easy to create graphs.

STANDARD FORMATS

Another important feature of spreadsheet software is that a spreadsheet can be used as a *standard format* into which data can be downloaded from the central computer facilities. In this process, data stored in a central database are requested through the user's terminal or microcomputer. The data are then modified and even summarized so that they can fit into the row-and-column format of a spreadsheet, and then they are entered into the spreadsheet.

This feature gives end-users a significant advantage. It means that business professionals with only spreadsheet skills can access centralized corporate data and process them according to their own needs. Without such a link, they might have to ask the central data processing department to obtain and process the data, an alternative that frequently takes more time and costs more money than the value of the data merits.

?   Q   U   E   S   T   I   O   N   S   ?

1. What types of problems can be represented by a spreadsheet?
2. Prepare a budget for your weekly expenses over the next four weeks. Is it in the form of a worksheet? Identify those cells containing labels, data, and calculated entries.
3. Return to Question 2. Suppose you just discovered that your entertainment costs in Week 2 will be $25 higher than expected. If you revised your spreadsheet, would the computation for weekly expenses be considered a calculation or recalculation? What advantage would a spreadsheet offer in this situation?
4. What is the difference between the numbers in row 8 and the numbers in row 3 of Figure 7-3?
5. Based on the spreadsheet in Figure 7-3, write a formula that computes total wages for the entire year. In what cell should you put this formula?
6. Return to Question 5, and write the formulas that compute the annual totals for each of the remaining expenses.
7. Can knowledge of how a spreadsheet is used be helpful in accessing data stored on a mainframe?

BUILDING A SPREADSHEET TEMPLATE

Building a template is the first step in developing a spreadsheet application. A **template** is a worksheet in which all the labels and formulas, but none of the data, have been entered for a particular application (Figure 7-6). It is a reusable shell. Once the template has been constructed and

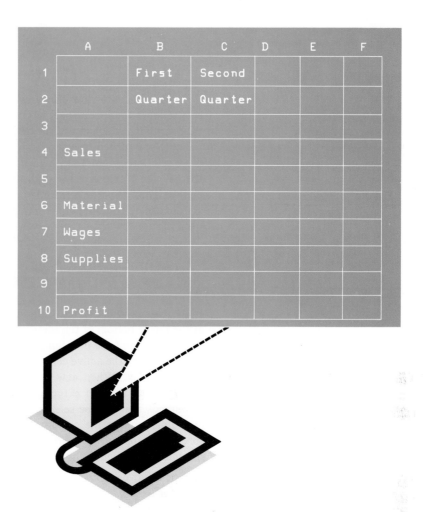

Figure 7-6.
Different users can retrieve a spreadsheet template and enter their own data directly.

saved, it can be used again and again. Only the data need be entered each time.

LOADING THE SPREADSHEET

When spreadsheet software is loaded into the computer, the first screen that appears will be similar to the one shown in Figure 7-2, a blank table waiting for entries. The cursor identifies where the data, entered from the keyboard, will be placed, a location called the **active cell.** Using the cursor movement keys, the cursor can be positioned at any cell of the spreadsheet. (Some of the terms used in this chapter, such as *cursor* and *cursor movement keys,* were introduced in Chapter 6.)

SPREADSHEET WINDOW

Any screen is limited in its display capacity. Some spreadsheet software, however, can store tables with thousands of rows and hundreds of columns—the actual number of cells is limited by the main memory available to the user. Clearly it would be impossible to show a table of this size on the screen. Instead, the screen is treated as a **window** on the larger spreadsheet (Figure 7-7).

To bring into view other segments of the spreadsheet, it is necessary to move the spreadsheet left or right or up or down. This is referred to as **scrolling,** which moves the cursor off any edge of the spreadsheet. If the cursor is moved to the right-hand edge, for example, and then one more cell to the right, the view will change: The first column of cells (on the left side of the screen) will disappear, and a new column will appear on the right side of the screen. If the cursor is moved again, the view will shift one more column to the right. Scrolling in this manner can continue until the window shows the very last column in the spreadsheet.

THE STATUS, ENTRY, AND PROMPT LINES

In most spreadsheet systems, the status, entry, and prompt lines appear at the top or bottom of the screen to provide information needed during the creation and use of a template (Figure 7-8). The *status line* shows the contents of the active cell, usually displaying the data in the cell and its coordinates. When new entries are made to a cell, the *entry line* displays what the user is typing. The *prompt line* displays the menu of commands that can be selected to construct and use the spreadsheet, including printing the contents of the spreadsheet, saving the current spreadsheet on a disk, loading previously saved spreadsheets into the computer, and even graphing the contents of certain cells. Often several

Figure 7-7.
Only a segment of a large spreadsheet can be viewed on the screen at one time.

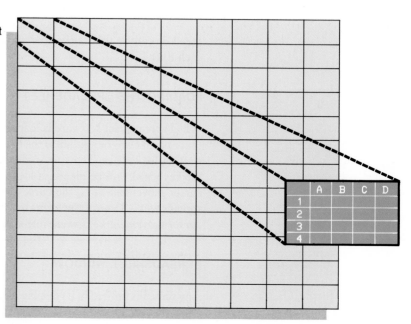

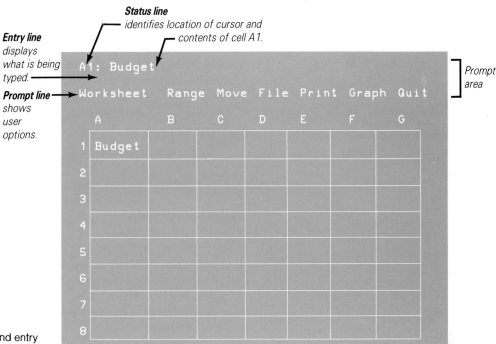

Status line
identifies location of cursor and
contents of cell A1.

Entry line
displays
what is being
typed.

Prompt line
shows
user
options.

Prompt
area

Figure 7-8.
The status line, prompt line, and entry
line.

menus are connected in a layered fashion. When a command is selected
from one menu, it may call another *submenu* or *pulldown menu* of commands.

ENTERING LABELS

As we stated earlier, spreadsheets differentiate among labels, numbers,
and calculated entries. Labels can be made up of any alphanumeric
characters, that is letters and numbers. An address, for example, is a
label. No arithmetic operations can be performed on labels. Most
spreadsheet software recognizes that a label is being entered if the first
character entered into the cell is a letter. But if the first character of a
label is not a letter, then it is necessary to enter a quotation mark (") to
allow the system to distinguish letters from numbers.

ENTERING NUMBERS

If the first character entered in a cell is numerical, the entry will be identified as a number. Few numbers, however, may be entered when the
template is constructed. Usually, numbers are entered when the template is used for a specific application or when it is tested to verify that
the template is working properly and producing the correct results.
Numbers may be displayed in several different formats, such as integer
(102), real (102.4923), and dollar (102.49).

ENTERING FORMULAS

Most spreadsheets recognize that a formula is to be entered when the first character is a plus sign, minus sign, or parenthesis. In a formula, arithmetic operations are indicated by using the following symbols:

*   Multiplication

/   Division

+   Addition

—   Subtraction

USING FUNCTIONS

Many of the formulas illustrated in Figure 7-4 reference several consecutive cells. For example, in cell B8, the formula sums the contents of cells B3 through B7. Most spreadsheet software packages include functions that simplify this and other mathematical procedures. In this case, a function called SUM might be used to sum the contents of cells within a specified interval:

     @SUM (B3:B7)

A symbol such as @ informs the software that a function is to be used. Conventions, however, vary according to the specific software package. Other functions include those for determining present value and internal rate of return, finding the maximum or minimum value in a range of cells, and looking up values in a table.

SAVING THE TEMPLATE

Saving a template is very simple. The save command is selected from the menu that appears in the prompt line. In Figure 7-8 the File command begins this process. The user gives the spreadsheet a file name, and the contents of the template is saved on disk.

     When the saved template is needed again, the user returns to the prompt line and selects the command for loading a file. The user enters the file name under which the data are stored; the disk is searched for the file; and the template is loaded into the CPU and displayed on the screen.

USING THE TEMPLATE

Templates are used by moving the cursor to blank cells and directly entering the appropriate number. In our budgeting example, the user enters the first number by moving the cursor to cell B3 and then enters the number 32 through the keyboard. Next, the user moves the cursor to cell B4 and enters the number 12. The process continues until all of the numbers have been entered. Once this process is completed, the final totals can be read in the bottom row.

SAVING SPREADSHEETS

In addition to saving templates, a complete spreadsheet may also be saved for later use. The procedure is the same as that for saving a template. First, the user selects the save command and then gives a name to the spreadsheet. This name must be different from the name used for the template; otherwise, the system would simply associate the name with the saved spreadsheet and the template would be lost. That is, the next time the user tried to load the template, the whole spreadsheet would be displayed, complete with numbers that would probably have little relationship to the ones used in the new application.

PRINTING

By selecting the print command from the prompt line, the contents of the spreadsheet can be printed. Because a spreadsheet can be quite large, and because some printers can print at most eighty columns across, it may be necessary to print the spreadsheet in separate segments. Fortunately, there are additional commands to indicate a particular range of cells to print. Once the different segments have been printed separately, they can be taped together.

OTHER SPREADSHEET FEATURES

Spreadsheet software has many other features that help make templates easier to construct and use. And it is on many of these additional features that commercial packages compete. These features are:

- Editing a label or formula without having to retype the entire entry.

- Copying formulas that may be used over and over again in several different cells.

- Sorting the data found in columns or rows into a desired sequence.

- Formatting the way in which cells display data (by using commas, decimal points, and dollar signs).

- Moving the cursor directly to a cell.

- Working with two separate spreadsheets at the same time.

- Protecting cell entries from any changes.

- Writing programs, called *macros,* that automate complex or repetitive spreadsheet activities.

SPREADSHEET GRAPHICS

As we mentioned earlier, some spreadsheet packages can also graph the data contained in the cells (Figure 7-9). The user can plot the data as a line or bar graph or as a pie chart.

Graphics are used when a visual picture of the data can communicate a message more effectively than can a column or table of numbers. This is an especially effective way to show trends or comparisons. Later, in Chapter 11, we will examine the role of graphics in an information system.

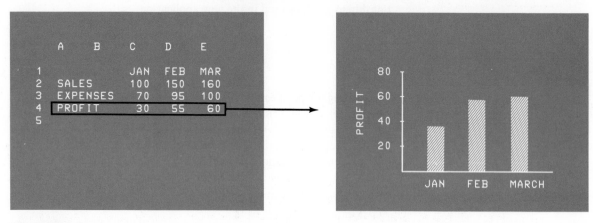

Figure 7-9.
The data in a spreadsheet can be shown graphically.

Alicia:

    As you can see, the figures for the next four quarters look good. The third quarter will be a record-breaker, but the fourth will suffer from our usual fall slump.

	Quarter 1	Quarter 2	Quarter 3	Quarter 4
Sales	105	125	175	160
Charges	30	35	45	40
Expenses	25	30	40	38
Profit contribution	50	60	90	82

    Let me know what you think about the profit projections. I feel they are realistic, possibly even understated.

        Regards,

        Martin

Figure 7-10.
Integrated software combines the features of spreadsheets, word processing, data management, and graphics. This memo shows how output from a spreadsheet can be incorporated into word-processing text.

INTEGRATED SOFTWARE

Chapter 6 showed that it is often desirable to tie together the output from spreadsheets, word processors, and graphics packages. *Integrated packages* make it possible to use these different software components and to move among them easily, usually with just a few keystrokes. Figure 7-10 illustrates how data pulled from a spreadsheet can be incorporated in the text of a memo. Without this feature, the user would have to run each software package separately and then cut and paste the results into a final report.

WINDOWING

When analyzing a problem, it is often necessary to review several documents at once. If you are not using a computer, you can do this by spreading the papers on the top of a desk. But some software allows this to be done on the screen. Windowing, a concept that is not unique to spreadsheets, allows the user to overlay portions of several different spreadsheets on the screen. The user can then compare the contents of several documents without having first to produce hard copy.

• •

E N D · U S E R   H I N T S

DESIGNING USEFUL SPREADSHEETS

The following hints should help you design effective spreadsheets.

1. Build a template first. Do not enter the data until the template does what it is you want it to do.

2. Make the assumptions in the template explicit by parametizing the spreadsheet.

3. Use blank rows and columns to make the template easier to read and use.

4. Use special characters ($-$, $=$, $*$, $\#$, and so on) to highlight data or to bring attention to certain sections of your template.

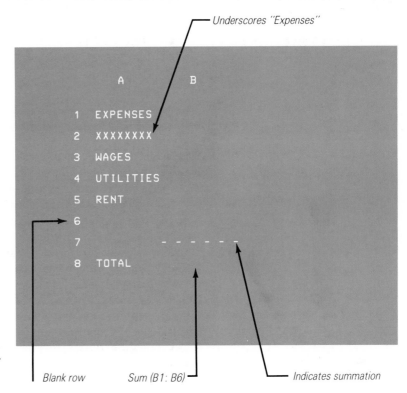

Underscores "Expenses"

Blank row   Sum (B1: B6)   Indicates summation

5. Always test your template by entering test data. Check to make sure that all calculations are correct.

6. Plan ahead. For example, it might be preferable to include one or more blank rows in the template so that an additional label and its associated data can be added. These blank rows can also be included in the @SUM function, making it possible to enter data into the new rows and have them added with the other data without changing the range of the @SUM function.

7. Always back up your template by saving an extra copy on a second disk.

8. When you design your template, keep in mind the possibility that it might be effective to display one or more columns or rows graphically. A picture is worth 10,000 words. Plan your template with graphics in mind!

9. Try to fit all of the output on one piece of paper. Although it might be necessary to tape several pieces of paper together for large spreadsheets, they will be harder for the user to understand than those that can fit on one page. Use condensed print, if possible. But remember the concept of information overload. Don't produce too much information!

10. Be aware that statistics can lie. When graphs are automatically drawn by spreadsheet software, they often do not begin at the origin of the X and Y axes. As a result the graph may be misleading. The sales graph to the left was automatically generated from a spreadsheet. Sales look like they are on the rise—they are, but only slightly. A graph where the user manually sets the scale to begin at the intersection of the X and Y axes (graph to the left) shows the data in a more realistic framework.

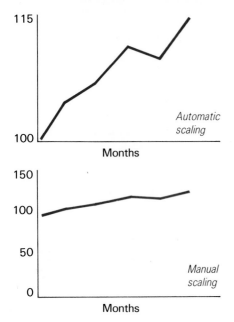

● ●

BUILDING A MORE GENERAL MODEL

The budget template constructed earlier may be adequate when the user is relatively certain about the data that will be used in the spreadsheet. There may be other decision-making situations, however, when the user is less certain about the data. Then a more general model may be more versatile, providing an efficient way of exploring a wide range of alternatives, the data associated with the alternatives, and their outcomes.

Consider the *pro-forma* profit-and-loss statement shown in Figure 7-11. *Pro-forma* statements are projections or estimates. This one, developed by a household appliances manufacturer, estimates the profits from a new electric toothbrush. The first entry is the sales estimate, and the next entries, from materials through promotional costs, are the expenses. Finally, on the last line, the profit contribution is computed by subtracting the expenses from the sales.

But this statement is only one outcome. Because the toothbrush will be sold in a competitive marketplace, other outcomes are also possi-

Pro-Forma Profit and Loss

                                        Electric Toothbrush

            Sales   300

            Materials   60

            Wages   24

            Shipping   3

            Promotion   21

            Profit contribution   192

Figure 7-11.
A *pro-forma* profit-and-loss statement
for an electric toothbrush.

ble. The model we shall develop will make it easier to examine these outcomes.

When the *pro-forma* statement in Figure 7-12 was developed, several assumptions were made about the relationship of costs to sales. These relationships, determined by studying the costs incurred by other similar products, are as follows:

■ Material costs are 20 percent of sales.

■ Wages are 8 percent of sales.

■ Shipping is 1 percent of sales.

■ Promotion is 7 percent of sales.

These relationships will be used to generalize the model.

GENERALIZING THE RELATIONSHIPS AMONG CELLS

Rather than relying on the user to enter the sales figure and each of the expenses directly into the appropriate cells, the template would be more useful if formulas expressing the expense relationships were used to calculate the cell values for each of the expenses. This is illustrated in Figure 7-12. The cell value that will be displayed in cell B5, for example, represents the cost of materials. Because the material costs are expected to be 20 percent of sales, the following formula is entered into cell B5:

+B4∗.20

The plus sign is necessary to indicate that a formula is to be entered. Then the formula instructs the spreadsheet software to multiply the contents of cell B4 by 0.20 (20 percent). The result of this computation will then be displayed in cell B5.

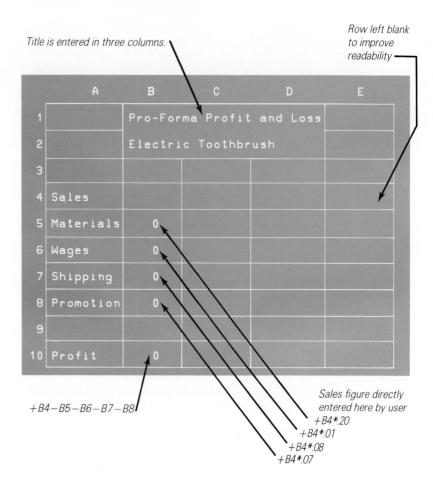

Title is entered in three columns.

Row left blank to improve readability

Sales figure directly entered here by user
+B4*.20
+B4*.01
+B4*.08
+B4*.07

+B4−B5−B6−B7−B8

Figure 7-12.
A template is generalized by entering the relationship between sales and the expense categories.

In a similar fashion, the remaining relationships are entered into the spreadsheet. Once the template is completed, the user needs only to enter sales in cell B4, and then all of the remaining cells—including profit—will automatically be calculated. In this way, various outcomes can be determined for sales figures ranging from pessimistic to optimistic.

PARAMETIZING THE TEMPLATE

One disadvantage of this template is that the assumptions made about the relationship between sales and the other expenses are hidden from the user. These assumptions could, of course, be uncovered by moving the cursor to the appropriate cell and reading the formula from the status line. But this would be clumsy and time-consuming.

There is an even greater drawback in the design of this template. If the user wants to explore the consequences of different relationships, then each of the formulas must be changed. For example, suppose that the user wants to find out how profit would be affected if wages increased to 35 percent of sales.

The user enters the numbers in this column.

This column of numbers is automatically calculated by the template.

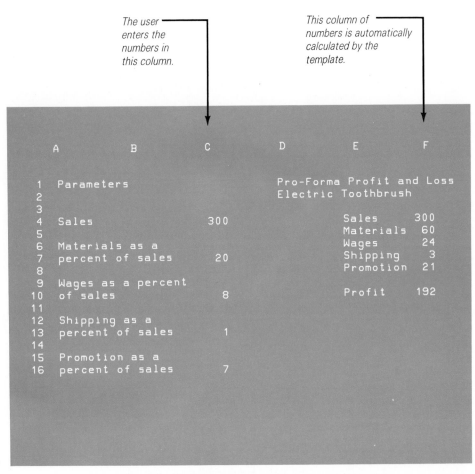

	A	B	C	D	E	F
1	Parameters				Pro-Forma Profit and Loss	
2					Electric Toothbrush	
3						
4	Sales		300		Sales	300
5					Materials	60
6	Materials as a				Wages	24
7	percent of sales		20		Shipping	3
8					Promotion	21
9	Wages as a percent					
10	of sales		8		Profit	192
11						
12	Shipping as a					
13	percent of sales		1			
14						
15	Promotion as a					
16	percent of sales		7			

Figure 7-13.
A parametized template

Both of these obstacles can be overcome by parametizing the template. A **parametized template** is one that contains a separate section for entering the assumptions and relationships on which the spreadsheet application is built. Then these assumptions are referenced in the main body of the template.

A parametized template for our problem is shown in Figure 7-13. It is best to visualize this as two separate but connected templates. The left-hand side is the part into which the user will enter the assumptions for one particular execution of the model. For instance, the user may enter a sales estimate of 300 in cell C4, a material cost of 20 percent in cell C7, a wage expense of 8 percent in cell C10, a shipping expense of 1 percent in cell C13, and, finally, an advertising and promotional expense of 7 percent in cell C16.

The estimates from the left-hand template are referenced in the appropriate cell of the main template. The entry in cell F4, for example, is +C4. This instructs the spreadsheet to use the entry from cell C4 as the value for cell F4.

The entry in cell F5 is

+C4*C7*.01

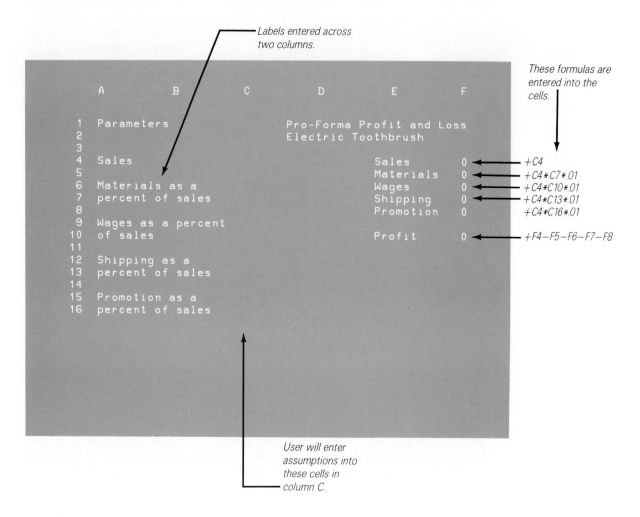

Labels entered across
two columns.

These formulas are
entered into the
cells.

	A	B	C	D	E	F
1	Parameters			Pro-Forma Profit and Loss		
2				Electric Toothbrush		
3						
4	Sales			Sales	0	← +C4
5				Materials	0	← +C4*C7*.01
6	Materials as a			Wages	0	← +C4*C10*.01
7	percent of sales			Shipping	0	← +C4*C13*.01
8				Promotion	0	+C4*C16*.01
9	Wages as a percent					
10	of sales			Profit	0	← +F4−F5−F6−F7−F8
11						
12	Shipping as a					
13	percent of sales					
14						
15	Promotion as a					
16	percent of sales					

User will enter
assumptions into
these cells in
column C.

Figure 7-14.
The relationships in a parametized
template.

First, the spreadsheet is instructed to multiply the value found in cell C4 by the value found in cell C7 and then to multiply this product by 0.01 (this converts a percent into a decimal). The other formulas for each of the remaining cells in the main template are shown in Figure 7-14.

The template is now a flexible vehicle for exploring a range of assumptions. And because the assumptions are clearly presented in the left-hand side of the template, the spreadsheet is self-documenting—that is, it is easier to understand.

SPREADSHEET APPLICATIONS

Learning what the capabilities of spreadsheets are and how to use the software on a computer is only part of the picture. Knowing how to apply them properly to a business application is also important. The following cases illustrate how several companies use spreadsheets for applications that range from operational planning to strategic planning.

SKY COOK—OPERATIONAL PLANNING

The Sky Cook Company is an airline caterer that serves 110,000 meals on one thousand flights every day. At O'Hare International Airport in Chicago, one of several airports at which it operates, Sky Cook provides meals over two hundred airline flights each day. To get the right number of meals to the right place at the right time is a difficult planning problem, and so Sky Cook uses Lotus 1-2-3, a commercial spreadsheet package, to help solve this problem. Their spreadsheet template supports the meal-planning process, keeps track of who gets what food, and even computes the costs of the meals. When meals have been delivered, the data are then used to bill the airlines.

BEAUTY CARE, INC.—STRATEGIC PLANNING

A leading manufacturer of hair coloring, hair care, and skin care products, Beauty Care, Inc., has its corporate headquarters in New York and its research and manufacturing facilities on both the East and West coasts.

Strategic planning, or planning for the long run, is often a neglected activity, even by Fortune 500 companies. Some undertake this process only yearly and others even less frequently. Beauty Care, however, prepares a long-range plan every six months and reviews the plan every month.

Using spreadsheet software, different scenarios and projections are entered into its template, and the results of these scenarios are carefully studied. Many "what if" scenarios are presented, which allows the planning staff to explore responses to changing market conditions.

When asked for the major benefit of this system, a user explained that one-shot plans are now a thing of the past. With monthly planning sessions, the company has discovered that plans are no longer locked in for long periods of time. When new data become available, new scenarios can be tested and, if necessary, strategies revised.

WESTERN BANK AND TRUST—OPERATIONAL CONTROL

The commercial loan departments at all branches of the Western Bank and Trust Company use spreadsheets to screen loan applicants. The lending group that specializes in oil and gas loans relies heavily on this software.

Because 80 percent of all gas and oil wells drilled do not pay off, those who review the oil and gas loan applications must analyze them thoroughly before approving them. Using spreadsheet software, the lending group enters many factors, such as the estimated productivity of a well over its remaining life, the expected price of oil or gas, the expenses the investor is likely to incur, and the taxes that must be paid. The spreadsheet then determines the investor's cash flow.

After cash flow has been estimated, the data are used to determine the investor's ability to repay the loan. For example, if the investor has applied for a $2-million loan to be paid back over ten years at 10 percent interest and wants to use 80 percent of his or her cash flow to repay the loan, the spreadsheet will be used to see whether indeed he or she can meet this repayment schedule.

But one of the most useful features of this cash flow analysis allows the loan officer to ask "what if" questions. What if the productivity of the well falls faster than expected? What if oil prices drop? What if the investor's operating expenses rise? Through sensitivity analysis, the impact of such contingencies on the investor's ability to repay the loan can be determined, and the lending institution can better understand its risk in approving the loan.

As mentioned earlier in the chapter, one characteristic of a spreadsheet is that it provides a format into which data from central computers can be downloaded. The next cases illustrate how spreadsheets are used in this way.

PACIFIC LUMBER—MANAGEMENT CONTROL

Pacific Lumber is one of the world's largest forest products companies. With sales of more than $4 billion, it employs over forty thousand people at two hundred production plants and distribution centers. In addition, it manages over four million acres of timber and large reserves of oil, gas, coal, and gypsum.

Every month general ledger data are collected from each Pacific Lumber division and uploaded into its centralized mainframe. Headquarters then downloads these data into a spreadsheet format and uses it to analyze, manage, and better control the organization. When one of the users was asked about the benefits of downloading the data into her spreadsheet, she replied that through the downloading process, she could have access to the information whenever she wanted and in the format she wanted, rather than waiting for the request to fit into central data processing's schedule.

VINE PICTURES—MANAGEMENT CONTROL

At Vine Pictures, company accountants use spreadsheets to conduct a monthly audit of all Vine film projects. First, they enter the list of all movies currently in progress into the corporate mainframe. Next, they download the gross profit and distribution data for these films into their spreadsheet. Finally, they make calculations on this spreadsheet and have the results printed in the form of a corporate report.

FEDERAL HOME LOAN BANK BOARD—
MANAGEMENT CONTROL

The federal agency that regulates and insures the savings and loan industry is called the Federal Home Loan Bank Board. Its function is similar to that of the Federal Reserve Board, which regulates all commercial banks.

The Federal Home Loan Bank Board monitors the financial strength of its member institutions, helps those in trouble, and insures depositors through an agency called FSLIC. In the event of a bank failure, FSLIC reimburses each depositor for up to $100,000 of his or her deposits.

But before a savings and loan institution gets into trouble, the Office of Examination and Supervision, a division of the Federal Home Loan Bank Board, tries to uncover potential weaknesses, by means of periodic audits. In this examination, the financial statement, which every savings and loan member is required to file and which is stored on the mainframe, is downloaded into a microcomputer spreadsheet. But not every field of the data is downloaded. The mainframe record is just too large, and not all of the data are necessary for an effective audit. Consequently, only certain fields and summaries are downloaded to the micro. Once the data are available, the field manager can compare and analyze the numbers in carrying out the examination.

SPREADSHEET ERRORS

Not all spreadsheet applications are as successful as the ones just described. In fact, there are a growing number of reports of how erroneous spreadsheet data have led to unfortunate decisions. Budgets have been approved, schedules finalized, and alternative projects chosen, all using bad data.

But spreadsheets can be deceptively simple to build and use. And those who are unfamiliar with their mechanics can easily get into trouble. Perhaps the user is unfamiliar with the assumptions made when the template was built. Or, unknown to the user, formulas, hidden from direct view, could have been entered incorrectly. Sometimes the user enters data incorrectly. And users may access centrally stored data that are inappropriate for use in a particular template.

Could it be that the widespread use and acceptance of spreadsheet technology has added a false sense of security to the output from these models? Certainly spreadsheet output—such as a table or graph—looks very professional. But a responsible user must go beyond the aesthetics and carefully check the assumptions of the spreadsheet template, the data, and the procedures which were used to obtain calculated entries.

? Q U E S T I O N S ?

1. What are some benefits of spreadsheets?
2. What advantage does a spreadsheet have over using pencil and paper to perform the same analysis?

3. What is the difference between numbers and calculated entries?

4. Explain how spreadsheets are used for recalculations. How does this benefit management decision making?

5. How does a spreadsheet benefit the process of downloading data into a microcomputer?

6. One of the advantages of a spreadsheet is that it can be used to store and retrieve data. Design a spreadsheet model that can be used to store the following data for a class of seven students:
   Name
   Address
   Telephone number
   Student ID
   Grade point average
   Adviser
   Credits earned in major
   Status (freshman, sophomore, junior, or senior)

7. Design a spreadsheet into which the following data for year 1 can be entered:

Sales	200
Cost of goods sold	50
Sales expenses	20
Adminstrative expenses	10
Other expenses	40

   Design the spreadsheet so that it computes profit (sales less cost of goods sold and less all expenses).
   Now design a new template. This time, however, enter the following relationships as formulas:
   Cost of goods sold is 25 percent of sales.
   Sales expenses are 10 percent of sales.
   Administrative expenses are 5 percent of sales.
   Other expenses are 20 percent of sales.
   Also design the template to compute profit.

8. Return to Question 7. Suppose that sales for Years 2 through 5 are expected to grow at a rate of 30 percent per year. Cost of goods sold will remain at 25 percent of sales; sales expenses will remain at 10 percent of sales; administrative expenses will remain at 5 percent of sales; and other expenses will remain at 20 percent of sales. Design a parametized spreadsheet.

9. Return to Question 8 and enter the model into a spreadsheet software package. Print the completed spreadsheet.

10. Return to Question 9 and make the following changes: Sales in the first year will be $300 and will grow at the rate of 10 percent per year (did you parametize "growth rate"? If not, return to your model and make the appropriate changes.). Cost of goods sold will increase to 30 percent of sales; sales expenses will decrease to 3 percent of sales; and other expenses will decrease to 12 percent of sales. Recalculate and print the results.

S U M M A R Y

- An **electronic spreadsheet**, or **spreadsheet** for short, is a table with rows and columns into which data are entered. Spreadsheet software makes it possible to enter, manipulate, and store data and to present results.

- Whenever a problem or situation can be organized into rows and columns, a spreadsheet can be used.

- The intersection of a row and column in a spreadsheet is known as a **cell**.

- Three different kinds of data are present in a spreadsheet: **labels, numbers,** and **calculated entries.**

- Labels and numbers are entered by the user, and the spreadsheet software computes calculated entries using a **formula.**

- An important feature of spreadsheets is that whenever new numbers are entered, the software can recalculate the results.

- Spreadsheet data can be stored and retrieved as necessary and presented in tabular or graphical form.

- Spreadsheets can be used as a standard format into which data from central computer facilities can be downloaded.

- A **template** is a worksheet in which all of a spreadsheet's labels and formulas, but none of the data, have been entered for a particular application.

- Data are entered into a spreadsheet from the keyboard into a location identified by the cursor and known as the **active cell.**

- The display screen is like a **window** on the full spreadsheet, which can be much larger than the screen. **Scrolling** is used to bring other segments of a spreadsheet into view.

- Status, entry, and prompt lines appear at the top or bottom of the screen to provide information needed during the creation and use of a template.

- Standard conventions govern the entry of labels, numbers, and formulas and the use of functions.

- Both templates and spreadsheets can be saved and reused.

- Printing a full spreadsheet may require printing different segments of it separately and then taping them together.

- Spreadsheet output is often summarized into a line or bar graph or a pie chart.

- Spreadsheet software is often combined with word processors, graphics packages, and data management software in an integrated package.

- To accommodate situations in which the data are less certain, a generalized spreadsheet model can be constructed to examine a range of outcomes.

- A **parametized template** is one that contains a separate section for entering the assumptions and relationships on which the spreadsheet application is built.

- Spreadsheets are used successfully in many applications, but reasonable precautions must be observed.

KEY • TERMS

The following list shows the key terms in the order in which they appear in the chapter.

Electronic spreadsheet (or spreadsheet) (p. 180)
Cell (p. 182)
Label (p. 183)
Number (p. 183)
Calculated entry (p. 183)

Formula (p. 183)
Template (p. 186)
Active cell (p. 187)
Window (p. 188)
Scrolling (p. 188)
Parametized template (p. 197)

FOR DISCUSSION

1. Why do business professionals find it necessary to ask "what if" questions?
2. A company's mainframe computer maintains certain financial data. Why might it be helpful to download the data into a spreadsheet?
3. Do you think that spreadsheets help a decision maker reach a better decision?
4. The Fox Company has developed a spreadsheet to collect and summarize product sales data. The marketing department, after using the system for four months, has found it too costly to maintain. It complained that the secretaries had to call distributors throughout the country and then enter over twenty data items from each call. What do you think the problem was? Should Fox abandon its spreadsheet system?

HANDS-ON PROJECTS

1. Go to the library and find an article describing a spreadsheet application. Why was a spreadsheet used? What do you think the designer hoped to accomplish that could not be done without a spreadsheet? If the article had enough information, describe the layout of the spreadsheet. How were the data obtained? Was the spreadsheet used just once or regularly?
Suggestions: PC Week, Business Computer Systems.

2. Apply a spreadsheet to an exercise in another class you are taking (accounting, finance, marketing, or another area). What features of the spreadsheet software were most helpful? Do you think using the spreadsheet improved your work?

3. Find advertisements for at least two different spreadsheet packages. Which features are these companies promoting?
Suggestions: Business Computer Systems, PC, Personal Computing.

4. Design a spreadsheet template to monitor the performance of an investor's stock portfolio. Enter the daily progress of each stock in the parametized section. The main body of the spreadsheet should include the following data for each stock:

- Price paid per share

- Number of shares

- Total cost (price paid times number of shares)

- Date purchased

- Dividend amount

- Current price

- Total investment in security (current price times number of shares)

At the bottom of the template, compute the investor's total investment for all securities.

C A S E · S T U D Y

WATER WORLD, INC.

Seacrest Beach is located on the New Jersey coast. At the center of the beach is an early-1900s wooden structure, the Seacrest Beach Casino, known in earlier times for showcasing the big bands of the 1930s and 1940s. Artists who played at the casino included Artie Shaw, Benny Goodman, Lionel Hampton, Glenn Miller, and Guy Lombardo.

Today the structure remains much as it was nearly ninety years ago. The ballroom section of the casino, on the second story, is now home for the casino nightclub. The lower floor contains about thirty small resort shops and a dozen amusement games. Parking for six hundred cars, at a cost of $5 per day, is available in the 2-acre casino lot in back of the main building. Parking for two hundred more cars, at the same price, is available in a smaller lot across the street.

The entire property, including the smaller parking lot, is located on land owned by the city of Seacrest. For fifteen years it has been leased by Fred Dennison who also operates and manages the property. He rents most of the stores, including the Casino Nightclub, to independent businesspeople. Mr. Dennison himself operates only the parking lots and a 2000-square-foot souvenir shop.

Dennison has felt for some time that the small lot across the street is too valuable to be used for parking. So, for the last few years, he has visited amusement centers, theme parks, and trade shows in search of an attraction for this space.

After screening several alternatives—ranging from small rollercoasters to children's rides—Dennison has decided on a water slide. The slide would be a massive structure, with fiberglass chutes built on a concrete base. At 80 feet high, it would be the tallest attraction on the beach.

The manufacturer of the slide has agreed to build the structure, including dressing-room facilities, on the site and lease the facility to Dennison for $31,800 per summer season (the total sum to be paid in equal installments of $10,600 in June, July, and August). The lease agreement would extend over a period of five years. At the end of the five-year period, the manufacturer would sell the slide to Dennison for $1.00.

Dennison would incur several expenses while the slide was in operation. The state would require four lifeguards on duty at all times, two at the top of the slide and two at the swimming pools where the chutes exited at the bottom. In addition, two people would be required to sell and collect tickets, and two more to patrol the women's and men's dressing areas. The wages for these eight people in the first year of the project would average about $5000 during June and $15,000 during July and August.

To advertise the facility, Dennison plans to purchase 30-second spots on several local radio stations and to run advertisements in six newspapers. For this exposure, he expects to spend $650 in June, $2500 in July, and $2000 in August.

The New Jersey Board of Health requires that each evening the entire slide be cleaned with a disinfectant. This and other maintenance would run approximately $1050 during June and $1800 per month during July and August.

The water bill during June would be about $500. For July and August it would increase to about $800 per month. Insurance—covering both the property and $1 million in personal liability—would cost $7550 per season. Telephone expenses would run about $200 in June and $400 per month in July and August; electricity, $450 in June and $950 per month in July and August; and miscellaneous supplies, $390 in June, $1500 in July, and $1200 in August.

For the first year, June receipts are expected to be $13,000; July receipts, $50,000; and August receipts, $40,000.

Questions

1. What alternatives is Dennison considering?
2. What criteria will he use to make his decision?
3. Construct an estimated profit-and-loss template (also called a *pro-forma* P&L template). Include a column for each of the months during the first season. You should have a row for sales receipts, a separate row for each expense category, and a row for the lease expense. (In this exercise, we will ignore taxes.) Profit should be calculated in the last row of the table. If a printer is available, print your results.
4. Parametize the template in the following way: Include a spreadsheet segment (in the upper left-hand corner) into which the user will later enter the sales figures for June, July, and August.

   Also parametize the following relationships: advertising expenditures as a percentage of sales and miscellaneous expenses as a percentage of sales. The other expenses—considered fixed expenses—are not expected to vary with either higher or lower sales revenues; consequently, it will not be necessary to parametize them. If a printer is available, print your results.
5. The estimates of sales receipts assume that the beach has an average summer. If the weather is cold, then sales may fall to $7000 in June, $30,000 in July, and $25,000 in August. An especially good summer could generate $20,000, $65,000, and $50,000, respectively. Bad summers occur in about three of ten years, and especially good summers occur in about two of ten years.

   Using your parametized spreadsheet, explore the consequences of the preceding scenarios. In each of these spreadsheets assume that advertising expenditures are 5 percent of sales and miscellaneous expenses are 3 percent of sales. What would you recommend? Should Dennison undertake the project?
6. Do you think that you have identified on your spreadsheet all of the risks in this alternative? If not, describe those that remain. Could you include them on the spreadsheet, or should they be considered after the results of the spreadsheet are available? Do you think these factors would significantly influence your decision?
7. Enter a row in the spreadsheet that will compute the year-to-date figures for each of the three months.

8. *Optional:* Expand your spreadsheet to include three-month periods for the next four years of the project. In the parametized segment of your spreadsheet, establish an entry for a rate of sales growth from one year to the next. Incorporate this growth rate into the body of your table. After you have entered this growth rate, the spreadsheet should automatically compute the revenue figures for the three-month summer periods over the remaining four-year life of the project. In addition, your new spreadsheet should also automatically determine the expense entries for each category, using the preceding guidelines for the variable costs and simply repeating the fixed costs for categories such as wages and maintenance. Print the results for a growth rate of five percent.

■ ■

8
DATA
STORAGE AND
FILE PROCESSING

O U T L I N E

O B J E C T I V E S

After studying this chapter you should understand the following:

■ *How magnetic disk and magnetic tape storage are used in a computer information system.*

■ *The principles of optical disk technology.*

■ *The main characteristics of the different types of file organization.*

■ *Which types of storage media and file organization are appropriate for particular types of applications.*

The computer's ability to store and retrieve data is at the core of almost every business application (Figure 8-1). Whether in inventory management, word processing, or posing "what if" questions to solve a management problem, the computer must be able to store and retrieve data in order to do the job. And *how* data are stored and retrieved can have a marked impact on how an application works—or how the data can be used. For example, if data are stored sequentially on magnetic tape, they can be used in many batch-processing applications, but they cannot be used in an on-line application, nor would it be practical to use them in a spreadsheet application.

Because data storage and retrieval are closely related to what can be done with the data, it is important for business professionals to know how data are stored and retrieved. This chapter will focus on the more technical aspects of these issues, including the media on which data are stored, the way that files can be organized to store data, and the way that files can be processed to retrieve data. Because the objective of this text is to present the material from a user's perspective, the technical details will be kept to a minimum as much as posssible.

Chapters 9 and 10 will build on the technical foundation developed in this chapter. They will introduce software that simplifies data storage and file processing. Chapter 9 will explore the use of file managers, a simple but handy type of software appropriate for small systems that business professionals may build themselves. Chapter 10 will describe database-management systems, more complex software that many business professionals find useful in the planning and control process.

First let us examine the different ways that computer systems store data.

Figure 8-1.
The storage and retrieval of data lie at the heart of computer information systems. This consumer service representative, employed by a public utility, can instantly access and store customer data.

Figure 8-2.
Secondary storage devices like these disk drives are used for the long-term storage of data and programs.

STORAGE TECHNOLOGY

Chapter 2 described a computer as containing a central processing unit and input, output, and secondary storage devices. The CPU temporarily stores data and programs in its main memory while the data are being processed. Because of the high cost of main memory as well as its volatility (if the power is lost, so are the data), permanent storage occurs in **secondary** (or **auxiliary**) **storage** (Figure 8-2).

There are various types of secondary storage technology, including magnetic tape, magnetic disk, and optical disk. Each has its advantages and disadvantages, which we will discuss in the next sections.

MAGNETIC TAPE TECHNOLOGY

The way that **magnetic tape** (or **tape** for short) is used to record, store, and play music in a home stereo system is similar to the way that it is used in a computer system. Both systems use tape made from flexible mylar plastic coated with a metal oxide capable of recording data through a magnetic process. Storage and access occur when the tape is passed over a magnetic head.

BINARY STORAGE ON TAPE

Figure 8-3 shows a cross-section of magnetic tape. Bits are represented by magnetic spots of metal oxide aligned in rows called **tracks.** If a spot is magnetized in one direction, it will represent a zero, and if it is magnetized in the other, it will represent a one. In Figure 8-3, eight bits are aligned in each vertical column and represent one byte of information. Records are separated by spaces known as **interrecord gaps,** which indicate where one record stops and the next begins (Figure 8-4). (For a refresher on terms such as *record* and *bit,* return to the "Data and Data Entry" section of Chapter 2.)

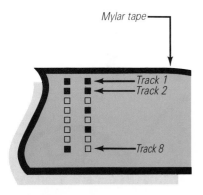

Figure 8-3.
Storage on magnetic tape.

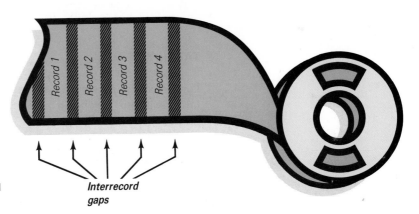

Figure 8-4.
Records stored on tape are separated by an interrecord gap.

ACCESSING DATA ON TAPE

Data stored on tape can be accessed only sequentially. So, if records are stored alphabetically by last name, they can be accessed only in this order. That is, to retrieve a person's name, every record in the file must be read and the name field examined until the correct name is reached. Later in the chapter we will examine the consequences of this approach.

BLOCKING

The computer reads and processes the data between one gap and the next and then between that gap and the one following, and so on, until it has processed the whole file. So, if a single record is written between gaps, then only one record will be processed at a time. Reading a single record, however, can be inefficient, because the tape must start and stop between each gap. In addition, the gaps themselves waste space on the tape. But these problems can be overcome by **blocking** together several records, with an interblock gap separating the blocks. Then the computer can read and process at one time a block containing several records, which is faster than working with individual records. The number of records blocked is called the **blocking factor.** Figure 8-5 shows a blocking factor of four.

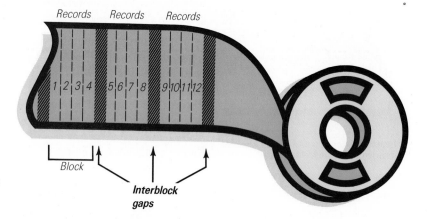

Figure 8-5.
Several records can be blocked together to speed data entry and to use secondary storage space more efficiently.

TAPE SYSTEMS

Until recently, most tape systems used reel-to-reel tapes. These tapes measure about 12 inches in diameter and can store about 180 megabytes (180 million bytes) of data. When writing to or reading from the tape, it is mounted on a reel-to-reel tape drive.

Many applications now use a cartridge that measures 4 inches square and stores 200 megabytes. The cartridge is inserted into a cartridge reader to read from or write to the tape.

Figure 8-6.
Storing data on disk.

MAGNETIC DISK TECHNOLOGY

Magnetic disks (or **disks** for short) were introduced in 1956 and in the 1960s came to dominate the data storage field. Since their introduction, the performance of disks has improved by a factor of 11 each decade!

BINARY STORAGE ON DISK

The recording surface of a disk is divided into concentric rings, also called **tracks** (Figure 8-6). Like magnetic tape, the disk is coated with a metallic oxide that responds to the magnetic recording process and stores data until they are erased. Each letter, number, or special character is stored as a set of eight magnetized spots along a track. The data are also blocked, as with tape, for more efficient entry and processing in the computer.

ACCESSING DATA ON DISK

The reason that magnetic disks dominate the storage market is that data stored on these devices can be retrieved by proceeding directly to the location where they are stored. In contrast, data stored on tape can be accessed only sequentially, that is, in the same order as the data were recorded. If a user needs a data item stored at the end of a sequential tape file, it may take several minutes to access it. But if the same item is stored on disk, access will take a fraction of a second. Later in the chapter we will explore the differences between sequential and direct access. First let us look at how these direct-access systems work.

ACCESS TIMES

To access data on a disk, three steps are required:

■   Moving the read/write head to the appropriate track.

■   Reading the record.

■   Transferring the data to the central processing unit.

The time it takes to complete all of these steps is measured in milliseconds (thousandths of a second), with the movement of the read/write head the slowest step in this process. In the following paragraphs we will explore each of these steps in more detail.

Moving the Read/Write Head   In the first step, the read/write head—which generally floats a few thousandths of an inch, at most, above the surface of the disk—must move to the appropriate track. The time it takes to make this move is called the *head movement delay.*

Reading the Record   In the second step, the read/write mechanism must read the records stored on this track until the record that has been requested rotates to a position under the read/write head. The length of time this takes is called the *rotational delay*.

Transferring Data   In the third step, the data are read from the disk and transferred to main memory. The length of time this step takes is called data the *data transfer delay*.

The average length of time for all three steps is between 16 and 300 milliseconds. At this speed, data can be retrieved in about 1/50 to 1/3 of a second. By contrast, early direct-access systems had access times of one second! A second may seem fast, but when a disk must be accessed thousands of times in a minute, the seconds add up quickly.

DISK SYSTEMS

Disk devices that store data and programs include floppy disk systems and hard disk systems. Each has different characteristics, capacity, and cost.

Figure 8-7.
A floppy disk is a popular and inexpensive medium for storing data on a microcomputer.

Floppy Disk Systems   Microcomputers generally include one or more disk drives into which **floppy disks** (also known as **diskettes** or **flexible disks**) can be inserted (Figure 8-7). These disks are constructed of a flexible mylar plastic. Data access time is between 175 and 300 milliseconds.

The storage capacity of a disk depends on two factors. The first is the number of tracks on the disk, measured in tracks per inch, and the second is the linear density, or closeness, of the magnetic particles, measured in bits per inch. Most microcomputer systems accept either a 3½-inch or a 5¼-inch diskette. The 5¼-inch diskette has forty tracks and stores around 300 kilobytes (300,000 bytes) to 1 megabyte (1 million bytes) of data. A 3½-inch diskette can store between 720K and 1½ MB of data.

One advantage of floppy disks is that they can be removed from the disk drive and stored for future use. Another advantage is that a disk can be used with other compatible computers. Consequently, users can share programs and data. And they are inexpensive!

A major disadvantage of floppy disks is that their capacity and access time compare poorly with those of hard disks.

Figure 8-8.
Winchester technology provides virtually trouble-free mass storage. The hard disk is permanently enclosed to prevent environmental contamination such as dust.

Hard Disk Systems   When additional storage and faster access are needed, **hard disks** (or **rigid disks**) are used. The base of a hard disk is an aluminum platter covered with a magnetic oxide or thin-film metallic medium.

Because the surface of the disk is hard and very flat, the read/write head can be positioned closer to the surface. This permits a higher linear density of bits and more tracks per inch. In addition, these disks rotate much faster than do floppy disks. As a result, more data can be stored on a hard disk, and they can be retrieved faster. A 5¼-inch hard disk system can store up to 30 megabytes, about ten to thirty times the capacity of a floppy disk. The average access time for these systems is about 30 milliseconds, with most systems in the range of 16 to 100 milliseconds.

Most hard disk drives for microcomputers as well as mainframes are based on Winchester technology. A **Winchester disk,** first developed in the early 1970s by IBM, is a nonremovable hard disk that is completely and permanently sealed to prevent environmental contamination, which can ruin disks. The performance record for these drives is quite impressive, many boasting about 15,000 hours between failures (Figure 8-8).

In mini and mainframe systems, whose demand for data storage is even greater, **disk packs** are frequently used (Figure 8-9). Disk packs combine several hard disks in one unit; all the disks rotate together at the same speed, and each has its own read/write head. Some systems use removable disk packs, and others use permanently installed disks. The capacity of some large units is from 2 to 5 gigabytes (a gigabyte is equal to 1 billion bytes). Some hard disk systems are designed with fixed read/write heads, a technology that uses one head for every track on each disk. As a result, access mechanism delay is eliminated. The benefit of this technology is clear, but the cost can be very high.

Figure 8-9.
Disk packs contain several hard disks and offer storage capacities of several gigabytes.

- -

E N D · U S E R   H I N T S

STORING PHOTOGRAPHS

Would you like to be able to store photographs with your computer? The answer from many users is yes. Real estate offices that store data on available properties, law enforcement agencies that store criminal records, companies that maintain employee records, and production facilities that store manufacturing and assembly drawings, are just a few of the examples of organizations that would find it useful to add a picture field to a record.

Only recently has the special hardware and software been created that makes it possible for users to store and access high-quality photographic images. With this hardware and software, the user can retrieve a record using its key and see the data from the record, including a photographic image,

displayed on the screen. With the right equipment, the image on the screen will be as sharp as that on a high-quality TV set, and in color.

In addition to a computer (usually a microcomputer), the following equipment is needed:

- A video source, such as a video camera, VCR, or videodisk.

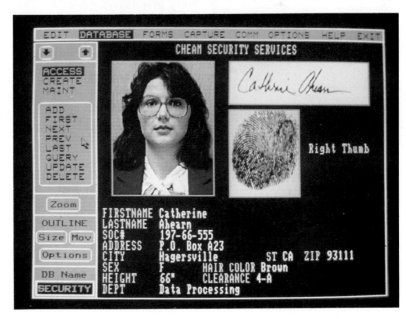

- A digitizer (also called a video board), which is a hardware device that converts a picture to digital form so that it can be stored just like other data.

- A high-quality graphics monitor so that the image

produced will be clear and sharp.

- Data management software.

With this equipment in place, a video camera can be focused on the subject and a picture can be "grabbed" and entered into the system. Or pictures can be taken

from tape as it is played through a VCR.

Why doesn't everyone store photos on their micro? These systems can cost between $10,000 and $20,000, and the digitized photographs require large quantities of disk storage space. Cost reduction and greater ease of use can be expected in the future.

● ●

WHERE IS THE TECHNOLOGY HEADED?

Will this disk technology continue to improve, as it has in the past? And because disks are basically a mechanical technology, will they become obsolete?

This next decade is expected to see further improvements in magnetic storage technology, with future products capable of storing even more data and with access times continuing to fall. Meanwhile, the emerging technology of optical storage may reach or exceed these same levels of capacity and speed. Although few anticipate the replacement of magnetic disks by optical disks in the next few years, it seems likely that optical storage will represent an appreciable share of the market by the year 2000. Let us take a moment to study these disks.

OPTICAL DISK TECHNOLOGY

In the late 1960s, work began on the development of an **optical disk** that could store large quantities of data. Now, some twenty years later, products are emerging that offer high storage capacity, reasonably fast access, and low cost.

There are three types of optical recording media: read-only, write once, and reversible.

READ-ONLY

Read-only optical disks, also referred to as CD-ROM (an acronym for Compact Disk-Read Only Memory), use the same technology as do the CD audio disks sold in the consumer audio marketplace. These disks are pressed from a master disk, in much the same manner as a phonograph record is pressed. And like a phonograph record, the data on a disk can only be read and cannot be changed in any way (Figure 8-10).

When the disks are pressed, the data are represented by a pattern of pits on the disk's surface. To read the disk, the user places the disk in

Figure 8-10.
This "read-only" optical disk can be used to read, but not to update, data.

an optical disk reader, and a laser system reads the intensity of light reflected from the disk's surface and sends these data, as a digital signal, to the computer.

Whereas an audio CD disk can hold up to 60 minutes of high-quality recorded sound on one side, a 5¼-inch CD-ROM used in a computer system can hold up to about 550 megabytes of data. Because this represents over five hundred times the capacity of a floppy disk, it is not surprising to find that this storage medium is especially useful when a large quantity of permanent data must be stored for later retrieval.

In business, this technology is suitable for storing large public databases, such as economic data. And it is also suitable for storing industrial catalogs, a company's policy manual, personnel directories, and procedure manuals. In all of these applications, the optical disk is pressed centrally and distributed to users periodically whenever the data need to be updated.

WRITE ONCE

Write once optical disk technology, also referred to as **WORM** (an acronym for Write Once Read Many times), allows the user to write data and programs into an optical disk a single time. After the data have been entered, they cannot be changed or rewritten. This technology is suitable for storing large volumes of data that need not be or must not be updated. For example, the Library of Congress uses one of these systems to maintain its inventory of 7.5 million card catalog records. The disk it uses is 14 inches in diameter with a capacity of 4.5 gigabytes.

■ ■

WHEN THE MAXWELL INSURANCE COMPANY UPDATED ITS DATA PROCESSING FACILITIES TO AN ON-LINE TRANSACTION-PROCESSING SYSTEM, the director of information systems, Bruce Dubins, had a difficult time convincing management that a WORM optical drive system should be used to store the accounting data. If approved, it would be the company's first use of optical storage technology.

Dubins argued that most accounting transactions are entered only once and are not changed. He also went on to explain that ensuring an accurate and complete record of each transaction (called an audit trail) is an important function of an accounting system. It is through these records that auditors trace the source of each accounting transaction.

"With a WORM system we will have two advantages," he explained to the vice-president of finance. "First, the disk will have a large capacity, and when it is full, we can simply remove it from the optical disk drive, store it as a permanent record, and enter a new disk. But if we use Winchester drives, we will have to write the data to tape when the disk is full. And then we will have to store these tapes in our underground vault, which is already running out of space."

"Second, and most important," he continued, "in WORM technology, the data can't be erased. Consequently, no one can make unauthorized or fraudulent changes once the original transaction is recorded. So the data in a WORM system will make a very reliable audit trail, much better than the erasable audit trail we would have on magnetic disk."

■ ■

REVERSIBLE

Reversible optical disks have optical qualities that can be switched endlessly, and they can therefore be used like a magnetic disk to record, erase, and rerecord over and over again. This technology remains quite new, and it still has some technical problems.

A reversible optical disk is coated with a layer of metallic alloy, over which another protective layer is applied. Like a magnetic disk, an optical disk rotates. The writing process, however, is quite different from that of a magnetic disk. In one approach, a thermomagnetic process is used (Figure 8-11). A laser beam is directed at one spot on the surface, and the heat from this source temporarily changes the properties of the alloy. Then a magnetic field is generated to change the direction of the alloy at that spot. When the magnetic field is applied in one direction, the spot points down and represents a zero, and when it is applied in the other direction, it points up and represents a one.

To read these disks, a laser beam is focused on the data. As the light passes through the disk (or, in some systems, is reflected from the surface of the disk), the laser beam is rotated slightly in one direction to represent a zero or is rotated in the other direction to represent a one. A photodetector is used to identify the direction of the rotation and to send these data in the form of digital information to the computer.

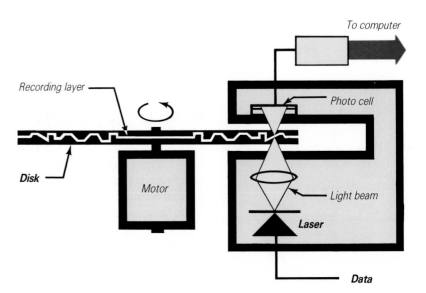

Figure 8-11.
The optical recording process.

Although the capacity of an erasable optical disk is impressive—550 megabytes on a 5¼-inch disk—the access time for currently available systems is slower than that for conventional magnetic disks. For example, the average access time for a microcomputer hard disk is about 50 milliseconds, but the access time for an optical disk is about 500 milliseconds.

?   Q U E S T I O N S   ?

1. Explain how data are stored on tape.
2. What is blocking? Why is it used?
3. Describe the steps to write data to, or to read data from, a disk.
4. What determines the storage capacity of a disk?
5. How does a floppy disk differ from a hard disk? How much data can be stored on each?
6. What are the advantages of removable versus nonremovable storage media?

7. What is a Winchester disk?
8. Will magnetic disks become obsolete in the near future?
9. Explain the difference between a read-only and a write once optical disk.
10. Does a write once optical disk have any advantages over a reversible magnetic disk?
11. How does a reversible optical disk work?
12. Compare the capacity of an optical disk with that of a magnetic disk.

FILE ORGANIZATION

When data are stored on secondary storage devices, the method of file organization chosen will determine how the data can be accessed. In turn, this will affect the types of applications that can use the data, as well as the time and cost necessary to do so. The two forms of file organization are sequential and direct, which we will examine next.

SEQUENTIAL FILE ORGANIZATION

With **sequential file organization,** records are stored in some predetermined sequence, one after the other. Their sequence, or order, is usually determined by one field, referred to as the primary key. A **primary key** is a field whose contents are unique to one record and can therefore be used to identify that record. Primary keys usually include

■ Person's name

■ Social security number

■ Part number

■ Account number

A company's payroll records, for example, might be stored sequentially by social security number. This file would start with the record that has the lowest number, and the remaining records would be arranged by ascending social security numbers. In the past, most sequential files were stored on tape, but today, they are commonly stored on disk.

PROCEDURES FOR SEQUENTIAL FILE PROCESSING

When records are stored on tape, the file *must* be processed sequentially. When a sequential file is stored on disk, however, it may not necessarily be processed in this way all of the time (later in the chapter we will explain how a sequential file can be processed directly using ISAM).

When using **sequential access** to reach a particular record, all of the records preceding it must first be processed. What this means is that if a record is stored toward the end of a sequential file, and if this record must be retrieved, then each of the records preceding it must be processed first. This can be slow. But if the entire file—or an appreciable portion of the file—must be processed at once, in sequential order, then sequential organization may be very efficient. Processing data using sequential access is referred to as **sequential file processing.**

Many payroll files are sequentially organized and processed. When a weekly payroll is processed, the first employee record in the file is accessed and the pay computed for that person; then the next record is accessed, and so on, until all of the records in the file have been processed. Once finished, the file will probably not be accessed for another week, at which time it will be processed once again in the same way.

If a sequential form of file organization is chosen, the process by which the file is maintained or updated is complex. The reason is that additional records cannot simply be inserted in the file, nor can old ones simply be removed. The same limitations apply to a stereo cassette: It is simply not possible to insert a song in the middle of a previously recorded tape.

By following the process used by the publisher of a well-established travel magazine, we can find out how a sequential file can be maintained and updated.

■■■■■■■■■■■■■■■■■■■■■■■■■■■■■■■■■■■■

AT THE END OF EVERY MONTH, when a new issue comes off the press, the subscriber file for the *Island Traveler* is processed sequentially, and mailing labels are printed. The labels are then affixed to the magazines, and they are mailed.

The subscriber file, referred to as a *master file,* maintains complete, up-to-date records on all subscribers. Every month, however, new

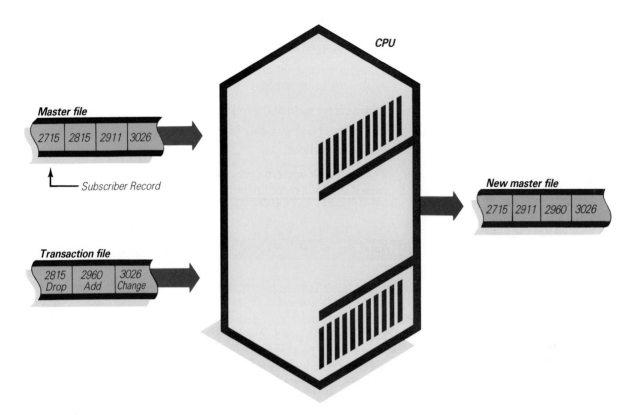

Figure 8-12.
A sequential file update. The sorted transaction file (arranged from lowest account number to highest account number) is merged with the master file to create a new master file.

subscribers must be added; the names of subscribers whose subscriptions have expired must be removed; and changes of address must be entered. These procedures are referred to as **file maintenance.**

To maintain the file, the records to be dropped, added, and changed are first collected in a temporary file called a *transaction file.* Then the transaction file is periodically processed together with the master file, and a *new master file* is created. This process is illustrated in Figure 8-12.

From this example, which is representative of the procedures that must be followed by all systems that maintain sequential files, we can conclude that additions, deletions, or changes to a sequential master file involve several steps.

ADVANTAGES AND DISADVANTAGES

There are many advantages and disadvantages of a sequential form of file organization. The advantages include the following:

■ Magnetic tape, the least expensive method of secondary storage, can be used.

- It is the most efficient form of organization when the entire file, or most of it, must be processed at once.

- Transaction and old master files act as a backup, should the new master file be damaged or destroyed.

The disadvantages include the following:

- The time it takes to access a particular record may be too long for many applications.

- The entire file must be processed and a new master file created, even if only one record requires maintenance or updating.

DIRECT FILE ORGANIZATION

In a direct file, unlike a sequential form of organization, the data may be organized in such a way that they are scattered throughout the disk in what may appear to be a random order. But it is this form of organization that supports **direct access** (also referred to as **random access**), in which records can be accessed nearly instantaneously and in any order. Once accessed, a record can be read or updated, and when this process is completed, the system is free to respond to another request. When using direct access, an application such as an on-line transaction-processing system for inventory control can be designed so that centralized data are not only instantly accessible but are always up-to-date. Processing data using direct access is referred to as **direct file processing.**

From a user's point of view, the procedures followed in direct file processing are more straightforward than are those followed in sequential file processing. Most applications do not use transaction files, and there is no reason to create a new master file when a single record is updated or when maintenance must be performed. Direct processing requires either magnetic disk or optical disk and cannot use magnetic tape.

PROCEDURES FOR DIRECT FILE PROCESSING

The sequence of steps followed in a direct-processing system to update a record is illustrated in Figure 8-13. In this application, data are entered directly into the system through a terminal that is in contact with the CPU of the central computer. The system locates the sought-after record in the master file and then updates it. As you can see, this is more straightforward than is the sequential update procedure we described earlier.

■■■■■■■■■■■■■■■■■■■■■■■■■■■■■■■■■■■■■■

PATIENTS' RECORDS AT THE GENERAL MEDICAL CENTER, a suburban hospital in the Midwest, are stored in a direct-access system. When a

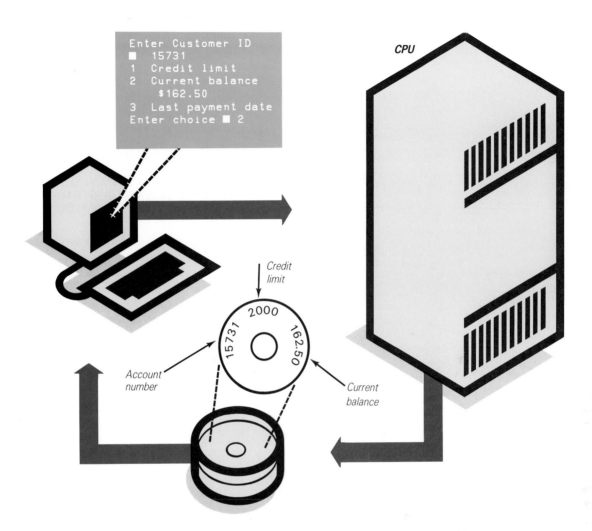

Figure 8-13.
In direct processing, records are accessed directly.

patient arrives at the hospital, a receptionist enters his or her name into a terminal. If that person has been a patient before, the billing record will immediately appear on the screen. If the patient is new, a new billing record must be created. And within seconds after the new one has been established, it will be available for access by any other user of the system.

■ ■

Direct-access systems do not search the entire file; rather, they move directly (or nearly directly) to the needed record. To be able to do this, they must have some way of determining where the record is stored. This is the principal challenge of direct processing.

Several different strategies are used to find a record, including relative addressing, hashing, and indexing. Each of these procedures will be covered in the following sections.

Relative Addressing   Perhaps the simplest method of finding a record is **relative addressing,** in which a record's primary key is associated with a specific physical storage location. The contents of the record are stored at this address. When the record must be retrieved, the user enters the key, and the disk operating system associates this number with the appropriate location on the disk. In some early banking applications, account numbers were actually changed to match the file address of a customer's record; that is, the key was made the same as the address.

When the record key cannot be made to match the physical storage location, then relative addressing loses its appeal. For example, the item numbers in a company's inventory system might have special significance and be impossible to change just to accommodate a data processing system.

Relative addressing can also create problems when many of the storage locations previously set aside are not used. Suppose that storage locations 0001 to 9999 have been set aside to accommodate an inventory system whose part numbers have been assigned to fall in this range. If most of the part numbers are in active use, then there is no problem; the system will be an efficient one. But if the company maintains only three thousand inventory items whose part numbers range from 0001 to 9999, then only 3000 records will be stored in a file that has locations set aside for almost ten thousand records. As a result, seven thousand storage locations will be left unused! Because disk storage is costly, this would certainly be considered an inefficient use of space. Wasted space is often considered one of the biggest problems with relative addressing.

Hashing   Another method for determining the physical location of a record is **hashing.** In this method a record key (such as a part number, employee number, or patient number) is processed mathematically, and another number is computed that represents the location where the record will be stored. Later, when a user needs to retrieve the record, its key is entered, and the hashing routine is used to determine where the record can be found.

The problem with this method is that different keys processed through the hashing routine can sometimes result in the same number or the same storage location, leading to "collisions." The second record must then be stored in an overflow area (Figure 8-14). This reduces the efficiency of the retrieval process, because the search for the right record becomes more complex through the use of overflow areas and thus becomes more time-consuming.

When a file has many keys that lead to the same physical storage location, then hashing may be inappropriate. And if it is occasionally necessary to process the file sequentially in ascending or descending key order, both the relative addressing and hashing methods, with their records stored randomly throughout the disk, also may be inappropriate. Nonetheless, both methods are often used when access speed is the primary consideration.

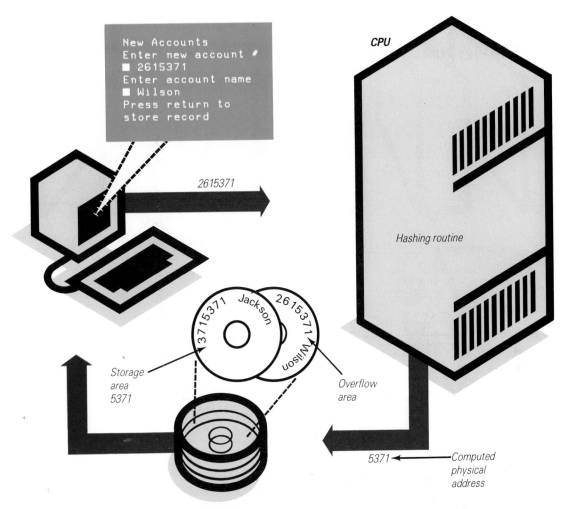

Figure 8-14.
A hashing routine determines a storage location from the record key. When there are collisions, the record is placed in an overflow area.

Indexing   Still another common procedure for locating a record in a file is for the system to store records randomly throughout the disk, but to provide one or more indexes to locate a particular record. We shall take a few moments to explain the **indexing** technique.

Primary index   A **primary index** associates a primary key with the physical location at which a record is stored. When a user requests a record, the disk operating system first loads the primary index into the computer's CPU and then searches the index sequentially for the key. When it finds the entry for the key, it then reads the address at which the record is stored. The disk system then proceeds to this address and reads the record contents.

     The use of an index is a familiar process, as library books are found in this way (Figure 8-15). First, the user finds the title of a book in the card catalog (which these days is often done using a display terminal rather than looking through drawersful of cards). The card catalog is analogous to an index. From the card, the user reads the physical loca-

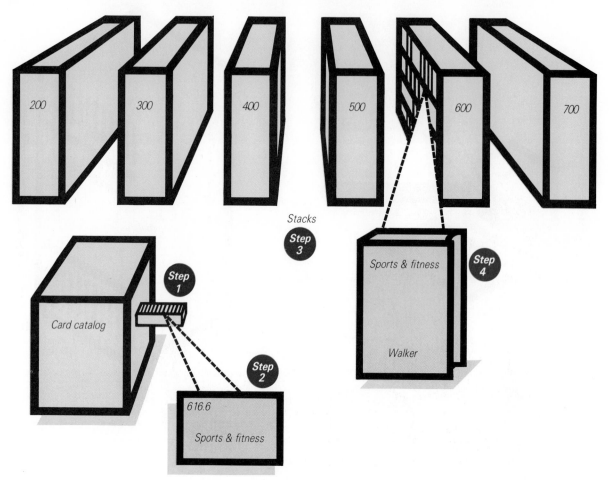

Figure 8-15.
A card catalog is an index, and the card indicates where a book is physically stored.

tion where the book is stored. Finally, the user walks to that location, identifies the book, and removes it from the shelf (or, in some libraries, fills out a slip requesting someone else to do this). Even though using an index is a two-step process, it is certainly more efficient than a sequential search—in which the user would start looking at the bottom floor of the stacks and continue down each aisle and up each floor until finding the book.

An example of a primary index is shown in Figure 8-16. The advantage of this index is that it contains only two pieces of information, the record key and the physical address of the record. The record, of course, includes many more fields of information. So, a search of a small index and then direct access to the record is much faster than is a sequential search of the data file itself. Nonetheless, this additional step in retrieving data does add to the computer's time burden.

Secondary index   In addition to a primary index, it is also possible to develop **secondary indexes,** which can be used to search a file on the basis of secondary keys. For example, an accounts receivable system might use the customer's account number as the primary key for constructing a

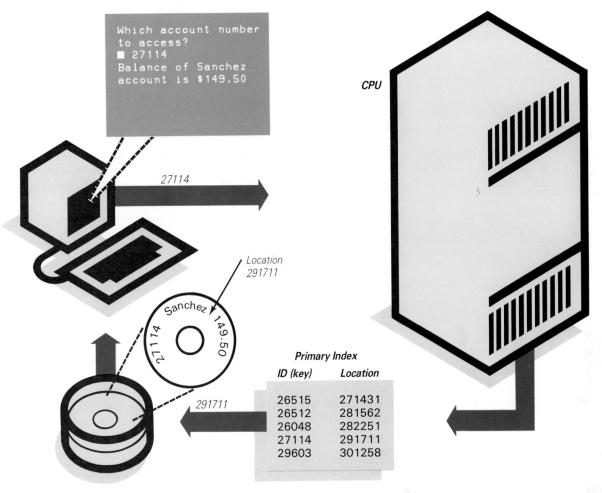

Figure 8-16.
A primary index is used to determine where a record is stored. When a record is requested, the user supplies the primary key. The key is located in the index; the track is identified; and this information is used to move the read/write head to the appropriate physical location.

primary index. But sometimes a user may need to access the data by another key. For example, it might be necessary to access a customer's file knowing only his or her name. In this case, a secondary index could be constructed with the customer name field as the secondary key. Then a user could access the system by either the customer number or the customer name.

Index sequential   Another method of direct processing combines the features of both sequential and direct access. In addition to a primary index, **index sequential access** establishes a secondary index in which all of the records are arranged by ascending or descending primary key. When the file needs to be processed sequentially, the index is followed from the first entry to the last, thereby processing the file sequentially.

But processing a file sequentially in this way is inefficient, because the index must be used to locate each record in the file. Furthermore, the read/write head may have to move continuously to different parts of the disk to read records in their desired sequence—recall that this movement accounts for most of the delay in reading a record.

To overcome this problem, still another method is used, in which the records are stored sequentially according to their primary key. And because they are stored sequentially, they also can be processed sequentially. But an index is also constructed so that a single record can be accessed directly. One variation of this approach, developed by IBM, is called ISAM (an acronym for **Index Sequential Access Method**).

■ ■

AT THE METROPOLITAN CABLEVISION COMPANY, serving subscribers in several Michigan locations, subscriber records are stored in an ISAM file. At the end of the month, the file is processed sequentially when the bills are mailed. But during the month the system also permits customer service representatives to directly access a customer's record and respond to questions that customers may ask on the telephone about their accounts.

■ ■

One problem with ISAM files is that adding new records to the file can be a problem. Because the records are organized and stored sequentially, where can new records be placed? To solve this problem, ISAM files maintain an overflow area for records added after a file is created. Pointers are used to find the records in their proper sequence when the file is processed sequentially. This does, however, slow the time necessary to process a file. When the overflow area fills up, an ISAM file can be reorganized, merging records in the overflow area with the records in the prime area to produce a new file with all the records in the proper sequence.

A more recent version of ISAM is known as VSAM (an acronym for **Virtual Storage Access Method**). The term *virtual storage* here should not be confused with the virtual storage described in Chapter 2. The only connection between the two is that the software for VSAM is so large that it may require virtual storage methods to enter the instructions.

VSAM does not use an overflow area when records must be added; instead, the new records are inserted into the appropriate place in the file, and the records that follow are shifted to new physical locations. The records that are shifted are logically connected through pointers located at the end of the inserted records. This is a much more efficient method for adding records than is the overflow method used in ISAM systems; VSAM files thus need not be reorganized as often.

ADVANTAGES AND DISADVANTAGES

The advantages of direct file organization include the following:

■ Data can be accessed directly and quickly.

■ Primary and secondary indexes can be used to search for data in many different ways.

■ Files can still be processed sequentially using a secondary index.

■ Centrally maintained data can be kept up-to-date.

The disadvantages include the following:

■ The use of an index lowers the computer system's efficiency.

■ Because all data must be stored on disks, the hardware for these systems can be expensive.

■ Because the files are updated directly and no transaction files are maintained, there may be no backup if a file is destroyed. Procedures must be established to ensure the regular creation of backup files.

CHOOSING STORAGE MEDIA AND FILE ORGANIZATION

STORAGE MEDIA

Tape As the Primary Storage Medium Several factors determine which media should be used for secondary storage. It is less expensive to store a given volume of data on tape than it is to store it on disk. And although a disk system can store a limited amount of data on-line, there is no limit to the size of a tape library.

Tape storage is frequently used to store historical data no longer needed on-line. Often this is called *archival storage*. For example, several days after a flight, airlines transfer their reservation data from disk to tape. Because the data at that point are historical and rarely used again, it makes no sense to keep them stored on more costly disk systems.

Banks are required by law to keep permanent records of deposit data. They, too, would find it prohibitively expensive to keep this information on disk. Consequently, many write such data to tape for archival storage after depositors have been sent their monthly statements.

Although tape has generally been the most economical medium for archival storage, optical disk technology is already beginning to challenge tape in some applications.

Tape As Backup Because the data stored on a disk are represented only by magnetized spots, it is possible for them to be lost. Therefore, tape is often used to store a backup copy of the data. There are two types of backup tape drives. *Streamers* rapidly make a mirror image of a disk. They copy an entire disk and cannot copy just a single file. *Start-stop* tape drives, on the other hand, can copy one or a few disk files. But when used to store the contents of the entire disk, start-stop drives take longer than streamers do. If only a few files need be routinely backed up, a start-stop system will be more efficient. But if the entire disk must be backed up once or twice a day, then streamers will be the better choice.

Disk As the Primary Storage Medium　Magnetic disk, as we have learned, provides nearly instantaneous access to records. Even though disks can be costly to install and maintain and the data stored on them can sometimes be lost, this is usually overshadowed by their speed. As a result, disks dominate most modern information-processing systems where the competitive environment demands accessibility to data in the process of producing and delivering goods and services to a firm's customers.

FILE ORGANIZATION

The choice of file organization and the methods used for direct access depend on five characteristics of the data: file volatility, file activity, file query needs, file size, and data currency.

File Volatility　When data are frequently added to or deleted from a file, the file is said to have a high *volatility*. Airline files are volatile files, as reservation transactions occur at the rate of hundreds or thousands per minute. But an employee master file for a company with a low employee turnover would have very low volatility.

When volatility is low, sequential or index sequential forms of file organization and access work well, especially when few queries are made against the file. But as the volatility increases, direct file organization becomes more suitable.

File Activity　The percentage of records in a file that is actually accessed during any one run is the *file activity rate*. In many applications, such as bank teller or hotel reservation systems, each transaction must be processed immediately. But in other applications, such as sending out invoices at the end of the month, transactions can be batched and then processed as a group.

When the file activity rate is around 60 percent or higher—meaning that 60 percent of the records in the file may be accessed at any one time—sequential techniques are often considered more efficient. For rates below 60 percent, direct techniques are recommended.

File Query　When information must be retrieved very quickly, then some form of direct organization must be used. Rental car reservation systems, inventory systems, and automatic teller machine systems all fall into this category.

File Size　When the records in a large file must be accessed immediately, then direct organization must be used. But if the size of the file is small—under about 100 kilobytes—then sequential file organization can be used. Files of this size can be read in their entirety into a computer's main memory. Once in main memory, the entire file can be searched quickly to find the needed record.

Data Currency   Data currency refers to the timeliness of data. If the data need to be up-to-the minute, then direct organization and processing will be required. Stock quote systems, airline reservation systems, and car rental systems all depend on timely data and therefore depend on direct systems.

?   Q U E S T I O N S   ?

1. Describe sequential file organization. How are sequential files accessed? Can they be stored on tape or on disk?
2. Explain why it is difficult to access a single record stored in a sequential file.
3. What is the benefit of direct file organization? Can it be used on tape or disk?
4. What are some of the ways to find a record stored in a direct file system?
5. How does an index work?
6. What are a primary and a secondary key?
7. How does an index sequential system work? What are its benefits?
8. Suppose a system is being designed to store inventory data. To make the system more flexible, users feel that data should be accessed not only by part number but also by item name. What type of index(es) should be used? Why?
9. What is the difference between file volatility and file activity?
10. When is it reasonable to store data on tape?
11. What data does a streamer copy?
12. When should disk storage be used?

S U M M A R Y

- The computer's ability to store and retrieve data is at the core of most business applications.

- Permanent data storage is in **secondary** (or **auxiliary**) **storage.**

- **Magnetic tape** (or **tape** for short) is used for secondary storage.

- On magnetic tape, bits are represented by magnetized spots of metal oxide aligned in **tracks.** Records are separated by **inter-record gaps.**

■ To speed the processing of tape, several records are often **blocked** together. The number of records per block is the **blocking factor.**

■ **Magnetic disk** (or **disk** for short) is a common secondary storage medium.

■ On magnetic disk, the surface is divided into concentric rings or **tracks.** Bits are represented by magnetized spots along a track. Records are blocked.

■ To access data on a disk, three steps are required: (1) moving the read/write head to the appropriate track, (2) reading the record, and (3) transferring the data to the CPU.

■ **Floppy disks** (also called **diskettes** and **flexible disks**) are frequently used with microcomputers.

■ **Hard disks** (or **rigid disks**) are used on computers of all sizes. A **Winchester disk** is a sealed, nonremovable hard disk. Disk **packs** combine several hard disks into a unit that is sometimes removable.

■ **Optical disks** can store large quantities of data.

■ **Read-only optical disks** (or CD-ROM) contain data, pressed on the disk by the manufacturer, that can be read but not changed.

■ **Write once optical disks** (or WORM optical disks) can be written on a single time by the user but thereafter can only be read.

■ **Reversible optical disks** can be used to record, erase, rerecord, and read data as often as desired. This technology is just emerging.

■ The method of file organization used on secondary storage devices determines how data can be accessed.

■ With **sequential file organization,** records are stored in a predetermined sequence, usually based on their **primary key.**

■ Records stored using sequential file organization must be accessed using **sequential access.** To reach a particular record, all the records that precede it must first be processed. Processing data using sequential access is referred to as **sequential file processing.**

■ With **direct access** (or **random access**), records can be accessed nearly instantaneously and in any order. Processing data using direct access is referred to as **direct file processing.**

■ Three procedures are used to establish the location of records in direct processing: **relative addressing, hashing,** and **indexing.**

■ With indexing, a **primary index** and one or more **secondary indexes** can be used to locate data. **Index sequential access** uses both. One variation is called ISAM, and another VSAM.

■ Several factors determine which media should be used for secondary storage. Tape is frequently used as backup. Disk is generally the principal storage medium.

■ The choice of file organization and file access methods depends on file volatility, file activity, file query needs, file size, and data currency.

K E Y • T E R M S

The following list shows the key terms in the order in which they appear in the chapter.

Secondary (or auxiliary) storage (p. 211)
Magnetic tape (or tape) (p. 211)
Track (p. 211)
Interrecord gap (p. 211)
Blocking (p. 212)
Blocking factor (p. 212)
Magnetic disk (or disk) (p. 213)
Track (p. 213)
Floppy disk (or diskette or flexible disk) (p. 214)
Hard disk (or rigid disk) (p. 214)
Winchester disk (p. 215)
Disk pack (p. 215)
Optical disk (p. 216)
Read-only optical disk (CD-ROM) (p. 216)
Write once optical disk (WORM optical disk) (p. 217)
Reversible optical disk (p. 218)

Sequential file organization (p. 219)
Primary key (p. 219)
Sequential access (p. 220)
Sequential file processing (p. 220)
File maintenance (p. 221)
Direct access (or random access) (p. 222)
Direct file processing (p. 222)
Relative addressing (p. 224)
Hashing (p. 224)
Indexing (p. 225)
Primary index (p. 225)
Secondary index (p. 226)
Index sequential access (p. 227)
ISAM (Index Sequential Access Method) (p. 228)
VSAM (Virtual Storage Access Method) (p. 228)

F O R   D I S C U S S I O N

1. Explain the difference between master files and transaction files.
2. Why must master files in a sequential tape system be completely rewritten when they are updated?
3. Why do you think records are processed in batches in a sequential file-processing system?
4. Which storage devices provide the fastest access? Which have the greatest storage capacity? What storage device would you recom-

mend to store on-line inventory data? To store historical government statistics such as regional unemployment data?

5. An automobile dealership wants to maintain records of both customers who have been into its showroom and expressed an interest in buying a car and of those customers who have made purchases. With this system, the dealership feels that it would have better control over its sales program and would be able to follow up on customer interest.

   The system would store the customer name, address, telephone number, date of last visit, model, price, and date of purchase. The dealership now has six thousand customers and is growing at the rate of 10 percent per year. Each record would be about 100 bytes long. What type of file organization would you recommend? What type of file access? Which field would you use as the key?

6. An electronics supply company maintains an inventory of over twenty thousand items. Until now, it has used a manual record-keeping system for inventory control. Errors with their system and continued growth of about 15 percent per year have convinced the company to develop a computer system.

   Each record in the inventory file will contain 200 bytes of data. The prices of the inventory items will be updated on the average of every three months. New items will be entered and old items will be deleted at the rate of five thousand annually.

   Inventory clerks should be able to access the data from terminals located in the inventory area. They should be able to determine how many items are in stock and when new orders are expected to arrive. Routine reports, including the amount invested in inventory and usage rates, should be produced each month.

   Compare the different file storage alternatives, and determine which one would be most suitable for this application. What type of file access would you recommend? What capacity is needed?

H A N D S - O N   P R O J E C T S

1. Visit a local business that uses computers. Identify one data storage application and describe the files and fields that you think it would contain.

2. Go to the data processing department at your local bank, hospital, or utility company. Does it use tape or disk for storage? What is the capacity of its system (in megabytes)? How are the files organized, direct or sequential? Are indexes used to speed access?

3.   Refer to several computer periodicals and write a short paragraph on the types of optical disk systems available. Include the access time in your description.
Suggestions: Computerworld, PC Week.

9
DATA MANAGEMENT AND FILE MANAGERS

O U T L I N E

O B J E C T I V E S

After studying this chapter you should understand the following:

■ *Why it is necessary to use additional software to manage data.*

■ *The main procedures followed in the data management process.*

■ *Where responsibility rests for the conceptual planning and design of data management systems.*

■ *How file managers can be used to create, modify, and query a file.*

Chapter 8 explained how data are stored on magnetic tape, magnetic disk, and optical disk. In addition, we discussed how files can be organized—sequentially and directly—and how they can be processed. But Chapter 8 suggested that to build and use a database would require knowing a wide range of details. Now, in Chapters 9 and 10, we will focus on data management software that takes responsibility for these details; it simplifies the design and use of databases.

This chapter will introduce the general procedures followed by those who use data management software. Then we will develop an application that illustrates these procedures for a very simple category of data management software, *file managers*.

Database management systems (DBMS) are more complex and will be covered in the next chapter. There are two advantages in waiting. First, many of the concepts of file managers are shared by database management systems. So this chapter will serve as an introduction to the next. Second, file manager applications are relatively easy to design and use, and so business professionals often find this software helpful in developing their own information systems to monitor operations and help make decisions.

WHAT IS DATA MANAGEMENT?

There are two basic forms of file organization, sequential and direct, as we saw in the last chapter. The direct method dominates most applications, because it offers instantaneous access to large quantities of data.

Regardless of which file organization strategy is chosen, however, a host of detailed instructions must be given to the computer system whenever data are stored or retrieved. Let us describe these instructions generally.

THE DETAILS OF THE STORAGE AND RETRIEVAL PROCESS

Assume that we have a file organized using the direct file organization method (called a *direct file* for short). Just to store a record in a direct file that uses a primary index to locate records, the system needs to be instructed to

■   Open the correct file.

■   Find an appropriate storage location on the disk for the record.

■   Add the record key together with its storage address to an index.

■   Write the new record to the file.

Complicated? Yes. And this example covers just a few of the details necessary in order to store a record in a direct-access system.

In the past, anyone using what we will call a **conventional file processing system** not only had to understand these details but also had to be able to express them in a computer program written in a traditional

Figure 9-1.
Regardless of the application, the data management process follows a sequence of common steps. Here a user is entering data that will be stored for later use.

computer language such as COBOL or BASIC. As a result, the only people with the skills necessary to interact with a firm's electronically stored data could be information system professionals, which placed the firm's data beyond the immediate reach of end-users. If business professionals wanted data or needed a report, they had no choice but to ask data processing professionals to carry out their request and then to wait.

COMMON CHARACTERISTICS

Fortunately, the detailed steps or procedures that must be followed are basically the same from one data management application to the next. For example, the steps to update an airline's reservation data when a new ticket is sold are not unlike the steps that need to be taken when a factory receives a shipment from one of its suppliers and the inventory system has to be updated (Figure 9-1).

SOFTWARE TO MANAGE THE DETAILS

Because data management procedures are similar even for very different applications, commercial software has been developed to take care of most of the details needed to store and retrieve data. Almost every modern information system uses this **data management software,** which consists of file managers and database management systems. It thereby removes an enormous burden from those who design and use computer information systems.

Data management software can be visualized as an additional layer of software in the computer system (Figure 9-2). So when a request is made to add a record to a file or to retrieve data from a file, the request is first processed by the data management software, during which the sequence and content of the details necessary to execute the request are determined.

As we shall discover, data management software has many advantages over using a conventional file processing system. Perhaps the biggest is that data management software has simplified the development and use of files to such an extent that it is not difficult for business professionals to learn how to use and, for some applications, even build their own data management systems.

PROCEDURES IN DATA MANAGEMENT

Regardless of the application and whether a file manager or database management system is used, data management systems support the following procedures:

■   Creating a new file.

■   Entering data.

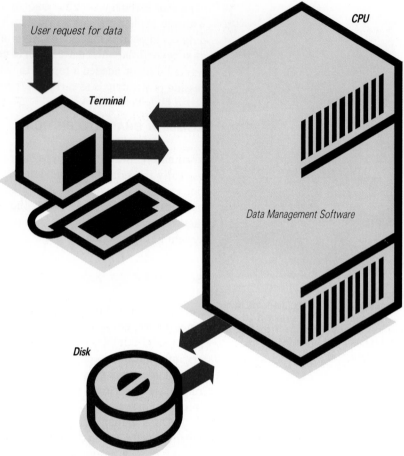

Figure 9-2.
Data management software exists
between the computer and user. It
facilitates the process of data management. With data management software, the user simply tells the computer what is needed, not how to do it.

- Retrieving data.

- Creating indexes for file access.

- Updating the file.

- Generating reports.

- Responding to queries.

- Maintaining the file.

Each of these procedures will be examined in the following sections.

CREATING A FILE

To create a file, the person designing it must first give the software a
general description of the file, called a **record format.** This description
usually includes

- Identification of each field in the record.

- The length of each field.

■   The type of data (numeric or alphanumeric) in each field.

■   Identification of the (primary) key field.

■■■■■■■■■■■■■■■■■■■■■■■■■■■■■

WHEN AN INVENTORY CONTROL SYSTEM WAS DEVELOPED FOR STAN-
DARD PLUMBING SUPPLY, a group including end-users from the purchasing and the stockroom departments determined the data they felt should
be contained in the database. Using this as a guide, a record format was
developed, as follows:

Field Description	Length	Type
Part number (KEY)	5	numeric
Description	20	alphanumeric
Balance	5	numeric
On order	5	numeric
Vendor	15	alphanumeric
Price	5	numeric

The part number field is identified as the primary key and will include
the number which uniquely identifies the part. The description field will
include a description of the item; the balance field will include the current balance of the items in stock; and the "on order" field will include
the units ordered but not yet received in stock. The vendor is the company from whom the item is purchased, and the last field will include the
price paid for the item.

The length of each field, in characters, is also part of the record
format, whose estimates are given in the preceding table.

With the exception of the description and vendor fields, which are
alphanumeric (sometimes called *text fields*), the remaining fields are
numeric fields.

■■■■■■■■■■■■■■■■■■■■■■■■■■■■

When the record format is entered, it is stored separately by the data
management software in a **data definition file.** This file then serves as the
framework into which specific values for each record can be fitted.

ENTERING DATA

After the record format has been entered, data entry for each of the records can begin. Each record must be entered into the system one data
field at a time. With a large amount of data, this can be tedious, and in
most large applications it can be an especially costly part of the project.

RETRIEVING DATA

A data management system also provides a means for users to retrieve
data already stored by the system. This process usually begins when one
or more characteristics of the data to be retrieved are entered into the

system. In a credit-card billing system, the person's credit card number would be entered. Often, as in this example, the characteristic is the record's primary key. After the key has been entered, the stored data are searched; the record or records that match the key are located; and the requested data are presented on the screen or printed in a report.

CREATING INDEXES FOR FILE ACCESS

In some very simple data management systems, files are organized and accessed sequentially. These systems are used only for applications with a relatively small number of records. If a system has thousands of records, even the most patient user would become annoyed with the long wait that a sequentially organized file would surely require for a search to retrieve a single record. Most systems, therefore, rely on direct file organization and direct-access methods with access to records through primary and secondary indexes.

Primary Index   Once the primary key field has been identified during the creation of the file, a primary index is automatically constructed by the data management system. It associates a specific primary key with the storage location at which the data for that record are stored. Whenever records are added or deleted, the index itself is automatically updated to reflect these changes.

To access a record, the primary key can be used as the basis for the search. In this process, (1) the user enters into the system the key for the record to be retrieved; (2) the index is then automatically searched for the key; (3) the physical address at which the record is located is read from the index; and (4) the disk operating system instructs the read/write head to move to the appropriate track. With the exception of the first step, these steps are executed behind the scene; the user is unaware that they are taking place.

■■■■■■■■■■■■■■■■■■■■■■■■■■■■■■■■■■

THE ACME INSURANCE COMPANY, with headquarters in St. Louis, maintains a direct-access system that stores data regarding its policyholders. Some of the fields contained in the file are illustrated in Figure 9-3. The file is accessed by a primary index similar to the one shown in Figure 9-4. When one of Acme's sales representatives needs information or customers request information about a policy they have purchased, the policy number is first entered into the system. Next, the location of the record is determined automatically from the primary index. Then the record is instantly retrieved, and its contents are shown on the screen.

■■■■■■■■■■■■■■■■■■■■■■■■■■■■■■■■■■

As we saw in the previous chapter, searching a file using a primary key may not be the only way that users need to retrieve information. They may also need to retrieve data using secondary keys. For example, an

Policy number	Policyholder name	Policyholder address	City	State	Policy type	Policy Amount (000)	Yearly premium
02165	Adams	25 Hunkins	Boston	MA	1	10	350
02321	Swenson	132 Main	Miami	FL	5	40	940
03157	Johnson	11 Pleasant	Los Angeles	CA	7	20	625
03322	Goldberg	5 Court	Philadelphia	PA	6	30	675
03657	Brown	17 State	Washington	DC	1	50	1475
04571	Sanchez	6 Richards	Atlanta	GA	5	50	1140
04602	Wu	1412 Ave A	San Diego	CA	6	40	830
04613	Alexander	11 Pine	Camden	NJ	6	10	225
04712	Wilson	32 Marcy	Omaha	NB	4	20	460
04714	Oleary	101 Silver	Sacramento	CA	3	40	800
04719	Caruso	16 Elm	Denver	CO	1	100	2350
04721	Batey	104 Meadow	Omaha	NB	6	30	675
04722	Henderon	1611 Main	Barston	CA	6	20	450
04723	Benson	221 Spruce	Denver	CO	7	10	350

Figure 9-3.
Data contained in Acme's file.

insurance company may regularly need to identify all policyholders who live in a certain state, or all policyholders with a certain policy type. To search on a basis other than the primary key, secondary indexes are used.

Secondary Index   A secondary index is used to efficiently identify all the records that satisfy a certain search criterion other than that of the primary key. Suppose, for example, that it is necessary to search the insurance company file shown in Figure 9-3 for all those policyholders living in California. To facilitate the search, the data management system can be instructed to build a secondary index using the state as the secondary key. The secondary index that the system itself will construct is shown in Figure 9-5. (Although the concept of a secondary index was introduced in Chapter 8, we did not mention that many secondary keys are not unique. For example, the state CA in Figure 9-3 appears in several records; thus state is not a unique key.)

UPDATING THE FILE

One of the most frequent activities performed in the data management process is a file update, usually in response to a business transaction. Here, the data management software takes the responsibility for executing the steps required to access a specific record and update one or more of its fields.

Policy number	Physical address
02165	0321
02321	0322
03157	0323
03322	0324
03657	0325
04571	0326
04602	0327
04613	0328

Figure 9-4.
Primary index for Acme's file.

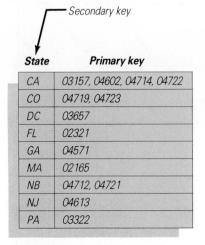

Figure 9-5.
A secondary index for the Acme file facilitates the search for policyholders who live in a given state.

In an inventory system, for example, it may be necessary to update the balance field whenever items are withdrawn from stock. In a hotel reservation system it may be necessary to update the room status field whenever a reservation is received. The data management software is responsible for all of the procedural details in this process.

GENERATING REPORTS

Of particular concern to business professionals is a data management system's ability to generate reports based on the data, and so most data management systems include comprehensive report-generating software.

Producing a report usually involves two steps. First, the format or layout of the report is described in some detail, and the data fields needed for the report are specified. In the second step, the report is produced according to these instructions.

Once a report format is developed, in most systems it can be saved as a separate disk file. This means that a user can produce an up-to-date report at any time by simply running the report format through the report-generating software. The software will access and use only the most recent data in the report.

Reports can be simple or complex. A simple report might list a company's customers in alphabetical order. A more complex report might "sort" or rearrange the data based on the contents of a certain field. In the report illustrated in Figure 9-6, used by a liquor distributor to maintain control over its inventory investment, the categories—which include beer, wine, scotch, vodka, and gin—are listed in descending order of dollar investment. Within each category the brands are listed in descending order of dollar investment. The ability to sort data in this manner is an especially useful feature of a report-generating system.

These reports represent a formal approach to producing information. Often the report may be designed so that comparisons and summaries make it easy for the user to understand and see patterns in the data. Usually they represent the backbone of an MIS system.

RESPONDING TO QUERIES

Although reports are generally used for routine and anticipated applications, more often the need for information is not anticipated, and so a formal approach for obtaining the information is not appropriate. In these situations, the business professional may need data in a simple form and need it quickly.

For example, a sales representative may need to know the names of the customers who have bought a specific product in the last two weeks. A personnel benefits manager may need to know how many employees have been with the company for more than twenty-five years and are earning over $40,000 per year. One way to obtain such information is by using a query language.

Beer	Gold Lite	5621
	Harvey's	3272
	Spitz Real Lager	2163
	Wohlsein	1714
Wine	Mr. Jug	7431
	St.-Etienne	3116
Scotch	Nutty-Sec	5904
	Penrod	4211
Vodka	A-OK	3714
	Olde Petersburg	1690
Gin	Martins	2050
	Steakeaters	1171

Figure 9-6.
A report generated from an inventory
file using a data management system.

A **query language** is a category of software that can understand a wide range of relatively informal end-user requests concerning data, each one expressed in a language that is not too unlike the everyday language we speak. By using a query language, a business professional can access a file and obtain responses without having to be an expert in a programming language. Once again, the procedural details are left to the data management software. Query languages are an important part of the DSS.

The skill level required to use the query language associated with any particular data management system varies, but none is too difficult to master. The goal, which has yet to be achieved, is to develop a query system that can respond to requests made in everyday English—a sys-

Figure 9-7.
Files must be maintained, a process that includes such activities as entering new records into the file, deleting inactive ones, and modifying those records that contain incorrect information.

tem that would require no training to use. Most systems currently in use, however, do require some training. Nonetheless, the direction is decidedly toward "natural language" query systems, systems that can understand the language we speak.

MAINTAINING THE FILE

After a file has been established and is in use, it often will be necessary to perform maintenance on it (Figure 9-7). The three most common forms of file maintenance are

- Adding a new record to the file.
- Deleting a record from the file.
- Modifying (correcting) a record in the file.

When a company acquires new customers, for example, new records must be added to the customer file. Or when a manufacturer buys an item never purchased before, new records must be added to the inventory file. Every data management system provides a mechanism for adding new records and at the same time automatically updating the appropriate indexes. Once these records have been added, they can be retrieved and updated as can any other record in the file.

Deleting records that are no longer active is another maintenance function supported by these systems. When a customer no longer makes purchases or when an inventory item becomes inactive, these records and their references in the index must be deleted. If they are not, then the file and indexes will grow unnecessarily large, increasing the length of time required to find the active records in the file. Moreover, the larger the file becomes, the closer it will move to its physical limit. It makes more sense, then, to delete unnecessary records, thereby making room for new ones.

Modifying, or correcting, a record is another form of file maintenance. Sometimes data have been entered incorrectly. Or the data may originally have been entered correctly but have changed since. For example, when a customer notifies the bank that her address has changed or when a credit-card customer notifies a department store that the address to which his monthly statements are mailed is incorrect, then the records for these individuals must be corrected.

PLANNING THE SYSTEM

As we have stressed, the details of data management are the responsibility of the data management software. However, the conceptual planning and design of an application is management's responsibility. Only management can decide what data should be stored, what reports should be produced, and how the system might be used.

The importance of careful planning and design should be emphasized. As the following example suggests, lack of attention to these aspects of the system can undermine its usefulness.

■■■■■■■■■■■■■■■■■■■■■■■■■■■■■■■

THE VICE-PRESIDENT OF RESEARCH AND DEVELOPMENT FOR GLOBECOM, a telecommunications company, decided that it would be helpful if a file were created of the operating, maintenance, and capital costs incurred by each of its communications centers. The file, he thought, could be useful when making replacement and upgrade decisions for the equipment installed in the field.

The project was assigned to the central data processing staff, and after a preliminary study, it became apparent that the effort required to complete the project would be substantial. One problem, for example, was that the data the system needed were dispersed in locations throughout the country, and integrating the data would be a huge task. At best, it would be a year before such a system could become operational.

How the system was to be used and the problems it would solve were not made clear. Indeed, it was not even clear exactly *what* data would be included or how they would be obtained. Even GlobeCom's vice-president had difficulty identifying the system's objectives or listing its benefits. Yet—illogically—he was confident that someone would find the data helpful once they were available.

The system—which actually required two years to develop—was hardly a success. Few people used it, and within a short period of time, it was discovered that the cost of keeping the data current was much higher than were its benefits.

■■■■■■■■■■■■■■■■■■■■■■■■■■■■■■

Indeed, planning must come first (Figure 9-8), as it is the only way to minimize the problems encountered by many organizations. And during the planning process, the management issues will probably be more important than the technical data processing issues. A number of questions must be answered:

■ What procedures or decisions is the system likely to support?

■ What data are currently used?

■ How are they used?

■ Should other data be used?

■ How will the data be collected and entered into the new system?

■ Who will be responsible for the system?

■ Will the system improve performance or lower costs?

■ Who will be authorized to use the system?

■ How can the system be protected from unauthorized use?

Figure 9-8.
Unless the system is carefully planned, it may not be useful.

Each of these questions—and other design questions raised in Chapters 12 and 13—must be answered. Only then can the designer solve the technical problems, to which we will turn next.

USING FILE MANAGER SOFTWARE

In the last section we learned that data management software must be able to create a file, update the file, generate reports, respond to queries, and maintain the file. In this section we will learn how file manager software can be used to perform these functions.

CHARACTERISTICS OF FILE MANAGERS

A **file manager** is a simple data management system that can perform many of the activities needed to manage single-file systems. For example, if a user needs to establish a single inventory file to maintain records for inventory items, then a file manager system may be appropriate.

In addition to the restriction that only one file can be accessed, file managers have other limitations when compared with the database management systems that we will cover in the next chapter. Nevertheless, there are many applications in which file managers perform very well. Indeed, file managers are some of the most popular software products purchased by business professionals.

It is worth noting that commercial software vendors sometimes apply the terms *database management system* and *file manager* somewhat loosely, and so many file managers are sold under the name of database management systems. Potential purchasers and users therefore should judge the product by what it does rather than what it is called. They are not the same!

DESIGNING THE SYSTEM

We will illustrate, by means of an example, how a file is designed and used with a file manager. We then will be able to show exactly what input the user is required to enter and the output that the system displays on the screen.

Carl Malm is a purchasing agent for Electromed, a manufacturer of medical diagnostic equipment. He is responsible for purchasing over three hundred items that his firm uses in its manufacturing processes. These items are obtained from over fifty-three vendors, and it is his job to ensure that the company is receiving the best possible quality and service at the lowest possible price.

Malm's job requires him to obtain periodic, competitive quotes on all three hundred items. As a rule, however, he is so busy with other responsibilities that a year or longer may pass between quotes. "Sometimes," he explained, "I simply lose track of when I last asked for a quote."

Then one day Malm discovered that one supplier—a respected blue-chip company—had sold him a circuit board laminate that cost 30 percent more than the price charged by other vendors. This incident convinced him of the need for a better method of control. His manual system needed to be replaced. Working with the microcomputer consulting group at his company, Malm decided to design a file manager system.

CREATING THE FILE

To begin the project, Malm determined the types of data he felt would help him control the purchasing process and make better decisions. This list included:

- Product identification code

- Product description

- Vendor from whom product is purchased

- Contact person at vendor's plant

- Current cost of the item

- Year-to-date quantity purchased from vendor

- Date last quote was received from vendor

- Vendor rating

Malm felt that these up-to-date items would be particularly useful because they included, in addition to on-line vendor information, a vendor rating that could be used when making purchasing decisions. Under this new system, vendors would be rated from a low of 1 to a high of 10, based on the experience of Malm and the other purchasing agents concerning the vendor's reliability, competitive pricing, and merchandise quality over the years.

To establish the file, Malm entered the record format. This procedure differs for every file manager, but the system Malm used (Figure 9-9) is representative of many. In this system the user first selects the design file option from the main menu. A second menu then appears, and the create file option is selected. The screen that now appears (step 3) is mostly blank, and into it the user enters each of the field names.

ENTERING DATA

Once the record format is established, each record in the file can be entered. Figure 9-10 shows a partial listing of the three hundred records that Malm must enter. To enter new records, the add option, illustrated in Figure 9-11, is selected from the main menu. The screen that appears includes each of the record's field names, automatically obtained from the data definition file. The cursor is moved to each field on the screen, and the data for that field are entered. When all entries are complete, the record is automatically added to the file.

Figure 9-9.
The steps necessary to enter the field names for Malm's purchasing system. The colon following each field name indicates the end of the name.

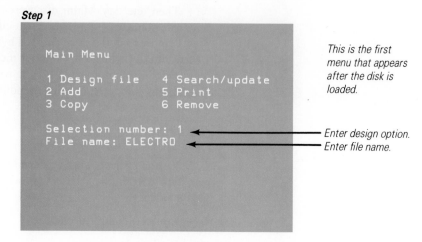

Step 1

This is the first menu that appears after the disk is loaded.

Enter design option.
Enter file name.

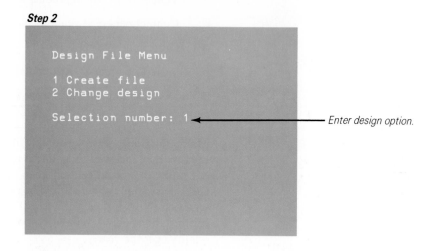

Step 2

Enter design option.

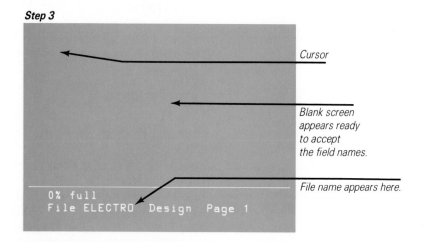

Step 3

Cursor

Blank screen appears ready to accept the field names.

File name appears here.

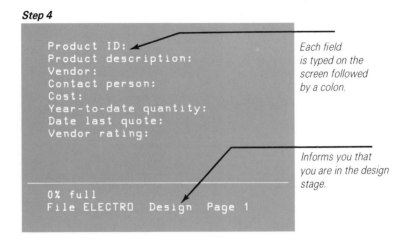

Step 4

```
        Product ID:
        Product description:
        Vendor:
        Contact person:
        Cost:
        Year-to-date quantity:
        Date last quote:
        Vendor rating:



        0% full
        File ELECTRO  Design  Page 1
```

Each field is typed on the screen followed by a colon.

Informs you that you are in the design stage.

Product ID	Product description	Vendor	Contact person	Cost	Year-to-date quantity	Date last quote	Vendor rating
21215	Chassis	Acme Metalforming	Dobbs	12.50	132	86/07/03	1
11196	Resistor	Allen Bradley	Thomas	0.40	562	86/01/21	2
17288	Variable capacitor	United Chips	Sharp	3.00	241	86/11/13	4
25261	Cable	Buffalo Wire	Jones	2.75	2422	86/06/12	3
51012	Processor	Techniboards	Raymond	45.00	324	86/11/12	3
10103	Processor	Wyoming Instruments	Brown	12.75	654	86/03/22	2
12962	Variable capacitor	Certified Electronics	Sharp	1.65	995	86/04/30	4
11041	Laminate	Allied	Jackson	8.75	4061	86/02/11	2

Figure 9-10.
A sample of the records found in
Malm's purchasing information system.

RETRIEVING DATA

To retrieve data from the file (Figure 9-12), the search/update option is selected from the main menu, and the file name is entered. A screen with all of the field names in the file appears next. The user then enters the criteria by which the record or records to be retrieved will be identified. If a user needs to know all of the parts supplied by Techniboards, for example, then he or she will enter Techniboards into the vendor field. When this information has been entered, the file manager software then searches the file and places the information from the first Techniboard record on the screen. If there are other records that meet this criterion, they can be viewed one after another on the screen.

Step 1

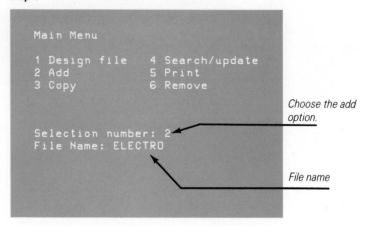

Step 2

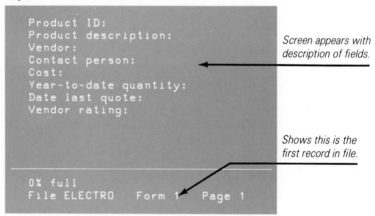

Step 3

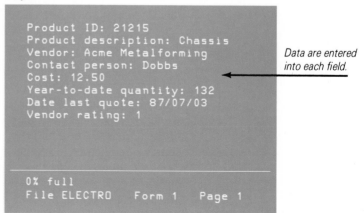

Figure 9-11.
Building the file.

Step 1

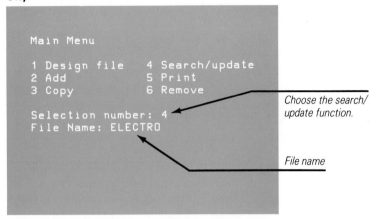

Choose the search/
update function.

File name

Step 2

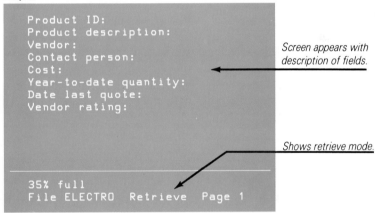

Screen appears with
description of fields.

Shows retrieve mode.

Step 3

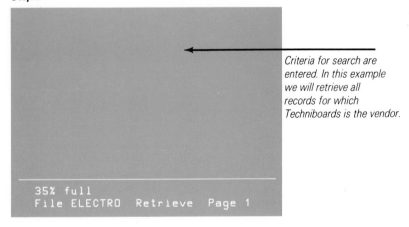

Criteria for search are
entered. In this example
we will retrieve all
records for which
Techniboards is the vendor.

Figure 9-12.
Retrieving records from the file.

●●

E N D · U S E R   H I N T S

A FILE MANAGER MAY BE ALL YOU NEED

Business professionals are finding that they seldom need the full-blown data management systems described in the next chapter. For many of their applications, file managers, which represent a much simpler approach, are all that is needed. File managers are much easier to learn and use. They are designed for the noncomputer professional.

File managers, also known as *flat-file managers,* are appropriate when only one file needs to be used at a time; situations in which the data in an application takes the form of a simple list. File managers are used to store customer lists, sales prospect lists, supplier lists, address and telephone files, department employee data, and simple inventory records. For these and other applications there is no need to look beyond a file manager.

File managers are capable of creating and maintaining a file, providing access, updating the file, producing reports, and answering queries concerning the file. Many have other capabilities as well. They can help the user control the accuracy and privacy of the data. Passwords, for example, prevent unauthorized users from gaining access, and the software often has the capability of checking data once they are entered to prevent data-entry errors from finding their way into the file. Some systems can even warn the user when certain required fields have not been filled in. And there are file managers that can also provide *automatic* data entry, such as date and time, when a record is created or a field updated.

File manager software is available from several companies, for example, pfs:File (Software Publishing Corporation); Rapid File (Ashton-Tate); Q & A (Symantec); Executive Filer (Paperback Software); and Nutshell (Nashoba Systems).

Before you turn to the more complex data management methods described in the next chapter, first determine if a file manager might be all you need.

●●

UPDATING THE FILE

To update a record, it must first be retrieved. Next, with the record on the screen, the user positions the cursor over the appropriate field and enters the new contents of that field. The new contents "overwrite" the old contents, thereby destroying the old contents (Figure 9-13).

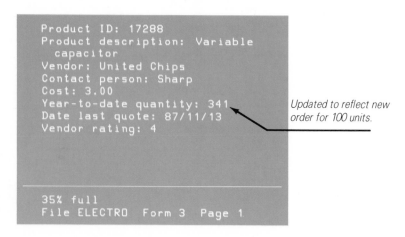

Product ID: 17288
Product description: Variable
  capacitor
Vendor: United Chips
Contact person: Sharp
Cost: 3.00
Year-to-date quantity: 341
Date last quote: 87/11/13
Vendor rating: 4

Updated to reflect new order for 100 units.

35% full
File ELECTRO   Form 3   Page 1

Figure 9-13.
Updating a file. First the record is retrieved using the sequence of steps illustrated in Figure 9-12. When the record appears on the screen, as shown here, the cursor is moved to the appropriate field, and the update is made.

QUERIES AND REPORTS

In a simple system such as this, some queries can be satisfied by simply retrieving a record. Once retrieved, the user can then read the needed information from the record. More complex queries can be accommodated using relational operators. A **relational operator** is an algebraic sign, such as < (less than), <= (less than or equal to), = (equal to), and > (greater than).

Suppose Malm needs to identify all vendors with a rating of less than 3. First he chooses the search/update option. Once again a screen appears showing the fields in the purchasing file. After moving the cursor to the vendor-rating field, Malm enters <3 (Figure 9-14). Now the query language software will search the file and locate all records that meet this criterion. The first one will be displayed on the screen; if there are others, Malm can elect to see them, one at a time.

In addition to viewing the outcome of a query on the screen, the user can also choose to have it printed. For example, a printout of the request made in Figure 9-14 would include the records for all of the products whose vendor rating was less than 3.

Keep in mind that this illustrates a very simple data management system, whose query and report capabilities are not clearly separated. In more sophisticated packages, there is a greater difference between the formality of designing a custom report and the informality of requesting data through the query language.

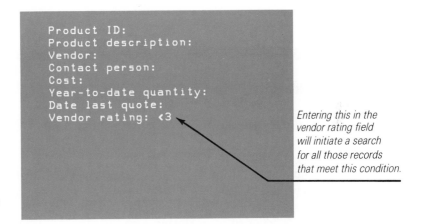

```
Product ID:
Product description:
Vendor:
Contact person:
Cost:
Year-to-date quantity:
Date last quote:
Vendor rating: <3
```

Entering this in the vendor rating field will initiate a search for all those records that meet this condition.

Figure 9-14.
Requesting the records for all vendors with a rating below 3.

MAINTENANCE

Maintenance in this simple file manager is performed by using the functions we have discussed. If a new record must be added to the file, for example, the add option is selected from the main menu, and the new record is added in exactly the same way that the original records were added when the file was first built.

To modify a record, it is first retrieved. Then the cursor is positioned over the field to be modified, and the correct data are entered over the incorrect data. Notice that this procedure is exactly the same as that for updating a record. But in more sophisticated systems, the procedures followed for updates and maintenance are different.

To delete a record, the remove option is selected from the main menu; the record is identified; and the system then automatically deletes it from the file.

USING A FILE MANAGER

As you can see from our example, file managers are relatively simple to build and use. Business professionals often find them adequate for relatively simple and limited applications in which a file helps maintain control over activities or make better decisions.

Concerning our example, when asked about the effectiveness of his system, Malm stated that it paid for itself many times over. Purchasing costs dropped and delivery performance improved. But useful as they are, file managers cannot begin to manage the volume of data that flows through a transaction or operational planning system. Instead, the database management systems described in the next chapter must be used. And if you have followed the principles of file managers, you are already well on the road to understanding their more sophisticated relatives.

? Q U E S T I O N S ?

1. Why is data management software necessary?
2. What steps or procedures are used in the process of managing data?
3. Give an example of a primary and a secondary index.
4. Which steps are followed in producing a report?
5. Give an example of a query. Can queries be made in everyday English?
6. What activities can be classified as file maintenance?
7. Describe some issues that must be considered when planning a data management system.
8. A travel agent accesses luxury liner reservation data and corrects the spelling of a passenger's name. This is an example of

■ Query

■ Update

■ Maintenance

■ Establishing a file

9. A customer calls and makes a reservation at a hotel for the following weekend. This is an example of

■ Query

■ Update

■ Maintenance

■ Establishing a file

10. A sales rep needs to know how many customers in the Northeast have ordered over $1 million of a certain product line. What would be the best way to obtain this information?

11. What is the difference between the way in which a query language and a report generator are used?

12. An investor wants to build a file of investment data. What questions should she ask before actually constructing the system on the computer?

13. Describe how a file is created in a file manager system.

14. Return to the illustrations of Malm's file-manager system. How would all records for "processors" be retrieved?

15. How would the records for all of those products that cost more than $2 each be retrieved from Malm's file?

S U M M A R Y

- In the past, users of **conventional file processing systems** had to understand how to handle numerous details concerning data storage and retrieval using traditional computer languages.

- **Data management software,** which consists of file managers and database management systems, removes this burden from those who design and use computer information systems.

- Regardless of the application, most data management systems support procedures to create files, enter data, retrieve data, create indexes, update files, generate reports, respond to queries, and maintain files.

- When a file is created, the person designing it provides the software with a general description known as a **record format.** This is stored separately by the software in a **data definition file.**

- To retrieve data, most large-scale systems rely on direct file organization and direct-access methods, often employing primary and secondary indexes.

- Output from a data management system can be in the form of reports or, less formally, in the form of responses to queries posed by the user in a **query language.**

- Management is responsible for the conceptual planning and design of data management applications. Lack of attention can undermine a system's usefulness.

- A **file manager** is a simple data management system that can perform many of the activities needed to manage single-file systems.

- File managers include provisions to create files, enter data, retrieve data, update files, pose queries (which often involve **relational operators** such as <, =, and >), generate reports, and maintain files.

K E Y • T E R M S

The following list shows the key terms in the order in which they appear in the chapter.

Conventional file-processing system (p. 238)

Data management software (p. 239)

Record format (p. 240)

Data definition file (p. 241)

Query language (p. 245)

File manager (p. 248)

Relational operator (p. 255)

F O R   D I S C U S S I O N

1. Do you think a file should have as many fields as possible, so that whatever data are needed will be available?

2. When the city of Russell built a file manager system that stored data on all the property owners in town, it expected the system to be used regularly. But after it was finished, the system found infrequent use at best. Now the city manager feels that the system should be abandoned, because it is too expensive to keep up. The city tax office believes that the system does not contain any useful information. The designer of the system, however, blames the city for never training anyone to use it. Where do you think the problem lies?

3. Pressroom Inc., a large printing company, needs a file manager system to store customer orders. The data in this system would include the customer's name, address, date an order is received, order number, number of copies, type of paper stock, color of stock, size of stock, ink colors, trimming instructions, binding instructions, due date, shipping instructions, and current job status. What procedures will be necessary to support such an application? Using the screens shown in Figures 9-9 and 9-11, show how this system would be designed. Give examples of the kinds of questions that a system like this could be used to answer (for example, "List all outstanding orders for the same customer.").

4. What are the similarities and differences between electronic spreadsheets and file managers?

H A N D S - O N   P R O J E C T S

1. Design a data management system similar to those discussed in this chapter that could be used to store the names and addresses of your friends. Before starting, consider for a minute the data fields you might find useful.

2. If you have access to file manager software, find out how to use the system, and build the personal address directory that you designed in response to the previous question.

3. If you have file manager software available, design a system that will store data describing the albums—records and tapes—that you have in your music collection. Use the following fields:

    - album name

    - artist or group's name

    - record company

    - year recorded

    - music type (soft rock, hard rock, jazz, classical, and so forth)

    Enter the data for ten albums and obtain a listing. Describe the different ways in which you might retrieve data (for example, listing all albums with the same group). Use one of these criteria for retrieving data. After you have built your file, add another album to it. Now you should have eleven in the file. Verify this with a listing.

10
DATABASE
MANAGEMENT
SYSTEMS

```
O   U   T   L   I   N   E
```

```
O   B   J   E   C   T   I   V   E   S
```

After studying this chapter you should understand the following:

■   *What a database management system can do.*

■   *The key characteristics of a database management system.*

■   *How hierarchical, network, and relational database management systems differ.*

■   *The types and functions of the different software modules in a database management system.*

■   *Why organizational and procedural controls are important to database management system design and use.*

Chapter 8 explained how magnetic tape, magnetic disk, and optical disk are used to store and retrieve data. It became clear in Chapter 9, however, that unless an intermediate level of software is used, managing and gaining access to the data stored on these media can be quite complex.

The use of file managers, described in the last chapter, is one solution to the problem. With this type of software, the user simply tells the system what is wanted, not how it must be done. As a result, the user is freed from having to know the details of file processing.

But file managers have some serious drawbacks. Data items belonging to different files cannot be related, because only one file can be accessed at a time. File managers, therefore, are suitable for only the simplest applications.

In this chapter, we will discuss a more powerful type of software, database management systems (Figure 10-1). They are capable of storing several files and, in addition, permit relationships to be established among files so that the data in these different files can be linked together, thereby producing useful information from several sources (Figure 10-2).

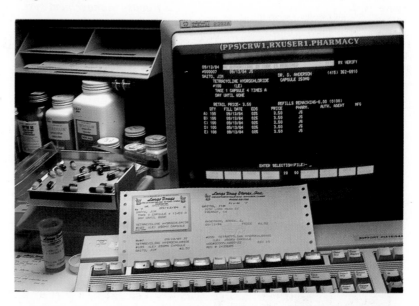

Figure 10-1.
Pharmacists at Long's Drugs, a retail chain in six Western States, use a patient profile database to serve their customers accurately and quickly.

DATABASE MANAGEMENT SYSTEMS

A **database** is a collection of all the data stored in one or more files. Generally a particular data item is stored in only one file but can be related to data in other files (Figure 10-3). Later we will see how this concept minimizes the need to store the same data item in more than one file.

A **database management system (DBMS)** is a set of programs that manages a database, providing the mechanisms through which data items can be stored, retrieved, and changed. Like file manager software, a DBMS is an additional layer of software between the computer and the user (Figure 10-4). But a DBMS offers many more capabilities than a file manager does, as we shall see.

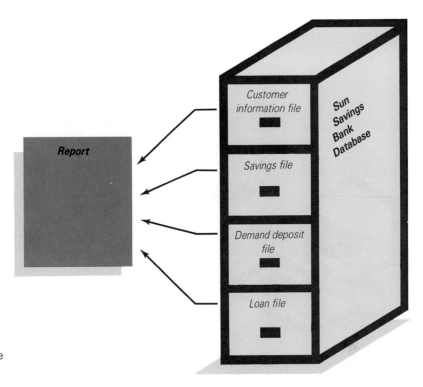

Figure 10-2.
A database management system permits the establishment of relationships among files so that the data in these files can be linked together, to produce a report, for example.

Figure 10-3.
A database is a collection of all the data stored in one or more files. This student database includes a student name and ID file, and a student grade file.

PHYSICAL AND LOGICAL VIEWS OF DATA

Because database management systems can manage a wide variety of data stored in different files, it is necessary to understand the difference between the physical view, or how data are stored in a computer system, and the logical view, or how data are viewed by designers and users.

PHYSICAL VIEW

The way that the computer actually stores data is called the **physical view** of data. The way that those who develop and use applications visualize the data is called the **logical view** of data. These views may be quite different.

For example, we might expect that all of the data for one particular file are stored on one contiguous path on a disk, in much the same way that data fields for a particular record are stored consecutively on a tape; but this may not necessarily be the case. The data items on a disk file may be stored on separate tracks, and if a disk pack is used, they may be stored on separate disks. A major factor that influences where on the disk data will be stored is the speed with which the data need to be retrieved. This is especially true for high-volume transaction applications, in which the inappropriate placement of data items can result in unacceptably long access times.

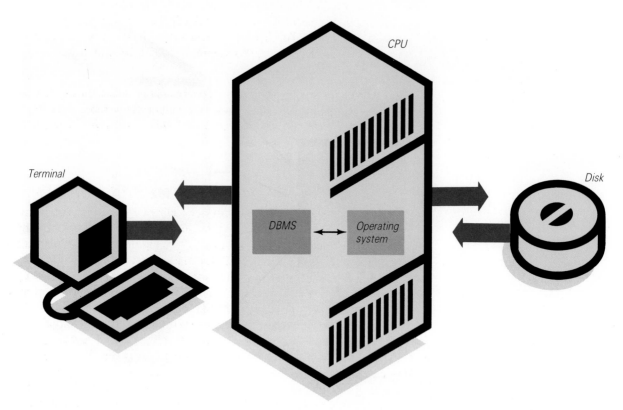

Figure 10-4.
A database management system serves as an interface between the computer and the user.

Although it is not necessary to know the details of the physical storage process, it is essential to understand that the logical view of data, which we will examine shortly, represents the way that we visualize data and not necessarily the way that data are stored. The linkage between our logical view and the physical view is one of the responsibilities of the database management system.

LOGICAL VIEW

The logical view of data, that taken by developers and users of the database, can be represented by schemas and subschemas.

Schema A **schema** is an overall representation or description of every data item to be included in the collection of files found within the database. It is the view taken by those who are responsible for the design, development, and maintenance of the database.

The schema for a database constructed by a rental car agency is shown in Figure 10-5. This file includes such data items as name,

Figure 10-5.
A schema is an overview of all the data items in a database.

Name	Address	Social security number	Driver's license number	Car model	Date rented	Starting mileage	Date returned	Ending mileage	Amount due

address, social security number, driver's license number, and date rented. This example illustrates a schema with only one file; we will shortly expand the concept of a schema to include several files.

Subschema   Usually a schema supports many subschemas. A **subschema** is a subset of the schema and includes only those data items needed for a particular application. It is the view that would be taken by one group of users.

■■■■■■■■■■■■■■■■■■■■■■■■■■■■■■■

DECIBEL INC., a New York importer of audio and video systems, maintains an inventory database that is used in several applications. The schema for this system, shown at the top of Figure 10-6, represents all the data items in the database. Below the schema are two subschemas. The first represents just four data items, accessed in a program used by the marketing department. The purpose of this program is to report on the availability of stock to meet customer demand. Because these are the only data items that the marketing department needs, this subschema represents this department's logical view of the file. The purchasing department, on the other hand, also needs to access the file. It is interested in the data in the second subschema, shown in Figure 10-6. Because this department is interested only in the item number, vendor name, cost, balance on order, and order due date for a particular part,

Figure 10-6.
Schema and subschemas for Decibel Inc.'s inventory system. The schema is the overall view. A subschema is one application's view of the data.

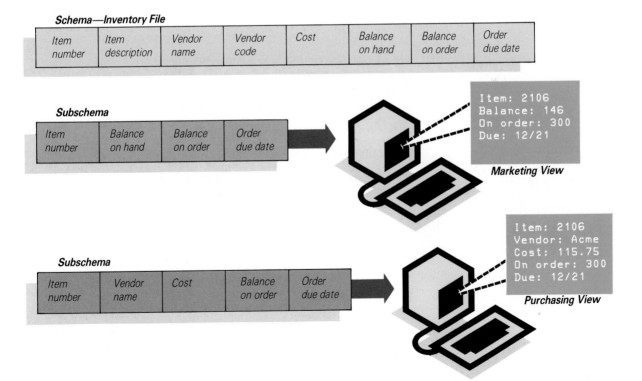

these data fields represent the purchasing department's logical view of the file.

■■■■■■■■■■■■■■■■■■■■■■■■■■■■■■■■■■■■

The Decibel Inc. example illustrates an inventory database. A large organization will also maintain accounting, finance, marketing, sales, and production databases. Each of these databases, in turn, can be represented by schemas, and each schema may support several subschemas.

We can conclude that a database is a collection of files that can be represented by schemas and subschemas, and that this representation is a logical view of the database. But physically, the database includes nothing more than a collection of data items, all under the control of the database management system.

CHARACTERISTICS OF A DATABASE MANAGEMENT SYSTEM

There are many characteristics of a DBMS that make this software package an especially valuable component in the computer information system. By examining these characteristics we will begin to learn how a DBMS works and how it can be used. A DBMS can

■ Maintain a collection of shareable data.

■ Establish relationships among data items.

■ Minimize data redundancy.

■ Maintain independence between programs and data.

■ Provide report-generating capabilities.

■ Offer query language access for unanticipated requests.

■ Provide a common and controlled approach for storing and retrieving data.

■ Facilitate the development of applications.

We will now examine each of these characteristics.

SHAREABLE DATA

A DBMS makes it possible for different applications to share data items in the database. In the following example, two departments share some of the same data.

■■■■■■■■■■■■■■■■■■■■■■■■■■■■■■■■

THE EMPLOYEE RECORDS FOR THE WHITING COMPANY, a milk processor and distributor, are stored in an employee database described by the schema shown in Figure 10-7. The first subschema represents the data used by an application in the personnel department. It includes such data items as the name, address, and telephone number of each employee. The second subschema represents the data used by an application in the employee benefits office and includes the name, address, and company benefits for each employee. Both subschemas share the name and address data items, and these items need to be stored only once in the database.

■■■■■■■■■■■■■■■■■■■■■■■■■■■■■■■■

RELATIONSHIPS BETWEEN DATA ITEMS

There often are relationships between data items. For example, each of the eleven manufacturing departments at the Midway Manufacturing Company employs several hourly workers. A department file in its computer information system maintains data about each department, and an employee file maintains data about each employee. We can say that there is a relationship between the data maintained for a particular department and the data maintained for each employee assigned to that

Figure 10-7.
The ability to share data is an important feature of a DBMS. Here, the personnel and benefits subschemas share employee name and address data.

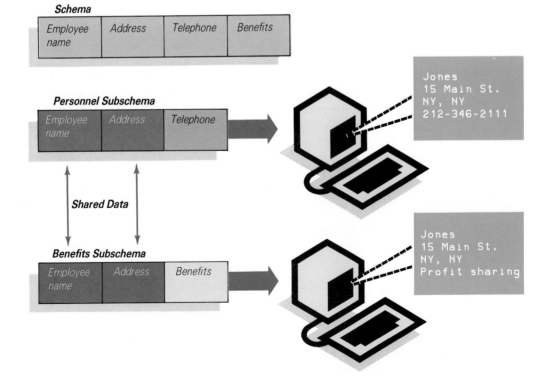

Figure 10-8.
Relationships are an important characteristic of data.

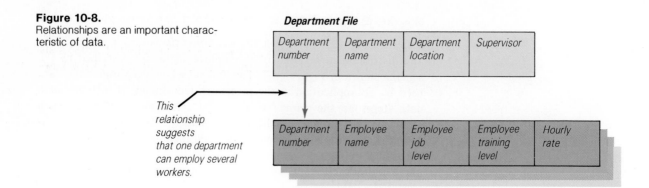

department. We can represent this relationship by the arrow shown in Figure 10-8.

For many reasons—one being to produce useful information—a DBMS must be able to establish such relationships between data items and use the relationships when users request certain types of data. For example, when the Midway Company needs a report that includes some information about each department and a list of its employees, the report can be produced only if the system can recognize the relationship between the department and the employee data. Later in the chapter we will see how and when relationships are specified with a DBMS. First, however, we must learn more about relationships.

Relationships can be described by returning to the concept of schemas and files. But to emphasize the fact that the files in a DBMS represent a logical rather than a physical view of the data, we will refer to a file as a conceptual file. A *conceptual file* is a designer's view of a collection of data items. A single database may include many conceptual files, but remember that they exist in our minds or on paper as a schema. On disk, only separate data items are stored.

The purchasing database system illustrated in Figure 10-9 is used by a manufacturer of commercial restaurant equipment. It keeps records of every purchase order issued and, in addition, maintains information on suppliers. The schema can be described as a set of three conceptual files, the purchase order file, the supplier file, and the line item file.

Figure 10-9.
A schema is comprised of conceptual files in which relationships are established through certain data fields in each of the files.

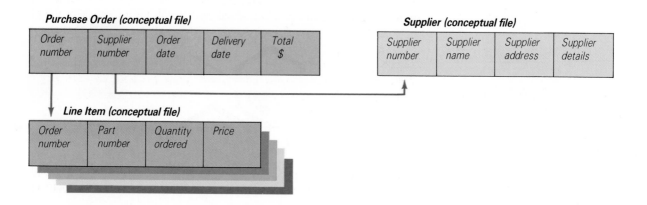

Before we see how these files are related, we should point out that the schema in this example actually contains eleven different data items. Remember that it is our description of the conceptual files that suggests how these data items are linked together. The data items are the following:

Order number

Supplier number

Order date

Delivery date

Total dollar amount

Supplier name

Supplier address

Supplier details

Part number

Quantity ordered

Price

In this purchasing system, the purchase order (conceptual) file maintains records on all outstanding purchase orders. Whenever a purchase order is written, a new record—which we can now call a *conceptual record*—in this file is established.

The line item (conceptual) file maintains separate records, which we again refer to as conceptual records, for every item that is ordered. So, if a purchase order is issued to one vendor for five different items, there will be one new (conceptual) record in the purchase order file—but it will be "related," through the purchase order number, to five new (conceptual) records in the line item file.

The third file is the supplier (conceptual) file. It contains information about the suppliers from whom the parts are purchased. Every purchase order is related to a single (conceptual) record in the supplier file through the supplier number.

A schema thus can be viewed as a collection of conceptual files in which relationships are established among certain fields in each of the files. Meanwhile, the data contained in these files are physically stored as separate data items, and it is through the DBMS software that these data items are eventually linked together. The following application shows how relationships are defined and used. In this case, and in the remainder of the chapter, the terms *conceptual file* and *conceptual record* will be shortened to *file* and *record*.

■ ■

HOLIDAY INTERNATIONAL IS ONE OF THE LARGEST GAMBLING CASINOS IN LAS VEGAS. The casino floor covers an area of 50,000 square feet and contains more than 1000 slot machines and 130 tables. On weekend nights and during holidays, the floor is packed with gamblers. The bright lights, colors, decor, show-business personalities, and holiday atmosphere tend to camouflage the scores of business decisions continuously being made behind the scenes. Many of these decisions are tied to the casino's main lifeblood, the flow of money.

Money, whether it is cash or credit, takes the form of chips. Chips can be obtained at either the tables or the casino's bank. Players can buy chips for cash or, having established credit, can draw chips against a line of credit. In some cases, players with large bankrolls deposit their cash into the casino's bank and draw against it when needed. When the players leave, they convert the chips back into cash.

Whenever a player asks for credit, the pit boss—who watches over several tables—uses a terminal to access the player's record from the casino's minicomputer. This record contains the player's credit limit and the amount of funds already drawn against this limit. Then, on the basis of this information, the pit boss makes a decision.

The information system is also used to distribute what the industry refers to as "comps." Big-spending gamblers expect to receive compensation, or "comps," for their extravagant behavior. These privileges range from a free meal at the casino restaurant or a pass to the casino's show to a room in the casino's hotel.

The casino's policy is to offer comps only to those who qualify. But enforcing this policy is not easy. Before the casino used computers, it was not unusual for players to be denied comps by one dealer only to be given them by another in the next pit. Some players, called "freeloaders," learned to stay at a table long enough to receive a comp and then to move their stack of chips to another table, where they would be given another comp; and so on. These practices, however, were difficult to stop, because the information available to one pit boss was seldom available to another.

Computers, however, have changed the way that these decisions are made. Now the pit bosses have access to terminals, and whenever a player requests a comp, they can access the database and see how often the player has visited the casino, how much money in chips has been drawn each time, how much has been drawn that day, how many comps have been awarded that day, and how much the player has won. On the basis of this information, the pit bosses can make better-informed decisions and better compare what is being given away with what is being received. No longer are these decisions based on guesswork.

At the center of Holiday International's information system is a database management system that provides the information the pit bosses need. The schema for the system is shown in Figure 10-10 and includes two files, the player profile file and the player daily log file. The player profile file contains general data on each player. In the player daily log file, one record is established for each day a player visits the casino. A player visiting the casino for five days in a month would have five records stored; another visiting for thirteen days during that month would have thirteen records stored; and so on. The player profile and the daily log files are related to each other through the player's ID number.

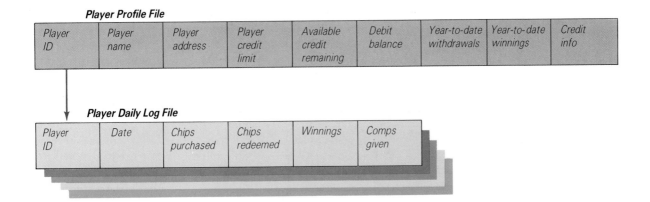

Figure 10-10.
Schema for the casino database.

The pit bosses are interested in only one part of this database. The subschema that defines the data fields they need is shown at the top left of Figure 10-11. When they request a report on a player, the player's identification number is entered into the terminal. Next, the DBMS refers to the relationships previously defined by the system's designer and produces the report shown in Figure 10-11.

■ ■

CONTROLLED REDUNDANCY

Conventional file processing systems—those that do not use either a file manager or a database management system—often must store the same data item in separate locations, because these systems are unable to establish relationships between data found in different files. When the same data item is stored in several different locations, it not only wastes storage space, but there also may be several different versions of what should be the same data item. For example, the item may be updated in one place but not in another. Before the advent of database management systems, this caused many problems, as illustrated in the following example.

■ ■

SUN SAVINGS BANK, in Jacksonville, Florida, offers its customers a range of banking services, including savings accounts, checking accounts, and loans. When Sun first decided to automate its transaction systems, it began with savings accounts. At that time the bank purchased a commercial software package designed especially for savings institutions. It did not, however, include a DBMS but instead used a conventional file processing system.

Two years after the savings account system was implemented, the bank automated its demand deposit and loan systems and purchased software from the same source. Each system, however, was completely independent of the other. No more than one file could be used at a time,

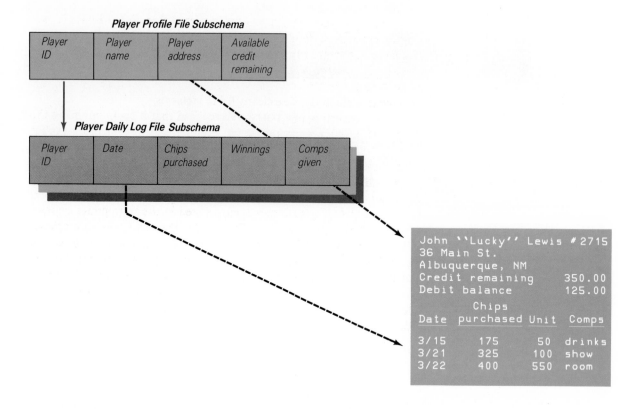

Figure 10-11.
Player report, containing data obtained from the relationship between the player profile and the player daily log files.

and as a result, it was not possible to establish and use relationships between the data.

Because the systems were independent, the files contained redundant data. Customer name, address, telephone number, and social security number were included in all three files (Figure 10-12). Therefore, if a customer used all three services, the data in two of the files would be redundant.

Figure 10-12.
Redundant data in a conventional multifile system.

Sun discovered that redundant data caused problems. Recently, one customer with a savings, checking, and loan account notified the bank of a change of address. The data-entry clerk, however, updated only the savings file. During the next several months, the savings statement went to the new address, and the checking and loan statements went to the old one. So, redundant data in this case clearly led to problems.

By converting to a DBMS, Sun realized that it could minimize the existence of redundant data and, in addition, benefit from several other features that this software offers. Figure 10-13 illustrates the schema and the relationships among the files in the proposed system. The customer information file, as you can see from this figure, is now the only location in which the name and address data are stored. Meanwhile, the data unique to the three services are stored in the appropriate savings, demand deposit, or loan files. The files in the new system are related through the customer's account number, which continues to appear in each file. Reports would therefore be prepared by accessing the customer information file and then accessing each of the other three files using the customer number as the link. Now, when the bank receives a change of address notice, it needs to enter the change only once, and the monthly statements and reports will use one address—presumably the correct one.

■ ■

As this case illustrates, a DBMS, because of its ability to establish relationships between data items in different files, can minimize the need to store redundant data.

INDEPENDENCE BETWEEN PROGRAMS AND DATA

Figure 10-13.
If Sun converted to a DBMS and used this schema, data redundancy would be minimized.

Application programs in conventional file processing systems must be linked very closely to the data that they use. This means that whenever a

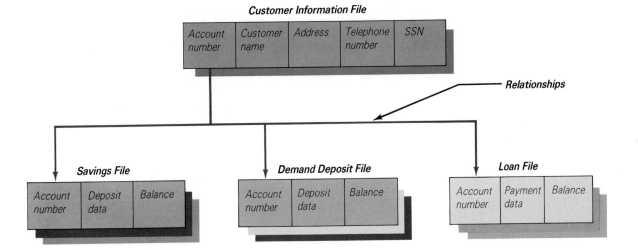

structural change in a file is made—such as adding an additional field to a savings account file—every program or report that accesses the data must be changed to reflect this modification.

If a DBMS is used, however, complete independence is maintained between application programs and the database. As a result, a modification of the database does not require a change in each and every application program that accesses the data. For example, with its new system Sun Bank can add a credit rating field to its customer information file, and the old programs that access this file would not need to be modified. But a system that does not use a DBMS would require every program that reads or updates the file to be changed. This takes time, costs money, and introduces new possibilities for errors.

REPORT GENERATION

An essential feature of any DBMS is its ability to produce a wide range of reports. Although file managers can also produce reports, those produced by a DBMS may be more complex, because they can draw data from several related files. The purchasing report shown in Figure 10-14 is an example. The report summarizes all of the purchase orders issued to one vendor. The data for the heading of the report, which includes the supplier's name and address, come from the supplier file, whereas the data for each purchase order are obtained from the purchase order and line item files.

■■■■■■■■■■■■■■■■■■■■■■■■■■■■■■■■■■■■

Figure 10-14.
A DBMS can generate a report by pulling together data from related files.

THE MANAGER OF MANUFACTURING AT TOOLEX CORPORATION, a defense contractor, needs a listing every evening of jobs overdue by three or

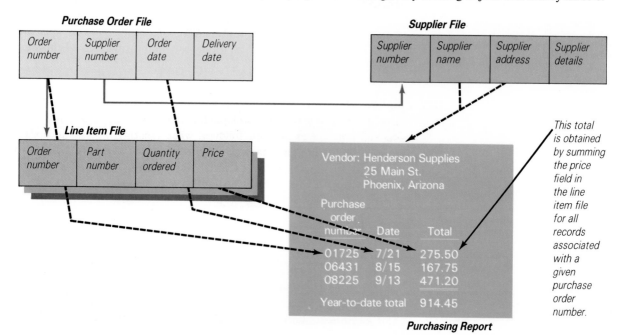

Purchasing Report

more days. Furthermore, to be useful, the report must be broken down into two categories: (1) overdue jobs with more than one week of work remaining and (2) overdue jobs with less than one week of work remaining.

The data needed to compile this report are managed by a DBMS. Using the report-generating software that is part of this system, a short series of commands was written to access the data and print the desired report. Then the commands were saved as a separate file and used to print an up-to-date report at the end of each shift.

■ ■

QUERY LANGUAGE ACCESS

A query system provides the mechanism for accommodating unanticipated requests. The last chapter pointed out that many query languages are approaching the capability of accepting and processing requests made in everyday English. This natural language capability is especially important in a DBMS, because it is through the query interface that most business professionals use the system. And the less training it takes to use the system, the greater will be its use. The following, for example, are several requests that suggest that indeed little training is necessary:

■ List January sales.

■ Give me a list of salespeople whose pay is greater than $40,000.

■ List all orders over $10,000 not shipped.

■ How many salespeople exceeded their quota?

■ How many compact disk players were sold in the northeast territory during January and February?

COMMON AND CONTROLLED APPROACH

Another characteristic of a DBMS is that it enforces a common and controlled approach to the development and use of applications. Well-defined procedures must be followed when creating, accessing, updating, or maintaining a database. Programmers and users are not free to design programs or use a database in any way they desire, which helps avoid the creation of poorly written programs that may not meet the standards of good design or that may not even work.

DEVELOPMENT OF APPLICATIONS

In addition to the advantages already mentioned, an application can be developed in much less time using a DBMS. Without a DBMS, the designer has to contend with all of the details in the storage and retrieval process—details that are automatically handled by a DBMS.

Although the purpose of a database management system is to manage data, the software is often flexible enough to permit a user to design an entire application using only the commands found in the database management language. In other words, a designer, and in some cases a business professional, can design a straightforward application by focusing on the data needed and working through the DBMS, without using additional software or learning its rules. In larger systems, however, an application program often must be written in a traditional programming language like COBOL or BASIC. Then, whenever file access is needed, the appropriate DBMS commands are used in the program (Figure 10-15).

Figure 10-15.
In large-scale applications, the user interfaces with a traditional application program, which in turn uses the DBMS whenever it is necessary to access the database.

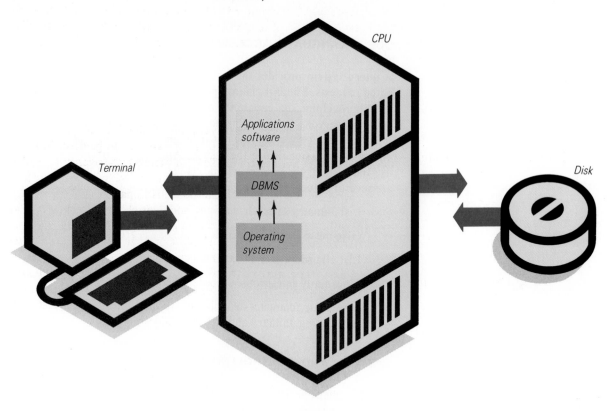

1. What is the major limitation of a file manager system?
2. What is a database?
3. How do physical and logical views of data differ?

4. What is the purpose of a schema?
5. Explain how data are shared in a DBMS.
6. Why were two files necessary in the Holiday International Casino example?

7. What is meant by redundancy? How can it be controlled?

8. Explain how Sun Savings Bank could eliminate redundant data by converting to a DBMS.

9. What is the benefit of keeping application programs independent of the data that they use?

10. How does a DBMS make it easier to develop an application?

TYPES OF DATABASE STRUCTURES

We learned earlier in the chapter that relationships, represented in the conceptual files of a schema, can play a central role in a database. Only two basic categories of relationships are needed to describe the possible types of relationships that can exist: the tree and the plex. Let us take a moment to examine each.

TREE STRUCTURES

The relationship between the player profile file and the player daily log file in the Holiday International Casino example can be described as a **tree structure.** A tree is composed of a hierarchy of elements, called **nodes.** A node represents a record. The highest level of a tree structure can have only one node, which can be called a **parent** (Figure 10-16). The parent, however, can have many nodes, or **children,** related to it at the next lower level. And each of these children can in turn become parents themselves and have several children of their own; and so on down the structure.

The distinguishing characteristic of a tree is the "one-to-many" nature of its relationships. In the casino example (Figure 10-17), there is only one player profile record (parent) for every player, but there are several daily log records (children) for a player.

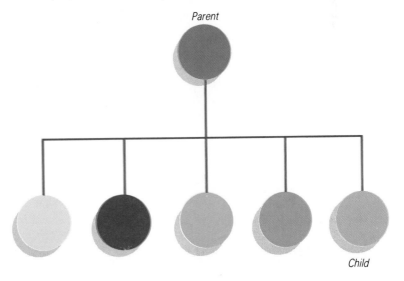

Parent

Child

Figure 10-16.
Tree structure.

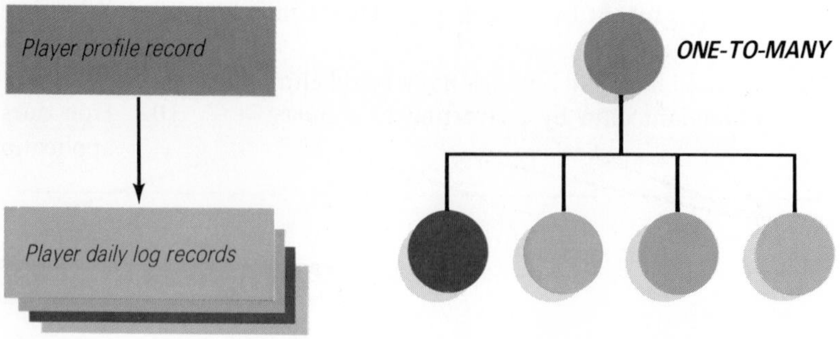

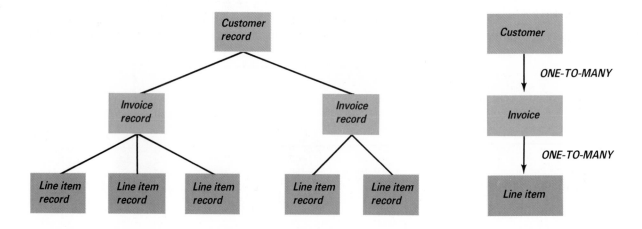

Figure 10-17.
The database for the casino example expressed as a tree structure.

An example of a more complex tree structure is a customer invoice system in which every customer master record is associated with one or more invoice records, and every invoice record is associated with one or more line item records, each representing a particular item on the invoice. An invoice that contained seven items would therefore have seven line item records related to it. The data structure for this situation is shown in Figure 10-18. Again, at every level we notice the one-to-many relationship that characterizes a tree structure.

PLEX STRUCTURES

In a tree structure, a lower node can have only one node above it. That is, in this structure, a child can have only one parent. But in the world of databases there are situations where a child does indeed have several parents. This configuration is called a **plex structure** (Figure 10-19).

For example, suppose a company purchases parts from more than one vendor. Supplier A, for example, might supply parts 1, 2, and 3; Supplier B might supply parts 1, 3, and 4; and Supplier C might supply parts 1 and 2. The plex structure of these relationships is shown in Figure 10-19. From this illustration we can see that each vendor supplies many parts, but in addition each part can be supplied by many vendors.

A school's course-enrollment database also can best be represented by a plex structure. Figure 10-20 illustrates how such a database

Figure 10-18.
A customer invoice database can be described as a tree structure.

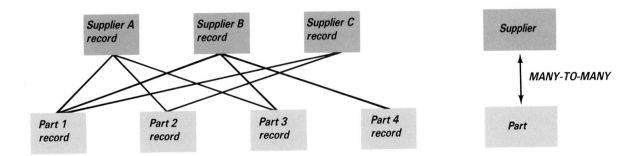

Figure 10-19.
In this plex structure, a supplier record may be related to many part records. In addition, a particular part record may be related to many supplier records.

would be set up. For every class there are many students, and every student can also be enrolled in many classes.

TYPES OF DATABASE MANAGEMENT SYSTEMS

The reason for differentiating between tree and plex structures is that some DBMS software packages can accommodate a plex structure, whereas others can accommodate tree structures. In fact, this is one of the characteristics that separates the three types of database management systems, which can be categorized as hierarchical, network, and relational database management systems.

HIERARCHICAL DBMS

Hierarchical database management systems accommodate data that can be represented in a tree structure, applications in which a parent may have many children, but a child can have only one parent. Because the data in the casino application (described earlier in the chapter) fit into this framework, a hierarchical DBMS can be used. But most hierarchical DBMS are found in large-scale computer systems, and so if the casino system were to be developed around a smaller system, then a relational DBMS might be used.

When a hierarchical database is first created, a description of the schema is entered into the system. At this time the designer must identify the fields in these files that are related. This means that when the

Figure 10-20.
A course-enrollment database can be described as a plex structure.

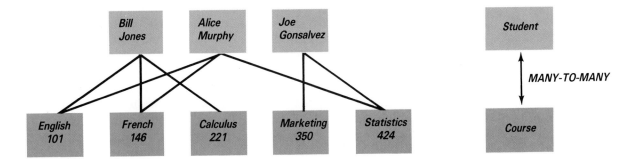

file is first created, the way in which it will be used must be anticipated.

NETWORK DBMS

A **network database management system** can accommodate plex structures, applications in which a child can have more than one parent. Therefore, structures like the course-enrollment database (Figure 10-20) can best be stored in a network DBMS. This type of DBMS is usually found on a large-scale computer system.

Just as the relationships must be identified when a hierarchical DBMS is created, they also must be identified for a network DBMS. And once again, the user must anticipate how the system will be used before these relationships can be identified.

RELATIONAL DBMS

A **relational database management system** is much more flexible than is either a hierarchical or a network DBMS and is often easier to design and use. First and foremost, a relational database management system does not require the designer to specify the nature of the relationships when the database is first created. These relationships need be specified only when the database is used to obtain information or when a procedure is written to generate a report.

This means that new applications can be added to the system that may link data in ways that were not even considered when the system was created. As a consequence, the database is more flexible and can be used to meet a variety of changing information needs.

Using relational database terminology, data are organized in the form of simple two-dimensional tables. These tables are basically a graphic representation of the data in a file. And any type of data, with the risk of some redundancy, can be expressed in this way. For example, consider the casino data shown in Figure 10-10. The data in the player profile and daily log files can be represented in two tables, as shown in Figure 10-21. In fact, data in any tree or plex structure can be represented as a set of related tables. Notice, however, that some redundancy in these tables is necessary, as each table must contain a data item that will tie it to another table, which must also contain the same data item.

Given the advantages of the relational model, it is not surprising to find that it is favored by decision makers. It should also not be surprising to find that most multifile DBMS systems available on microcomputers use this model. In fact, the relational model has become the *de facto* standard for microcomputers. But in large systems, network and hierarchical structures are still commonly used, because in high-volume applications they are the most efficient means of establishing links within the database. Access time, as a result, is shorter.

	Player ID	Player Name	Player Address	Player Credit Limit	Available Credit Remaining	Debit Balance	Year-to-Date Withdrawals	Year-to-Date Winnings	Credit Info
Player Profile	3571	Frank Lefave	Chicago	2500	2200	365	6340	9416	MC
	4275	Bill Donahue	Boston	6000	4321	1742	12142	2141	MC
	5105	Richard Yeaton	Miami	1250	1250	0	432	196	Visa
	6222	Albert Levinson	Houston	500	0	625	955	1231	MC
	7153								

	Player ID	Date	Chips Purchased	Chips Redeemed	Winnings	Comps Given
Player Daily Log	6222	10/6	350	525	175	Drinks Show
	4275	10/6	300	650	350	Show Room
	6222	10/7	300	125	– 175	Drinks
	3571	10/7	125	100	– 25	Drinks

Figure 10-21.
Relational view of the casino database,
with the data expressed in table form.

DBMS SOFTWARE

Every database management system relies on four major software modules to act as the interface between the user and the computer system. These modules are the data definition, data manipulation, report/query, and data dictionary modules (Figure 10-22). In this section we will take a closer look at these DBMS components.

DATA DEFINITION MODULE

The data definition module is the module through which the data structure, or record format, is defined. The field names, field lengths, and data type, among other pieces of information, all are entered through a **data definition language** (DDL) when the database is first created.

In hierarchical and network database systems, the nature of the relationships among the logical files must also be entered at this stage. When a relational database is used, however, relationships are not specified until the data are used.

Once the structural characteristics of the database have been entered, the DBMS establishes a **data definition file** in which all of this information is stored. This file is then used whenever data must be entered or retrieved—that is, the data definition file "overlays" the structure on the database, like a template. Otherwise the system would

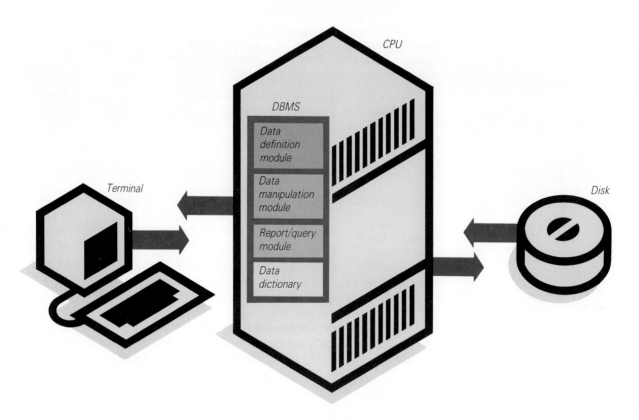

Figure 10-22.
DBMS software modules.

have no way of associating fields with files, as it simply stores a collection of separate data items. So, the data definition file therefore links the physical and logical views of data.

DATA MANIPULATION MODULE

The data definition module, as we have just seen, imposes the structure on the data stored in the database, whereas the data manipulation module makes it possible to use the database through a **data manipulation language (DML).** This is the command language through which a designer or user can access, process, and manipulate the database.

A data manipulation language is a type of high-level computer language and is far removed from the details that a traditional programming language like COBOL or BASIC must handle. Such languages are designed to be relatively easy to use, and they require only that the user specify what is needed rather than the complexities of how it must be obtained. Remember that it is the function of the DBMS software to figure out the details.

Data manipulation languages have a vocabulary of logically meaningful commands that provide the mechanism for performing all of the procedures necessary to use the system. These procedures, introduced in Chapter 9, include establishing, accessing, updating, and maintaining files.

The DML in one commercial DBMS, for example, can establish a file by using a "create" command. The "add" command can be used to add a record to the database, and the "delete" command can be used to drop a record from the database.

Most systems offer a wide range of commands, which gives the designer the flexibility to develop an application capable of meeting a variety of user needs.

REPORT/QUERY MODULE

The report/query module in the DBMS provides the framework and guidance to design a report. In one commercial report module, the design of the report begins with the layout of the report. In this step the designer enters or "paints" the titles, column headings, and other descriptive material to be included in the report on the terminal screen. Then the field names, which will identify the needed data, are entered into the system. Next, the place in the report where these data items are to be located is identified on the screen. Finally, the structure of this report is saved as a separate file. Whenever the report is needed, the report file will automatically access the most recent data from the database and display them in the format specified in the report file.

Query modules are usually designed to be useful to users who have had little training. Many of these systems boast natural language processing which understands simple, English-like commands. And as we mentioned in Chapter 9, the query module is an important tool in a DSS.

DATA DICTIONARY

Because a DBMS stores a collection of separate data items that users can share for different applications, it is important that some mechanism be used to provide information about these data items. This is the function of the **data dictionary.**

The data dictionary is a separate file that stores such information as the

- Name of each data item.

- Data structure for each item.

- Programs that use each item.

- Level of security for each item.

A user who needs to obtain some information from a database can refer to the data dictionary to find the name of the data item to be used in the search. And those designing an application can use the dictionary to determine whether a sought-after data item is already stored by the system and, if it is, the name by which it is called and the applications in which it is used.

The data dictionary is particularly useful in preventing data redundancy. Without it, users in different departments might store identical versions of the same data item in several locations, each one having a different name.

The data dictionary also maintains a list of the passwords that control access to the system. A **password** is a word or number, known only to a user, that authorizes access to the system. If a user attempts to access the computer by means of an invalid password, access will be denied.

Some database management systems support several layers of password protection. One user, for example, may be authorized to read only certain accounting data, whereas another may be authorized to read and update these data items. Still another may be authorized only to produce financial reports.

ORGANIZATIONAL AND PROCEDURAL CONTROLS IN DBMS DESIGN AND USE

Beyond the technical issues of a DBMS covered in this chapter, there are several organizational and procedural issues with which management must be concerned if the database is to be an effective organizational tool.

CONTROLLING DEVELOPMENT

Although the ability to share data is one of the major advantages of a DBMS, it also can be a source of problems. With shareable data, few applications can be developed in isolation of other users. To allow one user to design an inventory application and another, a sales application, and to allow each to use a different name for the same data item would result in the duplication of data, the very problem that a DBMS is intended to avoid.

To minimize the data redundancy problem, and other problems as well, many organizations will establish the position of **database administrator (DBA)**. This individual coordinates efforts among designers and between designers and users. The database administrator resolves the inevitable differences that occur because a common system is used to support a variety of applications. In short, the DBA serves as a central control point and clearinghouse for issues relating to the database.

For example, one critical point in the process of creating a new system occurs when the schema is developed. Here, the DBA must resolve conflicts over the data items to be included in the schema, the names of the data items, the primary and secondary keys, the field lengths, the data types, and so on. Resolving these conflicts may not be easy, as it may be difficult to secure agreement from individuals who need to use the data for different purposes.

Database administrators depend heavily on the data dictionary. They use it to determine whether a particular data item is stored in the system and, if it is, to identify its data name and other characteristics that describe the data item.

In large organizations "the" DBA might be an entire staff rather than one person. It also is quite common for DBAs to help educate both programmers and end-users concerning an organization's data resources and to offer consultation help both when an application is being designed and when problems arise.

CONTROLLING ACCESS

The fact that data will be shared and that natural language interfaces will be used also suggests that the data in the system will be easily accessible to a wide range of users. And this too can create problems. When data are accessible to a range of users—each accessing the data for a different purpose and each probably gaining access at different locations—the data become vulnerable to unauthorized use. As a result, it is management's responsibility to ensure that the system will be used only for authorized activities. This requires careful screening of employees, enforcement of password systems, and a working environment that emphasizes the protection of the information resource.

CONTROLLING DATA INTEGRITY

Because many users will have access to the data, controls must be instituted to ensure that the **integrity** of the data, or their accuracy and legitimacy, is maintained. Otherwise, careless, unauthorized, and even incomplete updates may sabotage the system and leave it relatively useless. Again, the database administrator should become involved in this process, helping to safeguard the system's usefulness.

● ●

E N D - U S E R   H I N T S

WHAT TO LOOK FOR IN A DBMS

What do professionals look for when they evaluate a database management system? A study conducted at Case Western Reserve University found these factors.

■ The DBMS should support both one-to-many and many-to-many relationships.

■ The DBMS should provide data manipulation languages of various types that can be used by end-users and system developers.

■ Data retrieval facilities must be available for end-users and system developers.

■ Backup and recovery facilities should be automatic.

■ Database administrator software should be included, to maintain and fine-tune the individual databases.

■ Data dictionaries must be available.

■ The DBMS should interface effectively with application software.

■ The DBMS must run efficiently on the computer, especially in a high-volume transaction environment. It turns out that some database management systems become bogged down when volume mounts, thereby sharply increasing user response time.

■ The degree of data independence from application software should be high.

■ Compatibility with other database management systems is important, since an organization may use more than one DBMS and require them to freely transfer data back and forth.

■ Training costs should be reasonable for both the casual user, who will probably use a query language, and the system developer, who will need a more comprehensive introduction.

■ Vendor support should be both strong and reliable.

● ●

?   Q U E S T I O N S   ?

1. What is the difference between a tree and a plex structure?
2. An accounts receivable system contains data on the customer who made the purchase, data on the sale such as the date and the clerk's name, and a list of all the items purchased. Is this data structure best represented as a tree or plex? Describe these data in a diagram.
3. What type of structure can a hierarchical DBMS accommodate? A network DBMS?
4. How are data organized in a relational DBMS?
5. Why do most microcomputers use relational database management systems?
6. What is the purpose of a data definition language?
7. Which sorts of procedures are performed with a data manipulation language? How does a DML compare with traditional computer programming languages such as BASIC or COBOL?

S U M M A R Y

■ A **database** is a collection of all the data stored in one or more files.

■ A **database management system** (DBMS) is a set of programs that manages a database, providing the mechanisms through which data items can be stored, retrieved, and changed.

■ The way that data are actually stored by the computer is called the **physical view** of data, which differs from the **logical view** of data, used by those who develop and use applications.

■ **Schemas** and **subschemas** are used to describe the logical view of a database.

■ A database management system is an especially valuable resource in the delivery of information services to an organization.

■ A database management system maintains a collection of shareable data, establishes relationships between data items, minimizes data redundancy, maintains independence between programs and data, provides report-generating capabilities, offers query language access for unanticipated requests, provides a common and controlled approach for storing and retrieving data, and facilitates the development of applications.

■ Relationships between data items in a database can follow a tree or a plex structure.

■ In the **tree structure,** the highest level can have only one **node,** which can also be called a **parent.** The parent can have many **children.** These children can in turn have many children. A one-to-many relationship characterizes a tree structure.

■ In the **plex structure,** a child can have more than one parent.

■ **Hierarchical database management systems** accommodate only data that can be represented in a tree structure and are used on large-scale computer systems.

■ **Network database management systems** can accommodate plex structures and also are used on large-scale computer systems.

■ **Relational database management systems** describe in two-dimensional tables the relationships among data. Simpler and more flexible to use, this type of database has become the *de facto* standard for microcomputers.

■ Every database management system relies on four major software modules: the data definition, data manipulation language, report/query, and data dictionary modules.

■ The data structure of a database is defined through a **data definition language** (DDL) and is stored in a **data definition file.**

■ Use of a database occurs through a **data manipulation language** (**DML).**

■ The **data dictionary** provides information about data items stored in a database, keeps track of what they are called and which applications use them, and helps avoid redundancy.

■ **Passwords** help control access to a DBMS. Often several layers of password protection are employed.

■ In many firms, the **database administrator** (DBA) coordinates use of the database among designers and between designers and users. The DBA's responsibilities include controlling database development, access, and data **integrity.**

K E Y • T E R M S

The following list shows the key terms in the order in which they appear in the chapter.

Database (p. 262)
Database management system (DBMS) (p. 262)
Physical view (p. 263)
Logical view (p. 263)
Schema (p. 264)
Subschema (p. 265)
Tree structure (p. 277)
Node (p. 277)
Parent (p. 277)
Child (p. 277)
Plex structure (p. 278)
Hierarchical database management system (p. 279)

Network database management system (p. 280)
Relational database management system (p. 280)
Data definition language (DDL) (p. 281)
Data definition file (p. 281)
Data manipulation language (DML) (p. 282)
Data dictionary (p. 283)
Password (p. 284)
Database administrator (DBA) (p. 284)
Integrity (p. 285)

F O R   D I S C U S S I O N

1. Design a relational database that could be used to keep track of the records, tapes, and compact disks in your music collection. Use one table to store general information about each album, such as the name of the album and the name of the record company. Use another table to store data for each track (song) on the album. Draw the schema. What fields did you include in the schema? What reports might you periodically obtain from your database? Give an example of a query.

2. Design a relational database that a professor would use to maintain records of the students in his or her class. Assume that the professor teaches several classes. Draw a schema illustrating the tables used and the fields in those tables. Give an example of a report that might be printed and a query that might be asked of the database. Describe the system you have designed using as many as possible of the key terms covered in this chapter.

3. The Kenmare Credit Corporation, a company that loans money to qualified individuals, has maintained a conventional file of customer data for over ten years. The new director of information processing has proposed that the company make a transition to a relational DBMS. Several executives have voiced their opposition to this proposal. They point out that the new system will be expensive, that their employees are used to the old system, and that the old

one is still doing its job. Kenmare's executives have many years of experience with the company. Do you think they are right? What arguments would you make in favor of the new relational DBMS?

H A N D S - O N   P R O J E C T S

1. Obtain literature that describes a mainframe commercial DBMS such as Cullinet's IDMS or IBM's DB2. Write a paragraph summarizing the features of this software.
2. Visit a travel agency or insurance agency. What type of data is stored on their system? How do they use this database? Can you draw a schema which might describe one of these databases?
3. Return to Discussion Question 2. After the Schema for the Music database has been designed, create a database using a DBMS system. Enter the data into the two tables. Following the instructions in your DBMS manual, intersect or join the tables. Finally print a report that includes data about one album, and data about the songs on that album. In other words your report will contain data from your two original tables.

C A S E · S T U D Y

STATE BANK AND TRUST

State Bank and Trust is a holding company that owns ten banks in the Southwest. With over $6 billion in assets and 3000 employees, it is the second largest bank in the region.

Managing Assets

In addition to commercial and consumer banking, State Bank and Trust also manages assets for large organizations. These managed assets include companies' pension funds, profit-sharing plans, and other benefit packages offered to employees.

The asset management service is sold by the bank's sales representatives. Because the assets that the bank proposes to manage can sometimes range in the millions of dollars and because the customer must be convinced that the bank can manage these assets well, the time it takes to sell this service can be quite long. Several contacts with the customer are usual before an agreement is reached.

The Problem

One of the more difficult problems that the bank's salespeople had in the past was tracking prospects. It was not uncommon for several different people to call on a single customer, and it was even more common for each salesperson to be unaware of the others' visits.

When Bob Schwartz was hired by the asset management group some five months ago, he learned of this problem during his first sales call. The customer had been contacted several times during the last year, but Schwartz had no knowledge of these contacts. He found this experience embarrassing and wondered how the bank could sell a million-dollar asset management program under such conditions.

After pondering this problem for several weeks, Schwartz proposed the development of a customer information system. The system, he explained, would use a relational DBMS software package and would be able to store up to two thousand records.

The Schema

The schema for the database that Schwartz proposed is shown in Figure 10-23. It contains three files: the company data file, the company contacts file, and a company plan file.

The first file, the company data file, would maintain general data for every prospect whom the salespeople felt could become a customer. The information in this file would be entered when the company was first contacted. Changes or additions to this file would be made infrequently if at all.

The company's name and address would be entered into the first two fields of the company data file. The types of assets—such as pension funds, profit-sharing, and benefit plans—that needed to be managed would be entered into the third field. The fourth field would contain the number of individuals covered by the plans. The name of the firm currently managing the company's assets would be entered into the next field. In the sixth field would be the name of the contact person at the customer's facility, and in the seventh field would be the date on which the record was added to the file.

The second file would be called the company contacts file. It would contain a record for every contact made between a salesperson and the customer. Because it was likely that several contacts would be made, one company data record, as illustrated in the schema, might therefore be related to many company contact records.

The first three fields in the company contacts file would include the name of the company, the date of the contact, and the salesperson's name. The fourth field would include the type of service discussed. Into the fifth field would be entered the likelihood of a sale. The sixth field would store the date when a decision would be made. The last two fields would contain the date when the next contact was promised and the type of contact—whether a visit or phone call.

In addition to the company data and company contacts files, the system would also maintain a company plan file. This file would store the details for each of the asset categories for which the customer's company was responsible. One company with several different categories would therefore have several different records in this file.

The company name would be entered into the first field of the company plan file. The second field would indicate the type of asset the record would describe. The third field would include a description of that asset.

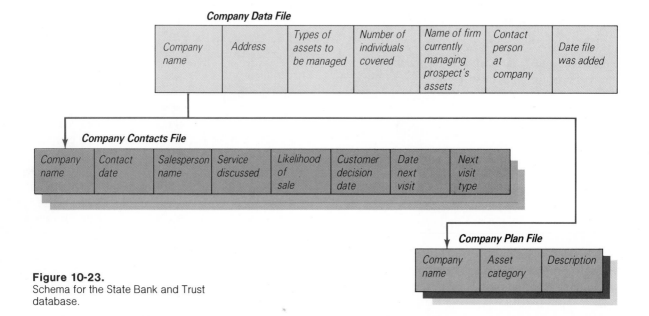

Figure 10-23.
Schema for the State Bank and Trust database.

Potential Uses of the System

"If the system is updated after every customer contact, it will be very useful," explained Schwartz. "Whenever a salesperson plans to make a sales call, he or she can query the database and determine when the last call was made, who made the call, what services were discussed, how close the customer is to making a decision, and what other services might be appropriate to discuss.

"Using the system's report capabilities, each salesperson can periodically request reports to help schedule sales calls. These reports will list all the customers in one state that a salesperson has promised to visit during the month and all the customers who plan to make a decision this month."

Opponents

Although Schwartz was convinced the system would work, others had their doubts. Cecil Mashpee said, "The only way it will work is if everyone cooperates, and we know how impossible that is. None of us has the time to sit at a terminal and enter the day's activities. What good will a system be that has some—but not all—of the data we need?"

Another opponent was Jane Bordeaux. "How can we all agree on the data that should go into the system?" she asked. "If Bob designs it, he's going to put in the data he thinks will be useful. And once it's designed, it will be like the rest of our systems . . . sealed in concrete. We won't be able to change it. I think our informal system is much more flexible. We should stay with what works!"

Questions

1. Describe the problem that the DBMS in this case was designed to solve.
2. What are the advantages of using a DBMS to solve this problem? Could a file manager system be used?
3. Describe the files that the schema contains. Explain how they are related.
4. Suppose a visit is made to a customer for whom a record already exists. What entries would be made to the system?
5. What records are established, and which data items are entered when a contact is made with a new customer?
6. Would there be any advantages in using a relational DBMS for this system rather than a hierarchical or network DBMS?
7. Should anyone be allowed access to this system, or should access be limited?
8. Cecil Mashpee suggested that it would be difficult for the sales force to keep the database up-to-date. Do you think this will be a serious problem? Can it be solved? Would this problem doom the project to failure?
9. Who should be responsible for keeping the data up-to-date?
10. Why does Bordeaux feel that the current system is more flexible? Do you think she is right? Do you think a new system could be developed that would overcome her objections?
11. Under what conditions do you think the new system should be developed?

11
MORE PRODUCTIVITY TOOLS

O B J E C T I V E S

After studying this chapter you should understand the following:

■   *How computer graphics are used to improve the performance of an information system.*

■   *The basic concepts of artificial intelligence and how AI systems are used.*

■   *How project management software can help schedule and manage the activities in a project.*

■   *The types of applications for financial modeling languages.*

Word processors, electronic spreadsheets, and database management systems—the main topics covered in Chapters 6 through 10—are three categories of software often credited with improving productivity in the workplace. Such software is sometimes referred to as **productivity software.** But word processors, spreadsheets, and database management systems are not the only productivity tools. Others also promise improvement, including computer graphics, artificial intelligence, project management, and financial modeling languages. In this chapter, our focus will shift to these new topics.

COMPUTER GRAPHICS

When designing an information system, it is important to think carefully about how the output can best be presented. Text output in many cases is just right. If a collection agency needs to list all the delinquent accounts in the Winnipeg area, then a list is exactly what should be produced. A query at a terminal concerning the status of a special order need not result in a bevy of sophisticated multicolor charts for a response—instead, a line of text and probably a few numbers will do it better. But for many applications it just does not make sense to present the user with pages and pages of textual output. To understand what this output means could take hours. Worse, the output could be misinterpreted.

When it is inappropriate to present volumes of textual data and when summary data and overviews are all that is necessary, the data are often best presented in graphical form.

Computer graphics, the presentation of computer stored data in graphical form, is relatively new. In early computer systems, data were harder to access, little if any graphics software was available, and the quality of the graphical output, when available, was poor.

But with the advent of end-user computing, DBMS, electronic spreadsheets, sophisticated graphics software, and high-resolution output devices, the use of graphics has increased dramatically as Figure 11-1 shows.

When computer graphics are the right choice for output, there are many benefits to be achieved, such as

- More effective conversion of data to information.

- Easier recognition of relationships and trends.

- Shortening of the time needed to make decisions.

- Better organization of output.

- Ability to focus attention on important issues.

- Capability of presenting ideas in an attractive format that may more readily receive attention.

Behind these benefits lies the fact that the mind can absorb information more rapidly from an effective picture than it can from words or num-

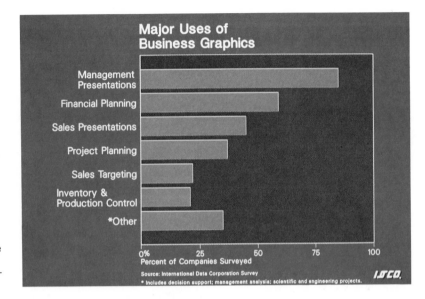

Figure 11-1.
Graphics are used in many applications. This bar chart, itself an example of computer graphics, shows how computer graphics are used in organizations.

bers. If they are used when appropriate, computer graphics can bridge the gap between computer data and the human mind. To the business professional this means more information in less time.

Using the graphics capabilities provided by integrated spreadsheet packages, data can be graphed in a variety of ways. Figure 11-2 shows a **bar chart** in the left half of the figure, illustrating the sales volume of a product line. The **pie chart** in the upper right side of the figure illustrates the forecasted profit, and the **line chart** in the lower right side of the figure shows the variance of forecasted data.

Although the graphics capabilities of integrated spreadsheet packages are very handy, some users need more. For example, it can be helpful to construct graphs from the company's central databases, to design

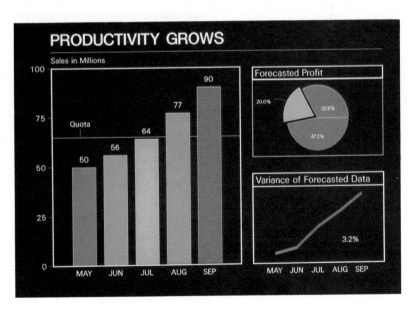

Figure 11-2.
Bar, pie, and line charts. In a bar chart, vertical bars are drawn to represent points. In a pie chart, a slice of pie represents its percentage of the whole pie. In a line chart, the data points are connected by a straight line.

more customized graphics than those offered by standard packages, and to use graphics for a wider range of applications than merely spreadsheets. And indeed, a host of more sophisticated computer graphics packages is available. Computer graphics software can be divided into two categories, presentation graphics and decision support graphics. We will briefly describe how each is used.

PRESENTATION GRAPHICS

Presentation graphics are used to communicate ideas to those who might be unfamiliar with a situation or who need a simple but highly effective overview of a topic (Figure 11-3). For example, presentation graphics might be used by a salesperson to show a customer how several insurance policies compare, by a marketing manager at a long-range planning session to show the change in market share between competitive products, or by manufacturing management at a budget session to give an overview of the expected work load in the next quarter.

Those who use presentation graphics need a system that can

- Produce high-quality illustrations.

- Produce a range of colors.

- Allow the user to choose among a variety of print styles or "fonts."

- Reduce and enlarge illustrations.

- Produce high-quality 35-millimeter slides or transparencies.

The data used in presentation graphics may come from different databases in the organization, from noncomputer sources in the organization, and from outside sources. Most illustrations are accompanied by

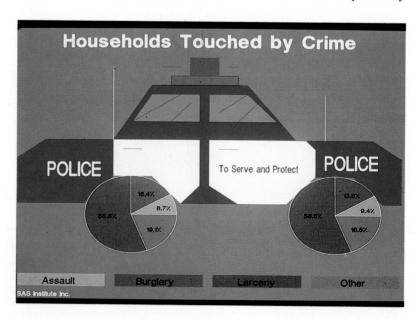

Figure 11-3.
In presentation graphics, the quality of the illustration is a key factor.

Figure 11-4.
The use of a commercial graphics package to produce a pie chart.

explanatory text, and so any graphics system must be capable of mixing text with graphics.

A simple example illustrates how a pie chart is constructed. The user first types the title for the chart on the keyboard and then enters the following information for each "slice" of the pie: label, value, whether or not the slice should be "exploded" out of the pie for attention purposes, color, and design code (texture). Provided with this input, the graphics software does the rest (Figure 11-4).

DECISION SUPPORT GRAPHICS

The second computer graphics category is **decision support graphics** or **analytical graphics.** Here, graphics are used as a vehicle for understanding patterns, trends, or relationships in data. Because the objective in using decision support graphics is to learn something about the data, the demands made on the quality of the graphics, the type of presentation, and the source of the data are quite different from the demands made on presentation graphics.

First, the quality of the illustration is not nearly so important as its ability to present the information in a way that can support the problem-solving and decision-making process. Second, color and special graphical effects are not usually necessary. Third, the data for decision support graphics usually come from spreadsheets, local databases, or the firm's central database. If the data are stored centrally, then the graphics system must be able to access the data and use them to produce graphs with a minimum of user involvement.

■■■■■■■■■■■■■■■■■■■■■■■■■■■■■■■

THE DAILY TIMES, a major newspaper in the Southeast, uses a graphics package to help identify new sales territories and prospective subscribers. In this application, a profile of the paper's current readers is compiled, and from this profile the group's demographic characteristics (such as age, income, and education) are summarized. Next, the *Daily Times* identifies a region in which it would like to increase its circulation. Then a collection of information, including street maps for the region, census data, and the profile of current readers, is entered into the computer. After these data are processed, maps are printed by the graphics package that show the density of target market households. These maps are then used to plan promotional campaigns.

■■■■■■■■■■■■■■■■■■■■■■■■■■■■■■■

It helps if a graphics package—decision support graphics or presentation graphics—is "smart." Users should not have to struggle with such problems as specifying dimensions for the figure; the software should determine what dimensions will fill the space. Nothing is more frustrating to the viewer than a large chart with the information squeezed into one very small corner of the available space, leaving the rest empty. A smart graphics system can also help the user select colors that complement one another, avoiding the gaudy combinations that many users come up with on their own when they suddenly find themselves with a wide palette of colors available. The attributes of an illustration, such as its color(s), should make the viewer want to look at the illustration rather than in the other direction. Smart graphics packages can make it easier for users to create charts that look professional rather than amateur.

The effective use of graphics offers finely "distilled" information for quick comprehension by decision makers. The speed of comprehension is not merely a matter of convenience but also of being able to make timely decisions. In the following example, the type of "detective work" described could have been performed with textual output—but would have taken so much longer that efforts to right the situation could have been too late.

■■■■■■■■■■■■■■■■■■■■■■■■■■■■■■

U.S. SOUND, a distributor of Japanese electronic equipment, regularly uses its graphics system to compare actual sales with sales targets. In one recent month (illustrated in Figure 11-5), the sales manager found that sales during the end of the month were beginning to fall off. By requesting a graph of product sales over this same period (Figure 11-6), she was able to conclude that sales of the compact disk player line were well below expectations. Determined to find the reason for this, the manager requested a graph of compact disk sales by division (Figure 11-7). And as you can see, she discovered that sales for the eastern, western, and southern divisions were all right, but that sales for the midwestern division were not. To narrow the problem even further, she then

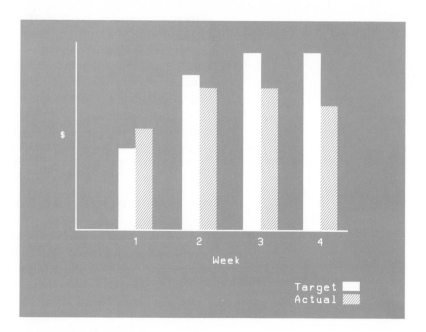

Figure 11-5.
Company sales for U.S. Sound.

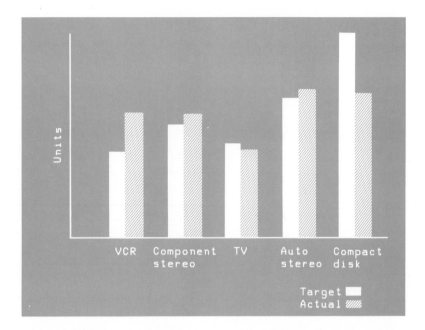

Figure 11-6.
Sales by product line.

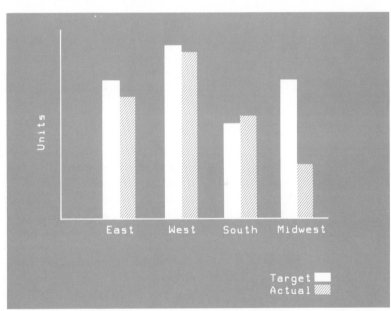

Figure 11-7.
Compact disk sales by division.

requested a graph that showed compact disk player sales for each of the wholesale distributors in the midwestern division (Figure 11-8). From this graph, it became clear that much of the problem could be narrowed to two distributors. Within a few minutes, she was on the phone with one of them. In fact, the entire process—from examining the first sales graph to making the first phone call—took less than thirty minutes.

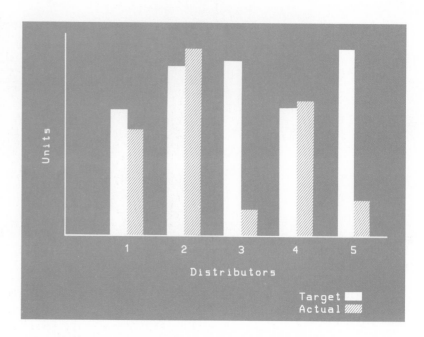

Figure 11-8.
Compact disk sales by distributors in the midwestern division.

GRAPHICS HARDWARE

The hardware used in a graphics system falls into several categories, including graphics terminals, graphics boards, graphics printers, and interface devices. The next sections describe these types of hardware.

Graphics Terminals   Conventional monitors and display terminals are usually not capable of producing high-quality graphics. Most are monochrome displays whose images are in a single color. Some produce pictures in shades of green, others in shades of amber, and still others in shades of black and white. But to produce high-quality graphics, in both monochrome and color, it is necessary to use special graphics hardware and software. **Graphics terminals** are capable of displaying a picture made up of many more lines of information, and as a result the user sees a much sharper, or "higher-resolution," image (Figure 11-9).

   Resolution is measured by the number of picture elements—called **pixels**—per line of information and by the number of lines of information that can be displayed on the screen. Standard monochrome resolution, as for a microcomputer monitor, is in the vicinity of 320 pixels by 200 rows, whereas top-quality monochrome monitors can reach resolutions of 720 by 350. Very high resolution color monitors designed for graphics applications have resolutions of 1000 by 800 or more.

Graphics Boards   When a microcomputer is used to produce high-resolution graphics, a **graphics board** is often necessary to act as an interface between the computer and the graphics device (Figure 11-10). The board, which provides additional circuitry for graphics applications, merely plugs into the computer.

Figure 11-9.
Graphics terminals can produce high-resolution images.

Graphics Printers   In many cases the graphics monitor is used to preview the finished product. Once approved, the output may be printed on paper, plotted on paper, or made into a transparency or 35-millimeter slide. Many different types of printers, plotters, and devices that output transparencies are used (printers and plotters were described in Chapter 2).

Dot-matrix printers can produce black and white as well as color graphics. Colors are produced using a multicolored ribbon. But most printers in this category are not capable of producing high-resolution graphics.

Ink-jet printers, which work by spraying jets of ink in one or more colors onto the paper, are often used if a relatively low-cost solution to the color graphics problem is needed. But without question, the technology that has revolutionized the production of graphics is the laser printer (Figure 11-11). Although more expensive, laser printers operate at easily sixty times the speed of a dot-matrix printer and offer excellent resolution. Only black and white reproduction, however, is possible.

With a complete graphics system including a laser printer, an organization can have many of the capabilities of a professional graphics

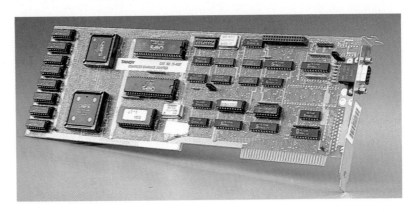

Figure 11-10.
Graphics boards are used to improve the quality of the image produced by a microcomputer.

Figure 11-11.
Laser printers can produce high-quality hard-copy graphics.

Figure 11-12.
A mouse is a graphics interface device that allows the user to paint a picture on the screen.

shop and printing company. Using these **in-house** or **desk-top publishing** facilities, letters can be printed complete with a firm's logo and illustrations. Brochures and sales material can be printed quickly and at a relatively low cost. This is not to suggest that professional graphics designers will no longer be needed. The options are available, however, for many end-users to design and print their own materials, saving the time and expense of involving others in the process.

Interface Devices   In addition to graphics printers and graphics boards, many systems include one or more interface devices. A **mouse** (Figure 11-12) is an interface device that is moved on a flat surface such as a desktop to guide motion of the cursor on the display screen. By moving a mouse over the lines of a drawing, a picture can be "painted" on the screen. Then, when the picture is completed, it can be incorporated into printed material or saved on disk. **Graphics pads** are used in a similar way: The user holds a pencil-like device and traces an image over a pad. The image simultaneously appears on the screen and can also be incorporated into printed material or saved.

A **digital scanner** is a cameralike device that scans a photo or illustration and converts the image into digital bits of information (Figure 11-13). The digital data are entered into memory and can then be stored for future use, presented on the screen, or printed on paper. For example, real estate offices use these systems to link the picture of a house with a description of the property together in the real estate database. When a prospective buyer requests information, the picture and description can be retrieved from the database and flashed on the screen or printed on paper.

GRAPHICS SOFTWARE

In addition to hardware, a graphics system needs software. It is the software that provides the capability of using different fonts, adjusting the

Figure 11-13.
By using a digital scanner, a picture can be "transferred" to a screen or paper.

size of the fonts, selecting colors, moving the image from one location on the screen to another, incorporating graphics into the text, and supporting the use of interface devices.

A wide variety of software packages is available. Many provide a standard set of line, bar, and pie charts; some offer the option of displaying these in three dimensions; and others allow several charts to be graphed on a single plot.

One of the main issues, however, is not necessarily the graphics software itself, but the system software that allows for a full integration of graphics with the remainder of the computer information system, especially the central database. The real power of a graphics system surfaces only when a user can access the central data. The graphics system must be integrated with the rest of the system to obtain this benefit. In Chapter 15 we will discuss the ways in which computer information systems can achieve this level of integration.

●●

E N D · U S E R   H I N T S

CHOOSING A GRAPHICS PACKAGE

Dozens of graphics packages are available. The problem: which one to choose? Here are some guidelines.

The package should be user-friendly. This means that the user should be required to specify only *what the graph should look like,* not *the details about how it must be drawn.* And the graphics package should understand simple English-like commands; the user should not be required to learn programming-level detail.

A good graphics package must be flexible. It should allow users to design graphs in the ways that best meet their own needs, rather than forcing users to work with a few standard designs. There must be a choice of formats, a choice of colors, and a choice of lettering styles.

The package should be capable of producing quality graphs. This means smooth lines, good colors, sharp colors, and effective shading to distinguish different areas on the graph.

With some graphics packages the user can plot several graphs on a single page; this feature is called multiple plotting. When information is compressed to one page, it is more likely to receive the attention of managers and colleagues who do not have the time to flip pages.

The graphics package should also be able to choose the scale on each axis so that the fit and format of each graph is automatically adjusted to the output device. It should be capable of choosing the best combination of colors to make a contrast and separate each graph segment. Alternatively, the user should also be able to specify axis scale and colors, overriding the automatic feature.

In addition, a good package should have the capability of storing custom designs and chartbooks for future use. A custom design, created by the user, specifies a chart in a desired format, with a given layout and certain titles. Once stored, these designs can be recalled and used with up-to-date data to produce timely graphs. It will not be necessary to go through the design steps again.

A chartbook is a collection of graphs that is used on a regular basis. One chartbook, for example, may include several charts that illustrate the sales performance and market share statistics of a company's product line. A good graphics package should be able to store these charts and then produce them with the most recent data using only a few keystrokes.

Finally, a graphics package should have the capability of retrieving data directly from central databases and producing graphs that summarize these data.

● ●

? Q U E S T I O N S ?

1. Define computer graphics.
2. Describe the differences among a line, bar, and pie chart.
3. What types of benefits can be obtained from using graphics?
4. How do presentation graphics and decision support graphics differ?
5. What is meant by a "smart" graphics package?
6. How is resolution measured?
7. What kinds of printers are used to achieve high-quality graphics output?
8. How is an interface device used in a graphics system?

ARTIFICIAL INTELLIGENCE

Ever since the development of the first digital computer, there has been considerable speculation over the possibility that one day computers could simulate human thinking and decision-making processes. What we have learned since those early days, however, is that this is more difficult than many had supposed. Although we are still a long way from building a machine that has the intelligence and common sense of a person, today we are capable of building "smart" systems. Smart systems are the products of an exciting new field called artificial intelligence.

Broadly speaking, **artificial intelligence** (AI) refers to the use of the computer in certain limited application areas to simulate some of the characteristics of human thought. It involves the ability of the computer system to learn, reason, solve problems, and understand ordinary language.

Artificial intelligence is one of the fastest-growing areas in information technology. Indeed, some experts believe that AI has already emerged as one of the most significant technologies of this century. They predict it will revolutionize the way in which computers are used. Although that remains to be seen, a lot has happened.

There are two classes of applications in AI: expert systems and natural language processing. Let's discuss expert systems first.

EXPERT SYSTEMS

Figure 11-14.
An expert system makes an expert's point of view available through the terminal of a computer system.

Expert systems are a category of computer applications that make an expert's point of view available to a nonexpert (Figure 11-14). They are designed by compiling some of the knowledge of the experts in a particular field and then using this knowledge to solve problems. The assumption is that with access to an expert's point of view, nonexperts will be better able to solve a specific problem or make a decision. To learn more about expert systems we need to see when they are used and then to examine how they work.

As a rule, the use of an expert system is considered when one or more of the following conditions prevail:

■ A difficult problem has already been solved by experts and will need to be solved regularly in the future.

■ The expertise that is needed to solve a problem is unevenly distributed in an organization.

■ A consistent approach is needed in solving difficult problems.

■ Complex problems in ambiguous environments must be solved regularly.

■■■■■■■■■■■■■■■■■■■■■■■■■■■■■■■■

AT THE GLENDALE COMMERCIAL BANK, an expert system has been designed to capture the expertise of the bank's senior loan officers. It is used by the junior loan officers to screen loan applicants. When the junior officers interview a loan applicant, data about the applicant are entered into the expert system. The data are then processed, and the expert system recommends whether the loan should be granted. While the output from this system is intended to be used as a recommendation, or as a check-and-balance on the decision process, in most circumstances, the junior officer follows this recommendation.

■■■■■■■■■■■■■■■■■■■■■■■■■■■■■■■■

Expert systems can be very effective when a specific expertise is not evenly distributed in an organization. For example, in the Glendale Bank example, the senior loan officers are located at the bank's headquarters, whereas most of the junior officers are located at the bank's branches. The expert system, then, brings the centrally located expertise to these remote locations.

In addition to bringing an expert's point of view to a nonexpert, these systems also impose a consistency on the decision-making process. With such a system, two decision makers with essentially the same data will seldom reach very different conclusions.

We learned in Chapter 3 that transaction systems are used in highly structured environments and are operated by people at the lower level of an organization. In contrast, expert systems are used at higher levels in the organizational hierarchy, from the tactical to the top management level. As a result, these applications can be classified as operational planning and control systems, management planning and control systems, or strategic planning systems. These higher-level applications focus on less-structured environments, in which there is likely to be a considerable degree of ambiguity associated with a decision. It might not be clear, for example, what alternatives should be considered, which criteria to use, and what outcomes may be associated with each alternative. Expert systems are often effective in dealing with these situations, as they capture the way in which the experts have dealt with these problems in the past.

Using an Expert System   Expert systems are developed by compiling and using the experience of one or more experts to establish a set of rules for processing data and reaching decisions. This experience, and the rules that describe the experts' behavior, are referred to as the system's **knowledge base.**

To use an expert system after it has been developed, the nonexpert first enters data that describe the specific decision that must be made or the problem that must be solved. The system then uses software, referred to as the *inference engine,* that applies the information in the knowledge base to the problem at hand. At the conclusion of this process, the expert system recommends a decision or a course of action.

Three types of expert systems are used:

- Problem-specific or off-the-shelf systems
- Shell systems
- Custom systems

Problem-Specific Expert Systems   **Problem-specific** or **off-the-shelf systems** include those systems that narrowly focus on a particular problem. Usually the knowledge base including the rules for the system have been developed by the software vendor, who has drawn on the knowledge of several sources, including industry experts, academic authorities, and published literature. No development is required to use such off-the-shelf systems. The user simply inserts a disk into the computer, enters the data that relate to a specific application, and has instant access to an expert's advice. In most cases those who use these systems would otherwise not find access to this level of expertise within their own organizations.

■■■■■■■■■■■■■■■■■■■■■■■■■■■■■■■

EASTERN DIGITAL SELLS COMPUTER INFORMATION SYSTEMS TO SMALL AND MEDIUM-SIZED COMPANIES. Although it sells several different turnkey systems to dentists, physicians, retail stores, and restaurants, at least 50 percent of its business is directed toward the development of customized systems.

Eastern sells in a very competitive marketplace. Because a system has an average cost of about $100,000, making a sale often requires the salespersons to invest a considerable amount of their time with their customers. To help them succeed, Eastern bought an off-the-shelf expert system designed to provide advice to their sales staff. Here is how the software works.

First, the system asks questions about the salesperson and then for details about the customer. Next, the system asks about the specific situation. It then refers to its own knowledge base of psychological data, which the developer obtained from experts in the field. Finally, the system recommends how the situation should be handled. In one application, the system suggested that the salesperson take a more aggressive stance, ask a higher price, and then at the end drop the price in response to the customer's apparent need for a bargain.

■■■■■■■■■■■■■■■■■■■■■■■■■■■■■■

Although most people who use problem-specific systems are quick to point out that they do not follow every piece of advice, they do find the information useful. For example, some users report that the advice acts as a check on their actions.

Expert System Shells   A different approach is required when users are unable to find an off-the-shelf software package that meets their needs and must become involved in the actual development of the system. Although an organization might find it necessary to have a system custom designed for their application, in most applications it is far more economical to use an expert system shell.

An **expert system shell** is a developmental tool for building an expert system. It can be visualized as a prefabricated general framework into which knowledge about an application can be placed. The user must do some of the work to develop the system for an application, but many of the details are left to the shell.

There are two types of shells. The first relies on the *induction method,* and the second relies on the *production rule method.*

Induction shells.   To use a shell that relies on the induction method, the knowledge base to be entered into the shell must be capable of being expressed in a decision-matrix format. A decision matrix is similar to the layout of a spreadsheet, in that it has columns and rows. First the factors that the expert considers when reaching a decision are entered into the decision matrix. Then several "training examples" are entered, illustrating how the expert used these factors to reach a decision. Next, the system's built-in inference engine uses the training examples to determine or "induce" the rules that the expert probably followed when making the decisions for those training examples. Once trained and once the shell has "learned" a set of rules, the system is ready for use. The following case study illustrates the process.

■ ■

JACK SIMMONS IS A SALES MANAGER FOR BEAUTY SPOTS, a costume jewelry manufacturer. Every week, ten salespeople submit their weekly expense accounts to him for approval. Until recently, this approval process took about two hours. During this time, he checked the days that were spent traveling, number of miles covered, mode of transportation used, salesperson's job category, and amount submitted. After looking at this information, he then weighed these factors and decided whether the expenses submitted were legitimate.

Several months ago, Simmons designed a system that now does most of this work for him. He used a commercial expert system shell that runs on his microcomputer. To develop the system, he

■ Verified that the problem would fit the framework of the expert system.

■ Specified the factors used when reaching a decision.

■ Entered training examples.

■ Tested the system.

First Simmons determined whether the commercial expert system could be used to capture the process he followed in reaching a decision. His system used the induction method and required that the decision environment be capable of being described in a spreadsheet-like format. He concluded that his problem could indeed be described in this way.

In this format (Figure 11-15), the factors he considered when reaching his weekly decision were listed across the top of the table. The decision to accept or reject the expense account was listed down the last column.

In the next step, Simmons entered several training examples into this framework, using data submitted in earlier weeks. For each salesperson's report, he entered the number of days, number of miles, transportation mode, job category, and dollar amount. In the last column he entered his actual decision either to accept or reject the expense account. The system's inference engine then used these examples, shown in Figure 11-15, to learn or "induce" the rules that Simmons had been following. Together with the data that he had already entered, these rules became the system's knowledge base.

In the next step, Simmons ran several test examples to see whether the system made the kinds of decisions he felt were appropriate. After entering several examples, Simmons was not satisfied with the way the system performed, so he entered more training examples. And with access to these additional training examples, the system increased its knowledge base and refined its ability to make appropriate decisions.

Number of Days Traveled	Miles Traveled	Mode	Job Category	Amount $	Decision
4	1500	1	3J	735	Approve
3	270	2	1J	175	Approve
2	320	3	1J	360	Reject
5	530	3	3J	565	Approve
1	50	2	4S	45	Approve
2	275	2	1J	190	Reject

Figure 11-15.
Examples given to an expert system. The software will induce the rules which the expert used to reach the decision shown.

Mode:
1. air
2. company car
3. rental car
4. other

After running several more tests, Simmons concluded that the system's rules were close to his own, because its decisions were what he too would have made.

Simmons's administrative assistant uses the system every week. It takes this person less than half an hour to make the decisions and permits Simmons to turn his attention to other, more productive responsibilities.

■■■■■■■■■■■■■■■■■■■■■■■■■■■■■■■

There are many applications, in addition to the one just described, that fit into this framework. The loan-granting process mentioned earlier in the chapter is an example. Factors such as a person's income, credit standing, and length of time on the job, together with the actual credit decision, can be entered into the system's spreadsheet-like format. The inference engine can then induce the appropriate decision rules from these data. Next, the expert system is evaluated using test examples, and when the system is approved, it is ready for use.

These applications illustrate the use of the inductive method. They are characterized by the fact that the inference engine finds the rules that best fit the data, which suggests that induction shells are used when the rules followed by the decision maker are not necessarily very clear.

Production rule shells. A second approach used by expert system shells is called the production rule method (also referred to as the if–then method). To use this approach, the expert must have some awareness of the rules followed in a decision-making process and also be able to express these rules in a logical if–then format. To develop these systems, first the rules are entered, then the system is tested, and once it meets the developer's approval, it is ready for use. To use the system for a specific application, the data are entered, and the shell's inference engine processes the data through the knowledge base of rules and recommends a course of action.

■■■■■■■■■■■■■■■■■■■■■■■■■■■■■■■■■■

FRANK PESO TEACHES A POPULAR COURSE IN AN ADULT EDUCATION PROGRAM IN THE MIDWEST. Because of increasing enrollments, Peso recently decided to build his own expert system to help him with his grading. After examining several shells that the school had available, he chose one that used the production rule method.

His first step was to identify the rules he used in grading. One of the first he entered was the following:

> IF the student has an exam average above 92, and IF the student has not missed more than 2 assignments, and IF the student has not missed more than 3 classes, and IF the student's class participation grade is higher than 3.5, THEN GRADE = A.

Once Peso entered all of his rules and tested the system with several examples, the system was ready for use.

To use the system he entered the data for a specific student. The expert system software then used its inference engine to process the student data through the knowledge base, eventually recommending a grade.

However, Peso did not rely completely on the expert system for assigning grades. First he manually computed a grade for the student and then compared it with the expert system's grade. Often, the grade recommended by the expert system made him go back and reconsider his own conclusion.

■■■■■■■■■■■■■■■■■■■■■■■■■■■■■■■■■■

Sometimes an expert's rules are only rules of thumb (also called *heuristic rules*) and may not have been consistently followed by that person from one application to the next. Does this mean that when an expert feels that a rule does not always apply, or applies in only some circumstances, it should not be entered into the system? The answer is no, for it is the ability to accommodate this ambiguity that is often what differentiates an expert system from a conventional Management Information System or Decision Support System. Expert systems are designed to handle this ambiguity; other systems are not. It is the job of the expert system to determine how the rules can best be applied in a specific instance.

To help the user understand why an expert system recommended a particular course of action, many shells have the capability of displaying the rules and the logic used to make a particular choice. In other words, they justify their decision. This gives the user the chance to approve or disapprove of the process and the conclusion. It is an especially useful feature when the user finds it difficult to understand how the expert system dealt with a particularly ambiguous or problematical situation.

■ ■

THE METRO GROUP, a financial planning consulting company, specializes in developing financial plans for large organizations. The company was founded by two individuals with over thirty years combined experience in corporate financial planning. As the company grew, newer and less-experienced professionals were added to the staff. To help support the complex decisions that these less-experienced professionals had to make for Metro's clients, the company hired a software firm to develop an expert financial planning system.

The software firm spent nearly a year on the project. It started by observing the senior consultants' decision behavior. First it learned how these individuals reached decisions concerning such services as risk management, pension planning, income tax planning, and employee benefits. Then the firm converted this knowledge into more than three thousand if–then rules.

During this development process, the experts were unclear on how they actually reached a decision in some circumstances. One expert, in fact, admitted to using lots of intuition and occasionally making "educated guesses." But the consultants explained that rules based on intuition and educated guesses were still important knowledge for the system to include, and that it was the shell's responsibility to use this knowledge in the best way possible.

In the next step of the development process, the rules were entered into the shell, and testing was begun. Once the system was approved by Metro's top management, it became operational.

With the new expert system, Metro's professional staff collects data about each client's operations and then enters these data into their terminals. The system processes the data through the knowledge base of three thousand rules and displays its recommendation on the screen.

■ ■

Custom Expert Systems　　There are many problem-solving situations for which neither a problem-specific expert system nor a shell expert system is suitable. In those situations, it becomes necessary to develop from scratch a **custom expert system,** using one of several artificial intelligence languages.

The languages used to develop AI systems can manipulate not only numerical data, as routine programming languages can, but also symbolic data. In *symbolic manipulation,* the system can process words and even graphics. The two AI languages most commonly used are LISP (short for LISt Processing) and PROLOG (PROgramming in LOGic).

But customized AI systems are very difficult to develop. To succeed, a company must have a staff of highly skilled AI professionals. Today, only the very largest of the Fortune 500 companies have this resource.

Custom applications are also expensive. Even the simplest application can cost $1 million. But we are continuing to gain experience from the applications that are being developed today, and the benefit from this experience should lead to lower developmental costs. Eventually, smaller organizations should be able to develop their own custom applications. For now, however, only problem-specific and shell systems are within reach for most organizations.

The Use of Caution Unlike the highly structured transaction applications such as payroll processing, in which correct data always produce a correct result, the heuristics or rules of thumb often used in expert systems suggest that their recommendations or decisions may not be correct in a specific application. That is, AI systems capture some, but not all, of the characteristics of the human thought process. Consequently, they must be used carefully. When the user is in doubt, the process by which the system reached the decision must be examined.

Underscoring the fact that these systems are far from perfect, the AI system used by the U.S. Department of Defense, according to one industry observer, has hundreds of times erroneously warned military personnel of a Soviet invasion.

NATURAL LANGUAGE PROCESSING

Natural language processing is another area in artificial intelligence receiving a considerable amount of attention. **Natural language processing** refers to the use of everyday language to access a computer system. This means that a person using a computer would require little if any training. Requests would simply be made using the language we speak every day. Indeed, most end-users would prefer to interact with computers in this way.

Perhaps the quickest way to appreciate the advantages of natural language processing is to see how it can be applied to an application with which we are already familiar, database management systems. In these systems, the natural language processing system can be visualized as an additional software layer over the database management system. The user interacts with the natural language system, which in turn interfaces with the database management system.

Using one natural language system, the user can ask such questions as "Who are the managers earning over $50,000?" Even if the question is asked in a different way ("List all managers who earn more than $50,000."), the same answer will be returned. And if the next question is "How many of them are women?" the system will be intelligent enough to know that the "them" refers to the managers.

But given today's state of the art, these natural language processing systems come with limited vocabularies; that is, it is not possible to ask the system just any question. Most vocabularies, however, can be expanded; the systems learn as they are used. For example, if you asked, "What was the profit for last year?" the system might not recognize the word *profit* and ask you to define it. You could respond with a definition of "sales minus expenses," and the system would add this to its vocabulary; it then would not have to ask for the definition again.

Natural language processing systems are also equipped to handle the ambiguities contained in any human language. So, when they are faced with some uncertainty about the question being asked, they will ask the user to rephrase the question or clarify a word.

We can therefore conclude that natural language processing makes it easier to use a computer system with little training. It has been especially successful in database management systems and has proved to be easier to use than are some query languages that are still more like programming languages than natural languages.

Although many natural language systems approach the way in which we use everyday language, most are still far from being able to respond to a totally untrained user's request. In all of these systems the user must still follow simple guidelines, be prepared to add new vocabulary words, and rephrase questions that the system does not understand.

?   Q U E S T I O N S   ?

1. Define artificial intelligence.
2. How is a problem-specific or off-the-shelf expert system used? Give an example.
3. For what type of problems can a shell expert system be used?
4. Describe the steps followed in developing an expert system that uses the induction method.
5. Is it necessary for an expert to understand how he or she uses rules to reach a decision, in order to submit these rules to an expert system?
6. Describe the steps followed in developing an expert system that uses the if–then format.
7. Are custom expert systems within reach of the average organization?
8. What is natural language processing? Would you describe this as an advanced or a developing technology?

PROJECT MANAGEMENT

A **project** is a collection of activities with a definite beginning and end. For example, building a house is a project. It begins when the land is cleared and ends when the occupants move in. Each step between the beginning and end is an activity. Clearing the land is one activity, pouring the foundation is another, and framing the house is another. In fact, the construction of a house involves hundreds of such activities.

Projects do not have to be a major undertaking, like building a house. They can be less ambitious, such as preparing a quarterly departmental budget or planning a presentation at a regional sales conference. But whenever a set of activities has a logical beginning and end, it can be classified as a project.

MANAGING PROJECTS

Projects can be difficult to organize and manage, for several reasons. First, a project may have many activities, and the job of juggling them can be difficult. Second, these activities may have to be carried out in a certain sequence. Third, projects usually require many resources, including equipment, materials, money, and labor. So projects must be managed in a way that ensures that the right activities are carried out at the right time in the right order with adequate resources available when they are needed.

In addition, as projects unfold, the conditions affecting the timing and completion of activities change. Some activities take longer to complete than expected; supplies and materials may not arrive on time; people may be needed elsewhere; and equipment may break down. And when these problems occur, plans may have to be revised for the entire project. Perhaps the completion of the project may be delayed; additional personnel may be needed; or overtime may be necessary. So, those who manage projects must not only develop plans at the beginning, but if the plans are to remain an effective tool, they must be constantly revised in response to changes that affect the completion of every activity.

PROJECT MANAGEMENT SOFTWARE

Project management software helps solve these problems. Project management software is used as a vehicle for collecting and organizing data and then providing management with the information needed to plan and manage the tasks associated with a project (Figure 11-16).

In general, project management software requires that the user supply four categories of data:

■   A list of activities to be completed.

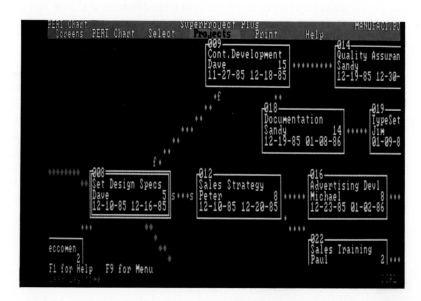

Figure 11-16.
Project management software is used to manage both large and small projects.

■ The expected time required to complete each of these activities.

■ The immediate predecessor(s) of each activity.

■ The resources required to complete each activity.

Once supplied with this information, the software produces several reports illustrating the relationship of activities in the project and summarizing activity and resource requirements.

AN EXAMPLE

Allen Davis, a salesperson for a major importer of automotive replacement parts, must begin to prepare for the semiannual distributors' meeting. The meeting, attended by approximately two hundred independent distributors, is an opportunity to present new products and provide new information on the old ones. Several activities must be completed before the meeting begins; including

■ Setting the meeting date.

■ Reserving food, lodging, and meeting room accommodations.

■ Notifying participants and receiving confirmations.

■ Designing and writing materials for the distributor packet.

■ Taking photos for the packet.

■ Printing packets for the confirmed registrants.

These activities are listed in Figure 11-17 and will be referred to by the activity number next to its description. The time required to perform these activities is also listed in the figure. For example, setting the date for the conference is expected to take one week.

Precedent Relationships   When activities cannot be carried out independently of one another, a "precedence relationship" must be followed. These restrictions are also identified in Figure 11-17 (right-most column). Activity 1, for example, has no predecessors and can therefore be scheduled at any time. Activity 2, however, requires that Activity 1 be completed before it can begin.

Figure 11-17.
The activities necessary to schedule a sales conference.

Activity Number	Activity Description	Activity Time in Weeks	Predecessor
1	Set date	1	—
2	Reserve accommodations	2	1
3	Notify participants	1	2
4	Design packet	3	—
5	Take photos	2	4
6	Print materials	2	5,3

Activities Chart   An activities chart is a useful way of illustrating precedence relationships. In such a chart (Figure 11-18), a line represents an activity, and a circle represents the end of one activity or the beginning of the next. Notice how the diagram accommodates the situation in which an activity such as Activity 6 has several predecessors. They all merge into the circle that represents the beginning of Activity 6.

Entering the Data   To enter these data into the computer, with most software the user types in the activity number, its immediate predecessor, the activity description, and the expected time to complete the activity. In more complex software systems, the resource needs for each of these activities can also be entered.

Reports   Once the data have been entered, several reports can be obtained, perhaps the most useful being a Gantt chart. A **Gantt chart** (Figure 11-19) shows the activities on a time scale. For example, the user can see that Activities 1 and 4 can begin during the first week of the project. Activity 2 can begin during the second week of the project (remember that Activity 1 is a predecessor of Activity 2, and so if Activity 1 is completed at the end of Week 1, then Activity 2 can begin at the start of Week 2). Activity 3 can begin at the start of Week 4 (it can begin only after Activity 2 has been completed). Activity 6 can begin at the start of Week 6 (it can begin only after Activities 3 and 5 have been completed).

Another useful report identifies those activities that are critical to the on-time completion of the project and the slack associated with each activity. When an activity can be delayed without affecting the completion of a project, it is said to have *slack*. Turning to Figure 11-20, we see that Activity 3 can be completed by the end of Week 4. But Activity 6 does not begin until the start of Week 6. Therefore, Activity 3 can be delayed one week without affecting the timely completion of the project by the end of Week 7. As a result, Activity 3 has one week of slack.

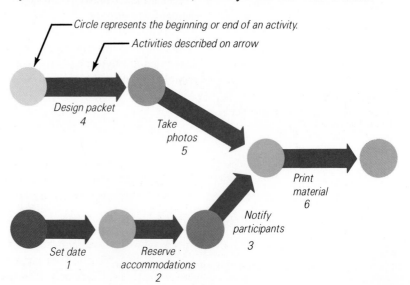

Figure 11-18.
An activities chart, which illustrates the precedence relationship among activities.

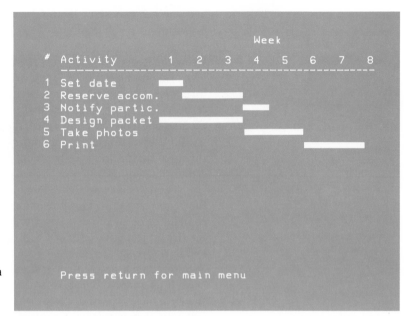

Figure 11-19.
A Gantt chart shows the timetable for a project. The bar for each activity begins at its earliest possible starting time.

#	Activity	Duration (weeks)	Begins (week)	Slack avail	Critical
1	Set date	1	1	1	
2	Reserve accom.	2	2	1	
3	Notify partic.	1	4	1	
4	Design packet	3	1	0	*
5	Take photos	2	4	0	*
6	Print	2	6	0	*

Figure 11-20.
Slack and critical activities are identified in this report.

When an activity has no slack, it is said to be *critical*. Critical activities are those that, if delayed, would delay completion of the project. So if Activity 5 were delayed by one week, the project would not be finished until the end of Week 8. All critical activities are said to form a **critical path** through the project diagram. The critical path for this project would therefore be Activities 4, 5, and 6.

Most project-scheduling systems also produce several different resource reports. One may show the resources required for each activity, and another may show the total demand made on the resources for all activities.

Using the Reports   These reports can be used in many ways. First, they help organize many of the details and relationships among activities that otherwise may not be noticed. Second, they can be used to identify the critical activities in a network that must be watched carefully if the project is to finish on schedule. Third, they specify the slack in each activity, so that users will know exactly how late an activity can be before it will threaten the project's completion date. Fourth, they can be used to establish closer control over the resources used in a project.

An especially useful feature of project management systems is that they can respond instantly to changes in the conditions that affect the completion of an activity. Suppose, for example, that the photo sessions for the project just described fall behind schedule and will require an extra two weeks. To determine the consequence of this on the project, the user simply enters the changed data into the computer and runs a new set of reports. The revised completion date of the project will be shown in these reports, together with revised estimates for slack and critical activities. In this small project, the revision process is simple, but in large systems with hundreds or even thousands of activities, this would be an enormous task if done manually. In either case, however, the computer reduces this process to a few seconds.

FINANCIAL MODELING LANGUAGES

Financial modeling languages are a type of programming language used primarily in financial analysis. They have been applied to the launching of new products, lease/buy decisions, mergers and acquisitions, and cash flow analyses.

Although spreadsheets and financial modeling languages can often be used to model the same problem, there are some basic differences in the way financial models are constructed and can be used. The principal difference is that spreadsheets mix together the model and data—they are really one—whereas financial models separate the model from the data. The advantage in separating them is that it becomes easier to run several sets of data through the financial model. One manufacturing company, for example, prefers a financial modeling approach because it can make a comparative financial analysis of several divisions by simply plugging the data for each division into the same model.

A financial model is written in a language that uses English-like statements. These statements logically express the sequence of steps that the computer must follow. For example, if it is necessary to express a gross profit computation at one point in the program, it can be written in the following way:

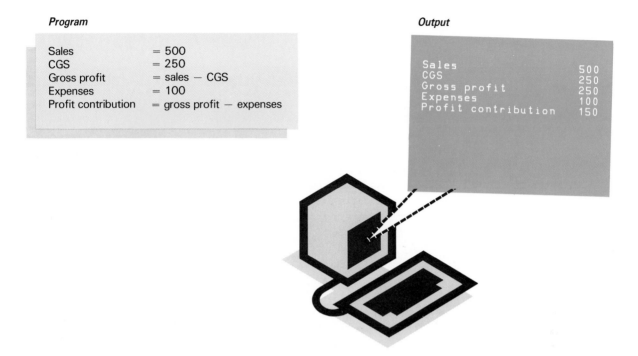

Program

Sales	= 500
CGS	= 250
Gross profit	= sales − CGS
Expenses	= 100
Profit contribution	= gross profit − expenses

Output

Sales	500
CGS	250
Gross profit	250
Expenses	100
Profit contribution	150

Figure 11-21.
A financial planning model is written as a series of programming statements. Unlike this simple example, the model in most applications is kept separate from the data.

Gross profit = sales − cost of goods sold

Using English-like statements makes this model easy to build and easy for others to follow (Figure 11-21).

In addition to the ability of financial modeling languages to perform simple arithmetic operations, they can also perform more complex operations, including calculating internal rate of return and present value. And financial modeling languages let the user design complex reports that contain bar, line, and pie charts. Many of these features, however, are also found in integrated spreadsheet packages, as we have seen.

Financial modeling is especially useful for performing sensitivity or "what if" analysis. The user can test the consequences of several different strategies (also possible using a spreadsheet model). For example, in Figure 11-22 we can see how a spreadsheet user would change the sales estimate to see the effect on profits. With financial modeling, however, the user can not only do this but also perform such analysis "backwards" by entering the desired result into the system; the model then determines the necessary conditions to achieve the result. This is known as *goal-seeking analysis* (Figure 11-23).

For example, in goal-seeking analysis a user might specify a sales target, and the model would then determine the advertising budget needed to achieve this outcome. Or profit goals could be specified, and the model would determine the sales necessary to reach the goal.

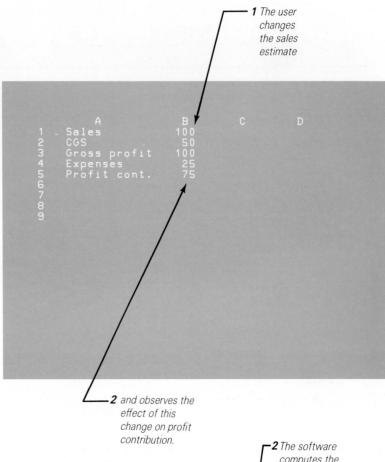

1 The user changes the sales estimate

```
          A              B        C        D
1 . Sales           100
2   CGS              50
3   Gross profit    100
4   Expenses         25
5   Profit cont.     75
6
7
8
9
```

2 and observes the effect of this change on profit contribution.

Figure 11-22.
In conventional ''what if'' analysis, like the kind found in most spreadsheet packages, the user changes a figure and observes its effect on the numbers below.

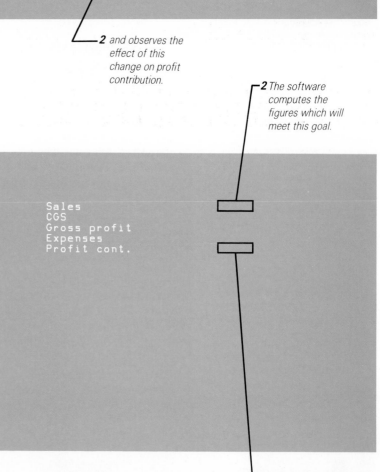

2 The software computes the figures which will meet this goal.

```
Sales
CGS
Gross profit
Expenses
Profit cont.
```

1 The user specifies a goal.

Figure 11-23.
In goal-seeking analysis, the user specifies a goal, and the model will compute the figures needed to achieve this goal.

?   Q   U   E   S   T   I   O   N   S   ?

1. Define a project.
2. Why are large projects difficult to manage?
3. What information is entered into a project management software package?
4. What types of relationships can be shown on an activity chart?
5. What is a critical activity? How is it related to a critical path?
6. Why can it be useful to know the slack associated with a particular activity?
7. What is a Gantt chart? How is one used?
8. What is the main difference between a financial planning language and a spreadsheet?
9. Give a definition and an example of goal-seeking analysis.

S   U   M   M   A   R   Y

- **Productivity software** includes programs that handle word processing, spreadsheets, database management, computer graphics, artificial intelligence, project management, and financial modeling.

- **Computer graphics,** or the presentation of output information in graphical form, is appropriate for some types of output.

- **Bar charts, pie charts,** and **line charts** are typical computer graphics produced by spreadsheet packages.

- **Presentation graphics** are used for those unfamiliar with a situation or who need a simple but highly effective overview of a topic. In contrast, **decision support graphics** or **analytical graphics** are used as a mechanism for understanding patterns, trends, or relationships in data.

- Graphics hardware includes graphics terminals, graphics boards, graphics printers, and interface devices.

- **Graphics terminals** are capable of higher-quality displays than are conventional monitors and display terminals. The **resolution,** measured in the number of picture elements or **pixels** per line of information and the number of lines of information is greater with graphics terminals.

- A plug-in **graphics board** is often necessary when a microcomputer is used to produce high-resolution graphics.

■ Interface devices commonly used to produce computer graphics include the **mouse, graphics pad,** and **digital scanner.**

■ **Artificial intelligence** (AI) refers to using the computer in certain limited application areas to simulate some of the characteristics of human thought. Applications can be classified as expert systems and natural language processing.

■ An **expert system** makes an expert's point of view available to a nonexpert. Expert experience is stored in a **knowledge base** in the system.

■ **Problem-specific** or **off-the-shelf expert systems** focus on a particular application.

■ **Expert system shells** are tools for building expert systems. The induction method is used to build induction shells, and the production rule (or if–then) method is used to build production rule shells.

■ **Custom expert systems** are built from scratch, using an artificial intelligence language such as LISP or PROLOG.

■ **Natural language processing** refers to the use of everyday language to access a computer system. The trend is in this direction, but systems still have a long way to go.

■ A **project** is a collection of activities with a definite beginning and end. **Project management software** can be used to help solve scheduling problems inherent in managing projects.

■ One useful report often produced by project management software is a **Gantt chart,** which shows activities on a time scale. Another report identifies a **critical path** composed of activities vital to a project's timely completion.

■ **Financial modeling languages** are a type of programming language used mainly in financial analysis. Although spreadsheets can perform some of the same functions, financial modeling languages separate model and data and perform more complex operations and goal-seeking analysis.

K E Y • T E R M S

The following list shows the key terms in the order in which they appear in the chapter.

Productivity software (p. 294)
Computer graphics (p. 294)
Bar chart (p. 295)
Pie chart (p. 295)
Line chart (p. 295)
Presentation graphics (p. 296)
Decision support graphics or
    analytical graphics (p. 297)
Graphics terminal (p. 301)
Resolution (p. 300)
Pixel (p. 300)
Graphics board (p. 301
In-house publishing or desktop
    publishing (p. 302)
Mouse (p. 302)
Graphics pad (p. 302)
Digital scanner (p. 302)

Artificial intelligence (AI)
    (p. 304)
Expert system (p. 306)
Knowledge base (p. 306)
Problem-specific or off-the-shelf
    expert system (p. 306)
Expert system shell (p. 307)
Custom expert system (p. 311)
Natural language processing
    (p. 312)
Project (p. 313)
Project management software
    (p. 314)
Gantt chart (p. 316)
Critical path (p. 317)
Financial modeling language
    (p. 318)

F O R   D I S C U S S I O N

1. How do computer graphics help business professionals solve problems and make decisions?

2. The First Regional Bank has been suffering from a deterioration in customer service for several years. Recently the bank noticed that its service has fallen so low that the bank was losing customers to its competitors. To reverse this process, the senior vice-president of marketing appointed a group to look into the problem and recommend a solution.

    The group identified one hundred quality performance indicators. One, for example, is the average time it takes to process a customer through a teller transaction. Another is the average length of the line waiting for teller service. A third is the length of time it takes to respond to a customer request for the transfer of funds over the bank's telecommunications network.

    They recommended that the data for each of these indicators be collected by the data processing department.

    Do you think this might be an application for computer graphics? If so, provide several examples of how a graph might be used. Do you think this would help identify trouble spots? Would this improve the bank's ability to spot trends before they become serious problems? Who should receive these graphs? One suggestion by a committee member is to send a representative sample of charts to its customers with their monthly statements. Do you think this would help the bank convince customers that something is being done about the problem?

3. Sammy's, a fast-food chain with over one hundred outlets, recently developed a computer system in which computers located in each of the restaurants send summary sales statistics over the telephone network to the central computer every night. These data are examined individually to determine the performance of each restaurant, and then they are grouped into the regional sales territories, so that the marketing department can follow the impact of regional advertising campaigns. Would graphics help communicate this information? If so, defend your position by drawing an example of how a graph might look.

4. Explain why it might be useful to use an expert system in medical diagnosis. Do you think such a system could replace the physician altogether? Why or why not?

5. Do you think an expert system could be used in the college admission process?

H A N D S - O N P R O J E C T S

1. Find an article in a computer or business magazine that focuses on the use of graphics in a business application. Summarize the article. How are the graphs used? Are they used to support operational planning and control, management planning and control, or strategic planning decisions?
Suggestions: PC, Computerworld, Business Week, Business Computer Systems.

2. Find an advertisement for a graphics package, and summarize its features.
Suggestions: PC Week, PC.

3. Ask an instructor in another course if he or she would consider using an expert system for grading. Be careful to explain how an expert system works and that it can accommodate ambiguity in the decision process. Summarize the instructor's response in a paragraph. What are his or her main objections? How would you respond if you wanted to convince the instructor that such a system could be helpful?

4. If you have access to graphics software, create a pie chart that shows the following distribution of expenses incurred by a company:

Cost of goods sold	25%
Wages	17%
Administrative	18%
Selling expenses	14%
Taxes	15%
Profit	11%

5.   If you have access to graphics software, create a line chart that shows the closing price of the Dow Jones Industrial Average over the last ten days.

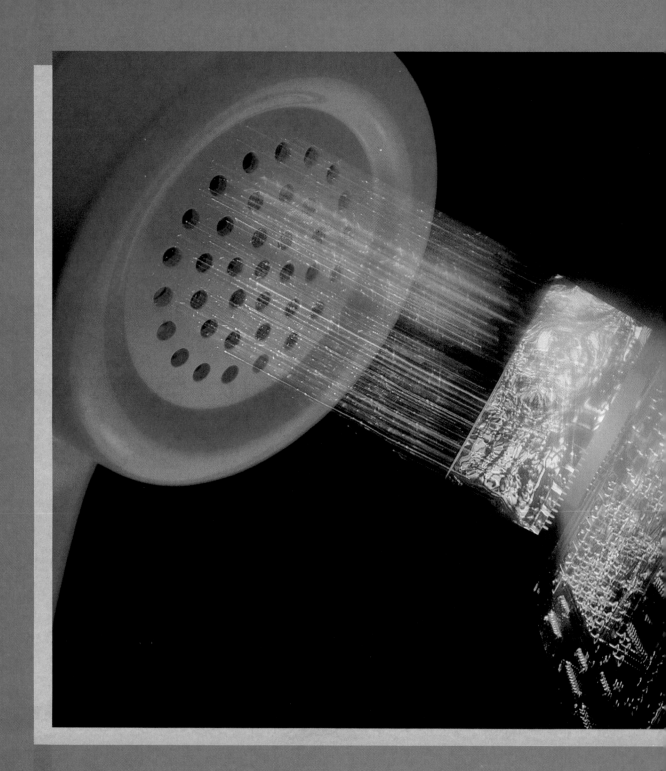

PART · FOUR

DESIGNING
INFORMATION
SYSTEMS

12
SYSTEMS ANALYSIS

O B J E C T I V E S

After studying this chapter you should understand the following:

■   *Who should be involved in systems development.*

■   *What a system is, and why it is advantageous to take a systems point of view.*

■   *Which phases comprise the systems development cycle.*

■   *The steps taken during a preliminary study.*

■   *The steps taken during detailed analysis.*

Figure 12-1.
The design and development of a successful computer information system requires careful planning.

In previous chapters you learned how computer information systems work and how they are used in both transaction processing and decision-making environments. Now, in this and the next chapter, we will examine the steps that are followed in the development of these systems, especially large systems.

This chapter will describe systems analysis. You will learn how preliminary studies of a proposed system are undertaken—whose purpose is to determine whether the system has any merit. Then you will see how a detailed analysis is performed—whose objective is to specify the system's requirements (Figure 12-1). In Chapter 13, the focus will shift to the design process and to the way in which the requirements for the new system are converted into working programs.

THE PEOPLE BEHIND THE SYSTEMS

Although it is usually clear who will use a computer information system, it may be less clear who should develop the system. Should it be left entirely to the professional data processing personnel, or should end-users, business professionals, and managers also be involved?

The success of every information system depends more on how it meets the needs of the job to be done than on how it takes advantage of the latest in hardware or software technology. And who knows more about the job to be done than those who will use the system? It therefore seems reasonable that any development effort should be oriented toward satisfying the needs and securing the approval of this group (Figure 12-2).

Often, however, users fail to become involved because data processing professionals may not be willing to listen to them, because users

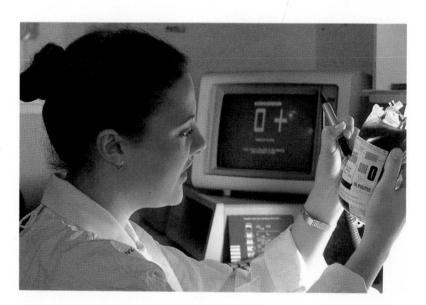

Figure 12-2.
The involvement of end-users in the development of a system is a must for success.

are not given the opportunity to spend time on the project, or because they resist the introduction of a new system altogether.

But users must become involved in system development, from the beginning through to the implementation of the new system, in order to ensure that the system created meets their needs.

To be effective participants in the system development process, users must be familiar with the concepts and techniques presented in this and the next chapter. In other words, end-users must know enough to be partners, not just bystanders, in the system development process.

The type of involvement varies. When large transaction processing or operational planning and control systems are developed, users are sometimes part of the development team or may be consulted intermittently to verify that development is on course. In some organizations a user heads the design team! And with a stand-alone, single-user microcomputer application, the user may well assume complete responsibility for the development of the application. Whatever the case, however, users—for their own protection—must be involved.

The development of large systems also requires the involvement of general management. Management must help plan the project, organize the resources—staff, equipment, and funds—that will be needed, and exercise general control over the project so that it achieves its objectives.

SYSTEMS

WHAT IS A SYSTEM?

A **system** can be defined as a collection of interrelated elements and procedures that interact to accomplish a goal. Computer information systems are a type of system with which, by this point in the book, we are very familiar. Computer information systems are a collection of interrelated hardware and software that responds to input from the environment, processes the input to meet certain objectives, and produces output that acts on the environment (Figure 12-3).

Using this definition as a guide, we can describe, for example, an on-line inventory system as a system in which an interrelated collection of hardware and software responds to such input as stock withdrawal and replenishment data, processes the data, and produces output such as stock balances and inventory status reports (Figure 12-4).

A SYSTEMS POINT OF VIEW

A special meaning is suggested in saying that a systems view of a problem is taken. A **systems point of view** implies that a problem is viewed from its widest practical consequences. What this means is that the designers are explicitly aware of the linkages between the particular system under study and other systems in the organization (Figure 12-5).

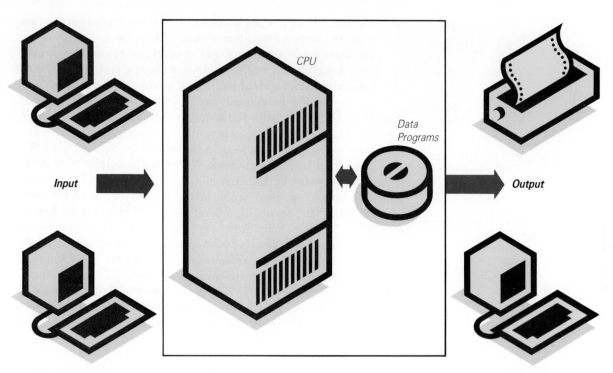

Figure 12-3.
Conceptual view of an information
system.

The following is an example of one company that did not take a systems point of view.

■■■■■■■■■■■■■■■■■■■■■■■■■■■■■■■■■

CASWELL COMPANY, a large manufacturer of parts for aircraft engines, maintains seven manufacturing facilities in North Carolina, Georgia, and Florida. Each site has its own computer information system. Personnel files, like most of the files in the system, cannot be shared among locations.

When there was a critical labor shortage in two of the locations, the personnel managers at these sites were not aware that people with the skills needed could have been obtained from the other plants. If a systems point of view had been taken when developing the employee information system, the need to provide some interface among the infor-

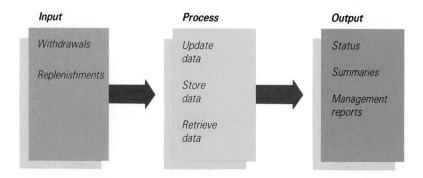

Figure 12-4.
Inventory application viewed as a
system.

Figure 12-5.
A systems point of view requires that linkages among the system under study and other systems within an organization must be considered.

mation systems in each of the plants would have become apparent. But instead the problem was solved piecemeal, each plant with its own independent system. Other systems in the plant also suggested the piecemeal approach. One visitor recently said that the entire data processing system consisted of "islands of automation all unrelated to each other."

■■■■■■■■■■■■■■■■■■■■■■■■■■■■■■■■■■■■■■

Why do companies like Caswell take a piecemeal rather than a systems approach? Many complain that a systems approach takes too long. Some find that technology may not be available to take a full systems view, that functional organization along division or profit-center lines interferes with a systems view, or that the staff or funds are lacking to implement such a strategy.

Nonetheless, those involved in a development project must at least consider the systemwide consequences of their efforts. And when it is feasible, systems must be designed to incorporate these linkages. In short, a systems view is a goal of system development, even though it may not be practical to link all of an organization's systems into a comprehensive information network.

THE SYSTEMS DEVELOPMENT CYCLE

UNDERSTANDING COMPLEX INFORMATION SYSTEMS

If you were to tour a computer facility (Figure 12-6) and listen to a description of its information system, the experience would probably

Figure 12-6.
Complex information systems can be understood only after careful study.

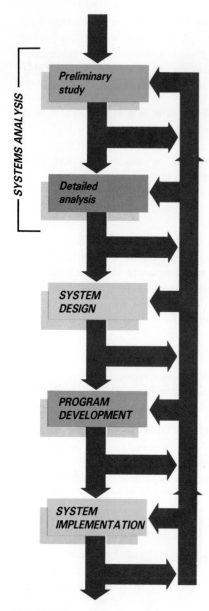

Figure 12-7.
The system development cycle.

leave you somewhat confused or even overwhelmed. How, you might think, could anyone have designed such a complex system?

The truth is that no system is developed overnight, and no individual alone can put together a large system. Rather, complex systems are developed by teams working for months or even years. And during this time, the development process is broken down into manageable segments: One problem is solved at a time, and each step in this process is related to other steps. Together, the steps make up the **systems development cycle** or **systems development process.**

THREE PHASES IN THE SYSTEM DEVELOPMENT CYCLE

Although the system development cycle for any two projects will never be exactly the same, the main characteristics are shared (Figure 12-7). Every project, for example, will pass through three major phases:

- Systems analysis
- Systems design
- Program development and system implementation

Systems analysis has two stages: a preliminary study and a detailed analysis. A preliminary study is usually a very broad-based study with little attention to detail. It determines whether the project is feasible and whether it warrants further consideration.

The second stage of systems analysis is a detailed analysis of the proposed system, including user requirements. Sometimes this stage is called requirements planning. In this stage, data are collected, and end-users are interviewed. Then the data are analyzed and alternative solutions explored. Finally, a report summarizing these findings is submitted for the approval of top management.

In systems design, attention turns to the details of the design problem. Output documents are designed, input methods are selected, processing methods are established, data storage strategies are chosen, and hardware and software decisions are finalized.

In the program development process, the specifications defined in the design phase are converted into working programs. Then the programs are tested, users are trained, and finally the system is placed into operation.

Although in theory the development process begins with systems analysis and moves steadily toward programming and implementation, the sequence of steps and the emphasis on each may vary widely. In fact, most projects do not proceed linearly from the first step in the development process to the last. Often the project returns to earlier stages when problems occur. Systems development, then, is not a strictly linear process.

In the remainder of this chapter, we will focus on the two phases of systems analysis, the preliminary study and detailed analysis. In Chapter 13, we will move through the remainder of the cycle.

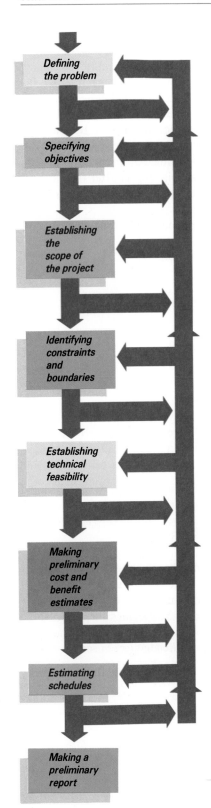

Figure 12-8.
The preliminary study.

PRELIMINARY STUDY

The first phase in the system development process is a **preliminary study** to determine the feasibility of the system (Figure 12-8). In this phase, the following steps are taken:

- Defining the problem

- Specifying objectives

- Establishing the scope of the project

- Identifying constraints and boundaries

- Establishing technical feasibility

- Making preliminary cost and benefit estimates

- Estimating schedules

- Writing a preliminary report

We will now look at each of these eight steps in turn.

DEFINING THE PROBLEM

Every request to develop a system represents a problem that someone feels must be solved. In this first step of the system development process, the objective is to define that problem as simply and clearly as possible.

■■■■■■■■■■■■■■■■■■■■■■■■■■■■■■■■■■

RICK SOMERSWORTH OWNS A CHAIN OF SIX CAMERA STORES LOCATED WITHIN A 30-MILE RADIUS OF SAN DIEGO. Each store is basically independent of the others and is responsible for maintaining its own inventory records. Although Somersworth finds this to be a reasonably good system, he is often frustrated by its shortcomings. He defines his problem as not having the up-to-date information to centralize the purchasing function, maintain tight control over inventories, and move inventory from one store that may have too many of an item to another that has too few.

■■■■■■■■■■■■■■■■■■■■■■■■■■■■■■■■■■

Somersworth's description of the problem clearly suggests a problem. Like any good definition, this one identifies what the problem is and sets the stage for the next step, specifying the objectives of the project.

SPECIFYING OBJECTIVES

Whereas the definition of a problem emphasizes "what is," the objectives of a project emphasize "what should be." But objectives are often stated vaguely. Some will say the objective is to reduce costs; others will say it is to improve performance; and still others will say it is to make better decisions. Yes, these objectives are certainly legitimate, but many of them need to be carried a step further and made more tangible by being expressed in quantitative terms, so that they can be measured.

For example, perhaps "better customer service" could be defined as a two-day reduction in average order-processing time. "Better marketing decisions" may be defined as a 2-percent increase in market share. "Better financial control" could be defined as a reduction by two weeks in the time it takes to obtain a financial report after the close of the quarter. Even if these estimates are rough, they will encourage a more thoughtful evaluation of the proposed system.

In general, objectives usually fall into one of the following categories:

- Higher revenues

- Reduced costs

- Better control

- Competitive advantage

- More efficient operations

- Faster decisions

- Better decisions

Most projects, however, have several objectives. A microcomputer investment system that monitors securities and identifies trading opportunities may have as its objectives a reduction in monitoring costs, an improvement in control over investment decisions, and a promise of both better and faster decisions.

ESTABLISHING THE SCOPE OF THE PROJECT

Once the problem has been defined and the objectives specified, the scope of the proposed system must be established. The **scope** is the range or ambition of the project and is affected by many factors:

- The information needed.

- The way that the proposed system is intended to be used.

- Changes that this system will impose on current methods and procedures.

- Technology available to build the system.

- Equipment that will be used.

- Size of the budget that can be allocated to the project.

- Willingness of people to change the way they work.

The scope, then, builds on the objectives of the new system and establishes the extent of the impact it will have on the organization. Little detail is needed at this stage. The emphasis is on general issues, not specific ones.

The scope can vary widely among applications (Figure 12-9). For example, the scope of an inventory system that will improve inventory control for one store is much narrower than is a system that will improve control for ten stores. The scope of a sales information system that will depend on weekly telephone calls from the sales force is different from a system in which every salesperson will enter daily sales data into a microcomputer and then transmit them automatically to the corporate mainframe. The danger at this stage is not that the scope of the project will be too narrow but, as the next case shows, that it will be too wide.

■ ■

J&J TRANSPORTATION, a common carrier located in southern New Jersey, was ready to buy its first computer, and Joe O'Brien was explaining what he wants to a sales representative from Garden State Computers. "Frank, we really need the computer to help us dispatch our trucks. Right now they go out of here half full, and sometimes they make the return trip empty. If the computer could assign loads to trucks so that they would be full most of the time and if it could keep track of our jobs so that another load would be waiting nearby when one load was delivered, then I would sign the sales agreement right now."

"Joe, I've got a commercial dispatching software package that you could use, but it would be dishonest of me to sell it to you."

"Why?" O'Brien asked impatiently.

"There is little or no computer experience at J&J. And you don't have a computerized accounting or billing system, which I consider the basic building block of a more sophisticated dispatching system. In my opinion you'd be in over your head."

Figure 12-9.
The scope of a multiuser system is usually much broader than is a single stand-alone microcomputer system.

"What do you mean?"

"The dispatching system will require you to use data that you probably don't use now; it will change the methods and procedures that your people follow; the software will be expensive; and we don't even know whether your dispatchers will be willing to use the new system."

"Joe, why don't you start with the general ledger accounting system? It's not as glamorous as a dispatching system, but it's a system you could handle. And once that system is up and running we could think about the next step, a computerized billing system. Let's not be too ambitious. How about one step at a time?"

■■■■■■■■■■■■■■■■■■■■■■■■■■■■■■■■■■■

IDENTIFYING CONSTRAINTS AND BOUNDARIES

Constraints   No development process can ignore the constraints on the choices that can be made. **Constraints** come in many varieties. Some are legal or governmental. Banks, for example, must keep depositor records on file for several years, and interest income must be reported to the IRS on a 1099 Form with a copy to the depositor. Regulated industries such as public utilities must use accounting methods approved by state or federal agencies.

There are also equipment constraints. The choice of additional hardware and software to expand an existing system, for example, may be limited to only those alternatives that are compatible with the old system.

Cost constraints are nearly always a factor. A system that solves the problem but is too costly may be no solution at all. Still other constraints, including time, staffing, and facilities, may restrict the freedom with which the development process can proceed.

Boundaries

The **system boundary** is the point at which one system interfaces with another. Most computer information systems in an organization, as shown in Figure 12-10, have many boundaries. Sometimes these boundaries are crossed. One distributor, for example, uses a system in which a withdrawal is entered into the inventory system, and as a direct result of this entry, another is automatically made into the accounts receivable system. But at another company, there is no such automatic entry; output documents from the inventory system are sent to the accounting department, where they are manually entered into the accounts receivable system.

Usually at this stage in the development process it is too early to determine whether boundaries should be crossed. What is important, however, is that they at least be identified.

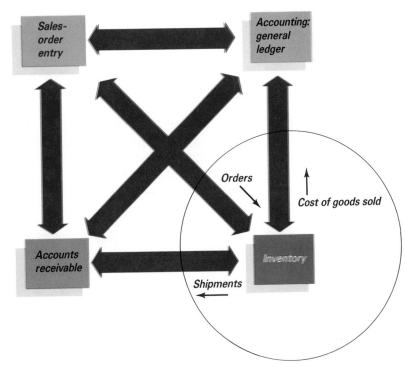

Figure 12-10.
The boundaries in an inventory system. In the development of any system, first its boundaries must be identified, and then the way in which these boundaries will influence the design of the new system must be settled.

ESTABLISHING TECHNICAL FEASIBILITY

Not every system that is requested can be delivered. Sometimes the application is simply technically infeasible.

■■■■■■■■■■■■■■■■■■■■■■■■■■■■■■■■■■■■

THE PERSONNEL GROUP AT THE SAFEWAY INSURANCE COMPANY WANTS TO ACCESS DATA STORED ON THE CORPORATE MAINFRAME, download them to their microcomputer, load them into a spreadsheet, and analyze them during its annual salary review period. The problem, however, is not that the data are unavailable; the mainframe stores volumes of personnel data. The problem is that the existing software cannot collect the data from the mainframe, summarize them, and then transfer them to the micro spreadsheet. This project will have to wait until the central data processing group can find software to link these two systems together.

■■■■■■■■■■■■■■■■■■■■■■■■■■■■■■■■■■■■

How does an organization determine whether the systems it proposes are feasible? One method is to consult with the design professionals that most computer manufacturers have on their staff. But there is still a risk of special interest on the part of the professionals. Whether knowledgeable people can be found within or outside the organization or whether research must be conducted by nonexperts, the time to find out that something will or will not work is now, before building the system (Figure 12-11).

MAKING PRELIMINARY COST AND BENEFIT ESTIMATES

At this stage in the development process, it should be possible to estimate the value of the benefits expected from the system and the costs necessary to bring the system into full operation. Often this can be a difficult task, because many benefits and even some costs can be hard to estimate.

Benefits can be tangible or intangible. **Tangible benefits** are those that can be measured, such as more revenue, lower manufacturing costs, reduced receivables, and higher interest income. **Intangible benefits** are the ones that are the most difficult to measure, such as better decisions, faster customer service, and more control.

The range of costs incurred by a system can be very wide. A partial list includes the costs of development, equipment, software, training, personnel, maintenance, and supplies. At this stage only rough estimates are needed.

After the benefits and costs are estimated, they are compared. If the benefits exceed the costs, then the system may show enough promise to be considered for a detailed analysis.

Figure 12-11.
Before deciding to connect computers in a network, the feasibility of the proposed application must be determined.

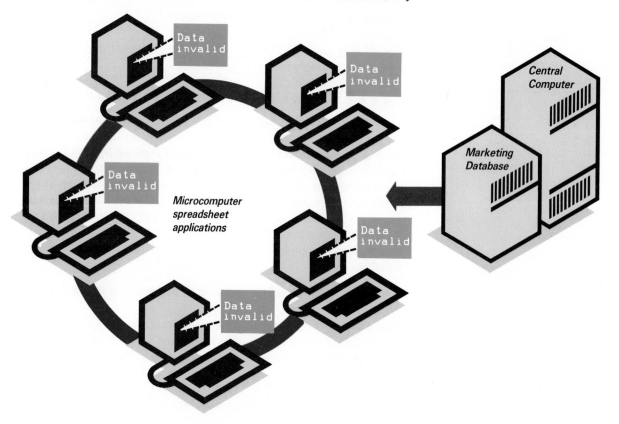

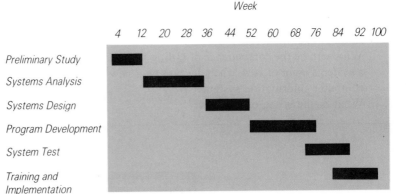

Figure 12-12.
A Gantt chart can be used to schedule the events in a project. Notice that some stages can begin before others are finished (training, for example, can begin before testing is completed).

ESTIMATING SCHEDULES

Before a preliminary report is prepared, a tentative schedule should be established. Gantt charts are often handy for this purpose (Figure 12-12). Gantt charts were described in the "Project Management Software" section of Chapter 11.

PRELIMINARY REPORT

At the conclusion of this preliminary study phase, the findings are often summarized in a written report. It should define the problem, specify the objectives, establish the scope of the project, identify the constraints and boundaries, establish technical feasibility, estimate benefits and costs, and include a tentative schedule. The very act of writing this report will often clarify issues and increase understanding.

Who should get the report? At least general management and some if not all of the users of the system.

Although the users' response to the report is important, general management plays the critical role at this point in the development process. Their responsibility is to review the report and then reach one of several possible conclusions: Continue with the next phase, return the report for additional data, postpone the project, or abandon it altogether.

?   Q U E S T I O N S   ?

---

1. Why is the topic of system development important to the business professionals?

2. How would you define a system? Is a university a system? Explain.

3. Define the three major phases in the system development cycle.

4. What is the purpose of the preliminary study?

5. Does the system development cycle ever return to a previous step, or does it proceed linearly through each phase?
6. What can be the consequence of failing to take a systems point of view when developing a new computer information system?
7. What is the scope of a project?

8. A manufacturing information system has been approved because it will reduce costs and improve deliveries. How can these vague objectives be expressed more tangibly?
9. What is management's role in systems analysis?

DETAILED ANALYSIS

The purpose of **detailed analysis,** the second stage of systems analysis, is to identify user requirements and to begin establishing the methods and procedures for the new system (Figure 12-13). A detailed analysis usually involves the following steps:

- Selecting a team
- Collecting facts
- Analyzing the facts
- Studying alternative solutions
- Making a preliminary choice

We will look at each of these steps.

SELECTING A TEAM

As we learned earlier in the chapter, no large project is undertaken by only one person. It would take too long, and the risk would be too high. In most situations, a team approach is used, and the people chosen for this team will depend on the nature and magnitude of the project.

The project team, especially for large projects, will include such information-processing professionals as systems analysts, system designers, and programmers. The **systems analyst** analyzes the current system—whether it is manual or computer based—and prepares a management report. The **systems designer** specifies the plans of the new system, and the **programmers** write the programs. In some companies, systems analysts are responsible for both the analysis and the design. In other

Figure 12-13.
Detailed systems analysis.

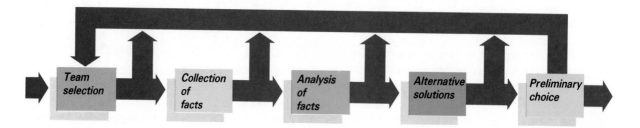

Figure 12-14.
Most large systems are designed by teams with representation from both the professional ranks of data processing and the end-users.

companies, a "programmer/analyst" might be responsible for all three functions.

As we also discussed earlier, users must be involved during the development of an application, and they are often included as members of the team (Figure 12-14). In the development of an inventory system at one company, for example, the inventory manager, two supervisors, and one inventory clerk were on the team. But not all members need be full time. Large groups can, after all, slow the pace of progress. Instead, some members can be assigned to a steering committee, which might attend only major review sessions. This would ensure wide participation and at the same time use these human resources economically.

When is the team selected? At the very latest it must be selected at the beginning of this stage. But in some projects it may be chosen at the beginning of the preliminary analysis stage. The timing depends, of course, on the project's nature, size, and consequences.

COLLECTING FACTS

If a completely new system is to be developed where none existed before, then it will be important to learn how the new system is expected to perform. But if an information system already exists (computer or manual) and the new one is being designed as an improvement, it will be important to understand the expectations for the new system and also to learn how the old one performs. In both situations, it will be necessary to collect some facts.

The Types of Facts Needed The facts describing a new or improved system can usually be grouped into five categories: output, input, processing, storage, and management.

Output facts describe the output that users see when a system is operating. Output facts are collected first, for several reasons. First, the system development process must maintain its focus on user requirements. Users will eventually rely on the output to initiate a transaction, solve a problem, or make a decision. The output, then, is the point at which the user interfaces with the system; that is, the system delivers what the user needs. Consequently, output is a critical element in the system. Second, to those who are designing the system, the output identifies what the system is or should be doing. This knowledge prepares the way for understanding the roles of the input, processing, and storage functions in the application.

The output facts that need to be collected include the identification of the end-user population, the data or information users obtain from the existing system, the data or information needed from the new system, the way the data are currently presented, the way they might be presented, how the information is actually used, how it is intended to be used, how often it is needed, and how up-to-date it must be.

Once the system's output has been studied, then attention can turn to the input required to produce the output. During this process, several questions must be asked. What data items does the system require? Where is the source of the data? How can the user collect or obtain the data? How can the data be entered? How can they be checked? How can exceptions be handled? What volume can be expected? Will this flow of data have peaks and valleys, or will it be steady?

Next, attention turns to the facts that describe the processing demands on the system. Detailed steps in the processing sequence will be considered later during system design, but at this point they should be described simply and briefly. For example, if a new inventory system is being designed, it should be pointed out that the application must be capable of maintaining an up-to-date inventory database by processing withdrawals and replenishments. In addition, it should be capable of processing inquiries about the balance of particular items.

The facts that will eventually be used to choose a storage and retrieval strategy must be collected: How are data currently stored; what is the level of file volatility and file activity; and how are data accessed?

Finally, facts are collected to help the designers understand the management context within which the new system will exist. These facts may help answer such questions as How is the organization structured? Will support come from the top? What incentive will users have to cooperate with the development and use of the new system? Will end-users resist the new system even if it has top management support? What skills will the system's users need? Will more highly skilled people be needed? What implications will this have for training activities?

Methods of Obtaining Facts   Several sources can be used to obtain the necessary facts, including

- Written documentation

- System input/output screens and reports

- Questionnaires

- Interviews

- Observation

When a system—either computer-based or manual—already exists and the new one is intended as an improvement, **documentation** may exist that can prove to be a valuable source of data (Figure 12-15). Sometimes, however, the documentation may be nearly impossible to understand or may be out-of-date. And at other times, there may be so much documentation that it may be difficult to know where to begin. If this is the case, then it will be important to narrow the material to only those sources that take a functional, not technical view of the system.

The system's input and output screens and reports can also prove to be an excellent source of facts. The input screen shown in Figure 12-16, for example, tells us that this purchasing information system collects data on a vendor's name, address, product line, contact person, and delivery performance. The output screen, illustrated in Figure 12-17, shows us that the system will generate a report that ranks all vendors by their delivery performance. From these screens, a picture of the system and how it is used begins to build.

Figure 12-15.
Sometimes there is a lot to be learned about a system by studying its existing documentation.

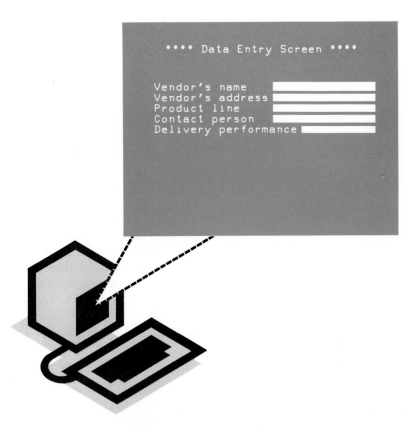

Figure 12-16.
Input screens help the systems analyst understand how a system works.

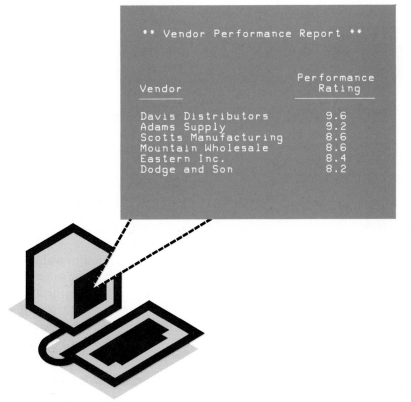

Figure 12-17.
Output screens help the systems analyst find out what types of output a system produces.

The **questionnaire** is a good vehicle for collecting facts when existing systems are improved or when new ones are designed. A wide spectrum of users can be given the opportunity to express their views of and insights into the system. If the potential users are dispersed across a broad geographic area, this may be the only way to obtain their involvement.

Closely related to the questionnaire is the **interview,** which also involves the users but has the advantage that particularly knowledgeable individuals can be given the opportunity to express their views in an open-ended format. In addition, interviews give the design team an opportunity to develop a good rapport with those who will eventually use the system.

If at all possible, it is useful to observe the performance of those activities the new system is to automate. One strategy is to follow several different transactions through every step of the process. This would be especially meaningful after the facts mentioned earlier have been collected. Then it can be determined whether the system really works the way people think it works. Usually there are a lot of surprises!

ANALYZING THE FACTS

Once the facts have been collected, they must be analyzed. An effective tool often used at this stage to organize many of the facts is the **system flowchart,** a diagram that depicts the flow of information from the input to the output stages of a system. These flowcharts are used to represent both existing computer information systems to be updated and new systems to be developed for the first time.

The symbols used to draw a system flowchart are shown in Figure 12-18. These are the symbols approved by the American National Standards Institute (ANSI) and used in nearly every professional flowchart.

The system flowchart shown in Figure 12-19 illustrates some of the steps included in a sales-order entry system. Order data are entered into the system and verified by comparing the part numbers with the numbers stored in the inventory file. Customer data are then compared with information stored in the customer file. In the next step, the customer's credit is checked. If credit is approved, the order data will be stored in the order file. The bottom of the flowchart shows that the system can generate reports and prepare the paperwork necessary to initiate the shipping process. In addition, users can obtain order-status reports on a screen.

It is important to realize at this stage that not every person will draw a flowchart in the same way. Flowcharting is not a science. Some people may include more detail, others less. But regardless of the level of detail, the system's input, processing, storage, and output stages must be shown, and in the proper logical sequence.

In addition to describing systems, a system flowchart may help identify such problems as

■ The duplication of tasks

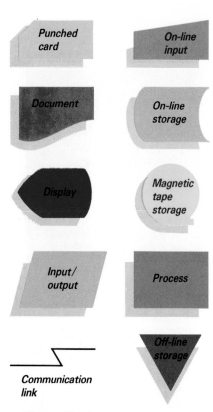

Punched card

On-line input

Document

On-line storage

Display

Magnetic tape storage

Input/ output

Process

Off-line storage

Communication link

Figure 12-18.
These symbols are used to develop system flowcharts.

■ Inconsistencies in work flow

■ Tasks that are not done

■ Delays

■ Information that is not saved

■ Insufficient verification of data

■ Unauthorized use of data

■ Lack of controls

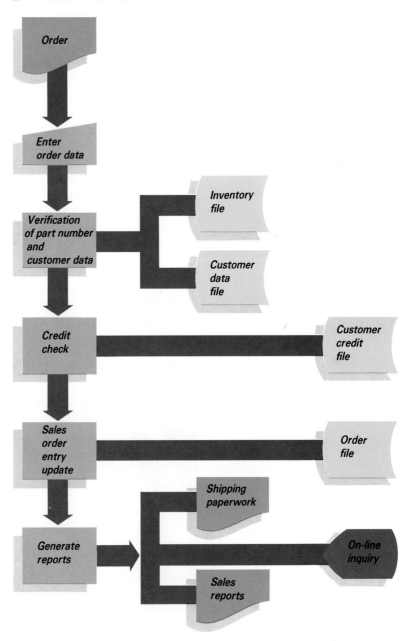

Figure 12-19.
A sales-order entry system flowchart.

As you can see, the system flowchart can be a valuable aid in the analysis of a system and in the search for better ways to meet the needs of its users.

STUDYING ALTERNATIVE SOLUTIONS

After the facts have been collected and analyzed, the development of the system can then take one of three directions. The direction will depend on whether (1) an off-the-shelf system, (2) an altered off-the-shelf system, or (3) a custom-tailored system is chosen. And this choice will have a significant impact on the remaining stages of the development process.

Off-the-Shelf Systems **Off-the-shelf systems** are a type of software developed by a commercial software vendor to be used almost exactly as it was written. The user can make few, if any, modifications in these systems. Most off-the-shelf systems are used in transaction-processing environments by small businesses. The problem, however, is that the software may use methods and procedures that do not correspond to those that an organization might otherwise follow. Often, then, the organization must adapt its methods and procedures to those required by the software. But the advantage is that little or no in-house technical expertise is required, and the systems are inexpensive to buy and maintain.

One category, called **turnkey systems,** is so-named because the user supposedly need only "turn the key," as in starting an automobile, and the system will be ready for use. These systems include or **bundle** together the software with the hardware. Turnkey systems are usually industry specific and are often found in hardware stores, auto parts stores, dental offices, and restaurants (Figure 12-20). Few turnkey systems are used in large organizations.

Figure 12-20.
Turnkey systems like the one in this flower shop are used to process customer transactions, control inventory, and provide sales reports.

Because an off-the-shelf system comes complete with all the programs, many of the steps in the system design and program development phases are unnecessary. But a few—including system implementation, testing, training, and maintenance—are still important.

Altered Off-the-Shelf Systems   An **altered off-the-shelf system** is a commercially designed system that is more flexible than an off-the-shelf system is. These systems permit purchasers to customize certain aspects of the system to their own particular environment. The end result is a system that appears to have many tailor-made features. Rarely can any one system meet all of the purchaser's needs. But for many, a reasonably good fit is a better alternative than building a completely customized system.

Because there is little if any conventional programming required by those who purchase these systems, many of the steps in the system design and programming phases are unnecessary. As a result, this approach appeals to companies without large professional programming staffs or to those already suffering from high programming backlogs. Not only is the cost of these systems highly predictable, but most can be demonstrated by the vendor before they are bought.

■ ■

SONOMA MANUFACTURING IS SEARCHING for a new accounting system to replace the commercial off-the-shelf package it has been using for five years. But this time it wants something that will meet its own special needs. Last week, when a sales rep showed Sonoma's design team his company's accounting system, the team became very interested. The software would allow Sonoma to customize the program in such a way that several profit centers could be established, reports could be designed to give Sonoma the kind of information it needs most, and financial statements could be configured to provide several levels of detail for each of these profit centers as well as several different kinds of consolidated statements. After attending a sales presentation, Sonoma's vice-president of finance commented that it was probably unnecessary for the company to write a software system of its own, as this package could be altered to meet most of its needs.

■ ■

Custom-Tailored Systems   It is probably fair to say that most companies prefer to have their own **custom-tailored systems.** Indeed, every application is different, and every company does things its own way. As one user put it, "Why should a vendor's software team in Phoenix decide how I should run my production-scheduling system?" The impulse to do it yourself is often difficult to resist.

But the cost of tailor-made software, for both large and small applications, can be very high. And because developing one's own software is not a straightforward and predictable process, costs can escalate well beyond early estimates. In many situations, nevertheless, this may be the only option.

Once a company has decided to develop a tailor-made system, it can take one of several different approaches. In a traditional approach, programs are written in a language such as COBOL. In a newer approach, programs are written in a **fourth-generation language (4GL).** These newer languages require the designer to specify only what is needed, and then the software will determine the necessary steps to meet this need. Sound familiar? Electronic spreadsheets and database management systems can be classified as examples of 4GLs.

Using a 4GL, programming is much faster, and development costs are therefore much lower. In the next chapter, we will look more closely at this approach.

E N D · U S E R   H I N T S

IS IT TIME TO REPLACE THE COMPUTER?

The relentless pace of technology has made many computers and their software packages old before their time. Although a computer may physically last for ten or more years, it often makes economic sense to replace it earlier.

As they get old, computers suffer from an increase in maintenance costs and, even more important, an ever-greater obsolescence. While software never wears out, it too can become obsolete. When is it time to update and buy new hardware and/or software?

No hard and fast rules can be given, but the following guidelines may prove useful. Consider replacement when one or more of the following factors applies.

1. The competitive business climate requires that data now difficult to obtain and available only periodically should be made available on-line.

2. The organization can gain a competitive advantage by using the data from a new on-line system to provide better service to its customers.

3. Transaction systems currently in operation are bogged down with heavy data requirements, access times are increasing, and users are becoming impatient with the system.

4. On-line storage needs are growing and will exceed the capacity of the system in the near future.

5. The maintenance costs of the present system are increasing as the system ages. Newer systems, especially if the user is moving from a mainframe to several interconnected minicomputers, could have lower maintenance costs.

6. The current system suffers from breakdowns, which have a significant impact on the efficiency and effectiveness of daily operations. Reliability as the system ages will deteriorate even faster.

7. New software such as database management systems can reduce the costs of building, maintaining, and accessing databases.

8. New software, such as fourth-generation languages (covered in the next chapter), can drastically reduce the time it takes to develop new applications.

9. New software, with features that make it easier to use, can accommodate applications at the management planning and control and strategic planning levels.

10. Creating a decentralized computing environment, which might include several distributed minicomputers or a network of micros, is considered an improvement over older and more centralized computing environments characterized by mainframe computers.

11. New commercial software systems, such as materials requirements planning systems and "just-in-time" inventory systems, can improve the organization's operating efficiency.

MAKING A PRELIMINARY CHOICE

Now with detailed analysis almost complete, it should be possible to identify the direction which the next phase of development will take. One company found that its problems were so unique that the only solution to a sales-order entry system was to develop a custom-tailored system. But the design team was able to keep development costs low by using a 4GL. A second organization, however, decided that it needed a new custom-tailored reservation system and that the system had to be written in COBOL. A third company found that a commercial software package would be the only economical solution to the fairly straightforward system requested by its personnel department.

DETAILED COST STUDY

Before a report on this phase of the project is prepared, a detailed cost study must be undertaken. Actually, this cost study is an extension of the cost estimates made during the preliminary analysis stage. But now many of the costs will be based on more substantial data and, as a result, will be somewhat more realistic.

    The estimate should also express the way in which costs will behave over the life cycle of the project. Figure 12-21 shows that the costs for a production scheduling project will reach $50,000 at the end of systems analysis, $200,000 at the end of system design, and $450,000 when the project is finally completed. A breakdown such as this serves as the basis for better cost control over the remaining phases of the project.

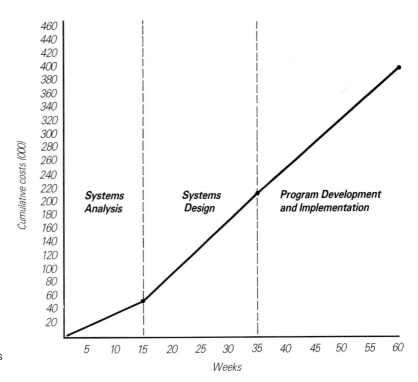

Figure 12-21.
The estimate of development costs made during detailed analysis should be more realistic than earlier estimates are.

ANALYSIS REPORT

At the conclusion of systems analysis, a report summarizing the work done up to this point is prepared. The report should include descriptions of the current system—if there is one—and a summary and analysis of the facts. Then the report should evaluate the three possible directions that future development may take and make a recommendation. In those cases in which off-the-shelf or altered off-the-shelf systems are recommended, the report may also include the vendor's promotional literature.

MANAGEMENT APPROVAL

Once again the written report is submitted to management, who must decide whether the progress made thus far deserves their approval to begin the next phase of the development process. If not, then the decision may be to return to earlier stages in the development process or to abandon the project altogether. If the go-ahead is given, the system development process will be ready to move to the systems design and program development phases, covered in the next chapter.

?   Q U E S T I O N S   ?

1. How does a detailed analysis relate to a preliminary study?
2. The marketing department of a Fortune 500 company wants to develop an information system to monitor the testing of new products in the marketplace. Who might be included on the project team?
3. What types of facts are needed to describe a system?
4. How are a system's input and output screens useful in learning how a system works?

5. What is the purpose of a system flowchart?
6. What is a turnkey system? Why would a small independent retailer find such a system an attractive choice?
7. What is the difference between an altered off-the-shelf system and a custom-tailored system?
8. Once the analysis report has been submitted at the conclusion of the systems analysis phase, what are management's choices?

S U M M A R Y

■ To develop a successful information system, it is essential that the users be involved throughout the process.

■ A **system** is a collection of interrelated elements and procedures that interact to accomplish a goal.

■ A **systems point of view** implies that a problem's widest practical consequences are taken into account.

■ The **systems development cycle,** or **systems development process,** consists of three main phases: (1) systems analysis, (2) system design, and (3) program development and system implementation.

■ **Systems analysis** has two stages: a preliminary study and a detailed analysis.

■ A **preliminary study** determines the feasibility of a system. The problem is defined, objectives specified, project scope established, constraints and boundaries identified, technical feasibility established, preliminary cost and benefit estimates made, and schedules estimated.

■ The **scope** is the range or ambition of the project.

■ A **system boundary** is a point at which one system interfaces with another.

■ Benefits of a system include **tangible benefits,** which can be measured, and **intangible benefits,** which cannot readily be measured.

■ In the **detailed analysis** phase a team is selected, facts collected, facts analyzed, alternative solutions studied, and some preliminary decisions made.

■ Team members may include a **systems analyst, systems designer, programmers,** and users.

■ In collecting facts about an existing system, **documentation** can prove a valuable aid.

■ **Questionnaires** and **interviews** are good vehicles for collecting facts about existing or new systems.

■ An effective tool for analyzing collected facts is the **system flowchart.**

■ Three directions that can be chosen at this stage are off-the-shelf systems, altered off-the-shelf systems, and custom-tailored systems.

■ **Off-the-shelf systems** are developed by a commercial software vendor and permit few, if any, modifications. One category, the **turnkey system, bundles** together software and hardware.

■ **Altered off-the-shelf systems** are also developed by a commercial software vendor but permit purchasers to customize some parts of the system.

■ **Custom-tailored systems,** which offer the greatest flexibility, are developed in house, often with a great expenditure of time and money. One way to develop a custom-tailored system is with a **fourth-generation language (4GL).**

■ When the systems analysis phase is completed and management approves further work, the system development process moves ahead to systems design and program development (covered in Chapter 13).

K E Y • T E R M S

The following list shows the key terms in the order in which they appear in the chapter.

System (p. 331)
Systems point of view (p. 331)
System development cycle or
    system development process
    (p. 334)
Systems analysis (p. 334)
Preliminary study (p. 335)
Scope (p. 336)
Constraint (p. 338)
System boundary (p. 338)
Tangible benefit (p. 340)
Intangible benefit (p. 340)
Detailed analysis (p. 342)
Systems analyst (p. 342)
System designer (p. 342)

Programmer (p. 342)
Documentation (p. 344)
Questionnaire (p. 346)
Interview (p. 346)
System flowchart (p. 346)
Off-the-shelf system (p. 348)
Turnkey system (p. 348)
Bundle (p. 348)
Altered off-the-shelf system
    (p. 349)
Custom-tailored system (p. 349)
Fourth-generation language
    (4GL) (p. 350)

F O R D I S C U S S I O N

1. Discuss the pros and cons of extensive user involvement in the system development process.
2. The inventory system used by the XYZ Corporation is not performing well. The balance of the items reported by the computer hardly ever matches the balance actually on the shelves in the stockroom. The central data processing personnel blame the end-users for not entering the data correctly and for not even submitting some stock withdrawal receipts when items are removed from inventory. The inventory personnel blame central data processing for not correctly entering into the system the data reported on the stock withdrawal receipts. The production manager has even blamed program errors.

   Which of these do you think could be to blame? How would you do a systems analysis to improve the system?
3. The student union and college bookstore at the State University operate on a cash-only basis. Items must be bought with cash or

check; no credit or charges are accepted. While attending a regional conference, the director of these facilities learned of an interesting new service that a few colleges were offering their students.

These schools were issuing a combination identification and credit card. With remote terminals located in the student union and bookstore, students could charge any purchase from a late-night snack to textbooks. The system bills the students monthly and extends credit to those who pass a simple credit test.

Upon his return to the campus, the administrator made an appointment with the director of administrative computing services at State to discuss the possibilities of this system.

■   What steps in the system development cycle should be followed to develop this system?

■   What factors would a systems view take into account?

■   Write a few sentences defining the problem.

■   Identify and discuss the objectives of this system.

■   Why might technical feasibility be an issue with this system?

■   What kind of costs and benefits would you consider in a preliminary cost and benefit analysis?

■   Do you think that the project is large enough to assemble a team, or could a single person design and implement this system? Should the end-users be involved?

■   What facts need be collected?

■   Which of the following do you think might be considered: an off-the-shelf, an altered off-the-shelf, or a custom-tailored system?

H A N D S - O N   P R O J E C T S

1.   You have just been asked by the university registrar's office to undertake a systems analysis of a project. The proposed system would replace the current system and allow students to register for courses at computer terminals across the campus. Registration would be on-line. A student would begin by entering the desired courses and sections. Next the system would refer to a central database and determine whether there was still space available in the courses and sections. If a section was filled, then the student would be notified on the screen and requested to select another

alternative. At the end of the scheduling session, which might last half an hour, the student would receive a printout confirming courses, sections, class meeting hours, and room numbers.

Describe how you would proceed through the preliminary study and detailed analysis stages. Speculate on their outcome.

2. You have been asked to develop a program that will maintain control of the food inventory in your school cafeteria. How would you begin this project? Who would be involved? State the objective. How would you determine technical feasibility? What would be the benefits and costs? What are the outputs in the system? The inputs? What processing occurs? Draw a system flowchart of the system you have in mind. What do you think would be your biggest problem?

C A S E · S T U D Y

SOX INC.

Sox Inc. is a leading manufacturer and distributor of women's hosiery. The company quickly gained market dominance several years ago when it revolutionized the way in which hosiery was packaged, distributed, and sold.

Sox's product is attractively packaged in a square plastic container. Although in the past hosiery was primarily sold in department and specialty stores, Sox began selling its product through point-of-purchase displays located in the high-traffic areas of supermarkets and drugstores. This strategy worked exceptionally well. Within a few years, it achieved a 45-percent market share of all hosiery sales.

Also contributing to Sox's success is the way that it distributes its product. Instead of relying on drugstore and supermarket clerks to place reorders with wholesalers, Sox employs a sales staff that travels to each retail location. These salespeople, assigned to one of five distribution centers across the country, drive vans that hold enough inventory to service the accounts on their route. The vans are actually warehouses on wheels. As a result, Sox also does not have to rely on the retail store clerks to keep the display stocked.

When the drivers arrive at a store, they see what stock is needed, go back to their vans, pull the items from the storage shelves, return to the store, and replenish the display. Then they fill out the paperwork, leave a copy with the store, keep one copy for themselves, and send a third copy to corporate headquarters in Atlanta using an overnight delivery service. Upon its arrival in Atlanta, the data are entered into key-to-disk machines and the central computer is updated in the batch mode. Shortly thereafter invoices are mailed to the stores.

Growth Problems

Sox has been extremely successful using these methods. Although several other competitors have tried to imitate it, few have achieved even a small market share. To ensure this market leadership position, Sox periodically introduces new products, most of them targeted to the fashion-conscious consumer. Because new products tend to be introduced into the line faster than old ones are dropped, the total number of items in the line is steadily increasing.

As this number increases, so does the problem of inventory control. With more products, a greater range of items must be carried in the vans. And as the sales of each product line also increase, the vans have to carry more of all items.

Recently the marketing department announced a new fashion line of hosiery. Production, it said, would begin within two months. The corporate distribution manager, Cassandra Williams, learned of these plans at a department heads meeting. At the meeting she was quick to point out that the vans could not possibly accommodate this increase, as they were already filled to capacity.

The Distribution Solution

Shortly after this meeting, Williams wrote a memo recommending that the corporation phase out its conventional vans (in which there was not enough room for a person to stand erect) and begin to acquire larger step vans (in which a person can stand). She explained that the new vans would have enough room to accommodate the new product line and would eliminate the crowded conditions in the conventional vans. She went on to say that this might help reverse a decline in driver productivity that had been plaguing the company over the last two years.

The Data Processing Solution

Chan Lee also learned of the new product line at the department heads meeting. Lee, manager of corporate MIS, stayed out of the discussion because he felt that this was strictly a distribution problem: If Williams got her step vans, then the problem would be solved. But later that day it suddenly occurred to Lee that Sox did not have a distribution problem at all; it had a data processing problem.

The next morning Lee asked Williams if she could wait three weeks before taking any further action. She agreed.

During this time Lee met with his senior systems analyst, the manager of inventory control, and two route drivers. After collecting many facts from them, he began to formulate a solution to the capacity problem. Bringing this group together at a meeting he began to unfold his plans.

"We already have historical sales data in our database for every product sold in every point-of-purchase display. The key to my idea is to use these data more effectively."

"Suppose," he continued, "that we generate a statistical forecast from the data. Take the Speedy Suprette location in Chattanooga as an example. The database might show that during the two-week period before the last visit, twenty-five pairs of our "sheer

brite" line were sold. In the two-week period before this restocking trip, the database might show that twenty-two pairs were sold. And in the two-week period before that trip, it might show that nineteen pairs were sold. This averages twenty-two pairs for the two-week period over the last three restocking trips. We could then use this average as the statistical forecast of the number of pairs we would have expected to sell since the most recent restocking trip."

"But I still don't see how this forecast would be used and how it would save storage space in our vans," asked Chuck Wilson, a van driver who had been with the company for six years.

"When a driver is scheduled to service a point-of-purchase display," explained Lee, "the distribution center closest to the driver's home base will produce a forecast from its database. This forecast will be used to estimate the demand since the last restocking trip. Next, the software will use this forecast to compute the quantity of each product to be included in a shrink-wrapped package. The computer will then print a picking document for the warehouse and also produce the paperwork for the driver, including an invoice to leave with the retailer. When the shipping department receives the picking document, it will pick the order, package it, and send it to the shipping dock."

"I'm beginning to understand," interrupted Gail Newsome, the senior systems analyst. "The drivers wouldn't have to keep a large stock of each product. They'd only carry prepackaged orders. And when they arrived at the retailer's location, they'd simply bring in the prepackaged order, unwrap it, stock the shelves, and give the paperwork to the store manager." Newsome paused. "But I see one major flaw in your system."

"What's that?"

"The package the driver delivers might not have the right number of items. In other words, actual sales since the last restocking trip might differ from our statistical forecast. So, the stock in the package for a particular point-of-service display might be more or less than is needed to restock the shelves."

Lee had thought about this problem, too. "The driver would actually use all of the items in the prepack. There would, of course, be times when it included too few items. Then it would not be possible to restock the shelves to the desired levels. And there would also be times when too many items would be included, and the shelves would hold more than was actually needed. But I don't think this would create a serious problem.

"What is important," Lee continued, "is that the driver complete an exception report. In this report, the driver would enter the amount by which the prepack includes too many or too few of an item. When the prepack includes the right amount, no entry will be necessary in the report. In this case, the forecast would have been perfect."

Lee then explained that each of the drivers would be issued specialized portable computers. At the end of the day, they would enter their exception reports for each point-of-purchase display and send these data through the telephone network to the district distribution center. At the distribution center, the data would automatically be entered into the database and would update the demand for the most recent period, so that when a forecast was prepared for the next delivery period, it would be computed using accurate demand data.

Although Lee was convinced that the plan was technically feasible, he was not sure of the economics; so he asked the group if they would help him prepare a developmental budget and an estimate of the savings that such a system would produce.

A week later they submitted a report showing that the system would cost approximately $4 million. This would include the computers needed by the drivers, new minicomputers at the five distribution centers, an increase in the storage capacity of the corporate mainframe, software development costs, and communications equipment needed to interface the portable computers with the minicomputers at the distribution centers.

They estimated that at a minimum, seventy-three data-entry personnel would no longer be needed to enter the data supplied by the drivers. These drivers would now enter their own exception data through portable computers in the field. In addition, the company would no longer need to spend several million dollars on new step vans. And another significant advantage would be an improvement of approximately two days in cash flow, because the retailers would now receive their bills when the order was delivered rather than waiting several days for the bill to arrive from Atlanta.

Their analysis suggested a rate of return on the investment of about 80 percent, and since most of the firm's projects produced a rate of return in the vicinity of 20 percent, they felt this project was a particularly attractive one. Furthermore, their estimates did not include the value that management would receive from access to a timely database that could be used for better control over operations, so the return would be even higher.

Lee was prepared to recommend that the project be completed in three stages. In the first stage, only the Atlanta district would be converted to the new system. If the results of this pilot study met expectations, then the second stage would be a conversion of the eastern divisions. Finally, the rest of the divisions in the country would be converted.

Questions

1. Write a short paragraph that defines Sox's problem.
2. Did Williams take a systems point of view in her solution to the problem? Did Lee? Explain.
3. How would you describe the objectives of the proposed computer system?
4. Does the project suggest a broad or a narrow scope? Explain.
5. Describe the inventory and accounting boundary in this proposed application.
6. Do you feel this system is technically feasible? Describe any concerns you might have.
7. What costs did the group consider in its preliminary estimate? What benefits did it identify? Do you think it overlooked any costs or benefits?
8. Do you think that Lee's preliminary schedule is reasonable? Would you recommend that the entire project be completed in one stage rather than three? Explain.
9. If you were to manage this project, who would you include on the team? Would you include the route driver? Why?
10. What type of facts might be collected in the detailed study of this system? How might these facts be obtained?
11. Do you think it would be necessary to develop custom-tailored software to implement this application? Explain.
12. Compare the solutions proposed by Williams and by Lee's group. Which one would you recommend? Why?

13. What should be the next step?
14. What role should general management play in this project?

15. Analyze the sequence of steps followed in the systems analysis process for this project. Where do you agree and disagree with the steps followed?

13
SYSTEMS DESIGN AND PROGRAM DEVELOPMENT

O U T L I N E

O B J E C T I V E S

After studying this chapter you should understand the following:

■   *What is meant by structured design and structured programming.*

■   *Some of the procedures followed in the design of output, input, and file-processing functions.*

■   *How complex systems are decomposed so that the system can be designed more efficiently.*

■   *The types of controls that can be built into an information system.*

■   *Structured methods used in program design.*

■   *The characteristics of the different levels of programming languages.*

■   *How systems are tested, installed, and maintained.*

The last chapter explained how to analyze a proposed system, to determine whether the system had any merit, and to identify user requirements. This chapter moves to the actual **systems design.** We will see how structured techniques can help guide this process, how controls can be designed into the system, and how programs can be tested, installed, and maintained.

OFF-THE-SHELF SYSTEMS

If an off-the-shelf system is being purchased, systems design and program development have already been performed by the vendor, and as a result the purchaser need not be concerned with these stages. Altered off-the-shelf systems, however, usually require some development and some programming (both types of software are discussed toward the end of Chapter 12). But purchasers of both types must still be responsible for the evaluation, testing, installation, and maintenance of these systems and so will benefit from an understanding of the topics in this chapter.

The in-house development of custom-tailored systems, on the other hand, requires the full-blown systems design and program development process described in this chapter. Although business professionals will seldom if ever be called upon to write programs for large systems, knowing something about design principles and programming languages will prepare them to be more informed partners with data processing professionals.

Then too, many of today's end-users do find themselves developing their own small-scale applications using spreadsheet, database, and graphics software, not as partners but as sole participants. When this is the case, every bit of knowledge will help.

STRUCTURED DESIGN

In the past it was not unusual for the development of a system to be a very personal and informal process. No two designers would approach a project in the same way. There were no standards of design, no guidelines. Each system was handled differently. And as a result, some were ill conceived, poorly executed, and difficult if not impossible to maintain. Indeed almost every large company—whose systems were developed in this way—can point to at least one example of a project that ran into trouble. A few can point to projects that were never used; projects that wasted tens of thousands of dollars.

Today, it is safe to say that the cost of developing a sizable application is so high that a more formal process of design must be used. The most prevalent formal approach is called **structured design** and uses some or all of the following guidelines, tools, and techniques:

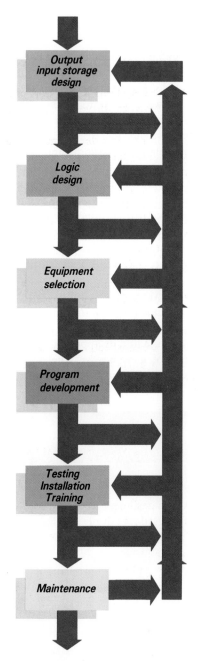

- **Top-down design,** in which the development process begins with the most general view of the application and progressively moves toward a more detailed view.

- Design of the output first and then design of the input and storage functions later.

- Tools such as structure charts to organize the design process.

- Division of the system into manageable segments called **modules.**

- Software such as database management systems.

- Data dictionaries to control the use of data items.

- Checks and balances on the design process through frequent reports, end-user involvement, structured walkthroughs, and management approvals.

Do all projects follow a structured approach today? Unfortunately, no. Some designers would rather leap to the last step in the processes and begin writing programs, even with little or no input from those who will use the application. To them the program is the system. Other designers support structured methods, but under the time pressure of project deadlines they too abandon the guidelines and principles of structured design, in order to meet these deadlines.

When structured design is used, the benefits usually overwhelmingly outweigh its drawbacks. The types of benefits an organization can expect are

- Higher level of involvement with end-users and general management during the development of the application.

- Prevention of a premature focus on the details of the project.

- Greater likelihood that the system will prove to be useful and effective.

- Reduction in errors during the design and programming stages.

- Lower life-cycle cost, as a carefully designed system is easier to build, modify, and maintain.

In the complex and rapidly changing world of computer information systems, structured design makes a great deal of sense.

OUTPUT, INPUT, AND STORAGE DESIGN

As you probably recall from the last chapter, the logical place to begin a detailed study of system requirements is with the output. Correspondingly, the output is also the logical place to begin the detailed design of a system. Then after the output has been designed, attention can turn to input and storage design. We will look at these steps in the following sections (Figure 13-1).

Figure 13-1.
The system design process.

OUTPUT DESIGN

If there is one cardinal principle of systems design, it is that output design must follow user requirements. So before output design can begin, the designers must be sure that end-user requirements are tied down; it must be clear to them what the users need to get the job done.

But if the individuals involved in the systems analysis phase follow the guidelines described in the last chapter; if they carefully define the objectives, scope, constraints, and boundaries of the system; if they collect and analyze the appropriate facts; and if management has approved this phase of the project; then it is reasonable to assume that the design team has a firm grip on these users' requirements.

Output design begins with output documents. The design team prepares samples of what the user will see when the system is in operation. So sample screens and reports are designed that represent the proposed output of the sytem, in enough detail so that those reviewing these documents will understand what it is the system will be doing and how it can be used (Figure 13-2).

Once prepared, the samples are shown to end-users, who should then be encouraged to examine them carefully. This gives them a chance to test the system early in its development and to determine how well the system meets their needs. If it does not, then now is the time for them to recommend changes, not later when the system is top heavy in developmental costs and any changes will be orders of magnitude more costly to make.

Management too must be involved. Management must approve the screens and reports. and in most large-scale projects, they must submit written approval for work to proceed beyond this point.

It should now be clear that output design and its approval by both users and management are requirements of good design. The importance of this point cannot be overemphasized! Output drives the design

Figure 13-2.
The output from an automatic teller machine must be carefully designed to lead the user through the steps necessary to complete a transaction.

of the rest of the system. As the next case illustrates, if the end-users and general management are not involved at this point, the finished product can miss the mark.

■ ■

WHEN THE DESIGN TEAM AT CAVANAUGH COMPANY, a large auto parts manufacturer, developed a production-scheduling system, they assumed that its users would find it helpful to have a printout that showed the whereabouts of every job in the system. This assumption was made without showing the users or management a sample of the report or consulting with them about how it might be used. When the system was up and running, few users took the time to look through the more than two hundred pages of computer output that was placed on their desk every week. It was relegated to a corner of the office and, after a decent interval, dumped out.

■ ■

INPUT DESIGN

The way that output drives the design of a system should become clearer as we now turn to the input design stage. Here we will determine exactly what data must be entered into the system to produce the output specified during the output design stage. For example, if a criminal records system must produce a report summarizing the length of jail sentences for all persons convicted of crimes in a given category, then the length of each sentence must be entered into the system as input after sentencing.

Even when an existing computer information system is modified, output drives input. The following example illustrates how inputs had to change once a change in the output format was required.

■ ■

WHEN COMMUNITY CABLEVISION, a regional cablevision company serving one million subscribers, decided to change the compensation of its sales staff from salary to commission, it had to revise its sales-reporting system. The current system simply kept an aggregate total of each salesperson's sales. Because commissions would now be based on the actual sales made in each of three product categories—each one with a different commission rate—Community Cablevision needed a system that would collect this detail for each sale and produce a monthly report (Figure 13-3) that would show these totals as well as compute and print the commission due.

■ ■

Once the design team ties down the input needed by the system, then sample screens can be prepared. They will include descriptions of

	Products	Sales	Total
Baxter	Basic	2,100	
	HBO	700	
	Cinemax	300	3,100
Demarco	Basic	2,700	
	HBO	940	
	Cinemax	200	3,840
Coombs	Basic	1,400	

Figure 13-3.
The design of a system begins with its output documents. Then input requirements are determined. Here the sales report suggests that the sales data for each of three product categories must be collected so that these data can be provided as output.

Figure 13-4.
Bar coding is the most cost-effective means of data entry for many applications.

the data that the users will be required to enter. Again, these screens need to move through an approval process which includes users and management.

Automated Versus Manual Data Entry One economic factor always weighs heavy in the data entry process cost.

Data entry costs can be one of the biggest expenses in the ongoing operation of an information system. So the way in which the mechanics of the data entry process are designed can have a lasting impact on the system's life-cycle costs.

Whenever possible, designers will choose source data automation methods. These include bar coding, other means of optical character recognition, and voice input. (Figure 13-4) (These alternatives are discussed in the "Data Entry" section of Chapter 2.) Remote terminals are used when data must be entered near the source of the data but when it is impossible to use more automated methods.

■ ■

THE NAUTICAL NAVIGATION DIVISION OF THE GENERAL SHIP COMPANY, located in Brooklyn, uses bar coding extensively.. When an employee requests a tool from the tool crib, for example, an optical wand is first used to read the bar code on the employee's badge, identifying the employee to the computer system. Then the wand is used to read the bar code on the tool, identifying the tool. When the tool is returned, the same procedure is repeated. Then at the end of each shift the tool crib attendant runs a report that lists all tools that have not been returned and the persons who borrowed them. From beginning to end, no manual data entry is necessary. And this application represents only one of the many found at General Ship, which has virtually eliminated all keyboard data entry on the shop floor.

■■■■■■■■■■■■■■■■■■■■■■■■■■■■■

In some transaction sytems it might be appropriate to combine input and output documents in a **turnaround document.** Many utility companies, for example, send their customers a two-part bill: The customer keeps one as a receipt and returns the other with the payment. When the payment arrives, the document is read automatically by optical reader recognition equipment, thereby eliminating the costly process of clerical data entry.

On-Line Versus Off-Line Data Entry   During the data entry stage the designers must also decide whether data will be entered on-line or off-line. When data are entered on-line, they are immediately processed by a CPU, but the central database may not be updated at this time. Instead, the data may be saved in a batch transaction file and the central database updated at a later time and in a more secure environment. This strategy is used in banking systems, in which it would be unthinkable to give a customer—through automatic teller machines—control over the centralized master files. But in many on-line data entry systems, like airline reservations, not only are the data entered on-line, but the central database also is immediately updated. If the central database in this application were not immediately updated, the airline might sell the same seat twice!

In off-line data entry the data are not processed immediately by a CPU. When this option is chosen, source documents, such as sales receipts, are collected and the data in these documents are entered into the system as a group using batch processing.

STORAGE DESIGN

As we learned in Chapters 8 through 10, data storage and access play a major role in the design of any computer information system. Indeed, this role is so big that storage options may be discussed during the "evaluation of alternatives" phase, covered at the end of the last chapter. Either at that time or now, storage media, file organization, and file access methods must be chosen.

Storage decisions depend on user requirements. And because these requirements are embodied in the output and input design documents already discussed, they will serve as the basis for determining what has to be stored and how accessible the data must be to the users of the system.

STRUCTURE CHARTS

After the output, input, and storage requirements have been decided, these requirements become the basis for designing the remaining details that will make this a functioning system. And it is at this point in the developmental process that we break the system into manageable segments. The tool used to guide this process is called a **structure chart.** Structure charts incorporate the philosophy of top-down design, mentioned at the beginning of the chapter. They begin with an overall view of a system and then expose more detail as the chart proceeds from top to bottom.

A structure chart is a mechanism for breaking up a system into a hierarchy of modules. In general these modules represent input, output, processing, or storage functions. Each module is designed to be self-sufficient and contains the steps necessary to perform an identifiable function in the system. At the top of a chart (Figure 13-5) is a module representing the whole system. Each lower-level module breaks down into more detail the module above it. For example, the sales-order entry system shown in Figure 13-5 contains a second level with modules that will accept a transaction entry, update the order file with the new data, generate output, and perform file maintenance. And at a third level are modules that decompose those above it into more detail.

Although it is not important to know exactly how to build a structure chart, it is important to understand the role of these charts in structured design. Because each module represents a self-sufficient function

Figure 13-5.
A structure chart of a sales-order entry system. The top module represents an overall view of the system, and each lower lever breaks down the system into more and more detail.

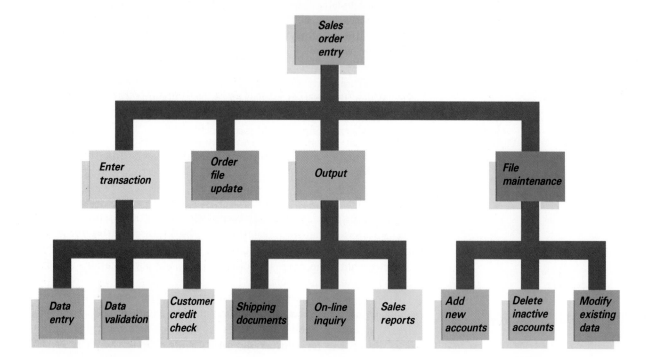

or identifiable segment of the system, the chart can be used to assign design responsibility. A group or individual is assigned a module—or in some cases several modules—of work. When the module is completed, it is tested. If it passes, it is combined with another tested module. Now the two modules are tested together, and later they are combined with other modules and tested. Using this pyramidlike approach, the modules are tested and combined until the entire system is functioning and ready for final system tests, a topic covered later in the chapter.

LOGIC DESIGN

After the project has been divided into manageable modules, each design group can begin the process called *logic design*. This process describes, verbally or graphically, the steps necessary for a module to meet its design objectives. Although the logic of an input or output module may be straightforward because it simply collects or presents data, the logic for some processing modules can vary from simple to complex. In a simple bank deposit system, for example, the module that processes a deposit may not be very complex: The new balance is computed by adding the deposit amount to the old balance. But sometimes the team responsible for the logic design of a module must unravel complex policies and conditions before they can proceed with the design.

■■■■■■■■■■■■■■■■■■■■■■■■■■■■■■■■■■■■■■■

WHEN ROSEMARY MCCARTHY, a systems analyst for Northeast Union Mutual Life Insurance Company, was assigned to design a computer system for processing auto insurance policies, she interviewed several of the staff in the underwriting department. She needed to know more about the rules used to determine how much a customer would be charged for different levels of coverage.

Jeff Demarco began to explain the rules. "If a person under twenty-five drives less than ten thousand miles per year and has had no speeding convictions or accidents in the last three years, and if the use of the car is for pleasure only, then we can insure that individual for up to $100,000 and the policy rate per thousand dollars of coverage will be $2.00. However, if that person is over twenty-five, still drives less than ten thousand miles per year, has no speeding convictions or accidents, but uses the car for business, then the maximum coverage can be $100,000 with a policy rate of $1.75 per thousand dollars."

Before Demarco could continue describing the remaining possibilities—of which there were many—McCarthy stopped him. "Jeff, I'm already confused. Why don't we start all over again. But this time I'll try to capture the logic in a table."

■■■■■■■■■■■■■■■■■■■■■■■■■■■■■■■■■■■■■■■

Decision tables, illustrated in Figure 13-6, are used to record and organize complex logical structures like the one McCarthy was trying to understand. These tables are divided into two sections. The top section contains the conditions and questions to be tested in reaching a decision. The bottom section identifies the action to be taken—in this case, the types of policy rules that apply. For example, you should be able to find out from the table that when a driver under twenty-five years of age with two accidents and no speeding convictions uses a car for less than fifteen thousand miles of pleasure driving, the maximum limit of the policy will be $50,000, and the cost will be $2.75 per thousand dollars of coverage.

As illustrated in this example, logic design can be complex in some processing modules. When appropriate, decision tables can help organize this complex process, thereby facilitating the design stages yet to come.

File-processing logic must also be considered during this phase. But most systems today rely on a database management system, and so many of the details of file-processing logic are the responsibility of the DBMS software (covered in Chapter 10), not the designer. When a database management system is used, the designer need only express what is needed, and the DBMS will determine the necessary logical steps.

Another responsibility that begins during this phase is overseeing the data items in the database. In most large projects this will be the job of the database administrator, who uses a **data dictionary,** described in Chapter 10, to keep track of these data items. The data dictionary stores the name of the data item, maintains descriptions of these items, and keeps records of the modules in the system that will share the data item. The database administrator thereby acts as a data coordinator, providing information to team members as data items are introduced in dif-

Figure 13-6.
A decision table identifies the action that needs to be taken when certain conditions are met.

	Auto Insurance Policy Coverage	Decision Rules								
Condition	Miles driven per year	<10,000	<10,000	<15,000	<15,000	<10,000	——	——		
	Age of youngest driver	>25	>25	<25	<25	<25	——			
	Accidents in last 3 years	≤1	≤1	≥2	≥2	≤1	——			
	Speeding convictions	None	None	None	None	None				
	Primary use	pleasure	business	pleasure	business	pleasure				
Action	Policy limit	100,000	100,000	50,000	25,000	100,000	——	——		
	Policy rate/$1000 of insurance	1.50	1.75	2.75	3.50	2.00	——	——		
	Type of policy	A1	F1	D1	H1	A2	——	——		

Adapted with permission from Murdick, Ross, and Claggett. Information Systems for Modern Management, Prentice-Hall Inc, 1984 page 283

ferent modules and preventing these designers from duplicating items in the database. Because many large systems contain more than five thousand data items, this function is crucial if data redundancy is to be minimized.

E N D · U S E R　H I N T S

MANAGING THE CENTRAL INFORMATION PROCESSING FUNCTION

With increasing frequency central information processing groups are under pressure to improve services, respond more to the organization's needs, and reduce costs. What this suggests is that central information processing, in many organizations, needs a fresh focus.

Here are some guidelines that, in the long run, can provide that focus.

■ Management must assure that the resources of the center are directed primarily to business problems rather than computer problems. Central personnel must regularly visit user areas, learn

what users need, and help them in accomplishing their objectives.

■ Managers must match the information center strategy to corporate strategy. They must be deeply involved in the formulation of organization strategy and tactics and then direct the information resources to support these goals.

■ Management must take the initiative to identify profitable projects. This means working with users and learning their business.

■ Central information-processing group personnel must take the responsibility for training a wide range of

users, from clerks who will follow standard operating procedures to business professionals who want to use micros to build spreadsheets or gain access to data kept by the mainframe.

■ The staff must undergo continual training, not only in technical subjects but business subjects as well. Learning how the organization works must be an important objective in any well-balanced training program.

■ Research must be emphasized. The pace of technology is so fast that an effort to stay up-to-date must be made part of a routine program.

SYSTEM CONTROLS

To ensure that the information system, once it is in operation, performs according to plan, controls must be built into the system, including

■ Control of data accuracy

■ Control of data security

■ Protection from unauthorized use

CONTROLLING DATA ACCURACY

In the ideal situation, data are collected and entered into the system without error. Seldom, however, can this be guaranteed. With data collected at remote locations, with a wide spectrum of users accessing the system, and with complex data to enter, the chances are good that errors will find their way into the database. To limit this problem, several techniques can be used, including verification, validation, and control totals.

Verification   With **verification,** data are checked by reading or entering the data a second time. If there are no differences between the first and second entries, the data will continue on their way. If there are differences, the errors will be corrected.

Validation   In the **validation** process, the computer is used to administer certain tests to the data. If a part number must contain six numeric digits, for example, then the computer can be programmed to test this condition. Thus, an entry such as 25A364 would fail, as not all six characters are numbers.

The validation process can also be designed to test for reasonableness. For example, it might be unreasonable for an item to be priced at less than $1.00 or more than $100. Entries into the computer system outside this range could be rejected for closer examination.

It is even possible to design a system in which an entry will not be validated unless every piece of data that the system needs has been entered. For example, an order-entry system might reject an entry that does not include the customer's name but does include the customer's purchase order number, order date, items ordered, and prices.

Control Totals   The **control totals** technique compares totals obtained at different points in the data processing cycle. In sales-order processing, for example, entry clerks can keep a running total in dollars of the orders processed during the day. Then, at the end of the day, this total can be compared with the total dollar volume processed by the computer. Differences in these totals would suggest that there has been an error somewhere in the processing cycle.

But these three data accuracy control methods certainly cannot uncover every error. If an entry clerk accidentally enters 5555 instead of 5545, if the number is not verified, and if it is in the reasonable range, then there is nothing that can be done to prevent this error from appearing in the database. In short, data accuracy controls offer some protection, but no guarantees.

CONTROLLING DATA SECURITY

To secure data from loss, every system must establish backup procedures. A **backup file** is a copy of a file, stored on disk or magnetic tape, that can be used if the primary file is lost or destroyed. In interactive processing, in which the file is updated continuously, it may be necessary to design procedures in which backups are made frequently, perhaps every hour.

PROTECTION FROM UNAUTHORIZED USE

One goal of most modern systems is that they be accessible to a wide variety of end-users. Some systems, however, are so accessible that unauthorized users may also be able to gain access easily. Although no system is perfectly protected against this eventuality, many employ security measures such as passwords, data encryption, and audit trails.

Most large systems use password protection. With this technique, users are assigned **passwords** that they must enter whenever access to the system is requested. Unless the system recognizes the password, access is denied.

Data are particularly vulnerable whenever they are sent between facilities over communications media. To prevent computer eavesdroppers from stealing or maliciously changing data, many systems code their data so that they cannot be recognized without knowledge of the coding scheme. This process is called **encryption.**

Still another method used to protect the data is to maintain detailed records of those who have either accessed or changed the database. This information is saved in a separate file and provides a form of **audit trail,** which can be used after something goes wrong, to help reconstruct where and how the problem occurred. In an accounting system, for example, the data entry clerks would have to enter some identification, such as a password or name, before the system would accept an accounting transaction. These data, stored in an audit trail file, can then be used to retrace the steps associated with this entry and to determine who had access to the system.

EQUIPMENT SELECTION

Although this chapter has focused on the logical issues of design, we cannot neglect the physical issues—choosing equipment.

Often a new information system will use existing hardware and so will need little new equipment. Sometimes, however, new equipment must be purchased. Although the exact time for beginning the search for new equipment will vary, it will occur at about this point in the development cycle (Figure 13-7).

Several steps must be undertaken during the search, including

- Describing the system's requirements.

- Submitting requests for proposals (RFPs) to vendors.

- Attending vendor presentations.

- Visiting user sites.

Figure 13-7.
An on-site visit often provides information about a system that cannot be obtained in any other way.

■   Establishing the credibility of vendor support and service.

■   Comparing vendor proposals.

■   Making the choice.

Seldom will the selection process be simple. Usually a range of hardware will be available, and the design team will have to spend a lot of time making the right choice.

?   Q U E S T I O N S   ?

1. What are some of the tools and techniques of structured design?
2. Why would an unstructured approach to a design problem be discouraged?
3. What is a module?
4. What is a structure chart? How is it used? What are its advantages?
5. In which order are the input, processing, and output modules for a system designed? Why?
6. A hotel reservation system can accept such transactions as making reservations and cancellations, printing reservation confirmations, responding to on-line inquiries, producing occupancy reports, and performing file maintenance. Draw a three-level structure chart similar to the one shown in Figure 13-5.
7. When are decision tables handy?
8. What is a data dictionary? How is it used?
9. What is the difference between the verification and the validation of data?
10. How are control totals used to control the data-entry process?
11. Name some of the techniques to help protect a system from unauthorized use.

PROGRAM DEVELOPMENT

Program development, which involves writing progams, begins after systems design has been completed. Again, the work done in previous phases is the foundation on which the work in this phase is built. And as long as systems design has followed the principles of structured design, the programming development phase will begin on the right foot. But if structured principles have not been followed and if the process has not been effectively managed, the results may be disastrous.

In the structure charts developed earlier, we saw that an information system can be decomposed into a group of related modules, each of which represents a self-sufficient function within the new system. This modular approach, together with certain programming guidelines and regular reviews, represent the fundamental working concepts of **structured programming.**

IDENTIFYING PROGRAMS

No large system has only one program; it has many—perhaps hundreds. And one reason for this is that many smaller programs are easier to write, modify, troubleshoot, and maintain than is one very large and complex program. The modular approach serves as the basis for identifying separate programs.

Although it is not always clear exactly which module or group of modules will be candidates for separate programs, at least every major input, process, output, and report module is usually considered a candidate.

The choices made for the sales-order entry system described earlier in the chapter (Figure 13-5) are shown in Figure 13-8. Separate programs have been identified for the entry of transaction data, order file updates, printing of shipping documents, on-line inquiry, printing of sales reports, addition of new accounts, deletion of inactive accounts, and modification of existing data.

Another designer might prefer to separate the entry of transactions into three programs: data entry, data validation, and credit check. If it is suspected that a program will be too long, then further decomposition may be appropriate. The choice also depends somewhat on personal preference. However, the number of programs cannot be determined by any rigid rule.

PROGRAM LOGIC AND FLOWCHARTS

As we move closer to the time when programmers will begin writing programs—called *coding*—the detailed logic behind each program is often expressed in program flowcharts, data flow diagrams, or in a more English-like form called pseudocode.

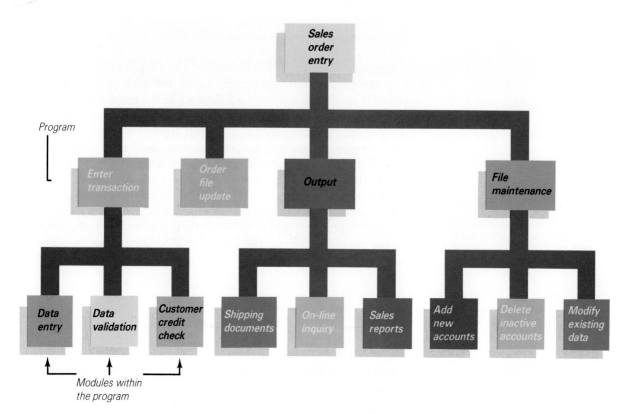

Figure 13-8.
The shaded rectangles represent the eight separate programs that will be written for this system. The detail below the transaction rectangle represents the modules within that program.

A **program flowchart** begins where a module in the structure chart ends. Whereas the module represents only the overall purpose of the task to be performed, the program flowchart is a detailed graphical representation of the logical flow of data within that module. It serves as the logical road map that the programmers will use to write programming code.

When following structured programming principles, the program flowchart must use the symbols illustrated in Figure 13-9 and certain guidelines concerning control structures which will now be described.

CONTROL STRUCTURES

Any program, from the simplest to the most complex, can be developed using only three basic control structures: (1) simple sequence, (2) if–then, and (3) do–while. Let us describe each.

Simple Sequence　　A **simple sequence structure** (Figure 13-10) is used when a series of steps must be carried out in linear sequence. These steps begin with the first and end with the last. Figure 13-11 shows a simple sequence containing some of the steps necessary to validate employee wage data, one module in a payroll system.

If–Then Structure　　The **if–then structure** (Figure 13-10) is used to transfer control from one point in a program to another. This transfer is

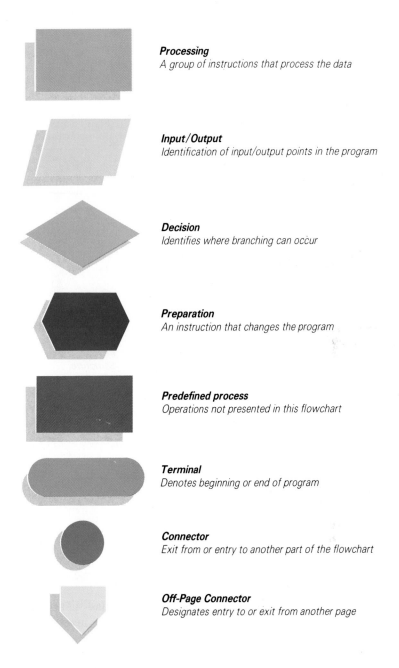

Processing
A group of instructions that process the data

Input/Output
Identification of input/output points in the program

Decision
Identifies where branching can occur

Preparation
An instruction that changes the program

Predefined process
Operations not presented in this flowchart

Terminal
Denotes beginning or end of program

Connector
Exit from or entry to another part of the flowchart

Off-Page Connector
Designates entry to or exit from another page

Figure 13-9.
Standard symbols are used to construct a program flowchart.

made only when a certain prespecified condition has been met. To state it differently, *if* a specified condition is met, *then* control will be transferred to another part of the program.

Suppose that a program must be written in which all employees with a job classification of 5 or greater are to be listed in a report. Figure 13-12 illustrates how the if–then structure can be used to perform this test. Notice that if the employee passes the test, then control will pass to the left-hand side of the flowchart, and the employee's name will be printed. If, however, the employee does not pass the test, then control

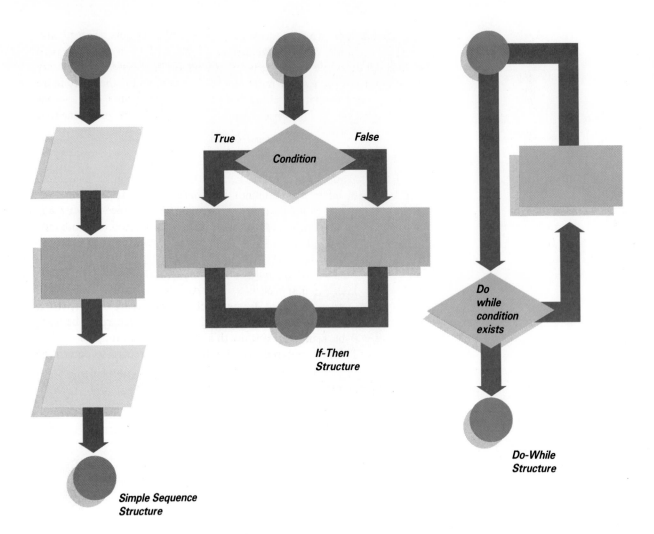

True   Condition   False

If-Then
Structure

Do
while
condition
exists

Do-While
Structure

Simple Sequence
Structure

Figure 13-10.
Three basic control structures are used
to develop structured program flowcharts.

will pass to the right-hand side of the flowchart, and no action will be
taken. The outcome of this logical sequence will therefore be a printed
list containing only the names of those passing the test.

Do–While Structure   The **do–while structure,** illustrated in Figure 13-
10, is used when it is necessary to loop through, or repeat over and over, a
sequence of steps. Looping begins when the structure is entered and continues *while* a prespecified condition still exists.

Often this structure is used when every record in a file must be
read. Reading begins with the first record and continues *while* there are
still records left to be read.

It is important to recognize that a do–while structure tests immediately for a prespecified condition and does not allow any processing
between the entry of the do–while structure and this test. Processing
within the structure can only be done after the test has been made and in
the line that returns to the top of the do–while structure. Therefore, a
record must be read before a do–while structure is entered for the first
time.

Figure 13-11.
A simple sequence structure example.

Figure 13-12.
An if–then structure example.

Suppose we want to access an employee file, read each record, and print its contents. As you can see from Figure 13-13, a record is read before the do–while structure is entered for the first time. Immediately upon entering, the test for more records is made, and if there are more records, then the contents of the first record will be printed, and another record will be read. The process continues until the last record—one that must specify that this is the end of file—is read. At that time, control passes out of the structure and to the next program step.

Combining Control Structures   Each of these three control structures can be combined to form complex flowcharts and complete programs. Figure 13-14 is a complete program flowchart for a process that reads accounts receivable records from a file and prints a list of all those customers whose accounts are more than ninety days overdue and whose balance is greater than $500.

The flowchart begins with the opening of the accounts receivable file, after which the first record is read. At Point A in the flowchart, a do–while structure is entered. Immediately after entering this structure, the test for more records is made. As long as there are records to be read, the loop will be repeated. Within this do–while loop are two if–then structures. The first, entered at Point B, tests the record to determine whether the balance due is over ninety days late. If it is, then control will passed to the next if–then structure, Point C, which determines whether

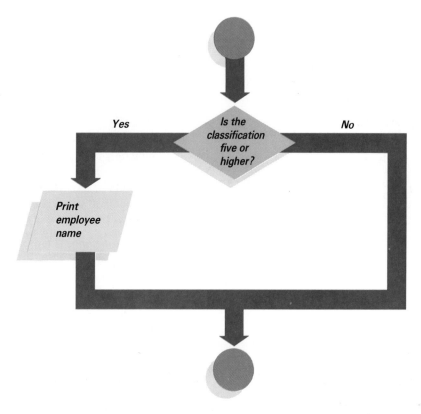

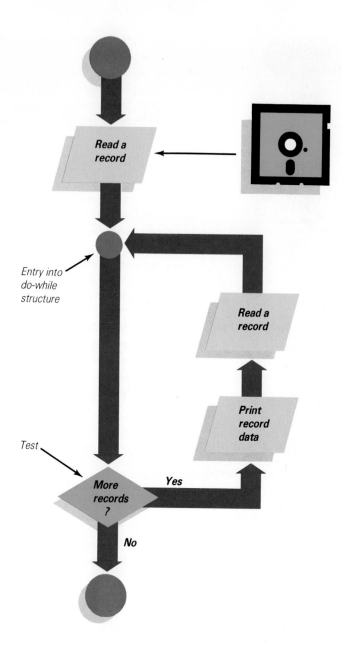

Figure 13-13.
A do–while structure example.

the balance is over $500. If both of these conditions are met, the company name and amount due will be printed. But if the conditions of either of these if–then structures are not met, control will pass to Point D, another record will be read, and the cycle will be repeated.

PSEUDOCODE

These program flowcharts illustrate the logic of a program. **Pseudocode,** often used as an alternative to this technique, expresses the logic of a

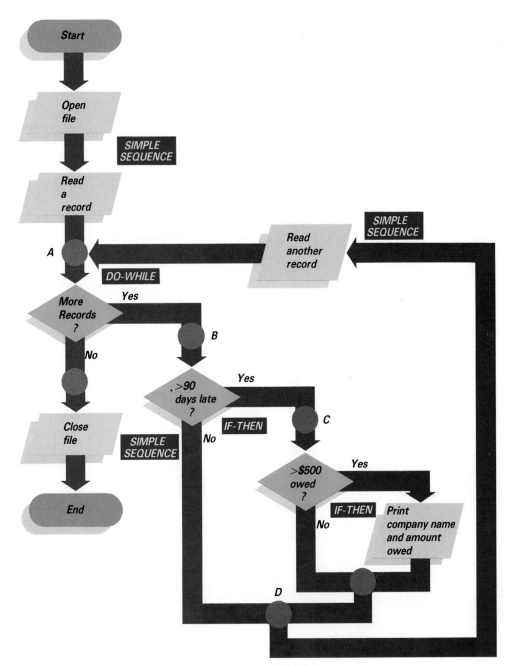

Figure 13-14.
A complete program flowchart.

program in English statements. It is a verbal rather than a graphic device.

The flowchart shown in Figure 13-15 is the same as that shown in Figure 13-13. It represents the steps necessary to read and print the contents of a file. Next to the flowchart is the pseudocode that represents the same logical process.

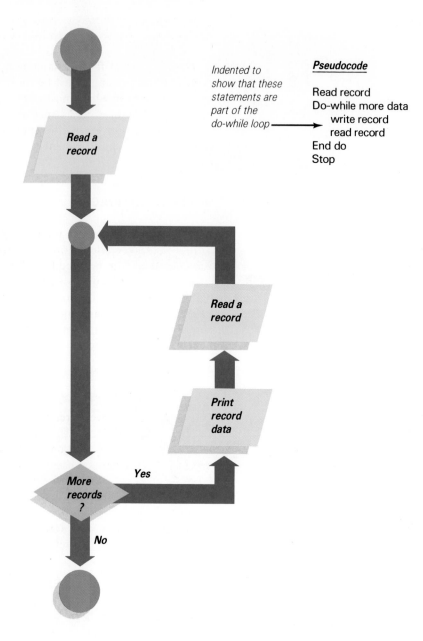

Figure 13-15.
Pseudocode and a flowchart equivalent.

One advantage of pseudocode is that it closely resembles the form that the actual programming code will take. Another advantage is that it is not necessary to spend time deciding how to lay out symbols on paper. In addition, pseudocode is easy to correct, whereas errors made on a flowchart often mean that the entire flowchart must be redrawn (programs are available for this purpose). The main disadvantage of pseudocode is that it does not give a graphic picture, and some designers prefer to see a program's logic rather than to read it.

PROGRAMMING LANGUAGES

After the program flowcharts or pseudocode have been completed, a programming language must be chosen. Often that choice will depend on the language in which most of an organization's other programs are written. This ensures consistency and eases the maintenance problem. Nevertheless, a number of different languages can be used. They can be classified as machine, assembly, procedural, or nonprocedural languages.

MACHINE LANGUAGE

A **machine language** communicates with the CPU using a string of ones and zeros, the computer's own binary language. Although all of the computer's power can be readily tapped with machine language, it is extraordinarily difficult to write long programs in it. In addition, the language varies from one machine to another. Today, few programs are written in machine language, although they once were, for the simple reason that other languages had not yet been developed.

ASSEMBLY LANGUAGE

Because it is so difficult to write programs in machine language, **assembly languages** were created. An assembly language rises above the detail of a machine language and uses symbols rather than binary numbers to represent a collection of programming instructions. Assembly language programming uses the machine more efficiently than do higher-level languages. But the programmer must still be familiar with the detailed steps the computer must follow to execute a program. Consequently, these languages are not far removed from machine language, are difficult to use, and vary from machine to machine. Few application programs are written in assembly language.

PROCEDURAL LANGUAGES

Procedural languages begin to look more like English. Programs written in these languages must be translated into a machine language by a compiler or interpreter before the computer can understand and execute their instructions (compilers and interpreters are described in the "Language Translators" section of Chapter 2).

Procedural languages are so named because the program's steps must correspond to the logical flow or *procedure* the computer must follow to convert input to output. Although these languages certainly do not get down to the machine level of detail, a procedural language must still specify how the computer is to carry out a job. Examples of procedural languages include COBOL (COmmon Business Oriented Language),

BASIC (Beginner's All-Purpose Symbolic Code), FORTRAN (FORmula TRANslation), and Pascal (not an acronym, but named after the French mathematician). Most of the massive inventory of computer programs used today by the business community is written in COBOL. This is in part because COBOL was one of the first procedural languages to be developed and standardized for business use; once an organization wrote its early programs in COBOL, it tended to continue doing so for the sake of compatibility, even though newer and more advanced languages emerged.

NONPROCEDURAL LANGUAGES

Nonprocedural languages, also referred to as **fourth-generation languages (4GLs)** are those farthest removed from the way in which machines process instructions. They are nonprocedural in that the user specifies *what* is wanted, not *how* it is to be obtained.

Electronic spreadsheets and database management systems represent fourth-generation languages, and many 4GLs can be used to develop high-volume transaction-processing and operational management systems as well. In some of these applications, a fourth-generation language has replaced COBOL.

Figure 13-16 illustrates the relationship between the different types of languages and the machine itself. Machine language is closest to the way the machine processes instructions. For this reason, machine language and assembly language are sometimes referred to as **low-level languages.** As we move away from machine and assembly languages to procedural and nonprocedural languages, we move steadily farther from the way that the machine processes instructions and closer to the way that people think. For this reason, procedural languages are sometimes referred to as **high-level languages,** and nonprocedural languages as **very high level languages.**

Figure 13-16.
As languages move away from the way in which the computer operates, they move closer to the way in which people think.

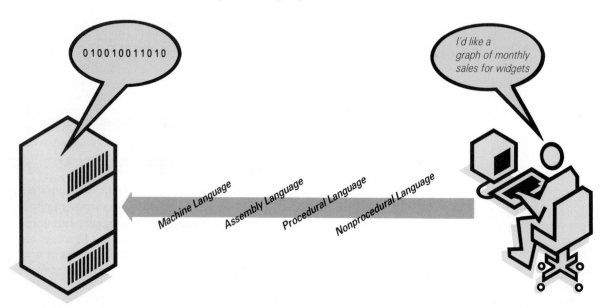

Because the use of nonprocedural languages is growing rapidly, we will take a closer look at them in the next section.

4GLS

We learned in the last section that when a nonprocedural fourth- generation language is used, it is no longer necessary to be concerned with the details of program flow. The designer need only specify the work to be done, and a nonprocedural language processor will then interpret these instructions and specify the details necessary to do the job.

Consider the following 4GL program that was written to produce a report. The report will show the total units sold for each product, by customer, in each month and year, with a subtotal for each customer.

```
TABLE FILE SALES SUM UNITS
BY YEAR BY MONTH BY CUSTOMER BY PRODUCT
ON CUSTOMER SUBTOTAL PAGE BREAK
END
```

If a procedural language such as COBOL had been used to produce the same report, it would have required five hundred to one thousand lines of computer code.

As you can see, the increases in programming productivity using a 4GL can be dramatic. And these increases depend on the particular category for which the 4GL is used. When the 4GL is used to develop reports, such as the one illustrated, or when it is used to query a database, the increase in productivity—compared with using a procedural language—can be in the range of 25 to 1 or more. When 4GLs are used to build complete applications, then productivity gains are reported to be in the range of 5 to 1.

■■■■■■■■■■■■■■■■■■■■■■■■■■■■■■■■■■■

SAFEWAY SECURITIES WAS A BROKERAGE FIRM THAT OFFERS ITS CLIENTS A FULL RANGE OF INVESTMENT SERVICES AT DISCOUNT PRICES. Growing at 20 percent per year, it was recently faced with having to update the information system that keeps records for all of its customers' accounts, including trading activities, orders, and statements. To develop the software, the progamming department decided not to write the system in COBOL, as it had in the past, but to use PROEASE, a fourth-generation development package used by several other firms in the brokerage business.

Once the programming department learned how to use the new 4GL, progress was fast. It developed the new application three months ahead of schedule and reported a productivity increase of 3 to 1, compared with writing in COBOL. Bob Tanner, the director of MIS, was so pleased that he decided that most new applications would be developed in the same way.

■■■■■■■■■■■■■■■■■■■■■■■■■■■■■■■■■■■

But 4GLs have a serious drawback in that they take more time to run on the computer than do those written in a lower-level language. Operations that will be performed many thousands of times, for example, would probably be better written in COBOL or even assembly language for the sake of computer information system efficiency.

Prototyping   One particularly productive use of 4GLs is called prototyping. **Prototyping** is the use of special-purpose application development software to develop a small-scale version or first approximation of a proposed program. The small-scale version, also called a prototype, can be built relatively quickly, and then it can be shown to users who can experiment with it and determine what changes or enhancements are necessary before it will meet their needs. For example, they can test transaction-processing procedures, produce reports, and update sample databases.

After the end-users have finished their test of the system, the design team can study the responses and rework the prototype. And by repeating this pattern, a prototype is eventually developed that meets the needs of users and obtains management's approval. In some situations designers may continue to build the prototype until it evolves into a full-scale system. Meanwhile at several stages in the design process, it can be submitted to users for testing. In other situations, once the prototype has been approved, it can be used as the model for the full-scale system, written in a third- or fourth-generation language.

The Influence of 4GLs on the Development Cycle   In the early stages of systems analysis, the development of a system which will use a 4GL will often parallel the developmental procedures described in the last chapter: The proposed system will be studied, the needs of the users identified, and its feasibility determined.

Once the systems analysis phase is completed, however, 4GLs can have a significant impact on many of the developmental stages that remain.

Recall that one of the first steps in systems design is developing output, input, and file-processing samples that the user then tests and eventually approves. Prototyping is especially effective here. It permits the designers to develop these samples quickly, build a small-scale version of the system around these samples, and then involve the user in a test of the "real thing." And when the users find problems and recommend changes, prototyping makes it relatively easy to incorporate the changes in the next version to be tested.

In the programming development phase, 4GLs can also have a significant impact. Not only do they cut programming costs, but they also reduce errors, simplify troubleshooting, and make maintenance easier.

But the use of 4GLs and prototyping in the development cycle does not replace the structured approach to system development. Rather, they are tools to be used as part of that process.

Figure 13-17.
Structured walkthroughs are used to detect errors. The earlier they are caught in the development process, the less costly it will be to correct them.

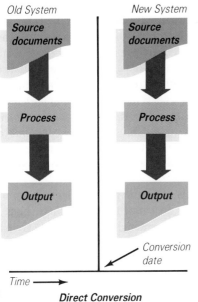

Direct Conversion

CONTROL AND FEEDBACK DURING THE PROGRAMMING PROCESS

The programming process, especially for large systems written in a procedural language, is often controlled through the use of a technique called a **structured walkthrough.** In a structured walkthrough, the logic of each program module is carefully examined by a group of programmers other than the ones who have written the program (Figure 13-17). Evidence has shown that this technique is especially useful in detecting errors before they become part of the larger system. Once in the larger system, any error becomes much more difficult and expensive to uncover and correct.

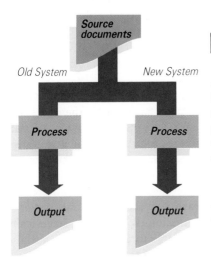

Parallel Conversion

Figure 13-18.
Direct and parallel conversion.

TESTING AND INSTALLATION

After the programs have been completed, they must be thoroughly tested before release for use. In a complex, multiuser system composed of a number of programs, this process may take a long time. Every program in the system must be subjected to a wide range of input over a variety of conditions. The design team must ensure, to its best ability, that the system does exactly what it was designed to do.

Two basic options for installing a system are available (Figure 13-18). In the first, the old system is abruptly terminated and the new one used in its place. This strategy is called a **direct conversion.** It is risky because the new system may have some bugs that are discovered only after the system is in operation.

In the second option, **parallel conversion,** both systems are operated side by side until there is enough confidence in the new one to discontinue the old one. This strategy is more conservative, giving the designers more room to work out the bugs, but it is more expensive, too.

Figure 13-19.
Good documentation makes a system easier to implement, use, and maintain. The documentation for many fourth-generation systems such as LOTUS 1-2-3 represents some of the best ever written.

Figure 13-20.
Training is an important part of the system development process.

DOCUMENTATION

Most systems have three levels of documentation: system, operational, and user (Figure 13-19). **System documentation** describes the design of the system and includes a general description, screen designs for all input and output, flowcharts, structure charts, a listing of all the programs, and even a listing of the data used to test each program.

The second level of documentation, **operational documentation,** is written for those people who will be responsible for implementing the system. It identifies the steps needed to bring the system to full operation and, once it is running, to keep it running. For example, the documentation that accompanies an altered off-the-shelf accounting system must identify the procedures to enter the chart of accounts and opening balances, establish profit centers, and design financial statements.

User documentation, the third level, is directed to the end-users. An accounting clerk, for example, must know how to make a sales entry, what measures to take if if data are entered incorrectly, and the procedures to follow when the books are closed at the end of the month. User documentation must explain each of these activities in a clear and easy-to-understand format.

Unfortunately, documentation is often the most neglected step in the development process. Once the project moves into its final stages, those people responsible for its development may be under too much pressure to spend time preparing good documentation. Even when time is available, the resulting documentation may be uneven in quality. For example, when several different people have been responsible for separate parts of the system and each document their own part, one section of the documentation might be clear and another unintelligible, depending on the people's writing skills. Worse, the details behind a system are sometimes kept in the heads of its designers rather than being documented. When these individuals leave, the organization can be in serious trouble.

TRAINING

Training is an important stage in the development process (Figure 13-20). During this stage, users must learn how the system operates and how they can use it to obtain the information they need. In large-scale multiuser systems, training may be given in a formal classroom setting. Instruction may be given by the central data processing staff or, if the software is purchased from a vendor, training may take place at the vendor's facilities.

SYSTEM MAINTENANCE

Rarely is a system developed, implemented, and forgotten. Every system must also be maintained. In fact, most large data processing departments budget over 50 percent of their time for maintenance! There may be changes in the legal or business environment, software errors, or modifications to improve the performance of the system. In each of these circumstances, design and programming changes must be initiated, and in some cases it will even be necessary to return to the systems analysis phase and proceed logically through many or all of the phases of system development as these changes are integrated into the new system. For this reason, the systems development process is referred to as a cycle—because in fact when the end is reached, the odds are good that at some point it will become necessary to return to the beginning.

?   Q U E S T I O N S   ?

1. How is a structure chart used in the program development process?
2. What is the purpose of a program flowchart?
3. What is the difference between an if–then and a do–while structure?
4. How does pseudocode differ from a program flowchart?
5. Revise the program flowchart in Figure 13-14, to produce a report that lists all customers whose bill is between thirty and sixty days late and for whom the balance due is over $1000.

6. What is the difference between a machine language and a procedural language?
7. How does a nonprocedural language differ from a procedural language?
8. What is a 4GL?
9. Suppose you bought an accounting software package. What categories of documentation would you expect to accompany the system? What category would you find most useful?
10. Do you agree with this statement: Most systems that are properly designed, developed, and tested need little maintenance.

S U M M A R Y

- In the systems development cycle, after the systems analysis phase comes **systems design.**

- **Structured design** is a formal approach to systems design, focusing on the details of the design process.

- A key to structured design is **top-down design,** whereby the design begins with the most general view and moves toward a more detailed view.

- Design begins with a focus on the output, then input, and finally storage methods.

- Source data automation offers an efficient alternative to manual data entry.

- Some transaction systems combine input and output documents in a **turnaround document.**

- **Structure charts** decompose a system into a hierarchy of manageable segments called **modules.**

- Modules can be classified as output, input, processing, and file-access modules.

- In working out complex logic to design processing modules, **decision tables** can be an aid.

- The **data dictionary** is used to oversee the data items included in the database.

- Data accuracy controls built into a system include **verification, validation,** and **control totals.**

- Data security control involves making regular **backup files.**

- **Passwords, encryption,** and **audit trails** provide some protection against the unauthorized use of a system.

- The **program development** phase follows the systems design phase. Structured concepts are used here, too, and are referred to as **structured programming.**

- A **program flowchart** identifies the logical flow of data through each step of a program.

- Program flowcharts, and programs themselves, can be constructed using three basic control structures: the **simple sequence structure, if–then structure,** and **do–while structure.**

- **Pseudocode** expresses the logic of a program in English statements and is often used as an alternative to flowcharts.

- **Machine language** communicates with the CPU using a string of ones and zeros. Because machine language is so difficult to work with, **assembly languages** were created, which use symbols rather than binary numbers.

- **Procedural languages** resemble English more closely than symbols or numbers do but the programmer still must specify the steps the computer must follow. Common procedural languages are COBOL, BASIC, FORTRAN, and Pascal.

■ **Nonprocedural languages** or **fourth-generation languages** (4GLs) are the farthest removed from machine operations. The user specifies what is wanted rather than how it is to be obtained.

■ Machine and assembly languages are sometimes referred to as **low-level languages,** procedural languages as **high-level languages,** and nonprocedural languages as **very high level languages.**

■ **Prototyping,** or the development of small-scale approximations of a proposed system, can improve the development process by involving end-users early in the process.

■ The programming process is often controlled through the use of a **structured walkthrough.**

■ Program installation methods include **direct conversion** and **parallel conversion.**

■ Most systems have three levels of documentation: **system documentation, operational documentation,** and **user documentation.**

■ The system development process is a cycle. Once a system is implemented, the need for system maintenance frequently makes it necessary to go through the cycle again.

K E Y • T E R M S

The following lists shows the key terms in the order in which they appear in the chapter.

FOR DISCUSSION

1. Suppose you are on a project team assigned to design a new accounts receivable system. At today's design review meeting, the programmers come up with a proposal to include the functions of all modules in one large program. They argue that if the system is designed in this way, the computer will operate more efficiently, and the response time for the end-user will be faster. Have they followed the principles of structured design? How would you respond to their proposal?

2. Have you used a third-generation language like BASIC, COBOL, or Pascal? Have you also used a fourth-generation language like LOTUS or dBASE? If so, describe how they differ.

3. The Berkshire Supply Company, a distributor of hotel supplies, recently commissioned a large public accounting firm to study its computer system. The accounting firm found that the controls imposed on Berkshire's payroll and accounts receivable systems were very weak. What do you think this implies? Why is it necessary for these applications to have tight controls? Should the controls imposed on these applications be tighter than the controls on others? Suggest one control that should be imposed.

4. The County Service Electric Company has decided to include a bar chart on the bottom of each monthly bill that will show the customer how monthly electric usage has varied over the most recent twelve-month period. Describe how this change might affect input, processing, storage, and output. Do you think that it will be necessary to write new programs? How would you organize the development of this project?

HANDS-ON PROJECTS

1. You are probably familiar with the output from many computer systems, such as automatic teller machines, microcomputer systems, supermarket checkout systems, or software packages used in your course work. Select one of these systems with which you are most familiar, and sketch the output that you have observed. Now look at this output, and describe any changes you might recommend. For example, perhaps the appearance of the report could be improved for easier reading; perhaps too much or even too little information is given; or maybe the information could have been presented in a different way. When you are through with your analysis, make a sketch of these new output screens. Then explain

how your change will affect, if at all, the system's input requirements.

2. Draw the top two levels of a structure chart that describe the computerized checkout system at your local supermarket.

3. Visit several businesses and describe the types of input devices that they use. Are these examples of source data automation? How could the efficiency of the organizations' data entry processes be improved?

4. Draw a systems flowchart of a computer system with which you come into contact regularly.

5. Find an administrator or secretary at your school who has used a commercial software package (such as a word processor or electronic spreadsheet). Ask him or her how much the documentation helped clarify the use of the software. What suggestions would this person make to improve the documentation?

C A S E · S T U D Y

DMV

"**W**hy can't we go back to our old system? At least we know it works! Maybe it can get us out of this mess." Bill Maloney, the state's attorney general, was on the phone with Mark Bridger. Bridger, the director of the Department of Motor Vehicles (DMV), was doing his best to cope with a crisis that was becoming worse by the hour.

Two months earlier, the state began using a new data processing system designed to streamline operations at the DMV. Although the cutover—direct conversion—to the new system was without incident, problems began to mount soon after the system was placed in operation.

Now the system was unable to cope with the work load. More than a million drivers had been unable to register their cars. To make the situation even worse, many of those who registered their cars after the system went into operation were incorrectly listed in the database as operating unregistered vehicles. And renewal notices—issued automatically by the new computer system—had been sent to the wrong drivers. In fact, so many drivers had been forced to drive without a registration that the attorney general, Bill Maloney, had ordered the state police to cease citing drivers for this offense. No one,

it seemed, had been spared: Even some of the vehicles operated by public works departments and local police forces throughout the state were registered to the wrong municipalities!

Background

When the system was first conceived, a little over three years ago, the DMV expressed a need for a more up-to-date information-processing system than the ten-year-old system it was using. The DMV especially needed a system with a strong DBMS, to have more flexibility in accessing data and in making changes in the application software. Its current system used a conventional file-processing approach.

In addition to performing all of the routine record-keeping functions such as maintaining automobile registration data, the DMV wanted the new system to automatically notify the state's five million drivers of license and registration renewals. It also wanted the system to be capable of allowing updates of the state's rating surcharge database to be made on a daily basis. This surcharge database keeps track of violation points against individual drivers and is used to penalize bad drivers by making them pay higher insurance rates. Under the old system, this database was updated periodically, but it was not unusual—due to inefficient update procedures—for the driver's record to be updated as much as three or four months after the conviction took place.

Political Factors

When the idea for a new computer system was originally suggested to the governor, he agreed that an effort such as this was long overdue. But he was not pleased to hear that it would take five years to develop and bring the project into full operation. It is alleged that he then asked DMV director Bridger to find a consulting firm to develop the system in two years so that the completed system would be finished in time to be used during his reelection campaign as an example of his administration's accomplishments.

The Consultants

Shortly after the governor's alleged request to expedite the development of the system, Bridger met with the information services division of Driscol and Russell, one of the country's leading public accounting firms. After studying the project's objectives, the manager of this division, Mike Price, suggested that the only way it could be completed in two years would be to use a fourth-generation language.

"We will still use a structured approach and build the system in modules," explained Price, "but the 4GL will save us a lot of time in programming, debugging, and testing the project."

Bridger was impressed with Price's confidence in his firm's ability to deliver the needed software and, above all, to deliver it on time. Within three months a $6.5 million-dollar contract was signed with Driscol and Russell.

The software development process went smoothly for the DMV. The senior systems analyst for Driscol and Russell spent six weeks at the DMV, during which time he learned about the current system and the characteristics of the new one. Once the systems analysis was complete and a preliminary plan approved, Driscol and Russell had few interactions with the DMV. According to the senior systems analyst at Driscol and Russell, the DMV preferred it this way, as the DMV was already overburdened with day-to-day problems.

The System Fails

The system was delivered right on schedule, and during the first few weeks, as the work load on the new system increased, it seemed to perform well. Data entry was made from on-line terminals, and users found the system efficient. As might be expected at the start, those who used the system complained a little about the new procedures, but no serious problems emerged.

But as more and more new tasks were added to the system, the operators began to report an increase in response time. When the system was finally in full operation, the response time became intolerable. At best, response times were in the five- to eight-second range and frequently took as long as one to two minutes. The original contract specified that response times were to be no longer than three to five seconds.

An increase in response time, however, was just the tip of the iceberg. First, it was not possible to process all of the jobs on the new system. Even an increase to a 24-hour-operation was insufficient to update the database. Within a few months, the backlog grew to such proportions that 1.4 million automobile registrations had not been processed. Meanwhile, when police stopped cars that did not have valid registrations, the drivers were arrested. As the protest from drivers began to mount, the attorney general's office stepped in and ordered the police to stop making arrests for invalid registrations.

Then an even more dramatic problem surfaced. It slowly became apparent that the database was contaminated with bad data, that the automobile registrations listed the wrong owners.

State Department of Data Processing

With the system in total chaos, the DMV director and the attorney general decided to call in Gail Hendrix, the director of the state department of data processing. Hendrix had known about this project since its inception, when she had been appalled not only that her department had been frozen out of the development process but that the bid had apparently gone to a company without the usual competitive bidding process.

Hendrix was not surprised at the DMV's problems. During her first meeting with Bridger and Maloney, she shed some light on the sources of the problem. "I can't understand why Driscol and Russell used PROWRITE. Everyone knew it was a new 4GL, that it had lots of bugs to be worked out, and that no one had really tested it on a large project yet. Not only that, but PROWRITE was developed to run smaller MIS jobs. I don't think it was ever meant to run transaction jobs where the system must handle several transactions per second."

Bridger asked, "How would you have developed the system?"

Hendrix replied, "I think COBOL should have been used for those modules that did the heavy processing. Then a 4GL, but not PROWRITE, could have been used for some of the other modules, especially the report-writing ones."

Finding a Solution

At the meeting with Hendrix and Bridger, Maloney insisted that they come up with a solution. "We've got our motor vehicle system in a shambles. To solve the problem tomorrow is even too late. What are we going to do?"

Bridger was in favor of holding a meeting with Driscol and Russell to determine what they could do to straighten out the situation. "Perhaps they could rewrite some of the transaction modules in COBOL, as Hendrix suggested."

Hendrix felt differently. "They've lost their credibility with me. I think we should write this software off as a complete loss and begin the development of a new system here in our own DP organization."

Maloney, however, was certainly not satisfied. "Look, why can't we bring our old system back into operation? At least we'll get the public and the politicians off our back."

"Bill, you asked me that on the phone last week, and I told you that it would take months to get the old software running again," replied Bridger. "And besides, we developed this new system to solve problems that our old software couldn't. I don't think yours is a reasonable solution."

Questions

1. Describe the DMV's problem.
2. What are the guidelines and techniques that should be used in the system development process? To what extent do you think Driscol and Russell followed them?
3. What were the new system's objectives? Were they reasonable?
4. How was the tentative schedule for the system's development established?
5. How does technical feasibility play a role in this project? At what stage in the development process must this be studied? Was this phase neglected?
6. Is there any evidence to suggest that the detailed analysis phase of the development project was neglected?
7. Describe what is meant by "breaking a system into modules." Can you describe one module that might be found in the system?
8. Give an example of one output required by the users at the DMV.
9. Give an example of an input.
10. Is it suggested that data entry in the new system is on-line or off-line? Explain the difference.
11. Do you think that source data automation could solve any of DMV's problems?
12. Describe, in very general terms, the use of files in this system.
13. Is there any evidence that inadequate system controls contributed to the DMV's problems?
14. What is the difference between a 4GL and COBOL? Do you think it was a bad choice to use a 4GL? Why?
15. Do you think that using a prototype in the development process would have saved the DMV from disaster?
16. What type of conversion strategy was followed? Which would you have recommended? Why?
17. Where in the development process would you place the blame for this system's failure?
18. If you were the DMV director, what would you recommend as the next step?
19. With increasing frequency, companies with large DP backlogs are turning to outside sources for help in developing applications. Using the insight gained from this case, what precautions would you take to minimize the kinds of problems that the DMV suffered?

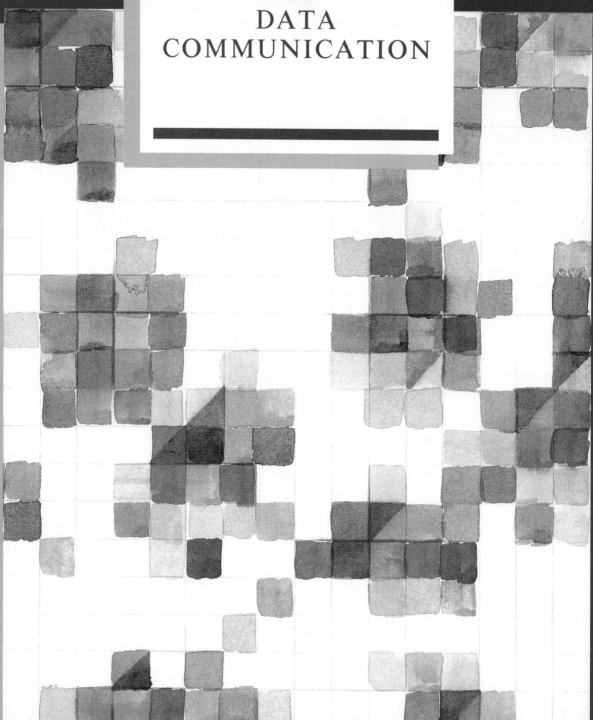

14
DATA
COMMUNICATION

O U T L I N E

O B J E C T I V E S

After studying this chapter you should understand the following:

■ *What data communication is and the purposes that it serves.*

■ *Why many information processing systems have come to depend on data communication.*

■ *The types (but not the details) of technical considerations in designing a data communication system.*

■ *Where data communication services can be obtained.*

Figure 14-1.
Data communication provides access from remote terminals to centralized facilities. Here, reservations for plays, concerts, and sports events are booked from the Seibu Department Store in Tokyo using microcomputers. The computers instantly update the central databases through a communication system.

Having reached this point in the book we know what computer information systems are and how they are developed. At several points we have seen that access to computer information systems often extends well beyond the central computer. In this and the next chapter, we shall address exactly this issue (Figure 14-1).

First, in this chapter, we will see how communications can tie remote terminals to a central computer, how these systems are used, and how they work. Then, in Chapter 15, we will see how a network of computers, tied together by a communications network, can share storage and processing functions.

DATA COMMUNICATION

Data communication is the process by which data are moved from one point in an information system to another. Whenever two or more devices that are geographically separated must communicate with one another, data communication is required (Figure 14-2). An automatic teller machine located at a supermarket, a microcomputer accessing stock market data, and an airline reservation terminal at a travel agency all require communication functions. Indeed, this is true of most modern computer systems.

APPLICATION EXAMPLES

Data communication applications can be simple or complex. The following example illustrates a fairly simple one.

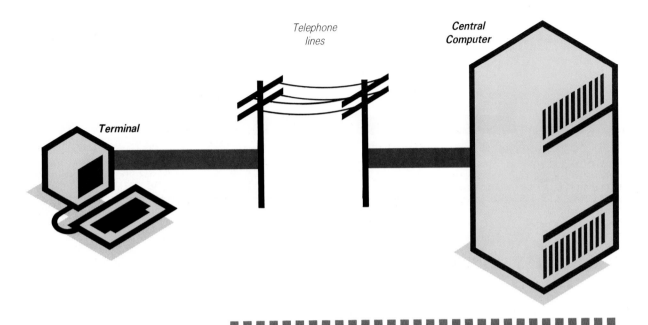

Figure 14-2.
A data communication system connects terminals or other devices to a central computer system.

CUSTODIO SANDOVAL IS AN ACCOUNT EXECUTIVE FOR SMITH AND ADAMS, an advertising agency in San Francisco. The agency maintains a large database of client and market research data that Sandoval often uses when creating advertising strategies for his clients. On his desk is a terminal through which he can gain access to the data. Sandoval, however, spends as much as 40 percent of his time traveling and, in addition, frequently works at his home in Cupertino. Without remote access the agency's data would often be out of reach.

Sandoval therefore carries with him a portable, 10-pound computer whenever he is away from his office. Because both the central computer and his portable unit are equipped with a modem, he can communicate with the central computer over conventional telephone lines. When Sandoval needs to access the agency's database, he simply plugs his portable unit into any telephone receptacle, instructs it to dial his office number, and, when he is connected, begins his work.

Sandoval's system illustrates how data communication can bring data right to the end-user. But this is a simple example; airline reservation and banking systems are much more complex.

For example, the system illustrated in Figure 14-3 is conceptually similar to many of the systems used in banking. Several different user groups may be connected to the central computer, which may not even be located at the bank's headquarters. The loan department may have several terminals, the accounting group several terminals, the branches several teller terminals each, and there also may be hundreds of automatic teller machines spread over a wide geographic area. And all of this equipment needs to communicate with the central computer.

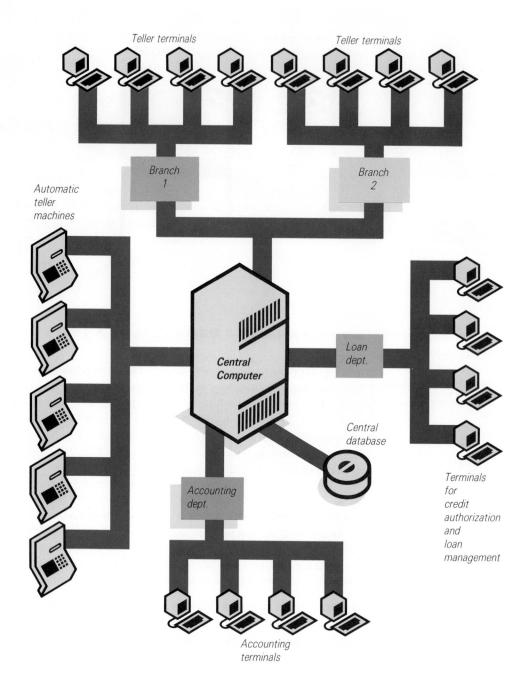

Teller terminals

Teller terminals

Automatic
teller
machines

Branch
1

Branch
2

Central
Computer

Loan
dept.

Central
database

Terminals
for
credit
authorization
and
loan
management

Accounting
dept.

Accounting
terminals

Figure 14-3.
A multibranch bank with automatic
teller machines and other terminals requires a sophisticated data communications network to connect all of its users to the central computer system.

FIRST INTERSTATE BANK OPERATES MORE THAN ONE THOUSAND
BRANCHES IN ELEVEN WESTERN STATES. In 1980 the bank began developing an elaborate communication network that would not only link
these branches' data processing activities to central computing facilities
but would also tie together their eight thousand automatic teller terminals. Today, with the network having been in operation for some time, a
customer can make a deposit or a withdrawal at any branch or teller

terminal location in the eleven-state region. The senior vice-president of marketing services claims that the development of this extensive inter-state communication network has helped First Interstate become a major financial institution. The communications network, he insists, has given the bank a competitive advantage over others in the region.

■■■■■■■■■■■■■■■■■■■■■■■■■■■■■■■■■■■■

The development of a complex data communication system such as the one used at First Interstate must be undertaken with the same care and organization used to develop a basic information processing system, described in the systems development chapters. In fact, communications design can be considered an additional stage in the systems development process. To understand the design of a communication system, we shall first explain how data can be transmitted.

TRANSMISSION SIGNAL

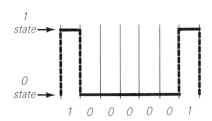

Figure 14-4.
Digital data move within the computer as a series of pulses.

Computers are digital devices. When data move from one place in a computer to another, they travel in the form of digital, or on–off, pulses. One such stream of digital data is shown in Figure 14-4. Although computers communicate within themselves in this format, they do not necessarily communicate with other computers or other peripheral devices in this way. For example, in some applications the most convenient way to tie a terminal in one location to a computer located hundreds of miles away is to use the same telephone network that carries conventional conversations. The problem, however, is that the telephone network was originally designed to accommodate only voice communication. And voice signals, as illustrated in Figure 14-5, are classified as *analog* signals. An analog signal takes the shape of a smooth wave in contrast to a digital signal with abrupt changes to peaks and valleys. So when a telephone network is used in data communication, digital information from a computer or a terminal must be transformed into an analog signal before it can be transmitted over the telephone network.

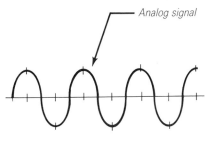

Figure 14-5.
The telephone network accommodates only analog signals. An analog signal is made up of a smooth wave instead of the sharp peaks and valleys in a digital signal.

The transformation from a digital signal into an analog signal occurs in a **modem** (short for modulator/demodulator). A modem is connected to the output of a computer or terminal and modulates, or converts, the digital signal into an analog one. Once modulated, the signal can then be transmitted over the communications network. When the signal reaches its destination, this process must be reversed: The signal must be processed by another modem and demodulated into a digital stream that the computer can once again understand and process (Figure 14-6).

When digital communication systems are used data are transmitted digitally between two points, with no conversion necessary to and from an analog signal. And when digital transmission is possible, the speed with which data can be sent increases dramatically.

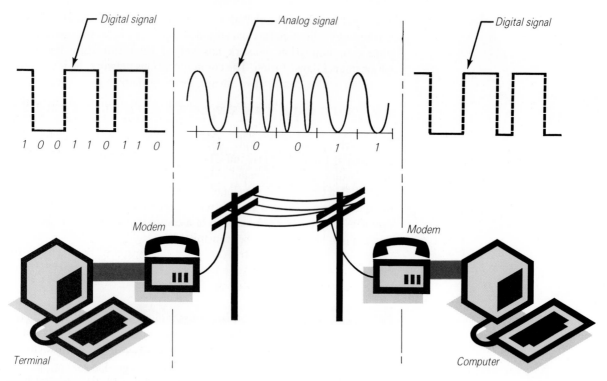

Figure 14-6.
To travel over the conventional telephone network, a digital signal from a
terminal is first modulated by a modem,
then transmitted, then demodulated at
its destination, and finally processed by
the computer.

TRANSMISSION MEDIA

Data can be transmitted over a variety of alternatives, including a simple twisted pair of wires, coaxial cables, microwave systems, and optical
fibers.

TWISTED-WIRE PAIR

Figure 14-7.
Most offices are already equipped with
twisted-wire pair for telephone communication, and as a result, these wires
are often used to connect computers
as well.

The oldest vehicle for transmitting data is the **twisted-wire pair** (Figure
14-7). It is the twisted-wire pair that runs from a telephone to a pole
outside and from there, bound together with other twisted-wire pairs, in
a cable to the telephone central office.

As we have just learned, twisted-wire pair was designed for voice
transmission, and so computer signals must be transformed from digital
into analog. Although not an ideal medium for transmitting data,
twisted wire has several advantages:

- The telephone network links the entire world.

- There is little additional equipment to buy.

- For many applications, it is the least expensive way to set up a
  point-to-point communication channel.

- Data transmission speed is fast enough for many applications.

Figure 14-8.
Coaxial cable, similar to the cable used by cable TV companies, can transmit data at a higher rate of speed than the twisted-wire pair can. Here, over twenty coaxial cables are combined in a protective casing.

For these reasons, twisted-wire pairs carry a significant portion of the world's data.

COAXIAL CABLE

Coaxial cable is a higher-quality transmission medium than is the twisted-wire pair (Figure 14-8). Unlike the twisted-wire pair, coaxial cable is relatively interference free, and so it can carry signals over longer distances without any deterioration in the quality of the signal. Coaxial cable also carries data faster than does twisted wire and can accommodate digital as well as analog signals.

MICROWAVE SYSTEMS

Microwaves are very high frequency signals that have the capacity to carry large quantities of data, both digital and analog, at high rates of speed. They are also used for the transmission of television and telephone signals.

A **microwave system** consists of towers located 25 to 30 miles apart on which are mounted dishlike antennas. Because microwave signals travel in a straight line and will not bend with the curvature of the earth, these towers must be within a line of sight from one another. When one tower receives a signal, it amplifies the signal and sends it to the next tower. About one thousand towers would be necessary to bridge the United States from coast to coast.

Communication satellites also use microwave technology (Figure 14-9). In these systems a signal is transmitted in a straight line from an earth station to a satellite in stationary orbit above the earth. When the satellite receives the signal, it amplifies it and returns it in another straight line to the receiving station on earth. You are probably familiar with this technology, because many home viewers use it to receive commercial television signals from satellites.

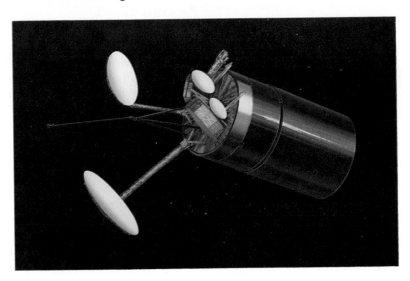

Figure 14-9.
Communication satellites are used in systems that transmit a significant amount of analog and digital data over a long distance.

Figure 14-10.
Fiber-optic cables are especially efficient for transmitting a high volume of digital data. Fiber-optic cable is already in place between most large North American cities.

FIBER-OPTIC CABLE

A **fiber-optic cable** is made from thousands of clear glass fibers, each about the thickness of a human hair (Figure 14-10). Data are transformed into light beams by a laser device and sent through the strands.

How do the different media compare? A twisted-wire pair can carry one voice channel; a coaxial cable can carry up to five thousand channels, and a fiber-optic cable can carry as many as fifty thousand channels simultaneously. The choice of medium depends on several factors, including the type of data to be transmitted, the speed desired, and the cost.

TRANSMISSION SPEED

The speed with which data are transmitted through a communications medium is measured in **bits per second (bps).** Some media such as fiber-optic cable can accommodate extremely high rates of transmission, while the twisted-wire pair in much of the telephone network can handle only a relatively slow rate of transmission.

Transmission speeds can be classified as narrowband, voice-grade, or wideband. The speed of **narrowband transmission** is between 45 and 150 bps, which is suitable only for telegraph and teletype communication.

Voice-grade transmission—so named because the media in this category can carry voice-quality communication—can reach speeds of up to 9600 bps. But to transmit at the highest end of the range, the lines must be "conditioned," a process that requires additional technology.

Wideband transmission, in which data can be transmitted digitally, is possible using microwave and fiber-optic technology. The speed of transmission is from 1 megabit per second (1,000,000 bits) to 1 gigabit per second (1000 megabits).

DATA COMMUNICATION CONVENTIONS

In order to communicate intelligibly, sending and receiving devices follow certain data communication conventions, which we will briefly describe next.

PARALLEL AND SERIAL TRANSMISSION

Data in a computer move around in 8-, 16-, or 32-bit channels. If the computer is a 16-bit computer (see Chapter 2), then the data will move around 16 bits at a time, or in 16-bit channels. If the computer is a 32-bit computer, then the data will move around 32 bits at a time, and so on.

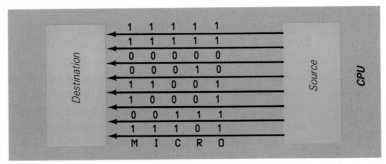

Parallel transmission

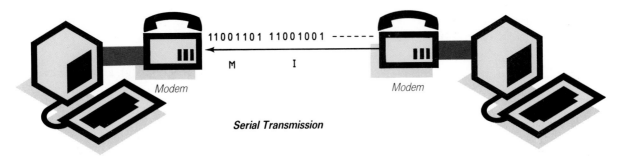

Serial Transmission

Figure 14-11.
Parallel and serial transmission.

Because these bits move in parallel (8, 16, or 32 bits at a time), this is called **parallel transmission** and is illustrated at the top of Figure 14-11.

Once outside the computer, data are usually transmitted on a single communications channel. **Serial transmission** must therefore be used, an approach in which one bit follows the next, as shown at the bottom of Figure 14-11. The biggest difference between these two methods is speed. Parallel transmission can obviously pass more information than can serial transmission. But parallel transmission is more expensive, as several channels must be used. Usually tape and disk devices communicate with the CPU in parallel, whereas modems communicate in serial. Serial communication can be categorized as *asynchronous* or *synchronous*.

ASYNCHRONOUS AND SYNCHRONOUS TRANSMISSION

In **asynchronous transmission** (Figure 14-12), each character is begun with a start bit and is ended with a stop bit. In between each pair of

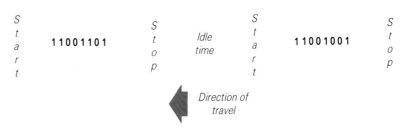

Figure 14-12.
In asynchronous transmission, each character is transmitted separately.

characters is a gap. Because of these added components, asynchronous transmission is considered relatively slow.

In **synchronous transmission** (Figure 14-13), another way to organize the data during serial transmission—a group of characters is transmitted over the line without start bits, stop bits, or gaps. The sending modem begins transmitting a block of data with a sync bit and follows this with a stream of characters. The receiving modem, which must know the speed of the originating transmission and the number of characters per block, begins reading when it receives the sync bit. It knows exactly how many bits to read for each character and, after breaking up the block, sends these characters, one at a time, to the computer. After it finishes, the modem listens for another sync bit and, when it receives it, begins the process again. Synchronous transmission is more complex and costs more but transmits data faster than does asynchronous transmission.

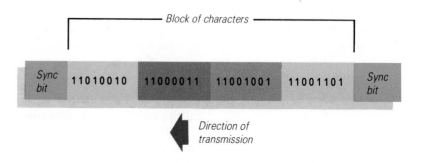

Figure 14-13.
In synchronous transmission, several characters are sent in a block.

DIRECTION OF TRAVEL

Another data transmission convention concerns the direction of travel. There are three possibilities: simplex, half-duplex, and full-duplex transmission (Figure 14-14).

In **simplex transmission,** data can be sent in one direction only. This alternative is seldom used, because even in such devices as a high-speed printer, an acknowledgement that the data have been received must be returned to the computer.

In **half-duplex transmission,** data are transmitted in both directions, but in only one direction at a time. This mode is often used when a microcomputer communicates with a mainframe. First the microcomputer transmits data to the mainframe; then the flow of data is reversed, and the mainframe transmits in the opposite direction. Common examples of this mode are intercoms and CB radios, on which two people cannot talk at once.

In **full-duplex transmission,** data can be transmitted in both directions simultaneously. No time is needed to reverse the flow of data. Consequently, this mode can transmit data very quickly.

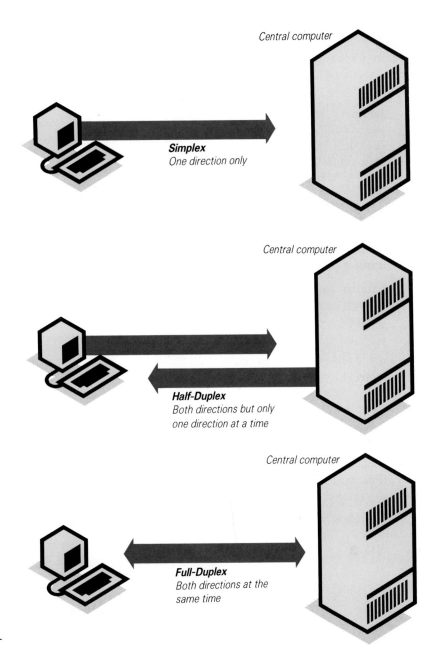

Figure 14-14.
Transmission in the simplex, half-duplex, and full-duplex modes.

● ●

E N D · U S E R   H I N T S

WHEN IS IT NECESSARY TO COMMUNICATE?

From a technical perspective, communications facilities must be used when computers, terminals, or other peripheral devices such as printers are geographically separated and must be connected.

From the end-user's perspective, here are some situations in which communications facilities are needed.

1. Internal company data, stored on-line but at another computer location or stored at a central facility in another geographical location, must be accessed or shared.

2. Data must be transferred among divisions of a company. Electronic funds transfer is an example.

3. External data, such as stock market, economic, or industry data, must be accessed.

4. Data from sources outside the company must be directly entered into the company's database through remote terminals. Examples include customer order data and airline reservations.

5. Data about a firm's operations must be made available to external organizations.

These data will be used to provide an efficient linkage between the two organizations. For example, manufacturing firms link suppliers directly to their production scheduling and inventory systems, so that the suppliers will know exactly when certain orders must be shipped. In this way the manufacturer can meet "just-in-time" objectives and avoid the costs of shipments that are either too early or too late to be useful.

6. Suppliers need to send invoice data directly from their computer to the customer's computer.

7. Business professionals use their portable computers outside the company, at home or away on a business trip, to upload or download data.

8. Reports need to be compiled that will include summary data from several divisions, each of which maintains its own computing facilities.

9. Salespeople must access a database using a portable terminal from a customer's location to answer questions about a product or service, or to provide the customer with price and delivery data.

10. Control over geographically dispersed operations is maintained by uploading batch data to a central computer. The point-of-sale terminals used in many restaurant chains, for example, are polled each evening. The machines at each site send summary sales data over communications facilities to central computers; corporate reports can then be produced the next day summarizing the previous day's sales results.

11. Electronic mail and computer conferencing systems are used.

MODEMS

Modems come in a variety of configurations. Some are built into the computer. Others, called **on-board modems** or **expansion card modems,** can be installed in the machine (Figure 14-15). A third type, **stand-alone modems,** are available as a separate unit that can be connected to the computer through a cable.

MODEM SPEED

Modem speeds range from 300 to 2400 bps and beyond. Most modems used with the switched telephone network operate at 300, 1200, or 2400 bps. Some operate as high as 9600 bps, under certain conditions. Slower modems cost less, but the data transfer rate is relatively slow. A 300-bps modem can transmit data at the rate of about 30 to 35 characters per

Figure 14-15.
This expansion card modem can communicate at speeds up to 2400 bits per second.

second, which is about 300 to 350 words per minute. Because a standard double-spaced typewritten page can hold about 300 words, it would take about 10 minutes to transmit a 10-page report.

This rate would probably not be acceptable for most business applications, as few people can afford to wait while data are being transferred. And because users generally work with relatively large data files, a modem should be capable of at least 1200 bps, with most users preferring 2400 bps.

■■■■■■■■■■■■■■■■■■■■■■■■■■■■■■■■■■■■

EAGLE BROKERAGE SERVICES OFFERS A FINANCIAL INFORMATION SERVICE, whereby customers can use their microcomputer to access up-to-the-minute stock reports and even enter orders to buy and sell stock from an account. Subscribers to the service pay a monthly flat fee and in addition are billed for the length of time they are connected to the service. They can choose between two speeds, 300 or 1200 bps.

Using one popular modem, the user enters Eagle's telephone number through the computer's keyboard. The modem then automatically dials the number. When the line is answered, the subscriber's modem "announces" its speed to the Eagle computer. Next, the caller enters an account number and then is given access to the system and the services.

When a customer buys a modem to access this service, he or she must choose either the slower or the faster one. Faster communication speeds mean less time to access information and lower long-distance bills. A subscriber who needs to update fifty stock prices in a portfolio might spend ten minutes on the line at 300 bps but less than four minutes at 1200 bps. The 1200 bps service, however, costs twice as much per minute as does the 300 bps service. But the data are transferred four times faster. Is a 1200 bps modem better? The answer depends on the cost differential between the faster and the slower modem, how often the system will be used, and the cost of long-distance calls.

■■■■■■■■■■■■■■■■■■■■■■■■■■■■■■■■■■■■

Figure 14-16.
This intelligent modem can automatically dial any number that it has stored in its memory and can automatically answer incoming calls. A salesperson can then call this computer using a portable computer at the customer's site and obtain sales information about that customer stored in the central computer.

INTELLIGENT MODEMS

Modems that include other features beyond the ability to transform signals from digital into analog or analog into digital are called **intelligent modems** or **smart modems** (Figure 14-16). With one feature, *auto-dial,* the modem can automatically dial one of several numbers stored in its memory. In addition, many modems also enable the user to redial automatically the last number, by pressing a single key, and others redial a telephone number until the line is answered. Using another feature, *auto-answer,* a computer can be called from a remote location, and the modem will automatically answer the call and initiate remote access. This feature enables a user to access an office computer from another unit, perhaps a small portable.

MODEM PROTOCOLS

Before one modem can communicate with another, both must be able to transmit and receive data in the same way; that is, they must share the same protocol. **Protocol** refers to the formal rules governing the flow of information in a communication system. To be compatible, both modems must

- Be either synchronous or asynchronous.

- Transmit at the same speed.

- Use the same error-checking methods (if any).

- Share other technical procedures in the transmission and reception of data.

?   Q U E S T I O N S   ?

1. What is data communication?
2. Why is data communication so important to such applications as airline reservation and banking?
3. Why is the telephone network used so often to carry computer data?
4. How do a digital and an analog signal differ?
5. Which transmission medium moves data the slowest? What moves them the quickest?
6. How does microwave transmission differ from fiber-optic transmission?
7. Which transmission media are capable of wideband transmission?
8. What is the difference between serial and parallel transmission?
9. What is the difference between half-duplex and full-duplex transmission?
10. How is the speed of a modem measured? What are three typical modem speeds?

MANAGING COMMUNICATION TRAFFIC

A large data communication system, serving hundreds of terminals, printers, data entry devices, and microcomputers, must be managed to coordinate the interaction of all the equipment and to ensure the efficient use of costly communication services. In the following sections we shall discuss how different types of hardware devices are used to manage these communication systems.

LINE CONFIGURATIONS

Two broad categories for describing the way in which communications lines are laid out, or configured, include point-to-point and multidrop.

In a **point-to-point** configuration, a direct line is established between the central computer and each device. While this method, illustrated at the top of Figure 14-17, is often chosen when periodic communication is needed, it is almost always chosen when constant and uninterrupted communication is needed between two points. The cost of this connection, however, can be high.

One example of a point-to-point configuration is found in the private telephone network within a company. These private networks are usually managed by a PBX (Private Branch Exchange), whose function it is to act as a switching center connecting the public telephone network

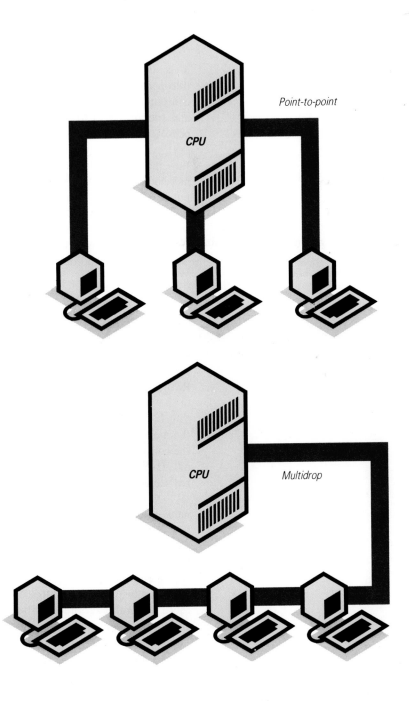

Figure 14-17.
Point-to-point and multidrop configurations.

outside the company with all the telephones inside the company. For example, when one employee dials another's telephone extension, the PBX will establish a point-to-point connection between the two parties. Or the PBX can route calls made from the private network to the public telephone network. While the initial purpose of a PBX was to connect telephone callers in a voice environment, this equipment is now made to handle the switching of both voice and data so that point-to-point connections can be established between computers and other computer devices. Some PBXs are designed to handle both analog and digital data signals and even convert analog to digital signals so the data, when they leave the PBX, can be sent over a digital network.

The second category for describing a communication layout is illustrated at the bottom of Figure 14-17. In this approach, called a **multidrop configuration,** several devices can share a common line to the computer. It is an efficient solution when a single terminal sends slow and sporadic data to the central computer and a dedicated line would prove to be too costly. Terminals in an order-entry department, for example, since they send relatively small amounts of data at relatively slow speeds, may be connected in this way. Each sales-order entry terminal would be tied to a central line which is then connected to the computer. The benefit from this approach is not only lower communication costs but less wiring. But the problem is that the central computer must manage the flow of data over this single line to prevent more than one user from accessing it at the same time (more about this in Chapter 15). This can add an additional burden to the computer.

CONTROLLERS

A **controller,** often a specialized minicomputer, is a device that is used to supervise and coordinate data traffic in a communication system. Rather than routing the data from a cluster of remote terminals directly to the computer, the data are first sent to a controller. The controller thus is a device for collecting signals from remote terminals and sending them on to the computer. And when data flow in the opposite direction, the controller is a device for routing the data back to the proper terminal. In a multidrop configuration, the controller also manages a terminal's access to the line.

Controllers are used because the job of managing a communications network is a complex and burdensome task, and assigning these functions to a central computer could impose a load too great for it to handle efficiently. But if the communications job is assigned to a controller, the central computer will be free to concentrate on user applications.

Front-end processors (Figure 14-18) are sophisticated controllers. They can be programmed to secure the system by limiting access only to those with valid account numbers, and they can also be programmed to validate or change incoming data. In short, they are sophisticated communications network managers.

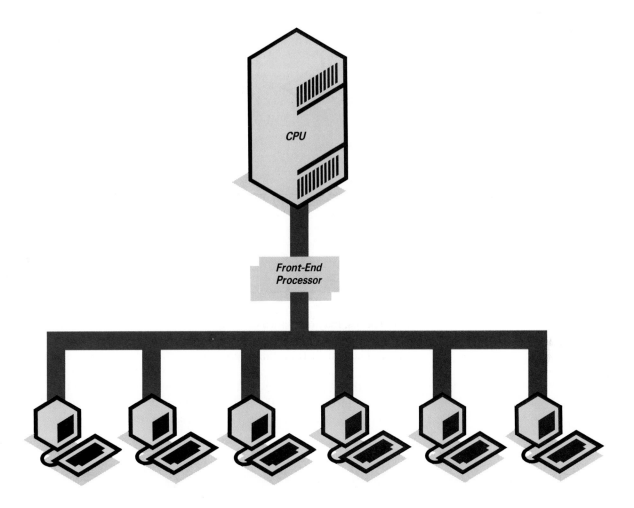

Figure 14-18.
Front-end processors are programmable controllers. They are used to coordinate the flow of data in a computer system and relieve the central computer from these tasks.

MULTIPLEXERS AND CONCENTRATORS

Some devices in a computer system need to communicate with the central computer at relatively slow rates of speed. Order-entry clerks, for example, work at speeds that are much slower than the speed at which a computer can process data. If a single communication line were dedicated to these slower devices, it would represent an inefficient and costly use of communication resources. It makes more sense, therefore, to combine the signals from several slow-speed devices and send them to their destinations at higher speeds over a communications network.

A **multiplexer** (Figure 14-19) is a device that makes this possible. The multiplexer first combines the slow-speed signals and transmits them over a single high-speed line. At the receiving end, another multiplexer converts or "demultiplexes" the signals. By sharing a single line, communications costs are reduced.

A **concentrator** combines slow-speed signals, and can be programmed. For this reason a concentrator is sometimes referred to as an *intelligent multiplexer*. In some applications, a concentrator is pro-

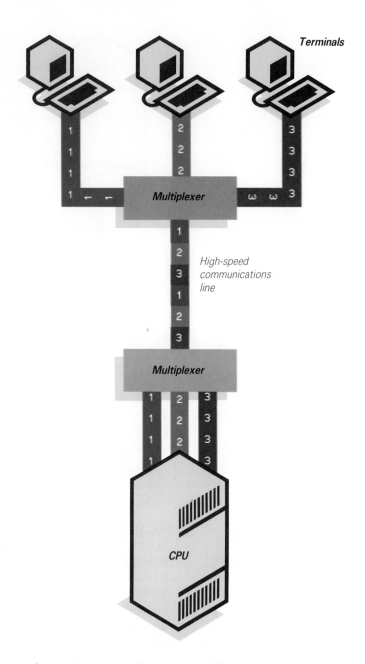

Figure 14-19.
Multiplexers combine signals from several sources and send them over a single high-speed channel.

grammed to pool messages from several different sources and save them for transmission all at once. This is especially economical for trans-Atlantic or transcontinental transmissions.

DATA COMMUNICATION SOFTWARE

Communication software is required when any computer—including a front-end processor—or peripheral device must send or receive data over a communications network. This software, considered part of the system software discussed in Chapter 2, is responsible for a range of functions, from establishing the connection between the equipment in the network to terminating the link when the transmission is completed. Because the computers and peripheral equipment in the network may be very different, the way each one packages and handles data may be different. As a result communication software must be able to convert the protocol of one device to the protocol of another. In effect, this communication software must act like an interpreter at the United Nations.

Because errors can be introduced during the transmission process, the communication software must also be able to detect these errors and, in some cases, to correct them.

Some communication software maintain a log of communications activity. Using this log, communications experts can determine how the network is being used. Such information is helpful when modifying the design to improve network efficiency.

OBTAINING COMMUNICATIONS SERVICES: THE ALTERNATIVES

There is a wide range of choices from which to select an appropriate communications network. At one extreme a user can choose to plug into the local telephone system, and at the other extreme a company may decide to construct its own private microwave communications network. First let us talk about the telephone system.

SWITCHED TELEPHONE NETWORK

Without doubt, the telephone network we use every day, called a **switched telephone network,** is the most convenient and accessible network available. Through it, communication channels can be established instantly between any locations in the world. All that is required is a telephone plug.

In some applications it is more economical to lease a nonswitched line, called a **private line.** These are leased from a **common carrier** such as a telephone company. Private lines provide a dedicated connection from one point to another. Rather than paying long-distance rates, which are based on time and distance, a flat fee is paid for the private line. But volume must be high for this alternative to be cost effective. Private-line users do, however, often enjoy another advantage: a better-quality connection than with a switched line, which makes it possible to use modems with higher transmission rates. Indeed, sometimes a private line is chosen for this reason alone.

SPECIALIZED COMMON CARRIERS

Specialized common carriers—such as MCI and ITT—have developed their own communications networks that are much more specialized than is the public telephone network. Their networks are capable of digital transmission at high speed and at a competitive cost. Companies that can't afford to develop their own networks lease time from these carriers and use their fiber-optic or microwave systems to send their own data. One limitation, however, is that these services are usually only offered between major international cities.

VALUE-ADDED CARRIERS

Still another source of communication services is the **value-added carrier,** such as Tymnet and Telenet. These organizations sell communications services to companies but may not necessarily operate their own communications network. For example, several carriers in this category receive customer data over the switched telephone network, temporarily store the data in "packets," send the packets over high-speed networks—which they lease from common carriers—to a facility in the vicinity of their destination, decompose the signal to its original format, and then complete the communication link over the switched telephone network to its final destination. Although the data stream has undergone additional processing, this may still prove to be a less expensive way to send the information than if the customer had used the switched telephone network for the entire link between its source and destination, for example.

PRIVATE NETWORKS

A **private network** is one that a company builds and operates for its own exclusive use. Microwave, satellite, and even fiber-optic systems, are very expensive and require heavy use before they can be cost justified. Nonetheless, there can be segments of an organization's communication system that are so busy, or that would require the purchase of such costly services from common carriers, that a private, custom-designed solution may be appropriate (Figure 14-20).

■ ■

AUTOJOB INC., an automotive subcontractor based in Detroit, installed a microwave system that connects three plants all located within a 30-mile radius. Each of the plants has its own minicomputer. During both shifts the computers continuously exchange and share data. Before the system was installed, AutoJob used private leased lines to carry the data among the plants, but the cost was high. Now, with microwave towers on each of the buildings, AutoJob has its own private communications system that will pay for itself in less than three years.

Figure 14-20.
Private communication networks are
feasible when the volume of voice and
data communication is high.

But this private network solves only part of AutoJob's data communication requirements. It continues to use the switched telephone network and a value-added carrier for less frequent transmission of sales and service data between five sales offices and its central facility.

■■■■■■■■■■■■■■■■■■■■■■■■■■■■■

THE DATA IN A COMMUNICATIONS NETWORK

DATA MUST BE ON-LINE

The demands made on data in a system that supports remote users are different from the demands made on data that can be accessed only at a central facility. First, the data must be on-line.

In systems that support remote access, it makes little sense to store data off-line. After all, one of the purposes of these systems is to offer users immediate access. If a user has to wait for a tape to be mounted and an entire file to be read, or to wait while a removable disk pack is mounted, the full potential of a data communication system will be lost. Consequently, most of these systems require that most of the data be stored on-line, which may mean very large capacity disk systems, in the range of several gigabytes.

DATA MUST BE ACCURATE

Because the data in these systems are accessible to a wide range of users, accuracy becomes a real problem. How is it possible to guarantee the integrity of data that may be entered or changed by users located hundreds or even thousands of miles from the central facility? How can it be possible to prevent an inventory clerk from entering a wrong number, an accountant from crediting the wrong account, a department store employee from entering the wrong product identification code, or a salesperson from entering the wrong customer ID number?

In Chapter 13, we learned that beyond verification, validation, control totals, and audit trails, there is little else that can be done. The major responsibility for data accuracy belongs to those using the system.

DATA MUST BE SECURE

Data communication is so successful in making data available to remote locations that control over the system can be lost. For example, if an auto-answer modem is tied to a microcomputer or even a mainframe system, then anyone who knows the telephone number may be able to access the system, change the data, and print reports. And as we will discover in Chapter 16, this is not an unlikely possibility.

To understand the vulnerability of data transmitted through communications networks, one has only to look at the two million homes that have sprouted dish-shaped microwave-receiving antennas for intercepting satellite TV signals. But these signals are not intended for home viewing. Rather, they are to transfer programming material from TV networks to their affiliated local stations and cable broadcasters. By using microwave dishes, however, home viewers can intercept 2500 cable news, information, and variety shows each week, without paying a cent.

In 1985, several of the cable networks—including HBO, ESPN, and the Disney Channel—began to put an end to the free buffet, by scrambling the signal sent through space.

The data that corporations send through the microwave and satellite networks are also vulnerable to interception. Therefore, they use a process somewhat similar to scrambling called **encryption,** which codes the data so that they are unintelligible without knowledge of the coding scheme; that is, the data must be decoded before they can be used.

As we mentioned earlier, the use of **passwords** is another technique for securing data. When used effectively they can prevent the unauthorized use of a computer system. And access can be made selective. An accounting clerk, for example, may be able to enter transactions but may not be given access to the inventory system. An inventory clerk, on the other hand, might be given access to the inventory database but denied entry to the accounting system.

ACCESSING PUBLIC DATABASES WITH A MODEM

One particularly useful application of data communication technology is access to public databases. There are many services available that offer such access, providing users with a wide spectrum of information. The cost is usually based on connect time.

■■■■■■■■■■■■■■■■■■■■■■■■■■■■■■■■

PENN TOY COMPANY, a toy manufacturer in Erie, Pennsylvania, periodically accesses an "electronic yellow pages" database maintained by Dialog Information Services of Palo Alto, California. This database, one of hundreds offered by Dialog, provides on-line directory listings for wholesalers in over 4800 cities in the United States. The listings, obtained from local yellow pages directories, include 500,000 entries and are updated semiannually.

The wholesalers are listed according to such categories as automotive parts, office furniture, housewares, lumber, toy and hobby supplies, electrical equipment, and farm and garden machinery. Each entry, or record, includes the company's name and address, its telephone number, the size of the city in which it is located, and the type of listing in the yellow pages ad (ordinary listing, boldface listing, or display ad). Penn Toy uses this database to obtain mailing lists of toy wholesalers and to find prospective buyers. And before a sales representative takes a trip, the marketing department refers to the database to print a list of all the wholesalers in the region to be visited. The list is sorted by the type of the ad. The marketing manager believes that larger companies have more expensive ads, and so sorting on this basis has helped rank these prospects by sales potential.

■■■■■■■■■■■■■■■■■■■■■■■■■■■■■■■■

To the Penn Toy Company, and others who use public databases, the primary advantage is access to external data without the need to be concerned with keeping the data up-to-date. It is the database company's responsibility to keep them up-to-date. The user simply needs a computer, a modem, and an understanding of how to use the database query language to search the database for the desired data.

?   Q U E S T I O N S   ?

1. What is the function of a controller?
2. How is a front-end processor used in a communication system?
3. What is the difference between a concentrator and a multiplexer?
4. Is it always cheapest to use the switched telephone network for data communication?
5. What is a value-added carrier?
6. When can a private network be cost justified?
7. Compare the differing demands placed on data sent through a communications network to remote locations and data that can be accessed only at a central facility.

S U M M A R Y

- **Data communication** is the process by which data are moved from one point in an information system to another.

- Computers are digital devices, and much data communication is carried by lines unequipped for digital signals; therefore, a **modem** is used to transform the signal from digital to analog and back. An increasing share of data, however, is carried digitally over specialized facilities.

- Data transmission media include **twisted-wire pair, coaxial cable, microwave systems,** and **fiber-optic cable.**

- Transmission speed, measured in **bits per second (bps),** is classified as **narrowband transmission** (45 to 150 bps), **voice-grade transmission** (up to 9600 bps), or **wideband transmission** (up to 500,000 bps and beyond).

- When a number of bits of data travel at the same time over parallel channels, this is known as **parallel transmission.** When data travel one bit at a time through a single channel, this is known as **serial transmission.**

- Serial transmission can be either asynchronous or synchronous. In **asynchronous transmission,** characters are sent one at a time and preceded by a start bit, ended with a stop bit, and followed by a gap. In **synchronous transmission,** characters are sent in blocks preceded by a sync bit.

- Concerning transmission direction, data can be sent with **simplex transmission** (in one direction only), **half-duplex transmission** (in both directions but only one at a time), or **full-duplex transmission** (in both directions simultaneously).

- Some modems are built into the computer. **On-board modems** or **expansion card modems** can be installed in the computer. **Stand-alone modems** are separate units connected to the computer with a cable.

- **Intelligent modems** are capable of doing more than transforming digital signals to analog and back again.

- **Protocol** refers to the formal rules governing the flow of information in a communication system.

- A central computer can be connected to remote devices by either a **point-to-point configuration** or a **multidrop configuration.**

- A **controller** supervises and coordinates data traffic in a communication system. **Front-end processors** are sophisticated controllers.

- A **multiplexer** combines signals from several slow-speed devices and sends them to their destinations at higher speeds. **Concentrators** are sophisticated multiplexers.

- Communications services choices include the **switched telephone network, private lines** leased from a **common carrier, specialized common carriers, value-added carriers,** and **private networks.**

- When data can be accessed by remote users rather than only at a central facility, the data must be on-line, accurate, and secure.

- **Encryption** and **passwords** are used to help reduce data vulnerability.

- One useful application of data communication technology is to tap some of the numerous public databases.

K E Y • T E R M S

The following list shows the key terms in the order in which they appear in the chapter.

Data communication (p. 398)
Modem (p. 401)
Twisted-wire pair (p. 402)
Coaxial cable (p. 403)
Microwave system (p. 403)
Fiber-optic cable (p. 404)
Bits per second (bps) (p. 404)
Narrowband transmission (p. 404)
Voice-grade transmission (p. 404)
Wideband transmission (p. 404)
Parallel transmission (p. 405)
Serial transmission (p. 405)
Asynchronous transmission (p. 405)
Synchronous transmission (p. 406)
Simplex transmission (p. 406)
Half-duplex transmission (p. 406)
Full-duplex transmission (p. 406)
On-board modem or expansion card modem (p. 408)
Stand-alone modem (p. 408)
Intelligent modem or smart modem (p. 409)
Protocol (p. 410)
Point-to-point configuration (p. 410)
Multidrop configuration (p. 412)
Controller (p. 412)
Front-end processor (p. 412)
Multiplexer (p. 413)
Concentrator (p. 413)
Switched telephone network (p. 415)
Private line (p. 415)
Common carrier (p. 415)
Specialized common carrier (p. 416)
Value-added carrier (p. 416)
Private network (p. 416)
Encryption (p. 418)
Password (p. 418)

F O R   D I S C U S S I O N

1. Do you think it would be possible for a competitor to intercept reports traveling through a communication system and use this information to sabotage a company's plans? How might this be prevented?

2. Suppose that a large regional bank has asked you for advice. The bank has recently received approval to merge with another bank in a neighboring state. Both banks have extensive data communications systems, including hundreds of automatic teller machines. The bank wants to know the following:

   ■ Whether the banks should consider merging their data communication systems.

   ■ What the advantages would be of this communications merger to their customers.

   ■ What the advantages would be to the company.

   ■ What the disadvantages would be.

   ■ What problems you can foresee in the process.

   ■ Whether a merger of the data communication systems could be used as a strategic advantage by the marketing department of the newly enlarged bank.

   After a brief tour of both data centers, you conclude that each bank approaches its data processing problems in very different ways. Explain how this might affect your approach to the problem.

3. Electronic Box Office Corporation sells tickets to sporting and other entertainment events through 200 remote terminal locations. At these locations the terminals are connected to the company's mainframe through the switched telephone network. As the system has been growing, the response time for each terminal has gotten longer. Sometimes ticket agents must wait for a minute or more before they can get a response. The company that sold the computer to Electronic Box Office said that it needs a larger one. A modem manufacturer, however, indicated that the system's response would be improved with a faster modem. Another vendor suggested a front-end processor, and still another recommended a multiplexer. Which of these alternatives makes the most sense to you? What would be your next step?

4. A manufacturing company with plants in four states requires that each of the plants enter production data using key-to-disk machines and then forward the disks by means of an overnight express service to headquarters, where the corporate database is updated. Corporate reports using these data are ready one week

after receiving the data. Design a new system that would improve the timeliness of the data. Describe your choice of input methods and communication facilities. Why did you choose them? What are the advantages and disadvantages of your system?

HANDS-ON PROJECTS

1. Find an article in a computer or business periodical that shows how data communication is used to tie together a computer system. What transmission medium is used? Is a private network used? What data communication conventions do you believe are employed? Do you think controllers and multiplexers are used?
    Suggestions: PC Week, Computerworld, Business Computer Systems, Business Week.
2. Find an advertisement for a modem, and summarize its features.
    Suggestions: PC Week, Byte, PC World.
3. Visit a travel agency, insurance agency, or car rental agency, and find out how data communication plays a role in its computer system. What transmission medium is used? Are modems used? At what speed do they operate? Does the system use the switched telephone network? If so, why? What is the response time? Does the system ever become so overloaded that the response time suffers?

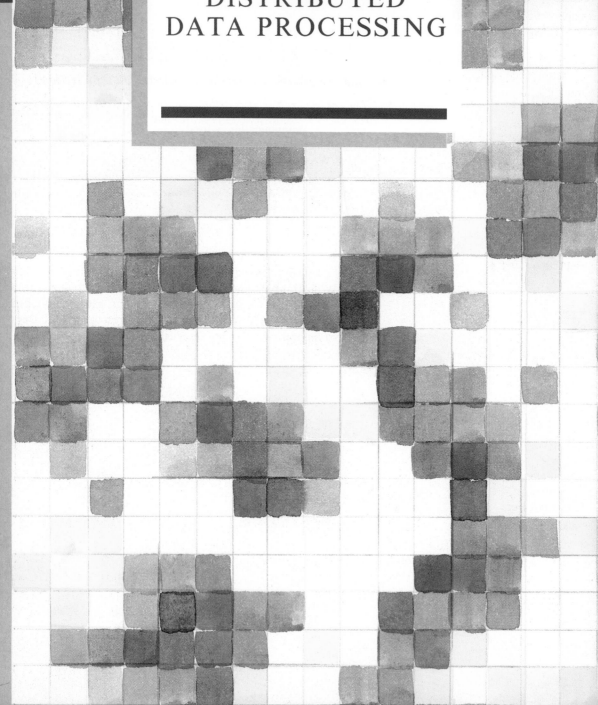

15
DISTRIBUTED
DATA PROCESSING

O U T L I N E

O B J E C T I V E S

After studying this chapter you should understand the following:

■ *The characteristics of distributed data processing and some representative uses by today's corporations.*

■ *The different forms of network topology.*

■ *Some of the problems associated with managing distributed data.*

■ *How local area networks function.*

■ *The role of departmental computing in a distributed computing environment.*

CENTRALIZED AND DISTRIBUTED DATA PROCESSING

In the last chapter we discussed how communications technology is used to tie together the hardware in an information system. All of the applications in that chapter were examples of **centralized data processing.** With centralized data processing, the CPU, storage devices, software, and the professional data processing staff are located in one central facility.

As you can see from Figure 15-1, all of the devices in centralized systems—including multiplexers, terminals, and printers—converge on one central computer, even though the users may work at distant terminals. All processing and storage take place at the central location.

But in some systems, the computers, storage devices, and even some computer professionals are distributed to separate locations throughout the organization (Figure 15-2). This is referred to as **distributed data processing** (or **distributed processing** for short). Processing and storage may occur at several locations in the computer system, now

Figure 15-1.
In centralized data processing, storage and processing are located at a centralized location. In some centralized systems, such as the one shown here, the users and terminals may be positioned at remote locations, but storage and processing are still confined to the central location.

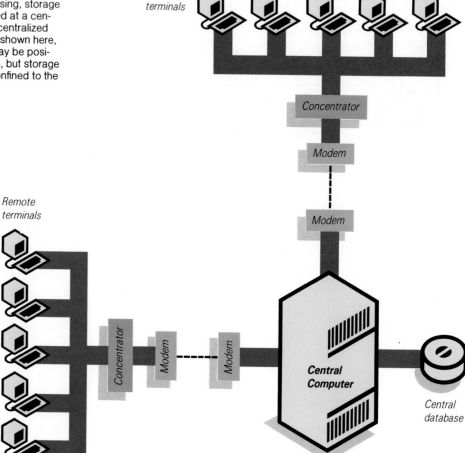

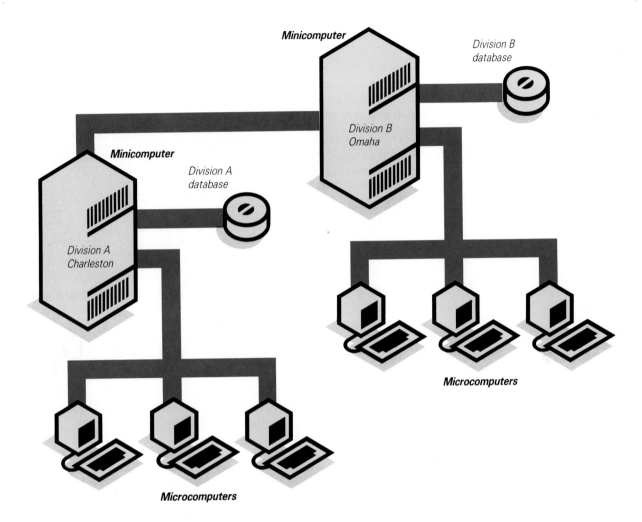

Figure 15-2.
A distributed data processing system decentralizes the information processing function by storing and processing data at those locations where the work is done.

called a **network.** Several computers, each located at a different point or **node** in the network, may be used. The communications technology described in Chapter 14 is used to tie together the computers.

Most organizations can benefit from using distributed processing. Such a system can be more responsive to its users' needs, and it may cost less to develop and maintain than a centralized system does.

This chapter will describe how distributed systems are designed, what hardware and software are used, how the hardware is connected, how data are distributed in the network, how data management issues change, and how organizations use these systems.

EXAMPLES OF DISTRIBUTED SYSTEMS

To understand how distributed systems are developed and used, we will begin by examining several examples.

DISTRIBUTING THE PROCESSING FUNCTION

The first examples show distributed systems in which the database remains centralized, but part of the processing function is distributed.

■■■■■■■■■■■■■■■■■■■■■■■■■■■■■■■■■■

JEFFREY SILVERMAN IS A TRADER ON THE FLOOR OF THE CHICAGO MER-CANTILE EXCHANGE. On his desk sits a microcomputer that is in continuous communication with a central computer that monitors all stock, bond, option, and commodity trades at the Merc as well as trading activities at other exchanges.

The mainframe downloads the trading data to Silverman's micro. These data are then stored on his 30-megabyte hard disk. Using his microcomputer, Silverman can obtain recent price quotes or process the data to obtain summaries, draw graphs, or prepare reports.

■■■■■■■■■■■■■■■■■■■■■■■■■■■■■■■■■■

In this application, the data are transmitted in just one direction. Data are sent, or **downloaded,** from the central computer to the micro; they are not sent in the opposite direction, from the micro to the central computer at the stock exchange. Nor are data shared among users at remote microcomputers. This is primarily a centralized database system with some sharing of the processing load at the local level.

Now let us look at another simple distributed system.

■■■■■■■■■■■■■■■■■■■■■■■■■■■■■■■■■■

THE WORLD TIMES, a newspaper printed in a major Northeastern city, uses a distributed network to collect and process news copy. Reporters, located throughout the world, use microcomputers or small laptop portables to write their stories. While writing, they work only with their personal computers. When they complete a story, they transmit it through a modem to the company's central system. At that point, there is additional processing as these and other stories are edited and combined to build the copy for the newspaper.

■■■■■■■■■■■■■■■■■■■■■■■■■■■■■■■■■■

In the *World Times* application, local computers collect data, process them, and then transmit or **upload** them to a centralized facility. Again, transmission is in just one direction, but this time from the micro to the central computer. And again, the database is centralized, and the data are not shared among the micro users.

DISTRIBUTING THE PROCESSING AND STORAGE FUNCTIONS

Although sharing the processing function distributes the computing load to computers away from the central computer, in most cases distributed data processing is chosen because storage too can be distributed. Furthermore, the data stored at the different locations can be shared among the users. The following case shows how these characteristics of a distributed system can help an organization use its data resources more effectively.

■■■■■■■■■■■■■■■■■■■■■■■■■■■■■■■■■■■■

LEN AND JERRY'S IS AN AUTO PARTS CHAIN LOCATED IN THE MIDWEST. The chain has sixteen stores, divided into three districts. Seven are located in the first district, four in the second, and five in the third. Each store has its own minicomputer, with 300 megabytes of hard disk storage. Connected to these minis are several terminals, many sitting right on sales counters and used as point-of-sale terminals into which the data for each sale are entered. Minicomputers are also located in each of the district offices and at corporate headquarters. The system is illustrated in Figure 15-3.

Each store is responsible for processing its own accounting, inventory, and order-processing data. Accordingly, the minis at these loca-

Figure 15-3.
This network of computers is configured as a hierarchy. Information is collected at each auto parts store and is transmitted to the mini at division headquarters. The summary data are, in turn, transmitted to the central corporate computer.

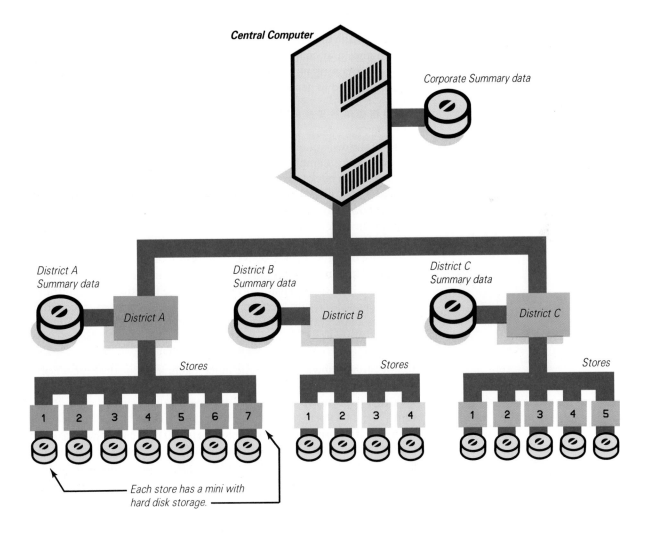

tions are equipped with the necessary software to accommodate these functions. And they all use exactly the same software.

But in addition to processing local data, the computer at each store can communicate with the computers at the other stores in its division. The sales clerks use this feature in the following way: When a customer requests a part that the inventory system reports to be out of stock, the clerk can ask whether the other stores in its division have it on their shelves. This inquiry is entered into the point-of-sale terminal, sent to other minis in the division, and the response returned to the minicomputer that originated the request. If the item is found at any of these locations and if the customer is willing to return in a few hours or the next day, the system will produce the paperwork necessary to have the part delivered by company van.

The computers at the division level of Len and Jerry's can access the minis at each store and monitor the sales, inventory, and purchasing data. In addition, these minis can aggregate accounting data and produce financial reports for the division. In other words, the division-level computers are used mainly for operational management and operational planning activities.

At the corporate level, the computer can access data from either the store or the division levels. Often the data are used to monitor actual performance and compare it with budget and sales goals, to negotiate purchasing contracts with vendors, to produce consolidated financial statements, and to generate data for management-planning purposes.

■■■■■■■■■■■■■■■■■■■■■■■■■■■■■■■■■■

Many of the distributed processing systems used in multibranch banking are even more complex than the system described in the preceding example. Turn back to the multibranch bank example in the last chapter (Figure 14-3). This system is centralized rather than distributed: The remote devices all converge on a central computer through a data communication system. Figure 15-4 illustrates one way that the processing load for that system can be distributed. In the new system, minicomputers are used at the branch banks and are responsible for the local processing of services such as savings and checking accounts and loans. Each machine uses duplicate software for these functions. A mainframe at the central facility performs all of the consolidated accounting functions and is responsible for processing both transactions through the bank's network of automatic teller machines and credit-card transactions.

Consider how the automatic teller machine application must work. When a customer initiates a withdrawal transaction, the data associated with this request are first sent to the mainframe. Then the branch at which the customer's records are maintained must be determined and the request forwarded to the appropriate branch minicomputer. The disk at this location is then searched to verify the customer's account and to determine whether the balance in the account is adequate. If there is enough money in the account, the depositor's record will be updated to reflect the withdrawal. Next, the data are returned to the automatic

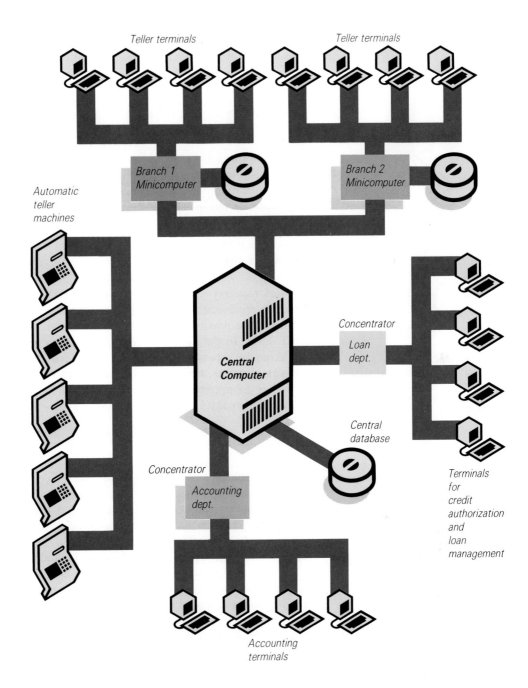

Figure 15-4.
A multibranch distributed processing system. Processing is done at each branch bank and also at the bank's central computer.

teller, and finally, the machine dispenses the cash and prints a receipt. All of this takes but a few seconds.

Many distributed systems, such as this banking example, are complex. Not only must the minicomputers in these systems perform as stand-alone machines, but they also must be able to interact with other machines in a network and share files.

In the next section we will examine the different physical layouts that can be used to connect distributed hardware. Then, in the following sections, we will see what system software is needed and how the data management process for these systems is affected.

DISTRIBUTED HARDWARE

The hardware in a distributed system may include mainframes, minis, micros, disk storage devices, printers, and other devices tied together by a communication system. Sometimes one computer may serve as a central computer; one or more may control communication; and others will be located close to where business tasks must be done.

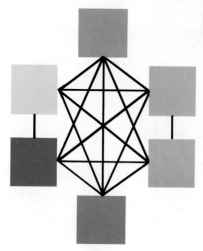

Figure 15-5.
If a line or cable were connected to every device in the system, each computer could have hundreds of wires connected to it.

NETWORK TOPOLOGY

Network topology refers to the way in which data are routed, or the way in which machines are positioned and physically interconnected, in a network. One possibility is to wire every computer and device to every other device in the network. You can see from Figure 15-5 that this would require extensive wiring. As the number of devices attached to the network increases, the number of wires or cables grows geometrically. Seldom is this approach used. Most distributed networks use a star, ring, or hybrid topology.

STAR TOPOLOGY

In a **star topology,** a point-to-point connection (see Chapter 14) is established between a centrally located computer and each of the system's other computers and devices (Figure 15-6). Usually the central computer functions both as a switching device or controller and as a central computer. As a switching device, it receives a message from one computer, identifies its destination in the network, and routes the message to its destination. In the example earlier in the chapter, the network at the *World Times,* with a central computer capable of being connected to the hundreds of micros used by its reporters is a star network.

The **hierarchical topology** is just a variation of the star design. A hierarchical topology is shown in the Len and Jerry's auto parts example (Figure 15-3). In this topology, large computers may be found at corporate headquarters, smaller minis at the division level, and micros and minis at the plant or sales offices.

RING TOPOLOGY

A **ring topology,** illustrated in Figure 15-7, is a configuration in which each computer in a network is connected to its neighbor. It is a variation of the multidrop configuration presented in Chapter 14. When a message is sent in the ring network, it is preceded by an address identifying

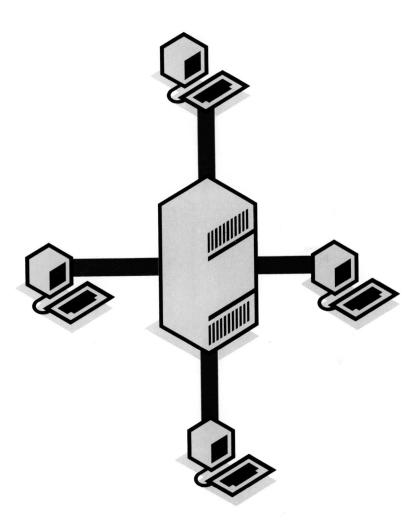

Figure 15-6.
In a star topology, the computer at the center of the network acts as a controller, receiving messages and routing them to their destination.

the destination. Each computer in the ring listens for its address before the message is passed to the next computer.

The disadvantage of a ring topology is that a breakdown in a single computer can disable the entire network. Nevertheless, this topology is frequently employed, especially in microcomputer applications.

COMBINATIONS

Networks are seldom limited to just one of these topologies; often, a combination is used. Such a network follows a **hybrid topology.** Perhaps the most common example—and one you are familiar with—is the telephone network. In it, local telephones that have the same first three digits (area code) are wired directly to the central office. This segment of the network can be classified as a star. Then, each of the local central offices is connected to the long-distance network. This segment of the system can be classified as a ring. When a call is made, the caller's telephone provides the instructions that the central office needs to link the

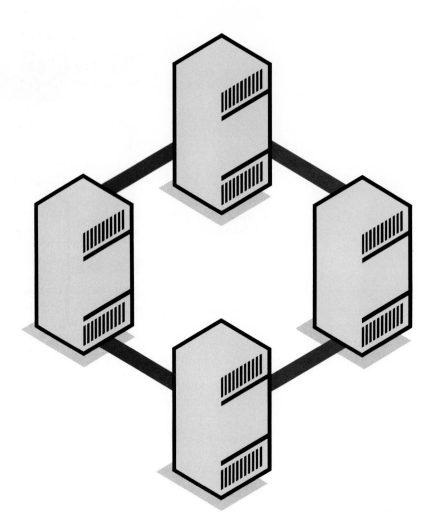

Figure 15-7.
In a ring topology, all computers and other devices are connected in a circle.

call first with the other appropriate central office and from there to the appropriate telephone in that local exchange.

SOFTWARE FOR DISTRIBUTED SYSTEMS

Stand-alone computers—those not used in a distributed network—need only manage the data processing activities in their own environment. But in a distributed network, data move beyond the single machine, and as a result, each computer in the network must have an additional layer of software in its operating system to contend with a wider range of input, output, and data management activities.

The system software must be able to recognize that the *data* a user needs may reside at another node in the network, and it must be able to determine how to locate those data. System software must also help the computers at each node recognize that their *output* may be intended for other computers or for storage devices other than the local disk drive. And each computer must be able to recognize that the input may be received not only from the local keyboard or disk drive but also from other computers and other storage devices in the network.

?   Q U E S T I O N S   ?

1. How does distributed data processing differ from centralized data processing?
2. Describe the difference between a centralized information system that might be used in a multibranch bank and a distributed processing system in the same bank.
3. What are the advantages of sharing files in a distributed system?
4. What is a network topology?
5. Describe the star topology. If a communications link to one of the computers in a star network malfunctions, do you think the entire network will be disabled?
6. Describe a ring topology.
7. What type of topology does the telephone network follow?
8. Why does each computer in a network need additional layers of operating system software?

DISTRIBUTED DATA

Although some of the issues and problems associated with managing data in a distributed environment are similar to those described in Chapter 10 ("Database Management Systems"), others are different. Those that need special emphasis include

■ Standardizing data names.

■ Deciding where data should be stored.

■ Replicating data.

■ Finding data.

■ Controlling data use.

■ Implementing backup and recovery strategies.

First we shall discuss the standardization of data names.

STANDARDIZING DATA NAMES

All applications used in more than one location or by many different users share the problem, uncovered in Chapter 10, that the data names must somehow be standardized. In a distributed system, data on a finished item, for example, may be requested by the inventory, accounting, sales, shipping, and field service departments. Each of these requests may be made by users at different distributed locations, and so the users must agree on how the finished item will be identified when the data are accessed.

DECIDING WHERE DATA SHOULD BE STORED

A major issue in designing distributed systems is where the data will be stored. Two possibilities exist: centralized and partitioned storage. If centralized storage is chosen, one of the computers in the network stores all of the data. The other computers then access this database for all of their data needs. This configuration has centralized data but distributed processing. The stock quote system used by security analysts is an example of this approach.

If the data are stored on several machines, then the data will be partitioned. A manufacturing firm with two computers, each responsible for storing and maintaining the data needed by its two divisions, is an example of partitioned storage. This configuration has both distributed data and distributed processing.

An advantage of a centralized database is that remote computers know where to find the data. They know that no other computers in the network store data, and so locating data is no problem. But in a partitioned database, the need to establish the location of data is an added burden placed on the software. We will return to this problem shortly.

A disadvantage of a centralized database is that response time may suffer as more and more users access the database. Indeed, at some point the system may become so bogged down with requests that its response time may test the patience of even its most devoted users. When data are partitioned, however, bottlenecks such as this are less likely to occur, as the demand for most of the data can be accommodated locally.

Another disadvantage of a centralized database approach is the lack of reliability. A malfunction in the equipment or in the communications network can bring the entire system to a standstill. Only a part of the system is lost, however, when a malfunction occurs in a partitioned system.

But pure centralized or partitioned solutions are the extremes: Many systems use a combination of both. Deciding which data will be centralized and which decentralized depends on the application. In some systems, for example, high-volume transaction data are centralized, and low-volume data associated with marketing, personnel, and finance are stored in a local environment.

REPLICATING DATA

Data stored electronically on disk can, of course, be lost. Thus another issue that must be considered is whether or not a second copy of the database should be maintained. If it is decided to duplicate or *replicate* the database using additional disk drives at other locations in the network, as is done in some fault-tolerant systems, then the system's storage requirement can nearly double. But sometimes this is not an unreasonable price to pay for security.

FINDING DATA

When data are partitioned, computers in the system must be able to find where the data are stored. This is done through a **data directory.** Sometimes the data directory is stored at a central location, and a request for data is first passed to this location before it is processed. In other systems, a directory is stored in every computer in the network. Regardless of the method, the operating systems in these networks must first reference a directory before the search for a data item can begin.

ESTABLISHING CONTROL OVER DATA USE

Controlling the use of a database, an issue discussed in Chapters 10 and 14, is more complex in a distributed environment. When data are stored at many locations, for example, the system must be prepared to handle situations in which some, but not all, of the updates for a particular transaction are completed successfully.

Consider a situation in which a manufacturing database is distributed over four locations. Three plants produce parts and subassemblies, and the fourth assembles these items into a finished product. When the order department receives an order, it is entered into the corporate sales-order entry system and from there is transmitted to each of the four plants. The plants in turn schedule their production according to this information.

Suppose there is a malfunction in the communications link or disk drive at one plant while the data are being transmitted from the corporate sales-order entry system. Three plants will receive the data, and the fourth will not. And if this error is not corrected, only two of the three items will be available when the product is supposed to be assembled.

Communications breakdowns such as this do occur. They are caused by malfunctions in computer equipment, breakdowns in the communication system, or interference with the flow of data by noisy communication lines. To avoid incomplete updates, many systems use a strategy in which the source computer waits for a verification from each destination to determine whether an update has been successful. If just one has been unsuccessful, then all of the related updates at the other locations in the network must be withdrawn and the changes held until they can successfully be made at some later time.

LOCAL AREA NETWORKS

Microcomputers are used in an endless number of successful stand-alone applications. Sooner or later, however, a user will need data that are not stored on the machine: They may be stored on another micro or even on the firm's minicomputer or mainframe.

Before micros can share data with one another, they must be integrated into a local area network. A **local area network** (LAN) is a distributed network that links several computers in a limited geographic area. Usually several microcomputers, printers, and hard disks are connected to a network, which might span the floor of a building, an entire building, or, in some cases, a few buildings (Figure 15-8).

A true LAN is a network that can connect many different devices. That is, it can connect different brands of microcomputers, even though they may use incompatible operating systems. But most LANs are not versatile enough to connect just any equipment and are limited to certain types of systems. Some local area networks, in fact, are limited to just one type of hardware and system software, but others can link a limited combination of both.

NETWORK TOPOLOGY

Although star, ring, and hybrid topologies are used in local area networks, most use a ring topology.

To obtain use of the single communication path in a ring, there must be some mechanism to prevent more than one user from commanding the use of the communications path. To prevent these possible "collisions," one of two general protocols are used in a LAN: token passing or carrier-sense multiple access (CSMA).

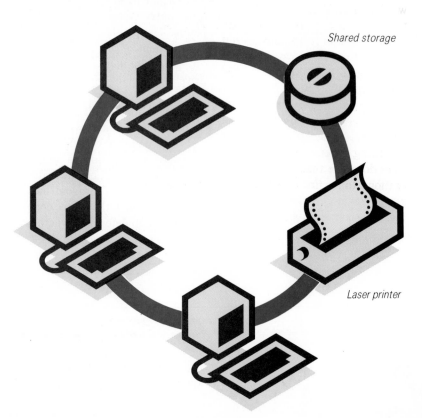

Shared storage

Laser printer

Figure 15-8.
Local area networks are used to connect microcomputers, printers, and disk storage devices, permitting the sharing of local computer resources.

In **token passing,** one of the computers is used as a server. Its function is to send a "token" or signal through the network. If the token is empty, a micro can grab it, specify the message's destination, attach a message, and send it on its way. Once the message has been delivered, the token is free to travel around the network until it is grabbed by another micro. Because only one micro can use a token at a given time, there is no chance for more than one micro to use the network at once. Hence, "collisions" between users are prevented.

Carrier-sense multiple access (CSMA) permits a micro to determine whether the network is in use by "listening" before it attempts to transmit. If it is apparent that a collision with another user would occur, the micro will wait a short period of time and then test the network again. When the network is clear, the message is sent.

● ●

E N D - U S E R   H I N T S

BUILDING A LAN: THE ECONOMIC ALTERNATIVE

Few companies today talk about stand-alone microcomputers. With increasing frequency they want to link them together in a LAN—or have already done so. LANs are not only economical but improve service to the end-user.

Although the initiative for the development of some LANs comes from groups or departments that need to have their computers and peripherals connected, other LANs are being developed as organizations downsize their computer operations. In the first case the group wants service; in the second, the incentive is primarily economic.

Better service is possible with a LAN because the microcomputer usually processes data in its local environment whenever possible. This means that a micro user can have something like 640 K available for his or her own exclusive use. Centralized processing resources, in many applications, do not have to be shared.

"Downsizing" is the process of moving from a mainframe or mini to a network of micros. And the economic incentive to downsize can be substantial. A microcomputer-based LAN can cost as little as one-fourth as much to purchase and operate as a comparable mini system.

Here is a comparison for a sys-

tem that can serve forty users. The disk storage in the minicomputer system is 480 M, divided equally over the forty terminals. The monthly lease and maintenance costs are divided among all of the workstations or terminals.

PC LAN

Workstation RAM	640 K
Disk storage	20 MB
Annual cost per micro	$500

MINICOMPUTER

Terminal RAM	4 K
Disk storage	12 MB
Annual cost per terminal	$2000

As you can see, economics are on the side of the LAN.

● ●

CABLING

The primary means used to connect equipment in a local area network are coaxial cable and twisted-wire pair.

Twisted-wire pair, the wire used to connect telephones, is inexpensive to install, but suffers from the fact that it has a very narrow bandwidth (Chapter 14), thereby limiting the amount of data it can handle.

In addition, the topology may be limited to a point-to-point configuration and the network can span a distance of no more than a few miles without the need for additional equipment.

Two types of coaxial systems include baseband and broadband. Both are used in ring topologies. In a **baseband** network a coaxial cable carries digital information along a single path (multidrop); like the way traffic moves on a one lane highway, with all cars moving in the same direction at the same speed. This can be a problem if many people must share the network. And the range is still limited; at most a distance of one-and-a-half miles can be spanned.

In a **broadband** network a single coaxial cable is still used, but the cable can be packed with hundreds of independent data paths and therefore is more like a multilane highway. It is a better solution when many users must share the network. With broadband, the data streams in these paths can move at their own speeds and over a range of thirty-five miles. A major advantage of this technology—the same technology that brings cable TV into your home—is that it can carry different services, such as voice, video, and high- and low-speed digital data. And adding computers to a broadband network can be relatively simple, in contrast to twisted-wire or baseband solutions. While we can conclude that broadband networks have more capacity and are more versatile than either twisted-wire or coax, the equipment required is more costly.

PROGRAMS

Earlier in the chapter we stated that when a computer is connected to a network, an additional layer of software is needed. This is, of course, also true for microcomputers in a LAN. The purpose of this additional software is to manage the complex input/output activities in this multicomputer environment.

In addition to the new operating system software, the application programs run on these computers must also be able to function in a distributed setting. For example, if a spreadsheet application is to be shared with other users in a network, then a multiuser version of the spreadsheet must be used. Or if a database application is to be shared, a multiuser version of the DBMS software must be used. The following example illustrates why a multiuser version of a database system is essential to a LAN.

Suppose that a user requests data from a specific inventory record with the intention of updating its inventory balance field. Furthermore, let us assume that the system does not have multiuser software. First, the request is sent from the user's micro to the common database stored on a hard disk. Next, the data are sent from the hard disk to the micro. Unknown to this first user, another user requests the same record. It is transferred to the second user's micro also. Both screens now show a balance of 300 units. The first user enters a depletion of 50 units. This brings the balance down to 250, which is written back to the central hard disk. The second user—completely unaware of what has just taken place—depletes the balance on her screen by 100. But this depletion is made from the balance retrieved earlier, 300 units. The second user's micro therefore assumes that the new balance will be 200 units and writes this over the previous entry on the hard disk. See the problem? The new balance should have been 150: the old balance of 300, less 50 depleted by the first user, and less 100 depleted by the second user. But because two users were allowed simultaneous access, the system overwrote the record updated by the first user. The database now stores the wrong balance.

Multiuser software is designed to prevent this and other problems. In this case, it could "lock out" other users once a file has been accessed. So if a user gains access to an accounts receivable file, no other users would be permitted access until the update has been completed. But in many transaction applications—especially accounting—several people may often need to access a file at the same time. Locking users out altogether would lead to long waits. Therefore, instead of shutting off an entire file, record lockouts enable several users to access simultaneously the same file but not the same record.

SHARING DATA

One of a LAN's major benefits is allowing its users to share data (Figure 15-9). For this reason, most LANs include a centralized hard-disk drive. But as we just noted, managing the data and access to them is complex. Accordingly, many data management functions are usually assumed by a **file server,** a separate computer that oversees the hard disk.

■ ■

THE WESTERN STARS, a professional basketball team, used a manual bookkeeping system to manage ticket sales and keep track of which seats had been sold to season-ticket holders. But the system did not work well.

Figure 15-9.
Local area networks allow users to share data, programs, and hardware resources.

It was often impossible to determine which seats had been sold for a game, and on several occasions, the same seat was sold to two or three season-ticket holders. Once the ticket office got so behind with the paperwork that it had to close off season-ticket sales for three days because it didn't know which seats were still available!

To help solve the problem, team officials decided to computerize the ticket-sales operation. A minicomputer would be expensive. And a stand-alone micro would not be adequate, because several people would need to have access to the system at the same time. So the officials selected a microcomputer LAN.

The network includes five IBM-compatible microcomputers and uses a token-passing ring topology. Each micro includes the system software needed to run in a network environment, and a network version of a popular database management system is used to manage the reservations database. Storage is maintained on a 30-megabyte hard disk managed by a micro that functions as a file server.

The new ticket system has been even more successful than the Stars expected. The vice-president of ticket sales, Buz Gibbons, thinks that the system has helped sell tickets. "We now can offer different season-ticket packages by breaking up a 44-game home season into four 11-game packages," Gibbons explained. "Fans can buy any one of the four packages, two packages, or the full-season package. Before we had the system, we couldn't have offered these promotions. Now we can spend less time on bookkeeping and more time on sales."

■■■■■■■■■■■■■■■■■■■■■■■■■■■■■■■■■

MICRO–MAINFRAME LINKS

The need to share data may extend beyond the local network; that is, it may be necessary to access data that are stored on a centralized mainframe or minicomputer. In fact, the data stored on these machines are often of most interest to decision makers (Figure 15-10). Accessing these data requires a micro–mainframe connection.

Types of Micro–Mainframe Connections   There are two basic types of micro–mainframe connections. When the first is used, the micro is equipped with a *terminal emulation board* and behaves much like a dumb terminal connected to a mini or mainframe. In this configuration, the micro can query the corporate database, request standard reports, and even access transaction-processing and operational systems. But none of the micro's storage or processing capabilities is used.

It is the second type of connection that most business professionals have in mind when they think of a mainframe connection. Here, the micro accesses the mainframe's data and downloads them to its own memory. And then once the data have been downloaded, they can be used in spreadsheets, graphs, microcomputer database software, and word-processing applications. Some users also need to be able to down-

Figure 15-10.
It is often necessary to access data stored in centralized mini or mainframe systems.

load mainframe data, process them locally, and then upload the modified data to the mainframe.

Difficulties with Micro–Mainframe Links   Many problems can stand in the way of successfully implementing a micro–mainframe link. All of them are related to the fact that a link often attempts to connect different computers, different operating systems, and different database management software—like a person who speaks only English trying to communicate with a person who speaks only French. Consider just one simple example: An IBM mainframe stores data in EBCDIC format, and an IBM PC uses ASCII format. And these machines are made by the same manufacturer! To solve these problems, an additional layer of software must be used to make this and other translations before machines can communicate. Actually, there are many software solutions for this problem. At one extreme are solutions tailor-made for specific hardware configurations at both the micro and mainframe ends of the link. Some vendors, using this approach, write system and application software that must be used, at both the mainframe and micro levels, on specific computer models. One major vendor, for example, sells a complete package, including mainframe database software as well as micro spreadsheet, database, and word-processing software. As long as certain IBM or IBM-compatible hardware is used at the mainframe and micro levels, users can expect a reasonable range of access to data for use on their micros.

There are other, more general solutions to this problem that allow different types of hardware and software to be connected. But connecting software and hardware in a multivendor environment can be extremely difficult and, in some cases, impossible. Although the ideal is to be able to connect any micro to any mainframe, download the data needed, process the data locally, and even upload the modified data to the mainframe, such a system is still not feasible in most computing environments. So, before deciding to link existing hardware and software in a micro–mainframe connection, the plan must be explored carefully to ensure technical feasibility.

Another problem in establishing a micro–mainframe link is that there are usually more data and more detail at the mainframe level than are needed at the micro level. In most applications the user needs only part of the data or summaries of the data. In fact, even if the user wanted to download the entire mainframe database, it would probably be too large for the micro system to accommodate. To solve this problem, the micro–mainframe software should be able to transfer only certain records or fields and to summarize some fields, so that fewer data need to be transferred to the micro.

DEPARTMENTAL COMPUTING

If a distributed environment includes micros and mainframes, then we can say that it has two levels of computing. With increasing frequency, however, organizations are introducing a third, intermediate level called **departmental computing.**

In departmental computing, general-purpose computers focus on those processing activities related to the performance of departmental-level activities. Usually these computers can be found in an office area or in such departments as manufacturing, marketing, personnel, and finance. Departmental computing occurs at a level between the micro and mainframe, with all of the computers linked through a hierarchical topology.

Although the mainfraime in this tiered environment is responsible for major applications that require its large storage capacity and high speed, departmental computers are used when a processing task falls between the micro's modest capabilities and the mainframe's considerable resources.

In addition to supporting an organization's department-level processing activities, departmental computers must also be able to respond to requests made by the micros below them and be able to access the mainframes above them. These links are made through the system software residing in the departmental computer.

A link between a microcomputer and a departmental computer will be needed, for example, whenever a user at a micro needs to run an application or needs data residing in the departmental computer. Although the departmental computer may be able to accommodate many of the end-user's requests, some may still require access to mainframe data and applications. In these situations, the user enters the request into the micro, the micro sends the request to the departmental computer, and from there it is forwarded to the mainframe. After the mainframe has been accessed, the response is them returned back through the network to the micro.

COMPARING CENTRALIZED AND DISTRIBUTED SYSTEMS

There are both advantages and disadvantages of distributed processing. Let us spend a few moments considering each.

ADVANTAGES

The advantages of distributed processing include

- Local control of local data
- Lower cost
- Modularity
- Better response times
- Ability to share data
- Greater reliability
- Direct user interaction

Local Control of Local Data   The comparison of decentralized and centralized information processing is not unlike the comparison in the management literature of the centralization or decentralization of organizations. A centralized organization is one in which the authority and responsibility for a wide range of business decisions rest with the central organization. A decentralized organization is one in which the authority and responsibility are delegated to local divisions or units.

The correct choice for an organization depends on which organizational structure is most likely to facilitate the achievement of the firm's goals and objectives. It is argued, for example, that in a decentralized environment, the organizational unit can be more responsive to local problems and opportunities. So if response to local problems is important, a decentralized organization may be the better choice.

Although a decentralized organization can be effective, it is not always necessary to decentralize all management functions. Some can still remain under central control. Just as a firm can decide to decentralize some or all of its management functions, it can also decide to support these functions by decentralizing some or all of the information resources. And the major benefit from a decentralized or distributed information system is local control of local data. This means that the local organization can take more responsibility for developing, scheduling, introducing, and managing applications. Above all, a local perspective can keep the information system more focused on the local organization's objectives. So decentralized organizations and decentralized information systems tend to go hand in hand.

Lower Cost   Often the hardware in a distributed system is less expensive than is the hardware in a centralized system. Several microcomputers or minicomputers cost less than one mainframe. And not only are these machines less expensive to buy, but they are usually less expensive to maintain.

Modularity   Distributed systems tend to be modular. As the demand for processing increases, most micros, minis, and other supportive equipment such as secondary storage devices and printers can be added to the network. In some local area networks, for example, when a new microcomputer needs to be added, it is simply plugged into the system. Within minutes it is a functioning part of the existing network.

Better Response Times   When only one centralized computer is used, the response time to a user's request can be delayed as more and more users make demands on the system. But in a distributed system, local processing is done on local machines, and in many systems, local machines only occasionally need to call upon the resources of others in the system. As a result, the response time as more users are added to a distributed network may slow relatively little.

Ability to Share Data   Another advantage of a distributed system is its ability to share data across the nodes in a network. Without a network, it is difficult or impossible to share data. Of course, the floppy disk from one micro can be taken to another compatible machine, and data can be shared in this way; but it is much more convenient if micros, minis, and mainframes can share one another's data through the electronic interface of a network.

Greater Reliability   Still another advantage is reliability. If a centralized mainframe system breaks down, the whole system will come to a halt. Networks, in general, are not subject to such catastrophes. If one micro or mini breaks down, the rest of the machines may not be affected, depending on the network topology.

Direct User Interaction   Another advantage is that users directly interact with the information system in distributed processing. This means that users will not consider the computer an unapproachable, mysterious black box located behind closed doors. Users may find it easier to identify with a readily available system.

DISADVANTAGES

Distributed networks have disadvantages, too, and these must be considered before a system is decentralized. They include

■ Technical problems of linking dissimilar machines

■ Need for sophisticated communication systems

■ Data integrity and security problems

■ Lack of professional support

Technical Problems of Linking Dissimilar Machines   Technical problems can be overwhelming, for a distributed system is much more complex than is a centralized one. As we have seen, additional layers of operating system software are needed to translate and coordinate the flow of data between machines. Sometimes a link between mainframes and microcomputers may be difficult, if not impossible, to establish.

Need for Sophisticated Communication Systems   Distributed processing requires the development of a data communication system. These systems, as we saw in Chapter 14, can be costly to develop and use. In addition, they present their own problems.

Data Integrity and Security Problems   Because data maintained by distributed systems can be accessed at many remote locations in the network, controlling the integrity of a database can be difficult. This issue, also discussed in the last chapter, is more marked in a distributed environment.

Lack of Professional Support   Finally, distributed computers are often placed in locations where little or no professional data processing support is available. Consequently, they will be run by nonprofessionals.

? Q U E S T I O N S ?

1. Identify and describe the problems that occur when data are distributed in a network.
2. Why would it be recommended to replicate the data in a distributed network?
3. How can a distributed processing network respond when some but not all of the updates to a distributed database have been made?
4. What is a local area network? Why is this type of network useful to business professionals?
5. Describe the network topologies used in a LAN. What is the difference between baseband and broadband cabling?
6. Why must data management software used in a LAN have file-locking or record-locking capabilities?
7. Do you think a stand-alone software package could be used in a LAN? If so, how would its use be limited?
8. What problems make a micro–mainframe link difficult to establish? How can these problems be solved?
9. When would a distributed system be better than a centralized one?
10. What are the disadvantages of a decentralized system?

S U M M A R Y

■ With **centralized data processing,** the CPU, storage devices, software, and the professional data processing staff are located in one central facility.

■ With **distributed data processing** (or **distributed processing**), computers, storage devices, and even some computer professionals are distributed among separate locations throughout an organization.

■ In distributed processing, the computer system is called a **network,** and the points in the network occupied by the different machines are referred to as **nodes.**

■ The processing function alone, or both the processing and the storage functions, may be distributed to different locations in a network.

■ Transferring data from a central computer to a smaller local computer is referred to as **downloading.** Transferring data from the smaller local computer to the central computer is known as **uploading.**

■ **Network topology** refers to the way that data are routed, or machines positioned and physically interconnected, in a network. Different possibilities include the **star, hierarchical, ring,** and **hybrid topologies.**

■ Computers in distributed processing require an additional layer of system software to contend with a wider range of input, output, and data management activities.

■ Managing distributed data raises problems concerning standardizing data names, deciding where data should be stored, replicating data, finding data, establishing control over data use, and implementing backup and recovery strategies.

■ The **data directory** is an aid to finding data in a distributed system.

■ A **local area network** (LAN) is a distributed network that links several computers, usually microcomputers, in a limited geographic area.

■ Star, ring, and hybrid topologies are used in LANs. With a ring topology, conflicts among multiple users are resolved using **token passing** or **carrier-sense multiple access** (CSMA).

■ Computers in a LAN can be connected with twisted-wire pair or with **baseband** or **broadband** coaxial cable.

■ Sometimes a separate computer, known as a **file server,** assumes the common data management functions in a LAN.

■ The need to share data often extends beyond a LAN, necessitating micro–mainframe links.

■ In **departmental computing,** another level of computers is placed at the departmental level between micros at the user level and the corporate mainframe.

■ For many applications, the advantages of distributed processing outweigh the disadvantages.

K E Y • T E R M S

The following list shows the key terms in the order in which they appear in the chapter.

Centralized data processing (p. 426)
Distributed data processing or distributed processing (p. 426)
Network (p. 427)
Node (p. 427)
Download (p. 428)
Upload (p. 428)
Network topology (p. 432)
Star topology (p. 432)
Hierarchical topology (p. 432)

Ring topology (p. 432)
Hybrid topology (p. 433)
Data directory (p. 437)
Local area network (LAN) (p. 438)
Token-passing (p. 439)
Carrier-sense multiple access (CSMA) (p. 439)
Baseband (p. 440)
Broadband (p. 440)
File server (p. 441)
Departmental computing (p. 444)

F O R   D I S C U S S I O N

1. A company currently maintains one mainframe, three minis, and over three hundred microcomputers. In its current configuration, none of the computers is integrated. They all perform as independent systems, each focused on different processing functions. The mainframe is primarily used for sales-order processing and accounting. The minis are used for manufacturing control, and the

micros are used for many purposes, ranging from budgeting to sales analysis.

■ Why might you recommend that this system be integrated into a distributed network?

■ What problems would have to be solved?

■ Do you think it would be best first to build a network including the mainframe and minis, then to build a local area network for the micros, and finally to combine both networks?

2. Under what conditions might it be appropriate for a company to consider offloading its information processing activities from a central computer to distributed computers?

3. What business factors do you think contribute to the trend toward distributed processing?

4. A fast-food chain uses point-of-sale (POS) terminals at the counters in their restaurants. These POS devices collect sales data that are then stored on each restaurant's 40-megabyte hard disk. Every evening the central computer automatically calls each of the restaurants and collects summary sales-and-cost data for the day. Once the data have been collected, the system prints management reports and distributes them to management through the firm's electronic mail system. Describe this system using the following terms: *on-line, batch, transaction system,* MIS, *data entry, distributed.*

5. Do you think systems development professionals should be distributed in a distributed processing environment?

HANDS-ON PROJECTS

1. Find an advertisement for a local area network, and summarize its features. What topology is used? Can any machine be connected to the network? What hardware and software are included? *Suggestions: PC WEEK, Byte, PC World.*

2. Find an advertisement in a computer magazine for software that will function in a LAN environment. Summarize the features of the software.

3. Ask the salesperson at a local computer store to describe the equipment necessary to build a LAN. Summarize in a few paragraphs what you learn.

CABLE INC.

Cable Inc. is a communications company that owns and operates twenty-five cable TV operations around Canada. Founded in 1971, the firm has grown at an average rate of 20 percent per year. The company's president, Larry Garland, maintains tight control over operations from his Edmonton headquarters.

Data processing at Cable Inc. is centralized. The large IBM mainframe supports over twelve hundred remote terminals located at the twenty-five cable operations. These terminals, used to answer customer inquiries as well as to add new subscribers to its customer database, are connected to the Edmonton mainframe through multiplexers and modems. Transmission between facilities is over the switched telephone network and leased microwave systems.

As the company has added cable operations and subscribers, the capacity of its central mainframe has come under increasing pressure. But it is not only the data processing function that is under pressure: Maintaining control over a company with twenty-five branches stretched from one end of the country to the other also has become increasingly difficult for Garland.

Two months ago, Garland began negotiations to enter five new TV markets. When he asked the company's MIS director, Felizia Gonsalvez, for her reaction to the plan, she was quick to respond that the company had no choice but to replace its 10-year-old mainframe with a larger system. Otherwise, she said, it would not have the data processing capacity to serve the new operations from Edmonton. Because such a replacement project would cost $10 million or more, Garland decided to bring in a consulting firm to prepare an independent opinion.

Consultants' Report

After an extensive two-month study, at a cost of $15,000, the consultants concluded that Cable Inc. should not replace its current centralized data processing facilities with a larger centralized facility. Instead, they recommended a distributed network of twenty-five minicomputers, with a smaller mainframe at company headquarters.

In their report, the consultants suggested that the centralized facility—which currently employs 155 people—be reduced to 60 during the transition period and finally to 20 people once the new system goes into full-time operation. These 20 data processing professionals would be responsible for such central functions as the development of new applications, consulting with users and data processing staff at the twenty-five remote locations, and the development of MIS applications for use by middle- and top-management personnel.

At each of the twenty-five cable operations, data processing would be controlled by the local business manager. This person would hire a small staff of one or two people who would be responsible for running software supplied from headquarters as well as developing specialized software that the staff might find useful in their market.

With computers at each of the cable operations, the report went on to say, "The response time would be shorter, communications costs lower, data integrity greater, and operating costs lower." Response time would be shorter because subscriber data would be stored at each cable operation, and queries to that database, as well as routine billing activities, would no longer need to access centralized facilities through multiplexers, modems, and a communications network.

Operating costs would be lower because the cost of purchasing and maintaining twenty-five minicomputer systems would be less than the cost of buying a single large mainframe system. For example, the report explained, the software costs would be significantly lower. The main reason that software costs would drop is that Cable Inc. would no longer write its own programs. Until now, the central DP group had written its own payroll, billing, and accounts receivable packages. The cost of developing these systems and maintaining them had been high. Customized, off-the-shelf software—which the consultants felt was adequate—would be purchased for the new system. This software, written for the communications industry, could be adapted or tailored to Cable

Inc.'s specific needs. Not only would the cost of the software be modest, but the software vendor would oversee the installation, training, and maintenance.

Another benefit expected from the distributed system is a decrease in downtime. Data would reside locally. As a result, if one computer broke down, the other computers in the network would not necessarily be affected. With the current system, a malfunction at the mainframe level brings the entire system to a stop.

Finally, the report mentioned that the new system would use a database management system (the current system uses conventional file processing methods) to manage the data at each computer site. Once a week, the central computer would dial up the local minicomputers, request summary data, and update the central database. Then, by using a query language, management would find it easier to obtain the information needed to manage and control the company.

MIS Reaction

When Gonsalvez read the report, she was amazed that a reputable consulting firm would suggest a system so unsuitable for Cable Inc. Gonsalvez has maintained that there is nothing wrong with the current system except its response time. And that can be solved with a bigger mainframe at headquarters.

She is particularly concerned about the recommendation to end the company's development of its own programs. "No one knows our business better than we do," she said, "and so we should write our own programs. And besides, we're doing the job economically. Each program we write is used at our twenty-five cable operations and most of our twelve hundred terminals."

Gonsalvez also points out that no one at the twenty-five operating locations has had much experience with computers and that it would be virtually impossible to run a company of twenty-five computers with only a handful of computer professionals.

Gonsalvez is especially critical of the operating companies' lack of technical expertise. "Our field managers, collection managers, service managers, and marketing managers all would have to change what they do. They—and the people who work for them—would have to learn how to use computers. And how could you do that with people who have

been with us for 15 years and are computer-illiterate?"

Gonsalvez is also concerned about security and data backup. She feels that if the data were stored at each site, it would be easier for unauthorized users to access the data, as the smaller, local facilities would probably not have the resources to enforce strict security measures. "And who would see that the backup procedures were followed when they're supposed to?" she asked. "If there was a disaster, all the data could be lost, probably never recovered, and thousands of dollars would go down the drain."

Data integrity too would suffer, she believes. Without a central organization to monitor the data entered into the computer, the database would become contaminated with bad data.

Questions

1. Describe the system that Cable Inc. now uses. Use the following words in your description: *centralized, mainframe, modem, switched telephone network, multiplexer, microwave, conventional file processing.*

2. Describe the system proposed by the consultants. Use the following words: *distributed, communications,* DBMS. Why would this system be classified as a distributed processing system? Would both processing and storage be distributed in the new system?

3. What are the major differences in the hardware and system software between the centralized and the proposed distributed systems?

4. How would the new application software differ from the old software?

5. Summarize the advantages and disadvantages of a new distributed processing system.

6. Summarize the benefits of an expanded centralized system.

7. What problems do you think Cable Inc. might have in implementing and operating a distributed system?

8. What are Gonsalvez's objections to the new system? Can you make any recommendations that would minimize the likelihood of these problems?

9. What type of network topology do you think would be suitable for this project? Explain.

10. Would it be possible to allow each of the twenty-five cable operations to design its own database

system and to choose its own names for the data fields? (For example, one cable operation might call the payables field *Pay,* and another might call it *Payable.*) Explain.

11. Larry Garland is a strong manager who likes to maintain tight control over his company. Do you think a distributed system would help or interfere with his management style?

12. What course of action do you think is best for Cable Inc.?

P A R T · F I V E

COMPUTERS IN SOCIETY AND THE WORKPLACE

16
COMPUTER CRIME
AND SYSTEM
SECURITY

O U T L I N E

O B J E C T I V E S

After studying this chapter you should understand the following:

■ *Why computer crime is a major problem.*

■ *How intruders break into computer information systems.*

■ *The different types of computer crimes.*

■ *What can be done to protect computer information systems.*

Just mention computer crime at an executive lunch: Heads will turn and conversations will stop. Unlike any other topic, this one is likely to strike fear into the hearts of those who are responsible for safeguarding organizational assets.

Today computer crime is an enormous problem. It can threaten the lifeblood of an organization, yet it often defies a simple solution.

In this chapter we will look at computer crime and system security. We will examine crimes that have been committed and discuss the measures that organizations can use to protect themselves.

THE INCREASING VULNERABILITY OF COMPUTERS TO CRIME

In the 1960s, computers began to change the way in which many businesses and other organizations kept their records. Rather than being kept manually, suddenly important data were maintained by computer. And with this shift came a change in the way that many crimes are committed.

Thirty years ago, a person intent on carrying out a crime against an organization needed either a gun or an accomplice who had access to the firm's manual record-keeping systems. Today, such a criminal needs less than $500 worth of computer equipment. The type of criminal has also changed. Now such crimes are committed by programmers, clerks, tellers, and even students. Indeed, they are committed by anyone who has some computer knowledge and is intent on breaking the law and who does not reflect on the possible personal and societal repercussions.

In the 1960s and 1970s, when most computer information systems were centralized, management thought that as long as the databases were centrally controlled, their security could be ensured. However, in 1973 a $2-billion fraud against the Equity Funding Corporation of America revealed the vulnerability of information systems and changed many minds. Although this crime was not entirely committed by computer, it did play a significant role.

Because of such incidents, by the mid-1970s it had become clear that a machine that stored records of an organization's assets as small, volatile magnetized particles could be an easy target for criminal activities.

Vulnerable as these centralized systems were in the 1970s, the subsequent movement toward distributed data processing and the explosion of end-user access in the 1980s increased the problem to critical proportions (Figure 16-1). What was once a centralized system accessible only to a few data processing professionals has now become a system accessible to nearly everyone in the firm. And in an increasing number of cases—in which, for example, computers are used to gain competitive advantage—the system is accessible even to the firm's customers.

Today's computer systems therefore are extremely vulnerable. Computer crime is on the increase, and so is management's concern about the problem.

Figure 16-1.
Decentralized systems have made access to centralized data very easy. Unfortunately, it is also easy for unauthorized users as well.

CRIME STATISTICS

It is difficult to estimate the magnitude of computer crime. Some claim the cost to North American businesses may be as high as $3 billion per year, but no one really knows. There is no clearinghouse for computer crimes, and in any case many crimes probably are never detected. In fact, one source estimated that the odds of uncovering a computer crime are 100 to 1 in the criminal's favor. And even if the crime is discovered, some companies will not prosecute for fear of bringing attention to their vulnerable systems and damaging their public image.

What is known, however, is that many companies are affected. In a 1984 survey conducted by the American Bar Association, half of the 233 businesses and government institutions it studied reported that they had been victims of computer crime in just the year preceding the study. One out of four respondents reported "known and verifiable losses in the prior 12 months." In addition, an equal number reported losses whose magnitude was not known or could not be measured in money terms. Those respondents who could measure the loss estimated the total for their businesses at between $145 million and $730 million.

TYPES OF CRIMES

Computer crime, or the use of a computer for illegal activities, can be divided into the following categories:

- Breaking in
- Theft of computer time
- Altering programs
- Altering data
- Theft of data
- Theft of programs
- Espionage
- Terrorism

In order to consider measures to prevent such crimes, we must first examine some representative crimes in these categories.

BREAKING IN

Breaking into a computer system is a crime in itself. It is also a necessary prerequisite to doing further damage to an information system.

Most minicomputer and mainframe systems are protected by several levels of authorized access. Some users may be authorized to read only certain types of data; others may be authorized to read and update the data; and so on. Most people are therefore restricted to only the kinds of data they need to perform their jobs. Only a few have the clearance necessary to roam free through an organization's database.

As we have already learned, the authority to access each level is controlled by the use of **passwords.** If a person has a password that carries with it the authority to gain access to a particular database, then access will be allowed; otherwise, it will be denied.

To gain unauthorized entry into a system, it is therefore necessary to obtain a valid password. Often this is not as difficult as it sounds. If the intruder already works for the company, then it may be easy to obtain the password from a careless user. All it takes is for one employee to leave near a terminal a piece of paper on which this number is written.

Sometimes passwords are quite simple: a person's birthdate or a social security number. So if the intruder knows someone who already has the appropriate clearance, figuring out the correct number sequence may be easy. Or obtaining a valid number may be as simple as finding out where these numbers are written and saved.

But if this information is not available, how can people break in? Some simply try a series of passwords until one works. In a system with thousands of authorized users, each with his or her own password, this may not take too long (Figure 16-2).

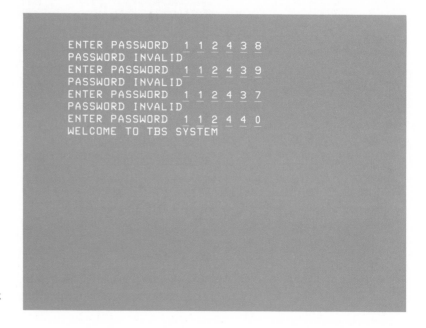

Figure 16-2.
In some systems it is possible to break in by trying a series of passwords.

TO DEMONSTRATE THE LACK OF SECURITY IN HIS COMPANY'S COMPUTER CENTER, Frank Smith, an employee of a large consumer goods company, called the computer center from his home one evening to explain that he had forgotten his password. At first the person who answered the phone refused to cooperate, but when Smith explained that the report he was working on needed to be submitted in the morning or his job would be in jeopardy, the computer attendant—who did not know Smith and could not possibly recognize his voice—looked up the number in the book and gave it to him.

■■■■■■■■■■■■■■■■■■■■■■■■■■■■■■■■■■■■

Although many of those who break into a computer system are employees of the company, others break in from the outside. They gain access by using a microcomputer and modem. First they dial a number that provides access to the firm's computer through a modem. Then, when they receive the high-pitched response tone over the phone line, they enter the password they have obtained illegally or simply try different password combinations until one works.

For some people, breaking into a system is the ultimate challenge. They will spend hours, days, and weeks trying different schemes in the hope of success. For example, the credit files maintained by TRW Information Services, the giant credit-reporting company that maintains records on 120 million Americans, have frequently been penetrated by **hackers,** a term used to describe people who are enthusiastic users. In one situation, hackers posted their methods for penetrating the TRW database on electronic bulletin boards that anyone could access using a modem and phone lines. TRW took action and shut down nine of these public bulletin boards and charged four youths with wire and credit-card fraud.

■■■■■■■■■■■■■■■■■■■■■■■■■■■■■■■■■■■■

PERHAPS ONE OF THE MOST DRAMATIC BREAK-INS—one in which thousands of unauthorized users were able to gain access to a system without being detected—occurred in a system operated by the U.S. Department of Agriculture (DOA). This system includes a communications center in Las Vegas into which data are entered and from which computer systems around the country are accessed.

The DOA maintains toll-free lines to its Las Vegas facility—anyone who knows the number can place a free call. Somehow hackers discovered this number, and because a tone is emitted upon making a call, it became clear that the number provided access to a computer.

After the hackers broke through the simple password system, they quickly learned that collect calls from the Las Vegas facility could be made to another computer in New Jersey. The New Jersey computer routinely accepted the calls. Once connected, the password protection system was easily circumvented again. From the New Jersey facilities it was possible to initiate prepaid calls to hundreds of other computer systems. In just one three-month period, 247 different corporate, educational, medical, and government computers were accessed using this approach.

It was eventually determined that unauthorized access to the DOA system came from up to forty different area codes. But even this information was very difficult to uncover. It would have taken an inordinate length of time to trace this information to the actual telephone lines through which the calls were placed. The identities of the intruders were never uncovered.

■■■■■■■■■■■■■■■■■■■■■■■■■■■■■■■■■

But examples such as this involve huge computer systems. What about local area networks with just a few computers, a modem, and a hard disk? Such systems indeed are a hacker's fantasy. Many are completely unprotected: All that is needed to break in is a telephone number.

THEFT OF COMPUTER TIME

If one is trusted with the use of or access to a computer system, there are various ways to violate this trust. One programmer used his company's computer and his own password to process a job for which a friend received cash. After he was caught, he insisted that what he did was not a crime. He found it hard to believe that using computer time in this way was theft. But his employer felt differently and fired him.

In another incident, an employee sold time on a communications network to a small company. The company had no idea how the connections were being made, but the price was right, and it did not ask questions.

More innocently, a group of employees used their company's computer to handicap horses at a local racetrack. They were not doing anything as brazen as selling time to outsiders, but merely engaging in an occasional office recreation which, it was true, might have turned out to yield a good tip. Like using the office typewriter to type up a personal letter, when computers are at hand in an office, they often are used for a few personal uses of this sort, which does not bother some employers. The line between "using" computer time and "stealing" it is not always easy to draw.

ALTERING PROGRAMS

Sometimes a small change in a program can make an unscrupulous programmer rich (Figure 16-3). Perhaps the best-known example is called **salami slicing.** Here is how it works.

Banks allocate monthly interest to savings account holders by multiplying the balance of the account by the monthly interest rate. So, if the rate is 0.66 percent and the balance of the account is $855, the interest to be posted for the month will be 855 × .0066 = $5.6430. Most banks follow certain procedures for rounding off this figure. As a result, the depositor might have $5.64 credited to his or her account, and the negligible sum of $0.003 stays with the bank.

Figure 16-3.
By altering a few lines of computer code, a computer criminal can defraud a company of tens of thousands of dollars.

Clever programmers have more than once discovered that if they alter the program just a little and transfer the fractional cent to a separate account, the change will probably never be detected. They then credit this fraction of a cent for each account to an account established under a fictitious name. A fraction of a cent is not much, but in a bank with 180,000 accounts at, say $0.003 per account, a programmer would accumulate $540 per month. Over several years, this could result in a significant fraud. What is especially striking about this crime is that the depositors lose nothing, but the bank does. And unless someone carefully examines a program that is thousands of lines long, or becomes suspicious in some other way, the crime can go undetected for years.

ALTERING DATA

Most companies and data processing professionals are concerned about the accessibility of sensitive data. They worry that unauthorized employees and others outside an organization can access and alter such data for their own benefit. What has made this problem especially troubling is the explosion in micro–mainframe links. Remote users can access and change a wide variety of data with little chance of detection. In the following example, however, the criminal was caught.

■ ■

DURING A ROUTINE FRAUD REVIEW AT MOUNTAIN STATES GENERAL LIFE INSURANCE COMPANY, examiners noticed a series of suspicious payments. They eventually discovered that a computer technician working through a remote terminal in Miami had entered over $200,000 in false claims to the company's IBM mainframe in Denver, Colorado. Over a period of eighteen months, she had sent herself forty-two checks! Soon after, she began serving two concurrent seven-year terms for computer crime and two concurrent five-year terms for grand theft and insurance fraud.

■ ■

There are many other examples of how data can be altered. A change in payroll records can give an employee an unauthorized raise. Accounts receivable entries can be wiped out, so that a customer is not charged for products received. Or the operation can be reversed—establishing accounts and charges in an accounts payable system for merchandise that a firm never received but for which it will then automatically pay when the bill comes due.

Finally, a fear of many corporations is the willful destruction of an entire database. This is exactly what happened to one Canadian company: An unauthorized user destroyed the firm's databases one by one. About 70 percent of the company's on-line files were affected. Fortunately, backup files had been maintained, and this enabled the company to restore most of the records, but not easily.

THEFT OF DATA

Stealing data is another problem that worries companies. Here is an illustration.

■■■■■■■■■■■■■■■■■■■■■■■■■■■■■■■■■■

THE MARKETING DEPARTMENT OF ABC CORPORATION, a large consumer products firm, was developing a marketing plan for a new product that it hoped would compete well against two established competitive products. The plan was stored on a spreadsheet package that ran on a network and to which the marketing staff had access. Because many employees worked at home or while away on business, the network was frequently accessed from portable units through a modem. Unknown to the firm, a competitor called into the system and downloaded a complete set of plans. As a result, the competitor was able to anticipate every one of ABC's moves, and so ABC's new product competed poorly.

■■■■■■■■■■■■■■■■■■■■■■■■■■■■■■■■■■

This story was told at a recent computer conference. Although the person who told it admitted that it was fictitious, those in the room agreed that crimes such as this probably do happen.

In a banking system, stealing data is stealing money. A former consultant for a major bank in Los Angeles managed to learn the bank's electronic funds transfer code and had $10 million diverted to a Swiss bank account. And with most of the funds in the world now transferred electronically, the incidence of this type of crime is likely to increase.

Many other kinds of valuable data can be stolen. How difficult would it be to steal a company's customer mailing list? If the list is maintained on a hard disk located on a local area network, it may be easy to steal. A clever thief would simply dial the telephone line connected to the modem, download the data, and print the mailing list.

THEFT OF PROGRAMS

Most software that is purchased or leased is legally protected by a **copyright,** an exclusive right to distribute and sell the product. Copyright law prohibits the purchaser from making more than a single copy, and that copy can be used only for backup purposes. The reason is simple: Whenever software is illegally copied and given to someone else, the firm that developed the software receives no revenues for the "pirated" version.

But everyone has heard of software that has been copied. In fact, it has been estimated that for every legal copy, at least one illegal copy is made. Computer games are notorious targets. Most high-school computer buffs can copy any game, and within hours of getting their hands on a new one, every friend has a copy. But this practice is not limited to game enthusiasts. Disks are copied by corporate personnel as well, and the magnitude of these crimes is greater. Whereas most games sell for

Figure 16-4.
The unauthorized copying of programs is a criminal offense.

under $50, business software can cost as much as hundreds of thousands of dollars (Figure 16-4).

In addition to legal copyright protection, most programs are also protected by software features that make them impossible to copy using the simple copy commands available on most systems. However, an industry has sprung up that sells software designed to break these very codes and make illegal copies. It seems that every time the software developers create a more sophisticated protection scheme, the code breakers are close on their heels with software designed to crack the new code.

Although this practice has been difficult to stop, software developers are beginning to enforce their protection under the copyright laws. BPI Systems, for example, filed a suit in Texas against Kwik-Kopy for selling only slightly disguised versions of their general ledger and accounts receivable software to Kwik-Kopy's network of more than 930 copying centers. BPI claimed that Kwik-Kopy's only changes were to delete both the BPI name from the software and the copy protection.

But using software that is electronically protected from being copied often interferes with its legitimate use. To load a software package onto a hard disk, for example, it must be able to be copied. In addition, if the hard disk is part of a network and if users on this network can download the software to their individual machines, then this means that many people should be able to use the software at the same time. Software vendors once insisted that users pay a software fee for each machine that uses the software. More recently, however, developers are offering **site licenses** that permit multiple users at each site.

There is also a growing group of software developers—some of whom sell inexpensive software—that no longer protects its software. Instead, these vendors permit unlimited copying and feel that this policy will lead to an increased use of their product and higher sales.

Nevertheless, many people feel that better protection schemes are necessary and that the laws must be more strictly enforced. They warn that if copying continues to be widespread, the price of software for honest users will increase, or many software developers will simply be unwilling to invest thousands of development hours only to find that their product can be copied for free.

ESPIONAGE

By **espionage** in a business context, we mean the misappropriation of company secrets. Usually such secrets are sold to competitors for a profit.

■■■■■■■■■■■■■■■■■■■■■■■■■■■■■■■■■

SEVERAL YEARS AGO, a West German tried to smuggle a Digital Equipment Corporation VAX 11/782 into the Soviet Union. The system included especially sensitive technology unavailable in the Soviet Union and useful for guiding intercontinental ballistic missiles, targeting anti-aircraft missiles, and manufacturing computer circuits. At least six phony companies were set up in South Africa to which crates containing computer parts were shipped. From there, the parts were forwarded to Sweden and West Germany. Thanks to a tip from an informant, the scheme was uncovered as the computers were being loaded on ships bound for Russia. Some of the earlier shipments, however, did make it through.

E N D · U S E R   H I N T S

COMPUTER SECURITY IS YOUR RESPONSIBILITY

Distributed processing, departmental computers, and microcomputers have made information almost too accessible. Although business professionals gain by this ready access, they must also accept some of the responsibility to protect that data from unauthorized use.

By answering the following questions, you will learn where and how you should become involved.

1. What are the threats to the data in your system?

2. How does the central data processing group help you to protect data?

3. Does your local area network provide protection from intruders?

4. Can you access the micro on your office desk from home or when on a trip by simply dialing an office telephone number? Can unauthorized users, perhaps competitors, also access the system in the same way?

5. Should you use cryptographic methods to code your data whenever they are sent between hardware devices?

6. Should data be stored in their encrypted format?

7. How effectively can noncryptographic methods—such as passwords, one-time passwords, and dial-back systems—protect data?

8. Are floppy disks, on which sensitive data are stored, handled carelessly? Are they left on the top of desks overnight? Can they be taken by an unauthorized person? Could a theft go undetected?

9. What about data backup? Are data on a hard disk routinely written to floppy disks or tape? Since the process of backing up a 30 MB hard disk on floppies can take several minutes, is tape back-up available? Will it be used on a regularly scheduled basis?

10. Should an audit trail be used? An audit trail would record each time a user logs on and how long an application is in use. It would also keep records of intentional as well as accidental security violations.

11. When you send sensitive memos and data over an electronic mail network, is the material protected from unauthorized eavesdropping? When the transmission of this material uses satellites or third-party services such as a value-added network (VAN), how is your material protected?

Unless the end-user becomes involved with the issue of data security, it is almost impossible to expect that a centrally directed effort in itself can protect the database. So the end-user must not only become aware of the importance of this problem but must also become committed to contributing to the process of protecting this important corporate resource.

SABOTAGE

Sabotage refers to the underhanded interference with work in an organization. Often the target is the computer system, and often the perpetrator is a disgruntled data processing employee who has been denied a raise or a promotion or who has been given a two-week notice to find another job. One common form of sabotage is called a **time bomb.** The employee, usually a programmer, adds several lines of code to a program such that the program will eventually destroy itself or the database or otherwise render the system inoperative.

TERRORISM

In recent years a new type of international terrorism has threatened computer manufacturers and users. Terrorist groups have targeted the computer as a symbol of modern business and have discovered that destroying computer facilities can bring a company's activities to a halt.

Although many of the attacks on computer facilities have occurred in Europe, there have been several incidents in the United States. Targets have included Motorola in Belgium and IBM in White Plains, New York. In the last ten years, over six hundred bombs have exploded in the capitals of Western Europe, many of them directed at computer facilities or suppliers.

The risk to a company depends on its business and where its facilities are located. The risks are greatest for multinational companies and other firms such as airlines and defense contractors.

Although most organizations are reluctant to talk about the steps they take to prevent such disasters, it is clear that most large firms do take some precautions. In fact, in an interview of users appearing in *Datamation* magazine, many of those interviewed were so concerned about this issue that they asked to remain anonymous.

COMPUTER SECURITY

As you can see from these examples, securing a computer information system from unauthorized access is absolutely necessary. No system can be left unprotected.

Many methods are used to secure these systems, including

- Procedural controls
- Technical controls
- Management controls
- Legal enforcement

PROCEDURAL CONTROLS

When an application is being developed, designers can integrate **procedural controls** into the system that will help safeguard its security. One control device is the use of passwords, perhaps the simplest way to restrict access to a system. Whenever a user wants access, he or she enters the password issued; it is compared with a table of valid passwords; and if there is a match, access will be approved.

Several problems result from the way this system is usually administered. First, passwords consisting of only a few numbers or letters are often used. This means that an intruder can try several at random and probably find one that works. Adequate protection usually demands that passwords be six or more characters long; because longer passwords reduce the mathematical odds of a lucky guess.

In addition to long passwords, it is necessary to change them frequently. This is especially true if users will be accessing financial or otherwise sensitive data. It only stands to reason that if numbers are valid for many years, the risk of their being discovered will increase.

Finally, it is important to use several layers of password protection. With this approach, access can be limited to only those segments of the system that a person needs in order to do his or her job. One user might be authorized by a password to read only inventory data, and another might be authorized to read as well as update the data. And one user may be authorized to update accounts receivable data but not to produce any reports, whereas another might be permitted to print aged trial balance reports but not to update any data.

In addition to passwords, other procedural controls can be used. Procedures to recover from natural disasters such as floods, tornadoes, and hurricanes, for example, should be established. This may involve the regular and routine backup of data that are then stored in a remote location. Even fires and power failures must be anticipated. Every organization needs written procedures for recovering the information system after such a disaster has struck.

TECHNICAL CONTROLS

Procedural controls are seldom enough to protect a system. As a result, several **technical controls** are also used. One such control is the **dial-back system.** With this approach, the communications front-end processor of a mainframe or minicomputer system automatically disconnects a call immediately after the user requests access and has finished entering a password. Then the system looks up the password, locates its authorized telephone number, and returns the call to see whether the user (or someone) is in fact there. This process takes only a fraction of a minute, and when the user answers, access to the computer begins. While unauthorized access with this approach is much more difficult, it is still not impossible.

There are many versions of call-back systems. Modem manufacturers now include this feature in their more sophisticated models. As a result, the simplest microcomputer configurations can be protected.

Even if computer access is secured with a dial-back system and the database is protected with passwords, the system is still vulnerable when data are transmitted across communication lines. By tapping into the lines, unauthorized users can intercept a transmission and download the data to their own facilities.

One method to protect against this possibility is to code or "encrypt" the data in a practice known as **encryption.** Most encryption systems require the user to enter a secret key. This key sets into motion a mathematical process that codes the data. Different keys result in different codes. Once encrypted, the data move through the communications network, and at the other end the code is "decrypted" after the proper key is entered. The key is not stored in the system, and so if it is lost, the data will become inaccessible even to the intended users.

Most data encryption systems rely on either a federal standard called **Data Encryption Standard (DES)** or the **Rivest–Shamir–Adleman (RSA) method** to code the data. Both are employed for all sizes of computer and are simple to use.

MANAGEMENT CONTROLS

Security is not limited to passwords and technical controls. **Management controls** are also required (Figure 16-5). Management must ensure that all job applicants are adequately screened before offered a job. People who can be readily identified as irresponsible do not belong in the company in the first place. Once employees have been hired, management also needs to ensure that they are properly trained. Training must stress the sensitive nature of the company's data and make it clear what the consequences are for unauthorized access.

Figure 16-5.
Management must assume responsibility for computer security. Those who are given access to the system must be carefully screened and trained.

In addition, management should see that information-handling tasks are split into several separate jobs so that no single person can access a process from beginning to end. When several people are involved, it is less likely that any one of them will be able to abuse the system. For example, the person who enters accounts payable information should be different from the person who authorizes payments for the accounts.

An effective audit system is another control mechanism that management can use to ensure that the system and procedures are used as intended. In an audit, transactions are selected at random and traced through the system from the very first data-entry step to the last output step. The auditor checks to see that routine methods and procedures were followed, and that those accessing the system had the authority to do so.

LAW ENFORCEMENT

To some extent, strict law enforcement can help discourage computer crime. With only a few exceptions, most states have laws that focus on computer crime. In one state, the law protects "electronically processed or stored data either tangible or intangible, or data which are in transit." Although violations of computer crime laws are considered criminal acts, the laws in different states vary widely in the acts they forbid and the penalties they impose.

Most data know no state, provincial, or even national boundary. In 1984 Congress passed the first federal computer crime law, the Federal Computer Systems Act. This law made the unauthorized access to classified national security information or information in certain financial records a federal crime.

In 1986 Congress passed a second computer crime law, the Computer Fraud and Abuse Act. This law extended the earlier computer crime law to include all computers operating in interstate commerce. As a result, federal laws protect the data sent by private companies and corporations across state lines. Now, computer information systems are protected by federal law against access with the intent to defraud when the loss is $1000 or more.

But the record of law enforcement as a deterrent to computer crime has been mixed. Of the firms surveyed by the American Bar Association, only one-third of those who had been the victims of a computer crime reported it to the authorities. Even fewer crimes were prosecuted. Companies often are reluctant to prosecute because the costs of court cases can be very high, and most companies do not want the negative publicity. If the company prosecutes, obtaining a conviction can be difficult. And even if convicted, a criminal may not go to jail. The FBI estimated that only one of twenty-thousand computer criminals goes to jail.

WHO IS ULTIMATELY RESPONSIBLE?

Whether the theft is of computer time, proprietary software, data, or whatever, we all are the ultimate losers, as the costs of prevention measures, lost revenues, and legal enforcement are borne by society as a whole.

The same hacker who copies programs for friends without a qualm—pleased at the ability to get around software-protection schemes as evidence of his or her technical prowess—would likely be mortified at the suggestion of stealing so much as a candy bar from a store. Yet a comparison of values makes the program theft far worse.

Computer crime will continue to rise until we educate people about their responsibility in a technological society. The modern thief who carries a spare password or two around in his or her head, is no less reprehensible than is the more familiar thief who breaks into a house and carries off the television set for quick "resale."

Everyone connected with processing information has a moral and ethical responsibility. This responsibility, simply put, is not to abuse the information any more than we would abuse the rights of individuals or property. This should be our goal. Better prevention and enforcement measures need to be devised only for those persons unimpressed with arguments of shared responsibility.

?   Q U E S T I O N S   ?

1. What factor has exposed computer information systems to more abuse and fraud?

2. Is the problem of computer crime widespread?

3. How can a computer criminal break into a computer system?

4. If an employee uses the company computer to keep a record of his or her stock portfolio, is it a crime? If so, what type of compensation or punishment do you think a firm should impose?

5. Is it illegal to copy a program? What consequences do widespread copying have on the companies that write commercial software and on the users who buy it?

6. Give an example of how altered data can be used to commit a crime.

7. Name three precautions that should be taken with the use of passwords as a security device.

8. What method can be used to help prevent unauthorized access to a computer system through the telephone network?

9. When data must be sent over communication links, what can be done to ensure that they are not intercepted? Explain how it works.

10. In what ways can management controls help minimize the occurrence of computer crime?

S U M M A R Y

- With the shift from manual to computerized record-keeping systems, organizations have become more vulnerable to crime. The shift from centralized to distributed data processing has further increased vulnerability.

- **Computer crime,** the use of a computer for illegal activities, affects many companies.

- Computer crime can be divided into the following categories: breaking in, theft of computer time, altering programs, altering data, theft of data, theft of programs, espionage, and terrorism.

- **Passwords** are used to provide levels of protection against unauthorized access. It is not necessarily difficult to figure out a password, however. Some **hackers** take pride in this type of activity.

- Programs can be altered to enrich criminals, as in the **salami slicing** of fractional monetary sums that add up over time.

- **Copyright** law and copy protection methods provide some safeguards against the theft of programs.

- Copy-protected software presents a problem to the legitimate user, however. Some developers are offering **site licenses** that permit multiple users at a site.

- **Espionage** has been directed toward obtaining company as well as technological secrets concerning computer systems.

- Computer systems are sometimes the targets of **sabotage,** as in the **time bomb,** a "present" left by a disgruntled or departing employee that renders a system inoperative.

- Methods used to protect computer systems include **procedural controls, technical controls, management controls,** and legal enforcement.

- Technical controls include the use of a **dial-back system** to help establish the right to access, and the use of **encryption** to protect the data being transmitted. Encryption generally follows the **Data Encryption Standard** (DES) or the **Rivest–Shamir–Adleman** (RSA) **method.**

- Laws are on the books today to apprehend computer criminals, but their effectiveness has been mixed.

K E Y • T E R M S

The following list shows the key terms in the order in which they appear in the chapter.

Computer crime (p. 459)
Password (p. 460)
Hacker (p. 461)
Salami slicing (p. 462)
Copyright (p. 464)
Site license (p. 465)
Espionage (p. 465)
Sabotage (p. 467)
Time bomb (p. 467)

Procedural control (p. 468)
Technical control (p. 468)
Dial-back system (p. 468)
Encryption (p. 469)
Data Encryption Standard (DES) (p. 469)
Rivest–Shamir–Adleman (RSA) method (p. 469)
Management control (p. 469)

F O R   D I S C U S S I O N

1. Do you think that computer crimes are easier to commit and easier to get away with than other types of crimes?
2. What organizations do you think are most susceptible to computer crime? What should they do to reduce their risk?
3. Do you think that the way to reduce computer crime is to enact tougher legislation, enforce current laws more vigorously, or improve the security systems that prevent unauthorized access?
4. Should accountants—and especially auditors—bear the major responsibility for safeguarding from criminal activities sensitive systems such as payroll and accounts receivable?
5. Why do you think computers are such tempting targets?
6. Would you report a computer crime?

H A N D S - O N   P R O J E C T S

1. Locate an article that describes a method for deterring computer crime, and summarize its main points.
   Suggestions: PC Week, Business Computer Systems.
2. Find an article in a newspaper or computer magazine about a computer crime. Write a short essay on the methods you would use to prevent further occurrences.
   Suggestions: Wall Street Journal, Computerworld.
3. Visit a local business that uses computers. Ask how it safeguards its system from unauthorized access. Then write a report suggesting improvements in this security system.

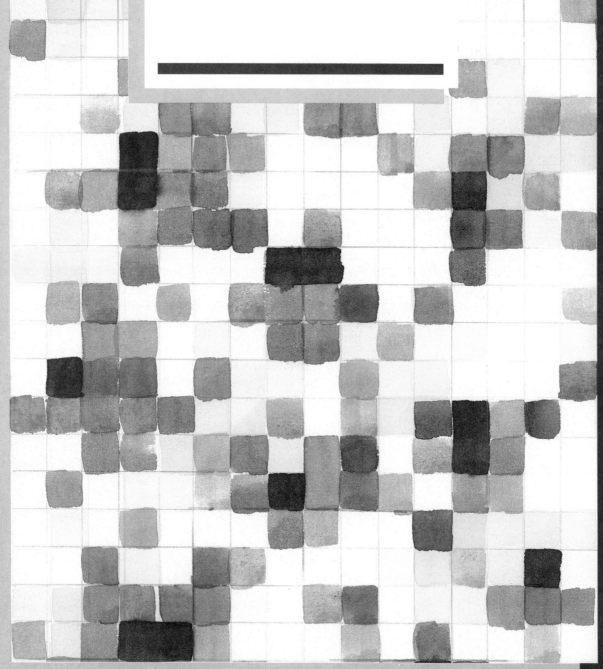

17
COMPUTERS AND SOCIETY

O   U   T   L   I   N   E

O   B   J   E   C   T   I   V   E   S

After studying this chapter you should understand the following:

■   *That computers have brought benefits to diverse areas of our lives.*

■   *How computers affect our workplace, jobs, standard of living, safety, education, and health.*

■   *That businesses and government store extensive personal data about us.*

■   *How businesses and government collect and use data about us.*

■   *How the collection and use of such data can violate our right to privacy.*

It is clear that computers have had a significant impact—perhaps even a revolutionary one—on business. But what about their broader impact? How have they affected our daily lives and the society in which we live?

This chapter will explore both the good and bad consequences of computers. It will explain how our jobs, health, education, safety, and standard of living have benefited. And it will also point out how some people have suffered by losing their jobs and how most people could be hurt by an invasion of privacy.

IMPACT ON SOCIETY

Few if any of us can escape the influence of computers on our lives. Sometimes the influence is direct, and at other times it is subtle and probably not noticed. However it occurs, this influence is widespread. It affects our workplace, employment, standard of living, safety, education, and health. Let us consider each.

WORKPLACE

Because most people will spend the greater portion of their lives working, the impact that the computer has on the workplace is a major societal issue.

Figure 17-1.
Computers have had a major impact on the workplace, as indicated by this automated warehouse.

Office There is no question that the nature of work has changed in just the last decade. Office workers—including secretaries, administrative assistants, professionals, and executives—all have had to adjust to the relentless pace of office automation. Those in factories have also seen their environments change. Factory automation has dramatically affected the way that jobs are performed and the way in which products are manufactured (Figure 17-1).

Earlier in the book (Chapter 6) we took a close look at office automation. We found a continuing trend toward easier access to information, fewer clerks and secretaries, and an increasing emphasis on the professional as a knowledge worker.

Telecommuting Another important trend in the office environment is that some work no longer needs to be done in the office but can be done at home or out in the field. This new way of working, with a computer or terminal at home that communicates with a central computer at an employer's office, is called **telecommuting.**

■ ■

IN HIGGINS GROVE, Colorado, the city government employs over three hundred office workers. About one hundred telecommute on a part-time basis, while twenty-five telecommute full time. And all seven city council members carry portable computers and keep in touch with city business through electronic mail.

■■■■■■■■■■■■■■■■■■■■■■■■■■■■■■■■

Although not all jobs are suited to telecommuting, it is frequently employed by field service technicians, engineers, sales representatives, and programmers.

●●

E N D - U S E R   H I N T S

HIGH STRESS IN HIGH TECH: WHAT CAN BE DONE?

Stress and *computers:* some people think these words go together. Programmers often work at a hectic pace, even through the night, to meet deadlines. Employees on the production floor struggle to meet computer-generated schedules. Professional staff work in environments where their performance may be monitored and controlled by computer-based information systems.

Certainly the computer has made it possible for firms to compete more effectively in local, regional, national, and world markets; but there have been costs. One is the increase in stress. Critics of automation argue that as a consequence of computer technology the workplace is a more stressful environment than ever before.

Indeed, some central data processing organizations even pride themselves on creating stressful environments. "We create stress because we work best this way," says one DP manager. "If we make

an error it could cost the company a million dollars," boasts one programmer. And a systems analyst suggests, "We are all workaholics in DP."

And the users of these systems—clerks, secretaries, business professionals, and customers—also suffer from high-tech stress. Consider the morning that the London Stock Exchange switched to a new computer-based trading system. Within half an hour it failed. How much stress do you think the clerks, traders, and customers felt as they were unable to obtain current trading data?

Or how much stress is felt by the tellers at a bank when the teller terminal system breaks down? Or by a credit card customer who for two months has been trying to clear up an error in a bank's computerized billing system? Or by sales-order entry clerks whose productivity, as they respond to telephone calls and enter order data into their terminals, is monitored on a screen by their supervisors?

It is impossible to avoid or eliminate all stress. In fact, some stress helps us to perform to the best of

our ability. Other stress, however—sometimes the kind we make for ourselves—can affect job performance and even threaten our mental and physical well-being.

To minimize stress imposed by the work itself, an individual might provide time for breaks between activities, change the pace of the activity from mental to physical, alternate creative and routine tasks, and learn to live with unfinished tasks.

When stress is self-imposed, individuals simply must learn to slow down. They must establish reasonable personal goals and then plan their day to accomplish these goals. Sometimes they must learn to adapt to a situation rather than resist it. Stress for these individuals is often the result of a feeling that they must be extremely competitive and complete tasks at lightning speed. Otherwise, they reason, it will not be possible to succeed. If they can learn to slow down and adapt to situations rather than resist, they discover that their stress level is lower and that they are more effective in their jobs.

●●

■■■■■■■■■■■■■■■■■■■■■■■■■■■■■■■■■■■■■

SPHINX LTD. IS A SOFTWARE DEVELOPMENT FIRM THAT WRITES SOFTWARE FOR SEVERAL OF THE MAJOR COMPUTER MANUFACTURERS. Its staff includes eighty programmer/analysts, each of whom telecommutes. They are divided into groups clustered around Princeton, New Jersey, New York City, Vancouver, and San Francisco.

Although Sphinx has very little in the way of office facilities, the employees keep in touch through telephone calls, electronic mail, and electronic conferencing facilities. To minimize the feeling of isolation, the programmers from each cluster regularly get together at local restaurants or the home of the local project leader. And several times each year, local project leaders take a trip to headquarters in San Francisco.

When asked about the benefits of telecommuting, the president, Alice Trane, said, "Productivity is as much as 10 to 20 percent higher; absenteeism is hardly a problem; our office-space costs are 50 percent lower; and our workers feel that the control over their lives as well as the quality of life has improved."

■■■■■■■■■■■■■■■■■■■■■■■■■■■■■■■■■■■■■

Robots On the factory floor, the impact of automation has been even more dramatic. Major auto manufacturers throughout the world now use "intelligent" computer-controlled robots to build automobiles. Many other companies use them in a wide range of manufacturing and assembly applications, from handling hazardous chemicals to assembling electronic equipment (Figure 17-2).

Figure 17-2.
Robotics has changed the way that products are manufactured.

The use of robots, called **robotics,** has many advantages over manual methods. Robots work faster and make fewer mistakes. They do not join unions, do not take sick days, and do exactly as they are told! On the other hand, of course, they are not much fun to sit down and have a chat with.

Robots come in many varieties. All are controlled by computers, but some have both visual and tactile capabilities. Those with visual systems use a small video camera to collect data. The data are converted to digital data and then compared with stored data that act as a reference for the system. In this way a camera can be used to scan parts as they move down an assembly line and watch for those with visual characteristics that do not match the standard.

Many robots also have tactile capabilities, the ability to collect and respond to information collected through their "hands." Although they certainly do not have the sophisticated tactile ability of a human, the robot's arm can still make adjustments in response to something that it touches. For example, a robot can screw the lid on a can to exactly the right degree of tightness. Or the robot can adjust its grip if it has not grasped a part correctly.

But the use of sophisticated computers in the factory does not stop with manufacturing. They are also used in the design process, in a field called **computer-aided design (CAD).** Using these graphics-oriented systems, the time it takes to design a product has been reduced from months to weeks. In some applications, CAD has improved productivity by as much as 400 percent (Figure 17-3).

So from design to production, computers and robotics are beginning to play a dominant role in an integrated engineering/factory/office environment. And it is safe to assume that as this parade of progress continues, more and more jobs will be affected.

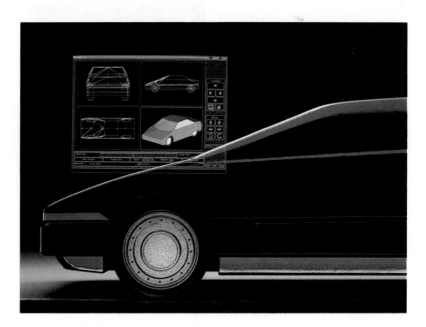

Figure 17-3.
Computers now play a significant role in the design of products.

EMPLOYMENT

How does factory and office automation affect jobs? Some jobs are lost. Some secretaries and administrative assistants lose their jobs to office automation; some production line workers lose their jobs to robots; and some accounting clerks lose their jobs to computerized accounting systems.

Not even computer jobs provide a lifetime of security. Until recently, data-entry operators were thought to have secure futures. These are the people who feed the computer's insatiable appetite for data and who use such equipment as key-to-disk entry systems. Now, however, many information systems are converting to source data automation, and so data-entry operators may become an endangered species (Figure 17-4).

Although some jobs are lost to the computer, others change, often for the better. Modern secretaries and administrative assistants, for example, no longer have to be as proficient in typing, spelling, and proofreading as they once had to be. However, the use of computer equipment and software has introduced a level of complexity to the secretary's work environment that far exceeds that found in the office just a few years ago. For many, this has made the job more interesting.

What this suggests is that a society heavily dependent on technology must expect not only many jobs to change but also some technological unemployment. Although financial assistance in the form of unemployment compensation can help in the short run, retraining and education are the keys in the long run.

Another side of technological progress is the new jobs that technology creates. Positions as programmers, systems analysts, database administrators, and communication specialists never existed before the computer age. And the evidence suggests that computer technology will create even more jobs in the future (Figure 17-5).

Has technology actually created more jobs than it has eliminated? Or are we on an upward spiral with higher and higher levels of unemployment? If we look to the past for an answer, it is unlikely that com-

Figure 17-4.
Although the future for data-entry clerks is uncertain, the future for other job categories in the computer field is bright.

Figure 17-5.
Although automation has certainly eliminated some factory jobs, other jobs in the computer and service industries have been created in their place.

puters and automation will lead to widespread unemployment. According to a 1981 U.S. Department of Labor study, computer-related job displacement for the preceding thirty years was compensated by the new jobs created and the increases in productivity.

Supporting this point of view, Tandon Corporation, a maker of computer peripherals, reported that its fourteen robots enabled it to slash costs and improve the quality of its products. As a result, order rates increased, leading the company to raise its employment from five to over two hundred workers.

Another company reported that it was able to accept bigger metal fabrication jobs after installing a robotics system. As a result, more workers had to be hired to accommodate the increase in orders that followed.

And there is another factor that must be considered as we balance the pluses and minuses of technology's impact on the job market. Robotics and office automation have eliminated many tedious and often hazardous jobs, and the new jobs are often considered to be safer and more interesting. Many feel this is a positive benefit to society, as it has helped improve the quality of the worker's life.

Finally, the impact of computers on product quality cannot be overlooked. In many areas employees now turn out higher-quality products than ever before.

SAFETY

Computers contribute to our safety. Robots perform dangerous tasks, including handling hazardous chemicals. In some cities robots are even used to inspect and defuse bombs. Computers control train and subway traffic, thereby reducing the chances of collision, and in automobiles, they are used to alert passengers to fasten their seatbelts, to check the car doors, and to turn on their lights.

STANDARD OF LIVING

The impact of computer technology on the office, product design, and manufacturing methods eventually reaches the price of goods and services we buy. As costs born by the producer are lowered, these benefits—through the competitive climate of business—are frequently passed to the consumer in the form of lower prices (Figure 17-6). So with the higher salaries that most people earn and the lower costs of some goods and services, everyone's standard of living is improved.

Also contributing to our standard of living is the convenience these machines bring into our daily lives. Cash can now be obtained at any hour of the day or night through an automatic teller machine, and computers enable credit-card purchases, mail-order shopping, and the purchase of tickets for theater and sporting events by telephone.

EDUCATION

The field of education also benefits from computers. When **computer-assisted instruction** (CAI) was introduced into the classroom in the late 1960s and early 1970s, it was used primarily to drill students in the skills of a new subject. For example, a fifth grader sat in front of a terminal and solved an endless stream of math problems until mastering that topic or passing a computer-administered test. Educators generally feel that this first wave of computer use in the schools did not live up to expectations. They point out that some of these systems were even abandoned.

But CAI has since become more sophisticated and is now moving away from a reliance on simple drill exercises toward more creative methods of learning. Many of the CAI packages, for example, now present a topic through the simulation of a realistic environment. And many new educational software packages are integrating videodisk technology

Figure 17-6.
The benefits from computer technology used in the design, manufacture, and delivery of goods and services are passed on to consumers in the form of lower prices.

Figure 17-7.
Computer-assisted instruction promises to improve the quality of education, make learning more interesting, and improve educational productivity.

with CAI. All of these developments will help make learning more fun and certainly more effective.

Although it is still too early to predict exactly how much of an impact this technology will have on education, many experts feel that we are just beginning to use it effectively and that CAI will play a major role in the classroom of the future. Meanwhile, the classroom of the present, from the elementary level upward, already has been invaded by a small army of microcomputers that are used to prepare papers, drill vocabulary, learn programming, and play educational games (Figure 17-7).

HEALTH

Computers also play a major role in the delivery of health care. Hospitals, clinics, and private physicians use computers in

- Financial record keeping

- Maintaining medical histories

- Dispensing and monitoring medications

- Monitoring vital signs (Figure 17-8)

- Formulating diagnoses

- Planning and monitoring treatment

The use of computers for medical diagnosis is particularly interesting. For example, it has been shown that in some applications expert systems can be designed to diagnose at least as well as medical experts can. As a result, remote communities that are unable to support a range of medical experts can have access to expert-like opinions through a computer.

Computers are also being increasingly used to help handicapped people function better. Many of the most highly skilled computer jobs, for example, are open to the blind and vision-impaired through the use of Braille or regular keyboards for input, coupled with voice output to explain what is happening on the screen.

Figure 17-8.
Computers play a major role in the delivery of health care. Here, a computer monitors a baby's heart and lung functions at the Mount Zion Hospital and Medical Center in San Francisco.

PRIVACY

Although computers have generally had a positive impact on the workplace, employment, standard of living, safety, education, and health, there is one area of great concern to many people: privacy.

What exactly is privacy? For our purposes, **privacy** is the assurance to individuals that the information gathered about them is accurate, will only be used as intended, and will somehow be protected from improper and unauthorized access and use.

Privacy is a complex issue. No one, of course, really wants his or her privacy invaded. But according to some critics, there may be little privacy left to invade. They maintain that computers already know a lot about us and are learning more at an alarming rate.

Although the U.S. Congress has tried to place a lid on this explosive problem, it has nearly failed. Today the problem is worse than it was in 1970 when legislation directed at the problem was first enacted.

There are, however, several legitimate reasons that little or nothing has been done. First, most people want and need the services that data-gathering activities provide. Second, it is sometimes difficult to determine when a person's privacy has indeed been invaded.

There are also several reasons that something should be done. Most of us have a fact or two that we would prefer to keep private: an incident from the past, perhaps concerning financial data, employment data, medical data, political opinions, or even criminal data.

DATA AVAILABLE ABOUT YOU

The data collected about you can be divided into two categories: (1) data collected by profit and nonprofit organizations and (2) data collected by local, state, and federal government agencies.

Some of the data maintained by profit and nonprofit organizations include credit information, medical data, employment history facts, and university records. Some of these databases are enormous. For example, the largest credit-reporting company, TRW Information Services, keeps credit histories on 120 million Americans.

Wherever a person has held a job, employment records exist. They reveal that person's employment history and salary and might even include performance evaluations. Sometimes employment agencies and companies maintain records on those who have simply *applied* for a job.

Records are also established as the result of visits to the doctor, hospital stays, administration of medications, tests, and so on. And you are certainly familiar with the records colleges keep: data on grades, recommendations, tuition payments, room and board charges, and scholarships. When elaborate computerized meal ticket systems are used, your college may even know what you had for breakfast.

Local, state, and federal record keeping is even more ambitious. At the state and local level, data are maintained on taxes, auto registration, voter statistics, and census facts. The federal data-gathering arm stores over four *billion* records on individuals that are maintained by such agencies as the IRS, Bureau of the Census, CIA, National Security Agency, Army, Navy, Air Force, Department of Defense, Secret Service, and FBI. There is no scarcity of data. It is not the volume of data, however, but the way in which they can be used that is the cause for concern.

CAN THE DATA BE MISUSED?

In 1967 the FBI created the National Crime Information Center (NCIC). At the heart of this system is a computer that maintains over fifteen million records, or one record for every fifteen Americans. The files include information on missing persons, arrest warrants, stolen property, criminal histories, registered guns, and registered vehicles.

Although many people accept the need for massive databases such as this and find little criticism with the way in which they are used, others take a different view. Their criticisms are directed at the widespread access that people have to these systems and the possibility that they can be misused. The NCIC center, for example, can be accessed from 17,000 terminals located throughout the country. The terminals provide the means by which 64,000 federal, state, and local police agencies, government prosecutors, and judges can access the system.

Many of those concerned about this and other large databases are worried that some users will combine information from different systems and build from this data-gathering exercise a profile of the individual that could easily be classified as an invasion of privacy. The following are several examples that have been reported in the press.

The motor vehicle departments from each state in the United States were asked to give to the Selective Service Administration the name, address, and social security number of all young men eligible for the draft. This was presumably to be used to cross-check with the SSA's list and identify those who failed to register. All but one state complied with this request!

In an effort to uncover tax cheaters, the IRS studied the possibility of matching lists of high-income households, obtained from a commercial marketing service, with its own records. The IRS reportedly did acquire a medical journal's subscription list to verify that all the doctors on it had indeed filed a return.

In the private sector, a large department store combined the information from several databases to identify a list of prospects that loosely met the characteristics of customers who would be likely to make certain large purchases. Armed with this list, the store began a person-to-person campaign that proved to be successful. This type of activity is not isolated.

Whether or not these applications do indeed violate one's right to privacy is a difficult question to answer. And the answer will probably depend on whether the data are used to fight crime, detect fraud, or sell time-share condominiums.

DO WE HAVE CONTROL?

What control do we have over the collection of data? Although some data are volunteered (Figure 17-9), other data are required. We voluntarily fill out questionnaires, return product warranty cards, answer telephone surveys, and complete job applications. But when it comes to bank and credit-card transactions, job histories, and medical histories, we do not really volunteer these data; rather, they are a requirement of the purchase or service. Nevertheless, they find their way into a database (Figure 17-10).

Whether volunteered or required, however, the real issue is this: Should the data about us become public, and should we have the right in some situations not to share the data? Should we be given a choice?

As an example of how the data about you can be used without your permission and how they can move from one user to another, try this experiment. The next time you fill out a subscription to a magazine or newspaper, add a new middle initial to your name. Soon after, you will begin to receive unsolicited mail addressed to this name with the new initial. How does this happen? The magazine has sold its mailing list.

ARE THE DATA ACCURATE?

Let us assume for the moment that data about you will indeed be accessible to a wide variety of users. If this is to be the case, then it would be reasonable to expect that the data be accurate and up-to-date. Unfortunately, the evidence suggests that this may not always be the case.

In one study, the U.S. Office of Technology Assessment (OTA) sampled NCIC arrest records only to discover that 27 percent of the records in the sample did not include information about the outcome of the

— STATEMENT OF CLAIM FOR GROUP HEALTH BENEFITS —

HOW TO FILE A CLAIM:

Complete this Side of Form and Top Portion of Reverse Side.
Have the Attending Physician Complete His/Her Portion of Reverse Side.

ABOUT YOU	Name & Address of Faculty/Staff Member ☐ Single ☐ Married ☐ Divorced ☐ Widowed ☐ Legally Separated Soc. Sec. # Date of Birth Please indicate if this is an address change ☐ Yes ☐ No This is necessary for claim identification.

ABOUT YOUR SPOUSE	Name of Spouse _____
	 Is Spouse Currently Employed? ☐ Yes ☐ No
	 Is Spouse Covered Under His/Her Employer's Plan? ☐ Yes ☐ No
	 Name & Address of Spouse's Employer _____
	 _____ Telephone # _____
	 If Spouse is not Currently Employed, when was
	  Spouse Last Employed? _____
	  Indicate Name and Address of Last Employer _____

ABOUT THE PATIENT	**THIS CLAIM IS FOR** 1. ☐ Myself—If disabled, 1st day not worked _____ Patient's
	 2. ☐ My Spouse Date of Birth _____
	 3. ☐ My Child-Name _____ Date of Birth _____
	    Is Child Employed? ☐ Yes ☐ No If Over 19 Years of Age, is Child a Full Time
	    If "Yes," for No. 3, please complete the following: Student? ☐ Yes ☐ No
	
	 Employer or School Name _____
	 City _____ State _____

ABOUT THE CLAIM	**THIS CLAIM IS DUE TO** **1. IS THIS CONDITION RELATED TO EMPLOYMENT?** ☐ Yes ☐ No **2A. AN ACCIDENT** Nature of Injury _____ How Did it Happen? _____ _____ Where? _____ When? _____ **(Complete Question 1, either 2a or 2b, and 3)** **2B. AN ILLNESS** Nature of Illness _____ When Did Symptoms Begin? _____ When Was a Physician First Consulted? _____ Name of Physician _____ Address _____ **3. IS THIS A SECOND OR THIRD SURGICAL OPINION?** ☐ Yes ☐ No

ABOUT OTHER INSURANCE	IS THE PATIENT COVERED BY ONE OR MORE OF THE FOLLOWING?
	 Any other group coverage? ☐ Yes ☐ No
	 Any federal, state or other governmental plan, or union welfare plan? ☐ Yes ☐ No
	 Any medical plan sponsored by a school or college? ☐ Yes ☐ No
	 Any other student health plan? ☐ Yes ☐ No
	 Any other No-Fault insurance? ☐ Yes ☐ No
	
	     Name of Insured Name & Address of Employer,
	 If "Yes" To Any of The Above _____ Group or School
	 Name & Address of Other Policy Number Providing The Plan
	 Insurance Company or _____
	    Certificate Number

Figure 17-9.
Most of the data collected on us are volunteered, as is true every time we fill out a health insurance form.

case. Other studies, of state criminal data, have shown that up to 75 percent of the records are incomplete or incorrect. What this suggests is that both innocent individuals *and* convicted criminals who have served their sentences may wind up as victims when an incomplete or incorrect record is pulled from the file.

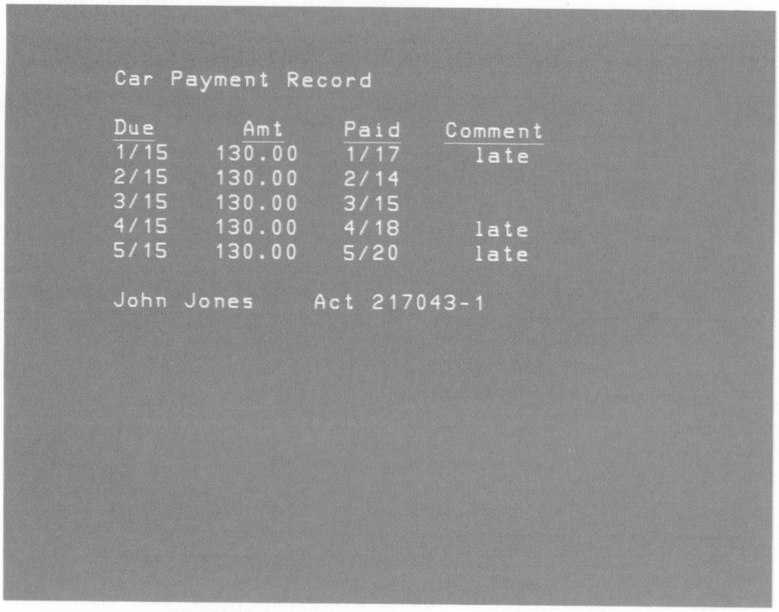

```
Car Payment Record

Due        Amt      Paid    Comment
1/15      130.00    1/17      late
2/15      130.00    2/14
3/15      130.00    3/15
4/15      130.00    4/18      late
5/15      130.00    5/20      late

John Jones      Act 217043-1
```

Figure 17-10.
Should these data be kept confidential?

In another study of the records maintained by the U.S. Veterans Administration, over half of the records were found to have faulty social security numbers.

Many consumers have been plagued at one time or another with credit-card billing errors. One woman was denied a mortgage from several banks because her credit-card company reported a balance long overdue. In fact, she had disputed a charge on her card and so had withheld this amount from her monthly payments. But because of this, her credit rating had plummeted.

DOES THE SSN MAKE IT TOO EASY?

Before the creation of large databases, information on us was scattered and unrelated. This worked in favor of privacy: It was difficult to pull enough data together to build a profile that might be considered an invasion of privacy.

Even after the development of large databases, the system for linking files together still needed one essential ingredient: a unique key by which all the records for a single individual could be related. A person's name was not enough, as many people have the same name. But social security numbers are, for all practical purposes, unique. And this number can link a lifetime of information.

Use of the social security number (SSN) as a "national identifier" has not gone unopposed. The 1973 report by the then U.S. Department of Health, Education and Welfare (now the Department of Health and Human Services) that led to many of today's privacy laws stated that

We recommend against the adoption of any nationwide, standard, personal identification format, with or without the SSN, that would enhance the likelihood of arbitrary or uncontrolled linkage of records about people, particularly between government-supported automated personal data systems. What is needed is a halt **to the drift toward a Standard Universal Identifier.**

The drift about which this report warned many years ago, however, has not slowed. In fact, the use of the SSN as an identifier is now standard practice. Universities use it as student ID numbers. And federal, state, and local agencies use it, as do credit bureaus, hospitals, banks, insurance companies, and employers.

HAS LEGISLATION HELPED?

Since 1970, several pieces of legislation have been enacted to protect citizens from computer abuses or an invasion of their privacy. The Fair Credit Reporting Act (1970) enables citizens to gain access to credit-bureau records and challenge inaccurate or out-of-date data. The Freedom of Information Act (1970) gives citizens the right to have access to the data about them gathered by federal agencies. But judging by reports, that access can be difficult to obtain. Nonetheless, this and the Fair Credit Reporting Act have been major victories for citizens and consumers.

The Federal Privacy Act (1974) makes it illegal for firms doing business with the government to maintain secret personnel files. It requires such firms to justify the need for collecting information about an individual and prohibits them from simply browsing through data in the hopes of finding "something." This act, however, has come under fire for being ineffectual. Critics claim that it is too broad and allows too many exceptions to the rules. And no agency or single person is in charge of enforcing it!

THE PROS AND CONS

Although there has been much criticism of public and private databases, it is important to keep in mind some of their advantages. They have been essential to providing consumers with the kinds of services they want and also effective in catching tax evaders, uncovering stolen property, preventing crime, and locating missing persons.

Perhaps the lesson that we can learn from this controversy is that society must continue to exert pressure on the trustees of vital data to ensure that they are accurate, that they are used only for legitimate purposes, that unauthorized access is not allowed, and that the data be kept up-to-date.

1. Describe some of the ways that computers have affected the workplace.
2. How have computers contributed to our safety? To our standard of living?
3. How were computers used in the past, in education? How are they likely to be used in the future?
4. What is meant by privacy?
5. Give examples of data that are collected about you by profit-making and nonprofit organizations.
6. What data are collected about you by local, state, and federal agencies?
7. Of the data items collected about you, which do you prefer to be kept private? Would you mind if some of the data were made available to a wide variety of users? If yes, which types of data?
8. Give an example from the text of files that can be linked together and used to discover information about an individual.
9. Give an example of how inaccurate or incomplete data about an individual might damage that person's reputation or invade that person's privacy.
10. What legislation has been enacted to support the rights of individuals? Has it helped?

■ Few people, if any, can escape the influence of computers.

■ Computers affect our workplace, employment, standard of living, safety, education, and health. In general, their impact has been positive.

■ **Telecommuting,** which moves the workplace into the home, is an important current trend.

■ In the factory and elsewhere, **robotics** is used in a wide range of manufacturing, assembly, and other applications.

■ Computers are used in **computer-aided design** (CAD).

■ **Computer-assisted instruction** (CAI) is now experiencing a rebirth in the classroom, from the elementary level upwards.

■ **Privacy** is the assurance to individuals that the information gathered about them is accurate, will only be used as intended, and will somehow be protected from improper and unauthorized access and use.

■ Profit-making and nonprofit organizations maintain data on individuals, including credit information, medical data, employment history facts, and university records.

■ Federal, state, and local government agencies maintain data on taxes, auto registration, voter statistics, and census results.

■ Over four billion records are stored about individuals by federal government agencies such as the IRS, Bureau of the Census, CIA, National Security Agency, Army, Navy, Air Force, Department of Defense, Secret Service, and FBI.

■ Concerns about these data center on their possible misuse, our ability (or lack thereof) to control the data, and their accuracy.

■ For all practical purposes, our social security number makes it possible to link together data about us gathered from numerous sources.

■ Federal legislation aimed at protecting citizens from computer-assisted abuses of privacy dates from the 1970s and includes the Fair Credit Reporting Act, the Freedom of Information Act, and the Federal Privacy Act.

K E Y • T E R M S

The following list shows the key terms in the order in which they appear in the chapter.

Telecommuting (p. 476)
Robotics (p. 479)
Computer-aided design (CAD) (p. 479)

Computer-assisted instruction (CAI) (p. 482)
Privacy (p. 484)

F O R   D I S C U S S I O N

1. Argue for using the SSN as a national identifier that enables the widespread access of databases to those who have a reasonable need for such information.

2. Argue against using the SSN as a national identifier to link databases for all but legal and criminal agency activities.

3. Should a company that collects information on its employees be required to secure the employee's approval before using the data, or should the company be free to use the data in any way it feels is appropriate?

4. What compensation (money or education) should a society give to those who lose jobs through technological obsolescence? What limits should be placed on these benefits?

HANDS-ON PROJECTS

1. Locate an article that illustrates how a computer information system has affected society (jobs, safety, education, health, or whatever). List the advantages and disadvantages of the system.
   Suggestions: Computerworld, New York Times, Wall Street Journal.
2. Find a friend or acquaintance who believes that his or her privacy has been invaded with the help of a computer system. Briefly write down the details.
3. List the databases that are likely to maintain records about you. Identify those data items that you would prefer to keep confidential. Do you think that you have any control over the use of these data? If not, should you be given such control?

CASE · STUDY

THE BILCO COMPANY

A manufacturer of replacement auto parts, the Bilco Company completed its automation program over a year ago. Both its manufacturing facilities and offices have been affected.

The office staff—including secretaries, business professionals, and managers—now rely on word processing, electronic mail, and electronic filing. Microcomputers are on every desk. They are connected through a local area network and then joined to the corporate mainframe through a gateway.

The manufacturing and distribution processes have also been automated. The latest in robotics is used to manufacture Bilco's line, which includes

spark plugs, condensers, and distributors. When the parts have been manufactured, they are automatically stored and retrieved using computer-controlled materials-handling equipment.

A manufacturing information system is used to schedule jobs. The system keeps a log of each job on the shop floor, and so the whereabouts of any part or finished product can be determined with just a few keystrokes.

Bilco's Competitive Position

Although the system had problems in the beginning, management now considers it a resounding success. Employment in the production and distribution departments has been reduced by 10 percent, from 1025 to 910. Although a similarly dramatic decrease in the office staff was not possible, employment in this area has dropped from 95 to 90. At the same time, the office staff is producing about 20 percent more work.

Job Security

When the project was first announced over three years ago, the employees resisted the idea of an automated plant. They were aware that it would change not only the nature of their jobs but also the ways that they worked and interacted with one another.

Economic reality, however, was instrumental in changing their minds. Bilco competes with several other domestic as well as foreign manufacturers, and when it announced the project, management made it clear that unless the employees accepted automation, the company could go out of business.

Better Control

Now with the system in full operation, management can control the entire operation from the offices to the shop floor. Productivity has increased, output is up, costs are down, and profit margins are higher.

But the improvement in control recently has become a major issue with the work force. Since the introduction of the new system, most employees feel that their performance is being monitored so closely that they are under an unreasonable amount of pressure.

Although the employees have never joined a union, a number of outspoken individuals suggested that a group of their representatives meet with top management and discuss their concerns. After some internal bickering, three representatives were elected: a secretary, an engineer, and a production-line supervisor. Top management agreed on a meeting, and a date was set.

Terminal Monitoring and Reporting System

At the meeting, the representative of the secretarial staff, Tammy Brown, was the first to speak. "It's not the computer system that bothers us," she began. "It's those weekly reports that keep us under so much pressure."

Brown was referring to the terminal monitoring and reporting system (TMRS), a software package

Bilco purchased with the new computer system. The software monitors the work performed at every terminal and microcomputer in the system and records this in a separate file in the database.

The TMRS works in the following way: Before any microcomputer or terminal can be used, the user must enter a password. As a result the TMRS software knows who is using the machine. The TMRS then categorizes the type of use—spreadsheet, filing, word processing, data access, data update, and so on—and also summarizes and stores several characteristics of the work session, including the length of time the machine is used. At the end of the week, these data are used in a report to managers and supervisors.

The report prepared for those who supervise the secretaries summarizes the number of letters each secretary typed, how long it took, and how many errors were made. The report also ranks secretaries by productivity.

Brown continued, "I have the feeling that this system is spying on me. Many of the secretaries, including me, wonder whether Bilco can do this to us."

"Some of us feel that the system is supposed to speed up our work but not give us any more money. If we haven't been working fast enough, there are other ways to get us to speed up. But we've been working as fast as we can, especially in the last few years with all the foreign competition. I doubt if any company gets more from its secretaries."

"And I don't think it's fair that we see the data for the first time at the end of the week. By that time we can't remember the circumstances when the data were collected. Don't you think we should at least be able to look at them when they are collected, so we can have them changed if they are wrong? It seems to me that after the data are collected and put into the computer, whether they are right or wrong, they're treated as fact."

Security Monitoring System

Charlie Lo, the production supervisor, was next to speak. "My people are ready to revolt over the new security monitoring system (SMS). They don't think the company should keep track of every move they make."

Lo was complaining about another controversial part of the new system: The company has installed automatic doors throughout the plant that require personal identification cards to be inserted into a card reader attached to the door before it can be opened. The card readers are actually remote terminals that collect data, including the person's ID number and time of day, whenever there is movement in or out of a secured area. The data are stored on disk and then used to update the security database every evening.

When it was first installed, management claimed that the security system was necessary to protect their new, state-of-the-art production facility from access by unauthorized persons.

The software is designed to compile from the security database a complete log of a person's whereabouts during the day. Weekly reports are issued to supervisors. As a result, a supervisor can reconstruct a worker's movements through the plant on any given day. The number of times an employee goes to the restroom can even be concluded from the data! According to Lo, several workers have already been reprimanded for being away from their workstations too often and wandering through the company.

Data Security

Maria Rodrigez, a design engineer, added her concerns. "The engineering staff also resents the use of this system by management to monitor the work we do at our workstations. Last week, in fact, an engineering manager spoke to one of our engineers about how he was working on a project and how long it was taking him compared with others on similar jobs. This never would have happened in the past. And this criticism was of one of our best engineers! For the first time since they came here, many of our engineers feel like every step they take is being watched. And this monitoring activity is not our only concern," Rodrigez continued. "With these remote terminals secretaries have apparently given personal data to people who have no business knowing them. In fact, I'm sure you heard about the incident last week when someone sent a public memo through the electronic mail system that listed every engineering manager's salary."

After pausing for a moment, Rodrigez stated, "It seems to me that you're interested only in keeping the company's secrets but feel it's OK to monitor what we do and violate our right to privacy."

Violation of Rights

Rodrigez concluded her presentation by reading a quotation from a spokesperson for the American Civil Liberties Union (ACLU), a private agency that keeps an eye on such privacy issues. The quotation states the ACLU's concerns about using computers to monitor work. If the monitoring is done to help the individual do a job better and improve productivity in the workplace, then the ACLU has no concern. But if the monitoring is used to speed the job to an unreasonable pace or if it creates new stresses in the workplace because the workers fear retribution, then the technology is being used incorrectly.

The Company's Response

After the group finished, Bilco's president, Scott Bilco, Jr., presented the company's position.

"I understand your concern," Bilco began, "but I can assure you that the reason we put in this system is to protect you. Several years ago, before we automated, I was worried about what the competition would do to our company. If you remember, I said that if we didn't improve our productivity, we all would be out of work.

"It's clear that the new system has given us a competitive edge," continued Bilco. "We are now in a stronger position than we have been in the last twenty years. I agree, some changes should be made. In fact, we are already changing the security measures for our payroll and personnel data. We don't want what happened last week to happen again.

"But I assure you, there are many ways the new monitoring system can help *you*. It helps your managers set *reasonable* productivity goals. It helps us discover problems *before* they become serious and respond to these problems with additional training or individual assistance. It helps us reward the high achievers, without showing favoritism. And it can help you reach many of your own productivity goals."

Questions

1. How did Bilco justify the new computer system?
2. Describe the problems that the employees have had with the new system.
3. Should employees have the right to examine data about them?

4. Is a company responsible for protecting the way in which sensitive employee data are used? Explain.
5. Justify Bilco's monitoring system.
6. Argue from the employees' point of view that employee monitoring is not justified.
7. In your view, should employee monitoring be limited? Does it violate the individual's right to privacy?
8. Did Bilco handle the situation well? If you were he, what would you do next?

■■

18
CAREERS IN INFORMATION SYSTEMS

O U T L I N E

O B J E C T I V E S

After studying this chapter you should understand the following:

- *The types of career opportunities available in information systems.*

- *Which information system jobs are available in companies that manufacture hardware and write commercial software.*

- *Which jobs are available in companies that use computers.*

- *The steps needed to prepare for a career in information systems.*

- *How to go about finding a job and, once found, how to maintain job skills.*

This book has addressed its readers as business professionals who will use computer information systems in their careers. The more the business professional knows about computers, the better, for a career path in business today will provide plenty of opportunities for significant interaction with, and planning of, computer information systems.

There is an inherent fascination in computing and its success stories, however, that leads some people to consider not merely using computers but making a career out of them. Accordingly, this chapter examines the career possibilities in information systems.

Indeed, the success stories are hard for anyone considering a career in computers to ignore. Steve Wozniak and Steve Jobs started in a garage and in a few years built Apple Computer Corporation, a major microcomputer manufacturer. In Cupertino, California, a dozen people left Hewlett-Packard and started Tandem Computers; in a few years, the company became the leader in fault-tolerant computing. And John Cullinane, founder of Cullinet Software, piloted his company very quickly to a leading position in database management software.

Entrepreneurs are not the only ones who have succeeded in an industry that has often grown at a double-digit pace. Scores of professionals have taken jobs with both large and small companies and found their services generously rewarded. For all of them, entrepreneurs and professionals alike, the computer industry has been a source of enormous opportunity.

This chapter will describe the different jobs available in information systems and will suggest ways in which those who are interested might prepare for a career in this exciting field.

CHOOSING AN INFORMATION SYSTEM CAREER

Business students choose information systems careers for many reasons. Some enjoy the challenge of working in a field that is rapidly growing and changing, and others enjoy using their minds to solve the kinds of problems found in a programming environment. Students sometimes find they are good at selling equipment that can improve a customer's operations or at working at jobs that help end-users become familiar with the ways that computer technology can help them solve their problems. A common thread is the opportunity to combine their interests in business and in information technology.

Whatever the reason, those who have chosen a career in this field have enjoyed a relatively strong demand for their skills. Behind this demand has been the increasing emphasis that organizations have placed on information as a corporate resource. And whenever new technology has proven useful, there has followed a new demand for specialists who can help bring this new technology into operation.

But it would be unrealistic to think that this steadily increasing demand for computer professionals is immune to setbacks. Several have already occurred, including those in 1975, 1981, and 1985. During these periods, jobs were sometimes hard to find and generous salary increases even harder.

Predicting the course of the industry in the future is difficult at best. If past employment trends are simply projected into the future, as experts have been known to do, then employment prospects for most jobs in the industry are indeed quite bright. But there are some ominous signs that a person making a career choice should consider. First, the manufacture of hardware—including semiconductors, disk drives, tape drives, disks, printers, communications equipment, and even computers—tends to move from North America to Asia, especially as the products mature. Second, the use of fourth-generation languages has made applications easier to develop and has shifted some programming development to end-users. Third, the competition among hardware and software companies has been intense: Many have been unable to keep up and as a result have failed.

In spite of problems, however, many experts predict that the computer industry will continue in good health and will be a significant source of new jobs in the future.

Computer-related jobs can be placed in two broad categories. The first includes jobs in companies that manufacture computer hardware, write commercial software, or do both. The second comprises jobs in companies that use computers. Let us look at each category.

JOBS WITH COMPUTER MANUFACTURERS

Companies that create hardware and software include major firms such as IBM, Hewlett-Packard, Digital Equipment Corporation, Cullinet Software, and Lotus Development Corporation, as well as numerous smaller and aspiring organizations. Many jobs available with these manufacturers and software developers require a degree in engineering or computer science, but some require business information system skills. The latter include

- Application programming
- Technical sales
- Customer support
- Technical writing

APPLICATION PROGRAMMING

Figure 18-1.
Computer manufacturers employ application programmers to develop programs that will work on their equipment.

Most manufacturers and software developers write application software that their customers will use to solve business problems (Figure 18-1). Consequently, they often need business information specialists on their development team. As a member of the team, each programmer must be proficient in a programming language. Although programs for large systems are often written in COBOL, an increasing number of projects use 4GLs, and programs for smaller systems are sometimes written in BASIC or Pascal. Consequently, those who want to be programmers will increase their opportunities if they master several languages.

TECHNICAL SALES

Technical sales combines an interest in information systems with an interest in sales and marketing. Those who choose this career path usually have strong social skills, enjoy meeting and working with people, and are self-motivated (Figure 18-2).

Before they can represent the company and its product line, technical sales personnel spend weeks or months in training programs. During this period they learn how products work, how technical support can be provided to the customer, how feasibility and system studies for the customers' systems can be prepared, how to arrange demonstrations, and how to make technical presentations.

Because those who sell large minicomputer and mainframe systems can have a significant influence on the design and performance of a customer's operation and because these systems often cost several million dollars, many vendors find it necessary to separate their sales force into specialties. Some reps will then become specialists in manufacturing systems, others in accounting systems, still others in hospital systems, and so on.

Figure 18-2.
The salesperson representing a computer line must understand not only how the system works but also how the system will meet the customer's needs.

CUSTOMER SUPPORT

Another category in which business students have found jobs is customer support (Figure 18-3). Computer manufacturers maintain customer support groups responsible for helping those who purchase their systems. Customer support specialists in this group have many responsibilities. At Wang Computer, for example, customer support personnel answer questions on the phone. Quite often they help the customer solve problems by accessing their computer through a modem and then working with the customer to determine the source of the problem. Sometimes the specialists even travel to the customer's site to help solve a particularly difficult problem. One employee remarked, "I enjoy working with so many different people and helping them solve their problems." And she went on to make a statement frequently heard from those who choose information systems as a career: "I can't believe how much I have learned in the year and a half since graduation."

TECHNICAL WRITING

Every commercial hardware and software system must be accompanied by several levels of documentation. Consequently, the companies that

Figure 18-3.
This customer-support specialist is helping a customer bring the system into full operation.

produce these systems must employ a staff of technical writers whose expertise is making technical material easy for the users to understand (Figure 18-4). These specialists work with hardware and software designers, learn the details of a system's operation, and then write program documentation, system documentation, user manuals, and even copy for marketing brochures. So in addition to understanding the technical issues, good technical writers must also have good writing skills.

JOBS WITH COMPUTER USERS

The second category of jobs is those with companies that use computers (Figure 18-5). This is clearly a larger category than the first, as today nearly every organization is a computer user. In fact, most students who specialize in information systems will probably find a job in this category.

Jobs with companies that use computers are in either central information system departments or in the functional areas of the business. The central information system department in many firms is managed by the manager of information systems, who is often at the vice-president level. Below the manager of information systems are many other groups or departments, each with jobs that often include business information specialists. We shall first discuss system development.

SYSTEMS DEVELOPMENT

Figure 18-4.
The responsibility of a technical writer is to prepare effective documentation.

The systems development group includes systems analysts and systems designers who are responsible for analyzing existing systems and designing new ones (Figure 18-6). Because the systems they design frequently have a strong end-user orientation, individuals with a business informa-

Figure 18-5.
Companies that use computers have the highest demand for those with information processing skills.

tion background are often included in these groups. Chapters 12 and 13 examined the kinds of work that systems analysts and designers do.

APPLICATION PROGRAMMING

Many large companies develop their own custom programs and so must maintain a staff of programming professionals. Usually this group includes people from both computer science and business information systems backgrounds.

Application programming is where many students who graduate from a business program begin their careers. Some companies first send their new hires through an extensive training program, to learn how to write programs that will meet the company's standards. Then, after completing the training program, the new employees are assigned to programming teams for their first project.

COMMUNICATION SPECIALIST

As we stated in Chapter 14, most computer information systems are not confined to one geographic area. Some even extend around the world. As a result, they must depend on communication technology to tie together all parts of the system.

Communication specialists are responsible for developing data communication systems; managing the flow of voice, data, and video traffic in the systems; and safeguarding them from unauthorized access. Communication specialists must work with hardware specialists, software experts, common carriers, private communications companies, and end-users (Figure 18-7).

Figure 18-6.
The system development people at a large organization are responsible for designing the systems used by their company.

Figure 18-7.
Communication specialists manage and control the flow of voice and data between computers in the company's information system.

Ten years ago there were few jobs in this speciality; today there are many. And with the growth in distributed processing, the need for people with skills in communication technology is sure to increase.

NETWORK SPECIALIST

Network specialist (Figure 18-8) is another career category that did not exist ten years ago. Those who choose this path will work with local area networks and even larger distributed networks that may span the globe.

In general, the job of a network specialist is to design and develop networks of computers and peripheral devices interconnected so that the networks enable the users to interact with certain equipment in the system. Because much of the interconnected hardware and software has not necessarily been designed to work together, specialists in this area spend much of their time solving interface problems.

As we mentioned in Chapter 15, there is a strong movement toward networking, and so the future for those choosing a career in this field is promising.

KNOWLEDGE ENGINEER

Artificial intelligence is a relatively new field, but already there is a strong and growing demand for those trained in it. The knowledge engineer's job is to work with authorities in a field and to design expert systems that incorporate their knowledge and problem-solving skills. After designing an expert system, these specialists must then work with end-users to modify, update, and maintain the system.

Figure 18-8.
Network specialists are responsible for the integration of the firm's computers into a functioning and useful information system.

Expert systems are now very costly to build, and so only the largest organizations can afford to experiment with them. Consequently, jobs in this field will probably be limited to large firms until the cost of developing these systems falls.

DATABASE SPECIALIST

With the explosion in the use of database software and the necessity for files to be linked together to form an integrated database containing an organization's data resources, companies now need people who can manage these large systems.

Database specialists are responsible for establishing logical data requirements, minimizing data redundancy, controlling access to the database, ensuring data security, maintaining systems for adequate backup protection, and preparing contingency plans for action when malfunctions occur or data are lost or inaccessible.

OFFICE AUTOMATION SPECIALIST

The job of the office automation specialist is to evaluate, implement, interconnect, and support the software products used in offices. Office automation specialists must be familiar with electronic filing, word processing, electronic mail, and computer conferencing systems. In addition, they must also be familiar with how mainframe, minis, micros, and peripherals all are linked through a communication system and how they can be used to give office workers access to the firm's data resources.

END-USER CONSULTANT

End-user consultants are the interface, or liaison, between central information system departments and end-users (Figure 18-9). They help users in setting up spreadsheets, establishing small database systems, arranging access to centralized data, and writing specialized reports.

COMPUTER OPERATOR

The computer operator's responsibility is to manage the operation of minicomputer and mainframe systems. Computer operators coordinate the utilization of central input and output devices, change magnetic tapes and disk packs when requested to do so, distribute output from central printing facilities, and schedule machine use for large jobs (Figure 18-10).

Figure 18-9.
End-user consultants help users design their own applications.

Figure 18-10.
Computer operators are responsible for monitoring and operating central computer facilities.

EDP AUDITOR

Because the computers and those who use them often process sensitive and vulnerable financial data, audits must be conducted periodically to evaluate the methods and procedures the computer system and its personnel use.

EDP (electronic data processing) auditors conduct such audits by tracing transactions through the computer system from the first point of input to the last output (Figure 18-11). They carefully note and explain any differences between documented procedures and the procedures they actually observe, and are always, of course, on the lookout for signs of abuse or fraud. Audits cannot be carried out by the same people who design and use a system; consequently the audit function is usually assigned to an accounting department group called EDP audit.

Those who choose this career field must be familiar with both accounting and business information systems. EDP auditing today often uses complex auditing software that runs concurrently with other applications; thus auditors must know how to use such programs. In addition, a good auditor possesses the kind of inquisitive mind that enjoys working with details and following a problem through to its logical conclusion.

Figure 18-11.
EDP auditors are responsible for ensuring the integrity of the systems and procedures used in an information system.

JOBS IN DISTRIBUTED ENVIRONMENTS

In addition to decentralizing computer hardware and software, some firms have moved toward decentralizing computer professionals as well. People are dispersed throughout an organization and assigned to accounting, finance, manufacturing, and marketing groups. Although they work in different areas, they are still basically computer professionals.

This approach has several benefits. First, the computer professionals are more likely to look at problems from the end-user's perspective. Second, they often become experts in an application area. Third, the group to which they are assigned usually obtains more control over information processing resources.

Jobs in distributed environments are especially suited to those who want to combine their business and computer skills. And because of their business training, these individuals will bring to the job a real understanding of functional problems. So a person assigned to an inventory department would bring not only computer skills to the job but also an understanding of the firm's inventory function.

COMBINING SKILLS IN BUSINESS AND INFORMATION SYSTEMS

Many business students combine a major in an area such as accounting, finance, operations, or marketing with their skills obtained from computer information systems courses. And these individuals consider themselves primarily business professionals rather than computer professionals.

Accounting Although the demand for accountants has always been strong, the demand for those that can combine accounting and information skills is even stronger. The reason: Most accounting systems are automated.

One obvious area in which the combination of accounting and computer skills is particularly effective is EDP auditing. It is the responsibility of professionals in this area to ensure that the procedures and controls used in the computerized accounting system are properly designed and followed.

Finance Because many of the decisions that are made in the finance area depend heavily on data, a background in information systems can be useful.

Spreadsheets, for example, are often used by finance professionals. And many finance users find it necessary to develop the skills necessary to access and then download centralized data into their spreadsheets. Some even learn how to use financial modeling systems.

Operations Few operational processes today function without a computer. As we pointed out in Chapter 3, operational decision making can be quite complex. To make effective decisions and to effectively control operational processes, being able to use a computer information system is essential.

Some students who choose this area will be involved with the company's manufacturing requirements planning system. To work effectively with such a system, the professional must understand the production-planning environment as well as the computer software used to help make planning decisions. Both can be complex.

Marketing Marketing in recent years has grown to depend on the timely information that a well-designed information system can provide. Those who can help create and use these systems usually find a stronger demand for their skills.

When a company is involved in a promotional campaign, for example, those marketing professionals who know how to use an information system and obtain information to monitor and control this campaign are likely to make faster and better decisions than are those who are not able to use the information system.

E N D · U S E R   H I N T S

IS A COMPUTER CAREER FOR ME?

Should you choose a career in computers? The answer to this question depends on a host of factors that relate to your interests and even your personality.

What have your interests been in the past? Have you enjoyed the challenge of a math, accounting, or statistics course? These focus on logical thought processes, as do programming courses. So if you performed well in such courses, then a career path that begins with programming might be worth further consideration.

Some students are interested in combining the structured skills of working with computers and the social skills of working with people. In this case, a career in computer sales or customer support may be appropriate. Jobs in this area range from extremely technically oriented sales and support positions to marketing jobs that rely almost entirely on interpersonal skills rather than detailed computer knowledge.

As a rule, salaries are higher for computer professionals than for lower-level business professionals. Salary, however, probably should not be the major consideration. Many surveys have indicated that money is not the key factor for most individuals; the job itself is. If you choose a job just for the money, you may quickly lose interest and even lose the job.

Although interests are an important factor in career choices, some students may be unclear about their interests and need to explore the issue in greater detail. Sometimes a comparison of one's own personality with that of others in a particular field can help. A person who shows interest in a computer career may find it useful to learn, for example, that his or her personality type is similar to others who have also chosen this career path.

A study by Sitton and Chmelir reported in *Datamation* (October 1984) showed that data processors usually are good at analyzing problems, have a high tolerance for complex situations, are always looking for new projects and activities, place a high value on innovation, and may ignore standard approaches and traditional ways of doing things. Although a commonly held stereotype of a computer programmer is of a person who enjoys working alone, this study found that many programmers are extroverts, focusing on the outer world of people rather than on the inner world of thoughts and ideas.

Programmers tend to be "thinking" people. Before taking action they carefully weigh a situation and consider all the possibilities. They are more logical than emotional in their decision-making processes.

Although the personality characteristics described here suggest that there is a particular type of person who is best at programming, this is not the case. If you share some of these characteristics and are interested in a career in programming, that may be a good sign. If you don't share these characteristics, a programming career may still be for you. It is your interest in computer information systems that is the most important factor.

PREPARING FOR A CAREER IN COMPUTERS

WHICH COURSES?

You can prepare for a career in computers by following one of at least two different paths. If you follow the computer science path, many of your courses will focus on the software that makes computers run, that is, systems software. If, on the other hand, you follow the business information systems path, most of your courses will emphasize how such systems are used. Some of the business topics often included are

- Introduction to information systems

- Systems analysis and design

- Database management

- Management Information Systems

- BASIC, COBOL, Pascal, and 4GLs

- Decision Support Systems

- EDP auditing

- Networks

- Communications

- Artificial intelligence

Because so many students are preparing for a career in computers, it is in your best interest to take as many computer courses as possible. And don't let the fact that you have lots of company discourage you. The old adage "There is always room for a good person," is especially true here.

HOW MUCH PROGRAMMING?

It is difficult to know how many programming courses a person who is preparing for a career in information systems should take. Most educators would recommend at least one course in a procedural language such as COBOL or Pascal. In addition, you should have experience in using a 4GL, especially a database language. If you are considering a career in programming, then you should take other languages as well. But if you are more interested in a career in one of the other specialized computer areas, then an introduction to these languages through a single course could suffice.

FINDING A JOB

You will probably discover that many companies—both computer man-ufacturers and computer users—will interview at your school. To be well prepared for the interview, you should prepare a resume that highlights your information system courses and also includes a statement of your career objectives (Figure 18-12). Most placement offices will help you prepare it.

To improve your chances during an interview, make sure to read at least the company's annual report. If you can find some other literature, that too will prove useful. And you might read periodicals such as *Computerworld,* a weekly newspaper containing recent news about hardware and software, or *Datamation,* a monthly publication analyzing current trends and issues. Above all, don't be afraid to use this information. It will help you stand out from the crowd.

But the traditional path—interviewing through the placement office—is not the only way to find a job. Newspapers are filled with ads for openings. Most are looking for experienced personnel, but a few might be willing to train recent graduates.

And don't neglect the open houses that many companies advertise in the newspaper. Usually held at a hotel or company headquarters, these events represent major recruiting drives. Again, they are targeted

Robert J. Thomas
201 North Main Street
Centerville, Ohio 35113

CAREER OBJECTIVE	Management position in information system department.
FIRST JOB	Programmer or programmer/analyst with a company that makes extensive use of computer information systems. Geographic preference: West coast.
EDUCATION	BS Business Administration, Ohio State. High school diploma, Centerville, Ohio.
WORK EXPERIENCE (summer)	* Assistant Programmer, King Company. Worked with team that was writing new sales-order entry system. * Manager, Frank's Lakeside Pizza Parlor. * Counselor, Camp Grenada.
SCHOOL ACTIVITIES	* Dean's list, Junior and senior year. * Treasurer, Business Club. * Racketball club. * AISEC. * Played trumpet in university concert band.

Figure 18-12.
To be prepared for your job interview, prepare a resume that highlights your computer information systems courses.

toward professionals with experience, but many students have made useful contacts and even landed a job in this way.

Also don't overlook summer jobs, internships, and part-time employment during the school year. These offer an opportunity to gain experience and get a foot in the door. Ask your placement office for details, or better yet, write the companies in which you are interested.

Finally, there are tens of thousands of small companies that cannot afford campus visits or open houses. Write them a letter, follow it up with a phone call, and ask for an interview. Many small firms, especially those in high-growth industries, can offer at least the chance of a fast ride to the top.

MAINTAINING YOUR SKILLS

One of the more subtle themes throughout this book is that the computer industry refuses to stand still. So if you plan a career in this field, you must also plan a lifetime of learning.

You can learn after you are out of school in many ways. Seminars scheduled in major cities can introduce you to the latest in hardware and software topics. Trade shows, such as COMDEX, provide an opportunity to see new equipment demonstrated and to attend sessions given by leading experts in the field (Figure 18-13). Vendors also hold training sessions to give their customers an opportunity to find out how their systems can be used. Some vendors, especially makers of mainframe software products, sponsor users' groups. These groups meet regularly and pro-

Figure 18-13.
Computer conferences give professionals an opportunity to learn about new developments in their field.

vide users with the opportunity to learn from one another and from the vendor.

Many professionals rely on professional associations and their publications to help them stay abreast of new developments. Professional associations include

■ The Data Processing Management Association (DPMA). Emphasis is on data processing management.

■ Association for Systems Management (ASM). Emphasis is on systems management and systems development in industry, business, and government.

■ Association for Computing Machinery (ACM). Devoted to a wide range of topics that support their members' advancement and continuing education.

?   Q U E S T I O N S   ?

1. Has every segment of the computer industry shown steady growth?
2. Describe some of the jobs available in companies that make computers or write commercial software.
3. Why is it necessary for a person hired in technical sales to understand the customers' problems?
4. Name some of the jobs available in companies that use computers.
5. Why should a large company's application programming group hire graduates with a business information background as well as those with a major in computer science?
6. Why are communications and network specialists in demand?
7. Explain the responsibilities of an office automation specialist.
8. What is the role of EDP auditors? Why do they usually report to the accounting department of an organization?
9. What does an end-user consultant do?
10. How do computer professionals stay abreast of their changing fields?

S U M M A R Y

■ Business students may choose an information system career because it is challenging and filled with opportunities.

■ The demand for information systems skills has been strong in the past, but it is difficult to say that this will always be so.

■ Information systems jobs can be found (1) in companies that make computer hardware and write commercial software and (2) in organizations that use computers.

- Companies that manufacture computers and write commercial software offer jobs in application programming, technical sales, customer support, and technical writing.

- Organizations that use computers (which means most organizations) offer jobs in system development and application programming and require the skills of communication specialist, network specialist, knowledge engineer, database specialist, office automation specialist, end-user consultant, computer operator, and EDP auditor.

- Many students choose to combine skills in business and information systems in such areas as accounting, finance, operations, and marketing.

- You can prepare for a career in computers by taking a computer science or a business information systems "path."

- Finding a job can entail preparing a good resume, reading company literature before an interview, interviewing through the school placement office, reading ads, writing letters, attending open houses, and working in summer jobs.

- Computer professionals maintain their skills in a variety of ways, including further education, trade shows, vendor training, and professional associations.

F O R   D I S C U S S I O N

1. How important is experience to finding a job? How can students gain experience?
2. Of the jobs described in this chapter, do you think that some require more interpersonal skills than others do? Why are these skills important?

H A N D S - O N   P R O J E C T S

1. Turn to the help-wanted section of a major metropolitan newspaper such as the *New York Times*. List the computer-related jobs. Which ones might a business information professional be interested in? What specialties seem to be in demand?

2. Read the help-wanted advertisements in the Sunday newspaper of a major city. Are there jobs for computer programmers? Take a moment to compare the number of ads for programmers with those for other job categories. Which languages are programmers expected to know? What are typical salaries?

GLOSSARY

Access time The time it takes to retrieve or store data on a disk, measured in milliseconds. (p. 213)

Accounting system A computer system that collects, stores, processes, and presents an organization's accounting data. (p. 105)

Accounts payable system A computer system that maintains records of purchases made from vendors. (p. 115)

Accounts receivable system A computer system that keeps track of the amounts owed by, and the payments received from, customers who make purchases on credit. (p. 112)

Activities chart An illustration showing the order in which the activities associated with a project can be undertaken. (p. 316)

Aggregate data Data in summary form rather than detailed form. (p. 78)

Alphanumeric Pertaining to characters which might include letters of the alphabet, numeric digits, and special characters such as arithmetic symbols. (p. 31)

Altered off-the-shelf system Commercially designed application software directed at a specific category of application that can be modified in limited ways to accommodate a user's specific needs. Commercial accounting software often falls in this category. (p. 349)

Alternatives The choices between which a decision maker must select when solving a problem or making a decision. (p. 135)

American Standard Code for Information Interchange (ASCII) a coding system used to represent characters in computers and to transfer data among computers. (p. 33)

Analog signal A means of electronic communication in which the signal takes the shape of a smooth wave. (p. 401)

Application software A collection of programs that direct the computer to perform user-related tasks such as payroll, inventory control, or accounting. (p. 45)

Arithmetic/logic unit (ALU) The function within the CPU responsible for performing arithmetic and logical operations on the data as specified by a program. (p. 41)

Artificial intelligence The use of the computer in certain limited application areas to simulate some of the characteristics of human thought such as reasoning, inference, learning, and problem solving. (p. 304)

Assembly language A low-level computer language that uses symbols to express the instructions a computer must follow to accomplish a task. (p. 383)

Assets Items of value to a firm such as cash or property. Records of these assets are usually maintained in the general ledger. (p. 105)

Asynchronous transmission Refers to the transmission of data in which each character in the transmitted stream of data is begun with a start bit and ended with a stop bit. (p. 405)

Audit trail A record of the details surrounding the use of an application (such as a person's name, date of use, etc.), maintained in a computer system as a separate file, which can be used to trace the use of an application and can also be used to reconstruct where and how a particular problem occurred. (p. 373)

Automated office an office that relies on the computer for many functions, such as word-processing and spreadsheets, to improve productivity in the workplace. (p. 18)

Automatic teller machine (ATM) A special-purpose intelligent terminal used in a computer banking system to interact with the customer for the purpose of processing deposit and withdrawal transactions. (p. 38)

Automation The automatic processing of work by machines with little or no human intervention.

Auxiliary storage *See* Secondary storage.

Backup file A duplicate file maintained on tape or disk to be used in the event that the original is lost or destroyed. (p. 372)

Balance sheet statement A report produced by a computer accounting system that lists the assets and liabilities of the organization. The data for the report are obtained from the general ledger accounts. (p. 110)

Bar chart An illustration that uses a vertical bar to indicate the value or quantity of a variable. (p. 295)

Bar code   A data input technology in which identification data—in the form of lines of varying thicknesses—are affixed to an item and read with an optical wand. (p. 36)

Baseband cabling   A coaxial cable that carries digital data along a single path, used in local area networks. (p. 440)

BASIC   Beginner's All-purpose Symbolic Instruction Code. A third-generation language used with microcomputers and sometimes with minicomputers. Considered easy to learn when compared to other third generation languages. (pp. 89, 384)

Batch processing   Operating system software that processes an identifiable job, such as payroll, as one work unit. Processing is done periodically. (pp. 47, 102)

Billing system   A (computer) system that bills customers for purchases of goods or services. (p. 111)

Binary   (1) Pertaining to a number system that uses 1s and 0s. (2) Pertaining to a choice or selection in which there are only two possibilities. (p. 32)

Binary digit   *See* bit.

Binary number system   A number system that uses combinations of 0s and 1s to represent decimal digits. (p. 32)

Bit   An abbreviation for "binary digit." A bit can have a value of 0 or 1. Combinations of bits are used to represent decimal digits. (p. 32)

Bits per second (BPS)   A measure of communication rate over transmission lines. (p. 404)

Block commands   A feature of word-processing software that permits the movement of text from one location in the document to another. (p. 163)

Blocking   Grouping or combining records to improve the efficiency of input, output, and processing operations. (p. 212)

Blocking factor   The number of records contained in a block. (p. 212)

Boundaries   The point at which one computer system or application interfaces with another. (p. 338)

Broadband cabling   A coaxial cable that can carry multiple data paths. Used in local area networks. (p. 440)

Business data processing   The use of computers to process business transactions. *See also* Data processing.

Byte   A group of adjacent bits that represents a decimal digit, a letter, or a symbol. (p. 33)

Calculated entry   Data in a spreadsheet cell that have been calculated by a formula and not directly entered into the cell. (p. 183)

CD ROM   *See* Read-only optical disk.

Cell   The intersection of a row and column in a spreadsheet. (p. 182)

Central processing unit (CPU)   The computer itself. It accepts data, stores the data in temporary storage, processes the data, and sends them to an output device. (p. 12)

Centralized data   Data maintained by an organization in a central data storage environment and usually under the management and control of centralized information processing professionals. (p. 132)

Centralized data processing   The organization of the data processing function in such a way that most of the activities are located and managed in a centralized environment. (p. 426)

Centralized storage   The storage of data in a central location usually under the control of central data processing professionals. (p. 426)

Character   A letter of the alphabet, a number, or a symbol. (p. 31)

Chart of accounts   The accounts in a general ledger system. (p. 108)

Coaxial cable   A transmission medium like the cable that brings cable TV into homes. It has a central core surrounded by a shield and can transmit large volumes of data in both an analog and digital format. (p. 403)

COBOL   Common Business Oriented Language. A third-generation computer language developed for business applications that require a significant amount of file processing. (pp. 88, 383)

Coding   A term used to describe the process of writing programs. (p. 375)

Communication system   The hardware and software that links computers with terminals, printers, and other computers. (p. 16)

Compiler   Part of the system software that translates an entire program—written in an english-like language—into a machine language the computer can understand. (p. 48)

Computer An electronic device that operates under the instructions of a program, and can accept data, process them, and present the results as output. (p. 9)

Computer-aided design (CAD) The use of computer hardware and specialized graphics software to facilitate the design of industrial and commercial products. (p. 479)

Computer-aided instruction (CAI) The use of hardware and specialized software to support the learning process. (p. 482)

Computer-aided manufacturing (CAM) The use of computers to automate the manufacturing process. (p. 478)

Computer conferencing The participation by users at different locations in an ongoing exchange of written ideas through their computers or terminals. (p. 173)

Computer graphics The presentation of computer output in graphical form. (p. 294)

Computer information system A particular kind of computer system used to collect, store, process, and present information to support an organization. (p. 4)

Computer system The computer itself together with support equipment, programs, procedures that users follow, and people who use the system. (p. 4)

Concentrator A hardware device that improves the use of a communication network by combining slow-speed signals from terminals or other devices and sending them over a high-speed line. Since it can be programmed, it is also called an intelligent multiplexer. (p. 413)

Conceptual file A designer or user's logical view of a collection of records in a file. Differs from a physical view which relates to the way the data are actually stored. (p. 268)

Conceptual record A designer or user's logical view of the data fields in a record. Differs from the physical view which relates to the way the data in the record are actually stored. (p. 269)

Controller A specialized computer used to supervise and coordinate data traffic in a communication system. (p. 412)

Controls *See* System controls.

Control structures Standardized logic configurations used to express the flow of data to accomplish a programming step or set of steps. They include simple sequence, if-then, do-while. (p. 376)

Control totals Statistics, such as the dollar value of orders taken during the day, used to verify that the computer system has processed the data correctly at each stage in the processing cycle. (p. 372)

Control unit A part of the CPU responsible for exercising control over the functions of the CPU. (p. 41)

Conventional file processing Use of traditional third generation languages—like COBOL or BASIC—rather than the use of a DBMS to process files. (p. 238)

CPU *See* Central processing unit.

Criterion A standard of judgment that is used to select among alternatives. (p. 141)

Critical path The activites in a project which if delayed will delay the completion of the entire project. (p. 317)

Currency Refers to the timeliness of data. (p. 231)

Cursor Small, often blinking, symbol that shows where you are on the screen. It usually shows where the next typed character will be inserted. (p. 161)

Custom-tailored system Software and sometimes hardware that has been developed for a specific application in a company. The development effort is usually major and requires careful attention to all of the steps in the systems analysis and design cycle. (p. 349)

Daisy-wheel printer An impact printer that uses a removable wheel on which the letters are embossed. A hammer strikes the letter and leaves the image on the paper. (p. 51)

Data Raw facts that are entered into the computer. (pp. 10, 30)

Database A nonredundant collection of data stored in one or more files. (pp. 32, 262)

Database administrator The position or job in an information processing organization with the responsibility to serve as a central clearinghouse for issues relating to the design and use of the database. (p. 284)

Database management system A set of programs that manages and controls a database, providing the mechanisms through which data items can be stored, retrieved, and changed. (p. 262)

Data communication The process by which data are moved from one point in an information system to another at a distant physical location. (p. 398)

Data definition file A file in a DBMS that stores the structural characteristics (record format) of a database, such as field names and data type. (pp. 241, 281)

Data definition module The module in a DBMS through which the data structure, or record format, is defined and entered into the system. (p. 281)

Data dictionary A separate file in a DBMS that stores such data as the name of each data item, data structure for each item, programs that use each item, and level of security for each item. Used to facilitate the development and use of a database. (pp. 283, 370)

Data directory A directory, maintained as separate file, that identifies the physical location in a network where a given data item is stored. (p. 437)

Data integrity The state of accuracy or legitimacy of data in a database. (p. 285)

Data management Software functions that are capable of storing, processing, and retrieving data in a database. (p. 239)

Data manipulation module The module in a DBMS which makes it possible for designers and users to use the database. Through it the database can be accessed, processed, and manipulated. (p. 282)

Data processing A systematic sequence of operations performed on data to accomplish an objective. (p. 9)

Data processing cycle The sequence of data processing events which includes the entry of data, its processing, and output of the results. (p. 9)

Decision support graphics Graphics used by decision makers to help them understand patterns, trends, or relationships in data. (p. 297)

Decision support system Provides business professionals and decision makers with the kind of information that is not predictably needed. (p. 7)

Decision table A table used to record and organize complex logical structures during the logic design phase of systems design. (p. 370)

Departmental computing A computer and its terminals or a network of computers dedicated to the computing needs of a department or small group of users. (pp. 158, 444)

Desktop publishing The use of specialized hardware and software to produce hard copy of a quality similar to that obtained by commercial printing. (pp. 167, 302)

Dial-back modem A modem that will return a call to an authorized number before permitting access to the person requesting access. This prevents unauthorized users who have obtained or stolen authorized numbers from accessing the system at unauthorized locations. (p. 468)

Digital scanner A cameralike device that scans a photo or illustration and converts the image into digital bits of information that can be stored in a computer system, retrieved, and reproduced on a screen or hard copy. (p. 302)

Digital signal An on-off pulse that represents the way in which communication within the computer occurs. Sometimes communication among computers and among computers and other peripheral equipment occurs in this way. (p. 401)

Direct access storage device (DASD) A storage device, like a magnetic disk, that can directly access and store data. (p. 44)

Direct access systems Computer systems in which data are stored on disk and can be accessed almost instantly. (pp. 44, 222)

Direct file processing Processing data using a direct access system. An approach to data processing in which the data are processed instantly. (p. 222)

Disk pack A unit, usually removable, that contains several disks and is mounted in a disk drive. (p. 215)

Distributed database The concept of distributing the contents of a database to the locations where the data are entered and/or used. (p. 436)

Distributed processing A computer system in which computers and storage devices—in different physical locations—are linked together for the purpose of sharing programs and data. (p. 426)

Document creation The process of entering text using word-processing software. (p. 159)

Documentation Written material, including illustrations and screen reproductions, explaining how an application has been designed and how it can be used. (p. 344)

Dot-matrix printer   A printer with a movable print head that encases a set of wires. When each wire is activated, the end of the wire presses against the ribbon and prints a small dot. Combinations of dots are used to represent characters. (p. 51)

Do-while   A control structure used in programming to repeat steps over and over again until a condition is met. (p. 378)

Download   The process of sending data and even programs from a central computer to a remote computer. (p. 428)

Dynamic data   Data such as bank balances which changes frequently. (p. 10)

Editing   The process of revising text after it has been entered into a word-processing system. (p. 162)

Electronic data processing (EDP)   Using computers to process data automatically. (p. 505)

Electronic filing   Creating, storing, and retrieving the documents in an office environment. (p. 169)

Electronic mail   A system in which documents are transmitted from one terminal or microcomputer to another terminal or microcomputer in electronic form. (pp. 18, 172)

Encryption   The process of coding data so they may be sent over communications facilities, thereby reducing the risk of malicious interference. (pp. 373, 418, 469)

End-user   Person who is using the computer information system for transaction or decision making purposes. (p. 90)

End-user computing   Solving problems using a computer oneself without involving programmers or other professionals. (p. 90)

Entry line   Shows what the user is typing when a new entry is made to a cell in a spreadsheet. (p. 188)

Expert system   A computer information system that uses knowledge obtained from experts and makes the experts' point of view available to nonexperts. (p. 306)

Expert system shell   A prefabricated general framework into which specific data surrounding an application can be entered after which the shell

itself develops an appropriate expert system. (p. 307)

Extended Binary Coded Decimal Interchange Code (EBCDIC)   A standard code used to determine how letters, numbers, and symbols are to be converted into binary format. (p. 33)

Fault-tolerant computer   Computers designed with special software and hardware to provide a high level of reliability. (p. 103)

Fiber optic cable   A cable used for communication that is made up from thousands of clear glass fibers about the thickness of the human hair. Transmission speeds approach the speed of light. Used in local area networks as well as long distance communication. (p. 404)

Field   A collection of one or more related characters, where a character can be a letter, number, or symbol. (p. 31)

File   A collection of related records. (p. 32)

File activity   The percentage of records in a file that is actually accessed during any one run. (p. 230)

File maintenance   The process of keeping a file up-to-date by adding, changing, or deleting data. (p. 246)

File manager   A category of data management software that is easy to use but permits only one file to be open at a time. Sometimes called "flat file manager." (pp. 20, 248)

File processing   Data processing activities that involve adding, changing, deleting, or updating the data in a file. (p. 220)

File security   The protection of files from use by unauthorized users. Passwords are often used for this purpose. (p. 169)

File server   A computer and its software in a local network that manages the data and controls access to centralized disk storage in the network. (p. 441)

File volatility   The frequency with which data are added to or deleted from a file. (p. 230)

Financial modeling languages   Computer software which facilitates the development of financial models in which the model or program is separated from the data. (p. 318)

Find-and-replace A process in which word-processing software will locate a specified word and replace it with a substitute, both of which are entered through the keyboard by the writer. (p. 163)

First-generation computers The first computers that were commercially available, beginning in 1953, which relied on vacuum tube technology. (p. 86)

Floppy disk A flexible magnetic disk enclosed in a protective envelope and used mainly with microcomputers. (pp. 43, 214)

Flowchart A graph showing the flow of data from an input function to an output function. *See also* System flowchart and program flowchart. (pp. 346, 376)

Forecasting A process in which data from the past is used to predict the future. (p. 137)

Formatting The process of controlling how a finished document produced by word-processing software will look. (p. 164)

FORTRAN FORmula TRANslation. A third-generation computer language used by the scientific community. (pp. 88, 384)

Fourth-generation computers Computers that became available in the 1970s and now rely on very large scale integration (VSLI) to store up to 1 megabyte on a silicon chip. (p. 89)

Fourth-generation language Languages that require the user to specify what is needed rather than the details of how it is to be done. (p. 350)

Front-end processor A sophisticated controller used to supervise and coordinate data traffic in a communication system. (p. 412)

Full-duplex Pertaining to two-way simultaneous communication by computers. (p. 406)

Functional view A view or classification of information systems in which the application is categorized according to the business function which it supports. Examples include accounting, manufacturing, and marketing systems. (p. 67)

Functions Prewritten routines that perform a series of operations or calculations quickly. When used in a spreadsheet, they become shortcuts that save users from having to specify several steps. (p. 190)

Gantt chart A chart which shows the duration of activities on a horizontal time scale. Used in project management. (p. 316)

General ledger The collection of accounts for maintaining records of an organization's accounting transactions. (p. 106)

Gigabyte One billion bytes or one thousand megabytes.

Goal-seeking analysis Computer analysis performed in financial modeling in which the user specifies the results (or goals) desired and the software determines the necessary conditions to achieve the goal. (p. 319)

Graphics The use of symbolic input or output from a computer including lines, curves, and other geometric shapes and forms. Requires terminals, plotters, printers, digital scanners, and other interface devices. (p. 294)

Graphics board A board that is plugged into an expansion slot of the microcomputer and supports high-resolution graphics applications. (p. 301)

Graphics terminal A terminal that is capable of displaying high resolution images used in presentation graphics. Available in black-and-white or color. (p. 301)

Hacker A term used to describe enthusiastic computer users. (p. 461)

Half-duplex Pertaining to two-way computer communication that can only take place one direction at a time. (p. 406)

Hard copy Computer output that can be considered permanent, usually referring to paper or document output. (p. 50)

Hard disk A magnetic disk built on a rigid base which has a higher storage capacity and faster access than a floppy disk. (pp. 44, 214)

Hardware The computer system's physical equipment. (p. 12)

Hashing The mathematical processing of a record key to obtain a number that will be associated with a physical storage location on a disk where the record will be stored. (p. 224)

Head movement delay The time it takes to move the read/write head to the appropriate track when data are stored or accessed, measured in milliseconds. (p. 213)

Hierarchical DBMS   A database management system that can accommodate data that can be represented as a tree structure, a structure in which a parent can have many children but a child can have only one parent. (p. 279)

Hierarchical view   A view or classification of an information system in which an application is categorized by the management level that uses the application. (p. 65)

Hierarchy of data   A logical view of data from the lowest level, called a field, to the largest aggregate form, called a database. (p. 30)

High-level language   A computer language that resembles the English language as opposed to a language that uses symbols. (p. 384)

Heuristic rule   A rule of thumb, often based on experience, used by managers to guide their decisions. (p. 310)

Hybrid topology   A description of the physical layout of a network that combines both ring and star topologies. (p. 433)

If-then control structure   A format used in programming to express a logical sequence in which control may be passed from one point in the program to another depending on the results of a test or comparison. (p. 376)

Impact printer   A printer that creates an image by bringing a printing element into direct contact with the paper on which the image will appear. (p. 51)

Implementation   The process of setting into motion a course of action. (p. 142)

Indexing   The use of a reference file in direct processing to find the location of a record stored on disk. The index stores the record's key and its physical location on disk. When records are accessed by users, the index is first searched to find its location. (p. 225)

Index sequential   A method of direct processing in which primary and secondary indexes are maintained to process the file directly and sequentially. (p. 227)

Index sequential access method (ISAM)   A method of file organization in which records are stored

sequentially according to a primary key, and an index is maintained. The file can be processed either sequentially or, by using the index, directly. (p. 228)

Induction method   A method for developing an expert system in which the factors used by the experts to make a decision are entered into the system. Next, several "training" examples are entered. Then the system automatically induces the rules that the experts probably used when making the decisions in these training examples. (p. 307)

Inference engine   The software in an expert system that uses the data and rules in its knowledge base to solve the problem at hand. (p. 306)

Information   Data that have been processed into a form that is useful for decision making or problem solving. (p. 10)

Information system   *See* Computer information system.

Ink-jet printer   A nonimpact printer that uses nozzles which spray liquid ink on a page. (p. 52)

Input   Term relating to a device or process involved in the entry of data into the computer information system, or to the data themselves. (p. 365)

Integer   A whole number, such as 150, with no fractional parts (in contrast to a real number, such as 150.45, which has fractional parts).

Integrated circuits (IC)   A miniature device made of silicon that stores data and programs in bit cells. (p. 41)

Integrated package   Word-processing, spreadsheet, graphics, and data management software combined into one package to permit the easy transfer of data between components. (pp. 166, 193)

Interface device   Hardware that is used to convert input data, usually in the form of a graph, picture, or illustration, to digital data, which a computer can store and process. (p. 302)

Internal data sources   The data collected by an organization in the process of doing its business. These data may be maintained centrally or locally. (p. 132)

Interpreter   Part of the system software that translates each program statement into a language that the computer can understand and then execute. (p. 48)

Interrecord gap The gap separating records on tape or disk. (p. 211)

Inventory system A (computer) system which keeps a record of the number of items stocked by an organization. (p. 116)

Job management A function of the computer's operating system that involves scheduling jobs waiting to be executed. (p. 47)

K-byte (also kilobyte.) 1,024 bytes. (p. 40)

Key A field used to identify a record.

Keyboard A typewriterlike device that is used to enter data into the computer. (p. 11)

Keypunch A hardware device used to punch cards. (p. 34)

Key-to-disk A data entry technology in which data are entered through a keyboard into a device which has a small memory. After they have been checked on a screen, and necessary corrections made, the data are then stored on disk, and eventually entered into the central computer. (p. 35)

Key-to-tape A data entry technology in which data are entered through a keyboard into a device which has a small memory. After they have been checked on the screen, and necessary corrections made, the data are then stored on tape, and eventually entered into the central computer. (p. 35)

Knowledge base Experience of experts stored by an expert system as data and rules. (p. 306)

LAN *See* Local area network.

Laptop The smallest microcomputers, usually weighing less than 10 pounds. (p. 16)

Large-scale integration A technology in which thousands of electronic ciruits are placed on a single silicon chip. (p. 89)

Laser printer A nonimpact printer that operates much like an office copy machine. Capable of high-quality black-and-white reproduction at high speeds. (p. 53)

Liabilities The firm's debts or sums owed to other businesses or individuals. Records of these liabilities are maintained in the general ledger. (p. 105)

Life cycle costs The costs of hardware, software, operation, and maintenance over the entire life of a computer information system. (p. 351)

Line chart An illustration in which a line connects a series of points to indicate the quantity or level of the variable. (p. 295)

Local area network A collection of computers, usually microcomputers, connected together within a limited geographic area, such as a building, for the purpose of sharing data and programs. (pp. 16, 438)

Local data Data collected, maintained, and used in limited environments—such as a department—within the firm. (p. 133)

Logical view The way in which users visualize data and data relationships, in contrast with the way data are physically stored in the computer and on secondary storage devices. (pp. 31, 263)

Logic design That part of the systems design effort that focuses on the logic associated with processing the data for a particular application. (p. 369)

Machine language A computer language—expressed as a string of 0s and 1s—in which the computer processes instructions and data. (p. 383)

Magnetic disk A flat circular platter on which data can be stored using a magnetic process and from which data can be retrieved. (pp. 12, 42, 213)

Magnetic ink character recognition (MICR) Technology that uses magnetic ink to print data and magnetic devices to read the data, used by banks to speed check processing. (p. 36)

Magnetic tape A flexible flat plastic ribbon on which data and programs can be permanently stored, and from which they can be retrieved. (p. 13, 44, 211)

Mail merge The process by which word-processing text and mailing lists are combined to produce form letters. (p. 166)

Mainframe The largest computer used by most organizations. Mainframes have the largest main memories, the fastest processing times, support massive secondary storage, provide access to many users, and are usually centralized. (p. 15)

Main memory That part of the CPU in which temporary storage of programs and data occurs while an application is processed. (p. 12)

Management hierarchy The levels of management necessary to plan, organize, coordinate, and control the activities in an organization to meet its goals and objectives. (p. 67)

Management information system (MIS) An information system that provides the kind of information that business professionals predictably need to manage an organization and make decisions. (p. 7)

Management planning and control system A computer system whose focus is the support of those activities needed to plan and control the organization's operational activities. It focuses on intermediate-range decisions needed to manage the firm's resources. (p. 75)

Master file A relatively permanent collection of records in a file. Examples include an employee master file and loan master file. (p. 221)

Megabyte One thousand K-bytes, or 1,048,576 bytes. (p. 40)

Menu A screen, or part of a screen, listing the program options that can be chosen. (p. 160)

Microcomputer A small self-contained computer with one or more disk drives for secondary storage. (p. 16)

Micro–mainframe link The connection between microcomputers and mainframes for the purpose of sharing data and sometimes programs. (p. 442)

Microwave system A high-frequency transmission system that uses dishlike antennas to send data and programs between two points. (p. 403)

Millisecond One-thousandth of a second. (p. 213)

Minicomputer A computer whose capacity and capabilities are between a mainframe and a micro. (p. 16)

MIS *See* Management information system.

Modem A device used to convert the digital output from a computer to an analog signal which can be sent over analog transmission lines. A modem is also used at the receiving end to convert the analog signal back to a digital one. (p. 401)

Module A design element in the structure chart that includes a collection of steps necessary to perform an information-processing task. A discrete and identifiable unit of hardware or software that is used with other units in the system. (p. 363)

Monitor A device like a television screen used to display computer output. (p. 11)

Mouse An interface device, moved in the palm of one's hand over a desk surface, and used to move or "point" the cursor to a menu selection. Also used to draw shapes or illustrations on a flat surface such as a desk. These shapes simultaneously appear on the terminal screen and can be stored for later use. (p. 302)

Multidrop A line configuration, or means of connecting computers and terminals, such that several devices can share a common line. (p. 412)

Multiplexer A device that combines slow-speed signals coming from several computers or terminals and transmits them over a high speed line. (p. 413)

Multitasking The ability of a computer system to perform many tasks at what appears to be the same time. Each task may require the use of a different program or several users may share the same program but be involved in different activities. (p. 103)

Multiuser software Software used in a network that permits several users access to the programs and data in the system. (p. 440)

Narrowband transmission A category of data transmission in which the transmission speed is suitable only for telegraph and teletype communication. (p. 404)

Natural language processing The use of everyday language to access a computer system. (p. 312)

Network An interconnected group of computers, terminals, communications equipment, and communications facilities used to support data processing activities. (p. 426)

Network DBMS A database management system that can support data structures in which a child can have more than one parent (p. 280)

Network topology *See* Topology.

Node Physical points or locations in a network where computers or other computer devices are located. (pp. 277, 427)

Nonimpact printer A printer that creates an image without direct physical contact between the printing mechanism and paper. (p. 52)

Nonprocedural language A computer language in which the user need express only what is wanted, not the details of how it is to be obtained. Spreadsheet and database management software include nonprocedural languages. (p. 384)

Off-line data entry The process of data entry in which data are grouped and entered as a batch into the computer system. Data entered when not under the control of the CPU. (p. 367)

Office automation The use of information-processing and communication technologies for writing, collecting, storing, organizing, retrieving, and communicating office data. (p. 156)

Off-the-shelf system Application software that has been developed by a software vendor for a specific commercial application and must be used exactly as written. (pp. 306, 348)

On-line data entry Immediate processing, by a CPU, of data entered into a computer system. (p. 367)

On-line processing An approach to processing data in which the data entered into the system or requested by the user are processed instantaneously. (pp. 47, 102)

On-line transaction processing (OLTP) An approach to processing transaction data in which the data entered into the system or requested by the user are processed instantaneously. (p. 102)

Operational planning and control system A computer system with a focus on the decisions that must be made to run the operational processes that deliver goods and services to the firm's customers. (p. 71)

Operating system Part of the system software that coordinates the functions performed by the computer hardware including the CPU, input/output units, and secondary storage devices. (p. 46)

Optical character recognition The process by which data written by hand or machine are optically read by input devices. (p. 36)

Optical disk Circular disk that stores data as microscopic patterns that can be read optically. Storage capacity is high but access time is slower than magnetic disk. (pp. 45, 216)

Output The results produced by a computer and presented on a screen, as hard copy or as a synthesized voice. (p. 11)

Parallel transmission The side-by-side movement of data through a computer. Data are moved in 8, 16, 32, or 64 parallel streams at a time. (p. 405)

Parametized template A spreadsheet that contains a separate section for entering the assumptions and relationships on which the spreadsheet application is built. (p. 197)

Partitioned data Data that have been distributed to several different direct access storage devices. Data stored in different locations. (p. 436)

Pascal A third-generation procedural language named after the French mathematician Pascal. (p. 384)

Password A set of characters, such as a number or word, assigned to an individual, which permits that person access to a computer or to a limited subset of applications on the computer. (pp. 284, 373, 460)

Payroll system System used to process a payroll. (pp. 115, 418)

PBX *See* Private branch exchange.

Physical view The way data are actually stored in the computer and on secondary storage devices, in contrast to the way they may be viewed by users. (pp. 31, 263)

Pie chart An illustration that uses segments of a circle (or pie) to illustrate the value or quantity of a variable. (p. 295)

Plex structure A data structure characterized by the fact that a child can have many parents. Applications that exhibit this data structure can be accommodated by a network database system. (p. 278)

Plotters Special-purpose printer capable of high-quality graphical output in color. (p. 53)

Point-of-entry terminal Data entry terminal located close to the source of the data. (p. 38)

Point-to-point wiring A method of connecting terminals to a central computer in which the central computer is directly wired to each terminal. (p. 410)

Precedent relation The relationship that exists when an activity in a project can only begin after one or more other activities has been completed. (p. 315)

Presentation graphics The use of computer graphics to communicate ideas to those who might be unfamiliar with a situation and need an overview of a topic. (p. 296)

Primary index An index, based on the primary key of a record, used to find the storage location of data on a disk. (pp. 225, 242)

Primary key A unique identifier of a record used to find that record in a file. (p. 219)

Primary storage *See* Main memory.

Printers Hardware devices for producing hard copy text and graphics. (p. 301)

Private branch exchange The switching center that connects the private telephone lines within a company to the outside telephone network. Many of the systems are capable of handling both voice and computer data. Some can handle digital data. (p. 415)

Procedural language Language in which the program steps must correspond to the logical flow or procedure the computer must follow to convert input to output. Examples include BASIC and COBOL. (p. 383)

Production rule method A method for developing an expert system based on the collection of the rules followed by the experts when previous decisions were made. Rules are stated in if-then format. (p. 309)

Productivity software Application software used by business professionals to improve performance on the job or to complete the job in less time. Examples include spreadsheets, word-processing, and data management software. (p. 294)

Profit-and-loss statement A report that summarizes the profit or loss associated with a specific accounting period. Data for the report come from the general ledger. (p. 109)

Program development The process of converting the detailed design of an application into working programs. (p. 375)

Program flowchart A flowchart expressing the steps, at program level detail, necessary to convert inputs to outputs. (p. 376)

Project A collection of activities that have a logical beginning and end. (p. 313)

Prompt line Displays a menu of the commands that can be selected to construct and use a spreadsheet. (p. 188)

Prototyping The use of special purpose application development software to develop a small-scale version of an application so that a project can be tested early in its development cycle. (p. 386)

Protocol The formal rules governing the flow of information among computers and other computer devices. (p. 410)

Pseudocode The use of English-language statements to express the logic of a program. An alternative to program flowcharts. (p. 380)

Punch card Cardboard card with holes punched in it to represent data. Used in early systems. (p. 34)

Pull-down menu Additional menu that appears in the menu area of a word-processing screen. Provides additional options once an initial choice is made. (p. 161)

Purchasing system A (computer) system that keeps track of purchases made from and payments due vendors. (p. 118)

Query The process of retrieving data or information from a computer system. (pp. 230, 244)

Query language A language, usually fourth generation, used by end-users to access a data base for informal requests. (pp. 245, 275)

Random access memory (RAM) Memory in the CPU that can be addressed, changed, and accessed. (p. 41)

Read only memory (ROM) Memory in the CPU that can only be read. It cannot be changed. Used when it is convenient to store programs permanently in CPU. (p. 41)

Read-only optical disk (CD-ROM) A disk that stores data using an optical process and whose data can only be read and not changed. Home audio disks are in this category. (p. 216)

Recalculation The process by which new or revised numbers are entered into a spreadsheet and the calculated entries automatically updated to reflect these changes. (p. 184)

Record A collection of related fields. (p. 31)

Record format A general description of a file that includes the identification of each field in the record, the length of each field, the type of data, and the identification of the primary key. (p. 240)

Redundancy The storage of the same data item in more than one physical location in a database. (p. 271)

Relational DBMS A database management system in which the data in a file are entered as tables and are related when the database is used or when reports are produced. Can accommodate both tree and plex structures. Standard database system used with microcomputers. (p. 280)

Relational operator An algebraic sign such as <, >, or =. Used, for example, in a DBMS when specifying the criterion by which records will be selected when a database is searched for data. (p. 255)

Relationship A term used in database processing to express the linkage between a record in one file and one or more records in another file. (p. 267)

Relative addressing A method of finding a record in a direct file in which the record is given a key that corresponds exactly to the physical location in which it is stored. (p. 224)

Replicated data The same data stored in more than one location in a distributed network. Improves data security. (p. 436)

Report module Software in a DBMS that is capable of accepting simplified instructions, which specify what the user needs and then translating these needs into the detailed steps that will produce a report based on the data in the database. (p. 283)

Resolution The clarity of output on a screen measured by the number of picture elements—called pixels and the number of horizontal lines. (p. 300)

Reversible optical disk An optical disk in which the data can be erased and the disk recorded over and over again. (p. 218)

Ring topology A network configuration in which each computer is directly connected to a common cable. The standard topology of local area networks. (p. 432)

Risk The range of possible outcomes to which a decision maker is exposed if a certain alternative is chosen. (p. 136)

Rotational delay The delay that occurs while the read/write mechanism in a disk drive waits for the data in a particular track to rotate under the read/write mechanism. (p. 214)

Schema An overall representation or description of every data item to be included in the collection of files found within a database. (p. 264)

Scope The range or ambition of a computer information systems project. (p. 336)

Scrolling The vertical or horizontal movement of data on the screen so that data from remote sections of the spreadsheet can be made visible. (p. 188)

Secondary index An index, based on a secondary key, that is used to find data on a disk. Secondary keys need not be unique, so a secondary index may have secondary keys that lead to several physical locations. (pp. 226, 243)

Secondary storage Storage on tape or disk. Storage not maintained in the CPU. (pp. 13, 42, 211)

Second-generation computers Computers that date from the late 1950s and use transistors in place of vacuum tubes. (p. 88)

Sensitivity analysis Exploring the consequence of "what if" questions on the outcome of an alternative. (p. 137)

Sequential access Data accessed in a specified sequence according to the order in which they have been stored on secondary storage media. (p. 44)

Sequential file organization Records stored in some predetermined sequence, one after the other. (p. 219)

Sequential file processing Processing data using sequential access methods. (p. 220)

Serial transmission A method of data transmission, used in communications, in which one bit follows the next. In parallel transmission bits move side by side. (p. 405)

Server A computer in a local area network that is dedicated to handling the communication needs of other computers in the network.

Shareable data Data stored in a database which can be shared by different users for a variety of applications. (p. 266)

Shell *See* Expert system shell.

Simple sequence A control structure in which a linear series of programming tasks is expressed. (p. 376)

Simplex transmission Transmission of data in one direction only. (p. 406)

Site license The right to use a single copy of a commercial software package in several computers. (p. 465)

Slack Project activities that are not on the critical path and that can be delayed for a given time without jeopardizing the completion of the entire project. (p. 318)

Smart terminal Terminal that contains some memory and processing circuitry to help perform such tasks as the formatting of data being entered. Dumb terminals contain no such aids. (p. 39)

Software The collection of programs used to provide instructions for the operation of a computer. (p. 12)

Source data automation The process of automating the data entry process in such a way that data are collected as close as possible to their source. (pp. 36, 101)

Spelling checker Software used to check the spelling in a document for errors. Used with word-processing software. (p. 165)

Spreadsheets A software package that accepts data in the form of columns and rows and facilitates their manipulation and presentation. (pp. 19, 180)

Star topology The physical layout of a network in which every computer or device is linked to a central computer which controls the sharing of resources in the network. (p. 432)

Static data Data such as a name and address that change infrequently. (p. 12)

Status line Located at the top (or bottom) of a word-processing screen and showing the name of the document and location of the cursor. In a spreadsheet application, the status line shows the contents of the active cell. (p. 161, 188)

Stockkeeping unit An item stored in inventory. (p. 116)

Strategic advantage A competitive edge over an organization's competitors. Computers are often used in achieving this advantage. (p. 6)

Strategic planning system A computer system that helps top-level managers make vital decisions that impact the future course and profitability of the organization. (p. 82)

Structure chart A chart in which a system is decomposed into a hierarchy of modules each containing a self-sufficient and identifiable function within the system. (p. 368)

Structured design The use of certain guidelines, tools, and techniques to ensure a disciplined and cost-effective approach to the development of an application. (p. 362)

Structured programming An approach to programming that uses certain guidelines and tools to ensure a cost effective and successful completion of the job. (p. 375)

Structured/unstructured view A view or classification of an information system in which the application is classified by the characteristics of the decision problem itself. When using a structured system a well-defined sequence of steps is followed by the end-user. This is not true of unstructured systems. (p. 67)

Subschema A designer's or user's view of a database for use in a specific application in which only selected fields of the schema are needed. (p. 265)

Supercomputer The largest and fastest type of computer, used in government, defense, and sometimes by large organizations. (p. 17)

Synchronous transmission A method of serial transmission in which a group of characters is sent over the transmission line without the need for start and stop bits between each pair of characters. (p. 406)

System a collection of interrelated elements and procedures that interact to accomplish a goal. (p. 331)

System control Safeguard built into an application during the development process to ensure data accuracy, data security, and protection from unauthorized users. (p. 371)

System flowchart A diagram that depicts the flow of information from the input to the output stages of a system. (p. 346)

System point of view Viewing a problem from its widest practical consequences. (p. 331)

Systems analysis A preliminary study of a proposed system to determine if the project has any merit, followed by a detailed analysis of the system's requirements. (p. 334)

Systems design The detailed steps necessary to convert the requirements of new systems into a collection of working programs, and to test and implement the new application. (pp. 342, 362)

System software A collection of programs that manages the resources of the entire computer system and provides supporting functions for the application programs. (p. 46)

Team Group of people assembled to develop a computer application. Includes individuals from several functional areas of the firm including information processing professionals. (p. 342)

Telecommunication The transmission of data between computers at different locations. (p. 172)

Teleconferencing The process of visually linking people at different locations. Sometimes video workstations, capable of data, video, and voice processing are used. (p. 174)

Template A worksheet in which all of the labels and formulas, but none of the data have been entered for a particular application. It then becomes a reusable shell. A master copy. (p. 186)

Terminal A device with a screen and keyboard used for both data input and output. (p. 38)

Text area The portion of the word-processing screen into which the user enters text. (p. 161)

Thesaurus Software used with a word-processing system to find synonyms. (p. 166)

Third-generation computers Computers of the 1960s which placed hundreds of circuits on a silicon chip. (p. 88)

Third-generation language A procedural language such as BASIC and COBOL. (p. 383)

Time series A progression of historical data points extending over a given number of time periods. Forecasters use this series to understand historical patterns and predict future patterns. (p. 138)

Top-down design The development of a system in which broad design issues are considered before more detailed issues. (p. 363)

Topology Pertaining to the physical layout of a network. (p. 432)

Track The physical location where data are stored on tape and disk. (pp. 211, 213)

Transaction file A temporary file for storing data. It is used to update the master file periodically. (p. 221)

Transaction-processing cycle A sequence that begins with the entry of transaction data, continues with the processing of data, and ends with output. (p. 99)

Transaction-processing system A computer system used to process the routine day-to-day information flows in an organization. (pp. 6, 68, 99)

Transfer delay The time it takes the read/write head to transfer data to the CPU once it has been read. (p. 214)

Transmission speed The speed with which data are transmitted through a communications medium. Measured in bits per second or BPS. (p. 404)

Tree structure A data structure used to express relationships between data in a database in which a parent can have several children but a child can have only one parent. A hierarchical and relational DBMS can accommodate this structure. (p. 277)

Twisted-wire pair A pair of copper wires like the wires used to connect telephones in the home or office. (p. 402)

Upload The process of sending data from a micro to a mini, from a mini to a mainframe, or from a micro to a mainframe. (p. 428)

Utility program Part of the system software that performs frequently required tasks such as merging files or copying the contents of one disk to another. (p. 49)

Validation A method for uncovering data entry errors in which certain tests are administered to the data to determine if they fall within a certain range of acceptability. (p. 372)

Value-added carrier Companies that provide specialized communications services. (p. 416)

Vendor The supplier from whom companies purchase the raw materials, components, and services that they need to produce their finished products or deliver their services. (p. 115)

Verification A method for uncovering data entry errors in which the data are entered or read for a second time and both versions are compared. (p. 372)

Very large scale integration (VSLI) Technology which is capable of storing in the range of 1 megabyte on a chip. (p. 89)

Virtual storage   Part of an operating system that makes it possible for a computer to handle larger programs and databases than it otherwise could handle. (p. 48)

Virtual storage access method (VSAM)   A file structure which permits both sequential and direct access. Records are stored sequentially, and an index is used for direct access. An overflow area is used to add records. (p. 228)

Voice-grade transmission   Transmission media capable of handling only voice or voice-like signals. (p. 404)

Voice input   The process of directly entering computer data or instructions using the human voice. System must be trained to recognize an individual's pronunciation of a specified and usually limited vocabulary. (p. 37)

Voice output   Use of synthesized speech to present output over loudspeakers, telephones, or headphones. (p. 54)

Wideband transmission   Data transmission method capable of transmitting data digitally and using microwave and fiber optic technology. (p. 404)

Winchester disk   A hard disk permanently enclosed to protect it from environmental contamination. (p. 215)

Window   The segment of a spreadsheet that is visible on the screen. (p. 188)

Windowing   The process of overlaying several applications on the screen at the same time. (pp. 54, 190)

Word processing   Use of the computer to create, edit, store, and print documents. (pp. 17, 159)

Wordwrap   The process of automatically placing complete words on a new line. A feature of word-processing software. (p. 162)

Workstation   A microcomputer with application software, or a terminal tied to a minicomputer or mainframe, which is dedicated to the functions performed in the office. (p. 158)

Write once optical disk   An optical disk on which data or programs can be written just once by the user, but which can be read any number of times. Also called write-once read many times (WORM). (p. 217)

INDEX

PHOTO CREDITS

CHAPTER OPENERS

Original art by Deborah Phillips.

PART OPENERS

Part One: Tom Grill/Comstock, Inc.; Part Two: Chuck Mason/Comstock, Inc.; Part Three: Mike and Carol Werner/Comstock, Inc.; Part Four: Stephen Marks/Stockphotos, Inc.; and Part Five: Michael Stickey/Comstock, Inc.

CHAPTER 1

Fig. 1-1a: Courtesy General Cinema Corporation; b: Courtesy Motorola, Inc.; c: Courtesy New York Stock Exchange, Inc. d: Courtesy Chemical Bank; Fig. 1-2: Courtesy Cullinet Software, Inc.; Fig. 1-3: Courtesy Hewlett-Packard Company; Fig. 1-4: Courtesy NCR Corporation; Fig. 1-5: Courtesy SAS Institute, Inc., Cary, NC, USA; Fig. 1-6: Courtesy Hewlett-Packard Company; Fig. 1-9: Courtesy Citicorp; Fig. 1-10: Courtesy IBM; Fig. 1-12: Courtesy Stratus Computer, Inc.; Fig. 1-13: Courtesy Hewlett-Packard Company; Fig. 1-14: Courtesy Amcodyne; Fig. 1-16: Courtesy IBM; Fig. 1-17: Courtesy IBM; Fig. 1-18: Courtesy Hewlett-Packard Company.

CHAPTER 2

Fig. 2-1: Courtesy New York Stock Exchange, Inc.; Fig. 2-7: Hewlett-Packard Company; Fig. 2-8: Courtesy Caere Corporation; Fig. 2-9: Courtesy Texas Instruments; Fig. 2-10: Courtesy Hewlett-Packard Company; Fig. 2-13: Courtesy Motorola, Inc.; Fig. 2-14: Courtesy Microscience International Corporation; Fig. 2-17: Courtesy Optimem, Sunnyvale, CA; Fig. 2-19: Courtesy Fujitsu Limited; Fig. 2-22. Courtesy Star Micronics; Fig. 2-22b: Courtesy Dataproducts Corporation; Fig. 2-23: Courtesy Juki Office Machine Company; Fig. 2-24: Courtesy Dataproducts Corporation; Fig. 2-25a: Courtesy Hewlett-Packard Company; Fig. 2-25b: Courtesy Hewlett-Packard Company; Fig. 2-26: Courtesy Hewlett-Packard Company; Fig. 2-27: Courtesy Xerox Corporation.

CHAPTER 3

Fig. 3-3: Courtesy Telenet Communications Corporation, A US Sprint Company. © 1986 Telenet Communications Corporation; Fig. 3-4: Courtesy IBM; Fig. 3-5: Courtesy United Airlines; Fig. 3-6: Courtesy

AMP, Incorporated; Fig. 3-7a: Courtesy United Airlines; b: Courtesy United Airlines; c: Courtesy United Airlines; Fig. 3-8: Courtesy Honeywell, Inc.; Fig. 3-9: Courtesy Hewlett-Packard Company; Fig. 3-10: FourByFive/L. Chiger; Fig. 3-11: Courtesy Hewlett-Packard Company; Fig. 3-15: Courtesy Hewlett-Packard Company; Fig. 3-16: Courtesy Dow Jones & Company, Inc.; Fig. 3-17: Courtesy Sperry Corporation; Fig. 3-18: Courtesy Sperry Corporation; Fig. 3-19: Courtesy IBM; Fig. 3-20a: Courtesy Intel Corporation; b: Courtesy Texas Instruments; Fig. 3-21a: Courtesy Apple Computer, Inc.; b: Courtesy Sperry Corporation; c: Courtesy Sperry Corporation.

CHAPTER 4

Fig. 4-1: Courtesy IBM; Fig. 4-2: Courtesy SAS Institute, Inc. Cary, NC, USA; Fig. 4-4: Courtesy Intermec Corporation; Fig. 4-5: Courtesy Computer Sciences Corporation; Fig. 4-6: Courtesy Honeywell, Inc.; Fig. 4-7: Courtesy Tandem Computers Incorporated; Fig. 4-8: Courtesy Hewlett-Packard Company; Fig. 4-20: Courtesy Motorola, Inc.; Fig. 4-21: Courtesy Integrated Software Systems Corporation.

CHAPTER 5

Fig. 5-2: Courtesy Chemical Bank; Fig. 5-4: Courtesy Data General Corporation; Fig. 5-7: Courtesy Hewlett-Packard Company; Fig. 5-8: Robert Burroughs; Fig. 5-9: Courtesy IBM; Fig. 5-13: Courtesy Xerox Corporation; Fig. 5-14: Courtesy Honeywell, Inc.

CHAPTER 6

Fig. 6-1: Courtesy AT&T Bell Laboratories; Fig. 6-2: Courtesy Xerox Corporation; Fig. 6-3: Courtesy Hewlett-Packard Company; Fig. 6-4: Courtesy Hewlett-Packard Company; Fig. 6-12: Courtesy Datapoint Corporation; Fig. 6-13: Courtesy Fairchild Industries, Inc.

CHAPTER 8

Fig. 8-1: 1985 Ron Villegas; Fig. 8-2: Courtesy Sperry Corporation; Fig. 8-7: Courtesy Dennison Manufacturing Company; Fig. 8-8: Courtesy Seagate; Fig. 8-9: Courtesy BASF Corporation; Fig. 8-10: Courtesy 3M; Fig. 8-17: Courtesy Hewlett-Packard Company.

CHAPTER 9

Fig. 9-1: Courtesy Sperry Corporation; Fig. 9-8: Courtesy Honeywell, Inc.; Fig. 9-7: Courtesy Dennison Manufacturing Company.

CHAPTER 10

Fig. 10-1: Courtesy Hewlett-Packard Company.

CHAPTER 11

Fig. 11-1: Courtesy Integrated Software Systems Corporation; Fig. 11-2: Courtesy Integrated Software Systems Corporation; Fig. 11-3: Courtesy SAS Institute, Inc., Cary, NC, USA; Fig. 11-4: Courtesy Integrated Software Systems Corporation; Fig. 11-9: Courtesy McDonnell Douglas Corporation; Fig. 11-10: Courtesy Tandy Corporation/Radio Shack; Fig. 11-11: Courtesy Hewlett-Packard Company; Fig. 11-12: Courtesy Apple Computer, Inc.; Fig. 11-13: Courtesy Eastman Kodak; Fig. 11-14: Courtesy Honeywell, Inc.; Fig. 11-16: Courtesy Computer Associates International, Inc.

CHAPTER 12

Fig. 12-1: Courtesy Hewlett-Packard Company; Fig. 12-2: Courtesy IBM; Fig. 12-6: Courtesy General Cinema Corporation; Fig. 12-9: Courtesy Xerox Corporation; Fig. 12-14: Courtesy AMP, Incorporated; Fig. 12-15: Courtesy Honeywell, Inc.; Fig. 12-20: Courtesy Hewlett-Packard Company.

CHAPTER 13

Fig. 13-3: Courtesy CashStream Network; Fig. 13-4: Courtesy Dennison Manufacturing Company; Fig. 13-7: Courtesy Honeywell, Inc.; Fig. 13-17: Courtesy Sperry Corporation; Fig. 13-19: Courtesy Hewlett-Packard Company; Fig. 13-20: Hewlett-Packard Company.

CHAPTER 14

Fig. 14-1: Courtesy Fujitsu Limited; Fig. 14-7: Frank Siteman/Taurus; Fig. 14-8: Courtesy AT&T Bell Laboratories; Fig. 14-9: Courtesy Hughes Aircraft Company; Fig. 14-10: Courtesy AT&T Bell Laboratories; Fig. 14-15: Courtesy Telebit Corporation; Fig. 14-16: Courtesy Hayes Microcomputers Products, Inc.; Fig. 14-20: Courtesy M/A-COM, Inc.

CHAPTER 15

Fig. 15-9: Courtesy Sperry Corporation; Fig. 15-10: Courtesy Honeywell, Inc.

CHAPTER 16

Fig. 16-1: Courtesy Hewlett-Packard Company; Fig. 16-3: Courtesy Texas Instruments; Fig. 16-4: Courtesy Xerox Corporation; Fig. 16-5: Courtesy Unisys Corporation.

CHAPTER 17

Fig. 17-1: Courtesy Harnischfeger Engineers, Inc.; Fig. 17-2: Courtesy General Motors Corporation; Fig. 17-3: Courtesy Apollo Computer, Inc.; Fig. 17-4: Courtesy Hewlett-Packard Company; Fig. 17-5: Courtesy General Motors Corporation; Fig. 17-6: Courtesy Hewlett-Packard Company; Fig. 17-7: Courtesy Apple Computer, Inc.; Fig. 17-8: Courtesy Hewlett-Packard Company.

CHAPTER 18

Fig. 18-1: Courtesy Hewlett-Packard Company; Fig. 18-2: Courtesy Hewlett-Packard Company; Fig. 18-3: Courtesy Honeywell, Inc.; Fig. 18-4: Courtesy Hewlett-Packard Company; Fig. 18-5: Courtesy IBM; Fig. 18-6: Courtesy Hewlett-Packard Company; Fig. 18-7: Courtesy Computer Sciences Corporation; Fig. 18-8: Courtesy IBM; Fig. 18-9: Courtesy AT&T Bell Laboratories; Fig. 18-10: Courtesy IBM; Fig. 18-11: Courtesy Sperry Corporation; Fig. 18-13: Courtesy Oscar & Associates, Inc.